Marketing Management and Administrative Action

McGraw-Hill Series in Marketing

Consulting Editor
Charles Schewe
University of Massachusetts

Britt and Boyd:	*Marketing Management and Administrative Action*
Buzzell, Nourse, Matthews, and Levitt:	*Marketing: A Contemporary Analysis*
DeLozier:	*The Marketing Communications Process*
Howard:	*Consumer Behavior: Application of Theory*
Lee and Dobler:	*Purchasing and Materials Management: Text and Cases*
Redinbaugh:	*Retailing Management: A Planning Approach*
Reynolds and Wells:	*Consumer Behavior*
Russell, Beach, and Buskirk:	*Textbook of Salesmanship*
Shapiro:	*Sales Program Management: Formulation and Implementation*
Stanton:	*Fundamentals of Marketing*
Star, Davis, Lovelock, and Shapiro:	*Problems in Marketing*
Stroh:	*Managing the Sales Function*
Wright, Warner, Winter, and Zeigler:	*Advertising*

Marketing Management and Administrative Action

Fourth Edition

Steuart Henderson Britt

Ph.D. in Psychology
Professor of Marketing, Graduate School of Management and
Professor of Advertising, Medill School of Journalism
Northwestern University
also President, Britt and Frerichs Inc.,
Marketing Research Firm, Chicago

Harper W. Boyd, Jr.

Ph.D. in Marketing
Dean, Graduate School of Business Administration
Tulane University

McGraw-Hill Book Company

New York St. Louis San Francisco Auckland Bogotá Düsseldorf Johannesburg
London Madrid Mexico Montreal New Delhi Panama Paris São Paulo Singapore
Sydney Tokyo Toronto

MARKETING MANAGEMENT AND ADMINISTRATIVE ACTION

1234567890DODO783210987

This book was set in Times Roman by Black Dot, Inc.
The editors were William J. Kane and Theresa J. Kwiatkowski;
the cover was designed by Albert M. Cetta;
the production supervisor was Leroy A. Young.
The drawings were done by J & R Services, Inc.
R. R. Donnelley & Sons Company was printer and binder.

Library of Congress Cataloging in Publication Data

Britt, Steuart Henderson, date comp.
Marketing management and administrative action.

(McGraw-Hill series in marketing)
Inclues index.
1. Marketing management. I. Boyd, Harper W., joint comp. II. Title.
HF5415.13.B7 1978 658.8 77-6434
ISBN 0-07-007923-4

Contents

Preface ix

I THE SCOPE OF MARKETING MANAGEMENT

1 *Marcology 101 or the Domain of Marketing*
Sidney J. Levy 3

2 *The Major Tasks of Marketing Management*
Philip Kotler 10

II ORGANIZING THE MARKETING FUNCTION

3 *The Changing Role of the Product Manager in Consumer Goods Companies*
Victor P. Buell 23

4 *Reorganize Your Company around Its Markets*
Mack Hanan 34

5 *A System for Managing Diversity*
Robert V. L. Wright 46

III ESTABLISHING MARKETING OBJECTIVES

A Determining the Marketing Objectives

6 *Corporate Strategy, Marketing and Diversification*
Harry Henry 61

7 *Concept of Strategy*
H. Igor Ansoff 70

B Predicting Behavior in the Marketplace

8 *Consumer Decision-Process Models*
J. A. Lunn 79

9 *The Behavioral Sciences*
Charles Ramond 102

10 *New Way to Measure Consumers' Judgments*
Paul E. Green and Yoram Wind 123

11 *A Model of Industrial Buyer Behavior*
Jagdish N. Sheth 135

C Segmenting the Market

12 *An Overview of Market Segmentation*
John C. Bieda and Harold H. Kassarjian 144

13 *Expanding the Scope of Segmentation Research*
Nariman K. Dhalla and Winston H. Mahatoo 151

14 *Market Segmentation: A Strategic Management Tool*
Richard M. Johnson 161

15 *Industrial Market Segmentation*
Yoram Wind and Richard Cardozo 170

IV DEVELOPING MARKETING STRATEGIES

16 *Marketing Strategy Positioning*
David W. Cravens 185

17 *A Strategic Perspective on Product Planning*
George S. Day 193

18 *Planning Gains in Market Share*
C. Davis Fogg 212

19 *Experience Curves as a Planning Tool*
Patrick Conley 224

V PUTTING THE MARKETING PLAN INTO ACTION

A Products and Product Lines

20 *Managing the Product Life Cycle*
Donald K. Clifford, Jr. 237

21 *The Marketing Importance of the "Just Noticeable Difference"*
Steuart Henderson Britt and Victoria M. Nelson 244

22 *Shift from Brand to Product Line Marketing*
Joseph A. Morein 246

23 *Targeting Prospects for a New Product*
Philip Kotler and Gerald Zaltman 256

24 *Why New Industrial Products Fail*
Robert G. Cooper 270

B Pricing

25 *The Myths and Realities of Corporate Pricing*
Gilbert Burck 282

26 *Techniques for Pricing New Products and Services*
Joel Dean 293

27 *A Decision-making Structure for Price Decisions*
Alfred R. Oxenfeldt 303

C Channels of Distribution and Physical Logistics

28 *Functional Spin-off: A Key to Anticipating Change in Distribution Structure*
Bruce Mallen 311

29 *A Frame of Reference for Improving Productivity in Distribution*
Bert C. McCammon, Jr., and William L. Hammer 320

30 *The Total Cost Approach to Distribution*
Raymond LeKashman and John F. Stolle 330

D Personal Selling and Management of the Sales Force

31 *Interaction and Influence Processes in Personal Selling*
Harry L. Davis and Alvin J. Silk 343

32 *The Computer, Personal Selling, and Sales Management*
James M. Comer 358

33 *Reactions to Role Conflict: The Case of the Industrial Salesman*
Orville C. Walker, Jr., Gilbert A. Churchill, Jr., and Neil M. Ford 367

E Advertising

34 *A Theorectical View of Advertising Communication*
Joseph T. Plummer 376

35 *Imagery and Symbolism*
Sidney J. Levy and Ira O. Glick 382

36 *An Attitudinal Framework for Advertising Strategy*
Harper W. Boyd, Jr., Michael L. Ray, and Edward S. Strong 389

37 *Media Approaches to Segmentation*
Albert V. Bruno, Thomas P. Hustad, and Edgar A. Pessemier 398

VI MARKETING INFORMATION SYSTEMS

38 *Marketing Information Systems*
Kenneth P. Uhl 411

39 *Modeling Marketing Phenomena: A Managerial Perspective*
David B. Montgomery and Charles B. Weinberg 423

40 *Environmental Information Systems for Strategic Marketing Planning*
William R. King and David I. Cleland 439

41 *Contingency Planning*
Michael J. Clay 447

Indexes 457
Name Index
Subject Index

Preface

This fourth edition of MARKETING MANAGEMENT AND ADMINISTRATIVE ACTION is *a new book.*

It is *a complete revision* of previous editions. Only 8 of the 41 selections* are from previous editions. The other 33 are new.

The dates of the selections (with two exceptions) are 1969 through 1976. Included are materials by Victor P. Buell, George S. Day, Joel Dean, Paul E. Green, Mack Hanan, Harry Henry, Harold H. Kassarjian, Philip Kotler, Sidney J. Levy, Bruce Miller, Alfred R. Oxenfeldt, Edgar A. Pessemier, Charles Ramond, Jagdish N. Sheth, Kenneth P. Uhl, Yoram Wind, and other marketing thinkers.

The major changes in this revision are in content rather than structure; and within each broad topical area a variety of management perspectives are presented.

We have kept in mind the same goal used in preparing each of the first three editions, namely, that the selections should help readers to understand and solve marketing problems.

The basic sections of the book are:

I The Scope of Marketing Management
II Organizing the Marketing Function

*Numbers 7, 12, 14, 19, 25, 30, 31, and 36.

III Establishing Marketing Objectives
IV Developing Marketing Strategies
V Putting the Marketing Plan into Action
VI Marketing Information Systems

We thank the 56 authors and coauthors of the 41 selections for their insightful materials which made the present book of readings possible. The affiliation of each author is indicated as of the date of publication.

We also appreciate the opportunity to reprint materials from the following sources:

Organizations
American Marketing Association
Arthur D. Little, Inc.

Periodicals
Business Horizons
Fortune
Harvard Business Review
IEEE Spectrum
Industrial Marketing Management
Journal of Advertising Research
Journal of Business Administration
Journal of Communication
Journal of Contemporary Business
Journal of Marketing
Journal of Marketing Research
Long Range Planning
Sloan Management Review

Book Publishers
The Dartnell Corporation
Harper & Row Publishers
Longman Group Limited
McGraw-Hill Book Company

Although as the editors we are responsible for the final selections, we thank the following for their useful suggestions:

Richard N. Cardozo, College of Business, University of Minnesota
Gilbert A. Churchill, Jr., School of Business, University of Wisconsin at Madison
Richard M. Clewett, Graduate School of Management, Northwestern University
George S. Day, Faculty of Management Studies, University of Toronto
Ralph L. Day, Department of Marketing, Indiana University
Edward L. Grubb, School of Business Administration, Portland State University

William F. Lewis, College of Business Administration, Xavier University
Robert A. Mittelstaedt, College of Business Administration, University of Nebraska–Lincoln
Edgar A. Pessemier, Krannert Graduate School of Management, Purdue University
Michael L. Ray, Graduate School of Business, Stanford University
Louis W. Stern, Graduate School of Management, Northwestern University
Frederick E. Webster, Jr., The Amos Tuck School of Business Administration, Dartmouth College
William L. Wilkie, College of Business Administration, University of Florida
Yoram Wind, The Wharton School, University of Pennsylvania

We also thank Darlene Hitchcock Nilges and Irene E. Peach for editorial and secretarial assistance.

Steuart Henderson Britt
Harper W. Boyd, Jr.

Marketing Management and Administrative Action

Part One

The Scope of Marketing Management

Marketing management is broader in both nature and scope than ever before.

Marketing used to be viewed as a subject area largely confined to a number of rather special activities—such as selling and advertising. But today more and more corporations are synthesizing their various marketing inputs into a strategic planning system which recognizes the interdependency of all marketing inputs.

Accordingly, marketing ought to be perceived as a force that pervades the entire business organization, and not just as the exclusive responsibility of the marketing department.

In today's world the growing importance of both the public area and the service area of the economy has raised substantive questions as to the appropriate roles of marketing in those areas. The growth of consumerism also raises some vital questions about the nature and scope of marketing in an industrial society.

The readings in this section are concerned not just with marketing by the business firm. They deal with what might be called the real domain of marketing, and with the real tasks of marketing management.

1

Marcology 101 or the Domain of Marketing

Sidney J. Levy

Current issues and attitudes within the field of marketing are discussed, particularly the general stigma attached to marketing, the territorial conflicts in defining marketing, and the tension between theory and practice.These problems are seen as arising partly from the confusions among ideas about marketing as a commercial activity, a universal phenomenon of exchange, and a field of study without adequate terminological distinctions.

The situation might be improved by distinguishing a field of study here termed the science of marcology.

INTRODUCTION

There seems to be a great amount of conflict and brooding going on over the state of marketing, reflecting both old problems and new ones. Discerning a crisis in one's field is a common ploy, but some times do appear to be more critical than others, and the recent agitation is unusually lively. It may help in the search for clarity to discuss some main controversial ideas.There are three central issues that are here cast in the form of three major criticisms of marketing.

1 Marketing is a general evil.
2 Marketing trespasses on other fields.
3 Marketing theory is irrelevant.

These three negative ideas generate a noticeable degree of heat, and challenge all marketing educators to examine their field and its basic nature, and to clarify response to these criticisms. The endeavor may be foolish—perhaps unnecessary for thoughtful and reasonable people and futile for others. Still, these ideas have repercussions, they repel good students, affect the support of marketing scholars, and hamper the free expression of inquiry seeking to understand the human actions, structures, and processes called marketing. These three problems radiate in many directions and involve numerous sub-issues and segments of society. They indicate that marketing is a controversial subject and source of conflict between marketers and non-marketers, among marketing thinkers, and between marketing thinkers and marketing doers.

The first proposition affects marketing in all its relations, stigmatizing it for existing in society; the second restricts its definition and application in a mean-minded and territorial fashion; and the third complaint denies the value of serious advanced study of marketing. The conflicts entailed are perhaps so deep and encompassing that they are ultimately irreconcilable, but they will probably gain from airing and dialogue, as Boris Becker [7] has pointed out, in our search for truth. Differences due to real opposed interests will undoubtedly continue, but those due to misunderstanding or confusion might be mitigated. It is not the purpose of this discussion to defend specific

Reprinted from Kenneth L. Bernhardt, *Marketing 1776–1976 and Beyond* (Chicago: American Marketing Association, 1976), pp. 577–581. At the time of writing the author was professor of behavioral science, Graduate School of Management, Northwestern University.

marketing actions against all comers, but to explore the issues and to suggest an ameliorative approach.

MARKETING STIGMATIZED

The general understanding of what constitutes marketing is both self-confident and negative. That is, most people do not doubt they know that marketing is the selling of goods and that the selling is conducted in a manner deserving of censure. This knowledge is ancient, going back to traditional attitudes toward those who sell. The root ideas of *mercari,* to trade, *mereri,* to serve for hire, *merere,* to earn, may seem neutral enough (or even positive, as in *merit*), but the use of these roots to form words such as *meretricious,* meaning like a prostitute, and *mercenary,* to indicate one who will do anything for money shows the early attachment of negative value judgments to ideas of selling. Aristotle agreed with the opinion of the day when he wrote that "retail trade . . . is justly censured; for it is unnatural, and a mode by which men gain from one another."

Basic Motives

It is interesting to speculate on the sources of the degradation of marketing. They are presumably deep-rooted in being so pervasive and enduring. A common assumption in condemning marketing is that the buyer is taken advantage of by the seller. Even when the marketing exchange is supposed to be equal in value to both participants, dissatisfaction often remains. The many reasons for this go on at various levels. One problem is that the equation is comprised of units whose values are either not easily determined or compared. If the buyer receives the product and satisfaction of his need and the seller receives the payment for his cost and mark-up ($P + S = C + M$), how can the two sides of the equation be judged truly equal? Even in a trade of goods where both parties are clearly buyer *and* seller, mutual suspicion may arise that one has yielded up a greater value than that received.

A second great source of difficulty relates to the perceived purposes of the seller, especially when a middle-man exists and when money is involved. The distributor becomes divorced from basic production and is associated more narrowly with the goals of gaining and accumulating money, supposedly as much as possible. This motive is taken as unusually egocentric and damaging to other people, and therefore deserving of less admiration than other vocational aims. Those who grow or craft goods, whose work is healing, study, salvation, artistry, appear to have a commitment that is direct and socially valuable—although they, too, become suspect if money looms too large in their aims. Because the professions are supposedly self-denying in this respect, they have been ennobled. If the merchant, the paradigm of the marketer, sought only to provide, to be the selfless, dedicated quartermaster to the community, then his endeavor too might be exalted.

But even the most loving provider (e.g., the nursing mother), thwarts the fundamental desire to receive without return. Resist as one may, society insists on *quid pro quo,* and socializes the young to believe it is more blessed to give than to receive, a precept that would not be needed if it were self-evident in one's feelings. But some giving becomes gratifying, a source of pride, sociability, greater receiving, and other benefits, so that not all exchange is condemned. Ideas of fair return become possible, as well as intellectual recognition of economic necessities relating to profit and accumulation of capital.

The Synechdochic Mechanism

Learning to adapt to the requirements of an elaborate system of giving and receiving, as society demands [9], leads to many complexities of outlook. In given economies, haggling may come to be admired, and bribery a way of life. In attempts to deny their own persistent desire to get, people do much blaming of others. Marketing is blamed for fostering materialism; and in case consumers seem overly fertile ground and for its attractions and too eager to embrace it, the products are deemed shoddy, and the seduction credited to lies and aggressive selling. Implying that in some state of nature (sans marketing) one would have only virtuous spontaneous needs and wants, marketing is accused of brainwashing, forcing, and manipulating people to want things they do not need and to buy things they do not want.

Certainly, there are marketers who make inferior goods, sell aggressively, and tell lies in their advertising. And it is no defense of them to cite equally culpable quick physicians, destructive politicians, cheating customers, faithless ministers, and ignorant teachers. But it is worth noting the overgeneralizing that occurs when all marketing is stigmatized and the term becomes synonymous with doing bad things. All group prejudice is a form of their overgeneralizing, or fallacy of composition. To identify it here, the way a part of marketing is taken for the whole is called the synechdochic mechanism. A synechdoche is a rhetorical device wherein the singular is substituted for the plural: here the disapproved marketer is being used to define the category, substituted for those others who strive to make a fine product, offer an excellent service, price fairly, sell helpfully, and communicate honestly.

To refer to such positive marketing probably arouses cynical reactions even in an audience identified with marketing. It illustrates the deep-rooted nature of the problem to observe within the marketing professions signs of self-hatred, acceptance of the stigma, and casual use of the rhetoric that makes marketing a bad word. For example, W. T. Tucker cites critics of the marketing viewpoint who equate marketing activities with exploiting motives, and "more gimmickry and packaging than substantive change." He seems to accept their criticism and the verb *marketed* as a negative one when he says that the student is a special person who "must not be marketed into doing what the organizations want" [14].

Thus, it is that marketing is stigmatized because it is associated with the many frustrations of wanting and giving—with material things and guilt over the desire for them, with money and its deflection of direct interest in providing goods and services—leading to the projection of these frustrations onto marketing and marketers, and to the synechdochic equation of the whole field with its worst manifestations.

THE DOMAIN OF MARKETING

Another level of explanation of marketings's poor reputation may lie in confusion or misunderstanding as to what marketing actually is. Perhaps the conventional notion of marketing is not a good or accurate one, and redefinition could assist in making some useful distinctions. Partly, this is an academic exercise. As Robert Oliver says, in trying to offer a definition of the field of speech,

> Knowledge does not lend itself readily to segmentalization. Departmentalization is decreed on our campuses not for investigative, but administrative, convenience. The boundaries established around the various academic specialties are not strong enough to contain human curiosity [12].

In the field of speech, Oliver finds the heart of the matter in one purpose: to deal with influence as exerted through oral discourse. He clings to this, despite his qualms.

> Like other professions, ours has been highly introspective, defensive, self-critical, and uncertain of its goals, its methods, and its boundaries. . . . When we replace the term "language" with

> the much more inclusive term "speech," the boundaries of our field tend to disappear. Yet within this complexity we must somehow establish our own identity of goals and methods. The task is appalling [13].

Territoriality

The marketing literature shows that marketing thinkers have trouble with finding their consistent locus, also, because their subject matter radiates so readily into and across other disciplines and ways of thinking about human behavior. In his discussion of "the identity crisis in marketing," Bartels raises this basic question:

> The crux of the issue is this; is the identity of marketing determined by the *subject matter* dealt with or by the technology with which the subject is handled? . . . Marketing has initially and generally been associated exclusively with the distributive part of the economic institution and function. In this capacity, marketing is identified by the *substance* and the *subject* of its area of concern [5].

Bartels seems open-minded about the issue, perhaps preferring the substantive definition rather than the methodological application one. He thinks the fresh interest in physical distribution, or *logistics,* may allow the word marketing to go on to refer to both economic and non-economic fields of application. Still, he sees marketing as but a species of generic behavioral activity, and one that is trying to trespass on someone else's territory: "From this standpoint, too, the idea that the fields of political campaigns, religious evangelism, or Red Cross solicitation are the province of marketers, rather than of social scientists, may also be questionable" [6].

David Luck also expresses his concern over the confusion of terminology and conceptualization created by the idea that "every sort of organization is engaged in marketing" [11], and hopes that an authoritative definition of marketing might come from a commission created for the purpose.

These territorial considerations are probably basically irrelevant. As Karl Popper says,

> All this classification and distinction is a comparatively unimportant and superficial affair. We are not students of some subject matter but students of problems. And problems may cut right across the borders of any subject matter or discipline [13].

That is, no one has any special right to a problem. Intellectual territoriality is not like the ownership of a piece of physical geography. Voting behavior may seem the province of political scientists, but that does not prevent sociologists from studying the behavior and need not inhibit marketers. That people like a particular food can be studied by biologists as a process of osmosis or hormonal secretions, by psychologists as a conditioned response or fixation due to trauma, by anthropologists as a cultural imperative, and by speech scholars as a reaction to the oral discourse, "Come and get it!" What makes sex political and politics sexual is the determined attention, analysis, and actions of feminists. To dismiss this as a "Feminist supremacy syndrome" (a la Luck's reference to those "with a sort of marketing supremacy syndrome") seems pointless and ostrich-like. To perceive or study the marketing content of a problem is not to say it is the marketer's province *rather than* the social scientist's, but that it is *also* the marketer's province.

Tucker implies that Kotler and Levy sought to broaden the boundaries of marketing in 1969 [10] in a desire to follow the action of important problems growing elsewhere [16]; but Levy studied such problems at Social Research, Inc. since starting his marketing research career in 1948. It may more properly be said that the action came to marketing for help rather than the other way around, as non-business managers recognized that the marketing point of view might be useful with their problems. In some ways, to resist or resent this fact is further agreement that marketing is an evil that socially virtuous causes ought not to turn to for help.

Exchange

It has been suggested above that the core issues in marketing arise from the coming together of *providing and needing or wanting.* That is, *exchange* comes about because one must always give something to get something one wants. The paradigm is the infant, reaching for anything available and trying to incorporate it. But experience soon teaches two conditions: one can't have everything, and one must give something in return. The first is the condition for making choices, and the second creates exchanges.

The issue of exchange has been much discussed—views have been presented by many, including Alderson, Kotler, Levy, and Zaltman [2], and two excellent recent articles by Bagozzi [3]. These will not be gone into here, except to reiterate and emphasize the latter's statement that marketing is "a general function of universal applicability. It is the discipline of exchange behavior, and it deals with problems related to this behavior" [4].

It seems important to insist on the issue of universal applicability, mainly because there seems no adequately consistent way to define marketing exchange that limits it short of universality. What is a marketing exchange as different from any other exchange? Some try to restrict marketing to the exchange of money for products, a distinction that fails immediately with consideration of markets in which money is exchanged for money, products for products, and money or products are exchanged for services. Then is there any way to limit which moneys, products, or services will be considered elements of marketing exchange, and which will not? Some use the word *economic* as the limiting adjective. But what is economic and what is noneconomic? Economics texts wrestle with such definitions and mainly retreat to notions of scarce resources, utilities, production, consumption; usually trying to stay as close to money as possible. But again, universality of reference is hard to avoid, as what is not a scarce resource, what is not a utility? These concepts are all interwoven. Money is a measure and surrogate for value, for one's labor; labor is a form of energy, skill and service. Anything can be a commodity. All "utility" is a form of satisfaction. In a world in which there is no truly free air (although optimistically cited by Samuelson as a non-economic good in his classic text on economics), in which all exchanges are economic choices and all are exchanges of satisfactions, there can be no nonmarketing exchanges. What is being exchanged may sometimes be hard to analyze, but marketing cannot be limited to being the science of *simple* exchanges.

It may be convenient, of course, to make distinctions between marketing exchanges that are culturally defined as commercial or economic, and other types. Some educators and most marketing practitioners in everyday business are more comfortable then. But that should not lead to the exclusion from marketing theory of the exchanges of goods and services in marriages, churches, politics, aesthetics, schools, government, and social causes.

MARKETING THEORY AND PRACTICE

Theorists and practitioners often develop tensions due to conflict of aims, procedures, concepts of scientific and professional standards, relevance, etc. Academic psychologists and clinical psychologists show this tension, and its recent flare-up in the marketing field is notable. For some time, marketing people have thought about the development of marketing as a science. Certainly, that ultimate state has not fully arrived; but various workers have been striving in that direction. The establishment of the Marketing Science Institute is one indication as well as numerous conferences, symposia, and articles, fretting over marketing as a science, an art, a pseudoscience, as having theory, metatheory, etc. [17].

In the classical extreme, practitioners see theorists (viz. academicians) as ivory tower thinkers, impractical people who do not know the realities of the marketplace, who have "never met a payroll," who teach because they can't do. The theorists return the compliment by regarding practitioners as concrete-minded people who are overly specialized and vocational, unable to generalize their experience, who want to know how-to-do-it rather than to understand why it works as it does. If a science is to work toward understanding, predicting, and controlling, the researcher and teacher tends to emphasize the first two aims, and the practitioner the last two.

The extremists write accusations about the uselessness of academic research or defend the validity and importance of the intellectual enterprise. Outstanding examples from the *Marketing News* are Newton Frank's rude and vituperative letter (March 14, 1975) on the uselessness of academic research, the letter (12/1/74) from James F. Engel in which he says that marketing is not a pure science, that publications should face this fact and judge their contents only by their practical value to the applied marketer. He defines marketing as akin to an engineering discipline that draws upon several underlying disciplines; and regards the proposal of Randall Schultz (11/1/74) that there be separate journals of study and practice as a perpetuation of the travesty of educators talking to themselves.

Between the extremes are such moderating, judicious suggestions as a broader dialogue, by Professor Becker (3/31/75) who, however, also believes that if practitioners are determined to be so ignorant, then it is time to go our separate ways. Richard E. Homans (8/15/75) offers an accomodating discussion explaining the benefits of academic research. Thomas Lea Davidson's article shows alarm.

> A schism exists today within the marketing community—with marketing academicians lined up on one side and marketing practitioners on the other. The continued growth of that schism—and it is growing—can only be detrimental to both sides.

His solution is indicated in the headline above this article:

> *One businessman's comments on marketing educators:*
> EDUCATORS MUST SEE MARKETING AS A 'DOING PROFESSION' AND ADD 'CLINICAL EXPERIENCE' TO 'CLASSROOM VACUUM' [8]

The pressure is to get more practice into the classroom by inviting businessmen to talk to classes, by urging practitioners to write for the *Journal of Marketing.*

THE SCIENCE OF MARCOLOGY

It is evident that many of the problems discussed above are real ones that will not easily be solved. Marketing will always be regarded as an evil by those who refuse to recognize its universality or do not want to countenance its demands for a return and often a profit. There are manipulative marketers, deceptive ads, and high pressure salesmen. There are sincere disagreements about discipline boundaries and preferred defintions, and about the value of theory. All solutions are partial—the calls for dialogue, a commission to define marketing, an article giving business persons 10 guidelines to follow when invited to speak to students, and another by a young man exhorting marketers to be honest.

One source of these problems and the struggles with them lies in the idea of marketing as an *activity.* It is not surprising that educators are urged to see marketing as a "doing profession," when *marketing* is a *doing.* When one is a seller and markets, one is a marketer who *does* marketing; and a buyer *goes* marketing. Thus, if educators teach marketing, they should teach how to do it and how to go to it; then no wonder Engel says they are acting as engineers of the marketplace. Then it is reasonable that textbooks tend to be prescriptive writing, oriented to help students to be profitable, successful marketers, good marketers who apply the marketing concept or virtuous marketers who consider their social responsibility in accordance with the latest ideas of how marketing ought to be done. Such prescriptions and applications are indeed not a "pure science," but the teaching of particular sets of marketing values, and they produce the faddishness and biases that Robert F. Agne deplores [1].

A marketing science should be demarcated that does not do *marketing research* but that does *research into marketing.* It should be a pursuit of knowledge, as distinguished from its application, candidly and proudly so. It should exist in relation to marketing as physics or chemistry are to their respective engineerings, as psychology is to counselling. Some have thought that marketing is applied economics, but economics shows little interest in marketing and marketing draws on economics mainly as it might on any other discipline—as sociology and economics draw on psychology and mathematics.

Marketing needs its own parent discipline and theoretical roots, its area of basic study. Despite being hampered by the confusions of being called marketers when they are trying to be teachers and researchers into marketing, such professionals have nevertheless been developing concepts, models, and a theoretical literature, and have doctoral students carrying out theoretical inquiries.

The name of such a science might draw on some appropriate linguistic roots and be called MARCOLOGY. Marcology could be the discipline of exchanges, operating at various levels of abstraction and in whatever contexts are of interest to the scholars. It could have its own focus and its interdisciplinary character, as all the behavioral sciences do. Marcology could study the history of exchanges, why marketing is evil, the various types of exchange, and such divisions of activity as commercial marketing, family or intimate marketing, social and political marketing—or their various marcologies. Abnormal or deviant marcology might study "unusual payments," as a study group recently called large-scale foreign bribery, without having to moralize about them. As *scientists,* marcologists should not teach their opinions about whether television or consumerism or emotional appeals or premiums or unit pricing are good or bad, but rather what these are, how and why they affect which participants in the exchange. They can study what is exchanged, by whom, where, when, and why, with what consequences personally, socially, nationally. They can do this like other scientists, *just to know,* and for those that wish, in order to share that knowledge without being condemned for having a journal that is not practical in character. And if they wish, like other scientists, marcologists can try to say what is likely to happen under given circumstances, so that practical people can learn from that and apply it as physics is applied to manufacturing and biology to medicine.

If there is to be a commission, let it convene marcologists to define their discipline and its curriculum. In this way, both marcology and the engineering activity that is marketing could be clarified, as well as the role identities that accompany the distinctions between research, teaching, and application.

REFERENCES

1 Agne, Robert F. "Businessman Proposes Conduct Code for Academicians," *Marketing News* (August 15, 1974), 4.

2 Alderson, Wroe. *Marketing Behavior and Executive Action.* Homewood, Ill.: Richard D.

Irwin, 1957; Kotler, Phillip. "A Generic Concept of Marketing," *Journal of Marketing,* 36 (April, 1972), 46–54; Levy, Sidney J. and Gerald Zaltman, *Marketing, Society, and Conflict.* Englewood Cliffs, N.J.: Prentice-Hall, Inc., 1975.

3 Bagozzi, Richard P. "Marketing as an Organized Behavioral System of Exchange," *Journal of Marketing,* 38 (October, 1974), 77–81; Bagozzi, "Marketing as Exchange," *Journal of Marketing,* 39 (October, 1975), 32–39.

4 Bagozzi. (October, 1975), 39.

5 Bartels, Robert. "The Identity Crisis in Marketing," *Journal of Marketing,* 38 (October, 1974).

6 *Ibid.,* 76.

7 Becker, Boris W. "Letters," *Marketing News* (April 25, 1975), 2.

8 Davidson, Thomas Lea. *Marketing News* (August 15, 1975), 1.

9 Firth, Raymond. *Symbols Public and Private.* London, England: George Allen and Unwin, Ltd., 1973, especially Chapter 11, "Symbolism in Giving and Getting," 368–402.

10 Kotler, Phillip and Sidney J. Levy. "Broadening the Concept of Marketing," *Journal of Marketing,* 33 (January, 1969), 10–15.

11 Luck, David J. "Social Marketing: Confusion Compounded," *Journal of Marketing,* 38 (October, 1974), 71.

12 Oliver, Robert T. "Contributions of the Speech Profession to the Study of Human Communication," in Frank E. X. Dance, ed., *Human Communication Theory.* New York: Holt, Rinehart & Winston, 1967, 266.

13 *Ibid.,* 265.

14 Popper, Karl R. *Conjectures and Refutations.* New York: Harper and Row, 1963, 67.

15 Tucker, W. T. "Future Directions in Marketing Theory," *Journal of Marketing,* 38 (April, 1974), 33.

16 Tucker, *ibid.,* 31.

17 Tucker, W. T. *ibid.;* Dawson, Leslie M. "Marketing Science in the Age of Aquarius," *Journal of Marketing,* 35 (July, 1971), 66–72; Bartels, Robert. *Marketing Theory and Metatheory.* Homewood, Ill.: Richard D. Irwin, 1970; Zaltman, Gerald, et al. *Metatheory and Consumer Research.* New York: Holt, Rinehart and Winston, Inc., 1973.

2

The Major Tasks of Marketing Management

Philip Kotler

Marketers engage in a variety of tasks which are not carefully distinguished from the literature but which are radically different in the problems they pose. Eight different marketing tasks can be distinguished, each arising out of a unique state of demand.

Whether demand is negative, nonexistent, latent, irregular, faltering, full, overfull, or unwholesome, a singular challenge is posed to the marketer's craft and concepts.

The popular image of the marketer is that he is a professional whose job is to *create* and *maintain* demand for something. Unfortunately, this is too limited a view of the range of marketing challenges he faces. In fact, it covers only two of eight important and distinct marketing tasks. Each task calls for a special type of problem-solving behavior and a specific blend of marketing concepts.

Marketing management may be viewed ge-

Reprinted from *Journal of Marketing,* vol. 37, pp. 42–49, American Marketing Association, October 1973. At the time of writing the author was Harold T. Martin professor of marketing, Graduate School of Management, Northwestern University.

nerically as the *problem of regulating the level, timing, and character of demand for one or more products of an organization.* The organization is assumed to form an idea of a desired level of demand based on profit maximization, sales maximization subject to a profit constraint, satisficing, the current or desired level of supply, or some other type of analysis. The *current demand level* may be below, equal to, or above the *desired demand level.* Four specific demand states make up *underdemand:* negative demand, no demand, latent demand, and faltering demand. Two specific demand states make up *adequate demand:* irregular demand and full demand. Finally, two demand states make up *overdemand:* overfull demand and unwholesome demand. These eight demand states are distinguished primarily with respect to the level of current demand in relation to desired demand; although two additional factors, the timing of demand (irregular demand) and the character of demand (unwholesome demand), are also important. The set of demand situations is fairly exhaustive and the order fairly continuous.

Each demand situation gives rise to the specific marketing task described in column 2 of Table 1. Negative demand results in attempts to disabuse it; no demand, in attempts to create demand; latent demand, in attempts to develop demand; and so on. Each of these tasks is given the more formal name shown in column 3.

All of these tasks require a managerial approach consisting of analysis, planning, implementation, organization, and control. Furthermore, they all utilize the two basic steps of marketing strategy development: defining the *target markets* and formulating a *marketing mix* out of the elements of product, price, promotion, and place. In these respects, all of marketing management has a unity, a core theory. At the same time, the eight tasks are not identical. They involve or emphasize different variables, different psychological theories, different managerial aptitudes. The eight tasks can give way to specialization. Some marketers may become especially skillful at developmental marketing, others at remarketing, others at maintenance marketing, and others at demarketing. Not all marketers are likely to be equally skilled at all tasks, which in one of the major points to be considered in assigning marketers to tasks.

A marketer in a given job may face all of these tasks as the product moves through its life cycle. At the beginning of the product's life, there may be only latent demand and the task is one of developmental marketing. In the stage of high growth, there may be overfull demand in relation to the firm's ability to produce, and some need for systematic demarketing. When facilities have been built up and demand reaches the maturity stage of the product life cycle, the task may be primarily one of maintenance marketing. When demand begins to decline or falter, it may be time to face some basic questions on reshaping it, or remarketing. Finally, the product may eventually fall into the category of being

Table 1 The Basic Marketing Tasks

Demand state	Marketing task	Formal name
I Negative demand	Disabuse demand	Conversional marketing
II No demand	Create demand	Stimulational marketing
III Latent demand	Develop demand	Developmental marketing
IV Faltering demand	Revitalize demand	Remarketing
V Irregular demand	Synchronize demand	Synchromarketing
VI Full demand	Maintain demand	Maintenance marketing
VII Overfull demand	Reduce demand	Demarketing
VIII Unwholesome demand	Destroy demand	Countermarketing

unwholesome either for the consumer or the company, and someone may undertake steps to destroy demand by countermarketing.

Thus the task of marketing management is not simply to build demand but rather to regulate the level, timing, and character of demand for the organization's products in terms of its objectives at the time. This view applies to all organizations. In the discussion that follows, each of the basic marketing tasks is developed and illustrated with examples drawn from profit and nonprofit organizations.

NEGATIVE DEMAND

Negative demand might be defined as *a state in which all or most of the important segment of the potential market dislike the product and in fact might conceivably pay a price to avoid it.* Negative demand is worse than no demand. In the case of no demand, the potential market has no particular feelings about the product one way or another. In the case of negative demand, they actively dislike the product and take steps to avoid it.

Negative demand, far from being a rare condition, applies to a rather large number of products and services. Vegetarians feel negative demand for meats of all kinds. Some Jews and Arabs feel negative demand for pork. Many Americans feel negative demand for kidneys and sweetbreads. People have a negative demand for vaccinations, dental work, vasectomies, and gall bladder operations. A large number of travelers have a negative demand for air travel, and many others have a negative demand for rail travel. Places such as the North Pole and desert wastelands are in negative demand by travelers. Atheism, ex-convicts, military service, and even work are in negative demand by various groups.

The challenge of negative demand to marketing management, especially in the face of a positive supply, is to develop a plan that will cause demand to rise from negative to positive and eventually equal the positive supply level. We call this marketing task that of *conversional marketing.* Conversional marketing is one of the two most difficult marketing tasks a marketer might face (the other is countermarketing). The marketer faces a market that dislikes the object. His chief task is to analyze the sources of the market's resistance; whether they lie largely in the area of *beliefs* about the object, in the *values* touched upon by the object, in the raw *feelings* engendered by the object, or in the *cost* of acquiring the object. If the beliefs are misfounded, they can be clarified through a communication program. If the person's values militate against the object, the object can be put in the framework of other possible values that are positive for the person. If negative feelings are aroused, they may be modifiable through group processes[1] or behavioral therapy.[2] If the costs of acquisition are too high, the marketer can take steps to bring down the real costs. The marketer will want to consider the cost of reducing resistance and whether some other marketing opportunity might be more attractive and less difficult.

NO DEMAND

There is a whole range of objects and services for which there is no demand. Instead of people having negative or positive feelings about the object, they are indifferent or uninterested. *No demand* is *a state in which all or important segments of a potential market are uninterested or indifferent to a particular object.*

Three different categories of objects are characterized by no demand. First, there are

[1]A classic discussion of alternative methods of trying to modify people's feelings is found in Kurt Lewin, "Group Decision and Social Change," in *Readings in Social Psychology,* Theodore M. Newcomb and Eugene L. Hartley, eds. (New York: Holt, Rinehart and Winston, Inc., 1952).

[2]New behavioral therapies such as implosive therapy and systematic desensitization are discussed in Perry London, *Behavioral Control* (New York: Harper and Row, 1969).

those familiar objects that are perceived as having no value. Examples would be urban junk such as disposable coke bottles, old barbed wire, and political buttons right after an election. Second, there are those familiar objects that are recognized to have value but not in the particular market. Examples would include boats in areas not near any water, snowmobiles in areas where it never snows, and burglar alarms in areas where there is no crime. Third, there are those unfamiliar objects which are innovated and face a situation of no demand because the relevant market has no knowledge of the object. Examples include trinkets of all kinds that people might buy if exposed to but do not normally think about or desire.

The task of converting no demand into positive demand is called *stimulational marketing.* Stimulational marketing is a tough task because the marketer does not even start with a semblance of latent demand for the object. He can proceed in three ways. One is to try to connect the object with some existing need in the marketplace. Thus antique dealers can attempt to stimulate interest in old barbed wire on the part of those who have a general need to collect things. The second is to alter the environment so that the object becomes valued in that environment. Thus sellers of motor boats can attempt to stimulate interest in boats in a lakeless community by building an artificial lake. The third is to distribute information or the object itself in more places in the hope that people's lack of demand is really only a lack of exposure.

Stimulational marketing has drawn considerable attack from social critics. Since the consumer had no demand (not even latent demand), the marketer has intruded into his life as a manipulator, a propagandist, an exploiter. The target group had no interest in the object until the marketer, using the whole apparatus of modern marketing, "seduced" or "bamboozled" the consumer into a purchase.

Two things, however, must be said in defense of stimulational marketing. The buyer does not buy because he is forced or coerced by the seller. He buys because he sees the transaction as creating more value for him than avoiding it. The object, while he did not conceive of it on his own, is now seen as related to some need which he does have. The basic need is not manufactured by the marketer. At most, it is stimulated, activated, given a direction and object for expression. Social critics would also have to hold that it is not right for organizations to attempt to activate people's needs.

This nonintervention thesis becomes more difficult in light of the positive benefits that stimulational marketing can confer. Stimulational marketing applies to efforts to get villagers in developing nations to take immunization shots to protect them from dreadful diseases; farmers to adopt better means of farming; mothers to improve their child-rearing practices; and teenagers to improve their nutritional habits. Stimulational marketing is also responsible for accelerating the adoption of many material inventions for which there was no initial market interest. Altogether, a blanket condemnation of stimulational marketing would consign many positive developments, along with the negative ones, to a state of limbo.

LATENT DEMAND

A state of *latent demand* exists *when a substantial number of people share a strong need for something which does not exist in the form of an actual product.* The latent demand represents an opportunity for the marketing innovator to develop the product that people have been wanting.

Examples of products and services in latent demand abound. A great number of cigarette smokers would like a good-tasting cigarette that does not yield nicotine and tars damaging to health. Such a product breakthrough would be an instant success, just as the first filter-tip cigarette won a sizeable share of the market. Many people would like a car that promised substantially more safety and substantially less pollution than existing cars. There is a strong latent demand for fast city roads, efficient trains, uncrowded national parks, unpolluted major cities, safe streets, and good television programs. When such products are finally developed and properly marketed, their market is assured.

The latent demand situation might seem not so much a problem in demand management as one in supply management. Yet it is thoroughly a marketing problem because the latent need must be recognized, the right product developed, the right price chosen, the right channels of distribution put together, and adequate and convincing product information disseminated. Such products as electric dishwashers and air conditioners were adopted slowly at first because people were not convinced that these products could do the job or were worth the price.

The process for effectively converting latent demand into actual demand is that of *developmental marketing*. The marketer must be an expert in identifying the prospects for the product who have the strongest latent demand and in coordinating all the marketing functions so as to develop the market in an orderly way.

In contrast to the substantial social criticism directed at stimulational marketing, most observers feel that developmental marketing is not only natural but highly desirable from a social point of view. Latent demand is the situation for which "the marketing concept" is most appropriate. It is not a question of creating desire but rather of finding it and serving it. The buyers and sellers have complementary interests. There is, however, one important qualification that has come to the surface in recent years. The sheer existence of a personal need may not be sufficient to justify its being served and satisfied. There are needs that people have which, if satisfied, are harmful to others or themselves through the spill-over effects of consumption. Satisfying those *needs* may hurt a lot of people's *interests*. Thus it is no longer sufficient for a developmental marketer to say that his new product is justified because there is a real need for it. He may have to show that the need is salutary and the product will not lead to more social harm than private good.

FALTERING DEMAND

All kinds of products, services, places, organizations, and ideas eventually experience declining or *faltering demand. Faltering demand* is *a state in which the demand for a product is less than its former level and where further decline is expected in the absence of remedial efforts to revise the target market, product, and/or marketing effort.*

For example, the natural fur industry is in deep trouble today as demand declines in the face of the trend toward more casual living, the emergence of artificial furs, and the attacks of ecologists who see the fur industry as preying on endangered species. Railway travel has been a service in steady decline for a number of years, and it is badly in need of imaginative remarketing. Many grand hotels have seen their clientele thin out in the face of competition from bright new hotels with the most modern, though somewhat aseptic, facilities. The downtown areas of many large cities are in need of remarketing. Many popular entertainers and political candidates lose their following and badly need remarketing.

The challenge of faltering demand is revitalization, and the marketing task involved is *remarketing*. Remarketing is based on the premise that it is possible in many cases to start a new life cycle for a declining product. Remarketing is the search for new marketing propositions for relating the product to its potential market.

Remarketing calls for a thorough reconsideration of the *target market, product features*, and *current marketing program*. The question of the appropriate *target market* is faced, for example, by a grand old hotel in Southern California whose clientele was formerly aristocratic and is now moving toward the comfortable middle class. Still, the hotel continues to try to attract its old clientele and to base its services and prices on this target market—an approach which neither attracts them back nor succeeds in building up the new clientele to its true potential.

The task of revising *product features* is faced by AMTRAK, the new semi-public corporation charged with the responsibility for revitalizing railway passenger travel. AMTRAK's initial temptation was to carry on a massive advertising campaign to get people to try the trains again. However, this would have been fatal because it would have shown people how really bad trains and train service have become. It is a marketing axiom that the fastest way to kill a bad product is to advertise it. This accelerates the rate of trial and the rate of negative word-of-mouth which finally puts the death knell on the product. AMTRAK wisely decided that mass advertising should come *after* product improvement. A sharp distinction must be drawn between *cosmetic marketing,* which tries to advertise a new image without revising the product, and *remarketing*, which calls for a thorough reconsideration and revision of all aspects of the product and market that may affect sales.

The task of overhauling the *marketing program* was faced by American Motors, whose auto sales sank to only three percent of the U.S. car market in 1967. A new management team undertook a major effort to overhaul the field marketing and sales organization and to prune out hundreds of low volume dealers. They also took a maverick approach to car warranties, product design, and advertising. These and other remarketing steps have reversed the decline in their sales.

Remarketing is similar to the physician's job of curing a sick patient. It calls for good diagnosis and a long-term plan to build up the patient's health. The marketing consultant who is good and experienced at remarketing is usually worth his fees because the organization has so much unshiftable capital tied up in the flagging business. In some ways, however, it might be charged that the skilled remarketer serves to slow down progress by trying to preserve the weaker species in the face of stronger competitors. There is some truth to this in that the product in faltering demand would probably disappear or stagnate in the absence of creative marketing respiration. In some situations, perhaps the organization simply should take steps to adjust the supply downward to match the demand. On the other hand, when the faltering demand is due to poor marketing premises and not to natural forces, able remarketing can make a major contribution to saving the organization's assets.

IRREGULAR DEMAND

Very often an organization might be satisfied with the average level of demand but quite unsatisfied with its temporal pattern. Some seasons are marked by demand surging far beyond the supply capacity of the organization, and other seasons are marked by a wasteful underutilization of the organization's supply capacity. *Irregular demand* is defined as *a state in which the current timing pattern of demand is marked by seasonal or volatile fluctuations that depart from the timing pattern of supply.*

Many examples of irregular demand can be cited. In mass transit, much of the equipment is idle during the off-hours and in insufficient supply during the peak hours. Hotels in Miami Beach are insufficiently booked during the off-seasons and overbooked during the peak seasons. Museums are undervisited during the week days and terribly overcrowded during the weekends. Hospital operating facilities are overbooked at the beginning of the week and under-utilized toward the end of the week to meet physician preferences.

A less common version of the irregular demand situation is where supply is also variable and in fact fluctuates in a perverse way in relation to demand. Imagine a kind of fruit which ripened in winter but which people yearned for in summer; or an animal species in which the mating instinct of the male peaked when the mating instinct of the female was at its nadir. Legal aid is more available to the poor in the summer (because of law students on vacations) but more in demand in the winter. Where demand and supply are both variable and move in opposite directions, the marketer has the option to attempt to (1) alter the supply pattern to fit the demand pattern, (2) alter the demand pattern to fit the natural supply pattern, or (3) alter both to some degree.

The marketing task of trying to resolve irregular demand is called *synchromarketing* because the effort is to bring the movements of demand and supply into better synchronization. Many marketing steps can be taken to alter the pattern of demand. For example, the marketer may promote new uses and desires for the product in the off-season, as can be seen in Kodak's efforts to show camera users that picture taking is fun on many occasions besides Christmas time and summer vacation. Or the marketer can charge a higher price in the peak season and a lower price in the off-season. This strategy is used in the sale of seasonal items such as air conditioners, boats, and ski equipment. Or the marketer can advertise more heavily in the off-season than in the peak season, although this is still not a common practice. In some cases, the pattern of demand will be readily reshaped through simple switches in incentives or promotion; in other cases, the reshaping may be achieved only after years of patient effort to alter habits and desires, if at all.

FULL DEMAND

The most desirable situation that a seller can face is that of full demand. *Full demand* is *a state in which the current level and timing of demand is equal to the desired level and timing of demand.* Various products and services achieve this condition from time to time. When this state is achieved, however, it is not a time for resting on one's laurels and doing simply automatic marketing. Market demand is subject to two erosive forces that might suddenly or gradually disrupt the equilibrium between demand and supply. One force is changing needs and tastes in the marketplace. The demand for barber services, engineering educations, and mass magazines have all undergone major declines because of changing market preferences. The other force is active competition. A condition of full demand is a signal inviting competitive attack. When a new product is doing well, new suppliers quickly move in and attempt to attract away some of the demand.

Thus the task of the marketer in the face of full demand is to maintain it. His job is *maintenance marketing.* This is essentially the task of the product manager whose product is highly successful. The task is not as challenging as other marketing tasks, such as conversional marketing or remarketing, in which creative new thinking must be given to the future of the product. However, maintenance marketing does call for maintaining efficiency in the carrying out of day-to-day marketing activities and eternal vigilance in monitoring possible new forces threatening demand erosion. The maintenance marketer is primarily concerned with tactical issues such as keeping the price right, keeping the sales force and dealers motivated, and keeping tight control over costs.

OVERFULL DEMAND

Sometimes the demand for a product substantially begins to outpace the supply. Known as *overfull demand,* it is defined as *a state in which demand exceeds the level at which the marketer feels able or motivated to supply it.* It is essentially the reverse of the situation described earlier as faltering demand.

The task of reducing overfull demand is

called *demarketing.*[3] More formally, *demarketing deals with attempts to discourage customers in general or a certain class of customers in particular on either a temporary or permanent basis.*

There are two major types of demarketing situations: general demarketing and selective demarketing. *General demarketing* is undertaken by a seller when he wants to discourage overall demand for his product. This can arise for two quite different reasons. First, he may have a *temporary shortage* of goods and want to get buyers to reduce their orders. This situation was faced by Eastman Kodak when it introduced its Instamatic camera in the early 1960s and faced runaway demand; by Wilkinson Sword in the early 1960s when dealers besieged it for the new stainless steel blade; and by Anheuser-Busch in the late 1960s when it could not produce enough beer to satisfy demand. Second, the seller's product may suffer from *chronic overpopularity,* and he may want to discourage permanently some demand rather than increase the size of his plant. This situation is faced by some small restaurants that suddenly are "discovered" but the owners do not want to expand; by the John F. Kennedy Center of the Arts in Washington which draws larger crowds than it can handle resulting in vandalism, damage to the property, and high cleaning bills; by certain tourist places, such as Hawaii, where the number of tourists has become excessive in terms of the objective of achieving a restful vacation; and by the Golden Gate Bridge in San Francisco, where authorities are urging motorists to reduce their use of the bridge. The Chinese mainland is engaged today in demarketing pork, a meat product which is historically more popular than beef in China but is in chronically short supply. U.S. electric power companies are demarketing certain uses of electricity because of the growing shortage of power generation facilities. Several of the far Western states are actively demarketing themselves as places to live because they are becoming overcrowded.

[3]See Philip Kotler and Sidney J. Levy, "Demarketing, Yes, Demarketing," *Harvard Business Review,* Vol. 49 (November–December 1971), pp. 74–80.

Selective demarketing occurs when an organization does not which to reduce everyone's demand but rather the demand coming from certain segments of the market. These segments or customer classes may be considered relatively unprofitable in themselves or undesirable in terms of their impact on other values segments of the market. The seller may not be free to refuse sales outright, either as a matter of law or of public opinion, so he searches for other means to discourage demand from the unwanted customers.

Many examples could be cited. A luxury hotel which primarily caters to middle-aged, conservative tourists resorts to selective means to discourage young jet-setters. A renowned university wants to discourage marginal applicants because of all the paper work and the wish to avoid rejecting so many applicants and creating bad feelings. A prepaid medical group practice wants to discourage its hypochondriac patients from running to them with every minor ailment. A police department wants to discourage nuisance calls so that its limited resources can be devoted to major crime prevention.

Demarketing largely calls for marketing in reverse. Instead of encouraging customers, it calls for the art of discouraging them. Prices may be raised, and product quality, service, promotion, and convenience reduced. The demarketer must have a thick skin because he is not going to be popular with certain groups. Some of the steps will appear unfair ways to ration a product. Some of the groups who are discriminated against may have just cause for complaint. Demarketing may be highly justified in some situations and ethically dubious in others.

UNWHOLESOME DEMAND

There are many products for which the demand may be judged unwholesome from the viewpoint of the consumer's welfare, the public's welfare, or the supplier's welfare. *Unwholesome demand* is *a state in which any positive level of demand is felt to be excessive because of undesirable qualities associated with the product.*

The task of trying to destroy the demand for something is called *countermarketing* or *unselling*. Whereas demarketing tries to reduce the demand without impugning the product itself, countermarketing is an attempt to designate the product as intrinsically unwholesome. The product in question may be the organization's own product which it wishes to phase out, a competitor's product, or a third party's product which is regarded as socially undesirable.

Classic examples of unselling efforts have revolved around the so-called "vice" products: alcohol, cigarettes, and hard drugs. Various temperance groups mounted such an intense campaign that they succeeded in gaining the passage of the 18th Amendment banning the manufacture of alcoholic beverages. Antismoking groups managed to put enough pressure on the Surgeon General's office to get a law passed requiring cigarette manufacturers to add to each package the statement: "Warning: The Surgeon General Has Determined That Cigarette Smoking Is Dangerous To Your Health," They also sponsored many effective television commercials aimed at "unselling" the smoker. Later, they managed to get a law passed prohibiting cigarette advertising on television. Antidrug crusaders have sponsored advertising aimed at unselling the youth on the idea of drug usage.

Unselling appears in other contexts as well. Peace groups for years tried to unsell the Vietnam War. Population control groups have been trying to unsell the idea of large families. Nutrition groups have been trying to unsell the idea of eating pleasing but nutritionally poor foods. Environmental groups have been trying to unsell the idea of being careless with the environment as if it were inexhaustible. Many manufacturers engage in campaigns to unsell competitor products or brands, such as a natural gas company trying to unsell electric heating or a compact car manufacturer trying to unsell large, gas-eating automobiles.

Unselling is the effort to accomplish the opposite of innovation. Whereas innovation is largely the attempt to add new things to the cultural inventory, unselling is the attempt to eliminate cultural artifacts or habits. It is an attempt to bring about the discontinuance of something. Whereas innovation usually ends with the act of adoption, unselling seeks to produce the act of disadoption. In the perspective of innovation theory, unselling may be called the problem of *deinnovation.* Many of the concepts in innovation theory might be usable in reverse. The countermarketer attempts to identify the varying characteristics of the early, late, and laggard disadopters so that unselling effort can be aimed at them in this order. He also considers the characteristics of the product that will tend to facilitate unselling, such as relative disadvantage, incompatibility, complexity, indivisibility, and incommunicability.

At the same time, every effort to unsell something may also be viewed as an effort to sell something else. Those who attempt to unsell cigarette smoking are attempting to sell health; those who attempt to unsell large families are trying to sell small families; those who attempt to unsell the competitor's product are trying to increase the sales of their own product. In fact, it is usually easier to sell something else. For example, instead of trying to unsell young people on drugs, the marketer can try to sell them on another way of achieving whatever they are seeking through drugs.

Efforts to turn off the demand for something can profitably draw on certain concepts and theories in psychology. In general, the effort is largely one of deconditioning or habit extinction theory. Instead of trying to build up a taste for something, the marketer is trying to break down a taste for something. Learning and reinforcement theory are suggestive in this connection. The marketer is trying to associate disgust, fear, disagreeableness, or shame with the use of the unwholesome object. He is trying to arouse unpleasant feelings in the potential or actual users of the product.

In addition to these psychological steps, the marketer also attempts to load the other marketing variables against the use of the product. He tries to increase the real or perceived price. He tries to reduce the product's availability through reducing or destroying channels of distribution. He tries to find an alternative product which is wholesome and which can be substituted for the existing product.

Clearly unselling is one of the most difficult and challenging marketing tasks. Unselling is an attempt to intervene in the lives and tastes of others. Unselling campaigns often backfire, as witness the popularity of X-rated movies and drugs whose evils are publicized. In its defense, however, two things must be said. First, unselling relies on exchange and communication approaches to bring about legal and/or public opinion changes. It is an alternative to violent social action. Second, unselling has as much social justification in a democracy as does selling. To set up a double standard where selling—say of alcohol and cigarettes—is allowable but unselling by those who object is not allowable would compromise the rights of free speech and orderly legislative due process.

SUMMARY

The marketer is a professional whose basic interest and skill lies in regulating the level, timing, and character of demand for a product, service, place, or idea. He faces up to eight different types of demand situations and plans accordingly. If demand is negative, it must be disabused (conversional marketing); if nonexistent, it must be created (stimulational marketing); if latent, it must be developed (developmental marketing); if faltering, it must be revitalized (remarketing); if irregular, it must be synchronized (synchromarketing); if full, it must be maintained (maintenance marketing); if overfull, it must be reduced (demarketing); and finally, if unwholesome, it must be destroyed (countermarketing). Each demand situation calls for a particular set of psychological concepts and marketing strategies and may give rise to task specialization. Managerial marketing, rather than a singular effort to build or maintain sales, is a complex game with many scripts.

The author wishes to thank the many people who responded to preliminary presentations of this paper, including Professor Sidney J. Levy (Northwestern University), who suggested discussing irregular demand, and Ralph Gallay (New York University), who suggested discussing negative demand.

Part Two

Organizing the Marketing Function

The ways in which a company is organized to accomplish its marketing tasks reflect how it seeks to accommodate the needs of its markets. The manner of organization also reflects the attitudes of company executives toward the planning process, and how the marketing executives should serve as planning agents.

In turn, this points up the firm's allocation plans for both products and markets. In fact, more and more firms are basing their organizational functions on product/market relationships.

An organizational system is required that generates specific plans for each such relationship—plans which will provide for the most efficient utilization of the firm's resources. The difficulties of optimizing across both products and markets are, of course, tremendous; and any organizational system will fall short in one respect or another. However, ways of organizing which yield acceptable results have been developed.

Articles in this section deal with the changing role of the product manager, plans for reorganizing a company around its marketing, and the development of a system for managing diversity in the firm.

3

The Changing Role of the Product Manager in Consumer Goods Companies

Victor P. Buell

A recent study examines the current status of the product manager's role, the changes it has undergone, implications for its future. Considerable attention is paid to the controversy surrounding the degree of control the product manager exercises over advertising.

What the proper role of the product or brand manager should be remains a troublesome question for the managements of consumer goods companies. It is particularly a problem for packaged goods producers, who are the most frequent users of this organizational device.

The role of the product manager has undergone several changes since the product management system was first introduced. That these changes have not produced entirely satisfactory results is evident in the continuing public debate on this topic. Titles of selected articles and papers illustrate the situation:

The Product Manager System Is In Trouble[1]

Has the Product Manager Failed? Or the Folly of Imitation[2]

Product Management—Vision Unfulfilled[3]

Brand Manager VS Creative Man: The Clash of Two Cultures[4]

Brand Manager VS Advertising Director—Must One of Them Go?[5]

Product Managers and Advertising—A Study of Conflict, Inexperience and Opportunity.[6]

The purpose of this article is to review the changes that have occurred in the product management form of organization since its introduction, to explore the reasons behind the continuing controversy, and to examine current changes in management thinking and their implications for the future. To this end, the author uses material from his recent study of several leading consumer goods manufacturers and major advertising agencies.

THE STUDY: BACKGROUND AND APPROACH

Much of the controversy has centered on the degree of control the product manager exercises over advertising. Under a grant from the Association of National Advertisers (ANA), the author studied the advertising decision-making process in companies with major advertising expenditures.[7] Although its overall purpose was broader, the study provided the

[1]Stephens W. Dietz, *Advertising Age,* June 2, 1969, pp. 43–44.

[2]*Sales Management,* January 1, 1967, pp. 27–29.

[3]David J. Luck and Theodore Nowak, *Harvard Business Review,* Vol. 43 (May–June 1965), p. 143.

[4]Ralph Leezenbaum, *Marketing Communications,* April 1970, pp. 40–43.

[5]*Advertising Age,* January 27, 1969, p. 53.

[6]James F. Pomeroy, paper presented to the Association of National Advertisers Workshop on Development and Approval of Creative Advertising, New York, April 2, 1969.

[7]Victor P. Buell, *Changing Practices in Advertising Decision-Making and Control* (New York: Association of National Advertisers, 1973).

Reprinted from *Journal of Marketing,* vol. 39, pp. 3–11, American Marketing Association, July 1975. At the time of writing, the author was associate professor of marketing, School of Business Administration, University of Massachusetts.

opportunity to explore management attitudes toward product management and to gather information on the restructuring this system currently is undergoing.

In-depth interviews were held during the summer and fall of 1972 with 63 executives in 20 leading companies which represented ten consumer industry classifications plus one miscellaneous category. Extensive interviews were also held with 23 executives in ten major advertising agencies.

Sixteen of the companies produced packaged goods primarily and four produced consumer durables primarily. Product management was the predominant form of marketing organization in fifteen of the companies; a functional form predominated in five. Some of the companies used one organizational form in some divisions and the other form in other divisions.

Survey Sample

The combined domestic sales of the 20 companies surveyed exceeded $60 billion, and their combined advertising expenditures were over $1.5 billion. Seventeen were among the 50 largest advertisers and 10 ranked among the top 20. The primary industry classifications of the consumer packaged goods companies included food; drugs and cosmetics; soaps, cleansers, and allied products; soft drinks; tobacco; paper; liquor; and one miscellaneous category. The consumer durable goods companies fell under the industry classifications of electric appliances, automobiles, and building products.

Participant companies were selected with the assistance of the Management Policy Committee of the Association of National Advertisers. Selection criteria included: (1) company commitment to a large advertising budget, (2) recognized leadership position in the company's industry, (3) management willingness to participate, and (4) multiple industry representation. Preference was given to companies that had extensive experience with product managers. Advertising agencies were selected from among leading agencies that served one or more of the 20 manufacturing companies. To encourage participation and frank discussion, participants were assured that neither companies nor individuals would be identified in the report.

Thirty-one corporate executives were interviewed, including chairmen, presidents, executive and group vice-presidents, and staff vice-presidents. Positions occupied by the 32 divisional executives interviewed included presidents, marketing vice-presidents, directors of marketing or advertising, directors of brand management, and group product managers.

The 10 advertising agencies in the study were among the nation's 20 largest and had combined U.S. billings in excess of $2 billion. Agency executives interviewed included chairmen, presidents, executive and senior vice-presidents, and vice-presidents.

Data Collection Method

All interviews were conducted by the author. Interviews were open-ended and ranged in length from one to three hours. Policies, procedures, and files were made freely available. Interviews with agency executives provided cross-checks on information developed with their clients.

The purpose of the study was to gain understanding of the reasons behind advertising and marketing management practices rather than duplicate the quantitative data developed by the more commonly used mail questionnaire. Because of the qualitative nature of the study, findings are reported primarily as the author's interpretations of prevailing management practices, attitudes, and intentions rather than in the form of statistical summaries. The findings have been reported to the participating executives and have been discussed in depth with several of them.

While the study provides the principal data source for this article, conclusions are based also on interviews with executives during other research projects by the author, reviews of product management literature, and recent reports of mail surveys.

Because of the selective sample, the findings are not representative of all companies. The findings are important in that they represent managerial viewpoints in consumer goods companies with leadership positions, most of whom employ large numbers of product managers.

HISTORICAL DEVELOPMENTS

The product management system, although introduced nearly 50 years ago, did not come into general use until the 1950s. The Association of National Advertisers, in a recent study among its members, found that the following percentages of participating companies used product managers: packaged goods—85% (93% of those with annual advertising expenditures exceeding $10 million); other consumer goods—34%; industrial goods—55%.[8]

Product management is a response to the organizational problem of providing sufficient management attention to individual products and brands when there are too many for any one executive to coordinate effectively all of the aspects of the marketing mix. Companies, or divisions of companies, with a limited line of products normally follow a functional plan of organization wherein departments such as sales, advertising and sales promotion, marketing research, product planning, and customer service report to a common marketing executive. When shifting from this purely functional organization, product managers are added to assist the chief marketing executive by assuming the planning and coordination for individual products or product lines.

Although the product manager has made possible greater management concentration by product, the position also has created new problems. Responsibility often has been assigned to the product manager for achievement of goals such as sales volume, share of market, and even profit in some cases; yet the product manager has no line authority over the functional departments that execute his plans.

Shift of Advertising Responsibility to the Product Manager

A key change in the original concept was made when companies shifted the management of advertising from the advertising manager to the product manager. In leading packaged goods companies that currently use product managers, one rarely finds an advertising department on the organization chart. If one is there, it is usually at the group or corporate level, where it provides services common to several divisions, such as media planning and coordinating media purchases.

The reasons for phasing out the separate advertising function were: (a) to reduce costs, which rose as the advertising department expanded to manage the advertising for increasing numbers of products and brands; and (b) to give the product manager more control over execution of a major marketing function. Such a move was possible because the advertising agency was available to develop and place advertising.

Figures 1 and 2 provide examples of typical functional and product management organizations. While details may vary from company to company, these charts reflect the main differences that exist between the two organi-

[8] *Current Advertising Practices: Opinions as to Future Trends* (New York: Association of National Advertisers, 1974).

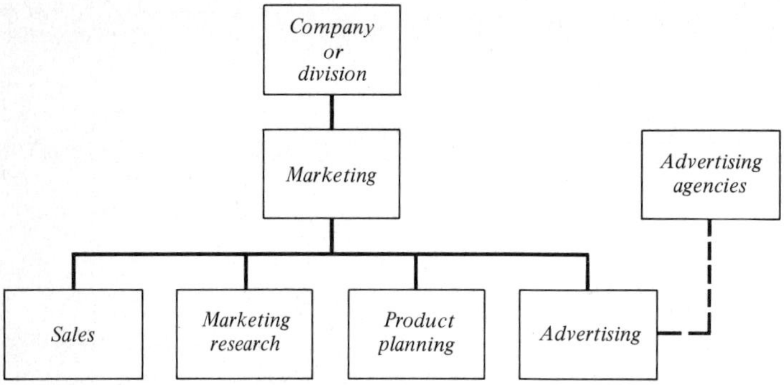

Figure 1 Functional marketing organization.

zational forms in the companies studied by the author.

Companies Assume the Planning Function

Concurrent with the growth of the product management function, companies began to assume the marketing planning and service functions—with the exception of creative and media—that had been performed for them by their advertising agencies.

As marketing grew in sophistication during the 1950s, much of the know-how was centered in the agencies. Gradually, however, companies expanded their own supporting service functions and the responsibility for initiating marketing plans became a key function of the product manager. This change has been made with little criticism. Agencies have accepted the idea that marketing planning should originate within the company, and they are aware of the growing effectiveness of the product manager as a planner.

Increases in Intervening Management Levels

As companies grow, the product manager becomes further removed from the real decision–making levels of management. When products were fewer in number product managers reported directly to higher–level executives, who had the authority to make broad decisions and implement programs. As product lines proliferated, and the numbers of product managers grew correspondingly, intervening levels of supervision became neces-

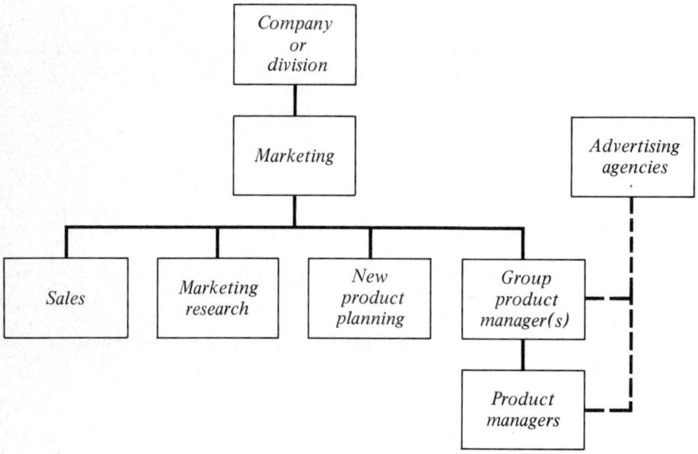

Figure 2 Product management organization.

sary. In large companies today, product managers may be anywhere from two to four levels below the executive who has the real decision–making authority and the clout to see that plans are carried out.

Due to rapid growth, companies also have shifted to filling product manager positions with younger, less experienced people. This relative inexperience, plus separation from the key decision maker, has increased management concern over the degree of authority that should be delegated to the product manager. These concerns are particularly strong with respect to advertising because of the magnitude of advertising costs and the importance of advertising to product success.

Continued Use of Functional Organization

The ANA study of its members found that 34% of the participating larger consumer durable goods companies used product managers, as compared with 85% of the packaged goods companies. Why do some companies stay with the functional form?

Pearson and Wilson believe there may be good reasons why a company should prefer the functional organization.[9] In fact, they think some companies have made a mistake in switching to product management before it was really necessary. They maintain that companies with a line of similar products, with one dominant product line, or with several large product lines (sufficient to support divisionalization) might be better off avoiding product management. It was not long after Pearson left McKinsey & Co. to become president of PepsiCo that the Pepsi-Cola division did away with product managers.[10] This division sells a related line of soft drinks with one dominant product—Pepsi-Cola.

Three of the consumer durable goods companies interviewed by the author had functional marketing setups. The major appliance group of an electrical company and the major division of an automotive manufacturer each had relatively few products although they accounted for large dollar sales. Both companies preferred to use advertising to build the overall brand name in addition to promoting individual products; they felt they could achieve better control through the functional advertising manager. The third company, a manufacturer of building products, organized its product divisions by markets and channels. Historically, the corporate advertising department has supervised the development of advertising and sales promotion for the various market sales managers, who appear to prefer this arrangement.

While there are good reasons why many companies do not use product management, there appears to be no significant defection by current users, as was implied in the article that featured the PepsiCo story.[11] Of the 211 companies surveyed by the ANA, 5% had adopted product management during the preceding three years, as compared with 1% who had abandoned it.[12] Clewett and Stasch, in a survey of 160 product managers and other marketing executives, found less than 1% who felt that product management was likely to be discontinued in their divisions.[13] In the author's study, none of the fifteen companies that used product management planned to change.

No doubt some companies will shift from product management from time to time for sound organizational reasons or out of sheer frustration. But there is no evidence of a trend

[9]Andrall E. Pearson and Thomas W. Wilson, Jr., *Making Your Marketing Organization Work* (New York: Association of National Advertisers, 1967).

[10]"The Brand Manager: No Longer King," *Business Week*, June 9, 1973, pp. 58–66.

[11]Same reference as footnote 10.

[12]Same reference as footnote 8.

[13]Richard M. Clewett and Stanley F. Stasch, "Product Managers in Consumer Packaged Goods Companies" (Working paper, Northwestern University Graduate School of Management, March 1974).

in this direction. If a trend exists it would appear to be in the direction of continued adoption of product management.

CURRENT MANAGEMENT ATTITUDES

Executives interviewed by the author were concerned about the product management system but were committed to making it work better. Their attitudes appeared to be changing with respect to the question of the product manager's responsibility and authority and his role in advertising. They also expressed concern over the scarcity of advertising specialists within their companies.

Disaffection with the "Little President" Concept

Almost all of the executives interviewed recognized that the earlier concept of the product manager as a "little president" or "little general manager," with profit responsibility, was unrealistic. As the manager of a paper products company said:

> We've gotten away from the concept of the guy who runs his own little company. We want our product managers to be profit conscious, but what we're really talking about is sales volume.

Remnants of the concept persist, however, as illustrated by excerpts from two recruiting brochures. The brochure of a household products company states:

> The Product Manager has responsibility for his brand. He is not only responsible for its management, he is accountable for its overall performance. . . . The Product Manager is not just a marketing manager, but in many respects a general manager of a good size business.

When this statement was pointed out to an executive of this company the author was told that it no longer represents management opinion; that, in fact, the company's product managers have no decision-making authority.

The brochure of a food company, after explaining the product manager's role in developing objectives and strategies, says: "The Product Manager is responsible for the execution and performance of the brands entrusted to him."

In describing the position, the marketing director of another food company probably came closest to prevailing management attitudes when he avoided mentioning responsibility for execution or performance:

> Our product manager's job is planning—objectives and strategy—monitoring progress, coordinating budget development and control, and working with other departments—Home Economics and Manufacturing, for example—on product cost and quality.

Clarifying the Advertising Role

Packaged goods executives pretty much agree that the typical product manager has insufficient training, experience, or skill to be entrusted with important creative decisions. They tend to share the view of the agency vice-president who told the author: "Advertising is too important a decision to be left in the hands of a product manager. His role should be planning and coordination—not advertising approval."

Agency critics complain that because of his inexperience the product manager is too cautious and too meticulous in judging creative work; he delays the development process and causes dilution of creative copy by requiring repeated rework; and, to compensate for his insecurity, he relies too heavily on copy testing, which normally produces inconclusive data. Company executives agree. All want the product manager involved in advertising decision making, but they are developing procedures that get agency recommendations up the line to the final decision maker as quickly as possible. Agencies, it should be noted, are reassigning responsibility for client contact to higher management levels to correspond with the client management levels making advertising decisions.

Current top management attitudes are reflected in the following comments. The president of a personal products company said:

> I want the best people in a profit center working on, and approving, marketing decisions. We try to set the atmosphere and tone so that our brand manager feels important, yet knows that advertising is too important to be decided at the bottom level.

The executive vice-president of a drug products company explained his company's position this way:

> We give much authority to the product manager other than the copy side—sales promotion, for example. But we let him know he is not to be the final authority on advertising. We say the person who knows the most about advertising should make the ultimate decision.

Companies, however, do make a distinction between *major* and *minor* advertising decisions. Figure 3 indicates the differences in executive levels that deal with decisions of varying importance. Major decisions may include almost anything to do with an important product or, for less important products, they may involve only significant matters, such as a change in strategy. The author's research showed that advertising decisions considered to be major were made most frequently at the division manager or division marketing manager levels, with some going to the corporate level. None of the companies believed *major* creative-type advertising decisions were made

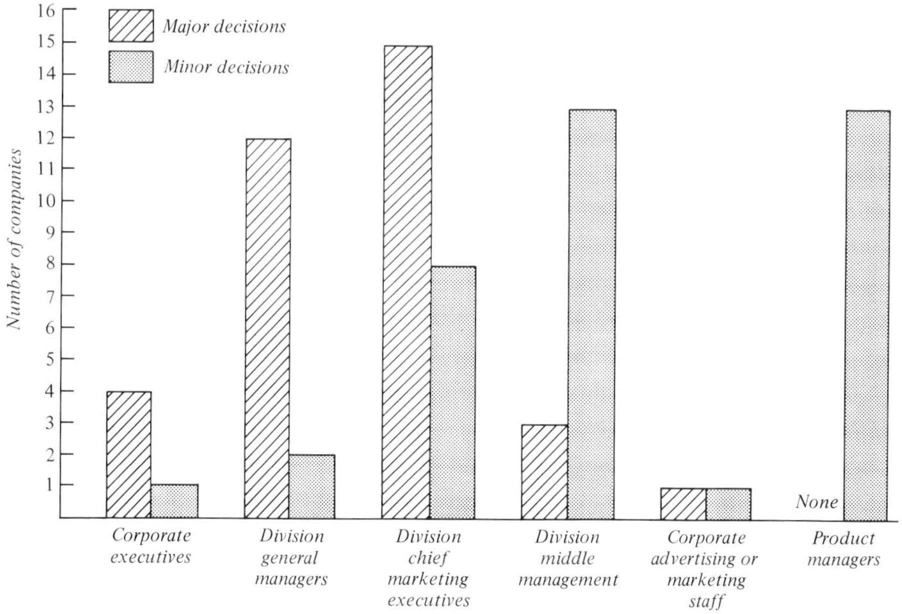

Figure 3 Where advertising companies say creative decisions are made. *Note:* The figure represented by the bars total more than the number of companies because decisions may be made jointly by two or more executives, decisions may be made by one executive in the absence of another, or the decision level may vary by degree of importance within the Major or Minor categories. [*Source:* Adapted from Victor P. Buell, *Changing Practices in Advertising Decision-Making and Control* (New York: Association of National Advertisers, 1973), p. 49.]

by the product manager. Decisions considered minor, on the other hand, most frequently were made at the product manager and division middle management (group product manager) levels. Understanding this distinction may help to clarify the sometimes confusing results of those mail surveys that indicate that the product manager makes advertising decisions: he does make some decisions, but usually not the major ones.

Considering the past sharp criticisms by agency executives it is worth noting that these complaints have been directed primarily at the product manager's role in the advertising approval process. In contrast, they agree with his role as the authoritative source of information and as marketing planner. An agency vice-president who works with both functional and product management organizations volunteered this comment:

> I would rather work with a product manager than with an advertising manager. The product manager has all the information, although he may be unaware of the broader strategies. But in the vertical organization, each person has only a part of the information we require.

Need for the Advertising Specialist

After several years of operating without advertising departments, many company executives now wonder whether they have any real advertising expertise left in-house. The normal promotion route provides added experience in judging advertising, and one learns from his mistakes and successes. But experience does not necessarily develop the kind of expertise in judging creative work that comes from long and intensive involvement in the development of advertising by talented people. Some marketing executives seem to have better creative judgment than others, but promotion up the line from product manager does not automatically guarantee success in this area.

To replace the skills that were lost with the demise of the advertising department, three companies have created a new position, staff advertising director, to provide creative counsel to product managers and others concerned with advertising decisions. Whereas the former advertising manager made the advertising decision, the new advertising director provides counsel to those charged with the decision-making responsibility.

Where this position has been introduced, it has usually been placed within the division marketing management organization. Executives report that product and other managers exhibit reluctance to avail themselves of staff counsel when it is located in corporate headquarters.

How Much Authority?

The persistent, unresolved question puzzling management is how much and what kind of authority the product manager needs. Luck, in discussing the many functional areas with which the product manager must interact, states: "Product managers are seriously hampered by ambiguity of authority in the execution of their plans and decisions. . . ."[14]

A common management attitude was expressed by the group vice-president of a liquor company, who said: "The brand manager's authority is the authority of his influence and knowledge." While true as far as it goes, this conclusion seems over-simplified. Several studies bear on the issue.

Lucas, in a mail survey of 60 product managers, found that four in five believed their degree of control over the decision areas of advertising, marketing research, and market testing was "adequate for their assigned responsibilities."[15] Smaller proportions reported that they had adequate control over the personal selling, production, and distribution

[14]David J. Luck, "Interfaces of a Product Manager," *Journal of Marketing,* Vol. 33 (October 1969), pp. 32–36.

[15]Darrell B. Lucas, "Point of View: Product Managers in Advertising," *Journal of Advertising Research,* Vol. 12 (June 1972), pp. 41–44.

functions and in the areas of legal affairs, advertising expenditures, and pricing. That these product managers did not consider their responsibilities insignificant is evident in the fact that two-thirds felt that they had major, or even 100%, responsibility for product profit.

The mail survey of 160 executives, primarily product managers and group product managers, conducted by Clewett and Stasch found product managers to be "less than major participants" in the decision areas of advertising, product, packaging, pricing, and personal selling.[16] They were reported to be "major participants" in marketing research and promotion. When tasks, as opposed to decision making, were considered this study reported that product managers had a "major role" in planning, budgeting, scheduling, communicating plans and maintaining enthusiasm for them, monitoring progress, revising plans, and reporting performance. The two studies appear to disagree only in the area of advertising decision authority.

Gemmill and Wileman report that in the absence of direct authority, product managers influence action by using reward power, coercive power, expert power, and referent (i.e., personal relationships) power.[17] They found that product managers who primarily employed expert/referent power were the most effective.

Dietz has identified at least two types of product managers: the *brand coordinator,* who has no entrepreneurial responsibility; and the *brand champion,* who has responsibility for making entrepreneurial recommendations.[18] Common to both types, he says, are the responsibilities for planning, securing approval of plans, coordinating the execution of plans by functional departments, and evaluating the results of the actions taken. Dietz suggests that the brand coordinator needs little authority to fulfill his responsibility but that the more aggressive brand champion reaches out for authority in frustration over the slowness with which higher levels of management arrive at decisions.

As mentioned earlier, the author's findings indicate that the product manager's authority varies with the relative importance of the decision and that his influence varies with his experience and competence. As a division president in a food products company said:

> The product manager system works well for us, but we don't have a set way of working with every product manager. Some are more experienced and some are more aggressive than others.

Consensus appears to exist with respect to the product manager's responsibility for planning, coordinating, and evaluating. Differences continue with respect to the questions of authority over execution and the authority to make decisions. The present answer for the last two would seem to be "it all depends."

As a result of these changing management attitudes, all companies interviewed indicated that they had made, or were making, changes in their product manager setups with respect to functions, authority, management decision-making levels, staffing, or length of time in the job. Eight indicated that they were acting in all of these areas.

Management accepts the system but believes it needs improvement. The president of a food company expressed the viewpoint of many when he commented: "There is nothing fundamentally wrong with the product manager system, but I don't think we operate it as well as we should."

Emphasizing Position Strengths—Deemphasizing Weaknesses

In redefining the job, management is emphasizing the functions that product managers can

[16]Same reference as footnote 13.

[17]Gary R. Gemmill and David L. Wileman, "The Product Manager as an Influence Agent," *Journal of Marketing,* Vol. 36 (January 1972), pp. 26–30.

[18]Stephens Dietz, "Get More Out of Your Brand Management," Harvard Business Review, Vol. 51 (July–August 1973), p. 127.

perform well and deemphasizing those aspects of the position with inherent weaknesses. Emphasis is being placed on the role of the product manager as the gatherer and synthesizer of all information about the product and its markets, as the developer of plans, as the communicator of approved plans, and as the monitor of performance. Management expects the product manager to have a deep personal commitment to the success of his product, while they recognize that he alone cannot be held responsible for achievement of sales and profits. Ultimate responsibility, they believe, must rest with the executive in a position to control all marketing activities.

The role of the product manager as decision maker is being deemphasized. The current trend is for decision-making authority to be given in accordance with the importance of the decision area and to vary with the experience and competence of the individual product manager. The product manager will remain involved with the decision-making process, but he will be encouraged to bring key decisions to his manager's attention. As one marketing director said, "The brand manager's job is to get good decisions made irrespective of who makes them."

Controlling Resource Allocation at Higher Levels

Management not only wants decisions made where the most competence exists, but it also recognizes the need to control resource allocations among products. The president of a liquor company put it this way: "Our brand managers make many decisions but they don't make the key ones. Someone at a higher level must look at the broad allocation of expenditures."

Obviously, the product manager is not in a position to see the overall picture. The more effective an individual product manager is, the better job he may do in obtaining a disproportionate share of functional resources. It is higher management's job to see that money and other resources are allocated on the basis of profit potential.

The idea that decision making should be moved up the line rather than down the line does not sit well with long-term advocates of decentralized management. However, most executives interviewed seemed to have come to terms with this issue. They recognized that on matters that have a major impact on profit, decisions should be made where all the necessary information is available and where competence exists to make the best judgment. This means that different decisions will be made at different levels, but it does not preclude participation by the product manager, who should have the most information about his product and market. Exceptions to this philosophy were found at the corporate level in three companies. Checks at the division levels in these companies indicate, however, that major advertising decisions were, in fact, being made at the marketing vice-president or division president levels.

Staffing with Marketing Experience

During the 1960s and early 1970s, a number of companies sought out the recent MBA graduate to fill the assistant product manager position. The graduate schools provided a selective recruiting source of people with broad management training. Though not unhappy with the quality of these recruits, managements have found that their limited training in marketing (particularly in advertising) and the usual absence of marketing experience are drawbacks for product management. They complain, also, that higher competitive compensation levels for the MBA tend to upset established wage patterns.

With the exception of two major packaged goods producers, the companies interviewed had reduced their reliance on the graduate business school as a primary recruiting source for product management. Five had eliminated this source entirely. They were recruiting instead from advertising agencies and other companies and were making internal transfers from sales, marketing research, and the like, in order to obtain people with marketing experience. Some of these people may already have their MBA degree, which is considered a plus, but the emphasis is being placed on marketing experience.

Slowing Job Turnover

Simultaneously, eight of the companies were upgrading the position and attempting to hold incumbents in the job for longer periods. This has not been easy, since the job attracts high-potential, well-motivated individuals who consider product management a stepping stone to higher management. To attract and hold good people, companies in the past have advanced them from assistant to associate to product manager to group product manager fairly rapidly. Switching to different product groups often occurred along the way.

This "churning" is felt to be undesirable. Incumbents do not stay with a product long enough to develop the desired product and market expertise. Furthermore, short-term assignments do not encourage the long-range planning that can enhance market position. Through different hiring practices and by providing incentives to remain with a product longer, the eight companies hope to increase product manager effectiveness. Other managements that would like to increase longevity in the job explain that they have been unable to do so because of rapid company growth.

FUTURE IMPLICATIONS

In summary, over the years the product manager system has undergone a number of changes and it is still in the process of change. Because the position corresponds to none of the classic line, staff, or functional positions it has never fit neatly into traditional organizational structure. Yet for companies with many products it affords a better means of product-by-product management concentration than does functional organization. For this reason—and despite its acknowledged problems—most companies that are using the product management system plan to stay with it.

It is too early to tell whether the current trend to emphasize planning and coordination, and deemphasize decision making, will resolve the major problems. The same can be said for attempts to improve staffing and to lengthen incumbent tenure.

In some ways the product manager system appears to be in tune with current organizational behavior theory, with its emphasis on group cooperation and participative decision making and its deemphasis of hierarchical authority patterns. The author found, for example, that those organizations with the longest product management experience appeared to be most happy with it, apparently because people throughout these organizations better understand the system. People seem to recognize the reasons for cooperating with the product manager in the absence of any formal authority on his part. The corporate advertising vice-president of one long-time user of product management emphasized this point:

> What makes our system tick is not organization or who makes the decision, but something more intangible—our people are trained in the company system and everyone knows how it works.

No doubt we have not heard the last of the product manager problem nor the last of change. Until a better idea comes along, however, we are likely to see continued use of the system and continued efforts to improve it. Product management has been, and will continue to be, an intriguing subject for organizational theorists and practicing managers alike.

4

Reorganize Your Company around Its Markets

Mack Hanan

A new term, "marketcentering," and, more importantly, a new concept in management are here introduced. The efforts some companies are making to organize their operations around the markets to be served rather than around production or other functions represents a significant advance in business thinking—as significant, some observers feel, as Alfred Sloan's decentralization philosophy or Procter & Gamble's brand management system.

This article analyzes the marketcentered approach from the standpoint of companies that might want to adopt it in whole or in part. First, the author describes the ways in which some leading companies are implementing the approach. Next, he examines the conditions that favor the adoption of marketcentering and the steps management should take if it elects to make the changeover. He then summarizes the operating features of a marketcentered organization and discusses the concept's impact on corporate growth.

Throughout the 1960s, market orientation was such a dominant business concept that it is surprising to find, a decade later, that few companies have found a way to organize themselves so that their customers' needs consistently come first. In most companies, the divisional structures are still determined by regions, organized around products, or structured to commercialize a process technology. It has been only over the past few years that a small number of companies have come to realize that:

- There is no substitute for market orientation as the ultimate source of profitable growth.
- The only way to ensure being market-oriented is to put a company's organizational structure together so that its major markets become the centers around which its divisions are built.

Some leading companies are emphasizing growth by gearing their organizational structures to their markets' needs instead of to their product or process capabilities. IBM's data-processing operations are segmented organizationally according to key markets, such as institutions like hospitals and retail establishments like supermarkets. Xerox Information Systems Group, which sells copiers and duplicators, has converted from geographical selling to vertical selling by industry. General Foods has adopted a market-targeting organizational style. Even the strict product orientation of some scientific companies is gradually giving way to a combined product and market orientation. In its electronics product marketing, for example, Hewlett-Packard has created a sales and service group that concentrates separately on the electrical manufacturing market while another group serves the market for aerospace. Still other groups sell to the markets for communications or transportation equipment.

In other companies steps are being taken to orient businesses to their markets. At Mead, broad market clusters are coming into being to serve customer needs in home building and

Reprinted from *Harvard Business Review,* vol. 52, pp. 63–74. At the time of writing, the author was managing director of Hanan & Son and president of the Wellspring Group.

furnishings, education, and leisure. PPG Industries has been examining the benefits of systematizing the marketing of its paint, ceramics, and glass divisions through a home environment profit center whose product mix could resemble the pattern shown in *Exhibit I.* Monsanto has organized a Fire Safety Center that consolidates fire safety products from every sector of Monsanto and groups them according to the market they serve: building and construction, transportation, apparel, or furnishings. Revlon is engaged in "breaking up the company into little pieces": as many as six autonomous profit centers are being created, each of which is designed to serve a specific market segment.

General Electric is well along in constructing strategic business groups for its major appliance and power-generation businesses. For GE, the process of reorganizing from a

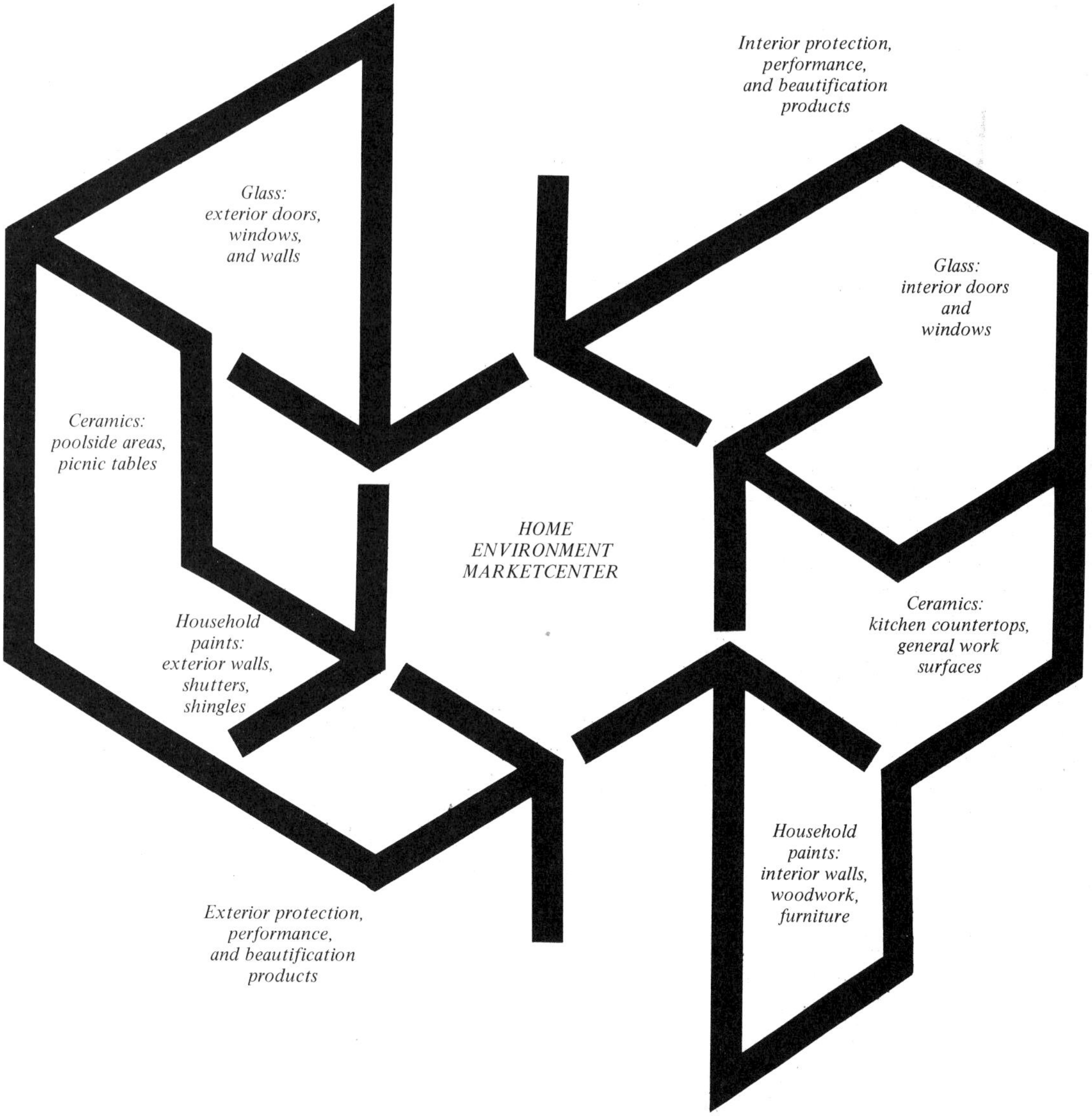

Exhibit I Product mix of a business marketcentered on the home.

product to a market orientation has been especially difficult. An average department contains three and one half product lines and may serve more than one business or, more frequently, only a part of a major business. Electric motors, for example, are divided among eight departments. Home refrigerators are split between two departments, even though the only significant product difference is the way the doors open. In such a setup, department managers have understandably become oriented to specific product lines rather than to the needs of a total market.

I use the term *marketcentered* (or marketcentering) to describe the wide range of corporate organizational forms that make a group of customer needs, rather than a region, a product line, or a process, the center of a business division. These forms include General Foods's "strategic business units," National Cash Register's "vocations," the "customer provinces" that some high-technology manufacturers are organizing as company-like units to concentrate on serving the needs of specific market groups, and the "financial need groups" through which some progressive banks serve the common financing needs of manufacturers of electronic systems, drugs, cosmetics, household products, and other items.

Marketcentering also describes the way some railroads are grouping their services around the common distribution needs of major customers so that they can provide a unique user-oriented service system for oil, chemical, and fertilizer shippers and a different system for grain shippers. These organizational formats are working so well that more railroads can be expected to adopt them.

WHEN SHOULD AN ORGANIZATION BE MARKETCENTERED?

Marketcentered describes an organization that is decentralized by markets—markets define the business. Organizing an enterprise in this way, which some companies think of as working backward from the points where they deal face to face with their customers, can yield many of the same benefits as decentralizing by processes, materials, or product lines. A marketcenter forms a natural profit center just as readily as does a materials center, such as Continental Can's Metal Operations group. A marketcenter may also be able to dominate the heavy users in its market to such an extent that it becomes the preeminent supplier, like such product centers as The Ansul Company's former Fire Protection Products division.

But marketcentering is not without some costs and inefficiencies. For example, when Coca-Cola was reorienting to its markets in the early 1960s, some of its veteran managers were moved to lament the passing of one of the most cost-efficient mass businesses of all time. Formerly, the company had manufactured a single product, made according to one basic formula and sold at one retail price, which was marketed with great economies in an internationally recognized bottle that conveyed instant product awareness. The managers saw this business give way forever to a diversity of sizes and prices and even to various companion products, all of which bore a considerable burden of their own administrative, operating, and marketing expenses.

Marketcentering an organization may incur other additional costs. In order to zero in on its market, management generally requires its own information bank of customer needs and its own exclusive sales force, which is intensively schooled to apply the data bank's resources to the center's customers. A company that has employed a single sales force before marketcentering may find itself recruiting, training, developing, and fielding several separate sales forces whose compensation plans and support services—to say nothing of product lines and channels of distribution—may be totally dissimilar.

Conditions Favoring Change

When, then, does marketcentering become an appropriate form of decentralization? Executives of companies that have been reorganizing around their markets suggested five particular situations that especially favor a marketcentered approach:

1 When market leadership is threatened by a competitor who has achieved sufficient product parity to deprive the leader of price superiority. Marketcentering can restore a competitive advantage with the more creative marketing techniques it develops from improved knowledge of customer, distributor, and retailer needs.

2 When new-product famine has afflicted the product-development function so that nothing, or only a crop of lemons, is being delivered, or when R&D has been foundering in its resource allocation because of a lack of market direction. Marketcentering can stimulate new-product winners by transmitting current knowledge of market life-styles or emergent needs to technical management. Marketcentering also enables innovative breakthrough thinking to replace a preoccupation with generating only marginal extensions of established product categories.

3 When a product manufacturer desires either to diversify into higher-margin services as a means of broadening his profit base or to market systems of correlated products and services in order to gain a lock on key customers. Marketcentering can group market needs into highly visible targets for systems, enabling the marketer to operate as a one-stop supplier to each center.

4 When a manufacturer who has been selling product-performance benefits shifts his marketing strategy to feature the financial benefits of customer profit improvement. Marketcentering makes it easier to amass the required knowledge of how customers make their profits. Each marketcenter is made responsible for compiling its own data resource.

5 When a marketer desires to attract a more entrepreneurial type of manager. Marketcentering offers candidates an enlarged scope of supervisory duties and full profit responsibility. In a multimarket company, a mobile young manager can often tackle diverse challenges by moving from one marketcentered division to another. He does not have to go to another company in order to obtain variety.

EASING INTO A MARKETCENTERED FORM

A major organizational change like marketcentering can be a shock to any company—especially to the traditional product manufacturer (who, paradoxically, may benefit the most from it). Companies have been experimenting with several ways of easing themselves toward a marketcentered approach, since the change is often best implemented by degrees. Along the way, a company can learn how much marketcentering it can stand at any given time and what particular form it should ultimately have. Three ways of beginning the transition have emerged thus far.

Marketcentering a sales force is the first way. It requires the least up-front commitment and the least alteration in the basic structure of a business. In addition, it succeeds in establishing the central relationship that earmarks all forms of marketcentered organizations: contact between customers with many varying needs and a sales force that can prescribe the most beneficial systems for those needs. In the romantic version of marketing, this interface takes place on a prolonged person-to-person basis in the marketplace. The reality, however, is that customer information is collected and analyzed at a data bank.

This is the approach that NCR has taken. Each sales staff is assigned a well-defined industry group to serve. The company's salesmen are trained to sell systems of different but interrelated products and services in a consultative manner. They consider market knowledge, rather than product knowledge, to be their principal resource.

General Foods has chosen a second way to ease into marketcentering. It has created a separate marketing division to serve each major market. This approach involves reclassifying major markets into new, more comprehensive groups and consolidating similar but differently manufactured products into product families to be marketed to each group. While the NCR sales-centered approach requires a single salesman to serve most or all of a customer's needs with many different products and services, the General Foods approach coordinates a wide range of products that are essentially alike for a single user segment.

The third way is to begin with either the first or second step and then proceed to achieve a thoroughly marketcentered structure by integrating manufacturing and all marketing functions, including sales, into a single division. Both the NCR and General Foods examples lend themselves to this end result, which IBM and Xerox have perhaps most fully achieved.

In the following sections, I shall examine some of the major characteristics of the NCR and General Foods approaches. Then I shall describe the key criteria of a marketcentered organization, the role of the business manager, and the service systems needed to support that role.

NCR'S APPROACH—SEPARATE SALES FORCES

NCR has been reorganizing its traditional product-line sales approach into a strategy of "selling by vocation" on an industry-by-industry basis. Each vocation is a broad industry grouping which forms a specific market definable by reasonably cohesive needs. NCR is focusing a separate sales force on each of the following vocational markets: financial institutions, retailers, commercial and industrial businesses, and computer customers in medical, educational, and government offices.

NCR's marketcentered sales organization is enabling the company to be more competitive, especially in the marketing of systems. In each market, the NCR salesman assigned to it can sell coordinated systems of numerical recording and sorting products. Previously, each salesman could sell only his own product line. Also, the decision maker in the customer company could be involved with several NCR salesmen, no one of whom could know the sum total of the customer's numerical control needs, let alone serve them. Under the new system, the same retail industry salesman who sells an NCR cash register to a department store can also search out and serve the store's needs for NCR accounting machines, data entry terminals, and a mainframe computer. If he needs help, he can organize a team with other NCR salesmen that can bring the required strength to his proposal. The product groups he sells are still manufactured separately; the centralized sales approach is the innovation that makes the difference.

By selling groups or systems of products through a single salesman or sales team, rather than selling individual products through many uncoordinated salesmen, NCR believes it can help customers achieve greater profit improvement. It can prescribe systems that solve comprehensive problems which would otherwise remain immune to single product solutions. Management also believes it can expand its profitable sales volume by selling larger packages and insulating its position against competition.

Each vocational market's full range of recording and sorting needs is becoming better known to NCR personnel. In turn, by specializing in seeking out and serving these needs, each of NCR's vocational sales organizations can become known for expertise in its market, almost as if it were an independent specialist company. Moreover, every sales group can utilize the total financial and technical resources of the company for professional counsel and support in developing, prescribing, and installing product systems.

Operations and Options

A vice president of marketing directs NCR's sales organization. The four vocational vice presidents report to him. Regional vocational directors supervise several states, giving a geographic underlay to the organization.

NCR's next step in marketcentering through its sales force is to specialize more precisely. This can logically lead to the appointment of retail specialists within the financial industry sales force, to mention one possibility. As additional ramifications of the new approach become apparent, NCR will be able to reorganize many other aspects of its corporate structure and operations, increasing its market orientation. Among the major options which will be open to the company are decentralizing staff services, bringing R&D and product development activities into closer vocational alignment, adding profit-making services to existing product systems, consolidating advertising and other promotional activities to appeal specifically to vocational needs, and combining the appropriate manufacturing and selling activities in marketcentered divisions.

GENERAL FOODS' APPROACH—SEPARATE MARKETING DIVISIONS

While NCR has been stimulated to reorganize by the increasing preferences of its customers for systems and by the relentless competitive pressures of IBM, General Foods revised its approach because of internal strains and frustrations. In the early 1970s new product winners either stopped coming out of product development at their former rate or carried an unreasonable cost. Better knowledge of the needs of its consumers was obviously required if the company's product developers were to harmonize their technologies with the new life-styles influencing the demand for processed foods. At the same time, the needs of the company's customers at the retail level required new responses. Competitive brands were proliferating, clamoring for shelf and display space, while an increasingly attractive profit on sales was making private-label products more acceptable to the major supermarket chains.

These events combined to place unprecedented strains on the company's divisional structure, which was the legacy of a generations-old policy of acquisition. General Foods's major food divisions—Birds Eye, Jell-O, Post, and Kool-Aid—had evolved historically, each according to the process technology which it brought into the company. As the scope of each division's product categories grew, it was inevitable that one division's consumer provinces would be impinged on by other divisions, and that any given market would be served in a fragmented rather than a concentrated manner. Divisional sovereignties frequently made it impossible for the company to dominate a market that was served by two or more divisions with related product categories but with different styles and degrees of commitment.

Often more damaging for new-product development was the way in which division managers respected a no-man's-land between their provinces, leaving gaps in product categories that could give competitors a clear shot or deny the company a chance to establish a position of category leadership. Beverages are a case in point. They were marketed by three divisions. If they were frozen, they were marketed by Birds Eye. If they were powdered mixes, the Kool-Aid division marketed them. Breakfast drinks had to come from Post. No centralized attack on consumer beverage needs could be made. In a similar fashion, puddings were marketed by two divisions:

Birds Eye had jurisdiction over frozen puddings while Jell-O was the steward division for powdered mixes. The pudding market as such had no general representative within the company.

Relating Products to Market Needs

The General Foods approach to marketcentering has been to reorganize its process-oriented divisional structure into separate marketing organizations known as "strategic business units" (SBUs). Each SBU concentrates on marketing families of products made by different processing technologies but consumed by the same market segment. As *Exhibit II* shows, the Food Products division coordinates the marketing strategy for all desserts whether they are in frozen, powdered, or ready-to-eat form. The exhibit also shows how the Beverage and Breakfast Food division markets breakfast drinks of three different processing techniques and how the Pet Food division centers the marketing of freeze-dried, dry pellet, and semimoist dog foods.

This scheme allows each SBU to take an overview of how an entire product family can best be related to the needs of both end users and retailers. Each SBU functions like a division and draws on the full range of corporate technologies. It also derives support services from a corporate pool where market research, production, personnel, new-product development, and sales are consolidated for use by all SBUs. A small amount of product-connected market research and new-product development is still left to the individual SBUs. But their primary mission is to engage in "pure marketing" as much as possible and to concentrate their resources on cultivating the market segments to which they have been assigned.

Among the benefits that General Foods believes it has gained so far from its form of marketcentering are an increasingly productive trade merchandising capability and improved ability to dominate a full consumer-

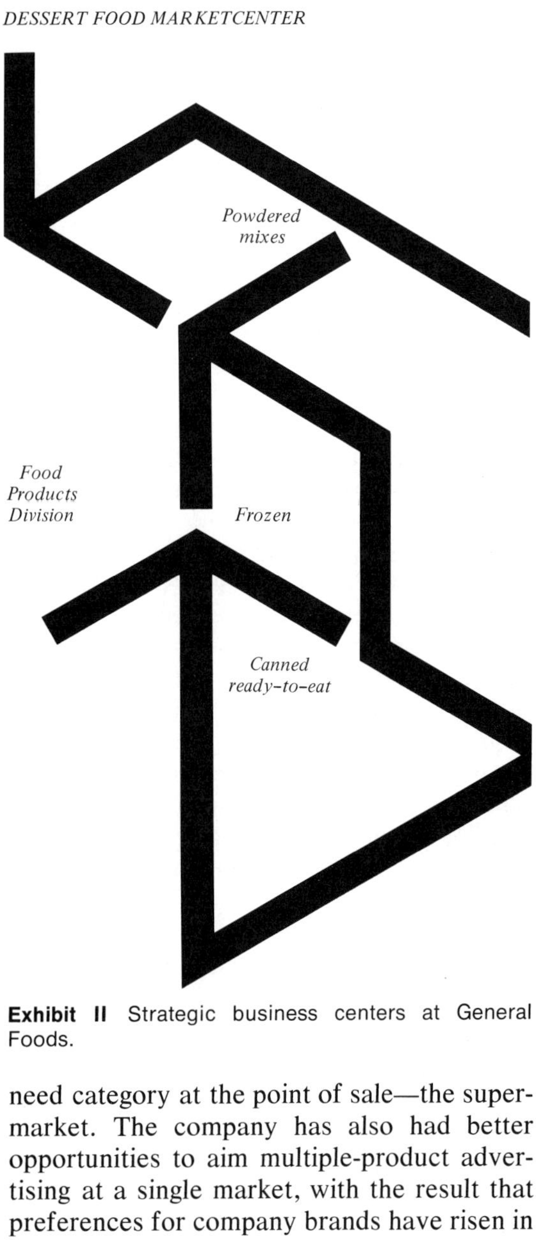

Exhibit II Strategic business centers at General Foods.

need category at the point of sale—the supermarket. The company has also had better opportunities to aim multiple-product advertising at a single market, with the result that preferences for company brands have risen in certain product categories.

Another benefit has been that new products can be launched with fewer problems of stewardship than before. To take a hypothetical example, suppose that skin care products were to become part of the corporate growth scheme. If one proposed item were to be

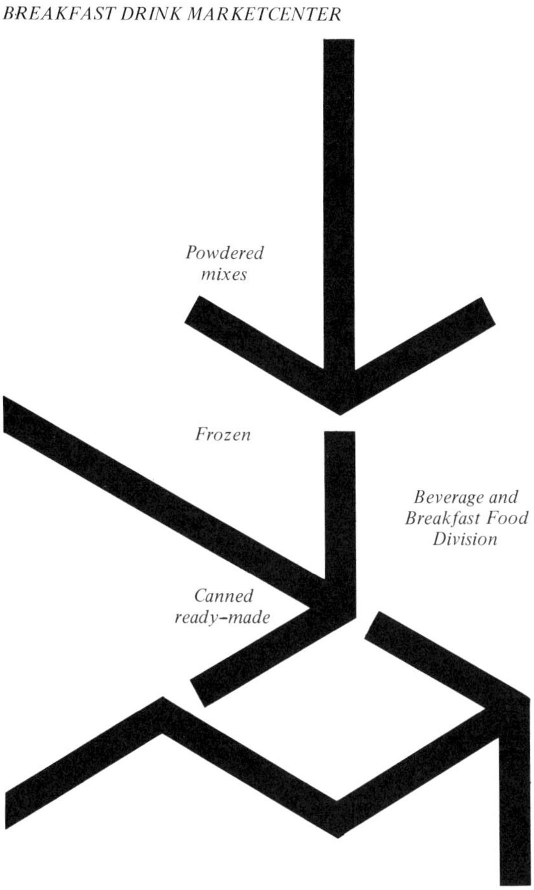

Exhibit II Continued.

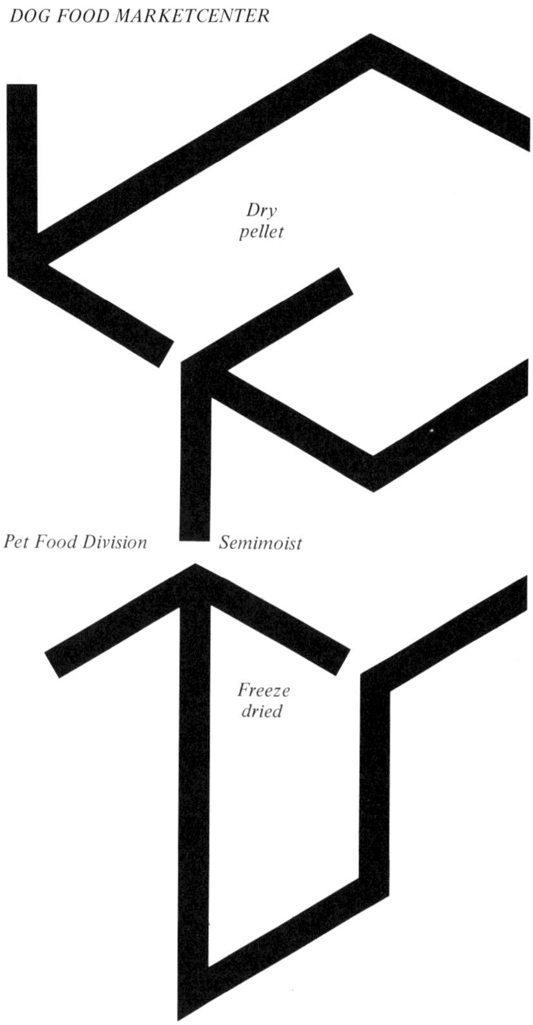

Exhibit II Continued.

packaged in frozen form, it would not have to start its market life in the Birds Eye division, as presumably would have been necessary in the past, and therefore labor under the potentially negative connotations of having vegetable origins. Or, if the new skin care product were to be a premoistened patty or a water-soluble pellet, it would not have to be marketed under the umbrella of the Gaines pet food division.

GUIDELINES FOR DEVELOPMENT

In sketching the main guidelines that product- or process-centered companies can use to change to a marketcentered approach, I shall place special emphasis on two areas. One is the key criteria of marketcentering. The other is the role of the manager who runs a marketcenter and the unique aspects of his supportive service system.

Key Criteria

When an organization is fully marketcentered, a market becomes the focal point of every one of the company's major operations. The objective of each business is to become its market's preferred center for fulfilling one or more principal needs. Such a business is the sum of its marketcentered divisions and should meet these five criteria:

1 It must be chartered to serve a market which is defined according to a system of closely related needs. This permits the market to be served by a diversified package of products and services that, taken together, supply a combination of closely related benefits. The business may market two or more related products in a single sale or market a package composed of products and their related services.

2 Because a marketcenter is operated as a profit center, it should be administered by an entrepreneur. I like to call this executive the *business manager* of the organization. Unlike most product managers or brand managers, or even market managers who are merely profit-accountable, a business manager is fully profit-responsible. He enjoys considerable authority in running his business. He commands the key decisions. He sets prices, controls costs, and is charged with operating his marketcenter for a satisfactory profit.

3 Business managers are the chief line officers in their marketcentered organizations. All other corporate functions must be repositioned as satellite supply services that support the business managers' operations. Business managers employ corporate staff services on a contractual basis, which gives them authority to refuse to do business with any service that cannot be competitive in pricing, quality control, or delivery.

4 Once a division is marketcentered, its storehouse of market information quickly becomes its key asset. Through marketcentering, a company grows by basing its future expansion on knowledge about its existing markets. A corporatewide market information center can be set up to store and give access to the market knowledge required by each division, or marketcentered divisions can create their own information centers.

5 Top management must position itself as a holding company or, as it is sometimes called, a central bank. This central bank acts as a council of portfolio managers who centralize corporate policy making and investment funding for their decentralized businesses. Top management's prime concern is usually to manage a balanced portfolio of businesses in which no single investment accounts for more than 50% of total corporate profit, or at least not for long. The business managers consult the central bank when they want money or need advice.

How the Business Manager Operates

A business manager may head up a single, large marketcenter or, if the operations are small or closely related, two or more such centers. His job is to manage the corporate investment in a center so that it will yield the maximum rate of return. At Textron, for example, a minimum pretax return on investment of 25% is mandated for every one of the company's businesses. At ITT, the manager's contribution must fall within the 10% to 12% annual range of increase in earnings.

As a result of his concentration on financial bogeys, a marketcenter's business manager tends to view himself as a profit creator rather than a curator of specific products or processes. He resists becoming addicted to any particular product line or acquiring a reverence for any technological process. "In my marketing mix, I recognize no such thing as an eternal product," one business manager told me. "Nor do I cherish any perpetual promotional appeals for them. Even the customer needs that I serve today will probably prove to be transient. Only my commitment to maximize the long-range profit of my marketcenter is everlasting."

Supportive Systems

While marketcentering decentralizes the management of operations, it centralizes many of the staff services which business managers use. As *Exhibit III* shows, up to four consolidated service functions may revolve around each business manager.

Development services combine new-market research and development with new-product R&D under a single director. In this way, the market orientation of R&D—historically one of the chief stumbling blocks in raising a company's level of consciousness to its customers—is accomplished organizationally. New-market needs, new-process technology, and new-product development are able to interact harmoniously rather than competitively. With marketcentering, the traditional vice presidential functions for marketing and R&D can be subsumed under the director of development's functions. There is generally

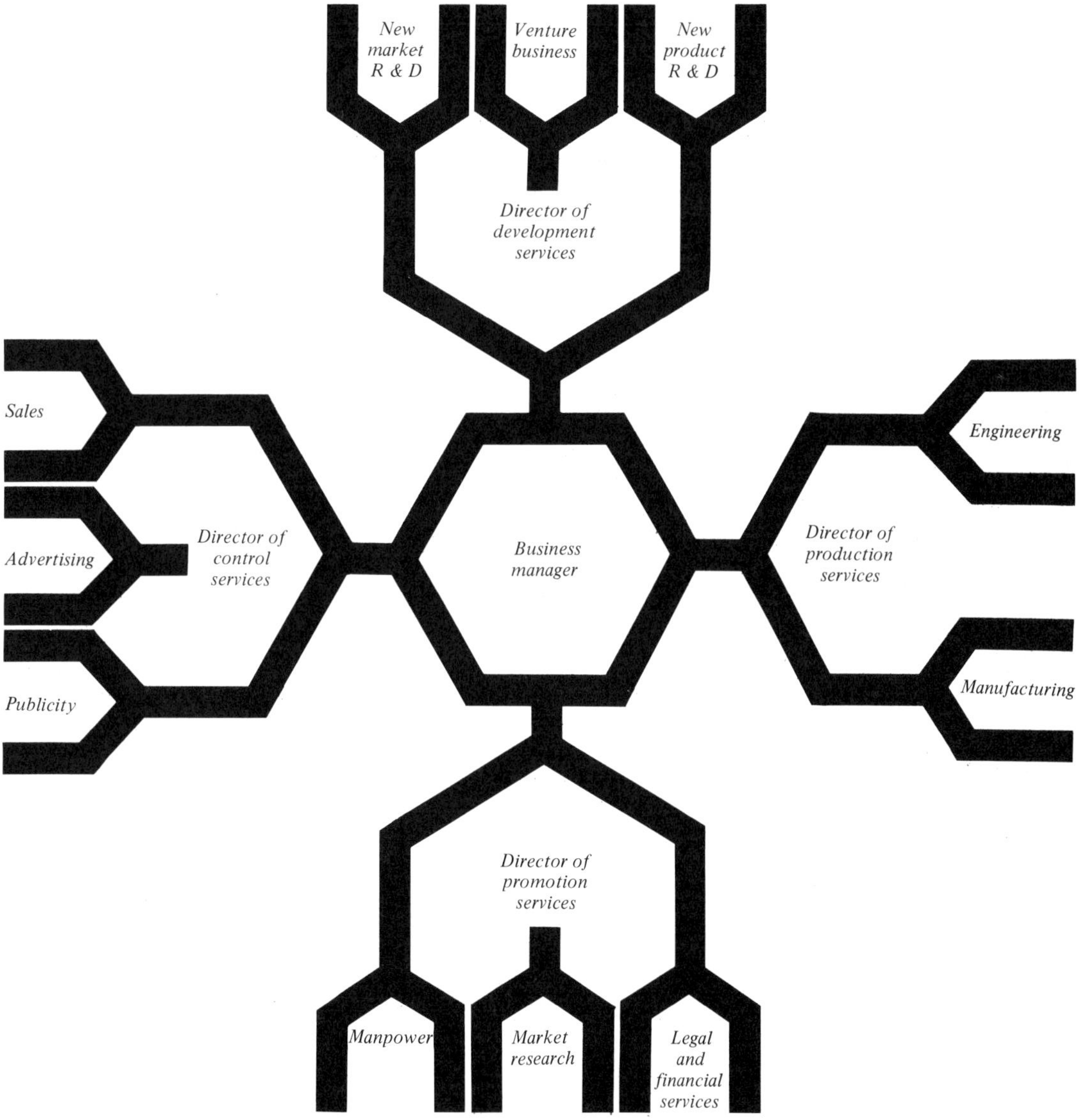

Exhibit III Supporting services available to a business manager.

no need for a vice president of marketing in such an organization because the entire corporate structure is market-oriented and each business manager must act as his own chief marketing officer.

Control services do the basic research to evaluate the effectiveness of established product and service-system marketing. They also provide the necessary recruitment, compensation and motivation, training and development, legal, and financial functions. *Production services* coordinate engineering and manufacturing operations. And *promotion services* combine sales, advertising, and publicity.

These four groups of services are supplied by top management on an elective basis. Whether and when they are used depends on the business manager. Should he elect to contract with the internal services, he negotiates with the service managers as if they were outside suppliers.

Contracting for Service

Any one, or all four, of his company's internal services may be retained, either in whole or in part, by a business manager. As the following position description indicates, the business manager is also chartered to employ outside services whenever he feels they can better help him meet his objectives:

> Through an annual contractual relationship with the director of production services, the business manager acquires a product supply to market. The business manager must, at minimal cost, negotiate for a dependable and sufficient supply of products, manufactured according to marketable specifications, that maintain maximum economies in production without impairing either market acceptance or corporate image.

Since the business manager has ultimate responsibility for profit, he must be free to negotiate with any strategic service that meets his product and market specifications at minimal cost. Much, if not most, of the time, these services will come from inside the company. But he can also buy them from outside and use them interchangeably with, or independently of, internal functions. In either case, the contractual form of doing business acts as his principal instrument of cost and quality control.

The service contract can also be an instrument of top management control. Making the use of internal services optional puts them squarely on their mettle. They must perform for the business managers, competing with alternate sources of supply in cost and quality terms, or be bypassed. If internal services are consistently selected by most business managers, top management can comfortably assume that they are competitive; if the services are rejected, that is a sign that they are not doing the job.

Ensuring Continued Service

From each business manager's point of view, being on the receiving end of a demand-feed schedule with contracted services is an almost ideal situation. Best quality at lowest price, every manager's dream, seems assured. But will there be chaos among the suppliers of services? To discourage an endless series of requests for custom-tailored variations in services, especially in production and promotion, a variance-request control system can be installed. Under this system, market-based justification can be required for all significant departures from contracted specifications.

However, it may be necessary to go further. What can be done to protect an internal supplier of services from having to react simultaneously to short-term strategy changes by several business managers? While a predictable problem area such as seasonal production peaks can be rather simply ironed out in advance, no service can fully anticipate a business manager's midcycle decision changes. He may need to alter his product mix in the face of sudden raw materials shortages. New corporate policies on allocating scarce ingredients or components may shut off his supply. Demand variations among his key customers may dry up one or more markets and force him to shift his product specifications to meet the needs of a previously less important customer group. Such stresses can disrupt R&D priorities, throw off manufacturing runs, scuttle cost estimates, and upset sales and advertising appropriations.

TWO-WAY GROWTH OPPORTUNITY

Some corporate executives feel that market-centering may come to rank with Alfred Sloan's decentralization of General Motors along market-segmented lines. They see themselves regaining a customer focus that often became blurred by Procter & Gamble's brand management system. While contemporary with Sloan's market awareness, brand management directed the styles of many corporate formats away from customers and back to products. When product and brand management were imposed on the traditional organization of the manufacturing division and on the pyramidal organization chart, which was adapted for the needs of commercial business from Von Möltke's general staff concept, progress toward marketcentering slowed for half a century.

In the mid 1960s, the beginning of a new thrust toward the customer was signaled by the advent of free-form marketing groups. They were allowed to cut across corporate pyramids whenever unusual market sensitivity was demanded in an operation. A variety of problem-solving task forces and project management teams came into being for much the same reason; they represented jerry-built improvisations to defeat a product-oriented or process-centered organizational system. In other instances, managers have had to depart from the accepted corporate framework and to create highly decentralized conglomerates of market-targeted businesses.

Since it is probable that these dislocations will be with us for some time to come, methods for coping with them are under experimentation. Some companies are establishing resource allocation groups, composed of the directors of development, control, production, and promotion services, who recommend to top management the most favorable distribution patterns in times of materials short-falls. Their suggestions are based on the central criterion of close-in contribution to profit but are naturally conditioned by short- and long-term considerations, such as maintenance of the traditional market position, potential for future growth, and possible preemptive reactions from competitors.

Because a marketcentered company expands chiefly by serving new needs in established markets where it is well franchised, its growth is relatively safe. By asking and reasking the key question, "What *other* needs of the markets we know so well can we serve profitably?" management can develop new business on the basis of the strength of its existing businesses.

Marketcentering a company can give it two-way flexibility for growth. Each of its major markets can be served *intensively*, once it is established as the center of a business. When growth on a broadened profit base becomes desirable, the same markets can be served more *extensively* by searching out their closely related needs and centering new businesses around one or more of them. Through these two approaches, the basic growth strategy of a marketcentered company can be defined as meeting the greatest number of interrelated needs of every market segment it serves.

5

A System for Managing Diversity

Robert V. L. Wright

Whether they like it or not, corporate managers must find better ways to manage diverse product-market relationships or settle for less than optimum performance. The author argues persuasively that there are more effective ways to manage diversity than those now used. These new methods are rooted in the development of comprehensive, differentiated strategy systems that not only recognize the unique potential of each business unit, but also enable corporate management to mesh the individual unit strategies to accomplish the objectives of the whole.

INTRODUCTION

It often seems that diversity is too much with us, but difficult as it is to manage, it is here to stay. There is no easy road back to the pre-diversified, pre-multinational world we once so enthusiastically left behind. Peter Drucker maintains that many companies would have been well-advised to restrict their urge to diversify, since more homogeneous companies tend to outperform those with many hard-to-integrate pieces. Reality is cruel, however. If those responsible for the fate of large multi-industry or multinational corporations are sometimes displeased with what they have wrought, they can make only minor or very gradual retrenchments: a major divestment program is usually too costly and has too many harmful reverberations. For the most part, managers must either find better ways to manage diversity or settle for less than optimum performance.

We believe there are effective ways to manage diversity, calling for new skills in strategic planning. The keys are (1) distinguishing the business units that comprise the diversified corporation and (2) conceptualizing what the composite of these units can and should be. A single-industry company can be likened to the wooden puzzle composed of irregular pieces that can be put together in only one way to form a sphere. The better the fit, the smoother the surface, the less friction, the more reliable and stable the performance, the greater the potential velocity. The single-industry company has a single goal—to optimize the exploitation of its market—and a single set of strategies and a uniform management system designed to achieve that goal.

The multi-industry company, on the other hand, seeks to fit the component pieces together in multiple ways, adding to them and varying their use in accord with evolving circumstances and goals. The resultant construct may be like a helicopter, a dirigible, or a jet aircraft, but not a round projectile. Each possible construct has its own characteristics and capabilities. The multi-industry company can pick and choose components (business units) to fashion a totality to meet specific performance requirements for speed, stability, or length of flight. For the single-industry company the ruling concept is to do things in "the one best way": for the multi-industry company it is to make skillful use of synergy, leverage, and balance. Unfortunately, too

Reprinted from Robert V. L. Wright, *A System for Managing Diversity* (Cambridge, Mass.: Arthur D. Little, Inc., 1974). At the time of writing, the author was a member of the staff of Arthur D. Little, Inc.

many managers still try to treat a diversified corporation as if it were still a single-industry firm.

To state the problem of diversification management is not necessarily to question the logic of diversification decisions. Many diversification programs undertaken in the sixties were financially and economically justified and have proven successful. Now, though, some of the corporations involved are beset by "diseconomies" of unwieldy management. This has led to some attempts at divestment, but also to a search for new approaches to management. Now that many companies have stopped acquiring businesses at the rate which characterized the late sixties, they are concentrating on managing what they have. The question before them is, "How?" They see the potential advantages of diversity—e.g., career opportunities, spreading of risk, and potentialities for economic self-renewal—but their multi-businesses are not amenable to traditional planning and managing approaches.

In attempting to encompass diversity, some companies have begun by trying to stretch their prediversification techniques for planning and control to cover all their units. They have increased surveillance by adding both more reports and greater rapidity of reporting, stepped up their management development efforts, and called for more detailed plans from each operating unit. Other companies have installed new planning systems to deal with their various business units, but have continued to rely on performance measurement and reward systems which treat all units uniformly—often without seeing the connection between this incongruity and the dysfunctional results. Even when this connection has been suspected, it has proved psychologically difficult to redesign already installed "total" management information systems, "comprehensive" business plans, or "uniform" compensation systems.

A growing number of companies, however, have understood the need for more far-reaching changes and have begun the process of developing comprehensive, differentiated strategy systems that recognize the full implications of diversity. They have started with a micro-economic business analysis which allows them not only to understand and manipulate the potential of each business unit, but also to orchestrate and dovetail unit strategies to accomplish the objectives of the aggregate. Each unit or "Strategy Center" is then managed with organization structures, controls, reporting, measuring, and reward systems appropriate to its own maturity, competitive position, strategies, and risk profile.

We believe that this is the most effective way to meet the challenge. It enables management to proceed without either sacrificing diversity or settling for ponderous suboptimization of the whole, and a growing number of executives are experiencing its merits first-hand.

A STRATEGY DEVELOPMENT SYSTEM

In recent years, we have counseled a large number of multi–industry corporations at home and abroad. An outgrowth of this work has been the development of a system for managing diversity. The elements of the system are not unfamiliar, but their configuration is new and provides a way of converting a traditional management system to one that is fully responsive to the needs of diverse businesses. We call it the "Strategy Center Development System," and it consists of four basic building blocks:

- A common method for identification and analysis of business units, reflecting an agreed-upon understanding of market dynamics and micro-economics;
- A common language, including but reaching beyond numbers, for dialogue across unit and functional boundaries;

- A process for developing multifunctional, interdependent strategies;
- A set of "congruency tests" for cross-checking the fit between market and financial performance information *and* between strategies and managerial systems.

The key steps in applying the system are as follows:

1. Identifying the *natural businesses* in which the corporation is involved,
2. Classifying them in terms of their industry *maturity,*
3. Characterizing their *competitive position,*
4. Selecting appropriate *unit strategies,*
5. Conducting financial and managerial *congruency tests,* and
6. Analyzing *risk.*

The basic ideas behind each step are outlined below.

Identifying Natural Business Units

The first step is to identify, for individual micro-economic analysis and strategy building, the natural business units, or "Strategy Centers," making up the corporation. Strategy Centers are not necessarily synonymous with existing divisions or profit center designations.[1] In different corporations, natural business units will be found to exist at different organizational levels.

A Strategy Center (or natural business unit) is composed of a product or product lines with identifiable independence from other products or product lines in terms of competition, prices, substitutability of product, style/quality, and impact of product withdrawal. It is around this configuration of products that a business strategy is designed. In today's organizations, this strategy may encompass products found in more than one division, and, on the other hand, some unit managers may find themselves managing two or more natural businesses. This does not necessarily mean that divisional boundaries need to be redefined; often a Strategy Center can overlap divisions and a division can include more than one unit.

The Chief Executive Officer, who holds ultimate responsibility for obtaining agreement on a definition of the natural business units in his corporation, is likely to find the task more difficult than it sounds. There are usually conflicting views within a company on such matters as who the relevant competitors are or what impact one product line has on the sales of other product lines. Traditional management attitudes can also complicate the process: divisional and profit center competitiveness, often deliberately fostered within corporations, make it difficult for one unit to see itself as linked strategically with other units and therefore called upon to react reciprocally and in an integrated manner toward a common competitor. The push for "entrepreneurship" at operating levels—an alluring but often misconceived motivational ploy—makes it difficult for some unit leaders to perceive benefits in synergy, cooperation, or integration.

Determining Industry Maturity

Once the Strategy Centers have been identified, the next step is to classify them in a way that will be useful for the purpose of strategy formulation. We have found it useful to place them in the matrix shown in Figure 1, classifying them by (1) industry maturity and (2) strategic competitive position.

Our choice of industry maturity as the initial basis for classification is based on our experience; although there are other ways to categorize businesses—for example, by capital intensity, product differentiation, or rate of industry growth—none has proved as useful to our clients as maturity. Maturity is determined by, and has impact on, certain observable

[1] See ADL publication, *Strategy Centers/A Contemporary Managing System,* by Robert V. L. Wright.

Industry maturity

Strategic competitive position	*Embryonic*	*Growth*	*Mature*	*Aging*
Dominant				
Strong				
Favorable				
Tenable				
Weak				

Figure 1 Matrix for categorizing business units.

business actions; therefore, it can be "tracked" by noting the level and rate of change in such things as technology, breadth of product line, rate of industry growth compared to GNP, degree of market concentration, and conditions of exit and entry.

The implications of the concept of industry maturity and the criteria for classifying industries cannot be treated in full detail here; however, in general terms, industries can conveniently be grouped into four stages of maturity. An *embryonic* industry (for example, laser measuring devices) is normally characterized by rapid growth, changes in technology, great pursuit of new customers, and fragmented and changing shares of market; a *growth* industry is one that is still growing rapidly, but customers, shares, and technology are better known and entry into the industry is more difficult (as illustrated by RCA's attempt to enter the computer business); a *mature* industry (like automobiles or paper in this country) is characterized by stability in known customers, technology, and in shares of market, although the industries may still be market-competitive; and *aging* industries (such as men's hats) are best described by falling demand, a declining number of competitors, and, in many such industries, a narrowing of the product line.

Some of our clients have added descriptive words to the four categories, such as spring, summer, fall, and winter; or sweepstake, stock, bond, and mortgage. Whatever terms are used, no value judgment on the characterization is implied. Each industry is what it is; each industry has a function and a role. A particular stage of maturity becomes "bad" only if the role assumed by or assigned to an industry participant is inappropriate to the nature of the industry or requires of the participant a performance at odds with what can reasonably be expected.

Determining Strategic Competitive Position

As a Strategy Center acquires certain attributes over time and in relation to its competitors, it gains or loses competitive advantage and can be classified at a given time as having a certain defined strategic position in its field: dominant, strong, favorable, tenable, or weak (or, in the worst case, non-viable). This is the other side of the matrix for categorizing business units.

Strategic competitive position is one of the most complex elements of business analysis and one of the least researched. In the face of this complexity, there is a temptation to fall back upon a single criterion such as share of market, but our experience tells us that competitive position can and must be treated as a multi-criteria problem embracing, for example, technology, breadth of product line, market share, share movement, and special market relationships. Such factors change in relative importance as maturity changes.

Selecting Strategies

Once each business unit has been located in the matrix of industry maturity and competitive position, a strategy can be formulated for each. In essence, a strategy directs resource investment to a series (or program) of related actions which together constitute a selected path to a certain objective—taking into account constraints on capital, expense, or time.

Most business managers and planners have a sense of the menu of possible choices of business strategies. We have compiled a "deck" of such choices, both for Strategy Centers within a corporation and for the corporation as a whole. With the matrix as a framework, the appropriate "natural" (or generically presumptive) strategies can be identified for each combination of maturity and competitive position. Strategies selected this way are the "first cut" at unit strategy determination. Subsequent refinement from the generic to the specific then leads to final strategy determination.

However, a unit is not always free to choose a natural strategy. A Strategy Center within a corporation, or a corporation which is itself a Strategy Center, may find its natural strategy precluded by internal tradeoffs or external competitive moves. When a *corporation's* long-term objectives conflict with full exploitation of a unit's market advantage, or when the company cannot appropriately fund all of its prime opportunities, a unit may be assigned a strategy which, though "unnatural" for its maturity and competitive position, is nevertheless appropriate for the corporate good. This is most apparent at resource allocation time, or when a corporation must change direction or emphasis.

Comparing Actual versus Expected Performance of Strategies

Unit strategy choice is obviously not a game of sheer preference or opportunity exploitation. Each and every strategy entails degrees of investment, returns, and risks; each strategy has its own pattern (rising or falling) of performance attributes, for example, the ratios of return on investment or earnings and sales. Because these patterns vary from one strategy to another, each strategy must be measured by its own financial "template," linking its salient performance characteristics to the Strategy Center's maturity/competitive position profile and the unit's actual performance. We call this process a testing for performance congruency.

Certain performance indicators (ratios) tend to move in certain directions during certain stages of maturity and are influenced by the actual strategy being executed, making it possible to see whether a strategy proposed is a strategy executed, and if so, how successfully. For example, a Strategy Center in a mature industry pursuing a long-term efficiency plan would normally show a declining ratio of inventory to sales. The widely prevailing practice of using a fixed set of indicators to track *all* units, whatever their strategies, maturity, or competitive position, results in serious suboptimization of performance and contributes to the familiar "diversity headache" which the Strategy Center approach has been designed to cure.

Choosing Managerial Systems

It is one of the clichés of contemporary design that form should follow function. This philosophy has led many organizations to question some traditional aspects of their managerial systems. In a multi-industry company, populated by many units in different stages of maturity and following different strategies, the diversity of such units creates a strain on uniform managerial systems, and vice versa. The logic of what is required in an administrative system to support a given strategy may be readily apparent, but it is very difficult to avoid the constraints of established corporate systems to allow all these different unit logics to be served at once. Examples of activities and functions that should be adjusted for different stages of maturity, and possible forms of that adjustment, are illustrated in Figure 2. A comparison of existing functional characteristics with the stage of maturity is what we call a "management congruency test."

MANAGEMENT ACTIVITY OR FUNCTION	*EMBRYONIC INDUSTRY*	*GROWTH INDUSTRY*	*MATURE INDUSTRY*	*AGING INDUSTRY*
Managerial role	*Entrepreneur*	*Sophisticated market manager*	*Critical administrator*	*"Opportunistic milker"*
Planning time frame	*Long enough to draw tentative life cycle (10)*	*Long-range investment payout (7)*	*Intermediate (3)*	*Short-range (1)*
Planning content	*By product/customer*	*By product and program*	*By product/market/ function*	*By plant*
Planning style	*Flexible*	*Less flexible*	*Fixed*	*Fixed*
Organization structure	*Free-form or task force*	*Semi-permanent task force, product or market division*	*Business division plus task force for renewal*	*Pared-down division*
Managerial compensation	*High variable/low fixed, fluctuating with performance*	*Balanced variable and fixed, individual and group rewards*	*Low variable/high fixed group rewards*	*Fixed only*
Policies	*Few*	*More*	*Many*	*Many*
Procedures	*None*	*Few*	*Many*	*Many*
Communication system	*Informal/tailor-made*	*Formal/tailor-made*	*Formal/uniform*	*Little or none, by direction*
Managerial style	*Participation*	*Leadership*	*Guidance/loyalty*	*Loyalty*
Content of reporting system	*Qualitative, marketing, unwritten*	*Qualitative and quantitative, early warning system, all functions*	*Quantitative, written, production oriented*	*Numerical, oriented to written balance sheet*
Measures used	*Few fixed*	*Multiple/adjustable*	*Multiple/adjustable*	*Few/fixed*
Frequency of measuring	*Often*	*Relatively often*	*Traditionally periodic*	*Less often*
Detail of measurement	*Less*	*More*	*Great*	*Less*
Corporate departmental emphasis	*Market research; new product development*	*Operations research; organization development*	*Value analysis; data processing, taxes and insurance*	*Purchasing*

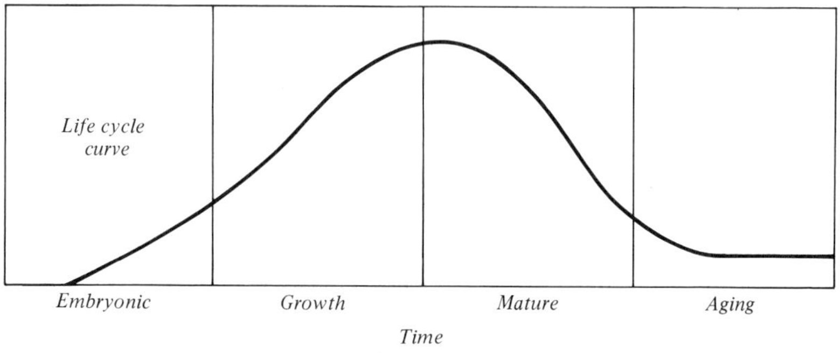

Figure 2 Management characteristics by stage of industry maturity.

Determining Strategic Risk

The entire Strategy Center Development System, in terms of strategy and administration, is conveniently summarized by the concept of strategic risk. The past predictability of performance (i.e., risk) of each business unit is a convenient cross-check on the logic of each business unit's intended strategies and results. It provides another congruency test. Essential to the management of diversity is an understanding of where to place one's bets with respect to anticipated rates of return. The individual Strategy Center manager and the corporation are both interested in the individual diverse risks, and the corporation is interested in the balance of risk.

Certain risks are associated with any particular industry; for example, women's contemporary fashions involves greater risk than does the retail food chain industry. Also, certain strategies are more predictable, and therefore less risky, than other strategies, and past performance and the level of expected future performance give strong clues as to risk. We have found that the inherent strategic risk of a Strategy Center is usually related to its place in the matrix of maturity and competitive position, as illustrated in Figure 3. In general, we find the unpredictability of performance (hence, the risk) is greatest for units with a weak competitive position in an embryonic business and least for those with a dominant position in an aging business.

A STRATEGY DEVELOPMENT PROCESS

Unit Profiling and Corporate Strategy Development

We have emphasized that the managing of diversity has at its core the micro-economic analysis of the corporation's business units or Strategy Centers. Our experience has taught us that this analysis must be done by the units using a common analytical framework, drawing upon the group efforts of those people who know the most about each business unit being analyzed. This calls for the involvement of the principal managers of all functions of the business unit. This is not to suggest that this group will know, initially, all that is needed to carry out the business analysis. It is they, however, who have the responsibility for beginning the strategy development process—the ultimate results of which they must live with.

The process of analysis, strategy development and communication we call "profiling,"

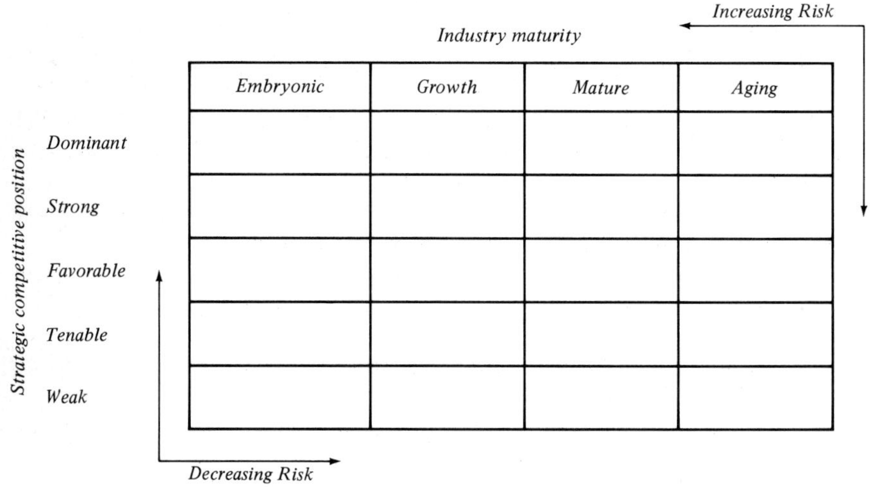

Figure 3 Risk matrix.

and the document we introduce to our clients for capturing and transmitting Strategy Center data and plans is entitled the "Strategy Center Profile." This is an outsized single sheet of paper on which is assembled all of the information needed to make the analyses described in this report. It includes past and planned performance, financial ratios computed from market statistics, and balance sheet and income statement data, as well as the information necessary to determine each unit's industry and market segment designations, industry maturity, competitive position, strategy selection, performance congruency tests, managerial system changes, and risk analysis.

A profile for a Strategy Center can be developed by the assembled management group of the unit in an intensive session usually lasting three days. This we have found is the normal time needed for the production of the initial strategic plan. In succeeding iterations, the process may take less time if conditions have not altered, or longer if a severe change in course is dictated either by market conditions or corporate needs. Prior to the profiling session certain basic materials are collected, and following the session details may need to be ironed out.

Our experience with clients leads us to conclude that it is best to have the profiling session led by someone outside of the unit being profiled. This trained outsider need not be from outside the company, but should not be there as a symbol of hierarchical authority; what is needed is intelligent naiveté about the unit.

In many instances we find that the management group has never before been assembled for the purpose of strategy development; or, if they have been together, it has been for the ritual of reciprocal deference to one another's special expertise. Usually the personnel manager, and in some instances the research director, will never before have participated in strategy development. Because of the use of a new common language denoting matrix positions, strategy types, congruency measures, and the other concepts inherent in the Strategy Center Development System—a language neither solely that of the controller nor that of the marketing manager—the group quickly traverses the learning curve for genuine interdisciplinary dialogue.

Of course, the purpose of analyzing business units is to categorize and evaluate them not only in terms of their intrinsic values for market and financial performance and their inherent risks, but also as elements of corporate strategy. The process of business analysis and strategy development at the Strategy Center level is guided continuously by the existence of the umbrella of a corporate strategy. However, in dealing with clients, we stress that in the initial development of both unit and corporate strategies the business units (Strategy Centers) should submit natural strategies without undue regard to an implied corporate strategy, and the corporation should remain aware of the possible trade-off imposed on the Strategy Center if the corporation does not allow the unit to select a natural strategy.

The end-product of the corporate strategy process as performed by our clients is a "Corporate Strategy Guideline Statement," subject to the periodic updating, revision, re-submission, and continuing analysis of the Strategy Centers' strategic plans. The specific objectives, strategies, policies, and admonitions making up this "Guideline" provide the framework for business planning. They are the basis for corporate review of the plans of each Strategy Center and for determination of whether a unit can follow its own "natural" strategy or whether a "revectored" strategy must be imposed by corporate direction or restraints.

A Client Case Example

To illustrate both the content and the process of the Strategy Center Development System, let us describe briefly a client situation. In this instance our client was a $2 billion multi-industry U.S. corporation with considerable overseas operations. (Our Strategy Center Development clients have been for the most part multi-industry or variated single-industry companies. All can be described as "multi-businesses." They have varied in size from $50 million to $12 billion.) A new Chief Executive Officer had just taken charge after the death of his predecessor. Notwithstanding his extraordinary abilities, he found himself managing a corporation made up of some thirty business units of varying size and health, in only two of which he had had any previous operating experience. He was in the market for what Peter Drucker has referred to as a "knowledge system"—an analytical framework which would allow him to understand his multi-business without having to acquire direct experience in each unit. He adopted the Strategy Center Development System to meet this need and to serve as the principal concept and device in the building of business unit strategies and an overall corporation strategy.

Prior to being invited to help install a new strategy system for the company, we identified and profiled two of its Strategy Centers as case studies in order to demonstrate the technique and acquaint key managers with what was involved. These two examples illustrated the profiling process to the operating hierarchy, trained in-house profilers who would subsequently help train others as well as serve their own units, and illustrated to the Chief Executive Officer how to use the resulting information as input to the development of a corporate strategy. The first two units produced their initial strategic plans within two months, and all thirty units had produced theirs five months later.

In parallel with this pilot profiling effort, we and the client's staff jointly began to assemble contextual economic, social, and political information, and began to design the process and tools for reviewing, revising, and integrating the proposed strategic plans of the units. All these elements converged as inputs to a corporate strategy, developed in an iterative series of interactions among the CEO, his principal officers, ourselves, and the assembled information.

Since the issuance of our client's Corporate Strategy Guideline Statement, the Strategy Center Development System has become institutionalized as part of the cycle culminating in budget submissions and approval prior to the beginning of the fiscal year. The process is staggered by units throughout the fiscal year to avoid congestion during the latter part of the year. This schedule allows the Strategy Centers to uncouple their thinking from the "tyranny of the accounting system" and gives the corporation time to review, discuss, and interrogate strategies on a less hurried basis. The conceptual and analytical framework of the system has given the corporation the flexibility to deal with units either sequentially or in parallel. For long-term financial forecasting, each unit has to submit current strategic performance numbers late in the third quarter, but no instant massive review of everyone's strategy has to be crammed as before into a constricted time frame.

The initial corporate strategy development sessions highlighted the need to ensure that standards of operating performance for the various units were adjusted to match their respective strategic requirements. Stemming from these discussions, a series of joint client/consultant assignments resulted in changes in the managerial compensation system, in reporting requirements, and in the organizational structure of two Strategy Centers.

Most importantly, the corporation took steps toward reshaping its assets and performance. It sold off certain businesses that either did not fit its long-term intentions or could not be managed effectively, and it wrote off certain low-return assets.

Key Management Skills

The kind of strategic thinking that is described here is concerned not just with what, but with why; not just with objectives, but with paths and relationships; not just with checklists, but with process. It goes beyond experience and received knowledge into the acquisition of knowledge and open-ended exploration. Our experience tells us that strategy knows no rank; the "mind set" and skills required to "strategize" are found in individuals exercising many different functions and holding many different ranks in an organization. Strategic thinking is neither a universal trait nor an exclusive attribute of marketing, financial, or planning staffs or a prerogative of senior management—particularly in a multi-business.

Because a track record of business success may act as an inhibiting factor in future attempts to succeed, and because those closest to today's opportunities are often those least disposed to consider the futurity of their present decisions, we urge our clients to open up strategy development and analysis to more functions and more ranks. This does not exclude the planning experts, but it increases the likelihood of hearing challenges and penetrating questions.

A predictable question in the area of strategic planning is "What should the role of the Chief Executive Officer be?" In approaching diversity through a strategic process, he must see it as a manageable, exciting, continuous and normal condition of his job. He must bring together the skills needed to solve strategic problems. He may not be (and often is not) the world's greatest strategist, but he must be adept as a leader, interrogator, debater, and conciliator.

The Outsider's Role

For business units and corporations in a state of transition, we believe that strategy development is accelerated and enhanced by the presence of a trained "profiler" from outside the unit to provide objectivity and insight. The contributions of consultants to strategy development can vary widely depending on the nature of the problem and the planning expertise available within the client organization. In our own assignments involving the Strategy Center approach, one of the most critical functions we have performed is to help the client think through and implement changes in managerial systems and behavior to ensure their congruency with the nature of each Strategy Center. These changes are not always obvious and are not easily brought about. For one member of a management team to suggest that other members change established systems in the name of "congruent balance" is usually much harder than for outsiders to demonstrate the needs and the benefits. For this reason we have built into our consulting teams individuals with the multidisciplinary skills needed to deal with the downstream effects of strategy decisions on measurement and control systems, compensation schemes, and organizational structures. Each of our teams also includes an expert in professional task force operations and in the "process skills" relating to organizational development and conflict resolution. Strategy development is a multidimensional process which involves externalities, internal political realities, micro-economics, sociology, and game theory—all in the context of a particular industry or set of industries. This calls for depth and diversity in the resources brought to it and for flexibility in the consultants' contribution.

Time, Costs, and Benefits

A Strategy Center Development system can be installed in a relatively short time. Our experience is that having once tested the system, the organization itself pushes for rapid installation, fully realizing that all units must use the same vocabulary and criteria for analysis if the system is to be effective. From introduction to full installation, the process has been completed by some clients within two years. This is not to suggest that it becomes part of the culture that soon, nor does it suggest that the process and its supporting systems are not being refined and balanced beyond that period. However, the concepts and methodology can be effectively applied to real-time question of resource allocation within this time.

One reason for the relative ease and rapidity of understanding and installing the system is that most operating managers in multi-business corporations already intuitively recognize that they need some such system. They have chafed under highly proceduralized, ill-fitting, and burdensome uniform planning systems. The reams of material prepared for, submitted to, and often unread by superior levels in the organization have converted many highly intelligent unit managers into anti-planners. Moreover, the resource allocation process and corporate decisions regarding acquisitions and appointment of personnel often seem somewhat arbitrary. Managers have always sought the underlying logic of corporate decisions, in order to assess the justice of resource allocations and strategy restraints. Lacking a convincing rationale, and seldom included in the process, they have been less than fully committed to official plans.

Even when the ratio of benefits to costs is high, the costs should not go unnoted. The greatest cost of learning and installing such a system is in terms of time. It takes less time than that required of the typical "comprehensive planning system," but still requires time of some considerable magnitude and involves more managers, initially, than do traditional systems. Consultant costs depend in large part on how much of a joint undertaking the effort is. We stress the value of close, bilateral effort by client and consultant team in order to hasten the transfer of knowledge and technique. Because this is challenging, difficult, and risky work, the costs are not trivial.

In Conclusion

Most companies are looking for better ways for dealing with "unique" situations. The single hurdle rate for capital investment is slowly being dropped, and the single performance measurement criterion is no longer being used with the same assurance that has been characteristic of the recent past. Increasingly, corporations are concerned that they maintain an organizational climate favorable to "corporate renewal"—one in which embryonic ventures can flourish. What has become apparent to them and to us is that if they are multi-businesses they need to be managed much differently than if they are not.

The receptiveness to new approaches also stems in part from an uneasiness about and disappointment in decentralization. In the past, the concept of decentralization served as a needed control device and as such was called upon as a tool for managing great size and a stimulus to motivate unit heads. Unfortunately, decentralization has not led automatically to corporate performance optimization, nor has it created a convincing climate of "entrepreneurship." Unit managers have realized that membership in the "club," large benefit programs, corporate funded research, well-established corporate brand identity, "across the board" resource cuts and program postponements have made their roles and their motives something less than those of true entrepreneurs.

Compounding the complexity of both the opportunity and problem of managing diversity are some increasingly potent external variables. It is not only necessary to resolve conflict between the economic ends and the internal values and culture of the corporation, but also to calculate the ever-changing cross-impacts and trade-offs among economic, social, and political forces.

Diversity, particularly in multinational companies, gives the Chief Executive Officer and his corporate strategists an opportunity to play what some have called the "ultimate matrix game"—dealing with the multiple impacts of multiple forces on multiple businesses in order to develop a corporate strategy. However, without a system for classifying and developing strategies for diverse business units, neither corporate strategy development, performance analysis, nor resource allocation can be carried out intelligently. More complex matrices are involved in managing a large urban area or a nation, but for the corporation, strategy development is the highest art form for the largest stakes.

Part Three

Establishing Marketing Objectives

What are the real objectives of the business firm?

In recent years the "customer" approaches advocated by Peter Drucker and by Theodore Levitt have challenged the traditional belief that the success of a firm should be measured by returns on capital invested. The "answer" probably is to be found by looking at a firm's objectives in a hierarchical context. At one level is the goal of profit maximization, while at another social responsibilities tend to serve as constraints to profit maximization.

Product/market relationships best describe the business in which a firm is engaged. Once such relationships are clearly planned and developed, a firm has a means of determining the best allocation of its resources. This calls for the study of buyers in each market segment to determine their probable responses to various marketing inputs.

Three different but related subjects are discussed in this section: determining the marketing objectives; predicting behavior in the marketplace; and segmenting the market. The determination of marketing objectives involves the development of corporate strategy and the concept of what strategy really is. Predicting behavior in the marketplace includes consideration of consumer decision-process models; of materials from the behavioral sciences; analysis of a new way to measure consumers' judgments; and methods of segmenting the market.

6

Corporate Strategy, Marketing and Diversification

Harry Henry

In order to understand the relationship between corporate strategy and the marketing concept the author postulates a number of questions which top management should ask itself. First, a company should decide what its objectives actually are; second, it should assess its existing product mix and market position and the probable shape of the future; third, in the light of these assessments, it should formulate its long-term corporate objectives.

This process of rigorous self-appraisal is a necessary prerequisite of successful strategic planning; and as a conceptual framework it may be applied to all companies in all situations.

The corporate strategy concept, being only about five years old, is currently extremely fashionable: the marketing concept, now almost twenty years old, has lost a good deal of its glamour. Since it is characteristic of most of us to seek for new management techniques which will give us better results without actually requiring us to modify in any substantial degree the way in which we conduct our businesses, we are naturally inclined to turn our enthusiasm to concepts which have not yet come to the crunch, in the hope that this will enable us to sweep under the carpet earlier concepts, the later stages of implementation of which are beginning to cause us some embarrassment. But the introduction of the corporate strategy concept in no way supersedes or vitiates the marketing concept. Indeed, it is largely meaningless without it, while a good deal of the difficulty involved in the implementation of the marketing concept arises from the fact that this latter needs to be viewed against the background provided by the corporate strategy concept itself.

Despite its relative novelty, the subject of corporate strategy has already accumulated a pretty massive literature, though it is difficult to avoid the impression that many of the contributions are saying the same thing in slightly different words. This is not because of any lack of insight or integrity on the part of their authors: it arises from the fact that there are relatively few main components of the concept, and that once they have been listed out it is virtually impossible to think of any others. But the complexity of the subject, and hence the opportunity it offers for reexposition, arises from the fact that most of its components can be seen as interacting with each other in almost any sequence or combination you care to select, and that one particular sequence and combination will attach different significance than another to a specific component.

What is meant by this will perhaps become rather clearer if we look at the very simplified hierarchical diagram of the corporate planning process, consisting merely of four questions:

1 What are our corporate objectives?
2 What business are we in?
3 What are our relevant strengths and weaknesses (internal and external)?
4 So where do we go from here?

The fourth question, of course, will automatically break down further into sets of options and plans, and the first three questions will prove on examination to be nothing like as

Reprinted from *Perspectives in Management, Marketing and Research* (London, Crosby Lockwood and Son Limited, 1971).

simple as they might seem at first sight. They will be discussed at a later stage: what we are concerned with at the moment is to indicate that we cannot answer the first three questions (and hence put ourselves in a position to tackle question 4) simply in the order 1, 2, 3; other orders could be just as relevant, or even more so.

Suppose, for example, one of the corporate objectives is set as a materially increased return on capital employed and the company is engaged in an industry where (*a*) capital employed consists largely of fixed plant, and (*b*) the market in which the industry operates provides only a low return. Unless the company can find some much more efficient method of operating, unknown to its competitors (which may be possible, but is improbable), such an objective might be unattainable until question 2 has been answered by saying 'some other business than our present one'. But before you can say this, you have to answer question 3, which covers not only the skills inherent in the business but also such things as the nature of the assets. Even if you decide to get out of the business, how do you do so? If you sell the assets on their earnings performance, you are no better off, and you can probably sell them on their capital value only if you are lucky enough to find some megalomaniac competitor obsessed with growth.

This is only one example: it is not too difficult to think of others which will equally well serve to illustrate that these three questions cannot meaningfully be answered in any fixed hierarchical sequence. And, obviously, if we run into this sort of difficulty in so simplified a model, the complications that arise when we start treating the concept more realistically, and therefore in greater detail, will increase exponentially.

CORPORATE OBJECTIVES

I have mentioned corporate objectives without so far attempting to indicate what these may be. I am not here suggesting what they *should* be: let us at this stage simply look at some of the areas which have been advanced as appropriate objectives for corporate strategy, starting off with what may be called the 'economic' ones, which are listed below. In most cases the word 'growth' may be assumed as being attached. What that means we can come to later.

Areas of possible economic objectives:

- return on equity
- return on assets (variously defined)
- price/earnings ratio
- volume of business
- size of operation
- liquidity
- flexibility
- risk reduction
- share of market

Not all of these necessarily belong in this list, but before we deal with them we might consider other objectives which, though non-economic and frequently not made explicit, can be just as significant to the management or the shareholders of a company. In practice they loom largest when the management *are* the controlling shareholds, but that is another matter.

Areas of possible non-economic objectives:

- survival of the business
- security for management
- security for personnel
- size of operation
- company prestige
- social responsibility

It may seem a little surprising that 'survival of the business' should be listed among the non-economic objectives, and that 'size of operation' should appear on both lists. But before these paradoxes are explained it would be as well for us to consider what we may be 'growth' and also to make reference to the question of time.

The investor who puts his money into equities, as against fixed-interest stocks, does so today for two reasons. One reason is as old as investment itself: he is putting his money at risk in the expectation that his foresight and judgement will be suitably rewarded, by a higher rate of return than he could hope for it he sought greater security—say in government bonds. The second reason, resulting from the general acceptance of the fact that we shall live for ever in conditions of regular inflation, is his desire to maintain his return at least constant in real terms.

Under present conditions in the money market the average investor does not attempt to separate in his mind these two components of his expectation: it is not at all certain that even the institutional investors do. But it is important that corporate managements should, in order that they may determine what degree of 'growth' they feel obliged to provide. Clearly they are required to furnish sufficient growth in return on equity to counter inflation: equally clearly they are required to provide some special return on equity to remunerate the shareholder for his risk. But whether that special return should itself be subject to growth—inflation apart—is by no means so obvious, particularly if such growth involves any increase in the size of risk.

Inflation underlines the time element involved in corporate objectives. But, even without this, corporate objectives must necessarily be long-range, taking into account not only likely changes in market needs and the probability of developments in production technology, both within the firm itself and outside, but also other external circumstances subject to change, and the consequences of the company's long-range strategy itself.

Indeed, at any particular moment of time corporate objectives must be determined by the nature, structure and situation of the company in question, and the criteria may differ not only quantitatively but also qualitatively. What is appropriate for a giant corporation with equity widely distributed in public hands may not be acceptable to the middle-sized company still basically in family hands: in the latter case particularly non-economic objectives may be of major significance. Further, such operating objectives as increased return on investment, growth in scale of operations, and reduction of risk, may often be incompatible one with another: how the company will choose among these must depend upon its current position and the requirements of its owners.

At this point we return to a more detailed consideration of the areas of possible objectives, beginning with the economic objectives. Growth in return on equity has already been discussed: an alternative objective might be growth in return on assets though there is vigorous controversy about which criterion is the better, and, indeed, about how 'assets' are going to be defined and I do not want to get involved in this.

It is unusual to list growth in price/earnings ratio as a possible corporate objective, but I think it legitimate at least to consider it in this context. Since a high P/E ratio reflects the judgement of the money market that a particular company has considerable growth potential still to be developed, it cannot be expected to be maintained for ever, but in the short term it may be of major importance to a company planning growth by acquisition and intending to use shares rather than cash for that purpose, or indeed, to a company planning to go to the market for more equity. Whether what is thus essentially a tool of growth may legitimately be regarded as an objective in its own right is an interesting philosophical point, but in practice it is difficult to separate the two, certainly over the sort of time-span we are considering. At the same time, a high P/E ratio is some defence against being taken over, and if the avoidance of takeover is a legitimate objective of the business—something we shall examine among the non-economic objectives—then the same considerations apply.

I have listed growth in the volume of business, along with growth in the size of the operation, as among the possible corporate objectives, because a number of people regard them in this light. I do not: growth for its own sake seems fairly pointless. It may, of course, provide the necessary mechanism for growth in profitability, but in this case it becomes a tactical manoeuvre, not a strategic objective. It may inhibit the growth of a competitor to a position of market dominance, but before such inhibition is accepted as a necessary corporate objective it is as well to be sure that the threat of competitive market dominance is real and not merely emotional or superstitious. Unless there is some reason to suppose the threat actually does exist, then growth in the size of the operation unrelated to growth in profitability ought really to be included among the non-economic objectives. And the same considerations apply to growth in market share, which is simply another aspect of the same subject.

It may be added that growth in volume of business, even if it does not result directly in any increase in the return on equity, could be conceived as likely to have beneficial side-effects, resuling from an increase in the over-all scale of operations. But this is looking at the matter through the wrong end of the telescope: if the over-all corporate objectives of the company entail a higher level of activity, then that higher level might be considered a means rather than an end in itself, as indeed might the effect of being in an expanding business on the morale of the executive staff and on the company's success in staff recruitment.

Liquidity and flexibility should perhaps be considered together. Whether or not a change in either or both is an appropriate corporate objective must depend entirely on the nature of the business, the industries in which it is operating, its existing capital structure, and the requirements of its owners in terms of both economic and non-economic objectives.

Let us now consider the examples listed of non-economic objectives, of which the first is survival of the business. Here we must define our terms: clearly it is no part of anybody's corporate objectives to run a company into bankruptcy. The economic objectives concerned with return on equity or assets look after this, however, and when we talk about the survival of the business otherwise we mean its survival as a separate entity, which is quite another thing.

It may well be to the economic advantage of the owners of a company—that is, the shareholders—that the company should be taken over at a good price and submerged in some other company. Indeed, a very considerable number of shareholders live in hopes that this will happen to some of their investments. In these circumstances the fight which managements put up to fend off takeover bids may sometimes be viewed with a jaundiced eye by at least a substantial minority of shareholders. On the other hand, the ultimate decision rests in the hands of the shareholders as a whole, and the question of the right of a board of directors to run a company in such a way that is not particularly attractive to a potential takeover bidder, so that the shareholders are not led into temptation, raises questions about the duties and responsibilities of directors which it would be out of place to discuss here. And while it is true that non-economic objectives of the type listed may sometimes be held by a mass of outside shareholders it is equally true that they are more usually found to exist in companies where the management holds equity control, and more particularly in family businesses.

In this context, the objective of security for management may simply mean that the family would rather have a given level of profit, and jobs, than a higher level of profit and no jobs. This is their right, as is their right to choose the other objectives listed. Size of operations and company prestige, in so far as they are not implicit in the company's economic objectives, fall into this same general category of decisions which it is the right of managements to take as a matter of personal preference when they are also the owners of the business but which are possibly beyond their proper powers when they are not. On the other hand, the questions of security for personnel and social responsibility are nothing like so easy to deal with in these terms, and open up major issues well beyond the orbit of corporate planning. All that can really be said here is that if these are regarded by the management of the company as legitimate objectives then the corporate planning procedure has no option but to accept them as constraints on the economic objectives.

The second question we asked in our simplified model of the corporate planning process was 'what business are we in'. This is the question on which the most popular attention has been focused in the recent literature of management, and it has produced some very odd answers, the basic philosophy underlying many of them being enshrined in Theodore Levitt's now classic article on 'Marketing myopia' in the *Harvard Business Review* of July–August 1960, and encapsulated in his observation on the buggy whip industry, which read: 'No amount of product improvement could stave off its death sentence. But had the industry defined itself as being in the transportation business rather than the buggy whip business it might have survived. It would have done what survival always entails, that is, changing.'

This particular example has so tickled the fancy of management enthusiasts that it is almost heresy to ask just what it means, or what is understood by 'the transportation business,' or who defined buggy whips as being part of it, or what the buggy whip makers were in a position to change to. Another example from the same article unconsciously underlines the difficulty even more strongly:

> The railroads did not stop growing because the need for passengers and freight transportation declined. That grew. The railroads are in trouble today not because the need was filled by others . . . but because . . . they assumed themselves to be in the railroad business rather than in the transportation business. The reason they defined their industry wrongly was because they were railroad-oriented instead of transportation-oriented; they were product-oriented instead of customer-oriented.

Now I yield to no man in my contempt for excessive product-orientation, but a market cannot really be defined except in relation to the products serving it, and the hard fact remains that railways are in the business of providing rail transportation, not transportation in general. If the market for their category of product is declining, so that they wish to invest elsewhere, then obviously it makes sense whether their existing railway operations and experience would give them a competitive edge in the airline business. If this is not the case, then there is no particular reason for them to choose airlines as a diversification.

Skills and Resources

Indeed, there is some case for suggesting that the business a company is in can only be defined as the business of meeting its corporate objectives. How it ought to go about this is something which derives, not from Cartesian definition-mongering, but from a meticulous appraisal of what means it has to that end: in current Corporate Planning terminology, what are its strengths and weaknesses.

These means fall into three main categories:

1 Production resources and skills.
2 Marketing structures and skills.
3 Financial resources and availabilities.

Production resources and skills include, of course, R and D facilities, and the financial resources and availabilities will naturally condition the two other categories. (It may be noticed that I have not included in this list anything that can be identified as 'general management skills.' This is because I personally do not believe that such generalised skills exist independently of the specialised skills already listed. General management has skills, of course, but these represent a mix, in various proportions, of the major business skills in production, marketing and finance. The thinking that sometimes leads companies into enterprises they do not know how to operate, that 'we understand the art of management' is perhaps on a par with that of those of us who came out of the services after the last war having as our only qualification 'I know how to control men.')

The means and resources existing within the company, or available to it, must then be measured against the markets to which these are appropriate, and against likely developments in those markets. In fact, the appraisal of the company's strengths and weaknesses, though it is likely to be time-consuming and to entail a lot of work, is conceptually the simplest part of the task. Where the real difficulty is encountered is in delimiting the relevant markets.

Here, as in so much else in management theory, we run straight into problems of definition. In the first place, we have to decide whether the word 'market' is defined by use or by geography: the question of geography is not unimportant, and we shall return to it later, but at this stage it is desirable to confine our definition to that of use.

But even at that we can find ourselves in some confusion, since whatever definitions are selected are likely to be either too narrow or too wide. What is the market for breakfast cereals? If we define it in terms of the present volume of consumption of the product category we have something which at least is clear-cut, but which is liable to have a very restrictive effect on our thinking. If, on the other hand, we try to define it in terms of the potential market, then there is no breakfast cereal market at all—merely a breakfast market, in which each brand of cereal battles for market share not only against all other brands but also against grapefruit, porridge, eggs, bacon, sausages and kippers—and, indeed, against nothing at all, an option always open to the commuter in a hurry. Similarly, should not the market for frozen vegetables be defined in terms of total market for vegetables—frozen, canned and fresh alike? We are back here, in effect, with the problem of whether the railways are in the transportation business or in the rail transportation business, and it is probably true to say that most manufacturers are inclined to take the narrower definition. On the other hand, some service industries adopt the much wider definition, and declare, for example, 'we are in the entertainment business' or even more widely, 'we are in the leisure business.'

The conceptual framework which has been put forward as providing a basis for decision in the light of corporate objectives and the company's resources, the product/market matrix, does not help a great deal with this problem. This, like so much else in corporate planning theory, is Professor Ansoff's, and takes, under his title of 'Growth Vector Component's, the form shown in Figure 1, though he uses the word 'mission' instead of 'market' for classification purposes, in order to make a distinction between the need being served and the actual customer.

This is possibly not the most useful break-

Product / *Market*	*Present*	*New*
Present	Market penetration	Market development
New	Product development	Diversification

Figure 1

down. A market can only be defined as the market for a product, and in this case the product itself defines the market. Thus a present product cannot be said to have the potential of a new market—that is, if we are ignoring the geographical sense of the term. A new market otherwise is only open to a new product. At the same time, however, there could sometimes be a case for considering a market as being defined by a certain type of distribution structure: we shall see an example of this later.

We might consider here an alternative matrix, based on the classification of present markets as 'saturated' or 'extensible.' Saturated markets are those where the total volume of sales is unlikely now to increase very rapidly whatever the industry does about it, such as toilet soap, or cigarettes, or toothpaste, so that a new product can only gain a foothold at the expense of existing products: extensible markets are those which can be regarded as capable of being expanded either through an increase in the number of consumers or an increase in the average *per capita* consumption. This is rather more in like with the realities of modern markets, and produces the schedule of growth vectors shown in Figure 2.

Product / *Market*	*Existing*	*New*
Saturated	Market penetration	Product development
Extensible	Market development	Product/market diversification
New		Diversification

Figure 2

At this point it is necessary to consider what difference is made if we take into our thinking the definition of markets in geographical terms. This approach is, of course, far more common in the United States than here, because of the much more regionalised nature of the US economy, and when we ourselves adopt it we normally do so in terms of export markets. Conceptually, however, it makes remarkably little difference: though the product may be an existing one so far as our production processes are concerned, it is a new product in marketing terms for the market in question, and though the particular vector thus involved might perhaps be better described as 'market extension' rather than 'diversification' yet the fact that we are probably going outside our established marketing structures and skills could well justify our continuing to regard the operation as a diversification.

The precise point at which a particular market ceases to be 'extensible' and becomes 'saturated' is, of course, likely to be very much a matter of degree and judgement. Nor is the distinction always clear between 'existing' and 'new' products: indeed, the difficulties here are likely to be not only conceptual but also practical. Continuous product improvement is the rule rather than the exception for most industries today, and the point at which such improvement turns an existing product into a new one is not easy to identify. Yet this can be of considerable importance in leading a company to decide which growth vector offers the greatest potential for the effort and resources likely to be involved. For an existing product in a saturated market, for example, market penetration can only come from more skillful marketing (broadly defined): a clear product improvement, however, could shift the operation over towards the product development vector, where the return might be materially greater. This problem becomes even more intractable when we turn to those industries which are in the habit of producing new models at reasonably frequent intervals, and possibly most intractable of all in connection with cars.

Selecting Vectors of Operation

It now remains to review briefly how we go about selecting which are the vectors in which we are going to operate, in the light of our corporate objectives and the production, marketing and financial resources and skills of which we dispose. The growth vectors are, as we have seen, identified by the interrelation between alternative product conditions along one dimension and alternative market conditions along the other. To a major extent the product conditions may be regarded as being under our control, in so far as we can lay down specifications and, according to our skill, have those specifications met at one price or another. But market conditions are largely outside the control of the firm, and have therefore to be taken as externally determined. It therefore follows that in any market/product interaction it is, with rare exceptions, the market which calls the tune, and it is to this fact that I refer when I point out that the corporate strategy concept in no way vitiates the marketing concept, but needs to take it in.

But in making it clear that the marketing concept should be subordinate to the corporate strategy concept we must not overlook the fact, already pointed out, that marketing considerations must always be important, and may well be dominant, in any implementation of corporate strategy. For product development requires that the product thus developed shall be acceptable to the consumer, by meeting a consumer need; market development assumes that the market for an existing product is extensible, because latent needs exist which can be exploited; diversification presupposes that a market/product organism can be found in an area of which the firm has no direct knowledge.

We have described the market/product vectors as growth vectors, but one at least of them need not be so unless we wish so to identify it. Market penetration, the vector made up of an existing product in a saturated market, does not necessarily imply growth. If the corporate strategy is simply to jog along as heretofore, in line with corporate objectives which are probably mainly non-economic, then no growth is called for. A considerable number of small and middle-sized firms remain quite happy with this situation and abstention from growth is equally possible in extensible markets, where market development potential exists but is regarded as of no particular interest. By the same token, product development in either saturated or extensible markets may not necessarily subsume growth for the firm as a whole: it may simply involve the updating or replacement of models which are becoming obsolescent.

If, however, the corporate strategy calls for growth, then growth potential can be found in any of the vectors we have considered, the size of this growth being a function of the external market conditions and of the production, marketing and financial resources and skill available.

Growth in market penetration, for example, will require in particular the application of marketing skills and of financial resources: the volume of these required may well need to be considerable, since within a saturated market increased market share can only be obtained at the expense of competitors, who will probably fight back. Market development, though it may involve less need to counter competition from other producers, may equally involve a heavy investment of marketing skills and financial resources to create the increased demand from consumers. In both these vectors, however, the enterprise will normally understand something about the dominant variable, the nature of the market, and it may sometimes be felt that companies are too prone to wander off into the more uncharted forms of expansion, and even into outright diversification, before there has been adequate exploration of the growth potential immediately to hand. Product development will call most heavily upon production skills, while product/market development calls upon all three of production, marketing and financial resources, and though the payoff may be correspondingly greater so may the risks.

In considering which growth vector to go

for, therefore, the firm has to examine what resources it has available which may be appropriate and how far their allocation is likely to be justified by the likely outcome, having regard to the long-term corporate objectives of the company. Leaving aside the question of financial resources, the decision frequently boils down to a choice between expansion along the production channel and expansion along the marketing channel.

A company which is making cars, for example, may decide to start making fire-engines. So far as production techniques are concerned, this is a logical development. But difficulties might arise because cars are sold to private individuals through car-dealers, whereas fire-engines are for the most part sold to public authorities direct, and the two sets of marketing skills required may have little connection. On the other hand, a firm which manufactures certain types of foods and sells them to grocers may decide that its most relevant skills lie not in its existing food-production technology but in its marketing structures, so that its expansion strategy lies in selling to those same grocers other foods of which it previously had no direct knowledge.

INTEGRATION

Within expansion vectors there is another sort of approach to the problem—that of integration, either horizontal or vertical. Both can be fitted into the corporate strategy mode, but they complicate it considerably and really form a subject of their own. I would say about vertical integration only that the judgement that it will serve the company's corporate objectives is frequently based upon an assessment of its appropriateness to the company's resources which is emotional rather than realistic.

Diversification

We have so far not dealt with the last of the growth vectors—diversification. The word itself is often used in a rather slipshod fashion and is frequently applied to activities which, in strict Ansoff terminology, are more accurately defined as expansion. But in the conceptual structure we are considering here 'diversification' is limited to the combination of new products with new markets, which in its purest form represents the entry of the firm into a market unrelated to its existing markets with a product unrelated to its existing products. It will be obvious that here in particular the appraisal of the company's strengths and weaknesses, and consideration of the appropriateness of its skills and resources, are of supreme importance. If my doubts as to the meaningfulness of the concept of generalised management skills (independent of the special skills which go to form the management mix) are accepted, it follows that the resources which a company can put into such a new venture must be viewed in specific rather than in general terms. Though the corporate objectives of the company may seem to call for diversification, very little purpose will be served by a diversification exercise which falls flat on its face because the company is unable to make a success of it.

Of course, the possibility always exists that the special skills required may be brought in. This assumes in the first place that the company understands enough about its new business to know what to buy, which is by no means always the case, but even if it reasonably successful in this the difficulty still remains that corporate management, with whom lies the ultimate responsibility, may not possess the skills necessary to manage the operation, and may not be able to acquire them in the necessary time-span.

This leads on, in fact, to that special form of multiple diversification which is the conglomerate. The problems of conglomerates are far too large a subject to be entered into here, but they do bring into focus the major distinction between 'control' and 'management'. Conglomerates control, rather than manage, and they do so by the application of their financial skills and resources rather than through the application of production and marketing skills, and the question which is beginning to nag is whether the warning financial signals arrive too late after the non-managed production and marketing errors have been committed for the damage to be easily repairable. In considering diversification of this order as a growth vector, therefore, the company whose corporate objectives call for growth will need to give very detailed attention to the question of whether it is not likely to run less risk by a policy of expansion in those areas with which its existing production and marketing skills have some sort of relationship.

Two points may be made in conclusion. The first is that corporate planning is *ad hoc*, of indefinite time-span, and involving top corporate management: this must be distinguished from long-range planning at the operating unit level, which is routine, of limited time-span, and decentralised to operating managements. The second point is that the conceptual framework is helpful and, indeed, probably indispensable as a background to any corporate planning operation. But the way in which any particular company chooses to go about the job in practice is likely to be unique, because the company's situation is unique: there is no system or routine which can be adopted as a general standard.

7

Concept of Strategy

H. Igor Ansoff

The author discusses devising a strategy which provides for a broad concept of the firm's business; he offers specific guidelines and supplements the firm's objectives with decision rules. He introduces the concept of "the firm's business and the common thread" and suggests useful specifications of "common thread" in marketing strategic tools such as the "product-market scope."

THE PROBLEM

During the past ten years the idea of strategy has received increasing recognition in management literature. Numerous papers have appeared dealing with product line strategy, marketing strategy, diversification strategy, and business strategy (1). This interest grew out of a realization that a firm needs a well-defined scope and growth direction, that objectives alone do not meet this need, and that additional decision rules are required if the firm is to have orderly and profitable growth. Such decision rules and guidelines have been broadly defined as *strategy* or, sometimes, as the *concept of the firm's business* (2).

It will be recalled from discussion in Chapter 2 that capital investment theory makes no use of the concept of strategy. The need for it arises from characteristics which are peculiar to the strategic problem: the fact that a firm needs direction and focus in its search for and creation of new opportunities and the fact that it is to the firm's advantage to seek entries with strong synergistic potential.

Reprinted from *Corporate Strategy* pp. 103–121. Copyright © 1965 by McGraw-Hill, Inc. Used with permission of McGraw-Hill Book Company. At the time of writing, the author was professor of industrial administration, Graduate School of Industrial Administration, Carnegie Institute of Technology.

The first two sections of this chapter are devoted to developing a concept of strategy which (1) provides a broad concept of the firm's business, (2) sets forth specific guidelines by which the firm can conduct its search, and (3) supplements the firm's objectives with decision rules which narrow the firm's selection process to the most attractive opportunities.

Next, the question is raised whether, and under what conditions, a firm needs to have a strategy. In the third section an answer is provided which relates the type of preferred strategy to the type of firm.

Definitions of strategy found in business literature are different from ours and are sometimes used interchangeably with the term "policy." The last section compares these definitions and relates them to different degrees of uncertainty under which business decisions are made.

CONCEPT OF THE FIRM'S BUSINESS AND THE COMMON THREAD

Objectives set the performance levels which a firm seeks to achieve, but they do not describe the business of the firm, unless statements such as "the firm is in 20 percent ROI business" or in "flexible position business" are constructed to provide the description. Levitt (3) has suggested that a more definitive description of the firm's role in the environment is requisite for growth and success. Such description should encompass a broad scope of natural extensions of the firm's product-market position, derived from some core characteristic of the present business. Thus railroads would view themselves in the "transportation business" and petroleum companies in the "energy business."

While plausible, such business concepts leave some unanswered questions. Does it follow from this concept that railroads should be in the long-haul trucking industry? The answer would seem to be yes. But how about taxicab or rental car business? These are also transportation industries, but at first glance would seem to have little in common with railroads. It is hard to see where the skills, facilities, and experience of railroad companies have anything to contribute to the latter areas. Consider the energy business for petroleum companies. Does it follow that they should diversify into fabrication of uranium fuel for atomic power plants, build the power plants, or retail electricity? The respective management, technical, production, and marketing skills are all different. Where is the common core capability?

The weakness with concepts such as "transportation business" or "energy business" is that they are too broad and do not provide what the investment community calls a "common thread"—a relationship between present and future product-markets which would enable outsiders to perceive where the firm is heading, and the inside management to give it guidance.

A separate question is how strong the common thread must be. Royal Little has built the successful Textron Corp. composed of consumer electronics, textiles, helicopters, work shoes, and satellite motors, etc.—all without a strongly apparent common thread.

Peter Grace took his company from bananas and shipping into chemicals, also with apparent success. The Du Pont Company, however, has built its great success by closely following a very clearly defined common thread.

In seeking to answer these questions it is useful to review how firms usually identify the nature of their business. Some firms are identified by the characteristics of their product line. Thus there are "transistor companies," "machine tool companies," and "automobile companies." Others are described by the technology which underlies the product line, such as "steel companies," "aluminum companies," and "glass companies." Each may sell a wide range of different products to different users, but a common thread is provided by a manufacturing and/or engineering technology.

Firms are also described in terms of their markets. Here it is useful to make a distinction between customers and missions. A *mission* is an existing product *need*; a customer is the actual *buyer* of the product; the economic unit (such as an individual, a family, a business firm) which possesses both the need and the money with which to satisfy it.

The usefulness of this distinction lies in the fact that sometimes the customer is erroneously identified as the common thread of a firm's business. In reality a given type of customer will frequently have a range of unrelated product missions or needs. He would not necessarily satisfy them through the same purchasing channels, nor use the same approach to buying. Thus, the individual consumer fills his food needs at the supermarket and his entertainment needs at a television dealer's. Since the product technology, the distribution channels, and the customer motivation are different, no strong common thread is available to a firm which would attempt to sell both food and television sets. Similarly, the Department of Defense is a customer for a very wide range of missions. A company which supplies weapon systems for combat missions of the Army would have a better common thread in supplying control systems to industry than in selling replacement parts for Army trucks.

In selecting a useful range of missions of a particular customer, a firm needs to find a common thread either in product characteristics, technology, or similarity of needs. Thus agricultural machinery firms supply a range of needs of the farmer. All of these are related parts of his overall mission of tilling and harvesting the soil. Similarly, a home appliance manufacturer offers effort-saving products for the home which may range from washing machines to electronic irons.

In this perspective it is easy to see why the term "transportation business" fails to supply the common thread. First, the range of possible missions is very broad; intraurban, interurban, intracontinental, and intercontinental transportation; through the media of land, air, water, underwater; for moving passengers, and/or cargo. Second, the range of customers is wide: the individual, family, business firm, or government office. Third, the "product" varies: car, bus, train, ship, airplane, helicopter, taxi, truck. The number of practical combinations of the variables is large, and so is the number of common threads.

While such a concept of business is too broad to be useful, the traditional identification of a firm with a particular industry has become too narrow. Today a great many firms find themselves in a number of different industries. Furthermore, the boundaries of industries are continually changing, and new ones are being born. For example, radio, television, transistor, home appliance, and atomic energy are all industries which did not exist fifty years ago. The need is for a concept of business which on the one hand will provide room for growth. We shall describe such a concept in the next section.

COMPONENTS OF STRATEGY

To the extent the respective objectives and goals are consonant with actual performance, they do provide an indirect description of a common thread. Thus, a firm which has shown a consistent rate of high growth is usually recognized by the investment community as a "growth firm," and a well-diversified one as a "broadly based" firm. Both of these descriptions can be constructively used by management as guidance in selecting new product-market areas.

However, this guidance is very weak and assures no common thread within the firm. Thus a "growth" firm may be simultaneously in pharmaceutics, banking, and industrial controls—areas which have no relationship to one another, except that they may all have attractive growth prospects.

A somewhat more positive specification of

the common thread is arrived at through the use of the *product-market scope.* This specifies the particular industries to which the firm confines its product-market position and it has the advantage of focusing search on well-defined areas for which common statistics and economic forecasts are generally available. However, many industries offer a range of products, missions, technologies, and customers which is so broad as to make the common thread very tenuous. For example, the electronics industry ranges from high growth in technologically sophisticated areas, such as optical electronics, to slow-growth consumer oriented product-markets, such as radio and television. To convey a common thread, description of the product-market scope frequently needs to be made in terms of subindustries which contain product-markets and technologies with similar characteristics.

Another useful specification of common thread is through the means of the *growth vector,* which indicates the direction in which the firm is moving with respect to its current product-market posture. This can be illustrated by means of a matrix shown in Table 1. *Market penetration* denotes a growth direction through the increase of market share for the present product-markets. In *market development* new missions are sought for the firm's products. *Product development* creates new products to replace current ones. Finally, *diversification* is distinctive in the fact that both products and missions are new to the firm. The common thread is clearly indicated, in the first three alternatives, to be either the marketing skills or product technology or both. In diversification the common thread is less apparent and is certainly weaker.

Specification of the common thread through the growth vector is complementary to the product-market scope, since it gives the directions *within* an industry as well as *across* industry boundaries which the firm proposes to pursue. As we shall see in the next chapter, it is a very useful tool in arriving at the basic diversification decisions.

A third way to see a common thread is to isolate characteristics of unique opportunities within the field defined by the product-market scope and the growth vector. This is the *competitive advantage.* It seeks to identify particular properties of individual product-markets which will give the firm a strong competitive position. Thus, a firm might seek acquisitions which are large enough to give it a commanding position in the new industry. Or it might insist on entries which enjoy strong patent protection. Or it might consider only "breakthrough" products which obsolete previously available products (just as the electric typewriter made the manual one obsolete and was in turn made obsolete by the IBM rotary head machine).

The triplet of specifications—the product-market scope, the growth vector, and the competitive advantage—describes the firm's product-market path in the *external environment.* The first describes the scope of search, the second the directions within the scope, and the third the characteristics of individual entries.

Mission \ *Product*	*Present*	*New*
Present	Market penetration	Product development
New	Market development	Diversification

Table 1 Growth vector components.

There remains one other alternative for describing the common thread, and that is *synergy*. As described in a preceding chapter, synergy is a measure of the firm's ability to make good on a new product-market entry. The common thread may be *aggressive*, requiring that new entries make use of an outstanding competence possessed by the firm (say, a nationwide chain of retail outlets or leadership in computer technology), or it may be *defensive*, requiring that new entries supply some key competence which the firm lacks. It may, of course, be both aggressive and defensive. Synergy is especially useful as the common thread in new growth areas where industry boundaries are ill-defined and changing. It is also a key variable in the choice of a diversification strategy.

The classification of common thread into product-market scope, growth vector, competitive advantage, and synergy is given added meaning when viewed in the light of the film's search for profitability. The first triplet of specifications describes the firm's search for *inherently* profitable opportunities in the external environment. The first sets the scope for the search, the second the directions within the scope, and the third the characteristics of outstanding opportunities. The firm may not realize the full profitability potential or may even lose money unless it has the capabilities required for success in the new ventures. This is provided by the fourth criterion, synergy.

The four characteristics are thus complementary, rather than mutually exclusive. We will call them, therefore, the *components of strategy*.[1] In conjunction with its objectives the firm may choose one, two, or all of the strategy components. For example, a chemical firm may specify the following:

1 Objectives: ROI: Threshold 10%, goal 15%
Sales Growth Rate: Threshold 5%, goal 10%

2 Strategy
- **a** Product-market scope: Basic chemicals and pharmaceuticals
- **b** Growth vector: Product development and concentric[2] diversification
- **c** Competitive advantage: Patent protection, superior research competence
- **d** Synergy: Use of the firm's research capabilities and production technology

Thus strategy and objectives together describe the concept of the firm's business. They specify the amount of growth, the area of growth, the directions for growth, the leading strengths, and the profitability target. Furthermore, they are now stated operationally: in a form usable for guiding management decisions and actions.[3]

IS STRATEGY NECESSARY?

To define strategy is not to prove that it is necessary for each firm. The question of the usefulness of strategy as a management tool must, therefore, be examined. We will do this by first examining the alternative to strategy. This alternative is to have no rules beyond the simple decision to look for profitable prospects.[4] Under these conditions the firm does not select formal objectives, performs no appraisals, formulates no search and evaluation rules. Instead, it would inform the business world, as did Socony Mobil Company, of its interest in "good" profitable opportunities; it would evaluate each new opportunity on the merits of its individual profitability.

Several reasons can be given in favor of this approach.

[1]In Chapter 9 we shall add another component: the "make or buy."

[2]This term will be defined in the next chapter.

[3]A different and interesting classification of business strategies has been devised by L. C. Sorrell (4). Among his strategies are the following: "strike while the iron is hot," "time is a great healer," "bore from within," "in union there is strength," "draw a red herring across the trail," "pass the buck," and "conserve your gunpowder."

[4]Example: Comment on diversification attributed to a vice-president of Socony Mobil's Center Division: "We'll find money to invest in any proposal that shows a promise of a substantial return" (5).

1 The firm would save the time, money, and executive talent which are required for a thorough strategic analysis. It will become evident in the following chapters that such savings can be very considerable.

2 The field of potential opportunities will be in no way restricted. Objectives and strategy limit the field of its search. Since strategy is based on uncertain and incomplete knowledge, there is a chance that some attractive opportunities will be missed. An opportunistic firm takes no such chances.

3 The firm reaps the full advantage of the "delay principle." By delaying commitment until an opportunity is in hand, it is able to act on the basis of the best possible information.

Counterposed to these are some weighty disadvantages.

1 In the absence of strategy, there are no rules to guide the search for new opportunities, both inside and outside the firm. Internally, the research and development department has no guidelines for its contribution to diversification. The external acquisition department similarly lacks focus. Thus the firm as a whole either passively waits for opportunities, or pursues a "buckshot" search technique.

2 Project decisions will be of poorer quality than in firms with strategy. Without a focus for its efforts, the staff will lack the depth of knowledge in any particular area needed for competent analysis. Without strategy criteria, it will lack tools for recognizing outstanding opportunities. As a result managers acting on such advice will be forced into extreme forms of behavior. Conservatives will refuse to take what under better information might be reasonable risks; entrepreneurs will plunge without appreciation of potential costs and dangers.

3 The firm will have no formal provision for partial ignorance. No yardsticks will be available to judge whether a particular opportunity is a rare one, or whether much better ones are likely to develop in the future. Thus there will be a danger of either premature over-commitment of resources or of failure fully to utilize the resources available within a budget period.

4 Without the benefit of a periodic appraisal, the firm would have no assurance that its overall resource allocation pattern is efficient and that some product lines are not obsolete.

5 The firm will lack an internal ability to anticipate change. Without a strategy, managers will either do nothing or risk the danger of acting at cross-purposes. For example, the director of marketing could assume that the growth will be attained through adding new products to the existing product line. He will proceed to expand and strengthen the present marketing organization. At the same time, the director of engineering could assume that progress is to be made by eliminating the obsolete product line and diversifying into brand-new markets. He would, therefore, take appropriate action to curtail support of existing products and initiate developments for radically new missions. The potential result would be a marketing organization with no products to sell and a product line without a marketing capability.

To summarize, the advantages of not missing any bets and of not committing the firm's resources until the last moment are pitted against the disadvantages of inefficient search, enhanced risk of making bad decisions, and lack of control over the overall resource allocation pattern.

It would seem that for most firms the advantages of strategy will outweigh those of total flexibility. However, strategy requirements will differ from one type of firm to another.

1 A type of firm which needs the most comprehensive strategy is a fully integrated operating firm. Since its product-market decisions have long lead times, it needs guidance for R&D, and it must be able to anticipate change. Much of its investment is irreversible, since it goes into R&D, which cannot be recovered, and physical assets, which are difficult to sell. It must, therefore, minimize the chances of making bad decisions.

2 A holding company has less stringent strategy requirements. It does not seek synergy among its subsidiaries, nor does it use

Strategy requirement / *Type of firm*	*P-M scope*	*Growth Vector*	*Synergy*	*Competititive advantage*	*Objectives*
Operating firm	√	√	√	√	√
Holding company	√(?)			√	√
Investment company					√

Table 2 Strategy requirements for different firms.

internal R&D as a primary source for diversification. Each subsidiary operates independently, and the common thread among them is primarily financial. The holding company does need objectives with threshold-goals type of provisions for partial ignorance. Its strategy would have no synergy component or growth vector component. It would include a component of competitive advantage, since it naturally prefers good, rather than average, acquisitions. Such a firm may or may not have a well-defined product-market scope to help focus, search and develop local expert knowledge of some industries. If present, the scope will reduce the chance of making bad acquisitions. However, some holding firms prefer to take the chance in favor of fully flexible choice. Although potentially costly, divestment from undesirable subsidiaries is feasible and widely practiced.

3 At the other extreme from a fully integrated firm is a company which primarily buys and sells. This may be an investment trust, a pension fund, or a real estate syndicate. Its position differs from the holding company in that the "portfolio" of holdings is widely diversified and is highly negotiable, and the transfer costs are relatively low (sales tax, commission fees, etc.). Because portfolios are widely diversified, such firms seldom have the depth of knowledge of individual industries to enable them to seek a specific competitive advantage. Their strategy-formulation requirements are usually confined to objectives which are established on the basis of generally available industry data. Thus, for example, investment funds choose between the role of a "growth fund" and that of a "current earnings fund."

The three types of company above were described in what might be called "pure form." In actuality there are various shadings of characteristics which make it difficult to place firms into one of the slots. There are different degrees of integration in operating companies, some companies act as holding firms in some respects and operating in others, and some investment firms *do* have industry experts and *do* specialize in certain industries. Therefore, each individual firm will have to determine its strategy requirement using the classification as a guide. The summary table [Table 2] may be useful for this purpose.

It can easily be seen from the table that the operating firm requires the most complex strategy.[5] The remainder of the development will continue to deal with the more complex case.

STRATEGY, POLICY, PROGRAMS, AND OPERATING PROCEDURES

The concept of strategy is relatively new to management literature. Its historical origin lies in the military art, where it is a broad, rather vaguely defined, "grand" concept of a military campaign for *application* of large-scale forces

[5]Investment funds which trade in listed securities have the additional advantage of knowing the full field of choice. There is no partial ignorance. This and low transfer costs permit an approach to the strategic problem which is much simpler than the present method (6).

against an enemy. Strategy is contrasted to *tactics*, which is a specific scheme for *employment* of allocated resources.

The bridge to business usage was provided in 1948 by Von Neumann and Morgenstern (7) in their now-famous theory of games. The theory provides a unifying viewpoint for all types of conflict situations, regardless of whether their origin is in war, politics, or business. The concept of strategy is given two meanings. A *pure* strategy is a move or a specific series of moves by a firm, such as a product development program in which successive products and markets are clearly delineated. A *grand* or *mixed* strategy is a statistical decision rule for deciding which particular pure strategy the firm should select in a particular situation.

Although game theory has not resulted in many practical applications, it has revolutionized ways of thinking about social problems in general and business in particular. One of the consequences was the increasing use of the concept of strategy in business literature. As one would expect, some business writers borrowed from game theory to define strategy as a set of specific product-market entries (8), while others have defined it in the military sense as the broad overall concept of the firm's business (9). In the latter sense strategy is often used interchangeably[6] with, or instead of, the term *policy*, which has long been a standard part of familiar business vocabulary.

In the business vocabulary, policy is also widely used in a very different sense in manuals of organization and procedures to denote a specific response to specific repetitive situations, e.g., "overtime reimbursement policy," "foul weather policy," "educational refund policy," "inventory writeoff policy." A contingent event is recognized, such as a periodic need to work overtime, or a snowstorm. What needs to be done and the outcomes of such contingencies are *well known*; the contingencies are repetitive, but the time of specific occurrences cannot be specified in advance. In view of this, it is not worthwhile to require a new decision on what should be done each time overtime is needed or each time it snows. A better and more economical procedure is to prescribe, in advance, the response to be made whenever a specified contingency occurs. This is done through a written statement of the appropriate policy and of accompanying procedures for its implementation. Since the management decision is thus made in advance of the event, a rule for behavior can be imposed on lower levels of supervision. Thus economies of management are realized, and consistency of action is assured.

When compared with our definition of strategy this meaning of policy is seen to be distinct and different. Policy is a *contingent decision,* where strategy is a *rule for making decisions*. Thus while implementation of policy can be delegated downward, implementation of strategy cannot, since last-minute executive judgment will be required. In technical terms, used by mathematical decision theorists, specification of strategy is forced under conditions of *partial ignorance,* when alternatives cannot be arranged and examined in advance, whereas under conditions of *risk* (alternatives are all known and so are their probabilities) or *uncertainty* (alternatives are known but not the probabilities), the consequences of different alternatives *can* be analyzed in advance and decision made contingent on their occurrence. The lower level executive merely needs to recognize the event and then act in accordance with his instructions.

As mentioned previously, condition of risk may mean assignment of probability either to the *occurrence* of an event or to its possible *outcomes*. When the occurrence is certain, but the outcome is either certain or uncertain, a different kind of decision, called a *program,* is possible; this is a time-phased action sequence used to guide and coordinate operations. When

[6]As for example in "Strategy of Product Policy" (10).

the occurrence of an alternative is not only certain but also repetitive, the decision takes the form of a *standing operating procedure.*

Thus, the several types of decisions commonly made within a firm can be ranked in the order of increasing level of ignorance: standing operating procedures and programs under conditions of certainty or partial risk, policies under conditions of risk and uncertainty, and strategies under conditions of partial ignorance.

There is an unfortunate coincidence in our definitions. We speak of "strategic" decisions,[7] where "strategic" means "relating to firm's match to its environment," and of "strategy," where the word means "rules for decision under partial ignorance." This coincidence should not obscure the fact that all four basic types of decision described above—strategy, policy, program, and standing operating procedure—occur in all three classes of problems: strategic, administrative, and operating. However, since conditions of partial ignorance are dominant in the strategic, but not the other two problems, the use of similar terminology is not entirely inappropriate.

It should further be made clear that all of the basic types of decisions may apply on organizations, such as research, development, finance, and marketing, have a strong interface with the outside environment and will frequently be faced with conditions of partial ignorance. Under these conditions they will require appropriate strategies, such as R&D strategy, finance strategy, marketing strategy.

[7]Perhaps a better term would have been *entrepreneurial.*

REFERENCES

1 C. H. Kline, "The Strategy of Product Policy," *Harvard Business Review,* vol. 33, no. 4, July-August, 1955; H. Igor Ansoff, "Strategies for Diversification," *Harvard Business Review,* vol. 35, no. 5, pp. 113-124, September-October, 1957; S. Tilles, "How to Evaluate Corporate Strategy," *Harvard Business Review,* vol. 41, no. 4, pp. 111-121, July-August, 1963.

2 T. Levitt, "Marketing Myopia," *Harvard Business Review,* vol. 38, no, 4, July-August, 1960; A. D. Chandler, Jr., *Strategy and Structure,* The M.I.T. Press, Cambridge, Mass., 1962; Tilles, *op. cit.*; F. F. Gilmore and R. G. Brandenburg, "Anatomy of Corporate Planning," *Harvard Business Review,* vol. 40, no. 6, November-December, 1962; and Ansoff, "A Quasi-Analytic Method for Long-Range Planning," presented at the First Symposium on Corporate Long-Range Planning, The Institute of Management Sciences, College of Planning, June 6, 1959, and the 6th Annual International Meeting, The Institute of Management Sciences, Paris, France, Sept. 9, 1959.

3 Levitt, *op. cit.* (ref. 2).

4 L. C. Sorrell, in W. H. Newman, *Administrative Action,* Prentice-Hall, Inc., Englewood Cliffs, N.J., 1951.

5 S. G. Walters, Vice President of Socony Mobil's Center Division, in *Time,* vol. 82, no. 5, Aug. 2, 1963.

6 G. P. E. Clarkson, *Portfolio Selection: A Simulation of Trust Investment,* Prentice-Hall, Inc., Englewood Cliffs, N.J., 1962.

7 J. von Neumann and O. Morgenstern, *Theory of Games and Economic Behavior,* Princeton University Press, Princeton, N.J., 1953.

8 Ansoff, *op. cit.* (ref. 2); Gilmore and Brandenburg, *op. cit.* (ref. 1).

9 Kline, *op. cit.* (ref. 1); Tilles, *op. cit.* (ref. 2).

10 Kline, *op. cit.* (ref. 1).

8

Consumer Decision-Process Models

J. A. Lunn

The current position in buyer behavior theory is reviewed, with particular reference to an increasingly popular approach which places major emphasis on consumer decision processes. The discussion is in three parts: the first briefly sketches reasons for the growing interest in theory; the second describes three main approaches to theory building prevalent in marketing research; the third indicates the practical value of theory for both day-to-day problem solving and basic marketing research.

THEORIES AND MODELS

A distinction is often drawn between theories and models, but the terms are used interchangeably here. As Lawrence (1966) has pointed out, the term "model" has a more practical ring to it, and it has been more widely adopted in marketing. However, both theories and models are concerned with providing a coherent and systematic structure for a field of study. Both involve (1) postulating a number of key variables (e.g., market forces such as advertising and price, or consumer characteristics such as motives and attitudes; (2) specifying causal relationships among these variables (e.g., the effect of advertising on attitudes); and (3) indicating the extent to which changes occur over time, either within the variables themselves or in their interrelationships. Both theories and models can differ in their objectives and in their level of generality: for instance, distinctions are made between macro and micro models and between descriptive and analytical models (Averink, 1970; de Jong, 1970; Fontela, 1970; Lambin, 1971). Again, Hendrickson (1967) presents his St. James's Model on two levels—at one he provides a conceptual framework of how advertising might work, at the other he presents a mathematical basis for calculating the relative importance of brand attributes.

Much activity to date—both published and unpublished—has involved building large-scale descriptive models of particular markets, using approaches heavily influenced by developments in operations research. See, for instance, the papers by Averink (1970), de Jong (1970) and Fontela (1970). These models are concerned mainly with the relative effects of different market forces on sales. Consumer characteristics tend not to be specified. Rather, they are lumped together into an undifferentiated "black box." Such models are valuable both for forecasting purposes and, especially when simulation procedures are used, for testing the likely results of future policy decisions (Lambin, 1971). But they provide relatively little explanation of how marketing activity can influence consumer behavior, hence only restricted guidance for the kind of action that may be called for in a particular market. By contrast, the models described in this paper specify key elements within the "black box" and are primarily aimed at providing diagnostic information to guide management decisions. The two approaches are, of course, complementary rather than contradictory, and it has been argued (e.g., Nicosia,

Reprinted from Jagdish N. Sheth (ed.), *Models of Buyer Behavior* (New York: Harper & Row, 1974), pp. 34–69. At the time of writing, the author was a staff member of the Research Bureau (Research International) Ltd., London.

1969) that true progress in marketing theory will arise only when they are applied simultaneously.

MODELS FOR PRACTICAL PROBLEM SOLVING AND FOR BASIC RESEARCH

The impetus behind theory development has arisen partly within the context of practical problem solving for marketing companies. This has occurred when marketing men, researchers, or both, have appreciated the need to conduct strategies and projects within a coherent framework rather than on a piecemeal basis. Even more important, however, has been the influence of "business academics"—that is, the growing number of researchers in business schools and the business departments of universities. "Business academics" in particular have been concerned with basic research in marketing. For them, the establishment of a coherent framework has been almost an end in itself or a means of guiding basic research. Practical problems solvers and basic researchers often have different perspectives, but their activities can be mutually beneficial. The issues outlined below concerning the need for and function of theory apply to both groups of people, if from different standpoints.

NEED FOR AND FUNCTION OF BUYER BEHAVIOR THEORY

It has often been claimed that marketing theory fulfills two main functions: description and prediction. An amplification has been suggested by Howard and Sheth (1969), whose schematic has been adopted, in modified form, in this section.

Description and Explanation

A major purpose of buyer behavior theory is to increase our understanding of the consumer. This is especially important because throughout their activities, both marketing men and researchers make *assumptions* about how the consumer ticks—about how he arrives at purchasing and usage decisions and about how these decisions can be influenced by marketing action. Marketing men make these assumptions when planning product strategies, when commissioning research, and when acting on its findings; so do researchers when designing, carrying out, and interpreting research projects and when developing new techniques. We all have a personal model of man. The problem is that most of these assumptions are implicit, few have any empirical foundation, and many are contradictory. A well-constructed body of consumer theory would at least help to make these assumptions explicit and would also enable some of the key ones to be tested. At the same time, it would provide a foundation for technique development; for instance, the development of advertising pretesting systems presupposes that we understand how advertising works. On a more day-to-day level, a good consumer theory would also increase the probability of relevant variables being included in specific market projects.

Explanation and description are closely related. A major part of theory building consists of identifying certain key variables and describing their interrelationships. As our *descriptions* became increasingly more detailed and sophisticated, we come to provide *explanations* of the phenomenon of interest—in this case, consumer behavior. During this process, we may generate hypotheses to account for the nature of the variables and their interrelationships and to specify the conditions under which these interrelationships may be expected to hold.

Delimitation

Description—and explanation—must operate selectively; they cannot include everything. To attempt to account for too many phenomena may lead to confusion. A primary function of a theory is to delimit the area being embraced—to clarify what aspects are being covered and what are not. One means of achieving this is to specify the key variables.

Integration

Buyer behavior may lack theory, but there is no shortage of data. Individual companies often have vast amounts of information available to them about particular markets gathered from their own past research and other sources. At the more general level, the published literature in marketing abounds with reports of studies dealing with a wide variety of issues, ranging from market segmentation to the influence of reference groups. Similarly, there is a great diversity in the concepts used to describe consumer behavior. To quote from Sheth's (1967) review of buyer behavior:

> What we really have, then, are a set of insular hypothetical concepts and a set of peninsular intervening variables reflecting a lack of formal science. What is more, they have lived an independent existence. Indeed, this reviewer has more than once felt that the situation resembles the seven blind men touching different parts of an elephant and making inferences about the animal which differ and occasionally contradict one another.

At all levels, there is a strong need for an agreed conceptual framework to integrate the plethora of disparate concepts and findings. This can be regarded as another prime function of buyer behavior theory. An example of this integrative role is given later in the paper in the discussion of Howard and Sheth's theory (1969).

A further benefit of integration should be better communication. Within the company setting, marketing men and researchers all too often mean different things by the same terms, and vice versa. The same is also true for researchers within the published literature: consider, for instance, the ambiguity generated by different definitions of the term "attitude" (Lunn, 1969b). Hopefully, an integrative framework will lead to clear and agreed definitions of central concepts.

Generation

The integrative function of buyer behavior theory is related to its role in generating ideas for future research. The act of drawing a variety of concepts and findings into a coherent system at once clarifies what we do know—or feel able to make firm assumptions about—and indicates where we are uncertain. This is especially true when a theory contains sets of fairly general hypothetical constructs and numerous combinations of relationships between these constructs. "A theory must stimulate hypotheses, or it must provide essential notions, hunches, ideas, and so on from which someone can create hypotheses which can then be tested" (Howard and Sheth, 1969). Marketing men should, as a result, obtain clearer guidance about the kind and amount of research needed for specific policy decisions; researchers should obtain guidance about priorities for future basic research.

APPROACHES TO BUYER BEHAVIOR THEORY

Attempts at developing buyer behavior theory have taken various forms. The writer has found it useful in previous papers (Lunn, 1969a, 1969b, 1971a) to categorize these under three headings, namely, a priori, empirical, and eclectic. These categories are a bit arbitrary, but they provide a useful schematic for discussing the various theoretical approaches.

The A Priori Approach

Researchers using the a priori approach have introduced concepts and theories from other disciplines, mainly the behavioral sciences and have explored their value for understanding the consumer. Well-known instances include the various manifestations of motivational research and such attitude theories as those of Festinger and Fishbein. This has sometimes involved giving the consumer an all-embracing label, such as "Economic Man," "Problem-Solver," "Learner" (Oxenfeldt, 1966), and, more recently, "Existentialist" (Christopher, 1970). For an overview of these contributions, see Sheth (1967) and Nicosia (1966).

Consumer behavior is, of course, a specific aspect of general human behavior, and the a priori approach is appropriate here because it attempts to harness existing knowledge and insights from behavioral science. But as traditionally applied, it has severe limitations. Many of the concepts adopted are still somewhat speculative. They have often been developed in contexts remote from consumer behavior—for instance, in laboratory situations with students as experimental subjects. Moreover, they have usually been developed to account for restricted aspects of human behavior (e.g., learning and perception). Nevertheless, protagonists of different theoretical positions have been all too ready to represent them as rival rather than complementary explanatory systems (McGuire, 1969b) and to overgeneralize their areas of application. Narrowness of perspective may help the advancement of academic knowledge, but it can be destructively limiting in a problem-oriented field such as marketing.

The Empirical Approach

A priori researchers have have attempted to fit consumer behavior to previously developed theoretical frameworks. Researchers in the empirical category have adopted the opposite approach. Consumer behavior itself has been their prime focus of study. They have attempted to derive laws from observations of patterns and regularities in this behavior, often though not invariably using consumer panel data. Both general laws of buyer behavior and deviations from these laws have stimulated interest.

A key exponent of this approach is Ehrenberg (1969), who has recently extended it to an examination of the attitude behavior issue (Bird and Ehrenberg, 1970). By and large, however, empirical theoreticians have been chary of working with other than "hard" behavior data and also of venturing too far into the realm of interpretation.

The strength of the a priori position lies in the firm and systematic basis of knowledge provided about certain aspects of the consumer. Its weaknesses lie in the virtual disregard of potentially illuminating theories from the behavioral sciences, and consequently, the relative lack of explanatory power.

The Eclectic Approach

The previous two approaches broadly encompasses the major attempts at consumer theorizing up to about 1964. More recently, however, a third, more eclectic approach has become increasingly popular. Basically, it attempts to incorporate the strengths of the a priori and empirical approaches but to avoid their weaknesses. Its distinguishing feature is the attempted synthesis of two sets of information: on the one hand, the theories, concepts, and findings in the various behavioral sciences that appear relevant to consumer behavior; on the other hand, the rapidly escalating findings from market research studies, whether commissioned in the marketing context for specific problem-solving situations or in the more generalized context of the business school.

The strength of this approach is the comprehensiveness of its perspective. But this comprehensiveness is also a potential source of weakness, for it imposes a herculean task on researchers. It is hard enough to establish an agreed outlook among specialists within a discipline (e.g., learning theorists within psychology). It is harder still to achieve among representatives of different aspects of a major discipline (e.g., learning theorists and psycholinguisticians), and even harder among representatives of quite different disciplines such as psychology, sociology, and economics. There is, moreover, a danger of undue complexity, of having too many variables and interrelationships.

Nevertheless, the eclectic approach offers considerable promise. Only by attempting to integrate the major influences on consumer behavior within a single framework—or series of related frameworks—are we likely to provide really illuminating guidelines for marketing action and for basic research. The challenge is to strike a balance between, on the one hand, the relatively narrow focus of the theory (i.e., market place and consumption behavior) and, on the other hand, the wide range of findings, concepts, and theories that may help to illuminate this behavior.

The next sections of this paper delineate some of the major features of the eclectic approach. This is done in two ways: first, by briefly summarizing some prominent published contributions; second, by drawing together some of their more important aspects. It should be emphasized that it is impossible to do justice to any of these contributions in the space of a short review paper; there has been space for only a few facets in each case. Consequently, the reader interested in the detail of any particular model is advised to read the original.

THE NICOSIA MODEL

Nicosia must be regarded as one of the leading figures in the eclectic approach. In a major work (1966), he produced one of the first large-scale reviews of findings and theories in the behavioral sciences relevant to consumer behavior. In his book he also evolves a conceptual framework, specifying the major elements and their interactions; the book concludes with an attempt to express the framework in mathematical terms, making particular use of differential equations.

A distinctive feature of Nicosia's approach is the shift of emphasis away from the purchasing act itself and toward the decision processes that both precede and follow this act. As he points out, "the act of purchasing is only one component of a complex, ongoing process of decision making—a process of many interactions among many variables over time. This emphasis on decision processes has become a hallmark of the eclectic approach; hence the title of this review paper.

In a subsequent paper Nicosia (1968), argues the case for computer stimulation and attempts to translate his model into simulation terms. Most recently (Nicosia, 1969), he has urged the synthesis of what he describes as behavioral and behavioristic models:

> In behavioral approaches the stress is on *behavioral* constructs (predispositions, opinions, images, attitudes, motivations, and social influences, and so on) which may intervene, in different ways, between environmental stimuli and the act of purchase, and/or may be affected by this act. In the other research approach, the stress is on *behavioristic* constructs; that is, on the object of choice (a store, a product, a brand) and related indicators of the choice-object (e.g., how much was spent, the package size, the deal, the time, the kind of store).

He has also speculated further on the thought and decision processes. In both recent works, he emphasizes the importance of combining conceptual elaboration with formal attempts at quantification of these concepts, by mathematical formulas and by simulation; that is Nicosia expresses the need to combine the richness of (often speculative) insights with the relative power and precision provided by mathematical formulation.

Nicosia's model (1966)—like those of the other two contributions summarized below—can be represented in terms of flow charts. These are presented together in Figure 1 in the appendix to this paper. The model can be expressed in terms of a series of fields, each one serving as both output from a preceding field and input to a succeeding one. Let us summarize a few major features.

First, like other eclectic theoreticians, Nicosia represents the consumer as purposive, seeking to fulfill certain goals through purchasing behavior and going through various decision processes that help him to at least approximate an optimum solution.

Second, there is the notion of the "funnel." Nicosia places much store in the idea of consumer predispositions moving from generality (very broad intentions) through the search and evaluation of alternative products and culminating in the selection of one particular brand.

Third, there is the crucial concept of feedback. Too many representations of the consumer have assumed a one-way process leading from marketing action to purchase and usage. In practice, the process continues with a feedback from consumer behavior. This feedback will affect marketing action itself, which may be adjusted in the light of reactions in the marketplace. It will also affect consumer predispositions that may be reinforced or modified in the light of experience with the product and also of the buying act itself.

Consumer predispositions are influenced by a variety of factors, some of them external to the consumer. External influences may be both commercial (e.g., media, point-of-sale factors) and noncommercial (e.g., word of mouth). For a full account, see Nicosia (1966).

It is possible to level a number of criticisms at Nicosia's work, and he himself would be the last to regard it as definitive. For instance, the search and evaluation process as represented is over-rational, and although applicable to infrequently purchased high-cost products, it has less relevance for frequently purchased low-cost goods. Moreover, the definitions of attitude and motivation seem to be unsatisfactory, and the attempt to formalize the model mathematically (Nicosia, 1966, chap. 7) appears as prematurely ambitious. An especially harsh criticism given by Ehrenberg (1966) is worth reading as an illustration of how a researcher with strongly empirical orientations finds it difficult to accept the eclectic approach.

However, for all the possible objections, Nicosia has provided an invaluable pioneering contribution.

THE ENGEL MODEL

A second major work is that of Engel, Kollat, and Blackwell (1968). The author's thorough documentation of research in the behavioral sciences relevant to marketing is worth reading in its own right. At the same time, they have elaborated a decision-process model that resembles Nicosia's in many respects and is explicitly linked to the various facets of behavioral science covered in the book. A flow chart of the model is given in Figure 2 in the Appendix. Some of the distinctive features can be summarized as follows:

1 Like Nicosia, Engel et al., portray an ongoing series of processes whereby products are sought and evaluated in terms of the consumer's goals and future purchases are influenced by previous experience.

2 They discuss the interaction of past experience and stored information with general predispositions such as personality variables. This interaction leads to the formulation of values and attitudes that are defined as "organizations of concepts, beliefs, habits and motives associated with a particular object." All these variables are contained within a central control unit. This unit produces response sets that play a key monitoring role throughout the decision process.

3 A distinction is made between the system itself, which consists essentially of a series of predispositions, and the arousal of the system on a specific occasion. Arousal can be triggered both by internal states, such as feeling hungry, or by external factors, such as advertising messages or point-of-sale displays.

4 Even when the system is active, the individual does not necessarily perceive all the stimuli to which he is exposed. He will filter out information that is relevant to his current motives and is consistent with his stored knowledge and expectations. Moreover, even when information is allowed into the system, it may be structured and distorted to make it consistent with existing predispositions.

5 Engel et al. suggest a series of processes that may follow the act of purchase. For instance, perceived doubt about the wisdom of the action can lead to a search for information to justify the decision.

Although the literature reviewed by Engel et al. is more thorough than Nicosia's, their model is less detailed and has not, to the writer's knowledge, been put in mathematical or simulation loop. It does, however, have heuristic value in pointing out some of the major factors bearing on consumer decision making. One specific criticism is that, as with Nicosia, the search and evaluation process is portrayed as highly rational. For an elaboration of decision strategies see the "Other Contributions" section of this paper.

THE HOWARD-SHETH THEORY

By far the most through, comprehensive, and well-articulated model of the consumer published to date is that of Howard and Sheth. It is distinguished by a richer specification of variables and their interrelationships, and it attempts a much deeper and more detailed integration of theoretical positions from several behavioral sciences. Seven instances of integration are listed by Howard and Sheth (1969, chap. 10). To quote just one (p. 396):

> Conduct arising from an ambiguous stimulus is one of the regulators of buyer attention and overt search behavior (Berlyne, 1966), as we saw in Chapter 5. Also, there we saw how it shapes the nature of how the buyer perceives whatever information he admits into his nervous system (Osgood, 1957b). Conflict in overt buying behavior—incompatible responses—also influences his attention and overt search behavior (N. E. Miller, 1959), as indicated in Chapter 8. Given that a buyer has well-formed Choice Criteria for a specified product class, the certainty (Confidence) with which he judges a brand in that class leads to a decrease in cognitive conflict. The cognitive conflict that occurs with low Confidence is manifested by search for information, for example, as postulated by one version of the consistency principle, namely, dissonance theory (Brehm and Cohen, 1962). "Inconsistency" is also used to describe cognitive conflict when it is manifested in attitude change. Furthermore, expectancy, as used by Lewin and others roughly to mean probability of payoff (J. W. Atkinson, 1964), implies conflict as a consequence of being unable to choose when certainty is low. "Inconsistency in the mind threatens to paralyze action" (R. W. Brown, 1965, p. 606). The behavioral manifestation of low "expectancy" (low Confidence) is vacillation (N. E. Miller, 1959). Thus by postulating the construct of Confidence we bring together (1) the processes by which the buyer obtains his *informational inputs,* (2) their *cognitive* consequences that will affect future purchases, and (3) their *behavioral* consequences for the current purchases. In using the concept of conflict to explain search effort we have developed a specific mechanism to explain what was postulated in an earlier version of the theory (Howard, 1963, p. 58), namely, that buyers further along the learning curve with respect to a brand are less inclined to seek information.

A flow chart of the theory is given in Figure 3 in the Appendix. A few of its main characteristics are outlined below:

1 As in the previously described models, the focal point is the individual consumer, whose "internal" states are treated as a system. In the tradition of econometric models, a distinction is made between *endogenous* variables (i.e., those that the theory is designed to explain) and *exogenous* variables (i.e., additional variables, largely, but not entirely, "outside" the consumer, which have a key influence on the system). In Figure 3, the seven exogenous variables—importance of purchase, culture, social class, and so on—are listed at the top. Within the book their respec-

tive influences are described and charted in detail.

2 Again, the core of the decision process is seen as the matching of products to the consumer's motives. However, there is a more detailed account of the nature and development of the "choice criteria" (e.g., attributes such as nourishment value and economy) whereby this matching occurs.

3 Choice criteria can be viewed from two standpoints: the extent to which the product or brand is believed by the consumer to possess the attribute in question, and the value of this attribute to the consumer—that is, the extent to which it represents a requirement sought from the product. This balance of perception and value characterizes the "means-end" approach to attitudes that has played a leading part in the theoretical developments of Rosenberg and Fishbein, among others.[1] It also figures prominently in the thinking of other decision-process theoreticians such as Hansen (1970b), who advances the case for relating value importance to the anticipated situation in which purchasing or consumption will take place. Hansen (1963) also makes some useful points about the various ways in which particular decisions originate, the extent to which they are reversible, and the extent to which they form chains along with other interrelated decisions.

4 Two crucial and related concepts are those of "product class concept" and "evoked set of brands." The former indicates that consumers do not necessarily perceive markets in the same way as manufacturers and that for the consumer, a product class is the set of brands or products that are broadly substitutable for a given set of motives (see also Lunn, 1969b, 1970). Product classes can be described at various levels (see Howard and Sheth, 1969, chap. 8). The evoked set concept postulates that the consumer does not necessarily choose, on any particular occasion, from all the alternatives that fall within his definition of the product class. Under some circumstances (e.g., when he is buying in an unfamiliar product field), the consumer may undertake a wide search for information about products and may select from among many possibilities. Under other circumstances, he may consider one or at the most two alternatives.

5 Perceptual processes are dealt with extensively. Key concepts here are the arousal (e.g., consumer hunger) as well as the directive (e.g., kind of food that is appropriate) value of the individual's motives, the ambiguity of the commercial stimulus (e.g., product display, advertisement), and the effects of these concepts on both the attention that will be paid to the stimulus and any distortion (perceptual bias) of the information to which he is exposed.

6 Like Nicosia and Engel et al., Howard and Sheth emphasize the importance of feedback, that is, the effects of the purchase act and usage experience on consumer predispositions toward particular products; here they incorporate the concept of satisfaction. However, they also explore the dynamics of the buying process in terms of a distinction adopted in Howard's previous work (1963) between (*a*) extensive, (*b*) limited, and (*c*) routinized problem solving.

Extensive problem solving is called for when the buyer is confronted by an unfamiliar brand in an unfamiliar product class. The choice criteria by which alternatives are assessed will be weak or nonexistent, and the buyer will search diligently for information, with both commercial (e.g., advertising) and noncommercial (e.g., consumer reports, discussions with friends) sources playing a part. Chapter 9 of Howard and Sheth (1969) provides an elaboration of the respective effects of these sources.

Limited problem solving applied to the situation of a buyer confronted with a new, unfamiliar brand in a familiar product class, usually where existing brands do not provide an

[1]See the collection of papers edited by Fishbein (1967), and a review article by McGuire (1969b), which puts this approach into perspective.

adequate level of satisfaction. Choice criteria will be better formed, but there will still be a certain amount of search and evaluation prior to purchase.

These first two situations accord with the somewhat rational accounts of the decision process propounded by Nicosia and Engel et al., although these authors would admit, along with Howard and Sheth, that decision processes may occur at the unconscious as well as the conscious level and may not always appear rational to the outside observer. Quite different is the *routinized problem solving* of the buyer who is purchasing familiar brands within a familiar product field and requires relatively little information. Under this situation, considerable brand loyalty would be expected.

No single model or theory can be fully comprehensive at this state of our knowledge. Nevertheless, the Howard-Sheth approach is a clearly admirable attempt. It has already guided research in a variety of product fields, and some of its propositions have been rigorously tested under the Columbia Buyer Behavior panel projects (Arndt, 1968a; see also Farley and Ring, 1970 and chap. 8 of this volume).

On the whole, the tests have provided favorable support for the theory. However, as Farley and Ring point out, they have also indicated certain weaknesses in the measuring instruments used in the Columbia Buyer Behavior project. This underlines an important issue: namely, the necessity of combining conceptual sophistication with methodological precision. Nicosia (1969) refers to "the problems of translating a construct (e.g., intelligence, attitude, etc.) into a measurable entity: this translation implies a number of methodological decisions: (*a*) choice of the construct dimension(s); (*b*) choice of indicator(s) for each dimension; and (*c*) choice of measuring instrument(s) for each indicator." As mentioned earlier in this paper, better theory is needed to guide technique development. Equally, to put theoretical developments to the test, we need adequate techniques of data collection and analysis.

OTHER CONTRIBUTIONS

So far we have been concerned largely with three representations of the eclectic approach. There are several other published contributions based on similar lines that should be referred to. These include the works of Arndt (1968a) and Hansen (1970a). In addition, the author, along with a number of colleagues in the Research International group, has evolved a conceptual framework of consumer decision processes that has helped to guide a program of basic research carried out for a multinational group of manufacturing companies (Lunn, 1969a).

There is no space to review any of the other approaches, even in outline. However, two more specific discussions of consumer decision making will be mentioned. The first is that of Cooper (1969), whose discussion of decision strategies provides valuable enrichment in this area. Cooper postulates two major dimensions underlying these strategies: rational—irrational and routine—dramatic. He then suggests eight different strategies based on the recognition that all decisions involve uncertainty and that, consequently, people making decisions face risk. Risk may involve wider considerations than money, including loss of self-esteem. "The decision-maker is, therefore, under considerable pressure to reduce risk and its accompanying anxiety, or otherwise to devise strategies for resolving risk." The eight strategies suggested by Cooper are the following:

> **a** *Scrutinize alternatives.* This is the solution of rational decision-making. The decision-maker assembles impartial information by using his or her own skills or through "expert" sources, in order to optimize the decision.

b *Use related cues.* For example, Price, Company Images, etc., are traditionally associated with value. This is a working solution where full information is not available.

c *Avoid hazardous decisions.* The decision-maker can rely upon past experience—"brand loyalty."

d *Wait.* Planning to spend, for example, on consumer durables, can pass through a lengthy "incubation period." To wait (saving) or to engage in "diversionary" activity (buying in a completely different product field), permits the consumer to resolve risk of when and what to buy.

e *Imitation.* Following other people's choices externalizes the risk. Mass media aid this solution by confirming widespread preferences.

f *Flirt with risk as in gambling.* That is, deliberately choosing an alternative with a high pay-off value, but which has little chance of success (bargains).

g *Ignore the risk.* Choose alternatives at random, irrespective of cost, pay-off, or value. Lack of time, other work, are often put forward as reasons for opting for this alternative.

h *Satisficing.* "Satisficing" refers to choosing that solution first encountered which meets minimal requirements.

The effects of risk on consumer decision making are also dealt with from a number of standpoints in the book of papers edited by Cox (1967). Here interrelationships are traced among variables such as consumer involvement in the product field, consumer self-confidence, methods of handling information, and persuasibility. However, neither Cooper nor the contributors to the Cox volume attempt to incorporate decision-making strategies into a broader framework of the total buying process.

SOME GENERAL FEATURES OF THE ECLECTIC APPROACH

Decision-process models can be discussed at many levels. At one extreme is the complex integration of theories from the various contributory disciplines (e.g., the study of learning, motivation, perception, cognitive structures, and attitude change). But the discussion can also be carried on at the level of systematized common sense, with a fairly general description of the main concepts and their interrelationships from the standpoint of the individual consumer. The latter approach has been adopted here. But it should be borne in mind that much of the value of eclecticism lies in the former, more complex account.

Decision-process models too, may have different purposes and referents. For instance, we may be primarily interested in the perceptual and communication processes as the background to devising an advertising pretesting system, in product innovation processes, in modeling the effects of promotions, and in illuminating the attitude-behavior controversy. Some of these specific issues are taken up later in this paper. For the moment, however, we are concerned with a global picture of the consumer, a picture that in any case is necessary as a context setter for more specific models. See, for example, the way in which Sheth has evolved models of attitude-behavior relationships (Sheth, 1971) and family decision processes (Sheth, chap. 2 of this volume) from the broader Howard and Sheth theory.

We now outline a series of propositions derived from the eclectic approach. It should be pointed out that these are hypotheses rather than proven facts. For a detailed discussion, and for an evaluation of the nature and status of supporting evidence from market research and the behavioral sciences generally, see Howard and Sheth (1969), Nicosia (1966), and Engel et al. (1968).

1. The consumer is not the defenseless or recalcitrant creature portrayed by many theoreticians. Rather, he is purposive and goal oriented. The needs and motives he seeks to satisfy through purchasing are of many kinds and exist at several levels of generality. They range from specific product field requirements (e.g., a margarine with a creamy texture) to such general values as experimentation and

economy-mindedness; from basic drives such as hunger to general aspects of personality such as extroversion (Lunn, 1971b).

2. Nor is the consumer a passive being, waiting to be influenced and manipulated by marketing men. He actively seeks information to satisfy his various motives, and he structures information coming from the environment as a guide to need satisfaction.

3. Nor is the individual's role as consumer pursued in isolation from the remainder of his life. Purchasing and consumption are carried out within the wider context of day-to-day living. Here the motion of plans, incorporated by Twyman (1969) into a model of the advertising process, is a useful one.

> They [i.e., G. A. Miller et al., 1960] suggest that an individual's behavior can be represented by a hierarchy of plans analogous to a computer program for living. The essence of these plans is that they are goal directed and the goals or objectives can be progressively broken down into a series of subgoals and plans to achieve them. The plans are arranged hierarchically in the sense that any single plan has been generated by a higher order plan and itself generates lower order plans which form a part of it. For example, one could postulate a housewife having a general plan or program to "look after the family" which would lead to various subplans to cover shopping and the preparation of meals and so on down to small subroutines for laying the table, cooking and serving the meal and washing-up after a meal and asking people if they had enjoyed it.

Twyman uses the concept of plan to hypothesize some of the different levels at which an advertisement for food might operate, for instance:

> **a** by suggesting something about the status of purchasers of a product
>
> **b** by appeal to plans concerned with care of self and family, e.g., health
>
> **c** suggesting new approaches to the form of meals, e.g., that convenience foods could be quickly prepared and served while watching television
>
> **d** by suggesting plans for ensuring that particular products are always kept in adequate supply in the home
>
> **e** by suggesting ideas for when and where to shop
>
> **f** by showing ways of using the product in meals at either the preparation or the serving stage
>
> **g** by suggesting advantages which might accrue from a more careful assessment of product qualities
>
> **h** by trying to create greater feedback of product qualities to the housewife from other members of the household

4. As described in the section on the Howard-Sheth theory, the individual establishes over time sets of choice criteria in terms of which he identifies and evaluates products. Choice criteria develop through learning and may be based on actual experience with the product, generalization from related experiences, and information derived from advertising, and so on, or from word of mouth. Choice criteria lead to the development of favorable or unfavorable attitudes toward products and of varying levels of buying intention. They also determine which products are perceived as substitutable for certain needs and which products will remain in the evoked set from which decisions are made on particular occasions.

5. In today's complex, highly developed society, the consumer is assailed daily by vast quantities of information. Only some of this is relevant to his purchasing goals. Even this, however, may be too much for any single person to pay serious attention to. The individual, therefore, in his role as consumer as well as in his other roles, develops strategies for dealing with information overload. These are often referred to as defense mechanisms. All involve the concept of selectivity.

Thus under some circumstances (e.g., extensive problem solving) the individual will deliberately seek out information and will selectively expose himself to advertisements. Under other circumstances he may adopt essentially negative strategies; that is, he may deliberately avoid certain advertisements or experiences. Similarly, he will pay selective attention to information about certain products in two senses: vigilance to those aspects he finds valuable or acceptable, and rejection of those that are unacceptable or of low value. Selectively does not stop here. Even when exposed to and paying attention to product information (e.g., an advertisement), the individual's defense mechanisms may lead him to restructure information in terms of already existing needs, attitudes, and expectancies: the advertiser may say one thing, the consumer perceive another. Selectivity also extends to the retention of information, with value and acceptability again determining whether particular messages are remembered or forgotten.

6. It was pointed out earlier that the decision-making situation itself is not invariably—if at all—a matter of consciously and rationally evaluating alternatives and settling for the product that provides the best all-round prospect. Sometimes (e.g., routinized problem solving) decisions may not, strictly speaking, be made at all. When they are, concepts such as confidence (in distinguishing between different brands and in the probability of the product performing as expected), involvement in the product field, and the extent of perceived risk may all play a part in the search and evaluation process. Moreover, in his day-to-day shopping, the consumer may adopt one or more of a variety of decision rules or strategies.

7. The ongoing nature of decision processes has also been discussed. The consumer's choice criteria are modified through past experiences with the product as well as by information and impressions from advertising. Search will continue when products are unsatisfactory. Search may also continue with the aim of providing reassurance that a good purchase has been made, particularly in ambiguous situations and when the consumer is highly involved but lacks confidence.

8. The above propositions have been stated in terms of a hypothetical individual. There are two fundamental qualifications here. First, individuals differ in respect to many of the characteristics listed, including decision rules as well as needs and motives. These differences have increasingly been recognized by marketing men and researchers and have been incorporated into market segmentation policies (Lunn, 1971b). Second, the individual makes and implements purchasing decisions within a social environment. Hence a variety of social influences bear on these decisions. Some of these are personal (e.g., other family members, neighbors, friends, workmates). Others are more impersonal—(e.g., people observed in the street or on television, reference groups and prevalent cultural values, such as the quest for youthfulness or the decline in authority).

To recognize the importance of social influences is not to devalue "internal" processes. The cornerstone of the eclectic approach is, of course, that sociological and psychological concepts should be brought together into a common framework.

Social influences have two distinctive functions. They help to formulate product awareness, choice criteria, attitudes, and buying intentions. They also help to mediate or modify the translation of these predispositions into actual behavior. For instance, a housewife who is highly predisposed toward certain exotic foods may buy other foods instead because of her husband's traditional tastes.

THE PRACTICAL VALUE OF DECISION-PROCESS MODELS

Earlier we outlined several functions of consumer models, including explanation, integration, and the generation of guidelines for research priorities. It was also pointed out that theory building can have a broad, long-term role in marketing by placing our knowledge and assumptions on a more scientific footing and enabling the latter to be tested. At the same time, theory can have a more specific function in day-to-day research projects by improving our interpretation of particular research findings and by suggesting which variables should be included, manipulated, and controlled. It is suggested that the eclectic approach, because it is problem focused but comprehensive, is more valuable for these objectives than either the empirical or the a priori approach in their respective extreme forms—although either of the latter might be equally suitable for particular problems and situations.

Four instances of the value of the eclectic approach are now outlined.

Market Segmentation

The explosive popularity of market segmentation studies has been reviewed elsewhere (e.g., Lunn, 1971a, 1971b). These studies have been increasingly useful in describing market structures and in guiding marketing policies concerned both with the maintenance of existing brands and products and with the identification of market opportunities. But a segmentation study can only provide a snapshot of a market at one period of time. For a complete perspective, these studies should be incorporated into a dynamic picture both of the market in question and of consumers in general. In addition, there is the crucial issue of which variables to include in segmentation projects, whether as "active" variables to help in the formation of target groups or as "passive" variables for cross-tabulation against these groups in an attempt to elucidate consumer behavior in the product field in question. In the writer's experience, the increasing insights into consumer decision processes gained in recent years can have immense benefits in these respects. For instance, "new" variables are suggested, such as the degree of involvement with product fields and the degree of problem solving (extended, limited, or routinized).

The Influence of In-Store Factors

Research Bureau Ltd. has recently carried out a major investigation into the influence of in-store factors upon purchasing intentions and actual behavior. An earlier project not based on a theoretical framework found few systematic results, despite the use of a large sample of shoppers and clear specification and recording of the in-store factors. Following this project, a consumer decision framework was developed within the Research International group (see "Other Contributions" section), which included a series of concepts of apparent relevance to the purchasing situation (e.g., the concepts of product class and evoked set, and different decision strategies). A second project was then carried out incorporating these variables: it has provided valuable evidence of in-store influence for a variety of product fields.

In addition, the project itself has contributed to the Research International conceptual framework—for example, through results that have extended the definition of purchases from the oversimplified dichotomy of planned and unplanned, postulated at the outset of the project. Moreover, through the use of factor and cluster analysis it has led to the development of six basic shopper types defined in terms of responses to basic attitudes salient to the shopping situation (e.g., the "happy, impulsive shopper," and the "reluctant, organized shopper").

An Advertisement Pretesting System

Advertisement pretesting is a major field of market research that has been the center of innumerable controversies and disputes between rival methodologists. This is not only because of deficiencies in particular techniques but because few pretesting systems have been based on a systematic conceptualization of how advertising might work. All too often when an underlying model has been adopted, it has been oversimplistic, such as the now-notorious hierarchy of effect schemata (Palda, 1966).[2] Lately this area has been examined more systematically. At an Esomar Workshop, Joyce (1967) attempted one of the first main syntheses of our knowledge about how advertising works. In the United States, Sheth (1969b) has applied the Howard-Sheth theory to a specific examination of the advertising process. Also in the United States, McGuire (1969a) has evolved an eclectic theory of the advertising process based on a variety of standpoints in the attitude change, persuasion, and communication fields. Both Sheth and McGuire point out that provided the hierarchy of effects paradigm is not regarded as irreversible or the sole form in which persuasion can take place, it can supply a valuable structure for assessing advertisements. But they also emphasize that different advertisements will probably have different effects at each point of the hierarchy (e.g., an ad with high attention value may have little persuasive power). However, quite different measuring instruments will be necessary at each stage.

Similar points have been made by Twyman (1969, 1970). Along with Juchen and colleagues from the Research International group, he has provided a review of the advertising field having two main foundations: an empirical review of existing advertising pretesting systems and an elaboration of consumer decision process theory. An integration of these two bases has led to a revised form of pretesting approach.

The Attitude-Behavior Controversy

The relationship between attitudes and behavior is an area that has recently undergone critical scrutiny in market research (e.g., Fishbein, 1972; Fothergill, 1968; Lunn, 1970; Wicker, 1969) and in the social sciences generally (e.g., Festinger, 1964; A. Cohen, 1964; Insko, 1967). "Attitude" has been a central concept in market research for many years and in psychology for even longer. Attitudes generally structure the way in which an individual perceives his environment, and they guide the ways in which he responds to it. Moreover, attitude data have a variety of practical applications in market research, including the following functions:

1 An essentially predictive function; that is, consumer attitudes are often treated as a kind of early warning system whereby changes of attitude are expected to anticipate changes in purchasing.

2 A derived predictive function; that is, attitudes are often included in product, advertisement, and similar tests; here the relative performance of different products, advertisements, and so on, are judged in terms of attitude measures on the assumption that attitude change in the test will be followed by corresponding attitude and behavioral change in the marketplace. In a sense, attitudes in the test situation are being used as surrogates for behavior.

3 An essentially diagnostic function; that is, attitude data are often used to indicate the kind of supportive or corrective action necessary for existing products and to provide guidance for new product development. For this function, attitude data may be gathered in several different kinds of projects (e.g., qualitative motivation research studies, quantitative market segmentation studies, and product and advertising tests). Here again it is assumed—often implicitly—that when marketing action succeeds in changing consumer attitudes, there will be subsequent changes in purchasing.

Unfortunately, there is, allegedly, little or no evidence that changes in people's attitudes toward an object (or person or situation) are in fact followed by corresponding changes in behavior in relation to that object (person or situation). This applies to social psychology as well as to market research. Indeed, it has been claimed that where relationships are to be expected they will be in the direction of attitude change following rather than preced-

[2] For example, Attention–comprehension attitude change–retention of change behavior.

ing behavior change (e.g., Festinger, 1964). As a result, some researchers have begun to despair of the value of consumer attitude data.

This is preeminently an area that demands a sound theoretical underpinning. Yet it is also one that has been characterized by naïve and oversimplistic conceptualization. The remainder of this section is largely devoted to an outline of some of the potential values of better theory.[3]

As a prelude to theory, a few points are made about research findings, definitions, and measurements.

Research Findings

Assertions about the low relationship between attitudes and behavior are somewhat misleading. The literature contains positive as well as negative findings. This applies to research in social psychology (e.g., Fishbein, 1972; Wicker, 1969) and in market research (e.g., Assael and Day, 1968; Day, 1970b; Sheth, 1971). Moreover, the studies purporting to show negative findings have been criticized on a number of counts, including research design measurement, and interpretation (Fishbein, 1972; Rokeach, 1968). As Fothergill (1968) pointed out—in a paper higly critical of certain market research studies that had reported positive relationships—it is hard to credit the notion that attitude will never precede behavioral change. The challenge for researchers is to identify the circumstances and conditions under which such change should or should not be expected, and both measurement and theory have a part to play.

Definitions of Attitude

Some of the problems in the attitude-behavior controversy have arisen because different researchers have used the term *attitude* to refer to quite different concepts. The writer has found it valuable to categorize the major uses in market research under two main headings: (1) perceptual and (2) motivational. The former refer to the consumer's reactions to a specific object, person, or situation; the latter to characteristics of the consumer that indicate the satisfaction sought through purchasing and usage behavior.

1 Perceptual
- **a** Overall evaluation
- **b** Buying intention
- **c** Specific evaluative beliefs

2 Motivational
- **a** Specific product field requirements
- **b** Consumer values
- **c** General personality

These distinctions have been discussed at length elsewhere (e.g., Lunn, 1969b, 1970), and just four points are made here:

1 There is a growing tendency in both psychology (Fishbein, 1972) and market research (Howard and Sheth, 1969), to restrict the term "attitude" to overall evaluation. The writer supports this but would argue that the crucial point is less one of terminology as such than of the need to preserve clear distinctions between different constructs.

2 Specific evaluative beliefs are a subset of the total collection of beliefs that a consumer holds about a particular object (person, or situation). As such they can be distinguished from descriptive beliefs—the latter have no motivational properties (unlike evaluative beliefs, which possess such properties by definition).

3 Evaluative beliefs and product field requirements represent the two facets of choice criteria (see above). That is, a consumer will hold certain beliefs about the attributes of particular products and will regard these attributes as more or less important.

4 When evaluating attitude-behavior relationships, it is important to ensure that the attitudes (or intentions, beliefs, etc.) being assessed are appropriate to the behavior in question. We return to this issue later.

[3]A thorough review of the attitude-behavior issue goes beyond the scope of this paper; and the topic has been covered by Sampson (1971) and by the writer at a recent Esomar Seminar (Lunn, 1970).

Measurement

It was pointed out earlier that good theory is inadequate without good measurement. Recent years have seen considerable advances in attitude measurement, and these have been described elsewhere (e.g., Lunn, 1968, 1969a). Two particularly important stages are:

1 Identification of the variables that are relevant to or determinative of (J. H. Myers and Alpert, 1968) the behavior that one wishes to predict or understand. Commonly used techniques are group discussions, extended interviews, and the Kelly Repertory Grid.

2 Development of measuring instruments for these variables that are at once sound (i.e., valid and reliable) and feasible to use in market research conditions. A commonly used technique is factor analysis, applied either to sets of bipolar phrases or "Likert" type agree-disagree scales.

These stages are especially important for the measurement of attitudes in the motivational category and for evaluative beliefs. Overall evaluation and buying intention are usually measured on single, quantitative scales, probably with five or seven categories. Especially for predictive purposes, however, more attention should be paid to their measurement; in particular, for buying intention, care should be taken over the phraseology—the more precise and specific the wording, the greater the probability of obtaining relationships with subsequent behavior—and the choice situation with which the consumer is likely to be faced.

Attitude Theory

Attempts by market researchers to introduce a more theoretical element into the attitude-behavior controversy fall neatly into the empirical–a priori–eclectic categorization outlined here. The *empirical* approach is illustrated by the work of Ehrenberg (1969) and a number of coauthors (e.g., Bird and Ehrenberg, 1970). This work has indicated some interesting relationships between attitude and behavior but has operated in too limited a manner to warrant detailed comment at this stage. Perhaps its major use for the moment is to warn researchers against interpreting too literally and superficially data involving general measures (whether of attitudes or of behavior) and against working with unsegmented samples of respondents.

The a priori approach has been the most popular to date. Many researchers have examined the explanatory power of psychological theories such as cognitive dissonance. Probably the most promising single theory adopted is that of Fishbein (1967, 1971), and it is still being developed. Particular strengths of Fishbein's approach include the following:

1 A precise definition of attitude (i.e., as overall evaluation) and the distinction of this concept from other related concepts such as beliefs and behavioral intentions (see above).

2 A recognition that when prediction is the main research aim, it is best achieved through precise measures of behavioral intention (rather than overall evaluation: an individual may have a high regard for an object but be in no position to purchase it), and also precise measures of behavior.

3 The incorporation of Rosenberg's value-instrumentality formulation (see above).

4 Recognition of the importance of social and situational factors.

In the writer's opinion, it is a mistake to treat Fishbein's theory (1967) as a ready-made model for consumer attitude data, excluding other approaches. Like other academic work, the model has been developed apart from the context of consumer behavior, and, in consequence, disregards certain key concepts relevant to this behavior (Lunn, 1970; see also below). It does, however, represent a useful foundation on which to build a consumer attitude model.

Nevertheless, it appears that the eclectic approach to consumer theory holds most promise for illuminating the attitude-behavior controversy. It is not that any single theory is rejected; rather, several possibly relevant theories are allowed to contribute to our understanding of consumer attitudes. In passing, it is worth noting that a more eclectic tradition is also developing among certain academic attitude researchers, especially in the United States. McGuire (1969b, 1970) is a protagonist of the approach. In the American Marketing Association paper, McGuire gives a fivefold classification of what he calls the guiding theories behind attitude change research, and he indicates some of the applications for the marketing area. The five theoretical paradigms are labeled Perceptual, Consistency, Learning, Functional, and Information Processing. In both papers McGuire insists that the various so-called rival theories are supplementary rather than conflicting. "Their assumptions about man and persuasion are quite different, but the difference resides in the tendency for each of the approaches to stress aspects of man and the social influence process which are neglected by other approaches." All the more reason, it might be argued, to incorporate a variety of these approaches into the study of consumer attitudes.

Sheth (1971) has presented a comprehensive conceptual model of attitude-behavior relationships, based on the work of several researchers including Dulany, Fishbein, Howard and Sheth, Rokeach, and Rosenberg. One of the aims has been to sort out the various dimensions of "attitudes" (see above), hypothesizing about their interrelationships and linking them to subsequent behavior.

A major contribution of Sheth's work has been to test this theory in a naturalistic setting, involving the choice behavior of a representative sample of 954 American housewives. The respondents formed a panel and recorded their purchases of several convenience foods, including instant breakfast (the object of the research), over five months. In addition, panel members were interviewed four times, with a questionnaire that included, in addition to relevant background data, a variety of attitudinal measures. The project monitored the launch of two new brands and the effects of these on sales of an existing brand. Since the study was longitudinal, time-lag analyses could be carried out on the same respondents.

Sheth's results, based on analysis carried out to date, include the following:

1 Evaluative beliefs are good predictors of overall evaluation and, to a lower extent, of buying intention.

2 Buying intention predicts subsequent behavior, although at a lower level.

3 Changes in behavior also predict changes in the various dimensions of attitude; that is, people appear to adjust their attitudes in the light of experience with the product. (It will be recalled that the interdependence between attitudes and behavior is a central tenet of consumer decision-process theory.)

4 Situational factors unanticipated by respondents at the time of stating buying intentions (e.g., competitive promotional efforts from two new brands with different appeals, the frequent unavailability of the new brands when the housewife went shopping) appeared to exert a significant effect on the predictive power of buying intentions.

To quote Sheth (1971, p. 121):

> All of this indicates that what is found to be a very high correlation between behavioral intention and behavior in the laboratory type experimental studies (Dulany, 1968; Fishbein, 1967) may be due to two factors, both of which are likely to be nonexistent in naturalistic situations. They are (1) contiguity of expressing behavioral intention and actual behavior and (2) lack of situational variations from one individual to the other and from one time period to the other because these are controlled in the experiment.

This ties in with the findings of the R. B. L. In-Store Influence project quoted above. Here a high relationship was observed between actual purchase and buying intention in relation to specific brands and products, established shortly prior to the shopping visit.

Sheth also raises problems surrounding the

definition and measurement of consumer behavior. His project used panel data, which should in general provide a relatively high level of accuracy and precision. However, the time interval problem can arise here. For instance, in the Columbia Buyer Behavior study that provided Sheth's data, many consumers did not buy even once between interviews, particularly in the case of the two new brands.

This leads in to a more general issue raised by the writer elsewhere (Lunn, 1970), namely, that in attitude-behavior projects, it has usually been assumed—if implicitly—that any weakness lay in the attitudinal rather than in the behavioral component. However, the behavioral questions used in market research field projects take various forms and often leave much to be desired. Not only do they lack precision (e.g., "brand usually bought") they also fail to recognize that consumers are by no means always single-brand buyers. Here the consumer decision-process concept of a repertoire of brands, all of which the housewife may regard as sufficiently satisfactory for her purpose, might provide more precise behavioral data. R.B.L. is currently experimenting with a technique that may contribute to a solution: the housewife is asked to estimate how many times she expects to buy each of a list of brands during her next ten purchases.

A further valuable theoretical consideration is that of attitude stability. Building on the work of Sherif, Sherif, and Nebergall, (1965), Day (1970a, 1970b) has developed measures of stability in terms of consumers' involvement in the product field and their confidence in brand purchases. He claims to have found higher relationships between attitude change and subsequent behavioral change where attitudes are stable than where they are unstable, as defined above.[4] This theoretical position could be related to that of Rokeach and others who have distinguished between central and peripheral attitudes. The former are more deeply held and have more relationships with other attitudes and cognitions. As a result they will be harder to change; but once changed, they might be expected to exhibit greater stability and closer relationships with behavior.

Day quotes his findings as an argument for analyzing attitude-behavior data within consumer segments (i.e., contrasting consumers with stable and unstable attitudes) rather than on aggregate samples. The writer would argue for extending the principle of segmentation to include additional variables. Market segmentation studies have firmly established the value of defining target groups of consumers in terms of needs and values relevant to the product field (e.g., Lunn, 1971b). It is probable that different levels of attitude-behavior relationships would be found within such target groups.

To conclude this section on the attitude-behavior controversy, we note that it has been argued that the published findings in this area are by no means as negative as is sometimes implied. Nevertheless, there is considerable scope for improvement if confidence in the value of consumer attitude data is to be maintained. Part of this improvement must occur in the area of methodology. Many published studies have used crude and inadequate measures of both attitudes and behavior.

There have also been conceptual weaknesses. For instance, general evaluations of particular objects have been related to specific future behavior in relation to these objects, regardless of the variety of additional variables that might be expected to determine behavior, including the situations in which it takes place. It is valuable here to distinguish the purposes for which attitude information is required. For prediction, buying intention would seem to be the most appropriate concept; but care should be taken over the phraseology of the measuring instrument and over the definition and measurement of behavior. For many consumer research problems, we

[4]Day used the same Columbia panel data as Sheth.

should attempt to represent the brand choice situation in our behavioral measure. For diagnostic purposes, specific evaluative beliefs and attitudes of a motivational kind (as defined above) will be most relevant.

A greater interest in theory has already led to the clearer conceptualization described in this section. But theory is, of course, playing a wider part by indicating some of the personal and social variables that intervene between consumers' attitudes—however defined and measured—and their behavior and in guiding the interpretation of attitude-behavior data—for instance, in recognizing the interdependence of these two variables. The promise of Fishbein's theoretical work has been referred to, but in the writer's opinion, it would be a mistake to restrict theoretical development to any single approach, especially one evolved outside the consumer context.

Finally, a distinction should be made between the requirements of basic research designed to advance our general understanding of the consumer and research for day-to-day practical problems. Basic research tends to be complex, and one project may involve the inclusion of a large number of variables (e.g., the Columbia Buyer Project). However, the point of such projects is to add to knowledge and to test our assumptions. This degree of detail and complexity would normally be inappropriate and unfeasible for day-to-day projects. At the same time, the inclusion of more rather than fewer variables is likely to "remove the noise from the channel" and to increase the precision of the results. It is a matter of deciding the optimum balance in each case.

CONCLUSION

This paper has reviewed the current position of decision-process models and has argued that they hold considerable promise for market research, on both a day-to-day level and a more basic level—not least because they help us to clarify our assumptions about how marketing action can influence consumer behavior. They have, moreover, an important part to play in identifying variables for inclusion in specific research projects. Here it is important to strike a balance between what may be gained in precision and what may be lost in complexity. Such models also draw attention to the needs for greater clarification of the concepts and measures we use in market research and for a greater use of longitudinal research designs and studies designed to replicate previous findings (Kollat, Engel, and Blackwell, 1970; Pellemans, 1971).

Consumer behavior is still a relatively young discipline, and all the models reviewed here contain considerable scope for revision and development. It is hoped that this development will come as much from market research as from researchers in the academic field.

APPENDIX

This appendix contains three flow charts representing the theories of Nicosia, Engel et al., and Howard and Sheth. There is no space here for a definition of the various concepts and interrelationships. Aspects of these theories are outlined in the main text and full descriptions can be found in the references given below. For Figure 1 (a flow chart of the Nicosia model), see Nicosia (1966); for Figure 2 (a flow chart of the Engel model), see Engel et al. (1968); for Figure 3 (a flow chart of the Howard-Sheth model), see Howard and Sheth (1969).

Where applicable, solid lines on the charts indicate flow of information; dashed lines indicate feedback effects.

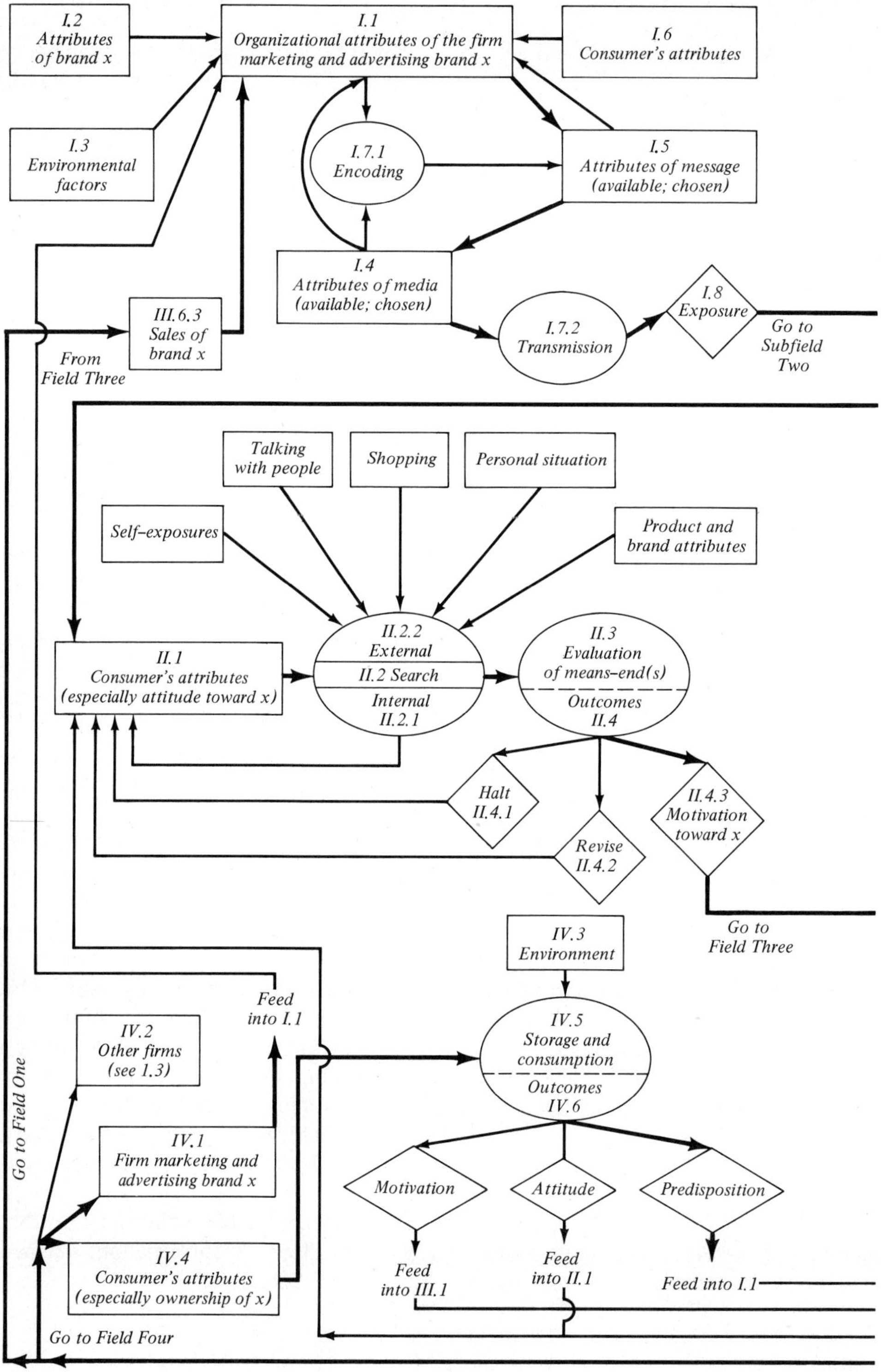

Figure 1 Comprehensive scheme of the Nicosia model.

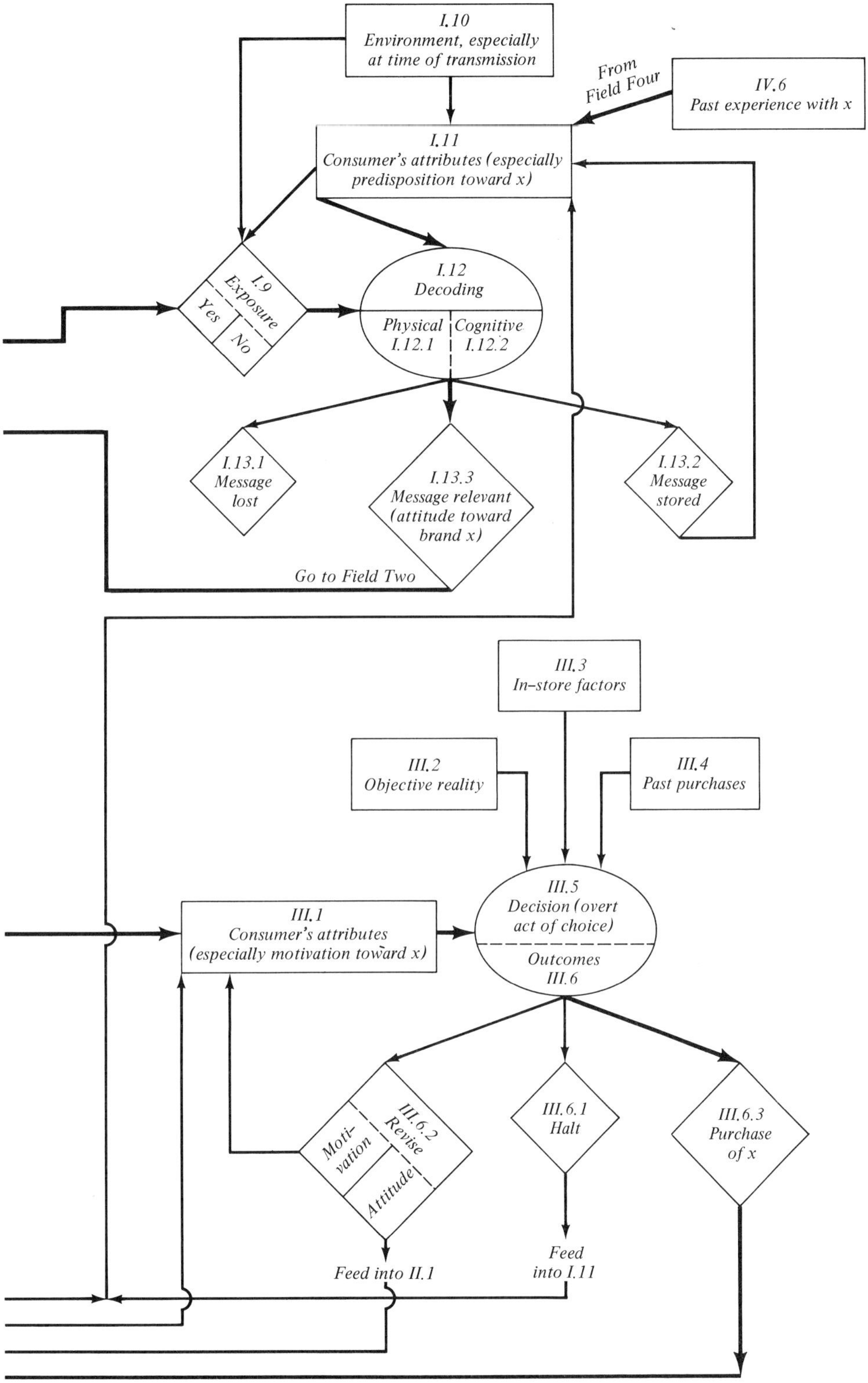

Figure 1 Continued.

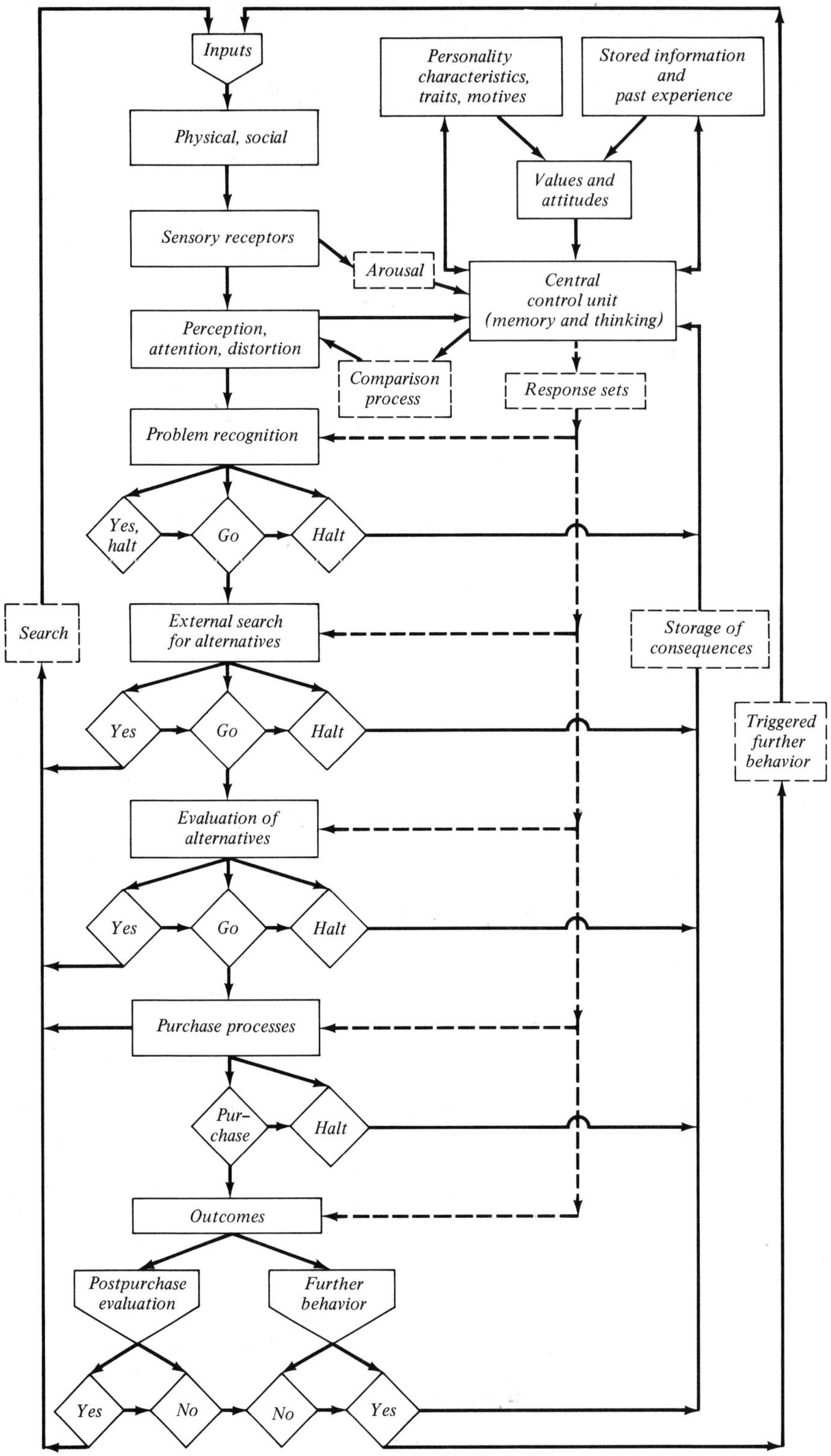

Figure 2 Complete representation of the Engel model.

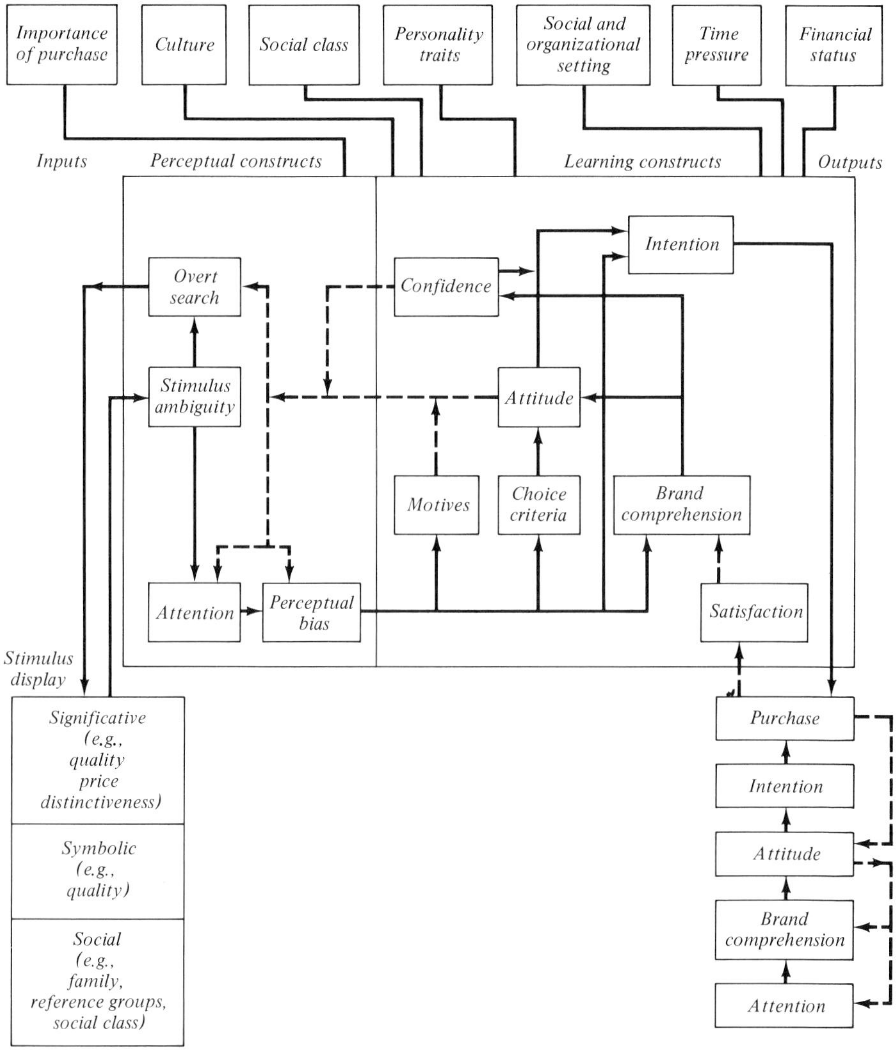

Figure 3 Simplified description of Howard-Sheth theory.

9

The Behavioral Sciences

Charles Ramond

Much of the art of using science involves knowing what other researchers have found, and how these findings have been turned to practical advantage. In this selection the author reviews certain literature of the behavioral sciences in search of contributions to marketing practice.

Unlike earlier reviews which were concerned essentially with techniques, this report deals with the concepts and laws that apply to consumer behavior.

BIASES OF BEHAVIORAL SCIENTISTS

Managers and scientists are more alike than either group admits. Both must act in the absence of adequate or sufficient information. Both use a complex dialectic, explicit or otherwise. Both operate through multilevel organizations. Both have as one goal the discovery of new knowledge about human behavior and as another the maintenance of certain schedules of rewards for themselves and the organizations they serve.

Division of Labor

The fact remains that marketing scientists have produced more laws of behavior than have marketing managers—to judge from publicly available materials. It is partly a question of who does what. If a great many experienced decision makers, half of them scientists and the other half marketing men, were confronted today with the problem of predicting a particular bit of human behavior, the chances are that they would assign the problem to the businessman, who would rely on the advice of a scientist, who in turn would base his recommendation on the results of research. It is this chain of command that Henry Kissinger had in mind when he observed that matters of policy have increasingly become matters of fact. Businessmen have not always been so open to advice, least of all from the nonexperimental social sciences. Their attitude was succinctly expressed by Henry Ford *père*: "History is bunk."

As administrators of science, businessmen necessarily observe behavior less than they theorize about it.[1] They use theories incessantly in such semantic disguises as policies, proverbs, and even jokes. A marketing plan inevitably makes assumptions about consumer behavior, many of which have never been tested or even carefully scrutinized. Beyond these written records lies a jungle of unverbalized, unexplored ideas. The manager's intuitions may or may not represent the real world more accurately than do most other people's; some say they must or he wouldn't be where he is.

In our culture businessmen are given the

[1]With notable exceptions. Kirk Parrish, president of Lanvin-Charles of the Ritz, regularly interviews women about the cosmetics they use. Vice-presidents of Imperial Oil used to be required by company policy to manage a service station for a few weeks each year. Executives on retail accounts at a major advertising agency periodically serve as sales clerks in client stores. Given the obvious value of such learning experiences, it is a shame they are so rare.

Reprinted from *The Art of Using Science in Marketing* (New York: Harper & Row, 1974), pp. 50–80. At the time of writing, the author was president of Marketing Control, Inc., and editor of the *Journal of Advertising Research*.

blame and credit for seeking power through individual action while scientists receive comparable blame and credit for behaving objectively, logically, and temperately. Like most stereotypes, these are convenient but misleading. The behavioral scientist has his own jungle of unexplored ideas, his own choice points, and is conditioned by the very thing he sometimes delights to point out in others, social motivation.

Behavioral Scientists and Society

Like the businessman, the scientist is politically and socially motivated, but unlike the businessman he ignores the implications of this fact for society. He has been too nearsighted to see the peculiar role society accords him and too farsighted to see the operation of certain dangerously powerful behavioral principles in his own decisions. When the behavioral scientist fails to see his own proclivities, this is uniquely threatening. It distorts society's official mirror. For this reason the layman has not only the right but the obligation to know what these distortions are. If he delegates to scientists his responsibility for knowing how he and others behave, this in itself is a political mistake. If he goes on to ignore the motives that govern the decisions of the scientist, he has nowhere to turn for understanding but to a source whose behavior he himself does not understand.

This seems less and less likely, however. Recently society as a whole has been more interested in the behavioral scientist's motives than the scientist himself. Society's incipient paranoia keeps it alert to any threat, real or fancied. This accounts for the success of a book like *The Hidden Persuaders,* in which a journalist who understood his audience was able to sell paranoia reduction.

At a more popular level the layman caricatures the scientist as the absent-minded professor, the genius ineffectual in practical matters, the man who can split the atom but cannot remember his umbrella. This image reassures anyone who fears that scientists know more than he does about controlling behavior. To the practicing amateur, professionals are less threatening if they seem to have compensating limitations.

In intellectual circles the scientist is recognized as the political animal he is. The intellectual who has met politically astute scientists sees them as becoming increasingly powerful (Rabinowich, 1962). In literature the stereotype becomes ever more threatening, progressing from Faust to Frankenstein to Dr. Strangelove. When B. F. Skinner said in *Beyond Freedom and Dignity* (1971) not only that behavior *could* be controlled but that it *should* be, the intellectual's worst suspicions were confirmed. Noam Chomsky's review (1972) was hailed by many as Skinner's official dismissal from the Intellectual Establishment.

Among intellectuals today the behavioral scientist has been relegated to a role akin to that of a hired killer. No one really wants his assignment—to discover the laws of human behavior—because it involves much that is unpleasant. Everyone would like to govern the behavior of others according to future knowledge, but not everyone wishes to govern his own: Who would care to know the exact moment of his death? We want to know nothing depressing or fearful about ourselves, just everything else.

It is not hard to understand why the average intellectual finds behavioral science a trifle *déclassé.* Fortunately he may leave it to others, but the result is not to his liking. As John Leonard, editor of the *New York Times Book Review,* said to the New York Academy of Sciences in 1973:

> We want to be Platonists, operating on an ideal scale of values—and along come these wonks with slide rules sewn into their sports jackets, these *utilitarians* with their impersonal instruments, their college board exams, weighing us as though each of us weren't *unique.* "They" are telling "us" that they can measure our merriment

> and our desperation and that we don't deviate very much from the norm.
>
> In other words, science tells us things that make us feel bad. It tells us that we aren't central but are peripheral to the business of the universe; that we aren't created in the image of God, but are rather a lucky concert of atoms; that we aren't masters of our fate or captains of our souls, but puppets of our past, jerking on strings attached to prior causes—"predestination without grace," someone called it. A gloomy truth.

Suggestions that this predestination be consciously interfered with are even less well received. When Kenneth Clark seriously proposed in his 1971 presidential address to the American Psychological Association that world leaders be given tranquilizers to reduce the threat of war, the press thought he was kidding. Since he glossed over the problem of who should administer the drugs, he was at once suspected of a naive demand for more "power to the psychologists." The press could not have imagined how isolated he was from the real world, the Intellectual Establishment, and the media themselves.

This involution of behavioral scientists has influenced their strategy and tactics. The victim must be dispatched (knowledge obtained) in only a few set ways; membership in the assassins' brotherhood is denied if the procedures are violated. In one of psychology's few passes at lighthearted self-criticism, Donald Bullock (1956) wrote a hypothetical letter to a journal editor complaining that he could not get his papers accepted because he used too few subjects, his experimental design showed lack of sophistication, and his data were not amenable to treatment by analysis of variance. The letter was signed I. P. Pavlov.

Such conformity, unfortunately, extends only to the behavioral scientist's methods. His subject matter is usually up to him and, at least in his early years, he exercises this freedom of choice with abandon. The object of the typical psychological Ph.D. dissertation seems to be much like the one Robert Frost assigned to a poem: to be as different as possible from every other. The few coherent collections of behavioral research have been stimulated by strong leaders. Freud, Jung, Piaget, Hull, Spence, Estes, Skinner, Lewin, Maslow, and others of their stature created coherent bodies of knowledge largely through the force of their own personalities.

A further problem, as shown by Orne (1962), is that human experimental subjects are to a striking degree controlled by the experimenter and his wishes. They will consciously or unconsciously attempt to help the experimenter obtain the results he expects. In another study it was found that student experimenters are able to confirm virtually any hypothesis they believe agrees with the teacher's viewpoint.

Perhaps because they suspect these realities, most corporate executives find behavioral scientists of little use in marketing (Feinberg and Lefkowitz, 1962). Retailers are no more receptive (Hollander, 1959). Businessmen are accustomed to dealing with persuasive communication both inside and outside their organizations, so it is not surprising that they doubt anyone who claims to observe and report behavior without introducing his own prejudices and biases.

These biases are not the same for all behavioral scientists. There are at least five behavioral subcultures—clinical, experimental, social, anthropological, and economic—each of which seems to want to do something different to man. The clinician wants to help him, the experimentalist to study him, the sociologist to recruit him, the anthropologist to play with him, and the economist to control him, preferably in large bunches. These viewpoints color their choices of what to study. Barkin (1961) reports that psychologists appear to have served management better than they have labor, probably because management is a better source of subjects. Lazarsfeld has observed that sociologists have just the opposite bias: Where better to organize than in a labor union?

In summary, then, we see that the scientist's

motives, particularly his need to be accepted by society and to assume a share of power in it, have colored his choice of subject matter, and his guildlike profession has colored his choice of methods to gather data. These are fairly fundamental limitations on the findings of behavioral sciences. There is no impersonal study of man, only man's own study of man.

PSYCHOLOGY

Perceiving

There is more to perception than meets the eye. What a person perceives depends not only on the energy changes transmitted from the physical world through his sense organs, but also on his past experience. He expects, wants, or is used to seeing some things more than others. The less information he gets from outside, the more he supplies from these expectations, needs, and habits. He also ignores or screens out threatening stimuli. In the language of the psychologist, perception is selective, organizational, interpretive, and defensive.

There are two basic parameters of a perceiving organism—range and sensitivity. His range begins at the smallest stimulus value he can perceive (absolute threshold) and ends when he can no longer perceive changes (terminal threshold). His sensitivity is the least energy change he can detect (differential threshold or JND—just noticeable difference).

Both of these parameters can be changed over time. The absolute visual threshold, for example, can be raised by prolonged exposure to a value 100,000 times as intense as is required after the eye has been in darkness overnight. In a marksmanship training study (Ramond, 1954) field measures found infantrymen's average vernier acuity—the ability to perceive two lines as joining or not—equivalent to the ability to see a fly on a telephone pole 100 yards away!

Just as human receptors can be extremely sensitive, especially after disuse, they can be correspondingly insensitive under conditions of constant stimulation. We become accustomed to the heat of a bath, the hum of a clock, or the dazzle of sunlit snow. This is the central fact about perception: that the sensory filters through which comes all our knowledge of the world change their properties with experience, not only their basic properties of range and sensitivity but also their less measurable characteristics of selectivity and organization.

While much of what we see is selected and arranged according to our needs and habits, it is never wholly unrelated to objective stimuli (except in hallucinations). One of the earliest and oldest laws of behavior relates changes in perception to changes in physical stimuli. It shows that the larger a stimulus, the more it must be increased for that change to be noticed. Weber's law states that this increment divided by the size of the organized stimulus is a constant: $\Delta I/I = k$. This is the first explicit statement of a profound psychological truth: that we respond not to absolute stimuli but to relations between them. Weber's law applies to such commercial phenomena as utility theory (Stigler, 1950), stock prices (Osborne, 1959), and consumer attitudes toward prices (Webb, 1961).

The late S. S. Stevens (1962) put forward a more general law that reduces Weber's fraction to a special case. Called the *psychological power law,* it states that any perceived psychological magnitude (Ψ) is a linear function K of the difference between the two physical magnitudes (α) raised to some power n determined by the sense modality involved. Symbolically,

$$\Psi = K\,(\alpha_0 \;\; \alpha_1)^n$$

The corresponding relationship from Weber's law would be logarithmic, hence would appear virtually the same except at extreme points. Stevens' power law has been confirmed in a wide variety of situations and may be taken as a fundamental part of any model of human behavior: Equal stimulus *ratios* correspond to equal sensation *ratios.*

This psychological law has many applications in marketing. One is in the testing of food products, where new tastes can be planned with greater efficiency if the psychophysical relationships are already known (see Chapter 6). Military contract specifications for food often include psychophysical tests as one criterion. Price changes, to be perceived as such, must be judged as a percent of the original price, not in absolute values. Container sizes should vary in the same nonlinear fashion. Often the variety problem (how many different sizes, colors, shapes, etc., shall I manufacture?) can be solved if the difference threshold can be estimated. The number of sizes of each product to display in a supermarket should be determined partly by psychophysical methods, and advertisements can be designed to be recognizable according to psychophysical recipes (Advertising Research Foundation, 1961).

Equally applicable are the more psychological laws of selective perception and perceptual defense. They serve as a warning to all advertisers that the consumer has powerful sensory mechanisms for "tuning out" advertising he doesn't like. They go far to explain loyalty in product fields where real differentiation is small.

But perception furnishes two fundamental concepts for marketing theory—threshold and adaptation. Broadly interpreted, these two explain most of the phenomena studied.

Expecting

When foreseeable events do not correspond to our expectations, we change our expectations to correspond to events. This axiom is central to what Leon Festinger calls *cognitive dissonance* (1957)—i.e., the hopes-versus-reality discrepancy. The reduction of cognitive dissonance explains much behavior marketers care deeply about and sometimes predicts behavior few of them would foresee from common sense. More to the point, dissonance reduction explains as much *executive* behavior as *consumer* behavior.

Festinger introduced his theory to laymen in the October 1962 *Scientific American.*

> Does some psychological process come into play immediately after the making of a choice that colors one's attitude, either favorably or unfavorably, toward the decision?
>
> Buy two presents for your wife, again choosing things you are reasonably sure she will find about equally attractive. Find some plausible excuse for having both of them in your possession, show them to your wife and ask her to tell you how attractive each one is to her. After you have obtained a good measurement of attractiveness, tell her that she can have one of them, whichever she chooses. The other you will return to the store. After she has made her choice, ask her once more to evaluate the attractiveness of each of them. If you compare the evaluations of attractiveness before and after the choice, you will probably find that the chosen present has increased in attractiveness and the rejected one decreased.

Students paid $1 to tell other students that a boring experiment was fun increased their own ratings of the experiment far more than did students paid $20 to do the same thing. The low-paid students had less justification for lying, so they experienced more dissonance, so they reduced it more by changing their minds. Children prohibited from playing with a toy by a mild threat downgraded the toy more than children prohibited by a severe threat. "Sour grapes" seem sourer when they are nearer but still unreachable. Dissonance produced by resisting temptation is greater the weaker the deterrent.

Analogous behavior by buyer and seller is easy to imagine. The man who agonizingly chooses a Chevy over a Ford suddenly finds more things right about the Chevy and more things wrong about the Ford. And he sees more car ads, too (Ehrlich *et al.*, 1957). The highly paid advertising manager still hates the taste of Goopo while his assistants really think they like it. And the larger the marketing decision made in the absence of information, the less doubt anyone has about it afterward.

The prolific Maccobys (1961a, 1961b) have extended the theory of cognitive dissonance to group behavior. They find that a person who has just changed his mind tends to talk to other people who support his new opinions; if he doesn't he reverts to his old ideas. Milton Rokeach (1960) describes the extreme case of cognitive homeostasis—the bigot—and shows that a dogmatism scale can predict how people attack and solve problems, including their ability to evaluate a message and its source separately (Powell, 1962.)

Apart from their immediate potential for generating hypotheses, these examples suggest some fundamental learning processes that ought to be understood by marketing management. Cognitive homeostasis is not unlike probability matching under conditions of partial noncontingent reinforcement, as will be seen in the next section.

Learning

If we ever understand the learning process, we will have the ability to predict virtually all behavior of practical interest. No process is more fundamental in psychology, and no problem has captured the attention of so many superior psychologists. Learning theorists, however, usually observe infrahuman behavior—that of rats, pigeons, cats, dogs, and monkeys—for the same reason that Galileo observed balls on an inclined plane: Simple controlled situations can provide basic principles that can then be tested elsewhere. In "A Case History in Scientific Method" (1956), Skinner criticizes this method as follows:

> It is perhaps natural that psychologists should awaken only slowly to the possibility that behavioral processes may be directly observed, or that they should only gradually put the older statistical and theoretical techniques in their proper perspective. But it is time to insist that science does not progress by carefully designed steps called "experiments" each of which has a well-defined beginning and end. Science is a continuous and often a disorderly and accidental process. We shall not do the young psychologist any favor if we agree to reconstruct our practices to fit the pattern demanded by current scientific methodology. What the statistician means by the design of experiments is design which yields the kind of data to which *his* techniques are applicable. He does not mean the behavior of the scientist in his laboratory devising research for his own immediate and possibly inscrutable purposes.

The organism whose behavior is most extensively modified and most completely controlled in research of the sort I have described is the experimenter himself. This point was well made by a cartoon in the Columbia *Jester* showing two rats in a learning apparatus. The caption read: "Boy, have I got this guy conditioned! Every time I press the bar down he drops in a piece of food."

Despite being a prisoner of his subject matter, the learning theorist has managed to observe a few phenomena of wide applicability:

Classical conditioning When a stimulus is paired with another stimulus that automatically elicits a response, the new stimulus will gradually come to elicit that response by itself.

Instrumental conditioning If a response is followed by an event that reduces drive or otherwise satisfies the organism, its probability of recurrence increases.

Stimulus generalization Other stimuli like that to which a response is learned will come to evoke the response (Mednick and Freedman, 1960).

Secondary reinforcement A previously neutral stimulus paired often enough with reward will itself come to reward and thus maintain a response (Myers, 1958).

Extinction If a response is not followed by a reward, its probability gradually falls to zero.

Partial reinforcement Responses not rewarded every time usually are acquired slower and extinguished slower than those that are (Lewis, 1960).

Fixed ratio schedule When every *n*th response is rewarded, the larger the *n,* the lower the response rate. The less frequent the payoff, the slower the work.

Variable interval schedules A response takes longer to extinguish if it was learned by being rewarded at varying time intervals.

Noncontingent schedules A response takes longest of all to extinguish if it was rewarded independently of the subject's behavior. Here Skinner writes the following:

> Suppose we give a pigeon a small amount of food every fifteen seconds regardless of what it is doing. When the food is first given, the pigeon will be behaving in some way—if only standing still—and conditioning will take place. It is then more probable that the same behavior will be in progress when the food is given again. If this proves to be the case, the "operant" will be further strengthened. If not, some other behavior will be strengthened. Eventually, a given bit of behavior reaches a frequency at which it is often reinforced. It then becomes a permanent part of the repertoire of the bird even though the food has been given by a clock which is unrelated to the bird's behavior. Conspicuous responses which have been established in this way including turning sharply to one side, hopping from one foot to the other and back, bowing and scraping, turning around, strutting, and raising the head.

Many human analogies of such "superstitious" behavior come to mind—Indian rain dances, knocking wood, lucky numbers. The less frequent the noncontingent reward, the longer the response will persist. Superstition lasts, not in spite of such "dry stretches" but *because* of them.

What Is a Response?

The traditional paradigm of rational choice (Chapter 2) makes three artificial slices in the natural passage of human behavior. It assumes that the organism is confronted by (1) discrete, simultaneous *alternatives,* (2) each of which has discrete, simultaneous *outcomes,* (3) each of which, in turn, has a probability and a value.

But if we assume alternatives, we delude ourselves if we fail to define them operationally. It is ingenuous to imply that we *see* the world so neatly packaged. As Tobin and Dolbear (1963) suggest, scientists should study how individuals and groups structure complicated situations in which they must make decisions whose outcomes they cannot control or predict.

The main methodological problem in modern psychology is the definition of an alternative or response (Ramond, 1964). One of the few empirically grounded solutions is that of Logan (1960), who suggests that we differentiate two responses when their respective rewards are differentially contingent. When tested under a wide variety of reward conditions contingent upon response speed or amplitude, Logan's rats learned the precise amount and duration of a response. If a food reward was greatest or quickest when the rat traversed the alley in exactly ten seconds, and less for faster or slower running, then the rat's running times converged on ten seconds: it learned to "make haste slowly." In this sense Logan suggests that we regard running fast and running slow as different responses.

We may properly wonder why theories of choice have existed so long without any agreed-upon definition of a response. The reason is dismaying because it stems from the nature of psychological experimentation itself. *Psychologists have almost invariably observed behavior in situations that preclude the subject's doing any searching or alternative-making whatever.* They give instructions that the subject is highly motivated to follow. The subject has a vast repertoire. He can do almost anything the psychologist suggests, especially taking as given the alternatives the experimenter proposes (Orne, 1963).

If by chance a psychologist had set out to

observe search behavior, or the *formulation* of alternatives in a complex situation, he would by now have died of boredom. As any rat runner knows, it is deadly dull to observe behavior euphemistically known as "habituation to the apparatus." Indeed, to observe the process of search may be antithetical to experimentation itself, where by experimentation we mean arranging or interfering with the environment so that we can see how it causes behavior. The essence of experimentation is control. The essence of behavioral experimentation to date has been control of the alternative responses available to the subject.

Search behavior can be crucial. My first job as an experimental psychologist was to improve the Army's marksmanship training program. Basic training before 1955 used bull's-eyes as targets, a good example of the experimenter's imposing fixed alternatives on his subjects and not simulating task realism in on-the-job training. This training had come under severe question when it was learned in Korea that many U.S. soldiers had never fired their rifles in combat. A subsequent survey found that the fault lay not in the soldiers' courage but in their training: they had never been shown how to find a target to shoot at. Filling this vacuum, our research team achieved noteworthy success by developing a course in target detection, since adopted as standard by the U.S. Army (Ramond and Mighell, 1954).

Managerial Choices

Laboratory studies of choice behavior are unrealistic for another reason. In any theory of choice the theorist must assume some form of functional relationship between the probabilities of choosing alternatives before and after one of them is chosen. In Luce's most realistic model (1960) this relationship is linear. Most laboratory studies of learning should get results that can be described by this linear operator for the simple reason that until recently psychologists have usually studied responses whose outcomes depended on the response. Contingent reward is the most commonly studied outcome in the laboratory, though it is the least common outcome of the choices a person makes in everyday life.

Life's rewards fall as randomly as rain, mostly on responses that did not cause them. To the observer this pattern of reward is indistinguishable from the random schedule Skinner used to obtain superstitious behavior in pigeons. This analogy is unjustified if an intelligent human can respond differently to a reward contingent on his own behavior than to other, irrelevant rewards. But can he?

We have some evidence from an unpublished experiment reported to the Operations Research Society of America (Bavelas, 1959). Engineers were individually confronted by an apparatus that flashed two-digit numbers every few seconds. Each was asked to guess the next number and was rewarded or not rewarded after each guess. Unknown to the engineers, they were being rewarded at a steadily increasing level no matter what they answered. The numbers were in random order.

At the end of the test, each engineer was asked if he had discovered any pattern in the numbers. Each said he had, and offered complex rules for guessing the next number in sequence. When told that the numbers were random and that his increasing rewards had been independent of his guesses, he was indignant and insisted that he had discovered the true pattern. Only after he was shown that the numbers were random was he convinced otherwise. Some were never convinced at all and even formed a committee to test the randomness of the numbers used.

We have to reckon with the wonderful capacity of the intelligent human being to reward himself (Farber, 1963). Suppose we must learn a game without knowing how well we're playing, and that as long as rewards for correct play occur at random we tend to increase the number of self-administered rewards. If each of us worked in isolation, there would probably be as many different patterns of play as there were people, each of us convinced that he had mastered the game. But if we worked together, many of us would simply follow the leader. This leader would not necessarily be the wisest of us but just the one who had the least tolerance for the agony of decision making in a group (Asch, 1955).

Marketing decision making often resembles this hypothetical game. The true consequences of choice are rarely well known. Rewards such as an upturn in sales or a raise in salary come independently of our decisions. Is it not possible that some executive decisions are as superstitious as the behavior of Skinner's randomly rewarded pigeons?

Some consumer decisions are certainly superstitious in this sense. Prices may well be set as a result of joint superstition. However many "unseen hands" are pushing and pulling so economic a phenomenon as price, the fact remains that all prices are agreements between the choice behavior of two or more individuals whose interests conflict. Prices are at bottom psychological phenomena.

Consumer Choices

A more obviously psychological choice is the one a consumer makes among brands. Economists may boggle at a psychological interpretation of price trends but not at such an interpretation of brand loyalty. Here the random reward schedule plus Luce's linear model implies that individuals are in fact indifferent to brands—i.e., that the outcome—experience with the brand—need not act in any consistent manner to determine the probability of choosing that brand again (Ehrenberg, 1973).

If we examine purchases on an individual basis, we do not see evidence of random reward. Too many people are habitual purchasers of the same brand. But if we examine these purchases in the aggregate by plotting the distribution of brand loyalty throughout the group, we find that many people will buy the same brand every time and fewer will buy different brands each pair of times. If these numbers of people were plotted for only two brands, we would find most people loyal to one or the other and very few indifferent to both. This familiar U-shaped distribution of brand loyalty can be derived from the assumption of random reward plus one absurdly simple constraint: that a person buys the brand he has seen most other people buy (Miller and Starr, 1960).

So many models can explain group choice behavior that there is no crucial experiment that will tell us whether a straight line, an equal sign, or a roulette wheel is the best mechanism to describe how the outcome of an alternative affects its probability of being picked again. But if we really want to find out, we must analyze choice behavior person by person rather than for the whole group.

So far we have shown that human learning is hard to unitize, a stochastic (random) process, and dynamic in that its progress depends on its outcomes. At the same time, human decision making is a function of other variables highly specific to the test situation. Hayes (1962) found that presenting more than four facts to the decision maker reduces both the quality and the speed of his decision. Wells (1963), on the other hand, found that subjects can readily choose the most frequent of several numbers presented through earphones, a phenomenon not unlike the probability matching ability reported so frequently by Estes (1963) and his students. Edwards (1963) similarly reported other situations in which men required to draw conclusions from fallible data did so very poorly. The same men could estimate accurately posterior probabilities from prior probabilities and additional information. He confirmed the notion that individuals differ in their preferences for various bets: Not only do men need certainty, but some need it more than others. Other external conditions affecting choice behavior are stress, variously defined, and social factors (Chenzoff *et al.*, 1960). We can conclude by noting that determination of the specific conditions of "optimal" choice can safely be postponed until we learn how to define alternatives and account for the stochastic and dynamic character of decision making.

Traits

Individual variability, like Mark Twain's environment, is very prevalent. When we find some way in which many people seem to vary, we call it a trait—a "psychographic," to use the neologism of the moment. This kind of logic has permeated men's minds since ancient days. In the absence of anything better, the trait has even served as an implicit theory of choice: Some people are naturally good choosers, others aren't. Hamlet, for example, was irresolute, his action "sicklied o'er by the pale cast of thought." Nicias and Alcibiades, according to Thucydides, were born opposites in this respect: Nicias was defeated because he delayed and Alcibiades slain because he rushed in.

But traits were thought of as *innate*. Barring better evidence, novelists usually believe that men do not improve the correctness of their choices. So do some businessmen. So, in fact, did the Internal Revenue Service, which used to let us deduct any business or entertainment expenses that might be "incurred by a prudent man in the exercise of his sound judgment." It did not explain how one tells who is prudent (Reston, 1962). This may be the *reductio ad absurdum* of a trait theory of business decision making. To deny that choice probabilities change with experience is to stretch the doctrine of free will beyond human size.

If traits do not explain *changes* in behavior, what good are they? They can serve as useful predictors in the same way that the question "Did you ever own a motorcycle?" served the Navy flight schools during World War II. The answer to this question predicted, better than any other item, who would make it through flight school.

Traits have been used in marketing primarily to characterize markets or brands. The thought has been that purchasers of different brands might differ from each other more in their personalities than in their demographic characteristics. A few years ago a marathon debate was waged over whether Ford and Chevrolet owners had different personalities (Evans, 1959; Evans, 1962; Winick, 1961; Westfall, 1962). Other investigators (Koponen, 1960; Compton, 1962; Greene, 1959; Tucker and Painter, 1961) found enough mild to strong correlations between brand or media consumption and personality so that the general principle is no longer open to question. The only questions left are: Do personality scores characterize markets (1) for *my product*, (2) better in combination with demographic factors than do demographic factors alone? The number of products for which the answers are both yes is probably very small (Massy, 1964).

Another use of trait theory in marketing is in the selection of salesmen (Yeslin, 1968; Pace, 1962; Kirchner and Mousley, 1963; Kirchner, McElwain, and Dunnette, 1960). Good salesmen tend to be articulate, between 30 and 40, highly motivated, and healthy. ("It may be psychology, but it ain't news.")

Two methodological uses are becoming increasingly frequent. The first measures the trait of "yeasaying" in order to remove from the variance of any correlation the part due to the respondent's natural tendency to say yes or be agreeable no matter what the question (Couch and Keniston, 1960; Wells, 1961; Solomon and Klein, 1963). This kind of technical hygiene can throw into sharper relief other relationships under study—for instance, that between media and product consumption. The other methodological application reports large differences between volunteers and nonvolunteers (Blair and Gallagher, 1960; Burchinal, 1960; Howe, 1960). This would argue against quota sampling of self-selected respondents, as in mail surveys where responses of oversampled categories are discarded.

Theoretical assists from trait theory are not likely. Its laws are static (one response correlated with another) rather than dynamic. Perhaps the best we can hope for is that a new typology developed for particular marketing problems will prove predictive of future purchase behavior.

SOCIOLOGY

> Much modern sociological theory seems to me to possess every virtue except that of explaining anything. . . . It consists of systems of categories, or pigeonholes, into which the theorist fits different aspects of social behavior. . . . The science also needs a set of general propositions about the relations between the categories, for without such propositions explanation is impossible. The theorist shoves different aspects of behavior into his pigeonhole, cries, "Ah-ha!" and stops. He has written the dictionary of a language that has no sentences. He would have done better to start with the sentences.

Nobody loves a sociologist, but it's not just because, in George Homans' words (1961), he can't explain anything. It's also because so many other kinds of people are explaining social behavior so much better. Does small-group research teach us much beyond Fred Allen's observation that "A committee is a group of men who individually can do nothing but who collectively can decide that nothing can be done?" Has a sociologist written more insightfully about the family than Thomas Mann in *Buddenbrooks,* about organizations than Cameron Hawley in *Executive Suite,* about social class than Louis Auchincloss in *The Rector of Justin*?

By the nature of their subject matter, sociologists observe nothing that is not frequently observed by someone else. They rarely experiment, travel, or go out of their way to spot the unusual. What they eventually report is presented sooner and better by the "pop-sosh" journalism of writers and TV reporters like Thomas Wolfe, Heywood Broun, Jr., and Gay Talese.

In 1963 Martin Mayer investigated for the American Council of Learned Societies the possibility of revamping high school curricula in social studies, following the superb example of Jerrold Zacharias and his fellow physicists in high school physics. Mayer's first step was to learn what social scientists wanted to teach high school children. The chairman of one committee of sociologists listed what he called "the basic concepts of my discipline." They were:

1 The behavior of individuals is in part a function of group forces on them.
2 Some of the strains and tensions in individuals are a function of conflicts in culture and social structure.
3 One's location in the social structure influences one's perception of the world.
4 Conformity is a function of the norms of the group, and different groups have different norms.
5 Elements of the social structure have latent as well as manifest functions.
6 Events have multiple causations.
7 You can study human behavior through the scientific method.

Mayer noted that these "concepts" are part of American common sense and concluded sadly: "The great bulk of what passes for sociology, not only before the public but within the field, is a tedious redefinition or quantification of common sense notions." He finds a glimmer of hope in that "somewhere, in the narrow range between the featureless visage of random accumulation and the waxed moustache of predetermined results, there is an intelligent human face to sociology; but it comes to view only occasionally." Some occasions when they have appeared are described here.

The Family

Mates, as everyone knows, are socially alike, but as maybe not everyone knows, they seem to be *psychologically* complementary. Winch (1957) lists four basic types of marriages: mother-son, father-daughter, master-servant girl, and docile man-mistress. This has the interesting implication for marketing that if the household has no consistent purchasing agent, or if by negotiation the consistent purchasing agent compromises all the time, then personality as a market-segmenting variable will not often be useful. The opposing personalities of the household, which is after all the buying unit for most products, may cancel out.

Small Groups

Argyle (1957) reports that a group discussion solves a problem better than averaging or otherwise combining individual answers under eight conditions that collectively produce a situation in which *learning* can take place. But Johnson (1955) says, "Four judgments are better than one for the same reason that four thermometers are better than one. The only consistent finding . . . is the trend toward homogeneity or reduction of variance." This gives an idea of the level of controversy in this field; thermometers, it may be noted, do not talk to each other.

Organizations

Those who like to see common sense confirmed quantitatively will welcome Sam Stouffer's confirmation of Sam Rayburn's advice to young congressmen: "To get along, go along." Stouffer (1949) found promotion of U.S. Army recruits directly related to their conformity scores as measured by a test. Amitai Etzioni (1961) suggests that there are three basic types of organizations: *normative* (religious, political), *utilitarian* (business), and *coercive* (military, custodial).

Social Institutions

"It is one of the best demonstrated propositions in social science that, in general, workers do not respond to the incentive to the full extent of their physical and mental capacities [but] . . . reach a point which they come to consider 'a fair day's work' and do not go beyond that point." So wrote William Foote Whyte and Frank B. Miller in Joseph B. Gittler's *Review of Sociology: Analysis of a Decade* (Wiley, 1957). This finding falls in the "explainable by simpler principles" department. Recall from the section on learning that on fixed ratio reward schedules rats worked slower when there were more trials between rewards.

Social Class

This variable is the sociologist's blessing and curse. It has powerful influences on much human behavior, but most of us know this already. The literature of social class is almost wholly descriptive, with few attempts at explanation. Pigeonholes are rife here (upper-upper to lower-lower, as used by Davis *et al., Deep South, Old City;* Lynd and Lynd, *Middletown;* Warner and Lunt, *Yankee City;* West, *Plainville, U.S.A.*), and the most common finding reported is a correlation between class and other behavior. The higher the class, the later the age at marriage; no upper-class children failed in school, but a quarter of the lower-class ones did; and so on.

More interesting is the observation that if society gives a low rating to what sociologists call a visible group (e.g., blacks, the military, etc.), that group develops increased status sensitivity *within itself* and makes more discriminations of status. This has implications for advertising and selling to such markets, since they should be particularly alert to status-conferring products.

An earlier example of sociological theorizing likely to be useful in marketing is provided by Lazarsfeld (1959).

> . . . People of low income prefer sweet chocolate, fabrics with a rubbery touch, and strong-smelling flowers; upper-class consumers favored what one might call more demanding sensory experiences: bitter-dry tastes, irregular weaves and less pungent fragrances . . . one can give a more psychological explanation: the lower-class person is starved for pleasant sense experiences; or a more sociological one: the upper-class indi-

vidual exhibits his "sensual" wealth by conspicuous nonconsumption of strong stimuli.

One concludes that there will always be a psychological *and* and sociological explanation for any bit of behavior.

MASS COMMUNICATION

> Advertising is not a science. Here and there it impinges on one of the social sciences, usually with stultifying effect. They pass each other like thieves in the night, sometimes with a tangential sideswipe, but the meeting is seldom firm enough for contagion.—*James Playstead Wood (1961).*

Not too long ago science sideswiped advertising in the form of epidemiological theory, and the contact was firm enough for contagion. This was one of the first really fresh ideas in the history of advertising research. If confirmed, it will render inaccurate the name "mass communication" because it shows that communications are transmitted like diseases, person to person, with many doublings back and recontacts and reverberating circuits—*not* like seed sown or shotgun pellets shot, two of the more traditional analogies.

Early studies of "mass communications" were very simply conceived (Cox, 1961). The "mass media" were thought to provide stimuli to which all individuals in the audience responded in much the same way. This conception had to be discarded, however, once survey techniques were available to measure the impact of such communications on good samples. It became clear that individuals were engaged in selective exposure (Ehrlich *et al.*, 1957) and selective perception (Kendall and Wolf, 1949; Hovland, Harvey, and Sherif, 1957). Those least likely to change were least likely to be exposed to a persuasive communication and, if exposed, most likely to ignore it. If a new piece of information contradicted existing ideas, it tended to be missed, ignored, or quickly forgotten; if it confirmed them, it was sought out, accepted, and remembered.

Studies have traced the flow of a new idea through a social network. Agricultural innovations, such as the introduction of hybrid corn (Ryan and Gross, 1943), showed that mass media can arouse interest but that interpersonal communication usually determines whether the innovation is adopted or not.

Benjamin and Maitland (1958) suggest that response to advertising may be analogous to physiological response to stimuli, to the law of diminishing returns, to the reaction of a population to increased dosage of a drug, or even to the charging of an electrical condenser. To inputs and outputs of advertising campaigns for vitamins, for military service, and for radio equipment they fitted logarithmic, cumulated normal, and exponential curves. The inputs were number of advertisements, magazine circulation, or number of direct-mail pieces distributed. The output was the number of inquiries during the campaign. Plots of these input-output relationships were best fitted by the logarithmic and cumulated normal curves.

Other observations of this personal-influence network are more ambiguous. It is still not clear, for example, whether innovators are also influencers or corroborators. Menzel and Katz (1955) found that new drugs are tried first by "lone wolves" and later picked up and spread by influential, gregarious doctors. Coleman (1957) found that the latter also are often the innovators. Cox (1961) sums up one interesting argument this way:

> Influentials may have considerable personal influence over others in the group, but they may enjoy this influence because they recognizably hold the norms and values of the group. If, as is often the case, the norms of the group favor the status quo, the influential have an investment in this status quo, hence are more likely to be resistant to change. Unless the norms of the group favor innovation (as in fashion or in some areas of the medical profession), the innovators

> are very likely to be the deviant or isolated members of the group, none too popular with the rest of the group, and with little direct personal influence over anyone in the group. However, the innovators may affect the behavior of others (including the influentials) through a process of "social influence by example."

One thing seems clear: There would be fewer conflicts among results if the latter were all based on observations of behavior rather than on verbal reports or attitude measures. Pioneering studies in this area (e.g., Katz and Lazarsfeld, 1955) were based on respondents' own estimates of exposure to personal advice and advertising, and the relative influence of each. This vitiates many of those personal-influence studies beyond salvage.

A person's personal influence may be better indicated by the number of social orbits in which he moves. This is not the same as the number of people he influences but the number he *personally* infects: the number of people he influences *minus* those who would have been influenced anyway (caught the disease) by someone earlier in that orbit. Thus someone near the head of a long, transitive pecking order would get a score of one on this dimension, while a more mobile, less "influential" person might make more contacts and score higher. The ship captain who operates only through his executive officer would score lower in personal influence than the ship's doctor, who sees everyone sooner or later.

ANTHROPOLOGY

Nothing will ever give us the power to see ourselves as others see us, if by "ourselves" we mean U.S. culture. Anthropology gives clues, however, by showing how differently things are done elsewhere. Of all the behavioral sciences, its perspective is the most chastening.

The late Clyde Kluckhohn once noted (1960) that "anthropologists of all branches have been so preoccupied with field work that the profession has not organized and assimilated what is in fact 'known.'" Any hypotheses for marketing from anthropology will have to come by analogy from specific cases like the following.

In the western Pacific Ocean, just east of New Guinea, lie the Trobriand Islands. We might never have heard of them but for Bronislaw Malinowski's *Argonauts of the Western Pacific*. By far the dominant activity of the natives of these islands is a system of tribal exchange called *Kula*. *Kula* is carried on by communities inhabiting a wide ring of islands, around which articles of two kinds, and only two kinds, are constantly traveling in opposite directions. Clockwise move long necklaces of red shell called *soulava*. Counterclockwise move arm bracelets called *mwali*. Each native has *Kula* partners on neighboring islands. With neighbors on one side he exchanges bracelets for necklaces. With neighbors on the other side he exchanges necklaces for bracelets.

Every movement of the *Kula* articles, every detail of the transaction, is regulated by traditional rules. One transaction does not finish the partnership, the rule being "once in the *Kula*, always in the *Kula*," and the same arm bracelets and necklaces have been traveling around the ring for generations. Yet neither the bracelets nor the necklaces have any practical or even ceremonial use. They are almost never worn and their value seems to lie merely in possessing them.

The decorum of the *Kula* transaction is strictly kept and highly valued. The Trobriand Islanders sharply distinguish *Kula* from exchange of the necessities of life such as food and axe blades. This barter they disparagingly call *gimwali*. When criticizing an incorrect or too hasty procedure of *Kula*, they will say, "He conducts his *Kula* as if it were *gimwali*."

Preparations for a *Kula* exchange are controlled by the natives' belief in magic. The magical rites are of three kinds: to make the sea-going canoes swift and safe, to insure fair weather, and to reach the mind of one's *Kula* partner in order to make him "soft, unsteady, and eager to give *Kula* gifts."

Just as the Trobriand Islanders divide trade into *Kula* and *gimwali,* so may we divide marketing into two parts—one ceremonial and one essential to survival. Clearly much of marketing is *Kula,* while production and research are mainly *gimwali.* Decisions made in the latter areas can usually be related to their immediate profits and losses. But marketing decisions, while they share the glamour and social acceptance of *Kula,* may rely for their value to the company on essentially social agreements among participants.

There is much *Kula* magic in marketing today. Just as the Trobriand Islander casts a spell over his canoe to ensure safe passage, so the marketer performs rituals to ensure the efficient distribution of his product to the consumer. Just as the native makes magic for fair weather, so the macroeconomist performs forecasts of consumer climate, though he knows they lack the observable certainty of cause-effect relationships. And just as the native utters mysterious chants to soften the mind of his *Kula* partner, so many an advertiser spends millions of dollars annually without knowing what they bring him in return.

The point of this analogy is not to denigrate as magical the marketing activities that for the moment cannot be based on solid foundations of observation and experiment. Rather the point is to show that social agreements about the future can perpetuate possibly unjustified behavior; that these agreements are understandable, since they reduce uncertainty about outcomes that cannot be accurately predicted from the data and resources available; and that these apparently ceremonial forms of behavior serve as the social mechanisms for maintaining other behavior more essential for the survival of the community or firm.[2] Though the Trobriand Islanders look down on it, *gimwali* or barter is always carried on during a *Kula* expedition. The superstitious native would hardly sail hundreds of miles in the open sea "merely" to exchange food and axe blades. Beyond these physical rewards, he requires the added incentive of the *Kula* gifts, incentives whose value is established by generations of agreement and whose mere exchange reduces his fear of uncertainty.

In few forms of economic exchange can a man be certain of the exact value of what he will get. But he can at least be sure, by observing customs, that he is behaving correctly in the eyes of society. This certain knowledge is a powerful reward indeed, so powerful that it may perpetuate ceremonial marketing in an affluent society. If infrequent, noncontingent real rewards can maintain certain kinds of behavior, then frequent, socially administered rewards must be operating in the absence of real ones. If these more frequent rewards take the form of social reassurance that one is doing the right thing—be it "right" according to *Kula* tradition or "right" according to the lore of mass marketing—then little curiosity remains about the marketing system. All that is necessary is a social or economic climate in which there is room for real error. If continually high seas prevented *Kula* expeditions, doubtless some other form of fear-reducing behavior would evolve. As the economic climate in this country worsened and became more competitive, U.S. marketers began to seek something more than traditional management acceptance or keeping up with competitors to justify their decisions.

[2]Another example of *Kula* must surely be the prices of "upper tier" stocks. They remain (*when* they remain) at such high multiples of earnings partly because the banks who own so much of them agree about the future of those earnings.

DEMOGRAPHY

Demography is no more an experimental science than economics or anthropology. Thus it was surprising to find some "if-then" laws in this field, based on fairly convincing natural experiments. For instance, if times are good the marriage rate rises (David and Blake, 1956) and the divorce rate rises as well. This can be explained by Luce's famous Axiom One (1960), that the ratio of probabilities of any two alternatives is independent of the total number of alternatives available. The better the times, the more options one has. The more options one has, the more likely *one* of them will be chosen in any interval, but the probability of the highest one is still the same multiple of the next highest. Thus increasing alternatives doesn't change the alternative chosen or make the choice any better; it just makes *some* choice more likely.

Of more interest to marketers is the birth rate, or fertility. Hauser and Duncan, in their inventory of population principles (1959), report that fertility is higher in stable times, in the fall, in underdeveloped countries, and when per capita income is up. While fertility varies with the business cycle, its swings are not so pronounced: From 1920 to 1958 a trend deviation of four percent in per capita income was accompanied by a trend deviation of only one percent in fertility. Fertility is also higher among members of large families, societies where women don't work, the lower and upper classes (today), families that don't move often, rural farm families, Catholics, and racial and national minorities in the United States. Most of these findings have been rendered obsolete by the The Pill.

The death rate (mortality) is lower in good times and advanced nations, and among upper classes, whites, women, and married people. Demographers have long wondered whether woman's longer life was a physical capacity or simply the result of her more sheltered life. Obviously no true experiment could be done to find this out. Madigan (1957) nevertheless made an ingenious test of the matter by studying mortality differentials among teachers and administrative personnel of Roman Catholic Brotherhoods and Sisterhoods engaged in educational work, thus eliminating "five highly significant sources of differential stress between the sexes": male service in the armed forces; greater male liberty to dissipate; the dissimilar roles of husband and wife; male employment in hazardous and life-shortening occupations; and employment of men and women in diverse occupations. The study clearly showed greater mortality among the Brothers and "indicates (1) that biological factors are more important than socio-cultural pressures and strains in relation to the differential sex death rates and (2) that the greater socio-cultural stresses associated with the male role in our society play only a small part in producing the differentials between male and female death rates." But the results can equally well be explained by the bias of self-selection: Perhaps weaker men chose to be Brothers while stronger women chose to be Sisters.

"Natural" experiments are never conclusive, but this one came close. If economists were as fortunate in finding natural control groups, they might be able to explain more consumer behavior.

ECONOMICS

Since marketing is composed of transactions, it may be divided into the behavior of buyers and that of sellers. In this section I review what economists think and know about each.

Buyers

Economists rarely observe behavior directly, especially that of the individual consumer. By and large, they would rather be telling someone *how* to behave, preferably the president of the United States or the chairman of the Federal Reserve Board. Few economists do not envy those who help determine national policy.

These understandable motives on the part of economists have left economics in sad shape to deal with marketing. Economics is usually divided into the normative and the descriptive, and into macro(national)economics and micro(business)economics. The normative-macro quadrant contains most of the economists and consequently most economic research. The other normative and macro quadrants take most of the remainder, leaving descriptive microeconomics neglected. It is no surprise that from this depressed area of the "economic economy" has come a theory that is itself a victim of empirical malnutrition.

Picture the following consumer: His preference patterns are constant. When he prefers A over B and B over C, he always prefers A over C. He knows all the products from which to choose and all their relevant attributes. This is easy because he can distinguish each product from every other—no two ever seem alike. He can buy any part of a product he likes—e.g., half a Cadillac. He is totally uninfluenced by other consumers. He has a fixed income. As he buys additional units of some product, he enjoys each additional unit less and less because he tends to become satiated and is forced to sacrifice more alternatives as he uses up his income in the purchase of the first product. He is happiest when he has allocated his income among products and quantities of products such that the additional enjoyment of the next unit bought of each product is proportional to the product's price.

If you don't recognize this consumer, it is because he doesn't exist. He is a figment of the ordinalist theory briefly alluded to in the section on learning, and his peculiar behavior is the ordinalist principle of diminishing marginal utility. It is this theory which assumes that consumers choose brands in order of preference, forming an interval scale. The theory is often represented graphically by the demand schedule or indifference curve showing how much of one product is worth how much of another. In fairness we should note that this is called "theory of the firm"—it does not aspire to be a theory of consumer behavior.

There are perils in using response-inferred constructs in theory construction—that is, explaining that Johnny plays the violin well because he has talent but inferring the talent from his playing the violin well. Utility in ordinalist theory has all the explanatory force of Johnny's talent. To say that the utility of what the consumer chooses must have been greater than the utility of what he did not choose is a tautology. It adds nothing to our understanding but a set of labels.

Even these labels have shortcomings: A person's utility function describing all of the products among which he chooses "is determined only up to positive monotonic transformations." This means that any other set of numbers (labels) would describe the consumer's utility function just as well—provided that the other numbers relate to the old numbers by any straight line or a curve that bends in only one direction. In other words, the utility function is a mere ordinal scale.

There are three kinds of scales in physical measurement—ratio, interval, and ordinal. Ratio scales have a zero point and a constant unit of measurement, like weight and money. Interval scales are unique up to a linear transformation and have a zero point but no necessary unit, like temperature and calendars. Ordinal scales, however, have no zero point and no constant unit, and for practical purposes amount simply to ranks. This is a roundabout way of saying that ordinal scales are not very useful. Their numbers cannot be multiplied or added and hence cannot be used as aggregate measures.

So all we have from the assumptions of the ordinalist is a rubber yardstick. It is a tribute to the rewards of rationalization that many economists continue to teach this theory even though its assumptions have been contradicted. Papandreou (1957) found that the assumption of transitivity was valid in a few simple choice situations, but Gulliksen (1957) and other psychologists have found A preferred over B, B over C, and C over A so often that they have named this particular phenomenon a *triad* and count triads in any preference study as an inverse measure of the internal consistency of the scale. Calvi (1961) found the buyer emphasizing any irrelevant aspect of the product to help him make what would otherwise be a difficult choice. This suggests the most frequent alibi made for intransitivity, namely that consumers may evaluate products on more than one dimension. Quandt (1956) dealt with this problem by requiring only that when A is preferred over B and B over C, C be preferred over A only a certain portion of the time. Other theoretical attempts to salvage conventional economic theory of choice are those of Modigliani and Brumberg (1954), who expanded the theory to include aggregates of products as well as individual products, and Basmann (1956), who attempted to deal formally with the fact of changing consumer tastes.

Aside from those just cited, there are few empirical studies of economic theory of consumer behavior and consequently few moves toward realism by theorists. The main body of consumer research is privately sponsored and unpublished. Most published consumer research concerns total consumer expenditures at the national level and the use of attitude surveys to predict these expenditures (Morrissett, 1957; Modigliani and Balderston, 1959; Katona, 1960; Juster, 1959; Paranka, 1960; Namias, 1960; Mueller, 1957; and the National Bureau of Economic Research, 1960).

There is one obvious reason why scientists have not concerned themselves with the study of buying decisions. As noted at the beginning of this chapter, these events are trivial to the consumer, so much less important than they are to the marketing manager or researcher that their very interest in him has a bearing on his behavior. Questions about brand choices create attitudes that were not there before and condition the respondent's next answer if not his next purchase. Panel membership may not change behavior (Ehrenberg, 1961), but only 50 to 70 percent of those invited will join a panel. The theorist interested in the sequence of brand choices (Lipstein, 1959; Maffei, 1960; Kuehn, 1962) may have a representative cross-section of choices or a nonrepresentative sequence of choices, but not a representative sequence. Present probabilities of switching from brand to brand can forecast future brand shares with great accuracy for the panel from whom the probabilities were obtained but not as well for a test market and still less well for the nation as a whole.

One popular model for analyzing panel data, the simple Markov chain, has been oversold. Its main assumptions cannot be met. Customers do not purchase at regular intervals, more than one brand may be bought at one time, transition probabilities are not constant, and most obvious of all, the buyer was not born yesterday: More brand choices than his last one determine his present choice. Hope lies mainly in complicating the model to bring it closer to reality. Ron Howard (1963) took a step in this direction by treating the interval between purchase as a separate datum, thereby eliminating arbitrary time periods. Kuehn (1962) assumed that repurchase probabilities increase with the number of consecutive purchases of the same brand, thus treating choice as a learning process, as does Luce. He found evidence in favor of his assumption, as did Frank (1962); but Frank pointed out that these results could equally well be explained by assuming that some buyers are just more loyal than others ("What about individual differences?"). Weak as it is, the modified Markov process is the strongest theory of buyer behavior around. If it can be adjusted as a result of experience, it may yet prove useful as part of a theory of marketing.

Sellers

Alfred Marshall, in his *Principles of Economics* (1890), said that a manager's decisions are guided by "trained instinct" rather than knowledge. The late Frank Knight noted (1921) that the mental operations of decision making are obscure and that neither logicians nor psychologists showed much interest in them. "Perhaps," he said, "it is because there is very little to say about the subject . . . when we try to decide what to expect in a certain situation, and how to behave ourselves accordingly, we are likely to do a lot of irrelevant mental rambling, and the first thing we know we find that we have made up our minds."

There is an even simpler explanation: that a decision is an exceedingly rare event. As voguish as it has become to equate management with decision making, the latter's rarity is known to any manager who has reviewed his own mental operations. Decisions are made, yes, but more often they are avoided, ignored, overcome, or postponed until events force a course of action. Dealing with uncertainty, the primary fact of business life, is usually what T. H. Weldon would call a difficulty: It has to be avoided because it cannot, like a problem, be translated into a puzzle and then solved.

This apparently pessimistic caveat rests, to be sure, on a narrowly specific definition of uncertainty. It excludes instances whose outcome distribution is known *a priori* or from experience. In such instances we can get rid of any real uncertainty by grouping cases, either by ourselves or through someone who agrees to pay back a large but uncertain loss in return for a smaller certain charge. Measurable uncertainty is insurable and is distinguished from true uncertainty by calling it *risk.*

Uncertainty in marketing is of a different kind. Here, as one so often hears, everyone's problems are different, and the same person's problems differ at various times. As Frank Knight noted (1921), "Business decisions, for example, deal with situations which are far too often unique, generally speaking, for any sort of statistical tabulation to have any value for guidance. The conception of an objectively measurable probability or chance is simply inapplicable."

But as Knight foresaw—I am quoting from his doctoral dissertation, written in 1921!—this "vicious usage" of probability has stuck. Subjective probability has become the subject of experimental study (Edwards, 1961) as well as of controversy between the classicists and the Bayesians, who would relax the distinction between subjective and objective probabilities.

There are still only four ways in which a business can deal with uncertainty: (1) by grouping cases, most useful in dealing with *a priori* or statistical probabilities (risks) but helpful with true uncertainties too when a common element can be found; (2) by specialization—e.g., assignment of the burden of uncertainty exclusively to certain persons; (3) by controlling the future; (4) by predicting the future. Knight defines free enterprise (as opposed to mere production for a market) as "the addition of specialization of uncertainty-bearing to the grouping of uncertainties." These bearers of uncertainty are traditionally the entrepreneurs, the managers, the speculators. In this century, in an economy of relative abundance, they are the marketing men as well. Fifty years ago Knight had already remarked "the separation of the marketing function from the technological side of production, the former being much more speculative than the latter."

Marketing management undertakes to reduce the buyer's uncertainty as well as the seller's. One means of reducing consumer uncertainty is advertising, which becomes a commodity with nominal utility of its own. Knight wrote:

> The morally fastidious (and naive) may protest that there is a distinction between "real" and "nominal" utilities; but they will find it very dangerous to their optimism to attempt to follow the distinction very far. On scrutiny it will be found that most of the things we spend our incomes for and agonize over, and notably practically all the higher "spiritual" values, gravitate swiftly into the second class.

One means of reducing manager uncertainty is through management consultants. Knight called them "the scientific managers of managers" and thought they probably paid their way, despite numbers of quacks, simply because they forced critical consideration of problems instead of blind tradition or guesswork. Knight resists the more straightforward interpretation: that they earn their way simply because they reduce management uncertainty and some managers are willing to pay for this.

Modern decision theory does not usually consider decisions in the face of true uncertainty. When objective probabilities can be assigned to the outcomes of the various alternatives, the decision is made under the long-range equivalent of certainty, expected value. When only subjective probabilities can be assigned to outcomes, the decision is made under *subjective* certainty, or what used to be known as faith. The creation of faith is a primary function of the modern corporation and serves to enhance its potential for survival.

One's subjective certainty in a decision should be about the same as one's confidence in the subjective probabilities of the outcomes, but this is not necessarily so. Mere processing of fallible information adds considerably to its capacity to induce faith, as hardened computer users will tell you. "Garbage in, garbage out," they say cynically, but they know that processed garbage leads to more decisions than unprocessed garbage.

This is unconventional wisdom in the best Galbraithian sense, suppressed out of fear because uncertainty is too awful to contemplate. Recently, however, two business economists mustered enough courage to contemplate it in depth. In *Behavioral Theory of the Firm* (1963), Cyert and March defined a theory as an exhaustive set of variables among which all relationships are specified. The variables that exhaust the system of the firm are, they say, those that determine its goals, expectations, and choices. Among these variables they postulate four "relational concepts": quasiresolution of conflict, uncertainty avoidance, the search for problems, and learning. In their theory the firm doesn't resolve all its conflicts but lets some of them lie; it avoids planning by attending only to pressing problems and trying to arrange a predictable environment; it searches for alternatives only when pressed, with the least possible effort, and in ways biased by the experience and needs of the searchers; it changes its goals as a function of its and its competitors' experience. This organization would bring happy tears to a psychologist's eyes: It is obviously run by real human beings.

In 100 simulations of firms in a stable market, the theory showed market share to be affected primarily by those forces which control the upward adjustment of sales effectiveness pressure (e.g., the availability of profits for advertising), and the upward and downward adjustment of sales promotion percentages. This model appears to agree with the actual findings of a Du Pont study of promotion (Buzzell, 1963), in which *change* in promotional level was a more important contribution to change in market share than was the absolute level of promotion used. Profit, in the Cyert-March model, was a function mainly of the rate at which the firm adjusted its sales goals to its sales results and the rate at which the firm learned to learn. This latter parameter determined adaptation speed of the sales goal and other adjustment mechanisms.

The Cyert-March theory of the firm resembles one psychological theory more than anything else considered in this review: Luce's model of individual choice behavior. Both the firm and the individual display unexecuted response tendencies (quasiresolved conflicts, unchosen alternatives) and learning (adaptation of goals, search rules, linear increment in probability of rewarded response). Luce's theory covers fewer contingencies, however, so it says little or nothing about motivation (uncertainty avoidance) or the search for alternatives beyond noting that the key problem in psychology is to develop a meaningful definition of a response or alternative. A theory of marketing could do worse than combine the mathematical elegance of Luce with the realism of Cyert and March. If successful it might even explain behavior on both sides of the transaction, the buyer's as well as the seller's.

SUMMARY

In this chapter I have tried to distill from the literature of the behavioral sciences the concepts and laws that accurately describe or explain the behavior of consumers or marketing managers. The resulting brew is not very heady, but we should not be surprised. Behavioral scientists and marketing researchers both study human beings, but any further similarity in their subject matter is hard to find. Almost all consumer behavior is relatively unmotivated compared to that typically studied by psychologists, sociologists, anthropologists, economists, and especially by demographers interested in fertility. The behavior of businessmen, on the other hand, is obviously highly motivated but by its nature remains relatively free from large-scale, naturalistic observation.

So we are left with a handful of concepts, an even smaller array of highly contingent principles, and the disturbing suspicion that even most of the techniques used so productively by behavioral scientists may not always be useful to marketing researchers in their naturalistic study of such relatively trivial responses as brand choice, repeat buying, and usage rate. Here are some of the most useful concepts, models, or techniques from each field of study.

Perception Absolute threshold; just noticeable difference; perceptual defense
Social Psychology Cognitive dissonance (sour grapes and sweet lemons)
Learning Reinforcement, especially noncontingent; stochastic models; traits ("psychographics")
Sociology Social class
Mass Communication Personal influence defined as orbits or networks
Anthropology *Kula, gimwali*
Demography Natural experiments
Microeconomics Transitivity; modified Markov models; risk versus uncertainty

In the chapters that follow we will see how these concepts or principles aptly insinuate themselves into the real-world cases reported. This will demonstrate how many new concepts and laws are needed and drive home the point with which we began the chapter: Marketing theory will have to grow out of the data of marketing research itself.

10

New Way to Measure Consumers' Judgments

Paul E. Green
Yoram Wind

When developing new products or services—or even when repositioning existing ones—a company must consider two basic problems. First, it must know its market; second, it must understand the nature of the product or service. It may find both problems hard to solve, especially when the product under consideration has several disparate qualities appealing to different customers with diverse interests.

Beyond the fundamental need that the product is to fill often lie several other needs that the marketing manager would do well to consider. But how should these needs be evaluated? How does the marketing manager determine which of the product's attributes the consumer sees as the most important? In order to market the product most effectively, marketing managers must have the means to answer such questions.

In this article the authors demonstrate one research technique that has been used in evaluating consumers' judgments, and they show how to apply the technique to a number of complex marketing situations.

Taking a jet plane for a business appointment in Paris? Which of the two flights described below would you choose?

- A B-707 flown by British Airways that will depart within two hours of the time you would like to leave and that is often late in arriving in Paris. The plane will make two intermediate stops, and it is anticipated that it will be 50% full. Flight attendants are "warm and friendly" and you would have a choice of two movies for entertainment.
- A B-747 flown by TWA that will depart within four hours of the time you would like to leave and that is almost never late in arriving in Paris. The flight is nonstop, and it is anticipated that the plane will be 90% full. Flight attendants are "cold and curt" and only magazines are provided for entertainment.

Are you looking for replacement tires for your two-year-old car? Suppose you want radial tires and have the following three options to choose from:

- Goodyear's, with a tread life of 30,000 miles at a price of $40 per tire; the store is a 10-minute drive from your home.
- Firestone's, with a tread life of 50,000 miles at a price of $85 per tire; the store is a 20-minute drive from your home.
- Sears's, with a tread life of 40,000 miles at a price of $55 per tire; the store is located about 10 minutes from your home.

How would you rank these alternatives in order of preference?

Both of these problems have a common structure that companies and their marketing managers frequently encounter in trying to figure out what a consumer really wants in a product or service. First, the characteristics of the alternatives that the consumer must choose from fall along more than a single dimension—they are multiattribute. Second, the consumer must make an overall judgment about the relative value of those characteristics, or attributes; in short, he must order them

Reprinted from *Harvard Business Review*, vol. 53, pp. 107–117. At the time of writing, Paul Green was Sebastian S. Kresge Professor of Marketing at The Wharton School, University of Pennsylvania. Yoram Wind was also professor of marketing at The Wharton School.

according to some criterion. But doing this requires complex trade-offs, since it is likely that no alternative is clearly better than another on every dimension of interest.

In recent years, researchers have developed a new measurement technique from the fields of mathematical psychology and psychometrics that can aid the marketing manager in sorting out the relative importance of a product's multidimensional attributes.[1] This technique, called conjoint measurement, starts with the consumer's overall or global judgments about a set of complex alternatives. It then performs the rather remarkable job of decomposing his or her original evaluations into separate and compatible utility scales by which the original global judgments (or others involving new combinations of attributes) can be reconstituted.[2]

Being able to separate overall judgments into psychological components in this manner can provide a manager with valuable information about the relative importance of various attributes of a product. It can also provide information about the value of various levels of a single attribute. (For example, if price is the attribute under consideration, conjoint measurement can give the manager a good idea of how sensitive consumers would be to a price change from a level of, say, 85¢ to one of 75¢ or one of 95¢.) Indeed, some models can even estimate the psychological trade-offs consumers make when they evaluate several attributes together.

The advantages of this type of knowledge to the planning of marketing strategy are significant. The knowledge can be useful in modifying current products or services and in designing new ones for selected buying publics.

In this article, we first show how conjoint measurement works from a numerical standpoint. We then discuss its application to a variety of marketing problems, and we demonstrate its use in strategic marketing simulations. The Appendix provides a brief description of how other research tools for measuring consumer judgments work, and how they relate to conjoint measurement.

HOW CONJOINT MEASUREMENT WORKS

In order to see how to apply conjoint measurement, suppose a company were interested in marketing a new spot remover for carpets and upholstery. The technical staff has developed a new product that is designed to handle tough, stubborn spots. Management interest centers on five attributes or factors that it expects will influence consumer preference: an applicator-type package design, brand name, price, a *Good Houskeeping* seal of endorsement, and a money-back guarantee.

Three package designs are under consideration and appear in the upper portion of *Exhibit I.* There are three brand names under consideration: *K2R, Glory,* and *Bissell.* Of the three brand names used in the study, two are competitors' brand names already on the market, whereas one is the company's present brand name choice for its new product. Three alternative prices being considered are \$1.19, \$1.39, and \$1.59. Since there are three alternatives for each of these factors, they are called three-level factors. The *Good Housekeeping* seal and money-back guarantee are two-level factors, since each is either present or not. Consequently, a total of $3 \times 3 \times 3 \times 2 \times 2 = 108$ alternatives would have to be tested if the researcher were to array all possible combinations of the five attributes.

Clearly, the cost of administering a consum-

[1]R. Duncan Luce and John W. Tukey, "Simultaneous Conjoint Measurement: A New Type of Fundamental Measurement," *Journal of Mathematical Psychology,* February 1964, p. 1.

[2]The first marketing-oriented paper on conjoint measurement was by Paul E. Green and Vithala R. Rao, "Conjoint Measurement for Quantifying Judgmental Data," *Journal of Marketing Research,* August 1971, p. 355.

PACKAGE DESIGNS

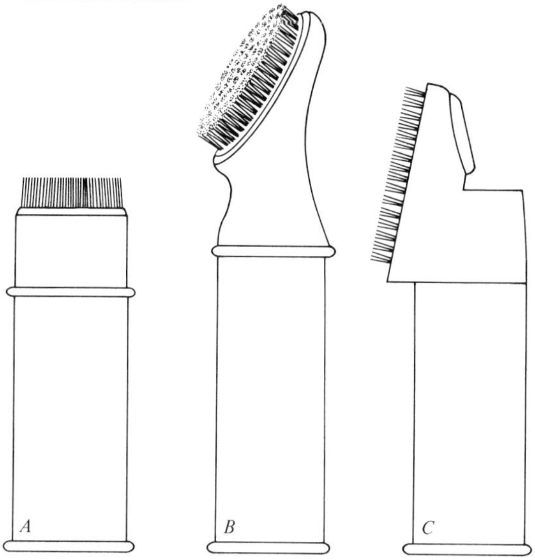

ORTHOGONAL ARRAY

Package design	Brand name	Price	Good Housekeeping seal?	Money-back guarantee?	Respondent's evaluation (rank number)
1 A	K2R	$1.19	No	No	13
2 A	Glory	1.39	No	Yes	11
3 A	Bissell	1.59	Yes	No	17
4 B	K2R	1.39	Yes	Yes	2
5 B	Glory	1.59	No	No	14
6 B	Bissell	1.19	No	No	3
7 C	K2R	1.59	No	Yes	12
8 C	Glory	1.19	Yes	No	7
9 C	Bissell	1.39	No	No	9
10 A	K2R	1.59	Yes	No	18
11 A	Glory	1.19	No	Yes	8
12 A	Bissell	1.39	No	No	15
13 B	K2R	1.19	No	No	4
14 B	Glory	1.39	Yes	No	6
15 B	Bissell	1.59	No	Yes	5
16 C	K2R	1.39	No	No	10
17 C	Glory	1.59	No	No	16
18 C	Bissell	1.19	Yes	Yes	1*

**Highest ranked*

Exhibit I Experimental design for evaluation of a carpet cleaner.

er evaluation study of this magnitude—not to mention the respondents' confusion and fatigue—would be prohibitive. As an alternative, however, the researcher can take advantage of a special experimental design, called an *orthogonal array,* in which the test combinations are selected so that the independent contributions of all five factors are balanced.[3] In this way each factor's weight is kept separate and is not confused with those of the other factors.

The lower portion of *Exhibit I* shows an orthogonal array that involves only 18 of the 108 possible combinations that the company wishes to test in this case. For the test the researcher makes up 18 cards. On each card appears an artist's sketch of the package design, A, B, or C, and verbal details regarding each of the other four factors: brand name, price, *Good Houskeeping* seal (or not), and money-back guarantee (or not). After describing the new product's functions and special features, he shows the respondents each of the 18 cards (see *Exhibit I* for the master design), and asks them to rank the cards in order of their likelihood of purchase.

The last column of *Exhibit I* shows one respondent's actual ranking of the 18 cards; rank number 1 denotes her highest evaluated concept. Note particularly that only *ranked* data need be obtained and, furthermore, that only 18 (out of 108) combinations are evaluated.

Computing the Utilities

Computation of the utility scales of each attribute, which determine how influential each is in the consumers' evaluations, is carried out by various computer programs.[4] The ranked data of a single respondent (or the composite ranks of a group of respondents)

[3]A nontechnical discussion of this special class of designs appears in Paul E. Green, "On the Design of Experiments Involving Multiattribute Alternatives," *Journal of Consumer Research*, September 1974, p. 61.

[4]As an illustration, see Joseph B. Kruskal, "Analysis of Factorial Experiments by Estimating Monotone Transformations of the Data," *Journal of the Royal Statistical Society,* Series B, March 1965, p. 251.

are entered in the program. The computer then searches for a set of scale values for each factor in the experimental design. The scale values for each level of each factor are chosen so that when they are added together the *total* utility of each combination will correspond to the original ranks as closely as possible.

Notice that two problems are involved here. First, as mentioned previously, the experimental design of *Exhibit I* shows only 18 of 108 combinations. Second, only rank-order data are supplied to the algorithms. This means that the data themselves do not determine how much more influential one attribute is than another in the consumers' choices. However, despite these limitations, the algorithms are able to find a numerical representation of the utilities thus providing an indication of each factor's relative importance.

In general, more accurate solutions are obtained as the number of combinations being evaluated increases. Still, in the present case, with only 18 ranking-type judgments, the technique works well. *Exhibit II* shows the computer results.

As can be observed in *Exhibit II,* the technique obtains a utility function for each level of each factor. For example, to find the utility for the first combination in *Exhibit I,* we can read off the utilities of each factor level in the five charts of *Exhibit II:* U(a) = 0.1; U (K2R) = 0.3; U($1.19) = 1.0; U (No) = 0.2; U (No) = 0.2. Therefore the total utility is 1.8, the sum of the five separate utilities, for the first combination. Note that this combination was ranked only thirteenth by the respondent in *Exhibit I.*

On the other hand, the utility of combination 18 is 3.1 (0.6 + 0.5 + 1.0 + 0.3 + 0.7), which is the respondent's highest evaluation of all 18 combinations listed.

However, as can be easily seen from *Exhibit II,* if combination 18 is modified to include package Design B (in place of C), its utility is even higher. As a matter of fact, it then represents the highest possible utility, even though this specific combination did not appear among the original 18.

Importance of Attributes

By focusing attention on only the package design, the company's marketing researchers can see from *Exhibit II* that Design B displays highest utility. Moreover, all utility scales are expressed in a common unit (although their zero points are arbitrary). This means that we can compare utility ranges from factor to factor so as to get some idea of their relative importance.

In the case of the spot remover, as shown in *Exhibit II,* the utility ranges are:

- Package design (1.0 − 0.1 = 0.9)
- Brand name (0.5 − 0.2 = 0.3)
- Price (1.0 − 0.1 = 0.9)
- *Good Housekeeping* seal (0.3 − 0.2 = 0.1)
- Money-back guarantee (0.7 − 0.2 = 0.5)

How important is each attribute in relation to the others? The lower portion of *Exhibit II* shows the relative size of the utility ranges expressed in histogram form. As noted, package design and price are the most important factors, and together they account for about two thirds of the total range in utility.

It should be mentioned that the relative importance of a factor depends on the levels that are included in the design. For example, had price ranged from $1.19 to a high of $1.89, its relative importance could easily exceed that for package design. Still, as a crude indication of what factors to concentrate on, factor importance calculations provide a useful by-product of the main analysis regardless of such limitations.

Managerial Implications

From a marketing management point of view the critical question is how these results can be used in the design of a product/marketing

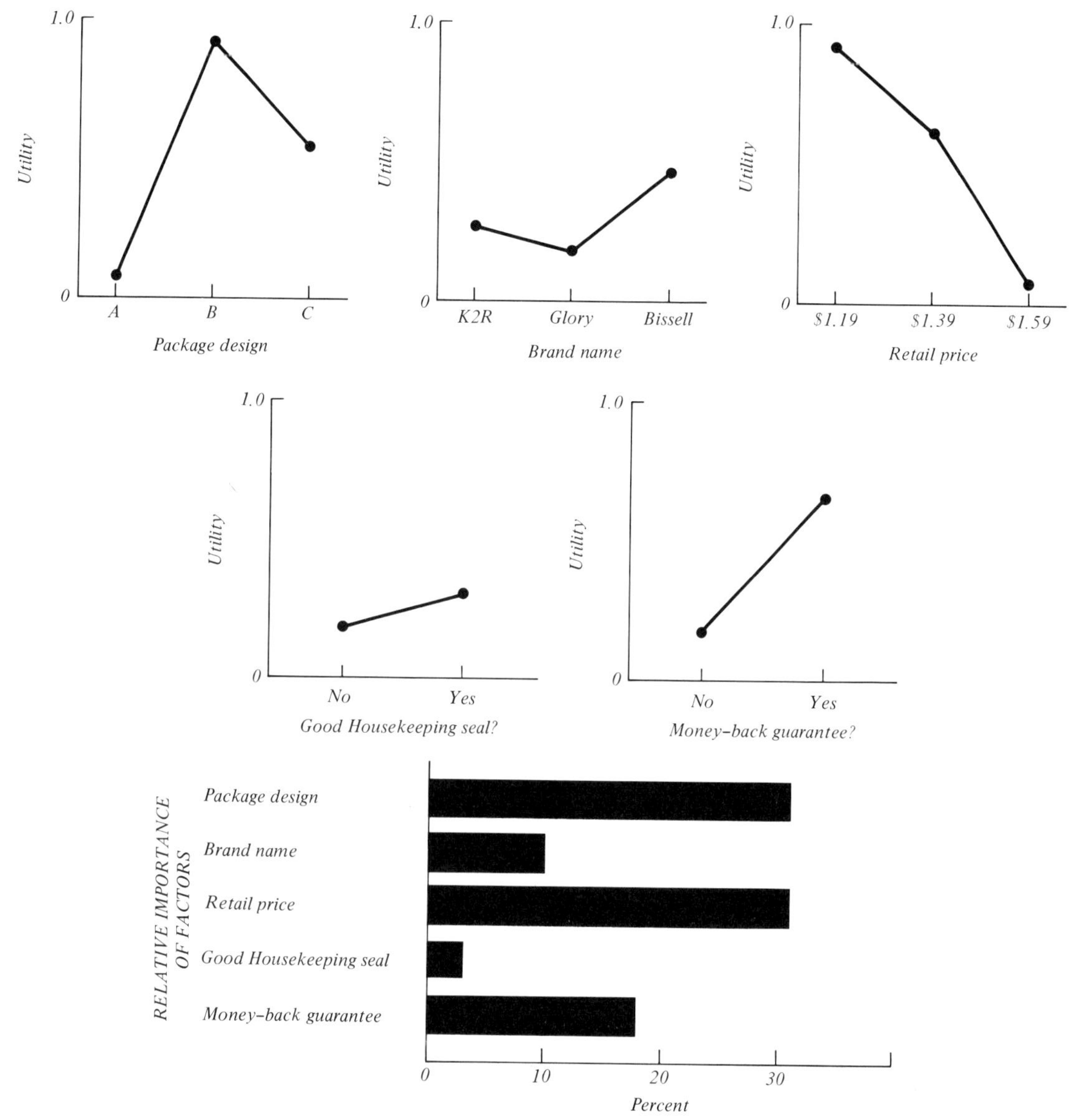

Exhibit II Results of computer analysis of experimental data for Exhibit I.

strategy for the spot remover. Examination of *Exhibit II* suggests a number of points for discussion:

- Excluding brand name, the most desirable offering would be the one based on package Design B with a money-back guarantee, a *Good Housekeeping* seal, and a retail price of $1.19.
- The utility of a product with a price of $1.39 would be 0.3 less than one with a price of $1.19. A money-back guarantee which involves an increment of 0.5 in utility would more than offset the effect of the higher price.

• The use of a *Good Housekeeping* seal of approval is associated with a minor increase in utility. Hence including it in the company's product will add little to the attractiveness of the spot remover's overall offering.

• The utility of the three brand names provides the company with a quantitative measure of the value of its own brand name as well as the brand names of its competitors.

Other questions can be answered as well by comparing various composites made up from the utilities shown in *Exhibit II.*

The Air Carrier Study

What about the two Paris flights you had to choose between? In that study, the sponsor was primarily interested in how air travelers evaluated the B-707 versus the B-747 in transatlantic travel, and whether relative value differed by length of flight and type of traveler—business versus vacation travelers. In this study all the respondents had flown across the Atlantic at least once during the preceding 12 months.

Exhibit III shows one of the findings of the study for air travelers (business and vacation) flying to Paris. Without delving into details it is quite apparent that the utility difference between the B-707 and the B-747 is very small. Rather, the main factors are departure time, punctuality of arrival, number of stops, and the attitudes of flight attendants.

The importance of type of aircraft did increase slightly with length of flight and for business-oriented travelers versus vacationers. Still, its importance to overall utility was never greater than 10%. It became abundantly clear that extensive replacement of older aircraft like the B-707 would not result in major shifts in consumer demand. On the contrary, money might better be spent on improving the scheduling aspects of flights and the attitudes and demeanor of flight personnel.

The air carrier study involved the preparation of some 27 different flight profiles (only two of which appear at the beginning of the article). Respondents simply rated each flight description in terms of its desirability on a seven-point scale. Only the order properties of the ratings were used in the computer run that resulted in the utility scales appearing in *Exhibit III.*

The Replacement Tire Study

The conjoint measurement exercise in the replacement tire study was part of a larger study designed to pretest several television commercials for the sponsor's brand of steel-belted radial tires. The sponsor was particularly interested in the utility functions of respondents who expressed interest in each of the test commercials.

The respondents considered tread mileage and price as quite important to their choice of tires. On the other hand, brand name did not play an important role (at least for the five brands included in the study). Not surprisingly, the most popular test commercial stressed tread mileage and good value for the money, characteristics of high appeal to this group. What was surprising was that this group represented 70% of the total sample.

This particular study involved the preparation of 25 profiles. Again, the researchers sorted cards into seven ordered categories. The 25 profiles, also constructed according to an orthogonal array, represented only one twenty-fifth of the 625 possible combinations.

POTENTIAL USES OF CONJOINT MEASUREMENT

The three preceding studies only scratch the surface of marketing problems in which conjoint measurement procedures can be used. For example, consumer evaluations can be obtained on:

• New product formulations involving changes in the physical or chemical characteristics of the product

• Package design, brand name, and promotional copy combinations.

• Pricing and brand alternatives

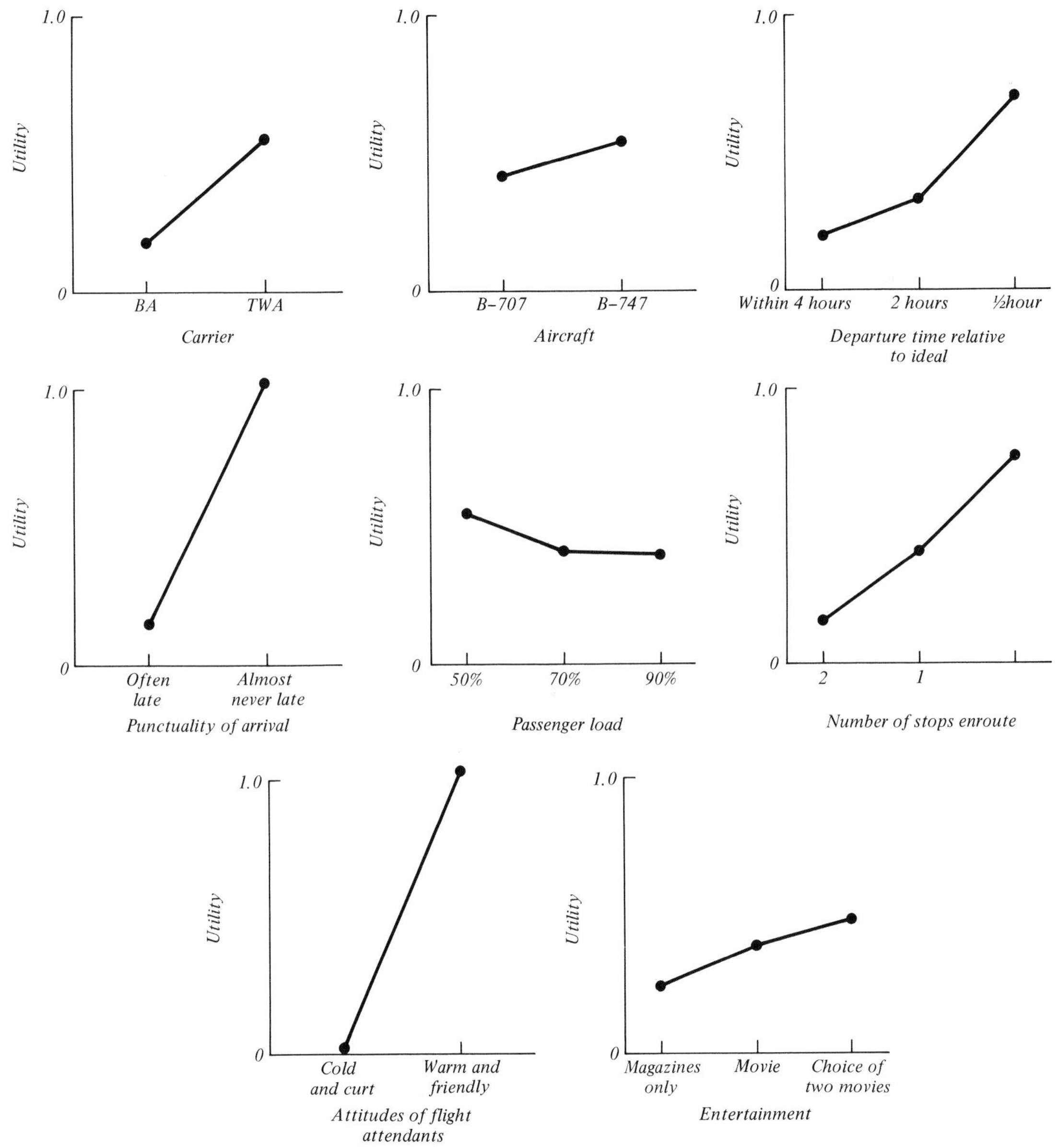

Exhibit III Utility functions for air travelers to Paris.

- Verbalized descriptions of new products or services
- Alternative service designs

Moreover, while the three preceding examples emphasized preference or likelihood-of-purchase orderings, any explicit judgmental criterion can be used. For example, alternatives might be ordered by any of these criteria:

- Best value for the money
- Convenience of use
- Suitability for a specified type of consumer or for a specified end use

• Ruggedness, distinctiveness, conservativeness, and other "psychological images"

Designing Bar Soaps

In one recent study researchers related the psychological imagery of physical characteristics of actual bars of soap to end-use appropriateness; this study was conducted for the laboratory and marketing personnel of a diversified soap manufacturer.

While the designing of a bar of soap—by varying weight, size, shape, color, fragrance type and intensity, surface feel, and so on—may seem like a mundane exercise, the fact remains that a cleverely positioned bar soap (for example, Irish Spring) can rapidly become a multimillion-dollar enterprise. Still, the extent of knowledge about the importance of such imagery is woefully meager. The researchers formulated actual bars of soap in which color, type of fragrance, and intensity of fragrance were constructed according to a design in which all possible combinations of the experimental factors appeared. All the other characteristics of the soap were held constant.

Respondents examined the soaps and assigned each bar to the end use that they felt best matched its characteristics—moisturizing facial soap, deep-cleaning soap for oily skin, woman's deodorant soap, or man's deodorant soap. The data were then analyzed by conjoint measurement techniques, leading to a set of psychophysical functions for each of the characteristics.

The study showed that type of fragrance was the most important physical variable contributing to end-use appropriateness. Rather surprisingly, the type of fragrance (medicinal) and color (blue) that appeared best suited for a man's deodorant soap were also found to be best for the deep-cleaning soap, even though deep-cleaning soap had been previously classed for marketing purposes as a facial soap. On the other hand, fragrance intensity played a relatively minor role as a consumer cue for distinguishing among different end uses.

In brief, this study illustrated the feasibility of translating changes in various physical variables into changes in psychological variables. Eventually, more detailed knowledge of these psychological transformations could enable a laboratory technician to synthesize color, fragrance, shape, and so forth to obtain soaps that conjure up almost any desired imagery. Moreover, in other product classes—beers, coffees, soft drinks—it appears possible to develop a psychophysics of taste in which such elusive verbal descriptions as "full-bodied" and "robust" are given operational meaning in terms of variations in physical or chemical characteristics.

Verbalized Descriptions of New Concepts

In many product classes, such as automobiles, houses, office machines, and computers, the possible design factors are myriad and expensive to vary physically for evaluation by the buying public. In cases such as these, the researcher usually resorts to verbalized descriptions of the principal factors of interest.

To illustrate, one study conducted among car owners by Rogers National Research, Inc. employed the format shown in *Exhibit IV.* In this case the researchers were interested in the effects of gas mileage, price, country of manufacture, maximum speed, roominess, and length on consumer preferences for new automobiles. Consumers evaluated factor levels on a two-at-a-time basis, as illustrated in *Exhibit IV.* Market Facts, Inc. employs a similar data collection procedure.[5]

In the Rogers study it was found that consumer evaluations of attributes were highly associated with the type of car currently owned and the type of car desired in the future. Not surprisingly, gas mileage and country of manufacture were highly important factors in respondent evaluations of car pro-

[5]Richard M. Johnson, "Trade-Off Analysis of Consumer Values," *Journal of Marketing Research,* May 1974, p. 121.

files. Somewhat surprising, however, was the fact that even large-car owners (and those contemplating the purchase of a large car) were more concerned with gas economy than owners of that type of car had been historically. Thus, while they fully expected to get fewer miles per gallon than they would in compact cars, they felt quite strongly that the car should be economical compared to others in its size class.

Organizations as Consumers

Nor is conjoint measurement's potential limited to consumer applications. Evaluations of supply alternatives by an organizational buyer are similar to benefits sought by the consumer.

What is more important to you? *There are times when we have to give up one thing to get something else. And, since different people have different desires and priorities, the automotive industry wants to know what things are most important to you.* *We have a scale that will make it possible for you to tell us your preference in certain circumstances – for example, gas mileage vs. speed. Please read the example below which explains how the scale works – and then tell us the order of your preference by writing in the numbers from 1 to 9 for each of the six questions that follow the example.*

Example:
Warranty vs. price of the car

Procedure:
Simply write the number 1 in the combination that represents your first choice. In one of the remaining blank squares, write the number 2 for your second choice. Then write the number 3 for your third choice, and so on, from 1 to 9.

Years of warranty

Price of car	3	2	1
$3,000	1		
$3,200			
$3,400			

Step 1 (Explanation)

You would rather pay the least ($3,000) and get the most (3 years). Your first choice (1) is in the box as shown.

Years of warranty

Price of car	3	2	1
$3,000	1		
$3,200	2		
$3,400			

Step 2

Your second choice is that you would rather pay $3,200 and have a 3-year warranty than pay $3,000 and get a 2-year warranty.

Years of warranty

Price of car	3	2	1
$3,000	1	3	
$3,200	2		
$3,400			

Step 3

Your third choice is that you would rather pay $3,000 and have a 2-year warranty than pay $3,400 and get a 3-year warranty.

Years of warranty

Price of car	3	2	1
$3,000	1	3	6
$3,200	2	5	8
$3,400	4	7	9

Sample:

This shows a sample order of preference for all possible combinations. Of course your preferences could be different.

For each of the six questions below, please write in the numbers from 1 to 9 to show your order of preference for your next new car.

Miles per gallon

Price of car	22	18	14
$3,000			
$3,200			
$3,400			

Miles per gallon

Maximum speed	22	18	14
80 mph			
70 mph			
60 mph			

Miles per gallon

Length	22	18	14
12 feet			
14 feet			
16 feet			

Miles per gallon

Roominess	22	18	14
6 passenger			
5 passenger			
4 passenger			

Miles per gallon

Made in	22	18	14
Germany			
U. S.			
Japan			

Price of car

Made in	$3,000	$3,200	$3,400
Germany			
U. S.			
Japan			

Exhibit IV A two-at-a-time factor evaluation procedure.

Thus, one can argue, these evaluations are among the most important inputs to industrial marketing strategy.

As an illustration, the management of a clinical laboratory was concerned with the problem of how to increase its share of laboratory test business. It had a study conducted to assess how physicians subjectively value various characteristics of a clinical laboratory in deciding where to send their tests.

Each physician in the study received 16 profiles of hypothetical laboratory services, each showing a different set of characteristics, such as reliability of test results, pick-up and delivery procedures, convenience of location, price range of services, billing procedures, and turnaround time. Utility functions were developed for each of these factors. On the basis of these results the management of the laboratory decided to change its promotion by emphasizing a number of convenience factors in addition to its previous focus on test reliability.

MARKETING STRATEGY SIMULATIONS

We have described a variety of applications of conjoint measurement, and still others, some in conjunction with the other techniques outlined in the Appendix, could be mentioned.[6] What has not yet been discussed, and is more important, is the role that utility measurement can play in the design of strategic marketing simulators. This type of application is one of the principal uses of conjoint measurement.

As a case in point, a large-scale study of consumer evaluations of airline services was conducted in which consumer utilities were developed for some 25 different service factors such as on-ground services, in-flight services, decor of cabins and seats, scheduling, routing, and price. Moreover, each utility function was developed on a route (city-pair) and purpose-of-trip basis.

As might be expected, the utility function for each of the various types of airline service differed according to the length and purpose of the flight. However, in addition to obtaining consumers' evaluations of service profiles, the researchers also obtained information concerning their *perceptions* of each airline (that is, for the ones they were familiar with) on each of the service factors for which the consumers were given a choice.

These two major pieces of information provided the principal basis for developing a simulation of airline services over all major traffic routes. The purpose of the simulation was to estimate the effect on market share that a change in the service configuration of the sponsor's services would have, route by route, if competitors did not follow suit. Later, the sponsor used the simulator to examine the effect of assumed retaliatory actions by its competitors. It also was able to use it to see what might happen to market share if the utility functions themselves were to change.

Each new service configuration was evaluated against the base-period configuration. In addition, the simulator showed which competing airlines would lose business and which ones would gain business under various changes in perceived service levels. Thus, in addition to single, ad hoc studies, conjoint measurement can be used in the ongoing monitoring (via simulation) of consumer imagery and evaluations over time.

PROSPECTS AND LIMITATIONS

Like any new set of techniques, conjoint measurement's potential is difficult to evaluate at the present stage of development and application. Relatively few companies have experimented with the approach so far. Capability for doing the research is still concentrated in a relatively few consulting firms and companies.

Conjoint measurement faces the same kinds of limitations that confront any type of survey, or laboratory-like, technique. First, while some successes have been reported in using

[6] Paul E. Green and Yoram Wind, *Multiattribute Decisions in Marketing Measurement Approach* (Hinsdale, Ill.: Dryden Press, 1973).

conjoint measurement to predict actual sales and market share, the number of applications is still too small to establish a convincing track record at the present time.

Second, some products or services may involve utility functions and decision rules that are not adequately captured by the models of conjoint measurement. While the current emphasis on additive models (absence of interactions) can be shifted to more complex, interactive models, the number of combinations required to estimate the interactions rapidly mounts. Still, little is known about how good an approximation the simpler models are to the more elaborate ones.

Third, the essence of some products and services may just not be well captured by a decomposition approach that assumes that the researcher can describe an alternative in terms of its component parts. Television personalities, hit records, movies, or even styling aspects of cars may not lend themselves to this type of reductionist approach.

While the limitations of conjoint measurement are not inconsequential, early experience suggests some interesting prospects for measuring consumer trade-offs among various product or service characteristics. Perhaps what is most interesting about the technique is its flexibility in coping with a wide variety of management's understanding of consumers problems that ultimately hinge on evaluations of complex alternatives that a choice among product presents them with.

APPENDIX: OTHER TECHNIQUES FOR QUANTIFYING CONSUMERS' JUDGMENTS

Conjoint measurement is the latest in an increasing family of techniques that psychometricians and others in the behavioral and statistical sciences have developed to measure persons' perceptions and preferences. Conjoint measurement can often be profitably used with one or more of the following:

Factor Analysis Factor analysis in marketing research has been around since the 1940s. However, like all the techniques to be (briefly) described here, factor analysis did not reach any degree of sophistication or practicality until the advent of the computer made the extensive computations easy to carry out. A typical input to factor analysis consists of respondents' subjective ratings of brands or services on each of a set of attributes *provided by the researcher.* For example, a sample of computer systems personnel were asked to rate various computer manufacturers' equipment and services on each of the 15 attributes shown in *Table I.*

The objective of factor analysis is to exam-

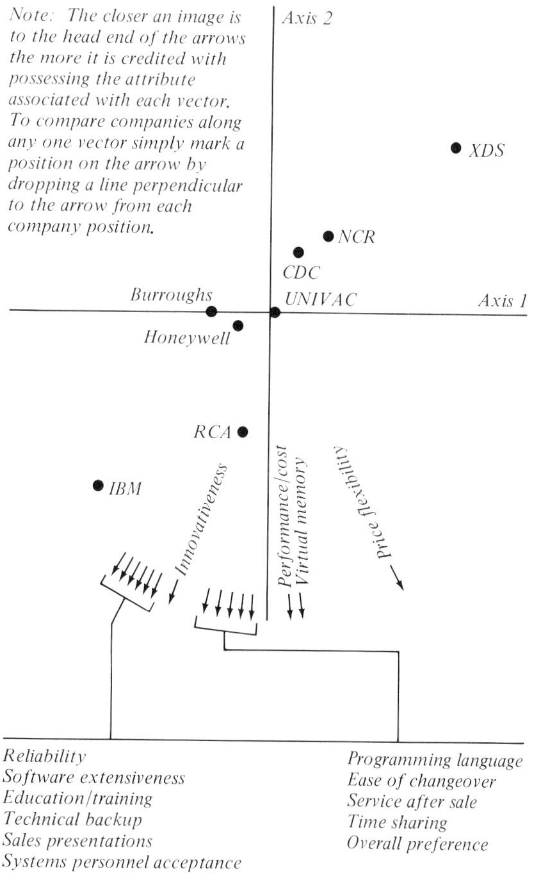

Table I Factor analysis of average respondent ratings of eight computer manufacturers' images on each of 15 attributes.

ine the commonality across the various rating scales and find a geometric representation, or picture, of the objects (computers), as well as the attributes used in the rating task. As noted in *Table I,* International Business Machines (IBM) was ranked highest on virtually all attributes while Xerox (XDS), a comparatively new entrant at the time of the study, National Cash Register (NCR), and Central Data Corporation (CDC) were not perceived as highly as the others with regard to the various attributes of interest to computer users.

The tight grouping of the attribute vectors also suggests a strong "halo" effect in favor of IBM. Only in the case of price flexibility does IBM receive less than the highest rating, and even here it is rated a close second. Thus as *Table I* shows, factor analysis enables the researcher to develop a picture of both the things being rated (the manufacturers) and the attributes along which the ratings take place.

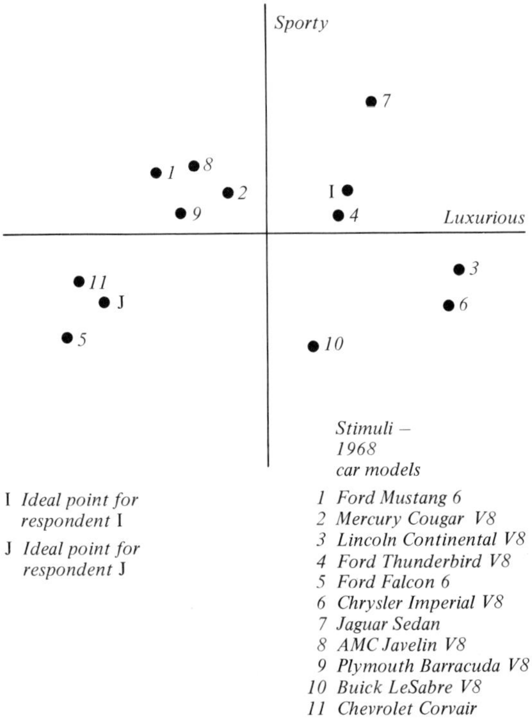

Table II Perceptual mapping of respondents' judgments of the relative similarity of 11 cars and two respondents' preference orderings.

Perceptual Mapping A somewhat more recent technique—also abetted by the availability of the computer—is perceptual mapping. Perceptual mapping techniques take consumer judgments of overall similarity or preference and find literally a picture in which objects that are judged to be similar psychologically plot near each other in geometric space (see *Table II*). However, in perceptual mapping the respondent is free to choose *his own* frame of reference rather than to respond to explicitly stated attributes.

The perceptual map of the 11 automobiles shown was developed from consumers' judgments about the relative similarity of the 55 distinct pairs of cars that can be made up from the 11 cars listed. The dimension labels of *luxurious* and *sporty* do *not* come from the technique but rather from further analysis of the map, once it is obtained from the computer. Ideal points I and J are shown for two illustrative respondents and are fitted into the perceptual map from the respondents' preference judgments. Car points near a respondent's ideal point are preferred to those farther away. Thus respondent I most likes Ford Thunderbird, while respondent J most likes Chevrolet Corvair. In practice, data for several hundred respondents might be used to find regions of high density for ideal points.

Cluster Analysis Still another way to portray consumers' judgments is in terms of a hierarchical tree structure in which the more similar a set of objects is perceived to be, the more quickly the objects group together as one moves from left to right in the tree diagram. Thus the words *body* and *fullness* are perceived to be the two most closely associated of all of the descriptions appearing in *Table III* that characterize hair. Note further that smaller clusters become embedded in larger ones until the last cluster on the right includes all 19 phrases. The words in this example were based on respondents' free associations to a set of 8 stimulus words. The researchers assumed that the more a stimulus evoked another word, the more similar they were.

Relationship to Conjoint Measurement
These three methods are best noted for their complementarities—both with each other and with conjoint measurement. Factor analysis and perceptual mapping can be used to measure consumers' perceptions of various products or services, while conjoint measurement can be used to quantify how consumers trade off some of one attribute to get more of another. Cluster analysis can be used in a variety of ways, either as a comparison technique for portraying the similarities of various objects or as a basis for grouping people with common perceptions or preferences. In short, all these techniques can—and frequently are—applied in the same study. As such, their combined use can heighten different aspects of the same general types of input data.

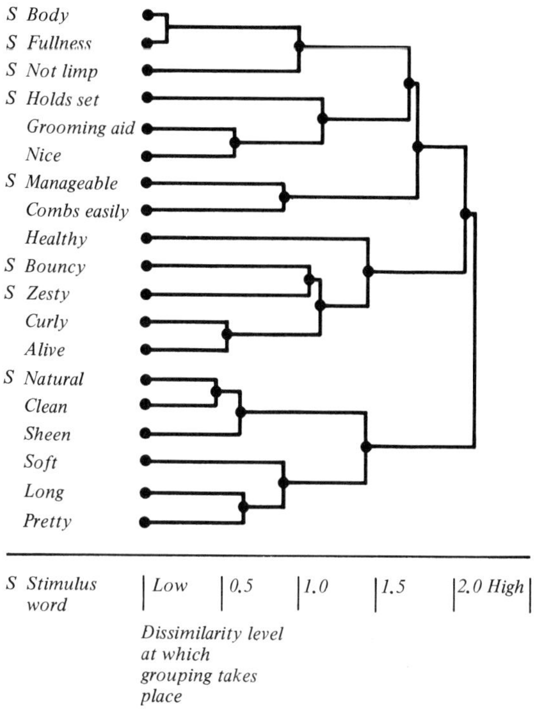

Table III Hierarchical cluster analysis of 19 phrases evoked in a free association task involving women's hair shampoos.

11

A Model of Industrial Buyer Behavior

Jagdish N. Sheth

Although industrial marketing research has generated large data banks on organizational buyers, very little from the existing data seems helpful to management. What is needed before more data are collected is a realistic conceptualization and understanding of the process of industrial buying decisions.

This article integrates existing knowledge into a descriptive model to aid in industrial marketing research.

The purpose of this article is to describe a model of industrial (organizational) buyer be-

Reprinted from *Journal of Marketing*, vol. 37, pp. 50–56, American Marketing Association, October 1973. At the time of writing, the author was professor of business and research professor at the College of Commerce and Business Administration, University of Illinois.

havior. Considerable knowledge on organizational buyer behavior already exists[1] and can be classified into three categories. The first category includes a considerable amount of systematic empirical research on the buying policies and practices of purchasing agents and other organizational buyers.[2] The second includes industry reports and observations of industrial buyers.[3] Finally, the third category consists of books, monographs, and articles which analyze, theorize, model, and sometimes report on industrial buying activities.[4] What is now needed is a reconcilation and integration of existing knowledge into a realistic and comprehensive model of organizational buyer behavior.

It is hoped that the model described in this article will be useful in the following ways: first, to broaden the vision of research on organizational buyer behavior so that it includes the most salient elements and their interactions; second, to act as a catalyst for building marketing information systems from the viewpoint of the industrial buyer; and, third, to generate new hypotheses for future research on fundamental processes underlying organizational buyer behavior.

A DESCRIPTION OF INDUSTRIAL BUYER BEHAVIOR

The model of industrial buyer behavior is summarized in Figure 1. Although this illustrative presentation looks complex due to the large number of variables and complicated relationships among them, this is because it is a generic model which attempts to describe and explain all types of industrial buying decisions. One can, however, simplify the actual application of the model in a specific study in at least two ways. First, several variables are included as conditions to hold constant differences among types of products to be purchased (product-specific factors) and

[1]For a comprehensive list of references, see Thomas A. Staudt and W. Lazer, *A Basic Bibliography on Industrial Marketing* (Chicago: American Marketing Assn., 1963); and Donald E. Vinson, "Bibliography of Industrial Marketing" (unpublished listing of references, University of Colorado, 1972).

[2]Richard M. Cyert, et al., "Observation of a Business Decision," *Journal of Business*, Vol. 29 (October 1956), pp. 237-248; John A. Howard and C. G. Moore, Jr., "A Descriptive Model of the Purchasing Agent" (unpublished monograph, University of Pittsburgh, 1964); George Strauss, "Work Study of Purchasing Agents," *Human Organization*, Vol. 33 (September 1964), pp. 137-149; Theodore A. Leavitt, *Industrial Purchasing Behavior* (Boston: Division of Research, Graduate School of Business, Harvard University, 1965); Ozanne B. Urban and Gilbert A. Churchill, "Adoption Research: Information Sources in the Industrial Purchasing Decision," and Richard N. Cardozo, "Segmenting the Industrial Market," in *Marketing and the New Science of Planning*, R. L. King, ed. (Chicago: American Marketing Assn., 1968), pp. 352–359 and 433–440, respectively. Richard N. Cardozo and J. W. Cagley, "Experimental Study of Industrial Buyer Behavior," *Journal of Marketing Research*, Vol. 8 (August 1971), pp. 329-334; Thomas P. Copley and F. L. Callom, "Industrial Search Behavior and Perceived Risk," in *Proceedings of the Second Annual Conference, the Association for Consumer Research*, D. M. Gardner, ed. (College Park, Md.: Association for Consumer Research, 1971), pp. 208–231; and James R. McMillan, "Industrial Buying Behavior as Group Decision Making," (paper presented at the Nineteenth International Meeting of the Institute of Management Sciences, April 1972).

[3]Robert F. Shoaf, ed., *Emotional Factors Underlying Industrial Purchasing* (Cleveland, Ohio: Penton Publishing Co., 1959); G. H. Haas, B. March, and E. M. Krech, *Purchasing Department Organization and Authority*, American Management Assn. Research Study No. 45 (New York: 1960): *Evaluation of Supplier Performance* (New York: National Association of Purchasing Agents, 1963); F. A. Hays and G. A. Renard, *Evaluating Purchasing Performance*, American Management Assn. Research Study No. 66 (New York: 1964); Hugh Buckner, *How British Industry Buys* (London: Hutchison and Company, Ltd., 1967); *How Industry Buys/1970* (New York: Scientific American, 1970). In addition, numerous articles published in trade journals such as *Purchasing and Industrial Marketing* are cited in Vinson, same reference as footnote 1, and Strauss, same reference as footnote 2.

[4]Ralph S. Alexander, J. S. Cross, and R. M. Hill, *Industrial Marketing*, 3rd ed. (Homewood, Ill.: Richard D. Irwin, 1967); John H. Westing, I. V. Fine, and G. J. Zenz, *Purchasing Management* (New York: John Wiley & Sons, 1969); Patrick J. Robinson, C. W. Farris, and Y. Wind, *Industrial Buying and Creative Marketing* (Boston: Allyn & Bacon, 1967); Frederick E. Webster, Jr., "Modeling the Industrial Buying Process," *Journal of Marketing Research*, Vol. 2 (November 1965), pp. 370–376; and Frederick E. Webster, Jr., "Industrial Buying Behavior: A State-of-the-Art Appraisal," in *Marketing in a Changing World*, B. A. Morin, ed. (Chicago: American Marketing Assn., 1969), p. 256.

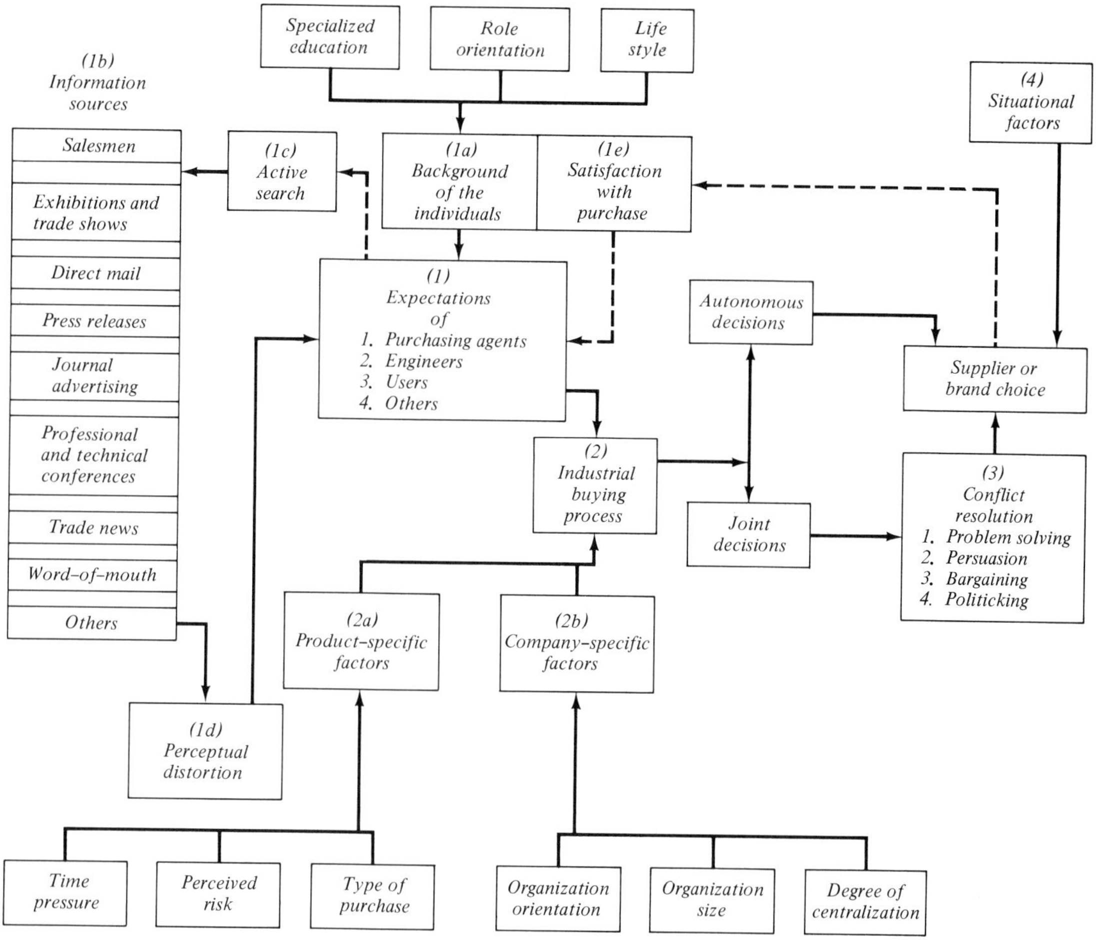

Figure 1 An integrative model of industrial buyer behavior.

differences among types of purchasing organizations. These exogenous factors will not be necessary if the objective of a study is to describe the process of buying behavior for a specific product or service. Second, some of the decision-process variables can also be ignored if the interest is strictly to conduct a survey of static measurement of the psychology of the organizational buyers. For example, perceptual bias and active search variables may be eliminated if the interest is not in the process of communication to the organizational buyers.

This model is similar to the Howard-Sheth model of buyer behavior in format and classification of variables.[5] However, there are several significant differences. First, while the Howard-Sheth model is more general and probably more useful in consumer behavior, the model described in this article is limited to organizational buying alone. Second, the Howard-Sheth model is limited to the individual decision-making process, whereas this model explicitly described the joint decision-making process. Finally, there are fewer variables in this model than in the Howard-Sheth model of buyer behavior.

[5]John A. Howard and J. N. Sheth, *The Theory of Buyer Behavior* (New York: John Wiley & Sons, 1969).

Organizational buyer behavior consists of three distinct aspects. The first aspect is the psychological world of the individuals involved in organizational buying decisions. The second aspect relates to the conditions which precipitate joint decisions among these individuals. The final aspect is the process of joint decision making with the inevitable conflict among the decision makers and its resolution by resorting to a variety of tactics.

PSYCHOLOGICAL WORLD OF THE DECISION MAKERS

Contrary to popular belief, many industrial buying decisions are not solely in the hands of purchasing agents.[6] Typically in an industrial setting, one finds that there are at least three departments whose members are continuously involved in different phases of the buying process. The most common are the personnel from the purchasing, quality control, and manufacturing departments. These individuals are identified in the model as purchasing agents, engineers, and users, respectively. Several other individuals in the organization may be, but are typically not, involved in the buying process (for example, the president of the firm or the comptroller). There is considerable interaction among the individuals in the three departments continuously involved in the buying process and often they are asked to decide jointly. It is, therefore, critical to examine the similarities and differences in the psychological worlds of these individuals.

Based on research in consumer and social psychology, several different aspects of the psychology of the decision makers are included in the model. Primary among these are the *expectations* of the decision makers about suppliers and brands [(1) in Figure 1]. The present model specifies five different processes which create differential expectations among the individuals involved in the purchasing process: (1a) the *background of the individuals,* (1b) *information sources,* and (1c) *active search,* (1d) *perceptual distortion,* and (1e) *satisfaction with past purchases.* These variables must be explained and operationally defined if they are to fully represent the psychological world of the organizational buyers.

EXPECTATIONS

Expectations refer to the *perceived* potential of alternative suppliers and brands to satisfy a number of explicit and implicit objectives in any particular buying decision. The most common explicit objectives include, in order of relative importance, product quality, delivery time, quantity of supply, after-sale service where appropriate, and price.[7] However, a number of studies have pointed out the critical role of several implicit criteria such as reputation, size, location, and reciprocity relationship with the supplier; and personality, technical expertise, salesmanship, and even life style of the sales representative.[8] In fact, with the standardized marketing mix among the suppliers in oligopolistic markets, the implicit criteria are becoming marginally more and more significant in the industrial buyer's decisions.

Expectations can be measured by obtaining a profile of each supplier or brand as to how satisfactory it is perceived to be in enabling the decision maker to achieve his explicit and implicit objectives. Almost all studies from past research indicate that expectations will substantially differ among the purchasing

[6] Howard and Moore, same reference as footnote 2; Strauss, same reference as footnote 2; McMillan, same reference as footnote 2; *How Industry Buys/1970,* same reference as footnote 3.

[7] Howard and Moore, same reference as footnote 2; *How Industry Buys/1970,* same reference as footnote 3; Hays and Renard, same reference as footnote 3.

[8] Howard and Moore, same reference as footnote 2; Levitt, same reference as footnote 2; Westing, Fine and Zenz, same reference as footnote 4; Shoaf, same reference as footnote 4.

agents, engineers, and product users because each considers different criteria to be salient in judging the supplier or the brand. In general, it is found that product users look for prompt delivery, proper installation, and efficient serviceability; purchasing agents look for maximum price advantage and economy in shipping and forwarding; and engineers look for excellence in quality, standardization of the product, and engineering pretesting of the product. These differences in objectives and, consequently, expectations are often the root causes for constant conflict among these three types of individuals.[9]

Why are there substantial differences in expectations? While there is considerable speculation among researchers and observers of industrial buyer behavior on the number and nature of explanations, there is relatively little consensus. The five most salient processes which determine differential expectations, as specified in the model, are discussed below.

Background of Individuals

The first, and probably most significant, factor is the background and task orientation of each of the individuals involved in the buying process. The different educational backgrounds of the purchasing agents, engineers, and plant managers often generate substantially different professional goals and values. In addition, the task expectations also generate conflicting perceptions of one another's role in the organization. Finally, the personal life styles of individual decision makers play an important role in developing differential expectations.[10]

It is relatively easy to gather information on this background factor. The educational and task differences are comparable to demographics in consumer behavior, and life style differences can be assessed by psychographic scales on the individual's interests, activities, and values as a professional.

Information Sources and Active Search

The second and third factors in creating differential expectations are the source and type of information each of the decision makers is exposed to and his participation in the active search. Purchasing agents receive disproportionately greater exposure to commercial sources, and the information is often partial and biased toward the supplier or the brand. In some companies, it is even a common practice to discourage sales representatives from talking directly to the engineering or production personnel. The engineering and production personnel, therefore, typically have less information and what they have is obtained primarily from professional meetings, trade reports, and even word-of-mouth. In addition, the active search for information is often relegated to the purchasing agents because it is presumed to be their job responsibility.

It is not too difficult to assess differences among the three types of individuals in their exposure to various sources and types of information by standard survey research methods.

Perceptual Distortion

A fourth factor is the selective distortion and retention of available information. Each individual strives to make the objective information consistent with his own prior knowledge and expectations by systematically distorting it. For example, since there are substantial differences in the goals and values of purchasing agents, engineers, and production personnel, one should expect different interpretations of the same information among them. Although no specific research has been done on this tendency to perceptually distort infor-

[9] Strauss, same reference as footnote 2.

[10] For a general reading, see Robert T. Golembiewski, "Small Groups and Large Organizations," in *Handbook of Organizations,* J. G. March, ed. (Chicago: Rand McNally & Company, 1965), chapter 3. For field studies related to this area, see Donald E. Porter, P. B. Applewhite, and M. J. Misshauk, eds., *Studies in Organizational Behavior and Management,* 2nd ed. (Scranton, Pa.: Intext Educational Publishers, 1971).

mation in the area of industrial buyer behavior, a large body of research does exist on cognitive consistency to explain its presence as a natural human tendency.[11]

Perceptual distortion is probably the most difficult variable to quantify by standard survey research methods. One possible approach is experimentation, but this is costly. A more realistic alternative is to utilize perceptual mapping techniques such as multidimensional scaling or factor analysis and compare differences in the judgments of the purchasing agents, engineers, and production personnel to a common list of suppliers or brands.

Satisfaction with Past Purchases

The fifth factor which creates differential expectations among the various individuals involved in the purchasing process is the satisfaction with past buying experiences with a supplier or brand. Often it is not possible for a supplier or brand to provide equal satisfaction to the three parties because each one has different goals or criteria. For example, a supplier may be lower in price but his delivery schedule may not be satisfactory. Similarly, a product's quality may be excellent but its price may be higher than others. The organization typically rewards each individual for excellent performance in his specialized skills, so that purchasing agent is rewarded for economy, the engineer for quality control, and the production personnel for efficient scheduling. This often results in a different level of satisfaction for each of the parties involved even though the chosen supplier or brand may be the best feasible alternative in terms of overall corporate goals.

Past experiences with a supplier or brand, summarized in the satisfaction variable, directly influence the person's expectations toward that supplier or brand. It is relatively easy to measure the satisfaction variable by obtaining information on how the supplier or brand is perceived by each of the three parties.

DETERMINANTS OF JOINT VS. AUTONOMOUS DECISIONS

Not all industrial buying decisions are made jointly by the various individuals involved in the purchasing process. Sometimes the buying decisions are delegated to one party, which is not necessarily the purchasing agent. It is, therefore, important for the supplier to know whether a buying decision is joint or autonomous and, if it is the latter, to which party it is delegated. There are six primary factors which determine whether a specific buying decision will be joint or autonomous. Three of these factors are related to the characteristics of the product or service (2a) and the other three are related to the characteristics of the buyer company (2b).

PRODUCT-SPECIFIC FACTORS

The first product-specific variable is what Bauer calls *perceived risk* in buying decisions.[12] Perceived risk refers to the magnitude of adverse consequences felt by the decision maker if he makes a wrong choice, and the uncertainty under which he must decide. The greater the uncertainty in a buying situation, the greater the perceived risk. Although there is very little direct evidence, it is logical to hypothesize that the greater the perceived risk in a specific buying decision, the more likely it

[11]Robert P. Abelson, et al., *Theories of Cognitive Consistency: A Source Book* (Chicago: Rand McNally & Company, 1968).

[12]Raymond A. Bauer, "Consumer Behavior as Risk Taking," in *Dynamic Marketing for a Changing World,* R. L. Hancock, ed. (Chicago: American Marketing Assn., 1960), pp. 389–400. Applications of perceived risk in industrial buying can be found in Levitt, same reference as footnote 2; Copley and Callom, same reference as footnote 2; McMillan, same reference as footnote 2.

is that the purchase will be decided jointly by all parties concerned. The second product-specific factor is *type of purchase.* If it is the first purchase or a once-in-a-lifetime capital expenditure, one would expect greater joint decision making. On the other hand, if the purchase decision is repetitive and routine or is limited to maintenance products or services, the buying decision is likely to be delegated to one party. The third factor is *time pressure.* If the buying decision has to be made under a great deal of time pressure or on an emergency basis, it is likely to be delegated to one party rather than decided jointly.

COMPANY-SPECIFIC FACTORS

The three organization-specific factors are *company orientation, company size,* and *degree of centralization.* If the company is technology oriented, it is likely to be dominated by the engineering people and the buying decisions will, in essence, be made by them. Similarly, if the company is production oriented, the buying decisions will be made by the production personnel.[13] Second, if the company is a large corporation, decision making will tend to be joint. Finally, the greater the degree of centralization, the less likely it is that the decisions will be joint. Thus, a privately-owned small company with technology or production orientation will tend toward autonomous decision making and a large-scale public corporation with considerable decentralization will tend to have greater joint decision making.

Even though there is considerable research evidence in organization behavior in general to support these six factors, empirical evidence in industrial buying decisions in particular is sketchy on them. Perhaps with more research it will be possible to verify the generalizations and deductive logic utilized in this aspect of the model.

PROCESS OF JOINT DECISION MAKING

The major thrust of the present model of industrial buying decisions is to investigate the process of joint decision making. This includes initiation of the decision to buy, gathering of information, evaluating alternative suppliers, and resolving conflict among the parties who must jointly decide.

The decision to buy is usually initiated by a continued need of supply or is the outcome of long-range planning. The formal initiation in the first case is typically from the production personnel by way of a requisition slip. The latter usually is a formal recommendation from the planning unit to an ad hoc committee consisting of the purchasing agent, the engineer, and the plant manager. The information-gathering function is typically relegated to the purchasing agent. If the purchase is a repetitive decision for standard items, there is very little information gathering. Usually the purchasing agent contacts the preferred supplier and orders the items on the requisition slip. However, considerable active search effort is manifested for capital expenditure items, especially those which are entirely new purchase experiences for the organization.[14]

The most important aspect of the joint decision-making process, however, is the assimilation of information, deliberations on it, and the consequent conflict which most joint decisions entail. According to March and Simon, conflict is present when there is a need to decide jointly among a group of people who have, at the same time, different goals and

[13]For some indirect evidence, see Strauss, same reference as footnote 2. For a more general study, see Victor A. Thompson, "Hierarchy, Specialization and Organizational Conflict," *Administrative Science Quarterly,* Vol. 5 (March 1961). p. 513; and Henry A. Landsberger, "The Horizontal Dimension in Bureaucracy," *Administration Science Quarterly,* Vol. 6 (December 1961), pp. 299–332, for a thorough review of numerous theories.

[14]Strauss; same reference as footnote 2.

perceptions.[15] In view of the fact that the latter is invariably present among the various parties to industrial buying decisions, conflict becomes a common consequence of the joint decision-making process; the buying motives and expectations about brands and suppliers are considerably different for the engineer, the user, and the purchasing agent, partly due to different educational backgrounds and partly due to company policy of reward for specialized skills and viewpoints.

Interdepartmental conflict in itself is not necessarily bad. What matters most from the organization's viewpoint is *how* the conflict is resolved (3). If it is resolved in a rational manner, one very much hopes that the final joint decision will also tend to be rational. If, on the other hand, conflict resolution degenerates to what Strauss calls "tactics of lateral relationship,"[16] the organization will suffer from inefficiency and the joint decisions may be reduced to bargaining and politicking among the parties involved. Not only will the decision be based on irrational criteria, but the choice of a supplier may be to the detriment of the buying organization.

What types of conflict can be expected in industrial buying decisions? How are they likely to be resolved? These are some of the key questions in an understanding of industrial buyer behavior. If the inter-party conflict is largely due to disagreements on expectations about the suppliers or their brands, it is likely that the conflict will be resolved in the *problem-solving* manner. The immediate consequence of this type of conflict is to actively search for more information, deliberate more on available information, and often to seek out other suppliers not seriously considered before. The additional information is then presented in a problem-solving fashion so that conflict tends to be minimized.

If the conflict among the parties is primarily due to disagreement on some specific criteria with which to evaluate suppliers—although there is an agreement on the buying goals or objectives at a more fundamental level—it is likely to be resolved by *persuasion.* An attempt is made, under this type of resolution, to persuade the dissenting member by pointing out the importance of overall corporate objectives and how his criterion is not likely to attain these objectives. There is no attempt to gather more information. However, there results greater interaction and communication among the parties, and sometimes an outsider is brought in to reconcile the differences.

Both problem solving and persuasion are useful and rational methods of conflict resolution. The resulting joint decisions, therefore, also tend to be more rational. Thus, conflicts produced due to disagreements on expectations about the suppliers or on a specific criterion are healthy from the organization's viewpoint even though they may be time consuming. One is likely to find, however, that a more typical situation in which conflict arises is due to fundamental differences in buying goals or objectives among the various parties. This is especially true with respect to unique or new buying decisions related to capital expenditure items. The conflict is resolved not by changing the differences in relative importance of the buying goals or objectives of the individuals involved, but by the process of *bargaining.* The fundamental differences among the parties are implicitly conceded by all the members and the concept of distributive justice (tit for tat) is invoked as a part of bargaining. The most common outcome is to allow a single party to decide autonomously in this specific situation in return for some favor or promise of reciprocity in future decisions.

[15]James G. March and H. A. Simon, *Organizations* (New York: John Wiley & Sons, 1958), chapter 5; and Landsberger, same reference as footnote 13.

[16]George Strauss, "Tactics of Lateral Relationship: The Purchasing Agent," *Administrative Science Quarterly,* Vol. 7 (September 1962), pp. 161-186.

Finally, if the disagreement is not simply with respect to buying goals or objectives but also with respect to *style of decision making,* the conflict tends to be grave and borders on the mutual dislike of personalities among the individual decision makers. The resolution of this type of conflict is usually by *politicking* and back-stabbing tactics. Such methods of conflict resolution are common in industrial buying decisions. The reader is referred to the sobering research of Strauss for further discussion.[17]

Both bargaining and politicking are nonrational and inefficient methods of conflict resolution; the buying organization suffers from these conflicts. Furthermore, the decision makers find themselves sinking below their professional, managerial role. The decisions are not only delayed but tend to be governed by factors other than achievement of corporate objectives.

CRITICAL ROLE OF SITUATIONAL FACTORS

The model described so far presumes that the choice of a supplier or brand is the outcome of a systematic decision-making process in the organizational setting. However, there is ample empirical evidence in the literature to suggest that at least some of the industrial buying decisions are determined by ad hoc *situational factors* (4) and not by any systematic decision-making process. In other words, similar to consumer behavior, the industrial buyers often decide on factors other than rational or realistic criteria.

It is difficult to prepare a list of ad hoc conditions which determine industrial buyer behavior without decision making. However, a number of situational factors which often intervene between the actual choice and any prior decision-making process can be isolated. These include: temporary economic conditions such as price controls, recession, or foreign trade; internal strikes, walkouts, machine breakdowns, and other production-related events; organizational changes such as merger or acquisition; and ad hoc changes in the market place, such as promotional efforts, new product introduction, price changes, and so on, in the supplier industries.

[17]Same reference as footnote 16.

IMPLICATIONS FOR INDUSTRIAL MARKETING RESEARCH

The model of industrial buyer behavior described above suggests the following implications for marketing research.

First, in order to explain and predict supplier or brand choice in industrial buyer behavior, it is necessary to conduct research on the psychology of other individuals in the organization in addition to the purchasing agents. It is, perhaps, the unique nature of organizational structure and behavior which leads to a distinct separation of the consumer, the buyer, and the procurement agent, as well as others possibly involved in the decision-making process. In fact, it may not be an exaggeration to suggest that the purchasing agent is often a less critical member of the decision-making process in industrial buyer behavior.

Second, it is possible to operationalize and quantify most of the variables included as part of the model. While some are more difficult and indirect, sufficient psychometric skill in marketing research is currently available to quantify the psychology of the individuals.

Third, although considerable research has been done on the demographics of organizations in industrial market research—for example, on the turnover and size of the company, workflows, standard industrial classification, and profit ratios—demographic and life-style information on the individuals involved in industrial buying decisions is also needed.

Fourth, a systematic examination of the power positions of various individuals involved in industrial buying decisions is a necessary condition of the model. The sufficient condition is to examine trade-offs among various objectives, both explicit and implicit, in order to create a satisfied customer.

Fifth, it is essential in building any market research information system for industrial goods and services that the process of conflict resolution among the parties and its impact on supplier or brand choice behavior is carefully included and simulated.

Finally, it is important to realize that not all industrial decisions are the outcomes of a systematic decision-making process. There are some industrial buying decisions which are based strictly on a set of situational factors for which theorizing or model building will not be relevant or useful. What is needed in these cases is a checklist of empirical observations of the ad hoc events which vitiate the neat relationship between the theory or the model and a specific buying decision.

C SEGMENTING THE MARKET

12

An Overview of Market Segmentation

John C. Bieda
Harold H. Kassarjian

The concept of market segmentation has triggered a considerable amount of discussion and articles. The authors present an overview of this interesting concept in terms of approaches to segmenting markets and of some research conducted on the subject. They imply that there is a real opportunity for a better understanding of the concept of market segmentation by use of a new series of multivariate studies.

Not unlike the fad of Motivation Research in the post World War II period, the concept of market segmentation has produced a phenomenal proliferation of articles, studies and papers in the past decade. The concept, itself, was first clearly articulated by Wendell Smith in a 1956 *Journal of Marketing* article,[1] a paper that by now has become a classic. And perhaps this should be so, for market segmentation has permeated the thinking of theorists, researchers and managers perhaps more than any of the other fashions and fads that marketing had passed through. Until very recently the controversial nature of the issue has been not whether or not segmentation leads to meaningful analysis as much as on what basis to segment.

To the earlier marketing manager, the natural segments of population were related to the socio-economic and demographic variables found in the U.S. Census of Population. From these variables one could distill our social class, the ultimate conglomerate in the determination of consumer behavior in the view of many. But the field was not to be left to the census analysts alone; for soon after, personality variables such as gregariousness, authoritarianism, inferiority, risk taking and self-esteem were to make their impact; and finally

[1]Wendell Smith, "Product Differentiation and Market Segmentation as Alternative Marketing Strategies," *Journal of Marketing*, Vol. 21 (July 1956), pp. 3–8.

Reprinted from Bernard A. Morin (ed.) *Marketing in a Changing World* (Chicago: American Marketing Association, 1969), pp. 249–253. At the time of writing, Mr. Bieda was assistant professor of marketing, Graduate School of Business Administration, University of California at Los Angeles. Mr. Kasserjian was professor of marketing at the same institution.

such concepts as usage rate, brand loyalty, channel loyalty, advertising susceptibility and even sensitivity were to make their debut.

The usefulness of any given technique for segmentation, of course, is the ultimate one of applicability. "In other words, a crucial criterion for determining the desirability of segmenting a market along any particular dimension is whether the different submarkets have different elasticities. . . ."[2] The determination of this criterion, according to Kotler,[3] depends upon several conditions.

The first of these is measurability, ". . . the degree to which information exists or is obtainable on various buyers' characteristics. Unfortunately many suggestive characteristics are not susceptible to easy measurement." The size of each segment that purchases toothpaste because of health fears, dislike of dentists, sex appeal, or because of habitual patterns inculcated by parents is difficult to measure.

A second condition is that of *accessibility,* the degree to which any given segment can be differentially reached. Unfortunately those starved for self-esteem, the hypochondriacal types, or heavy users of toothpaste do not cooperate by differentially exposing themselves to specific media, purchasing from different outlets or necessarily being willing to pay different prices.

Kotler's final condition is that of *substantiality,* the degree to which the segments are large enough to be worth subdividing for separate marketing activity.

TWO APPROACHES TO SEGMENTATION

As one reviews the literature on marketing segmentation, two approaches seem to emerge. On the one hand, the researcher starts with an existing product. The function of the researcher is to study the customers of that generic product to determine if there are differences between buyers of different brands. In this case the particular segment of the market that the brands are aimed at is determined empirically. Once such information is gleaned, better marketing decisions presumably are made, and perhaps further product differentiation is possible.

A great deal of the commercial research is undoubtedly of this sort answering such questions as, "Who is our market? and how can we better reach them?"

Evans' now often quoted study on the psychological and objective factors related to Ford and Chevrolet owners is an example of this type of approach. Starting with owners of Fords and Chevrolets he collected demographic and personality data and by the use of discriminant analysis attempted to predict the buyers of each make of automobile. His results parenthetically indicated that demographic variables did a better job of predicting brand choice than did the personality variables.[4]

The second type of segmentation research approaches the problem from the opposite direction. The research starts with preconceived notions of what the critical segmentation variables are—social class, personality, cultural variables, age and sex. Members of each group or segment are one way or another isolated, and product usage, brand and channel loyalty, or media exposure data, are then collected and analyzed. The question the researcher asks is of the sort, "How do young marrieds differ from older persons?" or "What products do southerners use as compared with northerners?" Rainwater's study on the Workingman's Wife is an example of this approach. He collected masses of data on

[2]Ronald E. Frank, "Market Segmentation Research: Findings and Implications," in Frank M. Bass, Charles W. King, and Edgar A. Pessemier (eds.), *Application of the Sciences in Marketing Management,* New York: John Wiley & Sons, 1968.

[3]Philip Kotler, *Marketing Management,* Englewood Cliffs, N.J.: Prentice-Hall, 1967.

[4]Franklin B. Evans, "Psychological and Objective Factors in the Prediction of Brand Choice," *Journal of Business,* Vol. 32 (Oct. 1959), pp. 340–369.

the behavior of working class and middle class housewives relating to their purchasing activities, attitudes, and so on, and made a number of significant comparisons.[5]

Another example of the precategorized approach to segmentation is Joel Cohen's study relating purchasing behavior to personality characteristics. Based on Karen Horney's tripartite conceptions of compliant, detached and aggressive styles of life, Cohen developed a questionnaire and attempted to divide his sample into these three groups of persons. Next he searched for and found some differences between groups on brand preference, usage rates and media exposure.[6]

The following overview of the literature in market segmentation includes further examples of both approaches.

AN OVERVIEW OF RESEARCH FINDINGS

Demographic Characteristics

That demographic variables are a useful method of segmentation has become almost axiomatic in marketing, and yet the research evidence is not at all clear. Evans, in his study on Ford and Chevrolet owners concludes, "The linear discriminant function of demographic variables is not a sufficiently powerful predictor to be of much practical use. . . . [They] . . . point more to the similarity of Ford and Chevrolet owners than to any means of discrimination between them. Analysis of several other objective factors also leads to the same conclusion."[7]

On grocery store products, the Advertising Research Foundation study in 1964 compared toilet tissue purchasing behavior with 15 socio-economic characteristics. The predictive efficiency of the characteristics was virtually nil.[8] Kopenen, using the same J. Walter Thompson panel data but on beer, coffee and tea, found very similar results,[9] while Frank, Massy, and Boyd using the Chicago Tribune panel data compared 57 product categories ranging from food to household products with demographic characteristics. The results were again similar with a very small portion of the variance being accounted for in the regression analyses.[10] Unfortunately, study after study throws doubt upon the direct usefulness of demographic characteristics as a predictor for product purchase.

Of course, this is not to deny that sanitary napkins are primarily purchased by women, razor blades by men, the influence of the purchase of sugar-coated breakfast cereals by children, and canned boiled peanuts in brine primarily by southerners. But nevertheless, other than very specific products aimed directly at a specific group, the empirical evidence seems to indicate that demographic measures, outside of education, are not an accurate predictor of consumer behavior.[11]

Social Class

Perhaps some of the most extensive work on market segmentation has been done in the area of social class.[12] Some differences do seem to emerge in spending patterns, product preferences and shopping habit. Martineau for example found some clear preferences between the lower and middle classes for types

[5]Lee Rainwater, Richard P. Coleman, and Gerald Handel, *Workingman's Wife,* New York: Oceana Publications, 1959.

[6]Joel B. Cohen, "An Interpersonal Orientation to the Study of Consumer Behavior," *Journal of Marketing Research,* Vol. 4 (August 1967), pp. 270–278.

[7]Same reference as Footnote 4.

[8]Ingrid Hildegaard and Lester Krueger, "Are There Customer Types?" as quoted in same reference as Footnote 2.

[9]Arthur Koponen, "Personality Characteristics of Purchasers," *Journal of Advertising Research,* Vol. 1 (Sept. 1960), pp. 6–12.

[10]As quoted in same reference as Footnote 2.

[11]Education taken as a univariate measure does seem to hold up as a segmentation variable as indicated in several studies and cannot as easily be brushed aside as most other demographic measures.

[12]E.g., James M. Carman, *The Application of Social Class in Market Segmentation,* Berkeley: Research Program in Marketing, Graduate School of Business Administration, 1965.

of retail stores.[13] Glick and Levy found preference differences in television programs with the middle classes preferring current events, drama and audience participation shows while the lower classes preferred soap operas, westerns and quiz shows. However, the degree of overlap is so great that a statistical prediction would be most difficult.[14]

Further, many of the social class studies are now several years old. By the 1970's what we will mean by lower class is perhaps not an income-occupation-education type of differentiation but more specifically Negroes, Indians and Mexican-Americans. Whether there is such a thing as a Negro market that is in fact different from the white market is still a controversial and not sufficiently researched issue. However, our expectation is that no such market exists. In any case, because of more exposure to the mass media consumption behavior differences between classes probably are disappearing.

Personality

Personality studies have been similarly disappointing. Westfall was able to find differences between convertible owners and sedans but the relationships were weak.[15] Kamen found no evidence to ascertain the consistency of food preferences among personality groups.[16] Koponen in the study mentioned above using J. Walter Thompson data found some minimal differences between smokers and nonsmokers on such variables as sex, aggression, achievement, dominance and compliance. However the percentage of variance accounted for both by personality variables and demographic variables combined was less than 12%.[17] Brody and Cunningham on reanalysis of the same data indicated that the personality variables measured by the Edwards Personality Preference Scale on both men and women heads of household accounted for a mere 15% of the variance.[18] Tucker and Painter similarly found significant but very weak relationships between measures such as responsibility, emotional stability, sociability and ascendancy and product preference. Among the products studied personality variables only differentiated between users of deodorants and cigarettes.[19]

Gruen found no relationship between product preference and inner- and other-direction,[20] and Kassarjian could not find differences in media exposure between inner- and other-directed subjects.[21]

To sum up the literature, personality as a variable has not been a useful mode of market segmentation. Perhaps it is too much to expect the forces of personality to be powerful enough to differentially produce the purchase of Colgate Toothpase over Crest or Gillette razor blades over Personna. Also it is possible that marketing has not yet found the right variables to measure, having no personality instruments of its own.

Buyer Characteristics

Finally turning to buyer characteristics such as brand loyalty and usage rate, the findings are not dissimilar. For example, Frank and Massy found no significant difference in elas-

[13]Pierre D. Martineau, "Social Classes and Spending Behavior," *Journal of Marketing*, Vol. 23 (October 1958), pp. 121–130.

[14]Ira O. Glick and Sidney Levy, *Living with Television*, New York: Aldine Publishing Co., 1962.

[15]Ralph Westfall, "Psychological Factors in Predicting Product Choice," *Journal of Marketing*, Vol. 26 (April 1962), pp. 34–40.

[16]Joseph M. Kamen, "Personality and Food Preferences," *Journal of Advertising Research*, Vol. 4 (Sept. 1964), pp. 29–32.

[17]Same reference as Footnote 10.

[18]Robert P. Brody and Scott M. Cunningham, "Personality Variables and the Consumer Decision Process," *Journal of Marketing Research*, Vol. 5 (Feb. 1968), pp. 50–57.

[19]William T. Tucker and John J. Painter, "Personality and Product Use," *Journal of Applied Psychology*, Vol. 45 (1961), pp. 325–329.

[20]W. Gruen, "Preference for New Products, and Its Relationship to Different Measures of Conformity," *Journal of Applied Psychology*, Vol. 44 (1960), pp. 361–366.

[21]Harold H. Kassarjian, "Social Character and Differential Preference for Mass Communication," *Journal of Marketing Research*, Vol. 2 (May 1965), pp. 146–153.

ticity between brand loyal and non-brand loyal buyers.[22] Although Twedt did find that heavy and light users can be moderately well distinguished on the basis of their different demographic characteristics, his findings, at best, indicated that the relationships are relatively modest.[23] Again using the J. Walter Thompson panel data, Massy, Frank, and Lodahl indicated that heavy and light buying households had virtually identical demographic and psychological characteristics.[24] To continue, Farley could not segment the brand-loyal customer,[25] and Frank and Boyd could not differentiate between the private label and manufacturer brand customers.[26] And finally Cunningham found little relationship between rate of purchase and brand loyalty.[27] However Brody and Cunningham found in a two brand discriminant analysis they were able to correctly identify 80% of brand choices.[28]

In general, the consistency of the results tends to indicate that the research to date in market segmentation has either been unsuccessful or if a relationship is shown, quite weak.

Turning back to Kotler's criterion for market segmentation, measurability, accessibility, and substantiality, it is clear that at least some of these conditions have not been met to date. In those cases where segmentation variables are measurable they do not seem to be related to purchasing characteristics. Or, even if the relationship is verified, too often the second condition, *accessibility,* is not a simple matter. Unfortunately media exposure, channel loyalty and purchase rate are not differentiated along the same variables as purchase behavior. To the everlasting frustration of the segmentation specialist, readers of *Argosy Magazine* and *True Experience* too often buy Cadillacs, while upper income professionals and businessmen too often shop at Macy's or Gimbel's in New York.

Perhaps then, the usual modes of segmentation are not sufficient. For example, Yankelovich argues that the analysis of various product markets should be made on the basis of several modes: patterns of usage, values derived from usage, preferences, aesthetics, and buying attitudes and motivations.[29] This view is enticing. Perhaps there are sufficiently substantial groups of people who on a multivariate set of dimensions can be considered a market segment. Unfortunately, Yankelovich does not present us with a method for such an analysis.

PROSPECTS

Although the results, to date, from studies on market segmentation have not been very encouraging, we might speculate on why so much of the research has been negative when the theory seems so logical and sound on an a priori basis. Perhaps the major problem of past research is that in an effort to segment markets we have lost sight of the basic premise of the theory: that different people have different needs and at different times these needs may change. Hence, a company's marketing program will have different elasticities when directed to groups of people where the needs in each group are relatively homogeneous and when the needs between groups are relatively heterogeneous.

[22]Ronald E. Frank and William Massy, "Market Segmentation and the Effectiveness of a Brand's Price and Dealing Policies," *Journal of Business* (April 1965), pp. 188–200.

[23]Dik W. Twedt, "How Important to Marketing Strategy Is the Heavy User," *Journal of Marketing,* (January 1964), pp. 71–72.

[24]As quoted in same reference as Footnote 2.

[25]John Farley, "Brand Loyalty and the Economics of Information," *Journal of Business,* Vol. 37 (October 1964), pp. 370–381.

[26]Ronald Frank and Harper Boyd, Jr., "Are Private-Brand Prone Food Customers Really Different," *Journal of Advertising Research,* Vol. 5 (December 1965), pp. 27–35.

[27]Ross M. Cunningham, "Brand Loyalty—What, Where, How Much?" *Harvard Business Review,* Vol. 34 (Jan.-Feb., 1956), pp. 127–137.

[28]Brody and Cunningham, *op. cit.*

[29]The conclusion is stated by Norman L. Barnett, "Beyond Market Segmentation," *Harvard Business Review,* Vol. 47 (Jan–Feb. 1969).

Consider for a moment the methodological logic of the past research. First, the researcher has arbitrarily selected a group of products or brands that he thinks are serving the same market. Then data on purchase behavior are collected for analysis. The analysis consists of using demographic, socio-economic, and psychological variables as independent variables in either a regression or discriminant analysis. The objective is to find out if buyers of different brands are related in any way to the independent variables. If a strong relationship is found a circular argument is used to establish cause and effect, i.e., because the person jointly had the characteristic and bought the product and because the person would not have bought the product unless he needed it, therefore, the characteristic must be the cause of the need for the product. But we never bother to extrastatistically establish the cause and effect relationship. We might ask at this point (1) what kinds of assumptions are made when this type of analysis is carried out and (2) are the assumptions realistic or are other assumptions more plausible?

First, it is assumed that because people have bought the same brand, they have bought it for the same reason, i.e., the same need, desire, tension. The alternative assumption that people buy the same product for different reasons seems more realistic. For example, one family might buy one brand of potato chips because the kids like ridges in them. Another family might buy the same brand because ridged potato chips do not break quite as easily as straight potato chips when served with a dip.

Second, it is assumed that all people perceive the same set of brands to be alternatives from which to choose. Some recent evidence would tend to indicate that this assumption may not be justified. Green, Carmone, and Fox[30] have shown that television programs were clustered differently, on the basis of similarity, by three groups of people. This would tend to support an alternative hypothesis that all consumers do not perceive the same set of products as competing with one another.

Third, it is assumed that each person has the same set of alternatives (brands) available from which to choose to satisfy his needs. But it is common knowledge to every housewife that all stores do not carry the same brands, therefore this assumption does not seem to be justified.

Fourth, it is assumed that people with the same set of characteristics, the same values of the independent variables, have the same needs, wants, and desires. This assumption may be reasonable; however there has been little, if any, systematic research to justify making this assumption on an a priori basis.

One final problem with past studies centers on the complete lack of integration into the segmentation analysis of information on the marketing mixes of the products and brands under study. This omission may have contributed to past negative findings if one or both of the following situations occurred.

Situation 1 Suppose that two brands, A and B, were essentially appealing to one set of needs and two other brands, C and D, were essentially appealing to another set of needs. If information on the marketing strategies of the four brands were not incorporated prior to using regression or discriminant analysis then the buyers of each of the brands would be considered a separate group, e.g., we would have a four-way discriminant analysis. This being the case, the regression or discriminant function would not be able to distinguish between the buyers of brands A and B nor between the buyers of brands C and D. In this situation we would probably conclude that the results were negative because we could not predict which brand consumers would buy based on the independent variables.

[30]Paul E. Green, Frank J. Carmone, and Leo B. Fox, "Television Programme Similarities: An Application of Subjective Clustering," *Journal of the Market Research Society*, Vol. 22 (January 1969), pp. 70–90.

Situation 2 Suppose that one brand was appealing to several segments using different marketing mixes for each segment. If this were the case then we would expect to find the brand satisfying a unique set of needs for buyers in each of the segments. When one or more companies follow this practice a discriminant or regression analysis would not be able to identify purchasers for the different brands because the buyers for each brand are aggregated even though they may belong in different market segments.

A next logical question is: What might we do to obtain more meaningful results on the subject? We would suggest attacking the problem as follows:

1 Determine what products or brands appeal which set of needs, wants, and desires by the following two-stage procedures. First, apply multivariate analytical techniques to similarity data, i.e., that data obtained by asking the consumers what products or brands they consider similar; then determine homogeneous groups (=clusters) of consumers that perceive the market in a similar manner, i.e., that see the same set of products as being similar. Second, for each of the homogeneous groups again use multivariate techniques to cluster products that are perceived to be similar. Then find out what basic set of needs are being met by each cluster of products. The works of Barnette and Stefflre,[31] Green, Carmone, and Robinson,[32] and Green, Carmone, and Fox[33] are significant contributions in this direction.

2 At this point it is proposed that preference data from the consumers be incorporated into the analysis, i.e., the data obtained by asking the consumer which product(s) he prefers. The preference data, in conjunction with the similarity data, provide a method of determining an ideal point for *each* individual in the homogeneous group obtained in the previous analysis. The ideal point for an individual would represent a product whose characteristics would be most preferred by the individual.[34] The ideal point for an individual would also serve an additional function as a reference point for determining how closely other sets of needs, represented by the clusters of products, match the needs of the individual. The degree to which the individual's needs and the needs being served by any cluster of products coincide should be an inverse function of the distance of the cluster to the ideal point, i.e., the more similar the two sets of needs the shorter the distance between that cluster and the individual's ideal point. Finally we should cluster the ideal points within each of the homogeneous groups. It would then be appropriate to determine if certain characteristics could meaningfully describe the consumers in each of these groups. This information would, of course, be used in determining future strategy for marketing to these segments.

It should be noted that the current approach takes into account differences in individuals' needs whereas previous work in this area has aggregated individuals over the entire market making it impossible to identify how different products or even the same product is related to individuals' differing needs.

The advantage of this approach is two-fold; first, we can study the basic needs of the consumers as they are currently being served by the market and, in doing so, we make no restrictions on the number or interdependence of the needs each brand can service; second, we can incorporate information on the marketing programs of the brands under study to determine the differential elasticities for each brand in each of the sub-markets.

[31]Norman L. Barnett and Volney J. Stefflre, "An Empirical Approach to the Development of New Products," unpublished manuscript, 1967.

[32]Paul E. Green, Frank J. Carmone, and Patrick J. Robinson, *Analysis of Marketing Behavior Using Nonmetric Scaling and Related Techniques,* Technical Monograph (Interim). Marketing Service Institute, March 1968.

[33]Same reference as Footnote 30.

[34]Green, Carmone and Fox, *op. cit.*

SUMMARY

In summary, although the concept of market segmentation has captured the imagination of marketers, the results of studies to date have not been very encouraging. Univariate studies on demographic, objective and psychological factors related to consumer behavior have on the whole leaned toward indicating that product choice cannot be predicted from these types of variables.

However, in recent months a series of multivariate studies have emerged that indicate a real potential for a better understanding of the concept of market segmentation.

13

Expanding the Scope of Segmentation Research

Nariman K. Dhalla
Winston H. Mahatoo

For segmentation research to be truly operational and profitable, it must cover more of the total marketing problem. This means not only obtaining more product-specific measures—including psychographics, communications behavior, attitudes, and usage—but also doing research to determine the response elasticities of the various segments to the firm's marketing plans.

Only if these goals are accomplished can management evaluate the profitability of its segmentation strategy.

Market segmentation helps the firm gear a specific product to the likes or requirements of a particular target group. For many companies, it is far better to capture bigger pieces of fewer markets than to scramble about for a smaller share of every market in sight.

The segmentation concept would be more meaningful to management if research were to cover the entire scope of the problem. This means the inclusion in the initial survey of product-specific measures on both psychographics and communications behavior in addition to the standard attitudinal and usage data. After the segments have been selected, a second-phase research should be conducted to estimate the response elasticities of different submarkets to the firm's communication mix. In this way, management will be in a firm position to evaluate the profitability of the segmentation strategy.

Most of the research undertaken at present does not adopt this two-fold approach. Even the initial survey is often unsatisfactory. In some cases, the criteria employed for grouping consumers are so general that they cannot discriminate among users of various brands within a product category. In other cases, these bases are so specific that they ignore the different nuances of consumer behavior and thus are not very helpful for developing marketing strategies.

A brief review of the published literature on

Reprinted from *Journal of Marketing*, vol. 40, pp. 34–41, American Marketing Association, April 1976. At the time of writing, Nariman K. Dhalla was associate research director in charge of economic and econometric research, J. Walter Thompson Company, New York City. Winston H. Mahatoo was professor of marketing at MacMaster University, Hamilton, Ontario, Canada.

the subject brings these problems out clearly and sets the stage for a detailed discussion of the proposed two-phase approach. A case history from the food industry illustrates the usefulness of this procedure.

PITFALLS IN EXISTING METHODS

As a rule, markets have been divided on the basis of two types of descriptor variables.[1]

1 *General variables,* which classify consumers by broad characteristics, such as demographics, personality traits, or life styles
2 *Situation-specific variables,* which group consumers on some pattern related to consumption, such as frequency of usage, brand loyalty, product benefits, or "perceptual maps"

Although both types of variables have proved useful to marketers, they also have certain drawbacks, as discussed below.

General Variables

Demographics provided the earliest basis for segmentation. Because of the severe limitations of demographics, however, many marketers turned to psychology and began to apply some well-established clinical tests. The Edwards Personal Preference Schedule, the Gordon Personal Profile, the California Personality Inventory, MMPI, and Cattell's 16-Personality Factor Inventory, among others, have all been used in a marketing context. The results have been disappointing.[2] These instruments were originally designed to measure major personality traits that underlie such psycho-social phenomena as racial prejudice, marital incompatibility, or proneness to commit suicide. It is a different story to use them to predict whether a shopper would buy a particular brand of toilet paper[3] or prefer a certain type of design on the package. The items that tend to discover psychological stability or imbalance do not have much relevance for mundane activities related to marketing.

Equally ineffective have been most attempts to use market-oriented sociological measures such as inner- and other-directedness,[4] self-actualization concepts,[5] cognitive needs and styles,[6] and activity-interest-opinion (AIO) items dealing with leisure, work, and consumption.[7] No doubt, the vast amount of research in these areas has led to deep insights into the basic processes of consumer behavior. In a majority of cases, however, the groups are far too broad to discriminate among users of different brands within a product category.

Sometimes such segments may even turn out to be misleading. A personality trait or a life style measure in its generalized form may not be related at all to the product under consideration. A buyer may be price conscious in making routine decisions but will still purchase the most expensive brand of wine or perfume. Similarly, an individual may perceive himself to be aggressive and act as such

[1]Ronald E. Frank, William F. Massy, and Yoram Wind, *Market Segmentation* (Englewood Cliffs, N.J.: Prentice-Hall, 1972), pp. 26–89.

[2]Harold H. Kassarjian, "Personality and Consumer Behavior: A Review," *Journal of Marketing Research,* Vol. 8 (November 1971), pp. 409–418.

[3]Advertising Research Foundation, *Are There Consumer Types?* (New York, 1964).

[4]Harold H. Kassarjian, "Social Character and Differential Preference for Mass Communication," *Journal of Marketing Research,* Vol. 2 (May 1965), pp. 146–153. See also, Arch G. Woodside, "Social Character, Product Use, and Advertising Appeals," *Journal of Advertising Research,* Vol. 8 (December 1968), pp. 31–35.

[5]B. Curtis Hamm and Edward W. Cundiff, "Self-Actualization and Product Perception," *Journal of Marketing Research,* Vol. 6 (November 1969), pp. 470–472.

[6]Stuart U. Rich and Subhash C. Jain, "Social Class and Life Cycle as Predictors of Shopping Behavior," *Journal of Marketing Research,* Vol. 5 (February 1968), pp. 41–49. See also, John Wilding and Raymond A. Bauer, "Consumer Goals and Reactions to a Communications Source," *Journal of Marketing Research,* Vol. 5 (February 1968), pp. 73–77.

[7]William D. Wells and Douglas J. Tigert, "Activities, Interests and Opinions," *Journal of Advertising Research,* Vol. 11 (August 1971), pp. 27–35.

in the office and at home, but he may never choose to express this aggressiveness in his driving behavior or in the type of car he buys.[8]

Situation-Specific Variables

Realizing the futility of adopting wholesale the concepts developed in the social sciences, marketing researchers recently have turned to certain situation-specific descriptors.

The segment that has the most intuitive appeal is the one that distinguishes between *heavy and light users.* But even here the findings have not been encouraging, because not all heavy consumers seek the same kinds of benefits from a product category. For example, heavy coffee drinkers can be divided into two groups: those who drink private brands because cost is an important factor, and those who drink premium brands because taste has greater significance. Obviously, these two groups, although they are both members of the "heavy half" segment, are not equally good prospects for any one brand; nor can they be expected to react favorably to the same advertising claims.[9] Similarly, some products may be heavily used for different reasons. For example, one segment uses a mouthwash to prevent sore throats, while another uses it to eliminate bad breath. Should the two groups have different life styles, the picture presented by the "heavy users" will be a mixture of the two.

Brand loyalty is another favored basis of segmentation, but its effectiveness is also reduced by confounding factors. Loyalty need not be based solely on high satisfaction with the brand. It may be due to sheer force of habit or to a desire to reduce risk associated with the purchase of unknown items.[10] Furthermore, instead of being confined to a single brand, it may extend to two or more brands in the consumer's "evoked set."[11] Because of this lack of within-segment homogeneity, it is not surprising to find that loyal customers do not, as a rule, differ from switchers either in their demographic and psychographic traits, or in their sensitivity to marketing strategies such as pricing, dealing, and retail advertising.[12]

In view of the lackluster performance of these "a priori" classifications, many researchers have turned to "natural" groupings by letting the figures speak for themselves. Thanks to the ready availability of computer software, multivariate methods can be used to extract segments latent in the data. *Benefit segmentation* is a good example of this approach. It uses statistical techniques to group respondents on the basis of the importance they attach to certain combinations of rational, sensory, and emotional benefits expected from the product.

This method is a great improvement over earlier attempts. On several occasions, it has proved valuable for developing new advertising copy or for suggesting alternative marketing strategy, such as the changes in product formulation.[13] Even here, however, the results are not always fruitful. By relying solely on natural groupings, the researcher runs the risk of arriving at purely spurious clusters, since most of the multivariate techniques are simply

[8]Joseph Pernica, "The Second Generation of Market Segmentation Studies: An Audit of Buying Motivations," in *Life Style and Psychographics,* William D. Wells, ed. (Chicago: American Marketing Assn., 1974), pp. 279–313.

[9]Russell I. Haley, "Benefit Segmentation: A Decision-Oriented Research Tool," *Journal of Marketing,* Vol. 32 (July 1968), pp. 30–35; and Haley, "Beyond Benefit Segmentation," *Journal of Advertising Research,* Vol. 11 (August 1971), pp. 3–8.

[10]Scott M. Cunningham, "Perceived Risk and Brand Loyalty," in *Risk Taking and Information Handling in Consumer Behavior,* Donald F. Cox, ed. (Boston: Graduate School of Business Administration, Harvard University, 1967), pp. 507–523.

[11]John A. Howard and Jagdish N. Sheth, *The Theory of Buyer Behavior* (New York: John Wiley & Sons, 1969), pp. 211–212.

[12]Ronald E. Frank and William F. Massy, "Market Segmentation and the Effectiveness of a Brand's Price and Dealing Policies," *Journal of Business,* Vol. 38 (April 1965), pp. 186–200.

[13]Same reference as footnote 9.

data-reducing tools and are not based on theoretical concepts of what the segments should look like. This is particularly true of low-salience, frequently purchased products. The brand-benefit profiles often are not sharp enough to permit successful segmentation analysis. Even when meaningful groups are extracted from the data, the benefits in most research studies are confined primarily to product attributes and do not cover the crucial areas of psychographics and communications behavior. Hence, one cannot be sure that a particular cluster selected will help increase sales.

Wilkie attempted to validate this method of segmentation using the Columbia University Buyer Behavior Panel.[14] He found that the classification based on intentions to buy predicted much better subsequent brand purchases than segments derived from the importance that consumers attached to certain sets of product characteristics.

Closely allied to benefit segmentation is *perceptual mapping.* Here a "map" is prepared of an individual's perceptions of competitive brands on certain product attributes. Then respondents with similar perceptual maps are grouped together. Finally, within each such group further segments are developed on the basis of preference scores. By combining both perceptual and preference data to analyze consumer behavior, the researcher can sometimes obtain unexpected insights into the psychological processes that consumers use for choosing brands.

Like benefit segmentation, however, this method has certain drawbacks. Frequently, the dimensions of the perceptual space cannot be easily interpreted. Also, the segments are derived from perceptions and preferences, and they totally ignore psychographics and communications behavior. Consequently, there is no guarantee that a favorable sales response will result from the marketing strategy suggested by the mapping procedure.

AN ATTEMPT AT SYNTHESIS

The poor performance of many segmentation criteria tested so far can be attributed to the fact that too often researchers are anxious to find a magic formula that will profitably segment the market in all cases and under all circumstances. As with the medieval alchemists looking for the philosopher's stone, this search is bound to end in vain. There is no single algorithm that can be employed across all market studies. Each case must be viewed as a unique and potentially different situation.[15]

Broad Classifications

A well-designed segmentation study, therefore, does not depend solely on one criterion for grouping consumers. It is flexible enough that one can examine the results from two or more alternative bases. These bases are very general, and it is within them that the segments are later developed. The selection of such broad classifications is governed by conceptual considerations that have bearing on the product under investigation.

In many cases, the theories of attitude reinforcement and attitude change, as formulated by social psychologists, can be of help. Since an individual's reaction to a brand is primarily a function of his overall predisposition, one possible preliminary step would be to have a broad "a priori" classification based on some attitudinal range. The extensive work of Sherif, Sherif, and Nebergall in this area can be effectively used here.[16] Adapting their approach, it may be hypothesized that a buyer,

[14]William L. Wilkie, "An Empirical Analysis of Alternative Bases of Market Segmentation" (Ph.D. diss., Stanford University, Graduate School of Business, December 1970).

[15]Joel P. Baumwoll, "Segmentation Research: The Baker vs. The Cookie Maker," in *1974 Combined Proceedings,* Ronald C. Curhan, ed. (Chicago: American Marketing Assn., 1975), pp. 3–20.

[16]Carolyn W. Sherif, Muzafer Sherif, and Roger E. Nebergall, *Attitude and Attitude Change: The Social Judgment Involvement Approach* (Philadelphia: Saunders, 1965).

in order to simplify his choice process, is likely to take any one of the following three positions with respect to the brand:

- Latitude of acceptance
- Latitude of rejection
- Latitude of noncommitment

In the noncommitment category, where ego-involvement is low, the consumer will accept without much difficulty a wide discrepancy between his own views and the communications stimuli (e.g., advertising message, point-of-sale display, salesperson's recommendation, etc.). On the other hand, if the brand falls in the latitude of rejection, such a message will be confronted with the mental roadblock of selective exposure, selective perception, and selective retention. In fact, the influence of this latitude is so strong that even when the communication per se does not deviate from the recipient's own point of view, it is likely to be perceived as being farther from his position than it is in reality (contrast effect). By the same token, there is a strong probability of an assimilation effect in the latitude of acceptance, and advertising or any other communication will be interpreted in a more favorable light than the contents justify. This behavior is on line with the consonance theory, and it has been confirmed by empirical research in both social psychology[17] and marketing.[18]

These findings suggest that the emphasis in research should be directed toward those consumers who are in the latitude of acceptance (mainly current users) or latitude of noncommitment (primarily other consumers who are not against the brand and may purchase it if properly persuaded). It is generally advisable to ignore those falling within the latitude of rejection. Since these consumers violently dislike the brand, the communications stimuli will be either censored from the mind or twisted out of shape.

This grouping is merely an illustration of how consumers can be clustered on some theoretical grounds. To cover all bases, the same study may also explore other product-specific classifications, such as heavy users versus light users, opinion leaders versus followers, and the like. Much will depend on the area under investigation.

For the information of a marketing strategy, however, all such classifications are far too general. Within these broad dimensions, the prospects need to be examined in greater detail—much more than is done in most segmentation studies. It is not sufficient to ask the usual product/brand questions, such as volume of usage, switching patterns, demographic profiles, and brand imagery. Information must also be gathered on psychographics and communications behavior. Since these two sectors tend to be ignored or glossed over in research, they are treated in some detail here.

Psychographics

Psychographics are crucial for discovering both the overt and the latent psycho-social motives that so often spell the difference between acceptance or rejection of the brand. However, the measures developed are meaningful only when they are situation-specific and not of a generalized nature. For example, instead of searching for the general trait of self-confidence, it is better to determine the extent to which consumers are self-confident in evaluating different brands within the product category. Similarly, anxiety as measured in personality tests does not have much meaning for businesspeople, but anxiety as connected with the physical or social risks involved in the purchase of a brand can have significant implications for marketing. The three key areas of psychographics are value orientations, role perceptions, and buying style.

[17]Muzafer Sherif and Carl I. Hovland, *Social Judgment: Assimilation and Contrast Effects in Communication and Attitude Change* (New Haven, Conn.: Yale University Press, 1961).

[18]J. Shable, "The Effects of Message Discrepancy on Attitude Change" (M.A. thesis, Ohio State University, 1968).

Value Orientations The term *value* is used here in the manner employed by social scientists, namely, as "an enduring belief that a particular mode of conduct or that a particular end state of existence is personally and socially preferable to alternative modes of conduct or end states of existence."[19] Thus defined, an individual's value system canalizes motivations, tells him what attitudes he should hold, and provides standards by which evaluations are made and goals are chosen.

Role Perceptions These refer to the manner in which an individual behaves in order to give positive expression to the type of person he is or perceives himself to be. This aspect of psychographics is important because brands today are the most universally acknowledged symbols of roles, and very often they are purchased not so much for their physical functions as for the impressions they convey about their owners.[20]

Buying Style This is the extension of value orientations and role perceptions to one special milieu, namely, shopping behavior. The premise is that there will be differences in buyers' reactions even when they are confronted with the same purchasing environment, and to some extent this is a consequence of the differences in buying style.[21]

Again it is essential to emphasize specificity. Since these three attributes tend to vary from one product category to another, the criteria used to measure them must focus on the product under investigation. Examples of these criteria with reference to a food product are given in Table 1.

[19]Milton Rokeach, "The Role of Values in Public Opinion Research," *Public Opinion Quarterly*, Vol. 32 (Winter 1968-69), pp. 547–559.

[20]Sydney J. Levy, "Symbols by Which We Buy," in *Advancing Marketing Efficiency*, Lynn H. Stockman, ed. (Chicago: American Marketing Assn., 1965), pp. 222–243.

[21]George S. Day, *Buyer Attitudes and Brand Choice Behavior* (New York: Free Press), pp. 75–79.

Table 1 Typical Examples of Value Orientations, Role Perceptions, and Buying Style, with Special Reference to a Food Product

Value Orientations

- Weight watcher—pays attention to calorie content of food
- Fond of cooking—loves to prepare food from basic ingredients
- Time saver—appreciates convenience foods
- Nutrition-prone—emphasizes salutary aspects of food
- Health-conscious—is concerned about the harmful effects of food
- Connoisseur—is fond of gourmet or exotic dishes
- Pro-ecology—dislikes chemical ingredients

Role Perceptions

- Social entertainer—frequently invites friends and neighbors to snacks or meals
- Home-oriented—spends a lot of time in the kitchen
- Home-avoider—wants to be emancipated and to escape from the drudgeries of the kitchen
- Creative—craves preparing novel dishes and finding new and interesting ways of serving food
- Achievement seeker—measures success on the basis of recognition obtained for skill in culinary activities

Buying Style

(related specifically to product type under study)

- Repeat buyer—sticks to the same brand through force of habit
- Loyal—repurchase decision is motivated by satisfaction with the brand
- Cautious—is high on "perceived risk," confining selection to well-known brands of large companies
- Cognitive—is sensitive to rational claims, evaluating brand on basis of weight and ingredients
- Value-inclined—is willing to pay premium for quality
- Impulsive—tends to buy on the spur of the moment
- Economy-minded—prefers low-priced to high-priced lines, or giant-sized to small packages
- Independent—notices very little difference between brands and switches a lot
- Time-pressured—is anxious to finish shopping as soon as possible
- Conformist—selects brands that friends and neighbors buy
- Hedonist—is affected by sensory benefits, such as attractive packaging
- Innovator—is eager to try new brands
- Variety seeker—changes brands for the sake of variety or novelty
- Bargain hunter—is susceptible to deals, coupons, and premiums, and shops around a lot to compare prices

Communications Behavior

To complete the segmentation study, it is necessary to explore the communications behavior of the prospects. The three main categories studied are: media habits, advertising, and decision-making process. (The types of questions that may be asked are shown in Table 2.)

Information on *media habits* may serve as a guide for the selection of media and of a particular vehicle within each medium. This is especially relevant when no one segment is large enough to be profitable. The advertiser can then aim at two or more segments with different appeals in different media, and avoid the danger of overlapping.

As regards *advertising,* some playback about prospects' reactions can be helpful in the effective execution of copy. The creative department is then able to use situational approaches that generate empathy and tune in well on the consumer's wavelength.

Equally important is knowledge about the prospects' *decision-making* process. Very often, consumers may be persuaded but may still feel the need to reinforce their judgment through personal interaction with their peers. It is then in the interest of the advertiser to direct the appeal to the opinion leaders.[22]

In certain cases, the "source" or corporate image can also play a major role. Consumers often select one brand over others because of their favorable predisposition toward its producer. If they like what the company stands for, then they choose to do business with it rather than with its competitors.[23]

Table 2 Typical Examples of the Area Covered by Communications Behavior

Media Habits
- Readership of representative newspapers and magazines.
- Preference for certain types of television programs.
- Favorite time periods for watching television and listening to the radio.

Advertising
- Amount of attention paid to advertising of the product category in various media.
- Level of confidence in brand advertising.
- Reaction to situational elements used in advertising.

Decision-Making Process
- Importance of advertising versus recommendations received by word of mouth or from salespeople.
- Role of opinion leaders in influencing brand selection.
- Perception of the manufacturer on such attributes as competence, trust, power, and likability. (The first two characteristics are important when purchase decisions are influenced by problem-solving needs, while the last two play a major role when psychosocial needs are in the forefront.)[a]

[a]Raymond A. Bauer, "Source Effect and Persuasibility: A New Look," in *Risk Taking and Information Handling in Consumer Behavior*, Donald E. Cox, ed. (Boston: Graduate School of Business Administration, Harvard University, 1967), pp. 559-578.

Development of Strategy

Segmentation study of this nature covers a very broad area. At first glance, the tabulation and analysis of the data would seem to be an almost superhuman task. Fortunately, it is possible to extract a few meaningful segments within the broad "a priori" classification by applying multivariate techniques (e.g., Q-type factor analysis) to most of the attitudinal psychographic, and communications-behavior measures.[24]

In most cases, because of media and budget constraints, only one segment is chosen for proper brand positioning. However, this does not rule out the selection of two or more segments, as long as they can be profitably exploited by the marketer. For example,

[22]For actual phrasing of questions, see questionnaire in the appendix of Elihu Katz and Paul F. Lazarsfeld, *Personal Influence* (New York: Free Press, 1955), pp. 340–352.

[23]Nariman K. Dhalla, "Look to Your Corporate Image," *Canadian Business*, September 1971, pp. 58–66.

[24]Nariman K. Dhalla, "How to Find a Winning Advertising Strategy," *Canadian Business*, November 1970, pp. 24–32, and December 1970, pp. 31–34.

through product and distribution differentiation, a firm may promote a low-priced line for one segment and a high-priced line for another. Similarly, one segment, which is price-conscious, may be cultivated by means of selective direct-mail couponing; while the other, which is sensitive to emotional appeals, may be won over by advertising that is in tune with its value orientations and role perceptions.

Second-Phase Research: How Much to Spend on Marketing?

Segmentation research by no means stops with the first survey. The financial aspects now enter the picture. Some guidelines are required on the amount of money that should be spent on marketing strategies so as to optimize profits.

One of the cardinal axioms of microeconomics is that profits are maximized when a firm allocates its expenditures in such a way that the incremental returns are equal for all subsets of markets. More money is spent on segments with greater potential until diminishing returns bring the incremental response down to the level for the less desirable segments.[25] In actual practice, budget constraint stops the process before equality can be achieved, and the less desirable segments are almost always ignored. However, even for a single submarket, the most advantageous procedure continues to be the same: the allocation of the marketing budget in such a way that marginal costs equal marginal revenues.

Consequently, as Frank and Massy point out, *"One crucial criterion for determining the desirability of segmenting a market along any particular dimension is whether the different submarkets have different elasticities with respect to the price and promotional policies of a firm."*[26] The same idea was expressed by Wendell Smith two decades ago: "In the language of the economist, segmentation is *disaggregative* in its effects and tends to bring about recognition of several demand schedules where only one was recognized before."[27]

This vital information on elasticity cannot be obtained from the first survey. It is necessary to know for each segment the percentage change in sales as a result of a percentage change in some element of the marketing mix, such as price or advertising. This calls for a *second-phase research program* in which weight tests are conducted for a certain period of time in the marketplace. For example, instead of having the same level of advertising or sales promotion all over the country, a few test markets are selected where controlled experimentation is carried out at different levels of expenditure. Data are collected not only on sales but also on extraneous elements that may affect purchase (e.g., competitive activities, socioeconomic differences, etc.) in order to factor out their influence mathematically. After all the results are in, multiple regression equations are fitted to obtain the elasticities of the variables tested, so that one segment may be meaningfully compared against the other.[28]

Generally, three options are open for performing the second-phase research. The most convenient way is to carry out the first segmentation study among members of a nationwide consumer panel, provided the sample size is sufficiently large to avoid gross instabilities by subcells. The segmentation strategy can later by validated by analyzing the purchases of selected segments of panel members

[25]Joan Robinson, *The Economics of Imperfect Competition* (London: Macmillan & Co., 1954), pp. 179–188.

[26]Same reference as footnote 12.

[27]Wendell R. Smith, "Product Differentiation and Market Segmentation as Alternative Marketing Strategies," *Journal of Marketing,* Vol. 21 (July 1956), pp. 3–8.

[28]It is not possible in this article to discuss controlled experimentation and the development of marketing models therefrom. This topic is covered in Seymour Banks, *Exprimentation in Marketing* (New York: McGraw-Hill Book Co., 1965). More detailed analysis may be found in William G. Cochran and Gertrude M. Cox, *Experimental Designs*, 2nd ed. (New York: John Wiley & Sons, 1957); and Karl A. Fox, *Intermediate Economic Statistics* (New York: John Wiley & Sons, 1968).

at different levels of marketing expenditures.

If no panel is available, a second option is to conduct the first survey with a large, well-dispersed random sample and then to contact the same respondents again after a certain lapse of time, preferably a year. On the second interview, questions are confined to attudinal data and brand usage, on the assumption that the interviewing period is too short to expect any changes in psychographic or communications-behavior variables.

When it is impossible or undesirable to go back to the same people, then an attitude and usage survey should be conducted with the same type of sample as in the first study. Although the respondents must be grouped anew into original segments, only those questions that were particularly discriminating in the first research (e.g., the ones with high loadings in the Q-type factor analysis) need to be asked.

AN ILLUSTRATION

The above procedure is now illustrated with the case history of a food product that had been promoted strictly on the basis of its strong and distinctive taste. Sales had been stagnant for some time, and the company needed to win over a portion of nonusers. A segmentation study was conducted, and the Q-type analysis of those respondents who fell within the latitude of noncommitment revealed the following five clusters: impulse buyers, social conformists, bargain hunters, time savers, and health promoters.

The decision was made to ignore the first four segments even though they represented about 70% of the "neutral" consumers. The impulse buyers were very volatile and did not provide a firm base for building the brand franchise. The social conformists were worrying too much about group norms, and it was unrealistic to expect that the brand's distinctive taste could win universal appeal. The thrifty were essentially bargain hunters, and it was not in the company's interest to compete on price. The time savers were primarily oriented toward convenience in food preparation, a benefit that the brand was not able to provide.

On the other hand, the health promoters held great promise. The housewives in this segment took very seriously their role as custodians of family health and well-being. Their brand selection was governed almost toally by this value orientation. Now it so happened that the strong taste of the brand was mainly due to certain "natural" ingredients, and the firm had a clear edge over competition in this respect. Furthermore, the media habits of health promoters were different from those of loyal users. The latter were primarily heavy viewers of situation comedy shows on television. The former, on the other hand, were fond of documentaries and also tended to be avid readers of certain magazines whose editorial content was slanted toward family health and well-being. As a result, the danger of overlapping of exposures was not serious.

New advertising was built around nutrition, wholesomeness, and natural ingredients. At the same time, in order to retain loyal users, the old 30-second spots, emphasizing strong taste, were continued as before on situation comedy shows.

The company already had on hand from a previous experiment on loyal users the following information on the diminishing marginal effects of advertising on sales:

$$Q_1 = 5.751 + 5.36A_1 - 1.2(A_1)^2 \quad (1)$$

where Q_1 = Quantity sold in millions of units
A_1 = Advertising expenditures in millions of dollars

(The subscript '1' refers to the first segment, that is, loyal users. The equation also included other exogenous variables, such as competitive advertising and number of prospects, but to simplify the exposition their estimated values have been incorporated into the intercept.)

An attempt was made to obtain a similar type of relationship for health promoters. A media-weight test was initiated in certain markets. and relevant data were collected from the respondents who fell within this segment. The results were then projected to the total universe to derive the following:

$$Q_2 = 3.9981 + 3.732A_2 - 1.24(A_2)^2 \qquad (2)$$

The gross margin per unit for the brand was \$0.50: the difference between the factory selling price of \$1.50 and the variable cost of \$1.00, excluding advertising.

Suppose management had only \$2 million available for advertising and wanted to know how much to spend on each segment to obtain the highest profit contribution for the brand, minus fixed costs. The problem could be solved by using the standard maximizing procedures found in differential calculus for constrained optima. The formula is:

$$P = M(Q_1 + Q_2) - A_1 - A_2 + \lambda (A_1 + A_2 - 2) \qquad (3)$$

where P = Profit contribution, excluding fixed costs, in millions of dollars
M = Gross margin (0.50)
λ = Lagrangian multiplier used for the calculation of constrained optima

The results obtained were as follows:

Variable	Loyal users ($MM)	Health promoters ($MM)	Total of the two segments ($MM)
Advertising	1.35	0.65	2.00
Unit sales	10.80	5.90	16.70
Profit contribution	4.05	2.30	6.35

If the company had spent the entire \$2 million of advertising on the loyal users, the profit contribution of the brand, according to Equation 1, would have been \$3.84 million, or \$2.51 million less than the amount generated by tapping health promoters. Segmentation research in this case may be deemed a success. Of course, as in all equations based on market experiments, the results are only approximations, subject to a margin of random error. Also, such weight tests are time consuming. Yet this approach helps to provide a fairly good yardstick for the profitability of a segmentation strategy.

SUMMARY AND CONCLUSIONS

A review of the segmentation criteria currently in use reveals the existence of two schools of thought: the behaviorally oriented school, which is interested in obtaining insights into the basic processes of consumer behavior, with only secondary consideration given to marketing needs; and the decision-oriented school, which focuses not so much on why there are differences among consumers as on how these differences can be exploited to increase the productivity of the firm's marketing programs.

Real progress can be achieved by fusing the concepts of these two schools. A viable marketing strategy can be formulated when the segmentation study examines all facets of consumer behavior as related to the product category under investigation. Also, the research must not stop with the first survey. Weight tests should be conducted to estimate the demand schedules of different submarkets.

This second research phase is essential because the theoretical route to profit maximization lies in equating marginal revenue with marginal costs. To obtain data on marginal revenue, it is necessary to have equations that show the response elasticities of different segments to the firm's marketing strategies. Only then is the firm in a position to judge the profitability of cultivating each submarket—and this, after all, is the object of all exercises in segmentation.

14

Market Segmentation: A Strategic Management Tool

Richard M. Johnson

In the past, marketing research has largely been restricted to tactical questions. However, with the advent of new techniques, marketing research can contribute directly to the development of strategic alternatives to current product marketing plans.

Like motivation research in the late 1950's, market segmentation is receiving much attention in research circles. Although this term evokes the idea of cutting up a market into little pieces, the real role of such research is more basic and potentially more valuable. In this discussion *market segmentation analysis* refers to examination of the structure of a market as perceived by consumers, preferably using a geometric spatial model, and to forecasting the intensity of demand for a potential product positioned anywhere in the space.

The purpose of such a study, as seen by a marketing manager, might be:

1 To learn how the brands or products in a class are perceived with respect to strengths, weaknesses, similarities, etc.

2 To learn about consumers' desires, and how these are satisfied or unsatisfied by the current market.

3 To integrate these findings strategically, determining the greatest opportunities for new brands or products and how a product or its image should be modified to produce the greatest sales gain.

From the position of a marketing research technician, each of these three goals translates into a separate technical problem:

1 To construct a product space, a geometric representation of consumers' perceptions of products or brands in a category.

2 To obtain a density distribution by positioning consumers' ideal points in the same space.

3 To construct a model which predicts preferences of groups of consumers toward new or modified products.

This discussion will focus on each of these three problems in turn, suggesting solutions now available. Solutions to the first two problems can be illustrated with actual data, although currently solutions for the third problem are more tentative. This will not be an exhaustive catalog of techniques, nor is this the only way of structuring the general problem of forecasting consumer demand for new or modified products.

CONSTRUCTING THE PRODUCT SPACE

A spatial representation or map of a product category provides the foundation on which other aspects of the solution are built. Many equally useful techniques are available for constructing product spaces which require different assumptions and possess different properties. The following is a list of useful properties of product spaces which may be used to evaluate alternative techniques:

1 *Metric:* distances between products in space should relate to perceived similarity between them.

Reprinted from *Journal of Marketing Research*, vol. 8, pp. 13–18, American Marketing Association, February 1971. At the time of writing, the author was a vice president of Market Facts, Inc.

2 *Identification:* directions in the space should correspond to identified product attributes.

3 *Uniqueness/reliability:* similar procedures applied to similar data should yield similar answers.

4 *Robustness/foolproofness:* procedures should work every time. It should not be necessary to switch techniques or make basic changes in order to cope with each new set of data.

5 *Freedom from improper assumptions:* other things being equal, a procedure that requires fewer assumptions is preferred.

One basic distinction has to do with the kinds of data to be analyzed. Three kinds of data are frequently used.

Similarity/Dissimilarity Data

Here a respondent is not concerned in any obvious way with dimensions or attributes which describe the products judged. He makes global judgments of relative similarity among products, with the theoretical advantage that there is no burden on the researcher to determine in advance the important attributes or dimensions within a product category. Examples of such data might be: (1) to present triples of products and ask which two are most or least similar, (2) to present pairs of products and ask which pair is most similar, or (3) to rank order *k*-1 products in terms of similarity with *k*th.

Preference Data

Preference data can be used to construct a product space, given assumptions relating preference to distances. For instance, a frequent assumption is that an individual has ideal points in the same space and that product preference is related in some systematic way to distances from his ideal points to his perception of products' locations. As with similarity/dissimilarity data, preference data place no burden on the researcher to determine salient product attributes in advance. Examples of preference data which might lead to a product space are: (1) paired comparison data, (2) rank orders of preference, or (3) generalized overall ratings (as on a 1 to 9 scale).

Attribute Data

If the researcher knows in advance important product attributes by which consumers discriminate among products, or with which they form preferences, then he may ask respondents to describe products on scales relating to each attribute. For instance, they may use rating scales describing brands of beer with respect to price vs. quality, heaviness vs. lightness, or smoothness vs. bitterness.

In addition to these three kinds of data, *procedures* can be *metric* or *nonmetric*. Metric procedures make assumptions about the properties of data, as when in computing a mean one assumes that the difference between ratings of values one and two is the same as that between two and three, etc. Nonmetric procedures make fewer assumptions about the nature of the data: these are usually techniques in which the only operations on data are comparisons such as "greater than" or "less than." Nonmetric procedures are typically used with data from rank order or paired comparison methods.

Another issue is whether or not a *single product space* will adequately represent all respondents' perceptions. At the extreme, each respondent might require a unique product space to account for aspects of his perceptions. However, one of the main reasons for product spaces' utility is that they summarize a large amount of information in unusually tangible and compact form. Allowing a totally different product space for each respondent would certainly destroy much of the illustrative value of the result. A compromise would be to recognize that respondents might fall naturally into a relatively small number of subgroups with different product perceptions. In this case, a separate product space could be constructed for each subgroup.

Frequently a single product space is assumed to be adequate to account for important aspects of all respondents' *perceptions.* Differences in *preference* are then taken into account by considering such respondent's ideal product to have a unique location in the common product space, and by recognizing that different respondents may weight dimensions uniquely. This was the approach taken in the examples to follow.

Techniques which have received a great deal of use in constructing product spaces include nonmetric multidimensional scaling [3, 7, 8, 12], factor analysis [11], and multiple discriminant analysis [4]. Factor analysis has been available for this purpose for many years, and multidimensional scaling was discussed as early as 1938 [13]. *Nonmetric* multidimensional scaling, a comparatively recent development, has achieved great popularity because of the invention of ingenious computing methods requiring only the most minimal assumptions regarding the nature of the data. Discriminant analysis requires assumptions about the metric properties of data, but it appears to be particularly robust and foolproof in application.

These techniques produce similar results in most practical applications. The technique of multiple discriminant analysis will be illustrated here.

EXAMPLES OF PRODUCT SPACES

Imagine settling on a number of attributes which together account for all of the important ways in which products in a set are seen to differ from each other. Suppose that each product has been rated on each attribute by several people, although each person has not necessarily described more than one product.

Given such data, multiple discriminant analysis is a powerful technique for constructing a spatial model of the product category. First, it finds the weighted combination of attributes which discriminates most among products, maximizing an F-ratio of between-product to within-product variance. The second and subsequent weighted combinations are found which discriminate maximally among products, within the constraint that they all be uncorrelated with one another. Having determined as many discriminating dimensions as possible, average scores can be used to plot products on each dimension. Distances between pairs of products in this space reflect the amount of discrimination between them.[1]

[1]McKeon [10] has shown that multiple discriminant analysis produces the same results as classic (metric) multidimensional scaling of Mahalanobis' distances based on the same data.

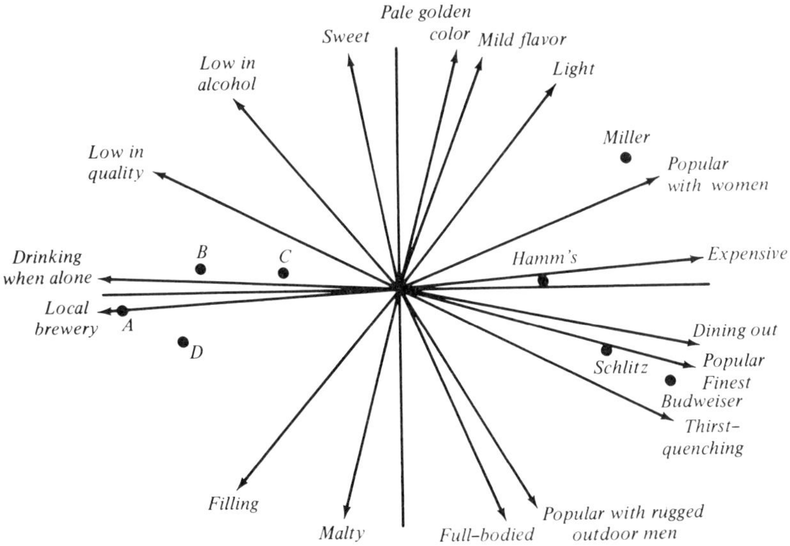

Figure 1 The Chicago beer market.

Figure 1 shows such a space for the Chicago beer market as perceived by members of Market Facts' Consumer Mail Panels in a pilot study, September 1968. Approximately 500 male beer drinkers described 8 brands of beer on each of 35 attributes. The data indicated that a third sizable dimension also existed, but the two dimensions pictured here account for approximately 90% of discrimination among images of these 8 products.

The location of each brand is indicated on these two major dimensions. The horizontal dimension contrasts premium quality on the right with popular price on the left. The vertical dimension reflects relative lightness. In addition, the mean rating of each product on each of the attributes is shown by relative position on each attribute vector. For instance, Miller is perceived as being most popular with women, followed by Budweiser, Schlitz, Hamm's, and four unnamed, popularly priced beers.

As a second example, the same technique was applied to political data. During the weeks immediately preceding the 1968 presidential election, a questionnaire was sent to 1,000 Consumer Mail Panels households. Respondents were asked to agree or disagree with each of 35 political statements on a four-point scale. Topics were Vietnam, law and order, welfare, and other issues felt to be germane to current politics. Respondents also described two preselected political figures, according to their perceptions of each figure's stand on each issue. Discriminant analysis indicated two major dimensions accounting for 86% of the discrimination among 14 political figures.

The liberal vs. conservative dimension is apparent in the data, as shown in Figure 2. The remaining dimension apparently reflects perceived favorability of attitude toward government involvement in domestic and international matters. As in the beer space, it is only necessary to erect perpendiculars to each vec-

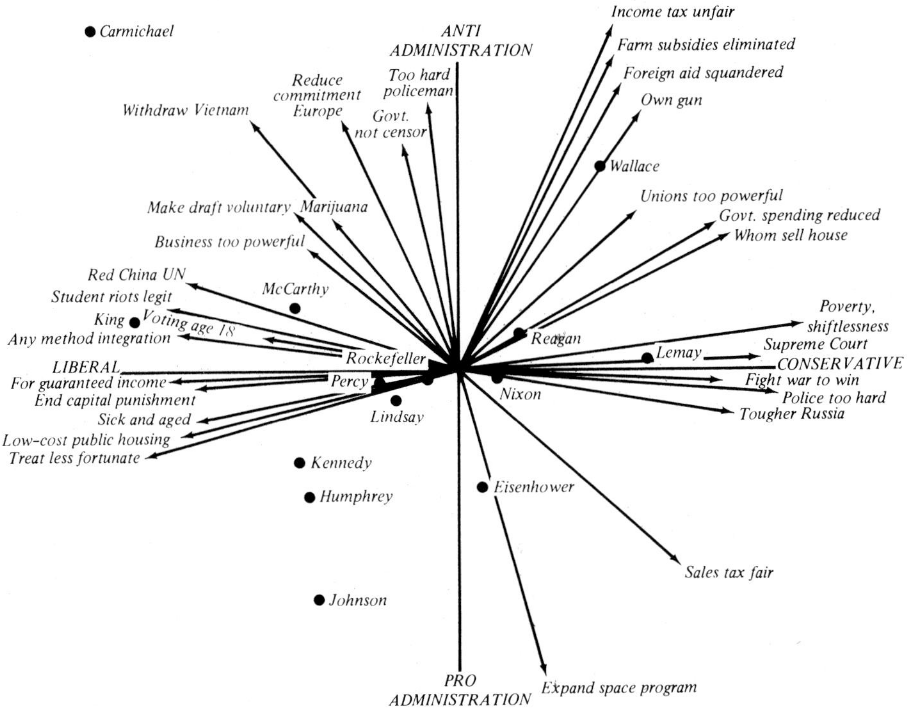

Figure 2 The political space, 1968.

tor to observe each political figure's relative position on each of the 35 issues. Additional details are in [5].

Multiple discriminant analysis is a major competitor of nonmetric multidimensional scaling in constructing product spaces. The principal assumptions which the former requires are that: (1) perceptions be homogeneous across respondents, (2) attribute data be scaled at the interval level (equal intervals on rating scales), (3) attributes be linearly related to one another, and (4) amount of disagreement (error covariance matrix) be the same for each product.

Only the first of these assumptions is required by most nonmetric methods, and some even relax that assumption. However, the space provided by multiple discriminant analysis has the following useful properties:

1 Given customary assumptions of multivariate normality, there is a test of significance for distance (dissimilarity) between any two products.

2 Unlike nonmetric procedures, distances estimated among a collection of products do not depend upon whether or not additional products are included in the analysis. Any of the brands of beer or political figures could have been deleted from the examples and the remaining object locations would have had the same relationships to one another and to the attribute vectors.

3 The technique is reliable and well known, and solutions are unique, since the technique cannot be misled by any local optimum.

OBTAINING THE DISTRIBUTION OF CONSUMER'S IDEAL POINTS

After constructing a product space, the next concern is estimating consumer demand for a product located at any particular point. The demand function over such a space is desired and can be approximated by one of several general approaches.

The first is to locate each person's ideal point in the region of the space implied by his rank ordered preferences. His ideal point would be closest to the product he likes best, second closest to the product he likes second best, etc. There are several procedures which show promise using this approach [2, 3, 7, 8, 12], although difficulties remain in practical execution. This approach has trouble dealing with individuals who behave in a manner contrary to the basic assumptions of the model, as when one chooses products first on the far left side of the space, second on the far right side, and third in the center. Most individuals giving rank orders of preference do display such nonmonotonicity to some extent, understandably producing problems for the application of these techniques.

The second approach involves deducing the number of ideal points at each region in space by using data on whether a product has too much or too little of each attribute. This procedure has not yet been fully explored, but at present seems to be appropriate to the multidimensional case only when strong assumptions about the shape of the ideal point distribution are given.

The third approach is to have each person describe his ideal product, with the same attributes and rating scales as for existing products. If multiple discriminant analysis has been used to obtain a product space, each person's ideal product can then be inserted in the same space.

There are considerable differences between an ideal point location inferred from a rank order of preference and one obtained directly from an attribute rating. To clarify matters, consider a single dimension, heaviness vs. lightness in beer. If a previous mapping has shown that Brands A, B, C, and D are equally spaced on this one dimension, and if a respondent ranks his preferences as B, C, A, and D, then his ideal must lie closer to B than to A or C and closer to C than to A. This narrows the feasible region for his ideal point down to the

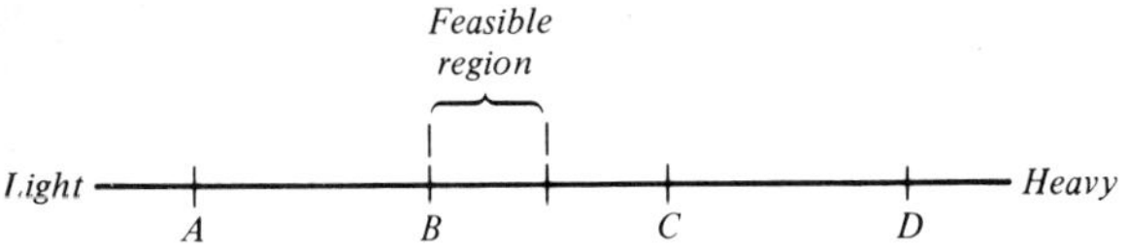

Figure 3 A one-dimensional product space.

area indicated in Figure 3. Had he stated a preference for A, with D second, there would be no logically corresponding position for his ideal point in the space.

However, suppose these products have already been given the following scale positions on a heavy/light dimension: A = 1.0, B = 2.0, C = 3.0, and D = 4.0. If a respondent unambiguously specifies his ideal on this scale at 2.25, his ideal can be put directly on the scale, with no complexities. Of course, it does not follow *necessarily* that his stated rank order of preference will be predictable from the location of his ideal point.

There is no logical reason why individuals must be clustered into market segments. Mathematically, one can cope with the case where hundreds or thousands of individual ideal points are each located in the space. However, it is much easier to approximate such distributions by clustering respondents into groups. Cluster analysis [6] has been used with the present data to put individuals into a few groups with relatively similar product desires (beer) or points of view (politics).

Figure 4 shows an approximation to the density distribution of consumers' ideal points in the Chicago beer market, a "poor man's contour map." Ideal points tended somewhat to group themselves (circles) into clusters. It is not implied that all ideal points lie within the circles, since they are really distributed to some extent throughout the entire space. Circle sizes indicate the relative sizes of clusters, and the center of each is located at the center of its circle.

A representation such as this contains much potentially useful marketing information. For instance, if people can be assumed to prefer products closer to their ideal points, there may be a ready market for a new brand on the lower or "heavy" side of the space, approximately neutral in price/quality. Likewise, there may be opportunities for new brands in the upper middle region, decidedly light and neutral in price/quality. Perhaps popularly priced Brand A will have marketing problems, since this brand is closest to no cluster.

Figure 5 shows a similar representation for the political space, where circles represent

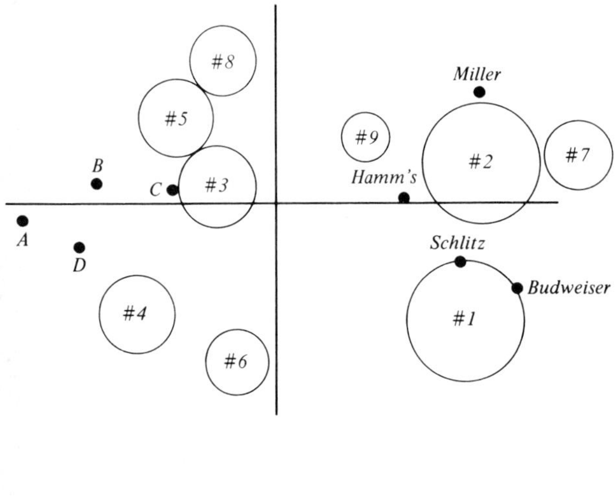

Figure 4 Distribution of ideal points in product space.

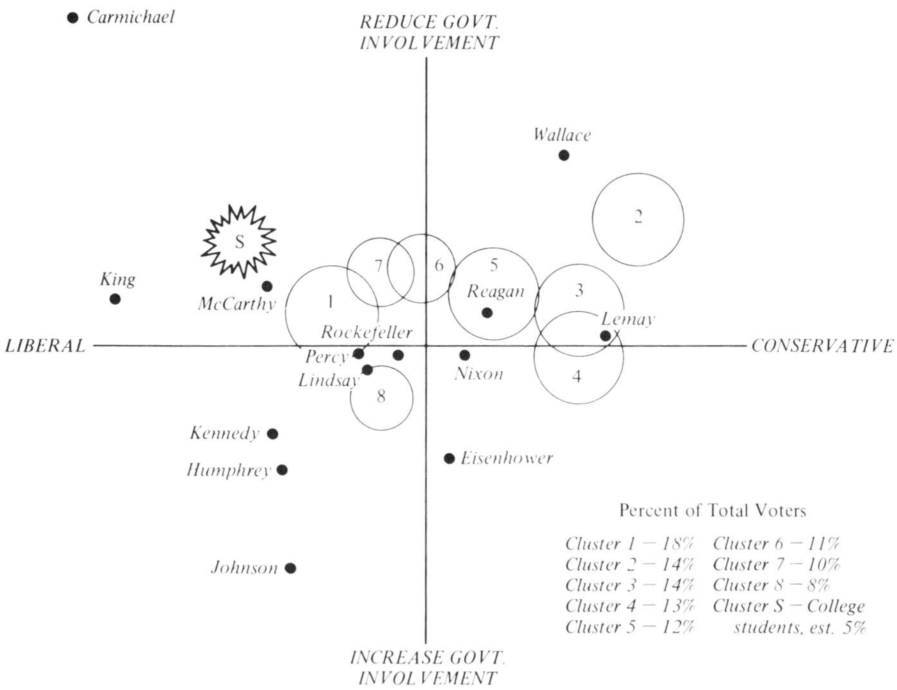

Figure 5 Voter segment positions relative to political figures.

concentrations of voters' points. These are not ideal points, but rather personally held positions on political issues. Clusters on the left side of the space intended to vote mostly for Humphrey and those on the right for Nixon in the 1968 election. Throughout the space, the percentage voting Republican increases generally from left to right.

It may be surprising that the center of the ideal points lies considerably to the right of that of the political figures. One possible explanation is that this study dealt solely with positions on *issues*, so matters of style or personality did not enter the definition of the space. It is entirely possible that members of clusters one and eight, the most liberal, found Nixon's position on issues approximately as attractive as Humphrey's, but they voted for Humphrey on the basis of preference for style, personality, or political party. Likewise, members of cluster two might have voted strongly for Wallace, given his position, but he received only 14% of this cluster's vote. He may have been rejected on the basis of other qualities. The clusters are described in more detail in [5].

A small experiment was undertaken to test the validity of this model. Responses from a class of sociology students in a western state university showed them to be more liberal and more for decreasing government involvement internationally than any of the eight voter clusters. Their position is close to McCarthy's, indicated by an "S."

STRATEGIC INTEGRATION OF FINDINGS

Having determined the position of products in a space and seen where consumer ideal points are located, how can such findings be integrated to determine appropriate product strategy? A product's market share should be increased by repositioning: (1) closer to ideal points of sizable segments of the market, (2) farther from other products with which it must compete, and (3) on dimensions weighted heavily in consumers' preferences. Even these broad guidelines provide some basis for marketing strategy. For instance, in Figure 4, Brand A is clearly farthest from all clusters and should be repositioned.

In Figure 5, Humphrey, Kennedy, and Johnson could have increased their acceptance with this respondent sample by moving upwards and to the right, modifying their perceived position. Presumably, endorsement of any issue in the upper right quadrant or a negative position on any issue in the lower left quadrant of Figure 2 would have helped move Humphrey closer to the concentration of voters' ideal points.

Although the broad outlines of marketing strategy are suggested by spaces such as these, it would be desirable to make more precise quantitative forecasts of the effect of modifying a product's position. Unfortunately, the problem of constructing a model to explain product choice behavior based on locations of ideal points and products in a multidimensional space has not yet been completely solved, although some useful approaches are currently available.

As the first step, it is useful to concentrate on the behavior of clusters of respondents rather than that of individuals, especially if clusters are truly homogeneous. Data predicting behavior of groups are much smoother and results for a few groups are far more communicable to marketing management than findings stated in terms of large numbers of individual respondents.

If preference data are available for a collection of products, one can analyze the extent to which respondents' preferences are related to distances in the space. Using regression analysis, one can estimate a set of importance weights for each cluster or, if desired, for each respondent, to be applied to the dimensions of the product space. Weights would be chosen providing the best explanation of cluster or individual respondent preferences in terms of weighted distances between ideal points and each product's perceived location. If clusters, rather than individuals, are used, it may be desirable to first calculate preference scale values or utilities for each cluster [1, 9]. Importance weights can then be obtained using multiple regression to predict these values from distances. If explanations of product preference can be made for *existing products,* which depend only on locations in space, then the same approach should permit *predictions* of preference levels for new or modified products to be positioned at specific locations in the space.

Models of choice behavior clearly deserve more attention. Although the problem of constructing the product space has received much attention, we are denied the full potential of

SUMMARY

Market segmentation studies can produce results which indicate desirable marketing action. Techniques which are presently available can: (1) construct a product space, (2) discover the shape of the distribution of consumers' ideal points throughout such a space, and (3) identify likely opportunities for new or modified products.

In the past, marketing research has often been restricted to *tactical* questions such as package design or pricing levels. However, with the advent of new techniques, marketing research can contribute directly to the development of *strategic* alternatives to current product marketing plans. There remains a need for improved technology, particularly in the development of models for explaining and predicting preferential choice behavior. The general problem has great practical significance, and provides a wealth of opportunity for development of new techniques and models.

REFERENCES

1 Bradley, M. E. and R. A. Terry. "Rank Analysis of Incomplete Block Designs: The Method of Paired Comparisons," *Biometrika*, 39 (1952), 324–45.

2 Carroll, J. D. "Individual Differences and Multidimensional Scaling," Murray Hill, N.J.: Bell Telephone Laboratories, 1969.

3 Guttman, Louis: "A General Nonmetric Technique for Finding the Smallest Space for a Configuration of Points," *Psychometrika*, 33 (December 1968), 469–506.

4 Johnson, Richard M. "Multiple Discriminant Analysis," unpublished paper, Workshop on Multivariate Methods in Marketing, University of Chicago, 1970.

5 ———. "Political Segmentation," paper presented at Spring Conference on Research Methodology, American Marketing Association, New York, 1969.

6 Johnson, Stephen C. "Hierarchical Clustering Schemes," *Psychometrika*, 32 (September 1967), 241–54.

7 Kruskal, Joseph B. "Multidimensional Scaling by Optimizing Goodness of Fit to a Nonmetric Hypothesis," *Psychometrika*, 29 (March 1964), 1–27.

8 ———. "Nonmetric Multidimensional Scaling: A Numerical Method," *Psychometrika*, 29 (June 1964), 115–29.

9 Luce, R. D. "A Choice Theory Analysis of Similarity Judgments," *Psychometrika*, 26 (September 1961), 325–32.

10 McKeon, James J. "Canonical Analysis," *Psychometric Monographs*, 13.

11 Tucker, Ledyard. "Dimensions of Preference, " Research Memorandum RM-60-7, Princeton, N.J.: Educational Testing Service, 1960.

12 Young, F. W. "TORSCA, An IBM Program for Nonmetric Multidimensional Scaling," *Journal of Marketing Research*, 5 (August 1968), 319–21.

13 Young, G. and A. S. Householder, "Discussion of a Set of Points in Terms of Their Mutual Distances," *Psychometrika*, 3 (March 1938), 19–22.

15

Industrial Market Segmentation

Yoram Wind
Richard Cardozo

This selection presents a conceptual approach to the segmentation of industrial marketing together with results from an exploratory survey of current segmentation practices in industry. Although segmentation is often claimed to have been used as a marketing tool, it could be that its main use is to explain results *after* marketing has taken place.

The authors present two examples to encourage appropriate use of market segmentation in planning and controlling marketing strategies. The approach is conceptual and also practical.

The purpose of this paper is to outline theoretically sound segmentation strategies, to explore the current market segmentation practices among manufacturers of industrial goods and services, and finally to contrast theoretically-derived strategies with current practice. It is our hope that understanding and questioning the current industrial segmentation practices in light of an "ideal" model may help identify promising areas for further study and encourage such explorations. The "ideal" model described here has been developed from the literature on market segmentation (which is primarily concerned with consumer markets), combined with pertinent literature on industrial buyer behavior.

The concept of market segmentation is a logical outgrowth of the marketing concept and economic theory, and is at least conceptually as applicable in industrial marketing as it is for the marketing of consumer goods. Daniel Yankelovich (1964) showed examples of the usefulness of segmentation in industrial markets. Knowledge of the size and heterogeneity of market segments may be essential to organizing for effective industrial marketing (Ames, 1971).

Recent texts and articles on industrial marketing (Alexander *et al.*, 1967; Rowe and Alexander, 1968; Wilson, 1968; and Dodge, 1970) include, however, no more than brief mention of market segmentation, and only cursory attention to the nature and behavior of the industrial buying decision making units. Given our initial statement that the concept of segmentation is conceptually a relevant (and even a crucial) ingredient in the design of industrial marketing strategies, the neglect of market segmentation in the industrial marketing literature can be explained if industrial firms do not follow a strategy of market segmentation, or, alternatively, if the introductory statement is wrong.

Our research indicates that industrial marketers by no means use market segmentation strategies as widely or effectively as they might. Segmentation appears to be largely an after-the-fact explanation of why a marketing program did or did not work, rather than a carefully thought-out foundation for market-

Reprinted from *Industrial Marketing Management,* **3**:153–166, 1974, with permission of *Industrial Marketing Management,* copyright 1974. At the time of writing, Yoram Wind was professor of marketing at The Wharton School, University of Pennsylvania. Richard Cardozo was professor of marketing and director of the Center for Experimental Studies in Business at the Graduate School of Business Administration, University of Minnesota.

ing programs. Yet two examples which will be described make it clear that market segmentation can indeed be a profitable strategy for industrial marketers.

THE CONCEPT AND IMPORTANCE OF MARKET SEGMENTATION[1]

A market segment is simply a group of present or potential customers with some common characteristic which is relevant in explaining (and predicting) their response to a supplier's marketing stimuli. For example, a market segment may consist of all firms whose annual purchases of steel exceed $5 million, but are less than $10 million. Buyers of noise-muffling equipment may be divided between those whose applications will be visible, in which appearance is important, and those in whose applications appearance is inconsequential. Buyers of many products may usefully be segmented into two groups: repeat buyers and first-time buyers, which differ with respect to the communications strategy which a prospective supplier might employ (Robinson and Faris, 1967).

As a marketing strategy, market segmentation involves first identifying particular segments, and then developing differentiated marketing programs for each of those segments. These programs may differ with respect to product design, communication or distribution channels used, and advertising and selling messages. To be useful to marketers, segments must be sufficiently different from one another and sufficiently large (and profitable) to make such tailoring of marketing programs worthwhile. Segments must also be accessible through specific communication and distribution channels. This accessibility may be, however, either via the media and distribution outlets reaching the segment (controlled strategy), via the message design (self-selection strategy) or in the most desirable case via both the media and message strategies. (Frank *et al.*, 1972). Sometimes identification may be very difficult or economically unfeasible, in which case the industrial marketer faces essentially one undifferentiated set of buyers. At the other extreme, each individual customer might conceivably constitute a segment. Unless the customers were few in number and each economically significant, the marketer would face an array of virtually unmanageable variety. The art of employing market segmentation, then, involves appropriate grouping of individual customers into a manageable and efficient (in a cost/benefit sense) number of market segments, for each of which a different marketing strategy is feasible and likely profitable.

Conceptually, the choice of segmentation as a marketing strategy for industrial goods and services is predicated on the same assumption and criteria as segmentation for consumer goods. The only differences, therefore, between consumer and industrial market segmentation involve the specific bases used for segmentation.

An "Ideal" Segmentation Model

Because some of these bases differ, we propose that industrial markets be segmented in two stages. The first stage involves formation of macrosegments, based on characteristics of the buying organization and the buying situation. The second stage involves dividing those macrosegments into microsegments, based on characteristics of decision-making units (DMUs). A flow chart which outlines this approach appears in Fig. 1.

This hierarchical approach enables an initial screening of organizations and selection of these macrosegments which, on the basis of organizational characteristics, provide potentially attractive market opportunities. Organizations which may have no use for the given

[1]Portions of this section are drawn from Frank *et al.* 1972.

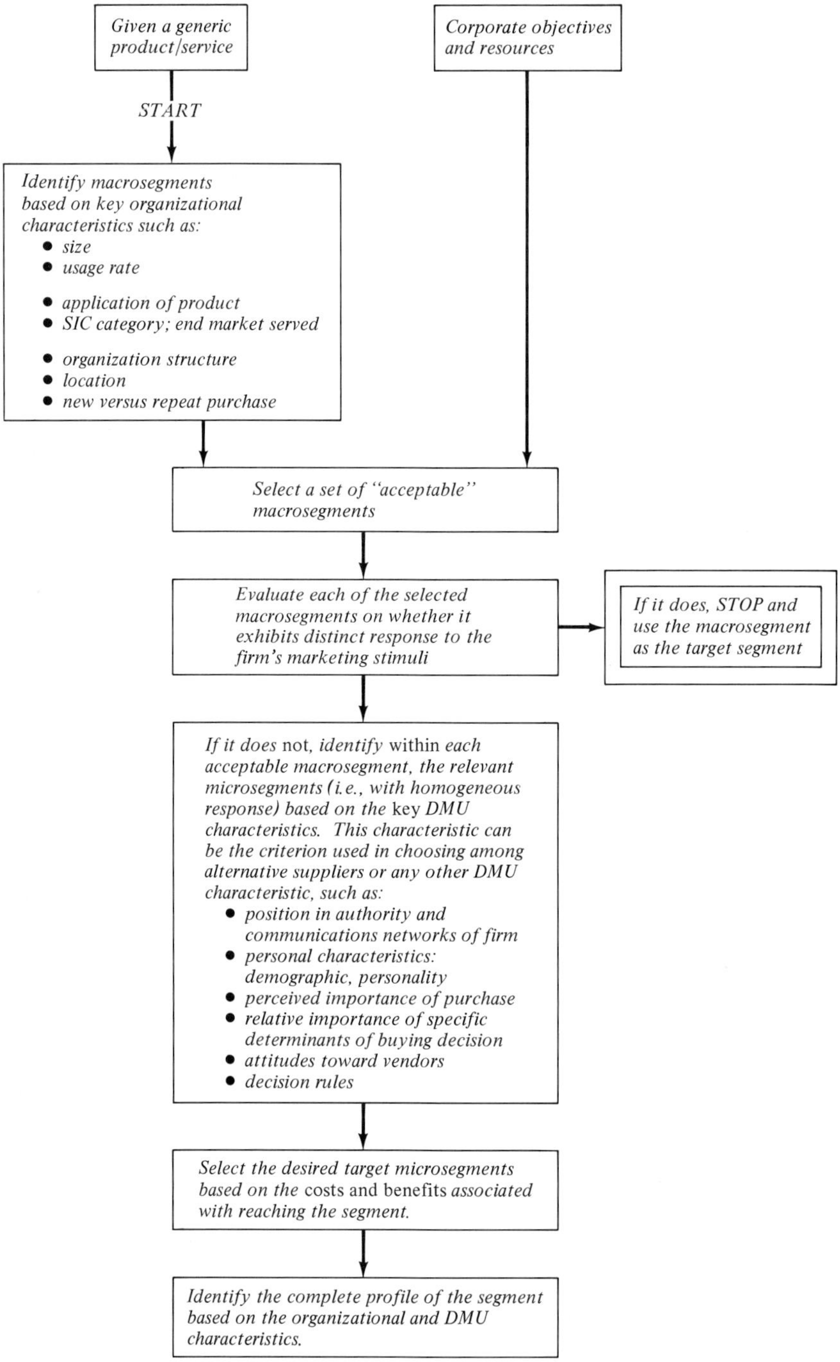

Figure 1 An approach to segmentation of organizational markets.

product or service can be eliminated. Starting with the grouping of organizations into homogeneous macrosegments also provides a reduction in the total research effort and cost. Instead of examining detailed buying patterns and attempting to identify the characteristics of the decision-making units in each organization individually, such analysis is limited only to those macrosegments which passed the initial screening. Furthermore, since most of the data for the initial screening can be drawn from available secondary sources (e.g., company files) and the screening procedure can be largely programmed, the research phase is relatively cheap and can be standardized as part of the firm's marketing information system.

In this first stage, a marketer may use a variety of bases, singly or in combination, to form macrosegments. Size of buying firm and rate of use of the particular product for which the marketer is planning can provide an estimate of potential sales.

Once the marketer has formed a set of acceptable macrosegments, he may divide each of them into microsegments, or small groups of firms, on the bases of similarities and differences among DMUs within each macrosegment. Information for this second stage of segmentation will come primarily from the sales force, based on salesmen's analyses of situations in particular firms, or from specially-designed market segmentation studies.

DMUs may differ with respect to the composition and position within a firm, and with respect to their decision-making behavior. Composition of the DMU may effect its position in the authority and communications networks of a firm. A DMU composed of relative newcomers to a buying firm, no one of which occupies a top or second-level position in his department, is likely to have little power to press its recommendations on others, and may not be fully integrated into the "informal organization" which may frequently be the network necessary to obtain acceptance of new concepts products or procedures. Clearly, such a DMU presents a more difficult task for a marketer with a novel offering than one composed of senior established corporate officials who have close contacts throughout the organization.

DMUs may differ with respect to the importance they attach to the purchase of a particular item; the relative weight they attach to such purchase variables as price, quality and service; their attitudes toward particular types of vendors; and the specific rules they employ to seek out and evaluate alternative offerings. DMUs which consider a specific product important, require prompt delivery and perhaps technical assistance, wish to deal with well-known vendors and seek a bid first from a supplier with which they have dealt previously, constitute a microsegment of considerable promise to a highly visible supplier with ability to meet delivery and service requirements, who has done business with firms in this microsegment. Such a supplier would have distinct advantage over a competitor who sought to enter this microsegment with a low-service, low-price product.

The output from this segmentation model should include (1) a key dependent variable on which firms can be assigned to segments, i.e., the *bases* for segmentation, and (2) a set of independent variables which allow a marketer to predict where along the key dependent variable a particular group of potential customers may lie as well as provide greater insight into the key characteristics of the segment, i.e., the *descriptors* of the segment. For example, a key dependent variable might be "criteria used to evaluate alternative suppliers." In one situation, a marketer found that "prompt periodic delivery of lots with less than five percent defects" was the paramount consideration used by some firms in choosing among suppliers for a particular component part. That same component was purchased by other firms almost entirely on a "lowest cost per thousand units" basis. After some investigation, the marketer discovered that three independent variables differentiated these two types of buyers, or segments: (1) size of firm, measured in number of employees; (2) SIC category; and (3) the type of individual most influential in the buying decision. Customers who insisted on adherence to delivery and quality standards were typically large firms in three SIC codes. Within these firms the most powerful member of the DMU was a quality control man or a purchasing agent with engineering training. In contrast, customers who bought on price were typically smaller firms, in half a dozen SIC codes, only one of which overlapped that of the first type of customer. Principle buying influences in these firms included purchasing agents without technical backgrounds, and production management personnel.

Selection of appropriate dependent variables should be based on the particular marketing problem the manager wishes to solve. In the preceding example, the problem was to reach new customers with a product which they had previously not purchased in appreciable quantities from any vendor. As users' requirements increased, they solicited numerous bids and began to set standards for reviewing those bids. Consequently, knowledge of those standards became the variable of key importance to the marketer. In another situation, knowledge of buyers' "switching rules" was of central importance. The marketer had lost a few previously loyal customers to competitors, and wished to know why. The key dependent variable of interest to him was "buyers' sensitivity to changes in competitors' offerings." He discovered that some buyers would switch for a price reduction of less than five percent, while others were reluctant to change suppliers until the price differential on this particular product exceeded 20 percent.

The art of market segmentation involves choosing the appropriate bases for segmenting industrial markets. The bases mentioned here have appeared in the marketing literature (Cardozo, 1968; Feldman and Cardozo, 1969; Frank *et al.,* 1971), and are presented as illustrative but by no means exhaustive of the bases which could be used. Because a marketer may choose key segmentation variables from an array of several dozen (or more), research to identify the most appropriate of those variables may be well worthwhile. Furthermore, because customers' needs and competitors' activities are constantly changing, a marketer must review his segmentation strategy periodically.

After identifying appropriate target segments, the marketer must analyze the profitability of differentiating his marketing program to reach multiple target segments. A first approximation of this cost/benefit analysis may often be made before detailed segmentation analysis is begun.

Relevant costs typically include those associated with product modification, selling and advertising. Although costs of making initial modifications of a particular product may be modest, the marketer will incur costs in carrying an additional product or line in inventory, and may incur hidden costs through confusion or misunderstanding on the part of salesmen and distributors. During the last several years many firms have proliferated their product lines to reach customers with highly individualized requirements. Today, many of those same firms look at product deletion (and not only new product introduction) as a source for increased profitability, hence eliminating the highly specialized and unprofitable offshoots of their principal products.

Sometimes an especially intensive selling effort may be required to reach a particular market segment. If this effort transfers salesmen from their routine calls, there will likely be a cost in terms of sales delayed or lost entirely. If headquarters personnel, in addition to field sales staff, are involved, the costs may be much greater. Because these costs typically involve no internal budget transfers and only modest out-of-pocket expenditures, marketing managers frequently overlook them.

The costs of advertising to reach a particular market segment ordinarily include preparation of separate copy and perhaps illustrations, as well as media costs. Because both types of charges may be highly visible, many firms underutilize differentiated advertising as a tool in a marketing segmentation strategy.

The Payoff from Segmentation

Two examples illustrate the potential payoff from following a marketing segmentation strategy. The first example describes a situation in which a fairly simple, single stage segmentation strategy yielded substantial profits. The second example describes a case in which the second stage of segmentation contributed to a substantial increase in profit.

Single-Stage Segmentation A marketer of spray painting and finishing equipment who had a new system to offer divided his markets into macrosegments on the bases of SIC category, size of buying firms and location. The marketer developed two distinct strategies: one for large firms in a particular SIC category, all of which were located within four states; another for smaller firms located both in those and in other states. The SIC categories of firms in the second segment overlapped, but were not identical with, those in the first segment. The marketer had observed that decision-making practices for capital equipment differed between the two segments. The large firms were receptive to cost-saving innovations in equipment, tested new equipment extensively, and willingly switched to new equipment which had proved its value in operating tests and benefit-cost analyses. Firms in the second segment were notably resistant to change, and historically had adopted new capital equipment innovations only after large firms—like those in the first segment—had done so.

Accordingly, the marketer concentrated his efforts on the first segment. Field salesmen, supported by headquarters staff, diverted their activities from smaller firms to concentrate almost exclusively on the larger ones. The marketer provided equipment for testing, and set up and helped to supervise test lines in plants of the largest manufacturers. Later, as this effort became successful, the field sales force reapplied its efforts to smaller firms, without, however, entirely discontinuing contact with the larger ones. These selling efforts to the smaller, more dispersed firms were supported with an advertising campaign which described installations in selected large firms and included endorsements by executives in these firms, but did not include provisions for extensive testing.

Results of this segmentation strategy included penetration of both segments, which had previously been dominated entirely by competitors. Company executives attributed their success to a good product and to following this segmentation strategy, citing instances in which other cost-effective innovations had not been accepted in these markets.

Two-Stage Segmentation In the preceding example, single-stage segmentation sufficed, because decision-making behavior was correlated closely and positively with size, SIC category and location. In the following example, decision-making behavior appeared not to be related to size of firm. Consequently, two-stage segmentation was necessary.

A small manufacturer of high quality metal components had traditionally segmented the geographically concentrated market which it served on the bases of SIC category and size of buying firm. The company concentrated its sales and sales support activities more on some SIC categories than on others, and followed a form of "key account" planning, which led to emphasis on customers with large potential volumes. Because sales potentials were frequently not attained, company officials and salesmen attempted to differentiate those customers which gave the company a high proportion of their business from those which gave the company only a small portion of their business. Results from this analysis indicated that the company enjoyed considerable success among customers who purchased its particular type of product simply by telephoning previous suppliers and placing the order with the first one which could meet product and delivery requirements ("satisficers"). The company fared poorly with customers which solicited bids, reviewed them and finally chose a supplier for this particular type of product ("optimizers").

These differences in "purchasing strategy", which crossed size and SIC categories, suggested a basis for forming microsegments within each SIC category. The company directed its sales and support efforts primarily at the first segment ("satisficers"), with which it had historically been more successful, and reduced its frequency of calls and sales support activities toward the second segment, ("optimizers"). As a result, the company experienced an increase in profits of more than 20 percent. Company officials attributed the increase almost wholly to the new market segmentation strategy.

These examples support the theoretical arguments for market segmentation strategy. With this initial empirical support for our belief that market segmentation was an economically viable approach for industrial marketers, we undertook an exploratory study to determine the extent to which market segmentation was employed by industrial marketers and the various ways in which segmentation was used.

INDUSTRIAL SEGMENTATION: SOME CURRENT PRACTICES

Data

To assess the extent and nature of industrial market segmentation, we first conducted a series of unstructured interviews with marketing managers of five Philadelphia-based industrial companies. Following these unstructured interviews we conducted structured interviews with marketing managers of 25 companies within the Minneapolis metropolitan area. The reporting units in the final sample included both operating divisions of large, decentralized corporations and independent firms. In sales volume, the size of these reporting units ranged from $3 million to more than $2 billion. More than 25 SIC codes were represented.

The interview schedule included questions about the use of different strategies in selling to different customers; the nature of the differentiated strategy, the bases used to segment one's market, the importance of the various bases for segmentation and company background data.

Methodology

The unstructured interviews and open ended questions of the structured interview were content analyzed. The structured parts of the questionnaire were then subjected to cross classification and multidimensional scaling analyses. This latter procedure was utilized to illustrate graphically the marketing managers' evaluation of the various bases for segmentation.

Results

The results of this study indicate that industrial marketers do differentiate their marketing programs among customers. But the differentiation appears less a conscious, explicit strategy of market segmentation, and more an explanation or concept applied *after* the fact to explain differences in the success of particular marketing programs. Detailed results are grouped under five research questions.

(1) To what extent is segmentation strategy used by industrial firms?

All the firms participating in the study indicated that they do use different strategies in selling to different customers. This overwhelming subscription to a policy of differentiation implies acceptance of—or at least lip service to—the concept of market segmentation. Nevertheless, examination of the specific examples given by the respondents suggests that segmentation is used primarily to describe ex-post events, and not as an explicit strategy which provides the foundation for the industrial marketing program.

(2) What is the nature of a segmentation-based industrial marketing strategy?

Industrial firms which differentiate their marketing offerings, to appeal to and reach different market segments, only rarely try to differentiate all their marketing variables. Nevertheless, more than half of the firms differentiated at least one of their marketing variables. Of the various ways in which a company can vary its marketing strategies to meet the needs of its target markets, elements reported as most important were the product and service mix (72%) followed by price (18%) and only in a very few cases by promotion (5%) and distribution (5%).

Most of the respondents modify or adapt their products to meet the requirements of particular customers. Product changes vary considerably and include technical as well as symbolic (e.g., changes from manufacturer to private brand) alterations. Quite frequently a firm's product strategy is supplemented, or replaced, by its service strategy—training, maintenance, warranties and technical information.

In addition to different products and services most of the firms offered a variety of pricing options to their customers. The reasons for such a policy were primarily volume and specific customer requirements.

The majority of respondents indicated that they emphasize different appeals (product benefits) to different customers. Yet, the examples presented suggest that such differentiation is accomplished "intuitively" by field salesmen, or that differentiation is an after-the-fact explanation of marketing activity, rather than a carefully designed strategy aimed at emphasizing for each segment the appropriate product benefits and usage situations. About 80 percent of the firms used a variety of promotional tactics—especially different media (trade magazines, direct mail, newspapers, general magazines, TV, radio and displays)—to reach their markets. No evidence exists, however, that the media selection or the message design decisions were based on an explicit analysis and understanding of the target market segments and the nature of the decision making units.

More than two-thirds of the firms used different channels of distribution in selling to different customers. The selection of the specific channel was based primarily on the nature of the customer (especially Government vs. non-Government clients), the nature of the products (components vs. systems), the geographical location of the buyers and the availability of particular channels.

(3) What are the bases used to segment industrial markets?

Organizational "demographics" such as size, SIC category, end use of product and geographical location were the most frequently used bases for segmentation. End use was generally thought to vary directly with the type of business in which the business firm is engaged.

Other bases used—considerably less frequently—by the responding firms to segment their markets were personal characteristics of the decision making units, such as the function of the buying unit, and the DMUs degree of source loyalty.

(4) How do industrial marketers evaluate various bases of segmentation?

Marketers group bases of segmentation into three clusters, which they evaluate on two different sets of criteria. The three clusters of bases for segmentation are (1) organization characteristics, (2) product characteristics and (3) DMU characteristics. Organization characteristics include type of industry, size of firm and geographic location. Product characteristics include usage rates, end use and product specifications. DMU characteristics include buyers' job title and personality, and pattern of source loyalty. The three clusters are displayed in a two-dimensional map in Figure 2. There were no clear differences in clusters (or in evaluation) among the different types of firms represented in our sample.

Marketers used two sets of criteria to evaluate these clusters. The first set included three

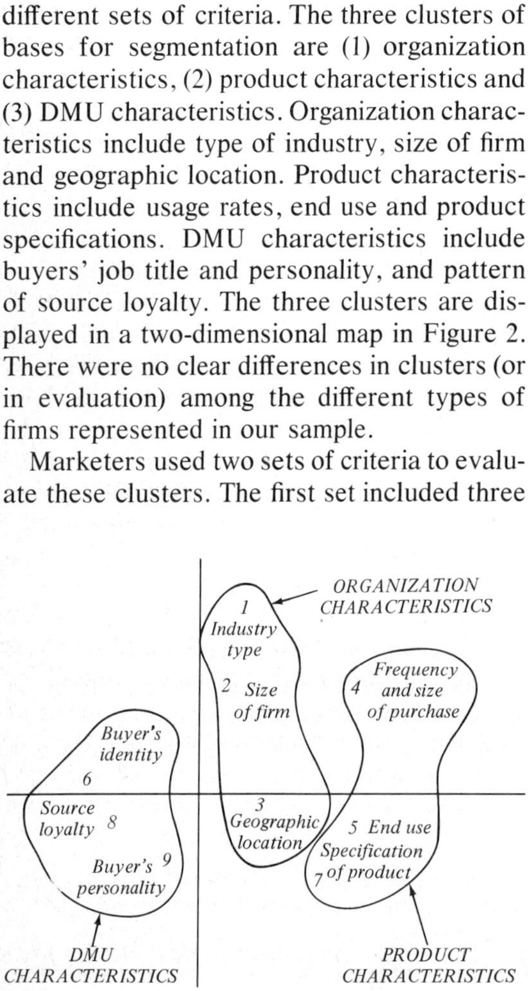

Figure 2 Two-dimensional configuration of nine bases for segmentation.

criteria: (1) cost of identifying segments and differentiating marketing programs, (2) acceptance of bases of segmentating by marketing personnel, and (3) ease of identifying segments and differentiating marketing programs. Of these three, cost was clearly the most important. The other set included one criterion—appropriateness—which respondents construed as a global evaluation, one which had normative futuristic implications.

The two sets of criteria correspond to the two dimensions in Figure 2. The vertical dimension can be viewed as the "difficulty of implementing" set of criteria. Given the grouping of the bases into 3 clusters, within each cluster the vertical spread of the bases reflect their perceived difficulty of implementing. For example, within the cluster of DMU characteristics the buyer's identity is the easiest to identify, the cheapest and the most acceptable of the three bases. The buyer's personality, on the other hand is viewed as the most difficult to identify, most expensive and least acceptable to marketing management.

The horizontal dimension can be interpreted, consistently with the second set of criteria, as the "appropriateness" dimension with the DMU characteristics as the most appropriate followed by organizational characteristics and the product characteristics perceived as the least appropriate.

The two sets of criteria result, therefore, in quite different evaluations of the three clusters. Marketers evidently now use inexpensive and acceptable means of segmentation, which they consider much less appropriate than what they'd like to use. For example, DMU characteristics are seen as very appropriate, yet are not currently used as bases of segmentation. Product characteristics, now used in some circumstances, are considered least appropriate as bases for segmentation. Organizational characteristics appear to be used more widely now than may be appropriate. Respondents'

Figure 3 Evaluation of Bases of Segmentation

Criteria	Bases of segmentation: Organizational characteristics	Product characteristics	DMU characteristics
Set 1: cost acceptability ease	Frequently used	Sometimes used	Not used
Set 2: appropriateness	Some are appropriate	Least appropriate	Very appropriate

evaluations of the 2 sets of criteria with respect to their appropriateness and frequency of usage are summarized in Figure 3.

(5) Which bases for segmentation may be used in the future?

More than 80 percent of the respondents thought that differences of industry type, geographic location, end use of the product, and specification of product (including cost and delivery) would continue to be important determinants of customer requirements and useful bases for segmentation. About 70 percent indicated source or brand loyalty as important factors, while only 62 percent mentioned the size of the firm. Slightly over 50 percent of the respondents thought that the identity of the buyer (e.g., engineer, purchasing agent) and the buyer's personality would be of some importance, while only 42 percent thought that the frequency and size of purchase would have importance.

(6) What criteria are used to evaluate segmentation-based marketing strategies?

Sales volume (33%), profits (23%) and market share (11%) are the primary criteria used by marketing managers to evaluate their marketing strategies. Growth (10%), image (5%), length of relationship with customers (5%), ability to meet customers' needs (5%) and cost (8%) were the other criteria used. These measures are not, however, applied separately to each segment. Consequently, marketing segmentation is not employed as a control strategy.

In summary, this study indicates that, while the concept of marketing strategy differentiation is widely accepted among industrial firms, there is little evidence to suggest that firms do follow a conscious segmentation strategy to plan or control their marketing activities. Although marketing managers are aware of the concept of segmentation, they appear not to articulate fully the concept of segmentation or to use the variety of possible bases for segmentation.

CONCLUSIONS

The concept of marketing segmentation has been one of major focuses of consumer research since the early Sixties. The concept has had a great impact on the thought and practice of marketing of consumer goods. These developments have had less impact, however, on industrial marketing management. Results from this study indicate that industrial marketers typically fail to employ market segmentation as a foundation for planning and control of marketing programs. At best, industrial marketers use only single-stage segmentation, and by no means employ or even examine some of the other bases of segmentation which might be employed profitably.

Articulation of the concept of market segmentation may by itself provide a basis for more precise marketing planning and for coordination of product development, selling and sales support activities. A marketer who accepts segmentation as the basis for his marketing strategy will have a basis for conceiving of and estimating potential profits from specific product modifications. Segmenting markets will enable field sales managers to direct their resources more efficiently at particular target firms or groups of firms in their geographic areas. At the same time, sales support materials and activities—including advertising—can be tailored to suit economically viable market segments.

We believe that industrial marketers who do not follow explicit segmentation strategies, planned in advance, either treat all customers alike or treat each customer differently. In the first case, marketers are losing opportunities for profit and laying themselves open to competitive inroads. In the second case, marketers undoubtedly are practicing unprofitable—and uncontrolled—segmentation in many instances. Interestingly, those marketers who permit sales (and sales support) men to treat each customer differently typically believe and state that they treat all customers alike. Those marketers generally lack adequate marketing planning and control techniques, they do not provide their sales force adequate support and typically have not thought about differences among their present and prospective customers.

Research into segmentation, therefore, is an essential precondition for intelligent marketing planning. Such research is feasible, and can readily be integrated with other marketing research projects. Once the marketing plan is fully developed, marketing operations may be controlled on a segment-by-segment basis. Such a control mechanism is more precise than most in use today and may be more responsive in a changing environment.

Once segmentation is accepted and articulated as a useful way of looking at markets, marketers can address the discrepancy, revealed in this study, between bases of segmentation which are considered appropriate, but too costly to implement, and those which are inexpensive but not always appropriate. One way to deal with this problem is to identify new, less costly bases of segmentation, perhaps by identifying particular types of behavior and their correlates. Another way is to develop advertising (media and message) and sales management plans, for example, which fit appropriate segments in particular markets. As a marketer gains experience in devising such policies, costs of differentiating marketing programs should decrease.

REFERENCES

Alexander, Ralph S., Cross, James S. and Hill, Richard M. (1967). *Industrial Marketing,* Homewood, Ill., Richard D. Irwin.

Ames, Charles B. (1971). "Dilemma of Product/Market Management," *Harvard Business Review.* Vol. 49 (March–April), 66–74.

Cardozo, Richard N. (1968). "Segmenting the Industrial Market." In King, R. L. (ed.), *Marketing and the New Science of Planning.* Chicago: The American Marketing Association.

Dodge, Robert H. (1970). *Industrial Marketing.* N.Y.: McGraw-Hill.

Feldman, Wallace and Cardozo, Richard N. (1969). "The 'Industrial' Revolution and Models of Buyer Behavior." *Journal of Purchasing,* Vol. 5, No. 4 (November).

Frank, Ronald E., Massy, William F. and Wind, Yoram (1972). *Market Segmentation.* Englewood Cliffs, N.J.: Prentice-Hall.

Robinson, Patrick J., and Faris, Charles W. (1967). *Industrial Buying and Creative Marketing.* Boston: Allyn & Bacon.

Rowe, David and Alexander, Ivan (1968). *Selling Industrial Products.* London: Hutchinson & Co.

Webster, Frederick E., Jr. and Wind, Yoram (1972). *Organizational Buying Behavior.* Englewood Cliffs, N.J.: Prentice-Hall.

Wilson, Aubrey (ed.). (1965). *The Marketing of Industrial Products,* London: Hutchinson & Co.

Yankelovich, Daniel (1964). "New Criteria for Market Segmentation." *Harvard Business Review,* Vol. 42 (March–April), 83–90.

Part Four

Developing Marketing Strategies

After identifying appropriate product/market relationships, executives of a company must plan how to maintain and—they hope—increase its market share in each such relationship.

Clearly this means determining the probable growth in each relationship as compared with the others, and the probable effect over time. Once the target markets are established, the planners must set up forecasts of probable market-share changes.

In sequence, this section deals with marketing strategy positioning, a strategic perspective on product planning, planning gains in market share, and experience curves as a planning tool.

16

Marketing Strategy Positioning

David W. Cravens

A variety of marketing strategy positions are outlined by the author. He presents guidelines for identifying and evaluating alternative strategies to be used as aids for management decision making.

Marketing strategy positioning provides an essential frame of reference for guiding management decisions. Rapid environmental changes, shifts in buyer preferences, new products and services, and increased competition demand that firms continually monitor their strategy positioning to capitalize on new opportunities and avoid potential pitfalls. An understanding of the concept of strategy positioning and its implications for marketing decision making is important for several reasons. First, changes in the marketing environment, both nationally and internationally, are increasing at a rapid rate, thus making strategy development significant to the success of an organization. Second, strategy positioning analysis yields important guidelines for marketing decision making and provides a basis for effectively linking corporate and marketing strategy. Third, appropriate shifts in marketing strategy must be based upon a thorough understanding of a firm's present positioning.

Consider, for example, the impact of energy shortages, in combination with a severe economic downturn in the mid-1970s, upon prevailing marketing strategies of many firms. Or consider the implications of the shift in the $1 billion hosiery market from panty hose to knee-highs, and the associated decrease in the size of the market which, in 1974, reduced profit margins, intensified price competition, generated claims of false advertising, and stimulated efforts for product differentiation and quality improvement.[1] Another example is the Wurlitzer Co., which had become an American institution over the past several decades, but in 1974 announced its decision to phase out of the jukebox business in the United States. These are but a few illustrations of changing conditions that directly influenced marketing strategies.

The challenge to top management and marketing decision makers is to:

analyze market-product position(s) currently occupied by the firm

identify desirable shifts in strategy positions, and avoid being forced into undesirable positions by external forces such as the government

determine how and when to accomplish desired shifts or whether to retain existing positions

Decisions can be facilitated by guidelines for strategy positioning that match different degrees of market-product maturity. This article examines the major types of marketing management decisions, reviews the concept of strategy positioning, discusses alternative marketing strategies, and presents an approach for analyzing shifts in such strategies.

[1] "The New Sag in Pantyhose," *Business Week*, 14 December 1974, pp. 98–100.

Reprinted from *Business Horizons*, vol. 18, pp. 53–68, December 1975. At the time of writing, the author was a faculty member in business administration, University of Tennessee.

CONCEPT OF STRATEGY POSITIONING

An enterprise's corporate goals delineate market-product boundaries which guide marketing decisions. Contrast, for example, the corporate mission of a multi-market-product firm such as General Electric with the single market-product orientation of the Wm. Wrigley Jr., Co. General Electric serves a variety of consumer, industrial and institutional users with a wide range of products. The Wrigley company manufactures chewing gum for a mass consumer market. Such differences in overall purposes and goals largely determine the nature and scope of marketing activities of various firms.

Marketing Decision Areas

Within the guidelines of the corporate mission, marketing decisions must be made in three major areas. They include an analysis of the *marketing environment* to identify opportunities and constraints; a *market opportunity analysis* to select target markets; and the design, implementation and control of *marketing strategy* to accomplish objectives in target markets.

Environmental analysis identifies, monitors and, where possible, predicts the impact of external forces, including economic conditions, technology, social change and government. Market analysis examines relevant markets to select specific target areas where the firm has the most favorable advantage over existing and/or potential competition. Marketing strategy encompasses the design, implementation and management over time of the total marketing effort as it relates to the product, channels of distribution, price, advertising and sales force.

Determinants of Strategy Position

A firm entering a new market with a new product or service faces a substantially different marketing challenge than one operating in an existing market with a line of established products. Thus, an essential first step in the marketing management decision process is an assessment of the marketing strategy positions already occupied by the company, or an assessment of the new situations into which it might move. Variations in the maturity of markets and products, coupled with the base of experience of a given firm, will substantially affect the specific activities of the marketing manager with regard to environmental analysis, target market selection and marketing strategy design and management over time.

Central to the need for strategy position analysis is a recognition of market-product dynamics. Clearly, the first half of the '70s has amply demonstrated that change will be a central element to be contended with in management decision making in the future. Within a general framework of societal change, certain possibilities suggest the need for ongoing marketing strategy analysis. For instance, modifications in a firm's marketing program may have to be made as its products move through different stages in the product life cycle. Contrast Polaroid's initial entry into the instant photography market with its recent introduction of the SX-70 camera. Firms may also decide to move into new markets. Consider, for example, Texas Instruments' move a few years ago into consumer markets, with electronic calculators.

Further, possible market-product gaps may offer new or expanded opportunities. Recall Lear Jet's move into the commercial jet aircraft market several years ago as a result of an assessed product gap. Changing environmental conditions such as energy shortages, inflation, international political unrest and declining birth rates may pose both opportunities and threats for particular industries and individual firms. Thus, marketing strategy position analysis is an essential frame of reference for the variety of specific marketing management decisions which must be made in an enterprise.

POSITIONING ALTERNATIVES

A firm's marketing strategy position is affected both by the prevailing market-product situations pursued by the firm, and by factors beyond the control of the firm, such as market-product life cycles, environmental forces and competition. An array of possible marketing strategy positions is shown in Figure 1.[2] Examples of market-product situations which illustrate different marketing strategy positions are shown in Table 1. The five alternatives, are admittedly arbitrary since a continuum of possible variations exists. Yet, this division seems appropriate in terms of characterizing the essential differences as they affect marketing decisions. Each strategy position will be described briefly.

[2]Related uses of product-market variations to array strategy positions are discussed in the following: H. Igor Ansoff, *Corporate Strategy* (New York: McGraw-Hill, 1965), pp. 122–38.

David T. Kollat, Roger D. Blackwell and James F. Robeson, *Strategic Marketing* (Holt, Rinehart and Winston, 1972), pp. 21–23.

John W. Humble, *How to Manage by Objectives* (New York: American Marketing Association, 1973), p. 75.

Balancing Strategy

In a balancing strategy position, a firm seeks to balance revenue-cost flows to achieve desired profit and market share targets. Both existing markets and products are typically at mature levels, and competition is well established. Management has accumulated a broad base of knowledge and experience about familiar markets and products. Relationships between functional areas of the firm are well established.

The focus of environmental analysis is on monitoring external influences to identify possible opportunities and threats. For example, an analysis of income trends, population growth and regulatory flexibility in the early 1960s, in combination with an assessment of market opportunities, precipitated movement

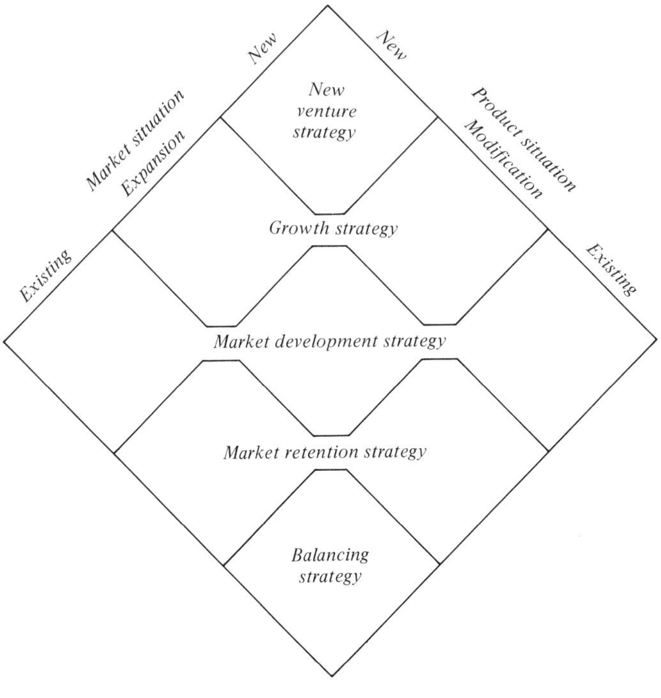

Figure 1 Alternative marketing strategy positions.

Table 1 Illustrations of Firms Occupying Alternative Strategy Positions

Balancing strategy

Strategy position occupied by railroads, electric utilities and various other mature industries

Holiday Inn's provision of motel services to its existing markets

Market retention strategy

Annual model changes of appliance manufacturers aimed at retaining market share

Introduction by Kentucky Fried Chicken of ribs to their food line

Modification of styles and models by automobile manufacturers

Market development strategy

Procter & Gamble's development of "Pringles" potato chips

Efforts of public transportation firms to lure people away from use of the automobile through modification of services

Movement of the large aluminum companies into automobile and beverage can markets for their products

Growth strategy

Offering (at a fee) first run movies on T.V. private channels in hotels and motels

Texas Instruments' move into consumer electronic calculator markets

Design and marketing of a low premium $1 million umbrella personal liability insurance policy for individuals

New venture strategy

Polaroid's introduction of the original Land camera

Xerox's pioneering development and marketing of copying equipment

Initial publication and marketing of *Playgirl* magazine

of progressive commercial banks from balancing strategies toward market retention, market development, and, in some cases, growth strategies. Of course, environmental analysis should not imply that strategy shifts are always desirable.

Market opportunity analysis within a balancing strategy is aimed at refining the firm's knowledge of its markets. Market segmentation strategies may often be appropriate to enable the firm to concentrate its efforts upon certain groups of product end-users, thus achieving advantage over competition through specialization. Consider, for example, American Motors' pursuit of the small car segment of the automobile market. Typically, a balancing strategy position necessitates setting clear priorities for subgroups of customers within a firm's aggregate market.

A firm's marketing program is well developed in this strategy position—only modest changes are normally made from year to year in advertising and personal selling methods. Distribution channels are established, as are pricing strategies. Emphasis is upon control as opposed to planning. Efficiency in the use of resources is critical since market growth is likely to be modest and competition for new customers is keen. Monitoring of product performance should be an ongoing activity to identify products which should be dropped.

Market Retention Strategy

This position relates to a situation in which a product is being modified or a market is being expanded; thus, it is a logical extension from a balancing strategy position, triggered by management's desire to improve corporate performance or to sustain historical sales and profit levels. It probably is the most typical strategy position occupied by established firms. Marketing activities and decisions are similar to those in balancing strategy positions, although the market opportunity analysis and marketing program design must take into account the firm's movement beyond existing market-product situations. For example, information about product modifications must be communicated to the firm's target markets. End-users in expanded markets must be reached through existing distribution channels or new channel intermediaries must be added to the firm's system.

Market Development Strategy

Pursuit of this strategy may extend an enterprise beyond existing market-product capabilities, and is likely to require realignments of organizational relationships and procedures. Additional financial resources and personnel are often required. Market development is a major undertaking, and is unlikely to fit neatly into existing operational patterns. New markets or new product commitments present key analysis and design uncertainties for marketing management. Careful assessment of the feasibility of pursuing this strategy should be made in terms of environmental influences, market potential, competitive situation, and financial viability.

Growth Strategy

A growth strategy moves the firm into higher levels of uncertainty than any of the three previously described strategy positions. Either a new product or new market is involved, in combination with a market expansion or product modification. Major new resources are needed to pursue this strategy, and a variety of new operating relationships must be established. Knowledge of prospective markets is crucial, indicating a possible need for acquiring information through marketing research and intelligence activities. Market segmentation may be difficult, due to lack of market experience and information.

In this strategy position, design of the marketing program presents a major challenge to marketing management. Assuming the firm occupies other strategy positions, it is doubtful that the growth strategy can be launched from the firm's existing marketing program base. The magnitude and deployment of resources among the various components of the marketing mix must be carefully planned; changes during the initial stages of program implementation may be necessary. For certain market-product situations, program implementation may occur in stages, for instance, by geographical area. This allows the gathering of market response information which can be useful in guiding subsequent efforts in other areas. Also, the use of marketing resources is not as "fine tuned" as, for example, in a market retention strategy position.

New Venture Strategy

The new venture strategy position represents a totally new undertaking by the enterprise. While decision making uncertainties and risks are at the highest level, the opportunities for success are typically very attractive. Direct competition often is not present. Established firms use various organizational approaches to cope with the overall management task of planning and implementing a new venture. The team concept has become popular in recent years. If the venture promises to be sufficiently large, a separate division may be established. For example, the Carborundum Co., in seeking to enter the pollution control market in the early 1970s, used this approach.

The market in a new venture situation is often not well defined. Refinements in management's understanding of customer characteristics and behavior must be developed over time, since a very limited base of historical experience frequently exists. Segmentation strategies often need to be deferred until the market gains some maturity and a sufficient degree of stability so that similar customers can be identified.

Design of the marketing program presents a major challenge in that the relative effectiveness of marketing elements in influencing target customers is difficult to determine. Experimentation may be necessary, such as using test marketing by consumer products firms. The program design involves major strategy decisions with respect to the type and intensity of distribution, the role of price in the marketing effort, and the relative importance of advertising and personal selling. Since these decisions may require modification over time, major changes in the marketing mix should be viewed as normal rather than exceptional in a new venture strategy position. Initial revenue-cost relationships may be unfavorable during the period that the firm is seeking to build market acceptance.

IMPLICATIONS OF POSITIONING

Analyses of the strategies pursued by many successful business firms indicate that managements seek to move firms away from balancing situations into positions where there are more favorable advantages over competition. New product/service development activities are widely used for this purpose. Similarly, continual searching for new and/or expanded market opportunities represents an alternative or complementary strategy shifting mechanism. Yet, continued shifting may be neither feasible nor desirable. A company particularly must avoid being shifted by uncontrollable factors into less preferable situations.

Multiple Positions

Firms often occupy multiple marketing strategy positions. In cases where the positions are widely separated, different marketing approaches may be appropriate. For example, a firm may pursue a new venture strategy for a particular market-product combination, and at the same time occupy a market retention strategy position. The characteristics and decision-making demands of widely separated strategy positions may vary significantly. Attempting to launch a growth strategy via a marketing organization built around a balancing strategy is a clear mismatch of capabilities and needs.

Many firms at their inception face new venture strategies. Few, if any, maintain this position for any length of time, although mature firms may undertake new ventures for specific market-product opportunities. Over time a new venture situation will inevitably shift into one of the other positions, since market-product life cycles mature. Similarly, a firm upon reaching a balancing situation may seek to occupy other strategy positions, and move away from the balancing strategy.

Marketing Decisions

Marketing decisions vary substantially depending upon the strategy position(s) occupied by a firm. For example, market segmentation may be difficult and unnecessary in a new venture situation. However, effective segmentation of a product or brand level market in a balancing strategy may be essential to achieving profit objectives. Positioning analysis provides guidelines for analyzing the environment, the market opportunity and the marketing program design, implementation and control. Similarly, the experience and qualifications of the marketing staff may vary according to strategy positions. For example, a marketing manager in a new venture situation should be a good planner with a strong entrepreneurial orientation. In a balancing strategy the chief marketing executive needs skills in analyzing and controlling resources, and the capacity to make tough retrenchment decisions when needed, such as sales force reductions and/or changes in deployment.

STRATEGY POSITION ANALYSIS

Considering the various strategy positions that may occur and the variety of controllable and uncontrollable influences, the need for strategy positioning analysis is clear. However, the determination of the need for strategy position shifts is not exclusively a marketing management decision; it should involve executives from the various functional areas. Nevertheless, because the marketing function is linked to the firm's markets in particular and to the external environment in general, the chief marketing executive must play a pivotal role in strategy position analysis.

A strategy position shift may be called for due to:

pending environmental threats

unsatisfactory performance in the present position(s) and limited possibilities for improvement

the identification of a potentially promising opportunity, such as a new product idea

management's desire to broaden the firm's market-product base to provide a more stable revenue and profit flow

innovations suggested by an aggressive, growth-oriented management group.

These are the influences which lead to consideration of strategy positioning changes. Of course, the result of this assessment may be a decision to remain in the present strategy position. If management desires to change or supplement an existing strategy, however, feasible alternatives must be identified and evaluated.

Identifying, Evaluating Alternatives

The most promising alternative market-product positions should be identified, taking into consideration present position(s) and the feasibility of moving into another position. Consider, for example, the three alternative multiple strategy positions shown in Figure 2. In the fragmented multiple strategy position (a), a firm's management capabilities and resources are spread over several market-product combinations. Movement toward market retention would extend the firm into yet another strategy position. Strategies of several of the multi-market-product conglomerates of the 1960s resembled fragmented strategy patterns. Some encountered serious problems, including bankruptcy, as a result of overextending financial and management resources.

Though a fragmented multiple strategy is not necessarily inappropriate, its use involves significant implications which should be recognized. Movement to adjacent positions

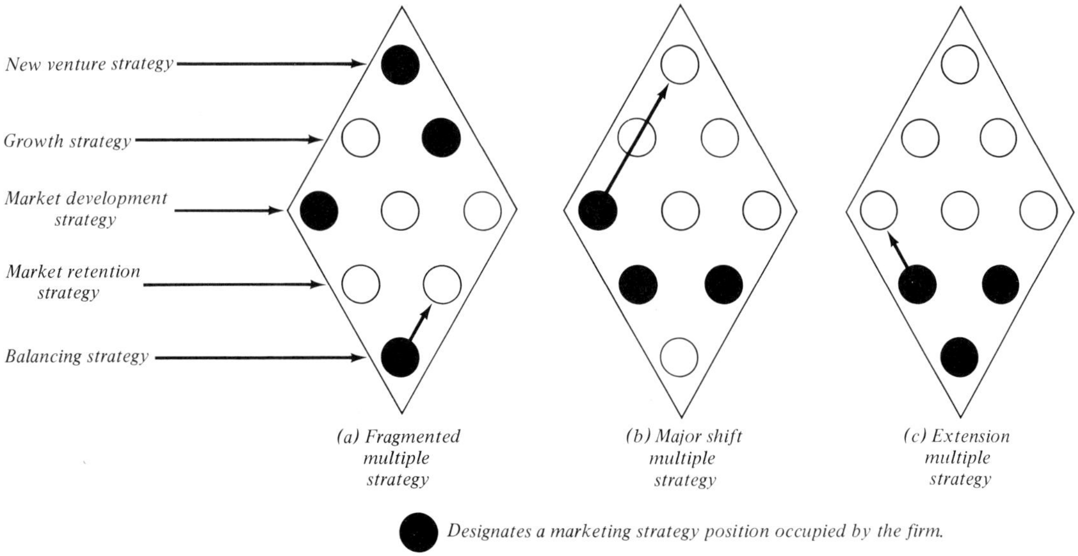

Figure 2 Illustrative multiple strategy positions.

from an existing extension multiple strategy position (c) is often more feasible than either the fragmented or major shift multiple strategies (a and b). The fragmented and extention multiple strategies represent quite different alternatives, and Table 2 outlines characteristics of them both.

After management has determined feasible alternative strategy position shifts, each should be assessed in terms of potential contribution to profits and other corporate goals, and in terms of competition, resource needs, impact upon current operations and risks. Depending upon the firm's existing strategy position and the alternatives being evaluated, certain areas of assessment may be more important than others. Management must weigh the various relevant criteria and arrive at a composite ranking of the alternatives. If only one possible strategy shift is considered, then it must be assessed in terms of whether moving toward it promises to make an acceptable contribution to the firm's goals.

Selection and Implementation

After selecting a new strategy position, specific plans must be developed to guide the implementation process. Our earlier examination of the characteristics of the various strategy positions provides guidelines for the marketing planning task with regard to environmental analysis, market target selection and marketing program design. Of course, the planning task should span the enterprise, since all areas of the firm will be involved in varying degrees, depending upon the particular market-product situation selected. For example, expanding the market of an existing product or service would place primary demands upon the marketing function. Alternatively, a new venture strategy would call upon the resources and capabilities of the entire firm.

Though marketing managers intuitively recognize differences in the various market-product situations confronting them, considerable insight into the marketing task can be gained by determining a firm's marketing strategy position. Through analysis of current position and evaluation of possible shifts, a sound basis can be developed for making needed changes. Perhaps most important, strategy position analysis provides clear support for the chief marketing executive when substantial resource increases are needed to implement a top management decision to pursue new market-product opportunities. By fo-

Table 2 Characteristics of Fragmented and Extension Multiple Strategy Positions

Fragmented multiple strategy	Extension multiple strategy
Adds to the demands upon possibly already overtaxed financial and managerial resources	The addition of a strategy position becomes a logical extension from the firm's existing market-product positions
Provides the firm with market-product situations at various life cycle stages	Multiple strategy tends to position the firm in a relatively narrow market-product maturity range
Enables extension to additional strategy positions from a wide range of possibilities	Options for additional strategy positions are relatively limited
Extension from an existing market-product combination provides certain of the same advantages of an extension multiple strategy	It is normally possible to pursue another strategy position with modest changes in existing organization and marketing program
Management must acquire a broad base of information about its markets and products	By concentrating in a limited range of market product situations, management can gain a strong, specialized base of knowledge and experience

cusing upon the variations in environmental analysis, selection of market targets and marketing program management resulting from different market-product situations, an attempt has been made to give direction to the marketing decision maker.

17

A Strategic Perspective on Product Planning

George S. Day

The pervasive nature of the resource allocation problem in relation to product planning is the subject of this article. Emphasis is placed on the role of new products and markets versus established ones, and the choice of areas of new product development to be pursued.

In this connection, an in-depth examination of the product portfolio is followed by a discussion of which search strategy to employ to locate desirable opportunities.

INTRODUCTION

The past decade has seen growing recognition that the product planning function within diversified companies of all sizes involves trade offs among competing opportunities and strategies. During this period the combination of more complex markets, shorter product life cycles and social, legal and governmental trends put a premium on minimizing the degree of risk in the product mix. More recently, managers have had to cope with severe resource constraints, stemming partly from weaknesses in the capital markets and a general cash shortage, and the triple traumas of the energy crisis, materials shortages and inflation.

Some of the manifestations of the new climate for product planning are skepticism toward the value of full product lines, unwillingness to accept the risks of completely new products, an emphasis on profit growth rather than volume growth and active product elimination and divestment programs.[1] Yet managements cannot afford to turn their backs on all opportunities for change and attempt to survive simply by doing a better job with the established products and services. Eventually all product categories become saturated or threatened by substitutes and diversification becomes essential to survival. Consumer goods companies are especially feeling this pressure as the productivity of line extensions or product adaptations directed at narrow market segments declines. Also the likelihood of regulatory actions directed at products, such as aerosols and cyclamates, points up the risks of having a closely grouped product line.[2] More than ever, long-run corporate health is going to depend on the ability of

Reprinted from *Journal of Contemporary Business*, Spring 1975, pp. 1–34, with permission of the *Journal of Contemporary Business*, copyright 1975. At the time of writing, the author was professor of marketing, Faculty of Management Studies, University of Toronto.

product planners to juggle those conflicting pressures of diversification and consolidation.

The pervasive nature of the resource allocation problem in product planning is the focus of this article. The emphasis is on the basic issues of the role of new and established products and markets and the choice of areas of new product development to pursue. The first issue is addressed in the context of the product portfolio, which describes the mixture of products that generate cash and in which the company can invest cash. A detailed examination of the product portfolio begins with its component parts, the product life cycle and the notion of market dominance, and then turns to the implications for strategic planning and resource allocation.

Once the role of new products has been established, the issue of where to look is addressed with an explicit statement of a search strategy. This statement defines the characteristics of desirable opportunities in terms that are meaninfgul to product planners.

STRATEGIC PLANNING AND PRODUCT PLANNING

There are as many concepts of strategy as writers on the subject.[3] Several of the more useful definitions for our immediate purposes are:

- Decisions today which affect the future (not future decisions)
- Major questions of resource allocation that determine a company's long-run results
- The calculated means by which the firm deploys its resources—i.e., personnel, machines and money—to accomplish its purpose under the most advantageous circumstances
- A competitive edge that allows a company to serve the customers better than its competitors
- The broad principles by which a company hopes to secure an advantage over competitors, an attractiveness to buyers and a full exploitation of company resources.

Following these definitions, the desired output of the strategic planning process is a long-run plan "that will produce an attractive growth rate and a high rate of return on investment by achieving a market position so advantageous that competitors can retaliate only over an extended time period at a prohibitive cost."[4]

Most strategic planning processes and the resulting plans show a distinct family resemblance, although the specifics obviously vary greatly. These specifics usually include[5]: (1) a statement of the mission of the strategic business unit (SBU),[6] (2) the desired future position the SBU and the corporation wants to attain, comprising measurable profitability, sales, market share, efficiency and flexibility objectives, (3) the key environmental assumptions and the opportunities and threats, (4) a statement of the strengths, weaknesses and problems of the SBU and its major competitors, (5) the strategic gap between the desired and forecasted position of the SBU, (6) actions to be taken to close the gap—the strategy and (7) the required resources and where they can be obtained, including financial resources such as net cash flow, the equity base and debt capacity and management capabilities. These are the main elements of the planning process that are relevant to product planning, leaving aside the issues of detailed implementation plans, contingency plans, which state in advance what modifications will be made if key environmental or competitor assumptions turn out to be false, and the monitoring procedures.

What is lacking in the planning process just described is a systematic procedure for generating and choosing strategic alternatives. One of the greatest weaknesses of current strategic plans is the lack of viable strategy alternatives which present very different approachs and outcomes. Too frequently top management sees only one strategy which the SBU has decided is best in terms of its own and the managers' personal needs and objectives. This ignores the interdependency among products (the portfolio aspect)[7] and the possibility that what is best for each SBU is not necessarily best for the entire company.[8] In recognition of this problem, the planning process shown in Figure I incorporates an analysis of the product portfolio. The remainder of this paper is devoted to the uses and limitations of the product portfolio and the implications for developing strategy alternates that optimize the long-run position of the firm.

THE COMPONENTS OF THE PRODUCT PORTFOLIO

Market share and stage in the product life cycle have long been regarded as important determinants of profitability. The contribution of the product portfolio concept is that it permits the planner to consider these two measures simultaneously in evaluating the products of an entire company or a division or SBU.

The Value of Market Share Dominance

The belief in the benefits of a dominant market share is rooted deeply in the experience of executives. It is reinforced by the facts of life in most markets:

- The market leader is usually the most profitable
- During economic downturns, customers are likely to concentrate their purchases in suppliers with large shares, and distributors and retailers will try to cut inventories by eliminating the marginal supplier
- During periods of economic growth, there is often a bandwagon effect with a large share presenting a positive image to customers and retailers.[9]

Of course, market domination has its own pitfalls, beyond antitrust problems, ". . . monopolists flounder on their own complacency rather than on public opposition. Market domination produces tremendous in-

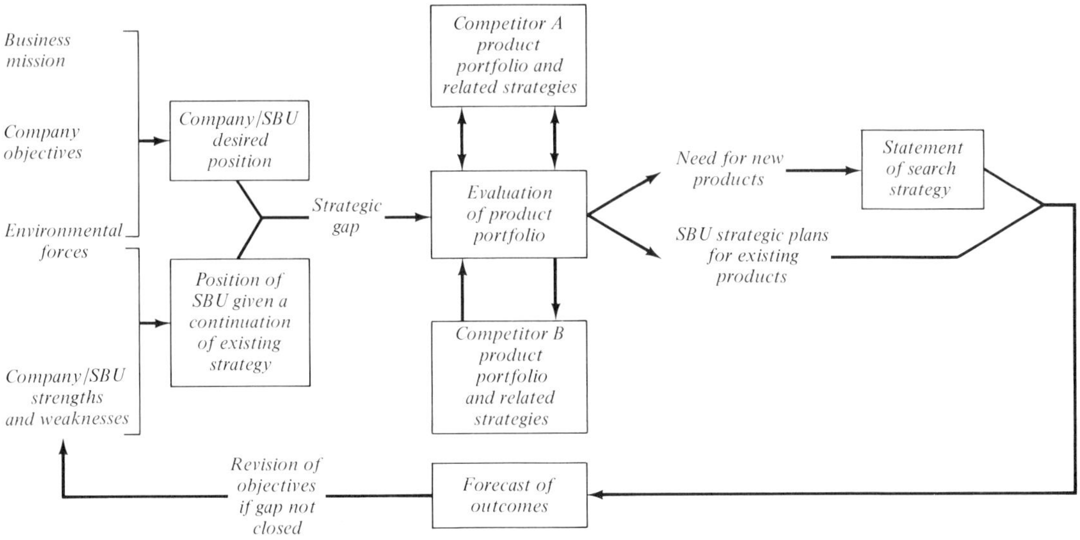

Figure I Highlighting product planning activities in the strategic planning process.

ternal resistance against any innovation and makes adaptation to change dangerously difficult. Also, it usually means that the enterprise has too many of its eggs in one basket and is too vulnerable to economic fluctuations."[10] The leader is also highly vulnerable to competitive actions, especially in the pricing area, since the leader establishes the basic industry price from which smaller competitors can discount.

The clearest evidence of the value of market share comes from a study of The Profit Impact of Market Strategies (PIMS) of 620 separate businesses by the Marketing Science Institute which, in turn, draws on earlier work by General Electric. Early results indicated that market share, investment intensity (ratio of total investment to sales) and product quality were the most important determinants of pretax return on investment, among a total of 37 distinct factors incorporated into the profit model.[11] On average it was found that a difference of 10 points in market share was accompanied by a difference of about 5 points in pretax ROI. As share declined from more than 40 percent to less than 10 percent, the average pretax ROI dropped from 30 percent to 9.1 percent.

The PIMS study also provided some interesting insights into the reasons for the link between market share and profitability.[12] The results point to economies of scale and, especially, the opportunities for vertical integration as the most important explanations. Thus high-share businesses (more than 40 percent) tend to have low ratios of purchases to sales because they make rather than buy and own their distribution facilities. The ratio of purchases to sales increases from 33 percent for high-share businesses to 45 percent for low-share (less than 10 percent) businesses. But because of economies of scale in manufacturing and purchasing there is no significant relationship between manufacturing expenses or the ratio of sales to investment and the market share. To some degree these results also support the market power argument of economists; market leaders evidently are able to bargain more effectively (either through the exercise of reciprocity or greater technical marketing skills) and obtain higher prices than their competition (but largely because they produce and sell higher-quality goods and services). The fact that market leaders spend a significantly higher percentage of their sales on R and D suggests that they pursue a conscious strategy of product leadership.

Experience Curve Analysis The importance of economies of scale in the relationship of market share and profitability is verified by the experience curve concept. Research, largely reported by the Boston Consulting Group, has found that in a wide range of businesses (including plastics, semiconductors, gas ranges and life insurance policies), the total unit costs, in constant dollars, decline by a constant percentage (usually 20 to 30 percent) with each doubling of accumulated units of output or experience.[13] Since the experience effect applies to all value added, it subsumes economies of scale and specialization effects along with the well-known learning curve which applies only to direct labor costs.

An experience curve, when plotted on a log-log scale as in Figure II, appears as a straight line. The locations of the competitors on this curve are determined approximately by their respective accumulated experience, for which relative market share is a good surrogate (this may not be true if some competitors recently have entered the market by buying experience through licenses or acquisitions). Then it follows that the competitor with the greatest accumulated experience will have the lowest relative costs and, if prices are similar between competitors, also will have

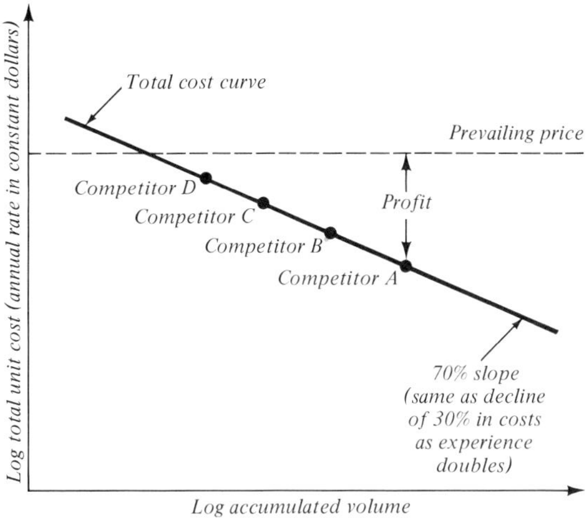

Figure II Cost experience curve showing relative profit levels of competitors.

the greatest profits. Of course, companies that fail to reduce costs along the product category experience curve and who are not dominant will be at an even greater competitive disadvantage.

Figure II shows a price prevailing at one point in time. Over the long run, prices also will decline at roughly the same rate as costs decline. The major exception to this rule occurs during the introduction and growth state of the life cycle, when the innovator and/or dominant competitor, is tempted to maintain prices at a high level to recoup the development costs. The high price umbrella usually achieves this immediate end because unit profits are high. The drawback is the incentive to higher cost competitors to enter the market and attempt to increase their market shares. In effect, the dominant competitor is trading future market share for current profits. This may be sensible if the early leader: (1) has a number of attractive new product opportunities requiring cash, (2) there are potential competitors whose basic business position will enable them eventually to enter the product category regardless of the pricing strategy[14] or (3) significant barriers to entry can be erected.

Product Life Cycle

That products pass through various stages between life and death (introduction → growth → maturity → decline) is hard to deny. Equally accepted is the notion that a company should have a mix of products with representation in each of these stages.

Thus the concept of a product life cycle would appear to be an essential tool for understanding product strategies.[15] Indeed this is true, but only *if* the position of the product and the duration of the cycle can be determined. This caveat should be kept in mind when considering the following summary of the important aspects of the product life cycle:

- Volume and profit growth attract competition during the early *growth* (or takeoff) stage of the life cycle. The product market is even more attractive if the innovator lacks the capacity to satisfy demand. However, these competitors may contribute to the growth of sales by their market development expenditures and product improvements.
- Purchase patterns and distribution channels are still fluid during the rapid *growth* stage. For this reason, market shares can be increased at relatively low cost over short periods of time by capturing a disproportionate share of incremental sales (especially where these sales come from new users rather than heavier usage by existing users).
- As a product reaches *maturity* there is evidence of saturation, finer distinctions in benefits surrounding the product and appeals to special segments.
- There is often an industry shake-out to signal the *end* of the rapid growth stage. The trigger might be an excessive number of competitors who have to resort to price cutting to survive; a dominant producer who seeks to regain share; or a large competitor buying into the market (and all these effects will be accen-

tuated by an economic slow down). The result is a period of consolidation during which marginal competitors either drop out, merge with other small competitors or sell out to larger competitors.

• During the *maturity* stage, market-share relationships tend to stabilize; distribution patterns have been established and are difficult to change. This, in turn, contributes to inertia in purchasing relationships and selling oriented toward maintaining relationships. Any substantial increase in share of market will require a reduction in a competitor's capacity utilization which will be resisted vigorously. As a result, gains in share are both time-consuming and costly. This is not necessarily the case if the attempt to gain shares is spearheaded by a significant improvement in product value or performance which the competitor cannot easily match. A case in point is the growth in private labels, or distributor-controlled labels, in both food and general merchandising categories.

• As substitutes appear and/or sales begin to decline, the core product behaves like a commodity and is subject to intense and continuing price pressure. The result is further competitors dropping out of the market, since only those with extensive accumulated experience and cost-cutting capability are able to generate reasonable profits and ROI's.

• The *decline* stage can be forestalled by vigorous promotion (plus, a new creative platform) and product improvement designed to generate more frequent usage or new users and applications.[16] Of course, if these extensions are sufficiently different, a new product life cycle is launched.

Measurement and Interpretation Problems

The concepts underlying the product portfolio are much easier to articulate than to implement.

What Is the Product-Market? The crux of the problem is well stated by Moran:

> In our complex service society there are no more product classes—not in any meaningful sense, only as a figment of file clerk imagination. There are only use classes—users which are more central to some products and peripheral to others—on a vast overlapping continuum. To some degree, in some circumstances almost anything can be a partial substitute for almost anything else. An eight-cent stamp substitutes to some extent for an airline ticket.[17]

Where does this leave the manager who relies on share of some (possibly ill-defined) market as a guide to performance evaluation and resource allocation. First he or she must recognize that most markets do not have neat boundaries. For example, patterns of substitution in industrial markets often look like continuua, i.e., zinc, brass, aluminum and engineered plastics such as nylon and polycarbonates can be arrayed rather uniformly along dimensions of price and performance. A related complication, more pertinent to consumer product markets, is the possibility of segment differences in perceptions of product substitutability. For example, there is a timid, risk-averse segment that uses a different product for each kind of surface cleaning (i.e., surface detergents, scouring powders, floor cleaners, bleaches, lavatory cleaners and general-purpose wall cleaners). At the other extreme is the segment that uses detergent for every cleaning problem. Thirdly, product/markets may have to be defined in terms of distribution patterns. Thus, tire companies treat the OEM and replacement tire markets as separate and distinct, even though the products going through these two channels are perfect substitutes so far as the end customer is concerned.

Perhaps the most important consideration is the time frame. A long-run view, reflecting strategic planning concerns, invariably will reveal a larger product-market to account for: (1) changes in technology, price relationships and availability which may remove or reduce cost and performance limitations, e.g., the boundaries between minicomputers, programmable computers and time-sharing systems in many use situations are becoming very fuzzy; (2) the time required by present and prospective buyers to react to these changes, which includes modifying behavior patterns, production systems, etc. and (3) considerable switching among products over long periods of time to satisfy desires for variety and change, as is encountered in consumer goods with snacks, for example.

Despite these complexities, the boundaries of product markets usually are established by four-digit Standard Industrial Classification (SIC) categories and/or expert judgment. The limitations of the SIC are well known[18] but often do not outweigh the benefits of data availability in a convenient form that can be broken down further to geographic markets. In short, the measure is attractive on tactical grounds (for sales force, promotional budget, etc., allocation) but potentially misleading for strategic planning purposes.

What Is Market Dominance? A measure of market share, per se, is not a good indicator of the extent to which a firm dominates a market. The value of a 30 percent share is very different in a market where the next largest competitor has 40 percent than in one where the next largest has only 20 percent. Two alternative measures which incorporate information on the structure of the competition are:

- Company share ÷ share of largest competitor
- Company share ÷ share of largest three largest competitors.

The former measure is more consistent with the implications of the experience curve, while the latter is perhaps better suited to highly concentrated markets (where the four-firm concentration ratio is greater than 80 percent, for example). Regardless of which measure is used it is often the case that the dominant firm has to be at least 1.5 times as large as the next biggest competitor in order to ensure profitability. When there are two large firms of roughly equal shares, especially in a growth business such as nuclear power generators, the competition is likely to be severe. In this instance, both General Electric and Westinghouse have about 40 percent shares and don't expect to be profitable on new installations until after 1977. Conversely, when the two largest firms have small shares, say less than 5 percent, neither measure of market dominance is meaningful.

Evidence of market share dominance, no matter how it is measured, will not be equally meaningful in all product markets. Results from the PIMS study[19] suggest that importance of market share is influenced most strongly by the frequency of purchases.

While the full reasons for this difference in profitability are obscure they probably relate to differences in unit costs and prior buyer experience with the available alternatives which, in turn, determine willingness to reduce risk by buying the market leader and/or paying a premium price. Also, the frequently purchased category is dominated by consumer goods where there is considerable proliferation of brand names through spin offs, flank-

Return on Investment

Share market	Infrequently purchased (< once/mon)	Frequently purchased (> once/mon)
Under 10%	6.9%	12.4%
10-19	14.4	13.7
20-29	17.8	17.4
30-39	24.3	23.1
Over 40	34.6	22.9

ers, fighting brands, etc. in highly segmented markets. Each of these brands, no matter how small, shares production facilities and will have low production and distribution costs, although they may be treated as separate businesses.[20] It is hardly surprising that the experience curve concept is difficult to apply to consumer goods. Most of the successful applications have been with infrequently purchased industrial products; relatively undifferentiated, with high value added compared to raw material costs and fairly stable rates of capacity utilization.

A further caveat regarding the experience curve concerns the extent to which costs ultimately can be reduced. The experience curve clearly does not happen according to some immutable law; it requires careful management and some degree of long-run product stability (and, ideally, standardization). These conditions cannot be taken for granted and will be threatened directly by the customer demand for product change and competitive efforts to segment the market. In effect, product innovation and cost efficiency are not compatible in the long-run.[21]

A related question concerns the relevance of the experience curve to a new competitor in an established market. It is doubtful that a new entrant with reasonable access to the relevant technology would incur the same level of initial costs as the developers of the market.

What Is the Stage in the Product Life Cycle? It is not sufficient to simply know the current rate of growth of the product category. The strategic implications of the product life cycle often hinge on forecasting changes in the growth rate and, in particular, on establishing the end of the growth and maturity stages.

The first step in utilizing the life cycle is to ensure that the product class is identified properly. This may require a distinction between a broad product type (cigarettes) and a more specific product form (plain filter cigarettes). Secondly, the graph of product (type or form) sales needs to be adjusted for factors that might obscure the underlying life cycle, i.e., price changes, economic fluctuations and population changes. The third and most difficult step is to forecast when the product will move from one stage to another. The specific problems are beyond the scope of this article. However, the range of possibilities is illustrated by these various leading indicators of the "top-out" point.[22]

- Evidence of saturation; declining proportion of new trier versus replacement sales
- Declining prices and profits
- Increased product life
- Industry over capacity
- Appearance of new replacement product or technology
- Changes in export/import ratio
- Decline in elasticity of advertising and promotion, coupled with increasing price elasticity
- Changes in consumer preferences

These measures generally will indicate only the *timing* of the top-out point, and each is sufficiently imprecise that it is strongly advisable to use as many as possible in combination. Forecasts of the product sales *level* to be achieved at the top-out point may be obtained by astute incorporation of the leading indicators into: (1) technological forecasts, (2) similar product analysis (where sales patterns of products with analogous characteristics are used to estimate the sales pattern of the new product) or (3) epidemiological models whose parameters include initial sales rates and market saturation levels estimated with marketing research methods.[23]

ANALYZING THE PRODUCT PORTFOLIO

The product life cycle highlights the desirability of a variety of products/services with different present and prospective growth rates. However, this is not a sufficient condition for a well balanced portfolio of products that will ensure profitable long-run growth. Two other factors are market share position and the need to balance cash flows within the corporation. Some products should *generate* cash (and provide acceptable reported profits) and others should *use* cash to support growth; otherwise, the company will build up unproductive cash reserves or go bankrupt.[24] These issues are clarified by jointly considering share position and market growth rate, as in the matrix of Figure III. The conceptualization used here is largely attributable to the Boston Consulting Group.[25]

It must be stressed that the growth-share matrix discussed here is simply one way of conceptualizing the product portfolio. It has been useful as a device for synthesizing the analyses and judgments of the earlier steps in the planning process, especially in facilitating an approach to strategic decision making that considers the firm to be a whole that is more than the sum of its separate parts. For these purposes, the arbitrary classifications of products in the growth-share matrix are adequate to differentiate the strategy possibilities.[26]

Product Portfolio Strategies

Each of the four basic categories in the growth-share matrix implies a set of strategy alternatives that generally are applicable to the portfolio entries in that category.[27]

Stars Products that are market leaders, but also growing fast, will have substantial reported profits but need a lot of cash to finance the

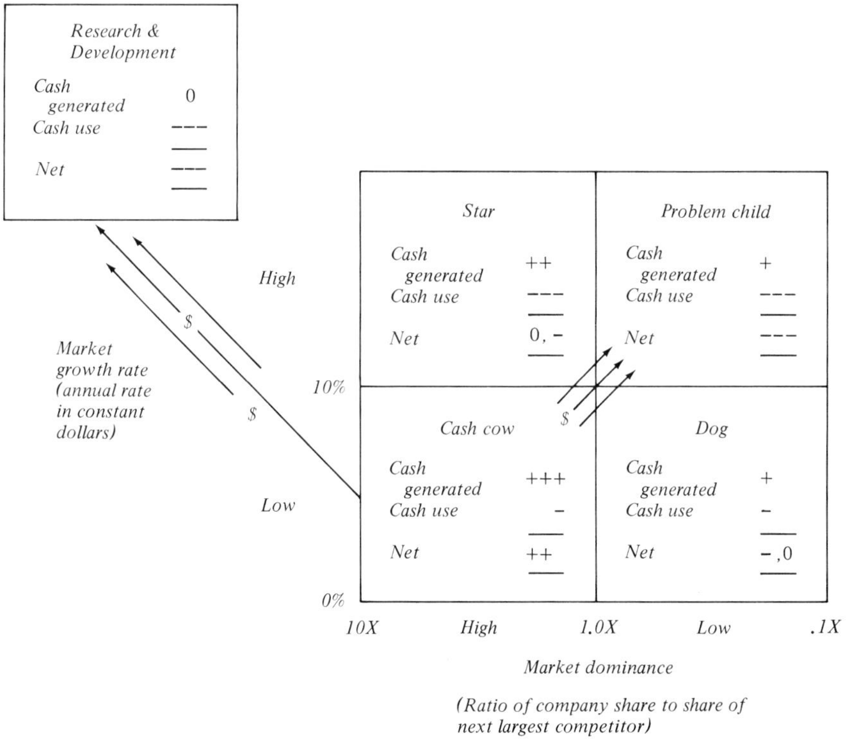

Figure III Describing the product portfolio in the market share growth matrix. (Arrows indicate principal cash flows.)

rate of growth. The appropriate strategies are designed primarily to protect the existing share level by reinvesting earnings in the form of price reductions, product improvement, better market coverage, production efficiency increases, etc. Particular attention must be given to obtaining a large share of the new users or new applications that are the source of growth in the market. Management may elect, instead, to maximize short-run profits and cash flow at the expense of long-run market share. This is highly risky because it usually is predicated on a continuing stream of product innovations and deprives the company of a cash cow which may be needed in the future.

Cash Cows The combination of a slow market growth and market dominance usually spells substantial net cash flows. The amount of cash generated is far in excess of the amount required to maintain share. All strategies should be directed toward maintaining market dominance—including investments in technological leadership. Pricing decisions should be made cautiously with an eye to maintaining price leadership. Pressure to overinvest through product proliferation and market expansion should be resisted unless prospects for expanding primary demand are unusually attractive. Instead, excess cash should be used to support research activities and growth areas elsewhere in the company.

Dogs Since there usually can be only one market leader and because most markets are mature, the greatest number of products fall in this category.[28] Such products are usually at a cost disadvantage and have few opportunities for growth at a reasonable cost. Their markets are not growing, so there is little new business to compete for, and market share gains will be resisted strenuously by the dominant competition.

The product remains in the portfolio because it shows (or promises) a modest book profit. This accounting result is misleading because most of the cash flow must be reinvested to maintain competitive position and finance inflation.[29] Another characteristic of a dog is that individual investment projects (especially those designed to reduce production costs) show a high ROI. However, the competitive situation is such that these returns cannot be realised in surplus cash flow that can be used to fund more promising projects. In addition there are the potential hidden costs of unproductive demands on management time (and consequent missed opportunities) and low personnel morale because of a lack of achievement.

The pejorative label of dog becomes increasingly appropriate the closer the product is to the lower-right corner of the growth/share matrix.[30] The need for positive action becomes correspondingly urgent. The search for action alternatives should begin with attempts to alleviate the problem without divesting. If these possibilities are unproductive, attention then can shift to finding ways of making the product to be divested as attractive as possible; then to liquidation and, finally if need be, to abandonment:

- Corrective action. Naturally all reasonable cost-cutting possibilities should be examined, but, as noted above, these are not likely to be productive in the long-run. A related alternative is to find a market segment that can be dominated. The attractiveness of this alternative will depend on the extent to which the segment can be protected from competition—perhaps because of technology or distribution requirements.[31] What must be avoided is the natural tendency of operating managers to arbitrarily redefine their markets in order to improve their share position and thus change the classification of the product when, in fact, the economics of the business are unchanged. This is highly probable when the product-market boundaries are ambiguous.
- Harvest. This is a conscious cutback of

all support costs to the minimum level to maximize the product's profitability over a foreseeable lifetime, which is usually short. This cutback could include reducing advertising and sales effort, increasing delivery time, increasing the acceptable order size and eliminating all staff support activities such as marketing research.

• Value added. Opportunities may exist for reparceling a product or business that is to be divested. this may involve dividing the assets into smaller units or participating in forming a "kennel of dogs" in which the weak products of several companies are combined into a healthy package. This latter alternative is especially attractive when the market is very fractionated.

• Liquidation. This is the most prevalent solution usually involving a sale as a going concern but, perhaps, including a licensing agreement. If the business/product is to be sold as a unit, the problem is to maximize the selling price—a joint function of the prospective buyers need for the acquisition (which will depend on search strategy) and their overhead rate. For example, a small company may find the product attractive and be able to make money because of low overhead.

• Abandonment. The possibilities here include giveaways and bankruptcy.

Problem Children The combination of rapid growth rate and poor profit margins creates an enormous demand for cash. If the cash is not forthcoming, the product will become a dog as growth inevitably slows. The basic strategy options are fairly clear-cut; either invest heavily to get a disproportionate share of the new sales or buy existing share by acquiring competitors and thus move the product toward the star category or get out of the business using some of the methods just described.

Consideration also should be given to a market segmentation strategy, but only if a defensible niche can be identified and resources are available to gain dominance. This strategy is even more attractive if the segment can provide an entree and experience base from which to push for dominance of the whole market.

Further Strategic Implications

While the product portfolio is helpful in suggesting strategies for specific products, it is equally useful for portraying the overall health of a multiproduct company. The issue is the extent to which the portfolio departs from the balanced display of Figure IV, both for the present and in 3 to 5 years.

Among the indicators of overall health are size and vulnerability of the cash cows (and the prospects for the stars, if any) and the number of problem children and dogs. Particular attention must be paid to those products with large cash appetities. Unless the company has abundant cash flow, it cannot afford to sponsor many such products at one time. If resources (including debt capacity) are spread too thin, the company simply will wind up with too many marginal products and suffer a reduced capacity to finance promising new product entries or acquisitions in the future.

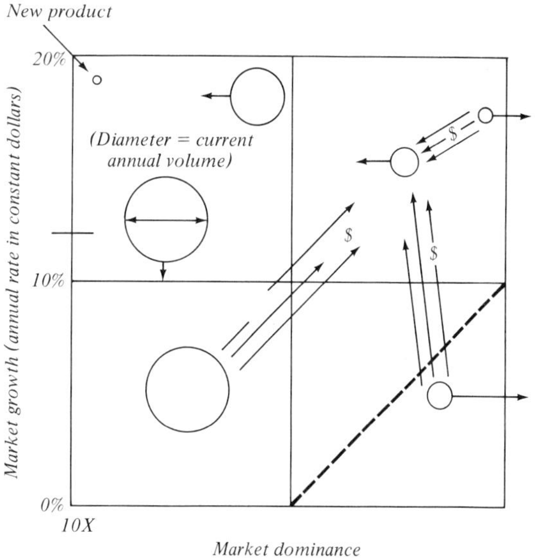

Figure IV A balanced product portfolio.

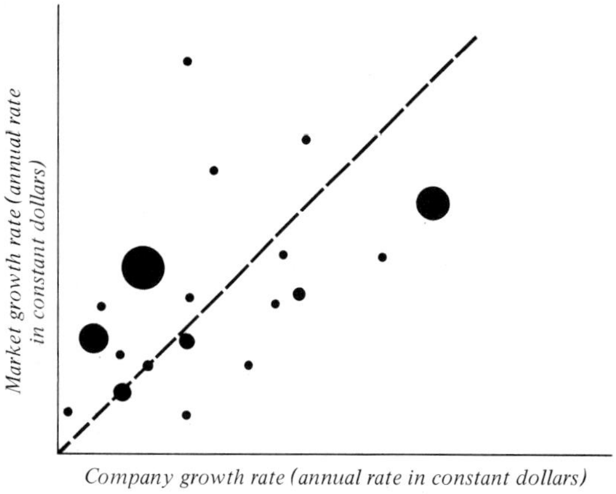

Figure V Market industry versus company growth rates. (Illustrative diversified company—diameters are proportional to current annual sales volume.)

Some indication of this type of resource misallocation can be obtained from a comparison of the growth rates of the product class and the company's entrant (as illustrated in Figure V). Ideally, nothing should be in the upper sector where market growth exceeds company growth—unless the product is being harvested.

Competitive Analysis Product portfolios should be constructed for each of the major competitors. Assuming competitive management follows the logic just described, they eventually will realize that they can't do everything. The key question is which problem children will be supported aggressively and which will be eliminated. The answer obviously will be difficult to obtain, but has an important bearing on the approach the company takes to its own problem children.

Of course, a competitive position analysis has many additional dimensions which must be explored in depth before specific competitive actions and reactions within each product category can be forecast.[32] This analysis, coupled with an understanding of competitive portfolios, becomes the basis for any fundamental strategy employing the military concept of concentration which essentially means to concentrate strength against weakness.[33]

Dangers in the Pursuit of Market Share Tilles has suggested a number of criteria for evaluating strategy alternatives.[34] The product portfolio is a useful concept for addressing the first three: (1) environmental consistency, (2) internal consistency and (3) adequacy of resources. A fourth criteria considers whether the degree of risk is acceptable, given the overall level of risk in the portfolio.

The experience of a number of companies, such as G.E. and RCA, in the main-frame computer business, points to the particular risks inherent in the pursuit of market share. An analysis of these "pyrrhic victories"[35] suggests that greatest risks can be avoided if the following questions can be answered affirmatively: (1) Are company financial resources adequate? (2) If the fight is stopped short for some reason, will the corporation's position be competitively viable? and (3) Will government regulations permit the corporation to follow the strategy it has chosen? The last question includes antitrust policies which now virtually preclude acquisitions made by large companies in related fields[36] and regulatory policies designed to proliferate competition, as in the airline industry.

Organizational Implications Although this discussion has focused on the financial and market position aspects of the product portfolio, the implications encompass the deployment of all corporate resources—tangible assets as well as crucial intangibles of management skills and time.

One policy that clearly must be avoided is to apply uniform performance objectives to all products, or SBU's, as is frequently attempted in highly decentralized profit-center management approaches. The use of flexible standards, tailored to the realities of the business, logically should lead to the recognition that different kinds of businesses require very different management styles. For example, stars and problem children demand an entrepreneurial orientation, while cash cows emphasize skills in fine tuning marketing tactics and ensuring effective allocation of resources. The nature of specialist support also will differ; e.g., R and D support being important for growth products and financial personnel becoming increasingly important as growth slows.[37] Finally, since good managers, regardless of their styles are always in short supply, the portfolio notion suggests that they not be expended in potentially futile efforts to turn dogs into profitable performers. Instead they should be deployed into situations where the likelihood of achievement and, hence, of reinforcement, is high.

Other Methods of Portraying the Portfolio

The growth-share matrix is far from a complete synthesis of the underlying analyses and judgments as to the position of the firm in each of its product-markets. The main problem of the matrix concerns the growth rate dimension. While this is an extremely useful measure in that it can have direct implications for cash flows, it is only one of many possible determinants of the attractiveness of the market. A list of other possible factors is summarized in Table I. (Not all these factors will be relevant to all markets.) The importance of each factor depends on the company's capabilities, but careful consideration will help to identify unusual threats, such as impending government regulations, that might significantly reduce future attractiveness. Similarly, market share may not provide a comprehensive indication of the company's position in each market; as in the case of a leader in a market that is rapidly fragmenting.

The qualitative aspects of overall attractiveness and position also can be incorporated into a matrix which portrays the product portfolio [see page 206]. This matrix does not have the immediate cash flow implication of the growth-share matrix, thus, it should be used as a complementary, rather than a replacement approach.

Table I Factors Determining Market and Industry Attractiveness

Market	• Size (present and potential) • Growth/stage in life cycle • Diversity of user segments • Foreign opportunities • Cyclicality
Competition	• Concentration ratio • Capacity utilization • Structural changes (e.g., entries and exits) • Position changes • Vertical threats/opportunities • Sensitivity of shares and market size to price, service, etc. • Extent of "captive" business
Profitability	• Level and trend of leaders • Contribution rates • Changes/threats on key leverage factors (e.g., scale economies and pricing) • Barriers to entry
Technology	• Maturity/volatility • Complexity • Patent protection • Product/process opportunities
Other	• Social/environmental • Government/political • Unions • Human factors

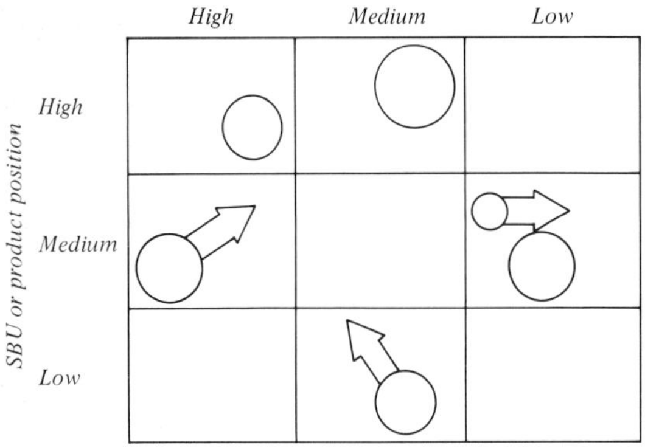

Industry or market attractiveness. (Arrow represents forecast of change in position. Diameter [of circles] is proportional to share of company sales contributed by product.)

NEW PRODUCT PLANNING

A product portfolio analysis identifies the need for new products or new markets and the probable level of available resources but does not indicate where to look. This presents management with a number of difficult questions:

- What degree of relationship to the present business is necessary and desirable?
- What are the possibilities for internal development versus acquisition?
- When is an innovation preferred to an imitation and vice versa?
- What are the characteristics of desirable new products?

These and innumerable other questions have to be answered before personnel in the product planning, corporate development or other responsible functions can pursue their tasks efficiently. In short, top management must decide how much growth is desired and feasible, the contribution of new versus established products and the broad direction as to how the growth will be achieved.

What is needed is a strategy statement that specifies those areas where development is to proceed and identifies (perhaps by exclusion) those areas that are off-limits. As Crawford notes, "the idea of putting definitive restrictions on new product activity is not novel, but use of it, especially sophisticated use, is still not widespread."[38] The major criticisms of a comprehensive statement of new product development strategy are that it will inhibit or restrict creativity and that ideas with great potential will be rejected. Experience suggests that clear guidance improves creativity by focusing energy on those areas where the payoff is likely to be greatest. Also, experience shows that significant breakthroughs outside the bounds of the product development strategy statement can be accomodated readily in an on-going project evaluation and screening process.

The New Product Development Strategy Statement

The essential elements of this statement are the specification of the product-market scope, the basic strategies to be used for growing within that scope and the characteristics of desirable alternatives. These elements guide the search for new product ideas, acquisitions, licenses, etc., and form the basis for a formal screening procedure.

Product-Market Scope This is an attempt to answer the basic question, "what business(es) do we want to be in" and is a specific manifestation of the mission of the SBU or company. There is no ready-made formula for developing the definition of the future business. One approach is to learn from definitions that have been useful in guiding successful strategies. For example, the General Electric Housewares SBU defines their present (circa 1973) business as "providing consumers with functional aids to increase the enjoyment or psychic fulfillment of selected lifestyles"—specifically those dealing with preparation of food, care of the person, care of personal surroundings and planning assistance. In the future their business will expand to include recreation, enhancement of security and convenient care of the home.

This statement of the future business satisfied one important criteria: that it be linked to the present product-market scope by a clearly definable common thread. In the case of G.E. Housewares, the common thread is with generic needs being satisfied (or problems being solved, as the case may be). Ansoff argues that the linkage also can be with product characteristics, distribution capability or underlying technology—as long as the firm has distinctive competency in these areas.[39]

Other criteria for appraising the usefulness of a description of the future business opportunities are: (1) specificity—if the definition of product-market scope is too general, it won't have an impact on the organization (e.g., consider the vagueness of being in the business of supplying products with a plug on the end); (2) flexibility—the definition should be adapted constantly to recognize changing environmental conditions (e.g., Gerber no longer can say that babies are their only business), (3) attainability—can be undertaken within the firm's resources and competencies and (4) competitive advantage—it always is preferable to protect and build on these strengths and competencies that are not possessed as fully by the competition.[40]

Basic Strategies for Growth At the broad level of a new product development strategy, the basic issues are the *growth vector,* or the direction the firm is moving within the chosen product-market scope, and the emphasis on *innovation* versus *imitation.*

There are almost an infinite number of possibilities for growth vectors. The basic alternatives are summarized in Figure VI.[41] There is no intention here to suggest that these strategies are mutually exclusive; indeed, various combinations can be pursued simultaneously in order to close the strategic gaps identified in the overall planning process. Furthermore, most of the strategies can be pursued either by internal development or acquisition and coupled with vertical diversification (either forward toward a business that is a customer or backward toward a business that is a supplier).

The choice of growth vector will be influenced by all the factors discussed earlier as part of the overall corporate planning process. Underlying any choice is, by necessity, an appraisal of the risks compared with the payoffs. The essence of past experience is that growth vectors within the existing market (or, at least, closely related markets) are much more likely to be successful than ventures into new markets.[42] Therefore, diversification is the riskiest vector to follow—especially if it is attempted by means of internal development. The attractiveness of acquisitions for diversification is the chance to reduce the risks of failure by buying a known entity with (reasonably) predictable performance.

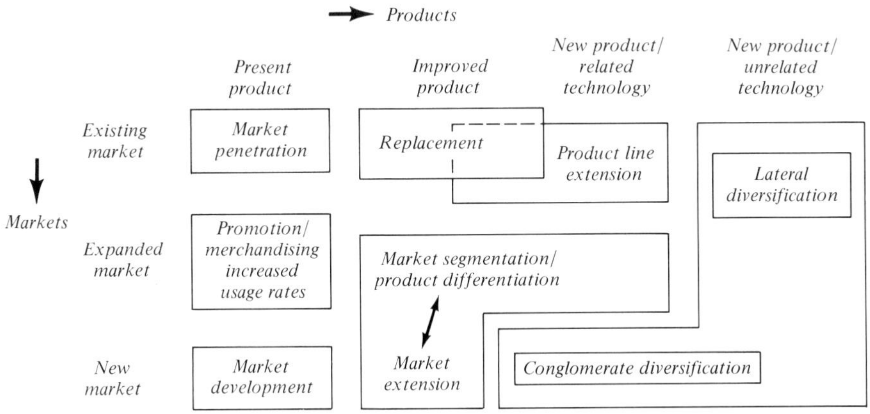

Figure VI Growth vector alternatives.

An equally crucial basic strategy choice is the degree of emphasis on innovation versus imitation. The risks of being an innovator are well known so few, if any, diversified corporations can afford to be innovators in each product-market. There are compelling advantages to being first in the market if barriers to entry (because of patent protections, capital requirements, control over distribution, etc.) can be erected, the product is difficult to copy or improve on and the introductory period is short. The imitator, by contrast, is always put at a cost disadvantage by a successful innovator and must be prepared to invest heavily to build a strong market position. While profits over the life of the product may be lower for an imitator, the risks are much lower because the innovator has provided a full-scale market test which can be monitored to determine the probable growth in future sales. Also, the innovator may provide significant opportunities by not serving all segments or, more likely, by not implementing the introduction properly.

The conscious decision to lead or follow pervades all aspects of the firm. Some of the important differences that result can be seen from the various strategic orientations to high technology markets discussed by Ansoff and Steward:

- First to market . . . based on strong R and D, technical leadership and risk taking
- Follow the leader . . . based on strong development resources and the ability to act quickly as the market starts its growth phase
- Applications engineering . . . based on product modifications to fit the needs of particular customers in mature markets
- Me-too . . . based on superior manufacturing efficiency and cost control.[43]

Characteristics of Desirable Alternatives

Three fundamental questions have to be asked of each new product or service being sought or considered: (1) How will a strong competitive advantage be obtained? The possibilities range from superiority in underlying technology or product quality, to patent protection, to marketing requirements. Another dimension of this question is the specification of markets or competitors to be avoided on the grounds that these situations would blunt the pursuit of a competitive advantage. (2) What is the potential for synergy? This asks about joint effects, or "the mutually reinforcing impact a product-market entry has on a firm's efficiency and effectiveness."[44] Synergy can be sought for defensive reasons, in order to supply a competence that the firm lacks or to spread the risks of a highly cyclical industry, as has motivated a number of mergers in the machine tool industry. Alternatively, synergy can utilize an existing competence such as a distribution system (notable examples here are Gillette and Coca Cola), a production capability, promotional skills, etc. In addition, "financial reinforcement may occur either because of the relative pattern of funds generation and demand . . . or because the combination is more attractive to the financial community than the pieces would be separately."[45] (3) What specific operating results are required? The possibilities here usually are expressed in terms of threshold or minimum desirable levels:

- Rate of market growth
- Payback period (despite its deficiencies it is a reflection of the risk level)
- Minimum sales level. (This is a function of fixed costs and scale of operations: the danger is that a product with good long-run potential will be rejected because of modest short-run sales possibilities.)
- Profit levels, cash flow and return on assets. (Each of these financial requirements must be developed in light of the firm's product portfolio.)

SUMMARY

Too often product planning is conducted as though each established product or service, and new product opportunity being sought or evaluated were independent of the other products of the firm. The implication is that corporate performance is the sum of the contributions of individual profit centers or product strategies.[46]

This article emphasizes the need to consider the interdependencies of products as parts of a portfolio described by market share dominance and market growth rate before overall corporate performance can be optimized. Only then can decisions as to resource allocation, growth and financial objectives and specific strategies be developed for established products and the need for new products identified.

There is little doubt that the future will see increasing acceptance of a broad systems approach to overall corporate strategy, in general, and to product planning, in particular. There are already a number of successful practitioners to emulate (who have gained a competitive edge that cannot be ignored).[47] More importantly, as the business environment becomes increasingly resource-constrained there may be no other choice for most firms.

FOOTNOTES

1 "The Squeeze on Product Mix," *Business Week* (5 January 1974), pp. 50–55, "Toward Higher Margins and Less Variety," *Business Week* (14 September 1974), pp. 98–99; E. B. Weiss, "We'll See Fewer New Products in 1975—Culprit Is Shortage of Capital, Resources," *Advertising Age* (2 December 1974); "Corrective Surgery," *Newsweek* (27 January 1975), p. 50; and Jack Springer, "1975: Bad Year for New Products; Good Year for Segmentation," *Advertising Age* (10 February 1975), pp. 30–39.

2 Barry R. Linsky, "Which Way to Move with New Products," *Advertising Age* (22 July 1974), pp. 45–46.

3 George A. Steiner, *Top Management Planning* (London: Macmillan, 1969); H. Igor Ansoff, *Corporate Strategy* (New York: McGraw-Hill, 1965).

4 David T. Kollat, Roger D. Blackwell and James F. Robeson, *Strategic Marketing* (New York: Holt, Rinehart and Winston, 1972), p. 12.

5 This description of the planning process has been adapted from Kollat, et al, *Strategic Marketing*; Louis V. Gerstner, "The Practice of Business: Can Strategic Planning Pay Off?" *Business Horizons* (December 1972); Herschner Cross, "New Directions in Corporate Planning," An address to Operations Research Society of America (Milwaukee, Wisconsin: 10 May 1973).

6 The identification of "strategic business units" is a critical first step in any analysis of corporate strategy. Various definitions have been used. Their flavor is captured by the following guidelines for defining a business: (1) no more than 60 percent of the expenses should represent arbitrary allocations of joint costs, (2) no more than 60 percent of the sales should be made to a vertically integrated (downstream) subsidiary and (3) the served market should be homogeneous; i.e., segments are treated as distinct if they represent markedly different shares, competitors and growth rates.

7 E. Eugene Carter and Kalman J. Cohen, "Portfolio Aspects of Strategic Planning," *Journal of Business Policy*, 2 (1972), pp. 8–30.

8 C. H. Springer, "Strategic Management in General Electric," *Operations Research* (November–December 1973), pp. 1177–1182.

9 Bernard Catry and Michel Chevalier, "Market Share Strategy and the Product Life Cycle," *Journal of Marketing*, 38 (October 1974), pp. 29–34.

10 Peter F. Drucker, *Management: Tasks, Responsibilities, Practices* (New York: Harper and Row, 1973), p. 106.

11 Sidney Schoeffler, Robert D. Buzzell and Donald F. Heany, "Impact of Strategic Planning on Profit Performance," *Harvard Business Review* (March–April 1974), pp. 137–145.

12 Robert D. Buzzell, Bradley T. Gale and Ralph G. M. Sultan, "Market Share, Profitability and Business Strategy," unpublished working paper, (Marketing Science Institute, August 1974).

13 For more extended treatments and a variety of examples, see Patrick Conley, "Experience Curves as a Planning Tool," *IEEE Transactions* (June 1970); *Perspectives on Experience*

(Boston: Boston Consulting Group, 1970); and "Selling Business a Theory of Economics," *Business Week* (8 September 1974).

14 "An example of this situation was DuPont's production of cyclohexane. DuPont was the first producer of the product but the manufacture of cyclohexane is so integrated with the operations of an oil refinery that oil refiners have an inherent cost advantage over companies, such as DuPont, without an oil refinery." Robert B. Stobaugh and Philip L. Townsend, "Price Forecasting and Strategic Planning: The Case of Petrochemicals," *Journal of Marketing Research,* 12 (February 1975), pp. 19–29.

15 Theodore Levitt, "Exploit the Product Life Cycle," *Harvard Business Review* (November–December 1965), pp. 81–94.

16 Harry W. McMahan, "Like Sinatra, Old Products Can, Too, Get a New Lease on Life," *Advertising Age* (25 November 1974), p. 32.

17 Harry T. Moran, "Why New Products Fail," *Journal of Advertising Research* (April 1973).

18 See Douglas Needham, *Economic Analysis and Industrial Structure* (New York: Holt, Rinehart and Winston); Sanford Rose, "Bigness Is a Numbers Game," *Fortune* (November 1969).

19 Buzzell, Gale and Sultan, "Market Share, Profitability."

20 An extreme example is Unilever in the UK with 20 detergent brands all sharing joint costs to some degree.

21 William J. Abernathy and Kenneth Wayne, "Limit of the Learning Curve," *Harvard Business Review*, 52 (September–October 1974), pp. 109–119.

22 Aubrey Wilson, "Industrial Marketing Research in Britain," *Journal of Marketing Research,* 6 (February 1969), pp. 15–28.

23 John C. Chambers, Satinder K. Mullick and Donald D. Smith, *An Executives' Guide to Forecasting* (New York: John Wiley and Sons, 1974); Frank M. Bass, "A New Product Growth Model for Consumer Durables," *Management Science,* 15 (January 1969), pp. 215–227.

24 Of course the cash flow pattern also may be altered by changing debt and/or dividend policies. (For most companies, the likelihood of new equity funding is limited). Limits on growth are imposed when the additional business ventures to be supported have too high a business risk for the potential reward and/or the increase in debt has too high a (financial) risk for the potential rewards.

25 Among the publications of the Boston Consulting Group that describe the portfolio are: Perspectives on Experience (1970) and the following pamphlets authored by Bruce D. Henderson in the general perspectives series; "The Product Portfolio" (1970); "The Experience Curve Reviewed: The Growth Share Matrix or the Product Portfolio" (1973); and "Cash Traps" (1972).

26 A similar matrix reportedly is used by the Mead Corporation; see John Thackray, "The Mod Matrix of Mead," *Management Today* (January 1972), pp. 50–53, 112. This application has been criticized on the grounds of oversimplification, narrow applicability and the unwarranted emphasis on investment versus new investment. Indeed the growth-share matrix is regarded by Thackray as primarily a device for achieving social control.

27 William E. Cox, Jr., "Product Portfolio Strategy: An Analysis of the Boston Consulting Group Approach to Marketing Strategies," *Proceedings of the American Marketing Association,* 1974.

28 It is also typical that the weighted ratio of average market share versus the largest competitor is greater than 1.0. This reflects the contribution of the cash cows to both sales and profits. It also accounts for the familiar pattern whereby 20 percent of the products account for 80 percent of the dollar margin (a phenomena generally described as Pareto's Law).

29 The Boston Consulting Group defines such products as cash traps when the required reinvestment, including increased working capital, exceeds reported profit plus increase in permanent debt capacity: Bruce D. Henderson, "Cash Traps," *Perspectives,* Number 102 (Boston Consulting Group, 1972).

30 The label may be meaningless if the product is part of a product line, an integral component of a system or where most of the sales are internal.

31 It should be noted that full line/full service competitors may be vulnerable to this strategy if there are customer segments which do not need all the services, etc. Thus, Digital Equipment Corp. has propsered in competition with IBM by simply selling basic hardware and depending on others to do the applications programming. By contrast, IBM provides, for a price, a great deal of service backup and software for customers who are not self-sufficient. "A Minicomputer Tempest," *Business Week,* (27 January 1975), pp. 79–80.

32 Dimensions such as product and pricing policy, geographic and distributor strength, delivery patterns, penetration by account size and probable reaction to our company initiatives need to be considered. See C. Davis Fogg, "Planning Gains in Market Share," *Journal of Marketing,* 38 (July 1974), pp. 30–38.

33 This concept is developed by Harper Boyd, "Strategy Concepts" unpublished manuscript, 1974, and is based on B. H. Liddel Hart, *Strategy: The Indirect Approach* (London: Faber and Faber, 1951).

34 Seymour Tilles, "How to Evaluate Corporate Strategy," *Harvard Business Review,* 41 (July–August 1963).

35 William E. Fruhan, "Pyrrhic Victories in Fights for Market Share," *Harvard Business Review,* 50 (September–October 1972).

36 "Is John Sherman's Antitrust Obsolete?" *Business Week* (23 March 1974).

37 Stephen Dietz, "Get More Out of Your Brand Management," *Harvard Business Review* (July–August 1973).

38 C. Merle Crawford, "Strategies for New Product Development: Guidelines for a Critical Company Problem," *Business Horizons* (December 1972), pp. 49–58.

39 H. Igor Ansoff, *Corporate Strategy.*

40 Kenneth Simmonds, "Removing the Chains from Product Policy," *Journal of Management Studies* (February 1968).

41 This strategy matrix was influenced strongly by the work of David T. Kollat, Roger D. Blackwell and James F. Robeson, *Strategic Marketing* (New York: Holt, Rinehart and Winston, 1972), pp. 21–23 which, in turn, was adapted from Samuel C. Johnson and Conrad Jones, "How to Organize for New Products," *Harvard Business Review,* 35 (May–June 1957), pp. 49–62.

42 According to the experience of A. T. Kearney, Inc., the chances of success are a direct function of how far from home the new venture is aimed. Specifically, the likelihood of success for an improved product into the present market is assessed as 0.75, declines to 0.50 for a new product with unrelated technology into the present market and to 0.25 for an existing product into a new market. The odds of success for external diversification are as low as 0.05. These numbers are mainly provocative because of the difficulties of defining what constitutes a failure (is it a product that failed in test or after national introduction, for example). See "Analyzing New Product Risk," *Marketing for Sales Executives* (The Research Institute of America, January 1974).

43 H. Igor Ansoff and John Steward, "Strategies for a Technology-Based Business," *Harvard Business Review,* 45 (November–December 1967), pp. 71–83.

44 Kollat, Blackwell and Robeson, *Strategic Marketing,* p. 24.

45 Seymour Tilles, "Making Strategy Explicit," in H. Igor Ansoff (ed.) *Business Strategy* (London: Penguin Books, 1969), p. 203.

46 Bruce D. Henderson, "Intuitive Strategy," *Perspectives,* No. 96 (The Boston Consulting Group, 1972).

47 See "Selling Business a Theory of Economics," *Business Week* (8 September 1973), "G. E.'s New Strategy for Faster Growth," *Business Week* (8 July 1972), "First Quarter and Stockholders Meeting Report (Texas Instruments, Inc., 8 April 1973); "The Winning Strategy at Sperry Rand," *Business Week* (24 February 1973), "How American Standard Cured Its Conglomeritis," *Business Week* (28 September 1974); "G. E. Revamps Strategy: Growth through Efficiency," *Advertising Age* (3 June 1974).

18

Planning Gains in Market Share

C. Davis Fogg

Marketing strategy often is defined in terms of a gain in share points. In turn, this raises the question of which tactics to use to accomplish such an outcome. This article presents a comprehensive approach to the process and to the problem of how to plan gains in market share.

Gaining market share is a key factor in reaching a leadership or number one position in any industry. It is particularly important to the achievement of a high volume of profits that can be used to expand a firm's business and pay dividends to stockholders, and to the attainment of leadership profit performance as measured by return on sales and return on investment. It is well documented that the higher a firm's market share the larger its cumulative production of a product, the lower its costs, and the higher its profitability.[1]

However, gaining significant share requires careful planning, thoughtful, well-executed market strategies, and specific account-by-account tactical plans. It requires a comprehensive, well-thought-out, and well-planned program. The purpose of this article is to present such a comprehensive program for gaining market share: to examine ways of increasing share, the key steps in planning market share gains, and the pitfalls that must be anticipated in implementing such a program.

[1]See the Boston Consulting Group, *Perspectives on Experience* (Boston, Mass.: The Boston Consulting Group, 1968). Additional unpublished work by The Boston Consulting Group concerning the automotive, brewing, aluminum, cosmetics, and mobile home industries, and using public data, conclude that the higher a firm's market share, the higher its profitability, and that the leader in market share in an industry is usually the most profitable.

WHEN TO PLAN MARKET SHARE GAINS

Typical situations where a business manager should seriously consider a plan to gain market share include: *poor market* position—share must be gained to increase profitability and profit volume; *new products* are being launched head-on against competition; significant *losses in share* have been suffered at the hands of competitors; a *new acquisition* is justified only if sales, profits, and market share can be significantly increased; *competition becomes vulnerable* by virtue of a strike, poor customer service, product shortage, financial difficulties, and the like.

WHEN SHARE GAINS ARE DIFFICULT

It should be noted, based on the author's experience, that gains in market share are particularly difficult under several key circumstances. One such situation would be when a firm has low share, is coming from behind, and is attempting to take share away from the leaders. It's easier to grow with the market than take share away from someone who "owns" it. Secondly, it's more difficult to gain share in a commodity market where there is little or no opportunity for a unique product and significant product differentiation. Finally and obviously, share gains are tougher when there is significant competition—competition

Reprinted from *Journal of Marketing,* vol. 38, pp. 30–38, American Marketing Association, July 1974. At the time of writing, the author was manager of market planning for the Electronic Products Division of the Corning Glass Works.

with an adequate product offering and good distribution channels and methods.

MEANS OF INCREASING MARKET SHARE

The author has found the following five key strategies to be most important for gaining market share in an industrial market.

1 *Price*—lower prices below competitive levels to take business away from competition among price-conscious customers.
2 *New Products*—introduce product modifications or significant innovations that meet customer needs better and displace existing products or expand the total market by meeting and stimulating new needs.
3 *Service*—offer more rapid delivery than competition to service-conscious customers; improve the type and timeliness of information that customers need from the service organization, information such as items in stock, delivery promise dates, invoice and shipment data, and the like.
4 *Strength and Quality of Marketing*—field a larger, better-trained, higher-quality sales force targeted at customers who are not getting adequate quality or quantity of attention from competition; build a larger or more effective distribution network.
5 *Advertising and Sales Promotion*—increase advertising and sales promotion of superior product, service, or price benefits to underpenetrated or untapped customers; advertise new or improved benefits to all customers.

Competitive price, new products, and service are all tangible benefits that are needed by, and can be evaluated by, customers. The marketing organization is a means of both communicating benefits and facilitating service. Advertising and sales promotion are means of communicating benefits to customers and increasing their awareness of a particular manufacturer's product line.

In addition to the five key strategies for gaining share, there are a number of lesser strategies that may be important in select markets and can be considered. These strategies include improving product quality, expanding engineering assistance offered customers, offering special product testing facilities, broadening the product line to offer a more complete range of products, improving the general corporate image, offering the facilities to build special designs quickly, and establishing inventories dedicated to serving one customer.

There are several key considerations that should be taken into account in using these methods to gain market share. First, one or more of these methods should be used only when significant (to the customer) distinct product, price, or service advantages over specific competitors can be found. The advantage must be sustainable for a sufficient period of time to gain targeted share and significant enough to cause target customers to shift their business from a competitor to the firm attempting the market share gain. If a distinct sustainable advantage cannot be found or if competition is extremely competent, aggressive, and expected to counter any attempt to gain share, then the cost of gaining share may far exceed the benefits. Under these circumstances, a firm should look for another business or product line in which to invest for share gain. Second, gains in market share will not only increase sales and profit volume, but will incur significant costs—the "cost" of decreased gross margins as prices are lowered, the cost of developing new products, the cost of new plant capacity to permit decreased delivery time, and the like.

Finally, the time that it takes to implement each method varies from strategy to strategy. Pricing changes can be quickly implemented. Improving delivery may take six to eighteen months if new plant capacity must be added. Strengthening, upgrading, and training of the sales force may take six to twelve months, and

Table 1 Strategies for Gaining Market Share

Strategy	When use	How apply in marketplace	Cost implications
1 Price	To gain share in a product line (a) where there is room for growth; (b) in launching a new product, preferably in a growth market	A Set general market price level below average ("catch share generally" strategy) B Lower prices at specific target customer accounts where reduced prices will capture high volume accounts and where competition is vulnerable on a price basis; lower prices enough to keep the business C Lower prices against specific competitors who will not or cannot react effectively	• Will lower gross margin by decreasing spread between cost and price for a period of time • Will lower cost as cumulative volume increases and costs move down the experience curve
2 New product	When a new product need (cost or performance) can be uncovered and a new product will (a) displace existing products on a cost or performance basis, or (b) expand the market for a class of product by tapping previously unsatisfied demand.	A Develop and launch the new product, generally B Target specific customers and market segments where the need for the product is strongest and competition most vulnerable, and immediate large gains in share can be obtained	• Cost of R&D necessary to develop product • Capital expenditures on plant to manufacture the product • Start-up operating losses • Promotion costs of launching the new product
3 Service	To gain share for specific product lines when competitive service levels do not meet customer requirements	A Improve service generally beyond competitive levels by increasing capacity for specified product lines B Target specific accounts where improved service will gain share and the need for superior service is high	• Cost of adding capacity and/or bolstering service systems • Cost of expanding the distribution system, including additional inventories required

developing and launching a new product may take one or more years depending upon the extent and difficulty of technical innovation required. A plan to gain share may, therefore, involve a number of different moves over a relatively long period of time.

Table 1 summarizes the circumstances under which each strategy can be used, how the strategy is applied in the marketplace, and the detailed cost implications of each strategy.

The Process of Planning Share Increases

There are eight key steps in the process of planning share increases. They are:

Table 1 Strategies for Gaining Market Share *(Continued)*

Strategy	When use	How apply in marketplace	Cost implications
		C Offer additional services required in general or at specific customers—information, engineering advice, etc. D Expand distribution system by adding more distribution points	
4 Quality/strength of marketing	When a market segment or specific customers are getting inadequate sales force coverage (too few calls/month) or inferior quality of coverage (poor salesmen or insufficient information conveyed by salesmen)	A Add salesmen or sales representatives to improve call frequency above competitive levels in target territories or at target accounts B Sales training programs to improve existing sales skills, product knowledge, and territorial and customer management abilities C Sales incentive program with rewards based on share increases at target customers or in target markets or products	• Salary and overhead cost of additional salesmen or representatives • Cost of training or retraining • Cost of incentive program
5 Advertising and sales promotion	(a) When a market segment or specific customers are getting inadequate exposure to product, service, or price benefits compared to competition (b) A change in the benefits offered is made and needs to be communicated	A Select appropriate media to reach target customer groups B Set level and frequency of exposure of target customers high enough to create adequate awareness of benefits and counter level of competitive efforts	• Cost of creative work to create campaign • Production and media costs

1 *Information Collection*—collect critical market and competitive information necessary to establish market share goals and strategies for reaching them.

2 *Competitive Analysis*—define which competitors are vulnerable to specific strategies, why, and what their likely reaction will be to attempts to gain share by different methods.

3 *Product Line Segmentation*—divide current (or proposed) product lines into groups where there is room for: (a) no gain in share; (b) share gain using nonproduct strategies—such as price, service, or strengthened marketing; and (c) new product and product innovations to gain share.

4 *Establish Overall Share-Gain Goals and Strategies* for each product line marketed.

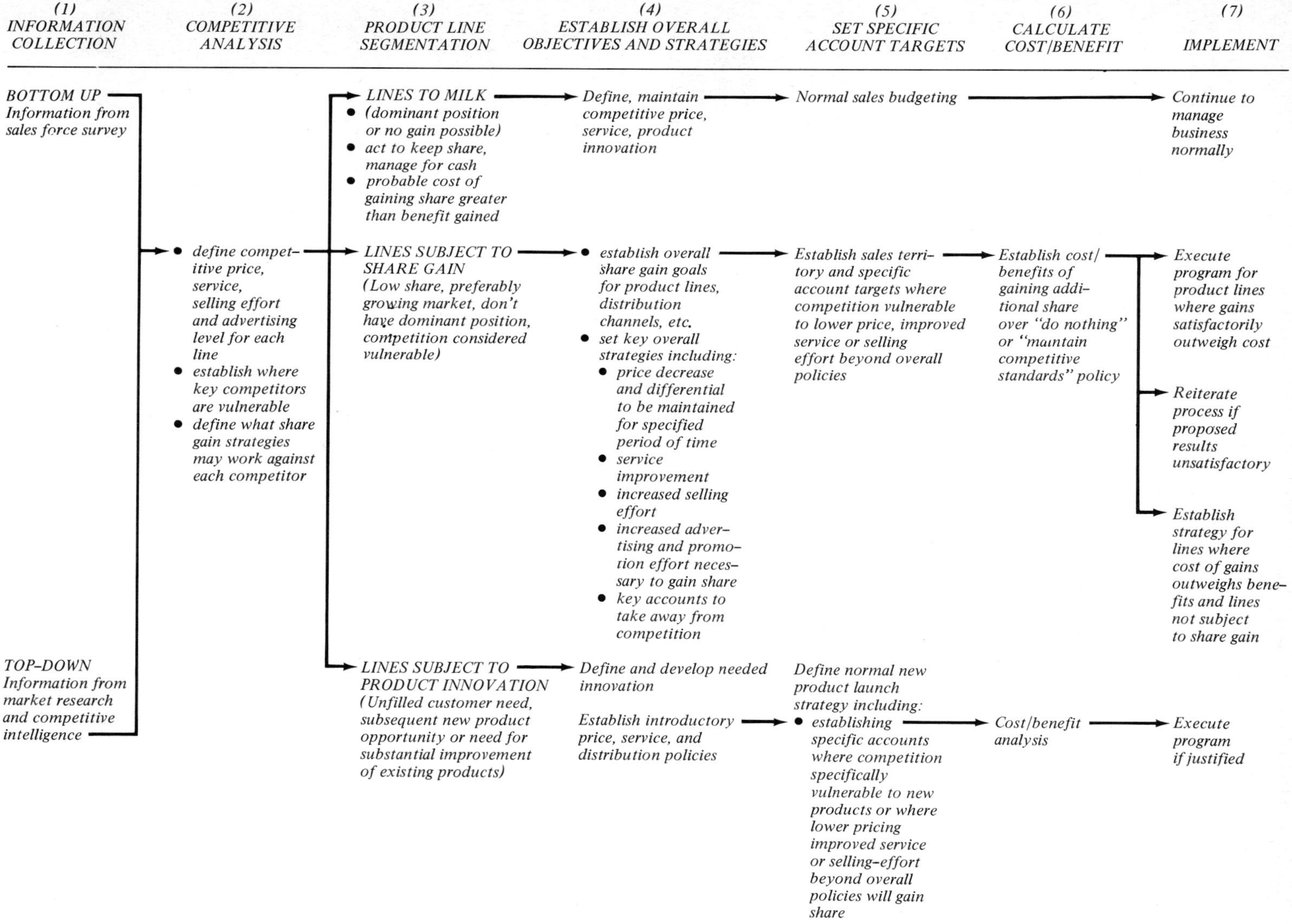

Figure 1 Schematic diagram of the process of planning market share gains.

5 *Key Account Analysis*—identify where competition is particularly vulnerable at specific key accounts; establish key account goals and share-gain policies, particularly if they deviate from general policies applied nationally throughout the market.

6 *Cost/Benefit Analysis*—calculate the expected share and profit gains, the costs of achieving these gains; judge whether or not the cost/benefit ratio is satisfactory; repeat steps 1 through 6 until the cost/benefit ratio is acceptable.

7 *Execute the Plan.*

8 *Monitor Results* and modify goals and action, if necessary, to combat competitive reaction or to react effectively to changes in the marketplace.

Figure 1 graphically depicts the planning process. The remainder of the article is devoted to methods of obtaining and analyzing information necessary to implement the process of planning share gains.

INFORMATION COLLECTION

The two types of information required to properly plan share gains are: "bottom-up" information typically obtained from salesmen, sales representatives, and industrial distributors; and "top-down" information typically obtained by market research and competitive intelligence activities.

Bottom-up research will accomplish three objectives. First, it will establish overall national competitive practices and patterns, including competitive pricing policies, product line strengths and weaknesses, sales force type, strength and quality, strength of distribution, market penetration, and the like. Second, it will define how vulnerable each key competitor is to moves against him and the extent to which share can be taken away for each distinct product line. Third, it will identify key large volume accounts where business is held by competition, and estimate how much business can be taken away from competition by what means.

In a bottom-up survey, salesmen basically are asked what they feel is needed in price, service, nonproduct benefits, or new products to gain and maintain share in their district or territory. This information can be effectively obtained—either by drawing on the salesman's prior knowledge of, or having him conduct a direct field survey of, a specified sample of accounts. The survey sample normally will include all key large accounts and distributors and a random sample of moderate to small accounts. Salesmen are then asked to identify what each competitor's share is, at which key accounts, what strategies can be effective in taking share away and keeping it for each product line, and how much (for example, in price) is necessary to effect a change in share. They are also asked, based on previous experience or speculation, to predict what each competitor's probable reaction will be to specified moves such as price cuts, new products, increased field sales coverage, and the like. Such surveys require excellent sample design, a good information-processing system, and careful design of questionnaires to be administered to salesmen in the field and to be administered by salesmen to sample accounts. The number of accounts to be sampled and the amount of information requested must be kept small to avoid overburdening the sales force with information collection.

Top-down research is also important. Professionally conducted surveys of select customers, distributors, and key salesmen can both identify key new product concepts that can be developed and used against competition and confirm or expand on findings from the bottom-up survey. Normal competitive intelligence activities can monitor a competitor's financial condition and ability to respond to an attack on his market, his probable new product policy, and his probable reaction,

Table 2 Simplified Competitive Analysis

Competitive dimensions			Us	Competitors A	Competitors B	Competitors C	Comments on data
1 *Product position*	Market size	Growth per year	Market share				
Line 1	$15MM	0%	65%	20%	10%	5%	1 Not subject to share gain, manage for cash.
2	$30MM	10%	25%	40%	15%	20%	2 Subject to share gain, *A* most vulnerable, *B, C* less so.
3	$20MM	15%	10%	25%	30%	35%	3 Subject to share gain, *A, B, C* equally vulnerable. Substantial unfilled need for a new product.
2 *Pricing strategy*							
H = Price for margin		Line 1	C	C	C	H	*B* and *C* will be easiest to take share away from on price, and it will be least expensive to maintain share taken away. *A* is more competitive, will require larger price differentials to gain and maintain share, and it is therefore more costly to take share away.
C = Price with market		2	C	L	C	C	
L = Price leader or very agressive		3	C	L	C	C	
3 *New product policy*							
L = Leader		Line 1	L	L	F	F	Expect new products first from *A*, monitor market carefully to identify what they're working on—expect *A* to imitate earliest any new products introduced.
F = Follower		2	F	L	F	F	
		3	L	L	L	F	
4 *Overall marketing strength*							*A* strongest and equal to us. *B* and *C* vulnerable to more intensive selling effort offered by us.
No. Representatives		Line 1	5	10	15	15	
No. Distributors		2	40	35	30	30	
No. Salesmen		3	25	20	10	7	
5 *Geographic strength*							
No. Salesmen and Reps							We may be weak in district G and should consider adding salesmen, otherwise are equal or superior to competition.
Territory	E		9	7	7	6	
	F		7	7	6	6	
	G		5	8	7	6	
	H		9	8	6	4	
6 *Distributor strength*							
No. Distributors							
Territory	E		12	10	8	7	*A* approximately equal in strength. *B* and *C* weaker and definitely vulnerable.
	F		10	9	7	8	

based on historical information, to each type of share-gain move being contemplated.

COMPETITIVE ANALYSIS

An in-depth analysis of competition based on survey results is required to identify those product lines where share gain is thought possible and pinpoint where and how much each competitor is vulnerable to specific share-gain strategies. Table 2 provides a simplified example of such an analysis and the key conclusions derived from the data.

PRODUCT LINE SEGMENTATION

Management judgment based on the competitive analysis should tentatively divide product

Table 2 Simplified Competitive Analysis *(Continued)*

Competitive dimensions	Us	Competitors A	B	C	Comments on data
G	10	9	7	7	
H	8	7	6	6	
7 *Delivery norm* (weeks)					Delivery improvements necessary in 1, 2 to be competitive. Improvement beyond competitive levels will not gain share. Improvement in line 3 will gain advantage against *A, B* and *C* according to sales force survey.
Product 1	6	6	4	7	
2	6	3	4	4	
3	6	6	7	9	
8 *Penetration by account size %*	$ Market—all products				
40 Large	40%	30%	15%	15%	We're weak in medium and small accounts, need program to improve penetration and coverage there.
15 Medium	15%	30%	25%	30%	
10 Small	10%	30%	20%	40%	
$65MM					
9 *Probable reaction* to:					
• Lower price	*A*—Immediate retaliation, continued price reduction to gain share back. *B, C*—Weaker response. Will try to hold large accounts.				Cost in taking share away from *A* on price will be high. *B* and *C* more vulnerable.
• New product	*A*—Will immediately match new product offering. *C*—May match immediately. *B*—Eventually match.				*B* and to some extent *C* vulnerable to new product offering.
• Increased sales coverage	*A*—Will match. *B, C*—Some increase.				*B* and *C* vulnerable in some measure to sales coverage, particularly if a new product is launched.

Key strategic conclusions

1 *Product Policy:* Focus on lines 2 and 3 where gain is possible by increased penetration and growth with the market and product modification for product 3.

2 *Competitive Strategy:* Focus on taking share away from *B* and *C*, who are vulnerable to lower pricing and a new product innovation requested by salesmen. Selectively take business away from competitor *A*—only up to the point where expensive price retaliation is expected.

3 *Marketing Strategy:* Add three salesmen to territory G and one to F to build strength against key targets—*B* and *C*. Shift call pattern and develop mktg. programs for medium to small accounts where penetration is poor. Develop distributor promotion program to capitalize on advantage over *B* and *C*.

4 *Service:* Invest in capacity to lower delivery time in product 2 to level competitive with *B* and *C*. Maintain competitive standards in other lines.

lines into three basic categories—product lines where there is:

- No room for share gain
- Room for product innovation and subsequent share gain
- No room for product innovation but room for share gain with existing products

In general, there is *little room for share gain* when competition is highly competent—is equal or superior in strength and ability to penetrate the market, and has significant or dominant market share. There is often little room for gain when a firm has achieved dominant stable market share (usually 35% to 70% of the market) or the market for a product line is stable or declining. In each of these circumstances, the cost of gaining market share will probably outweigh the additional benefits provided by a gain in share. The principal strategy under these circumstances is to manage the product line to produce cash: price only to maintain market share and make only the minimum required investments in product changes, plant and equipment, and marketing. If there is some doubt that a product line falls into this category it should be treated as a product where share gain is possible, and a detailed plan and calculations should be prepared to substantiate whether or not share gains are worth the cost.

There is room to gain share by *product innovation* where significant unfilled needs can be identified in the market, where it is technically feasible to develop a product to meet those needs, and where the product advantage in the market is sufficient to gain substantial share. In this case, the strategy is to undertake prototype product development and prove that the product is technically feasible before developing a plan to launch the product and gain share.

Finally, there is generally *room for a share gain* when a firm has less than dominant share and survey information indicates that a competitive advantage can be obtained in price, service, or selling and distribution methods and systems. This is particularly true where the product market is rapidly growing and competition is weak, fragmented, or known to be sluggish in reaction to aggressive moves by competitors. In this instance, a detailed plan for gaining share is called for as outlined below.

ESTABLISHING SHARE-GAIN GOALS AND STRATEGIES

The competitive analysis will permit establishment of overall share-gain goals and the strategies to be implemented in general in the marketplace and against each key competitor.

After preliminary overall strategies have been established, the two most difficult subsequent tasks are to establish how much change must be made (in price and service, for example) to gain share and approximately how much share gain a given change will produce. Estimates of the sensitivity of market share to proposed changes can be obtained in several ways. First, historical records document share changes based on previous moves by or against competition. Second, and perhaps best, salesmen can estimate the sensitivity of share in their territories and indicate the amount of change necessary to take business away at specified key accounts. Finally, knowledge of competitors, judgment of their probable reactions, and the percentage of share they will permit to be taken away before retaliation should put a limit on expected share gains.

How much share a competitor will allow to be taken away is a function of several factors. The first is his financial condition and ability to retaliate by building additional capacity or investing cash in other means of gaining back share. Second is his business philosophy concerning the product lines in question: does he want profits and incoming cash now, or is he willing to defer current financial return for future, larger returns resulting from maintained or increased share? Finally, the importance of the product line under attack to the firm's total business will influence a competitor's reaction. If the product is of minor importance in the competitor's business, attempts to maintain share are less likely than if the product line constitutes a major portion of his business.

It is important, in addition, to realize that all of the share initially gained during an assault on competition probably cannot be maintained indefinitely, and a portion of the share may have to be "given back" to stabilize the market.

Table 3 is a typical objective and strategy matrix showing overall share-gain goals by product line and detailed strategies by type of product for products sold direct to original equipment manufacturers. Each cell in a strategy matrix will normally include:

- Share (or sales) to be taken away from competition
- Specific accounts where share is to be gained
- Key strategies—price, product, promotions, change in call patterns, and the like

The simple product line vs. competition matrix in Table 3 assumes that strategy will vary only by competitor and product line. A more complex analysis will be necessary when share-gain strategy is expected to vary along other dimensions such as size of customer, customer's end market (industrial, consumer, computer, etc.), different distribution channels, and the like.

Territory Goals Specific goals are then set for each territory and for key accounts that salesmen have targeted for share gain. The potential share gains are totaled and discounted to factor in probability of success to see if reasonable account and territory goals add up to the overall share-gain goals established in the previous step. These goals become territory and account action steps if the share-gain program is accepted.

Cost Evaluation and Analysis Once program goals are established, the costs and

Table 3 Competitive Matrix for Products Sold Direct to Original Equipment Manufacturers*

	Competitor			
Product	***A***	***B***	***C***	**Overall goals**
1	No change	No change	No change	Maintain 65% share, competitive pricing. Manage for cash. Improve service to competitive levels.
2	Take away 3% Focus on accounts X, Y, and Z with below average pricing	Take away 6% Focus on accounts L, M, and N—below average pricing	Take away 6% Focus on accounts Q, R, and S	Increase share from 25%-40% by: • Establishing competitive service and capacity • Price 3%-7% lower than market
3	Take away 5% Focus on accounts X and Y where need for product modification great	Take away 10% Focus on accounts L, M, N, and X with lowered pricing on conventional product	Take away 10% Focus on accounts Q, R, S, and M—mix of modified product and low price on conventional product	Increase share from 10%-35% by: • Product modification • Cutting price on established product 3%-7% • New plant with superior service

Overall Strategies for All Products
1 Add salesmen to territories F and G where weak.
2 Shift call patterns to call on more medium to small size accounts.
3 Increase overall advertising level 25% during share-gain period.
4 Maintain competitive service in all lines.

*The same type of matrix could also be used for products sold through different distribution channels.

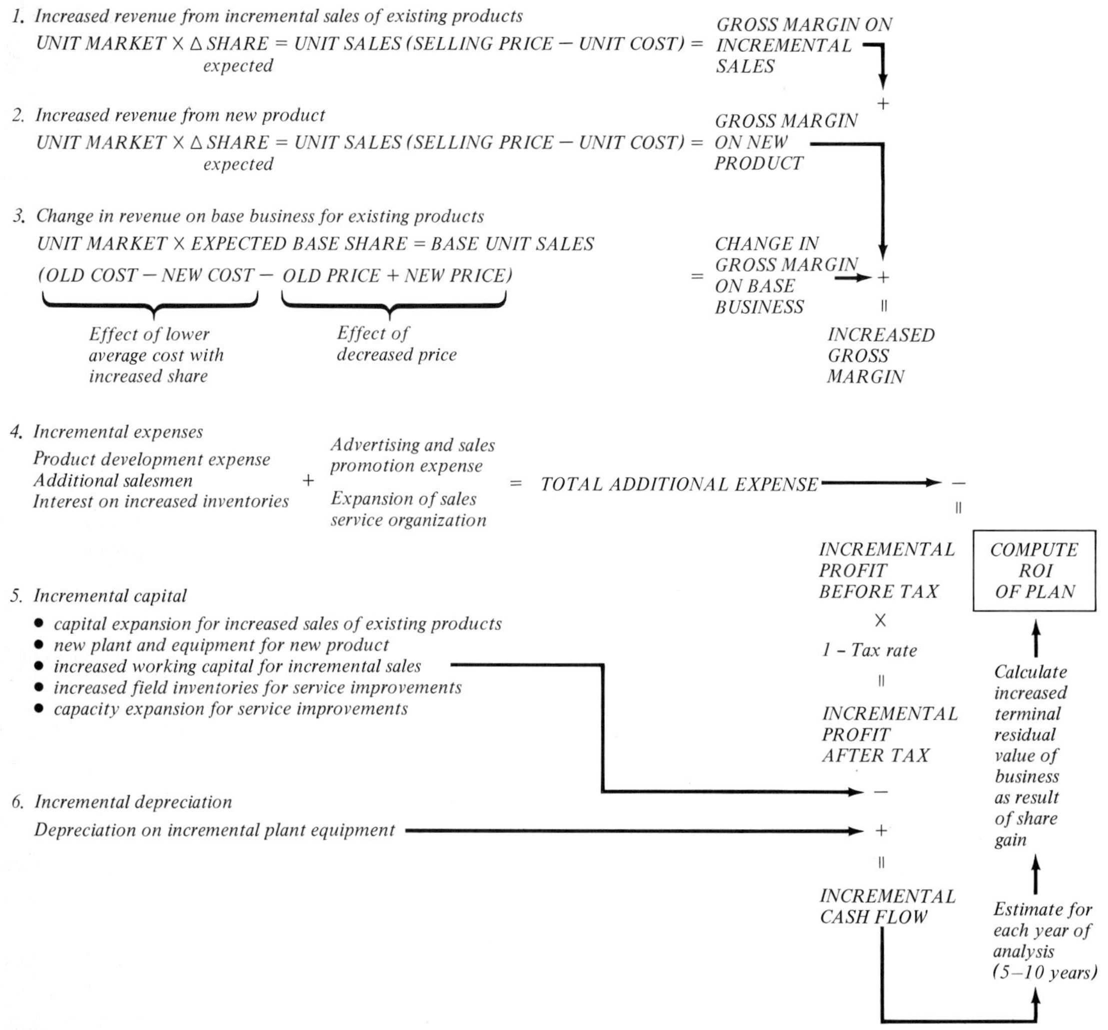

Figure 2 Schematic flow of calculation to compute ROI and cash flow of a share-gain plan. *Note:* See the Boston Consulting Group, *Perspectives on Experience* (Boston: The Boston Consulting Group, 1968), for a method of calculating the present value of market share gains accounting for the effects of decreasing prices, decreasing unit costs, and increasing unit volume.

benefits of the proposed plan must be carefully evaluated. Figure 2 is a simplified flow diagram for calculating the incremental costs, benefits, cash flow, and return on investment (ROI) for a firm intending to gain share by a combination of lowered prices on existing products, introduction of a new product, additional field sales coverage, and improved service. The chart lists most of the key items that will have a positive or negative effect on cash flow. The analysis isolates both the gain in profits from newly acquired share and the change in profitability of the base business—that business that would have been obtained without a share-gain plan—as a result of decreased prices and lowered costs as production costs move down the experience curve with increased cumulative volume. This type of analysis is easily adapted for computer calculation.

Assessing Risk A "source of sales analysis" is useful in assessing the risk and realism of a share-gain plan. In general, the higher the portion of a firm's five- to ten-year cumulative sales expected to come from disruptive moves against competition—lowered price, improved service, and new products—the higher the risk of the plan and the greater the advantage over competitors necessary to succeed.

Monitoring and Follow-up An intricate share-gain plan requires careful monitoring and control if it is to be effective. It is particularly important to insure that key account sales targets are being met, and the cost goals are on target and new product introductions are on schedule. Timing is also important. Once implementation begins, competitors will be aware of the threat to their market share; rapid, timely implementation of share-gain plans can catch competitors unaware, and share gain can take place before competitive retaliation.

It is also important to monitor competitive reaction to moves to gain share. Competitive moves should have been anticipated in the plan, figured into the market share targets, and calculations and plans prepared to defend held or gained share with continued price and cost reductions and product innovation.

Finally, it is important to recognize when attempts to stabilize competitive market shares should take place. When it is apparent that goals have been met, and/or the costs of gaining additional share obviously outweigh the benefits, it is important to attempt to stabilize shares by reverting to competitive—not aggressive—price, product, and service policies.

Pitfalls

There are five key pitfalls in implementing a plan to gain share. They are:

1 *Moving Too Slowly* and giving competition time to regroup and retaliate. Pricing, product, and service moves must be made quickly.

2 *Not Doing Enough* and being timid and conservative in moves against competition. Price cuts must be more than adequate, product advantage great and clear, and so on. It does not pay to do "just a little bit" to see if it works.

3 *No Follow Through*—neglecting the tools necessary to sustain share once gained, such as sustained cost reduction and ability to lower price or sustain excellent service or develop new products. One must be willing to stick with the battle to gain share over a long period of time.

4 *Underestimating Competition* and their ability to react, resulting in higher than forecast costs of gaining share; forgetting to figure the costs of combating competitive reaction in the share-gain financial plan.

5 *Don't Know When to Quit*—sometimes competitive reaction will be too strong; it is too costly to gain share, and giving up and concentrating on another business is the best policy.

Legal Implications of Market Share

Finally, before planning significant market share gain and seeking a dominant industry position, plans should be reviewed with legal counsel to insure that planned action is within established antitrust laws and government guidelines. In general, the government will not challenge high market share if it is attained by internal growth and legal competitive activity in the marketplace. The government may challenge market dominance if it is thought to significantly lessen competition in the industry in question or if significant share gains are obtained by acquisition rather than by internal growth.

If one attains a dominant position in a given market, the strategies appropriate to maintain or augment that position must be carefully scrutinized from the legal point of view. Aggressive, competitive action permissible for a firm seeking to improve its position in a fragmented market may be viewed quite differently by the Justice Department if undertaken by a dominant firm seeking to augment or merely defend its position in a concentrated market. A firm that dominates must guard against the possibility that in defending its dominant position, it is accused of predatory conduct that constitutes an abuse of an alleged monopoly position.

Summary

Gaining and keeping significant market share is considered by many to be the single most important key to high, long-term profitability and substantial profit volume. Market share gains must be carefully planned. The vulnerability of competition to changes in price, product, service, marketing and distribution methods, and advertising must be assessed. Potential advantages vis-à-vis competition must be identified and the costs and potential benefits of a plan to gain share carefully evaluated. Overall share-gain goals and strategies must then be translated into sales territory and individual sales account goals for implementation. Although the process of planning share gains is time consuming and costly, the profit rewards can be substantial.

19

Experience Curves as a Planning Tool

Patrick Conley

If experience improves performance, it should follow that the company that has produced the most widgets will be the most efficient widget producer. This implies that market share is vital in determining potential profitability and that new products, whether developed internally or acquired outside, are doomed to lackluster financial performance unless they capture a dominant market position.

Any study tool that can help managers understand and predict industry and company trends in price and cost, and that can also help them explain and predict product profitability, is obviously capable of greatly enriching planning. Like most tools, however, the utility of the experience concept lies in its imaginative application. It is no substitute for management, but it can help managers in determining business strategy.

The experience concept is related to the well-known *learning-curve* effect. Since its discovery by the commander of Wright-Patterson Air Force Base in 1925, the interesting "learning" effect has been highly developed and widely used in certain segments of industry.[1-3] The aircraft and electronics industries often use it to guide both their cost control decisions for assembly operations and their pricing policies. The Department of Defense procurement officers use the learning-curve effect in setting cost targets in cost-based contracts.

It is surprising, however, that more companies have not realized the value of the concept. Although it has been observed and applied by the chemical industry and occasionally by other manufacturing enterprises,[4,5] the

Reprinted by permission from *IEEE Spectrum*, vol. 7, no. 6, June 1970, pp. 63–68. At the time of writing, the author was vice president of The Boston Consulting Group, Inc.

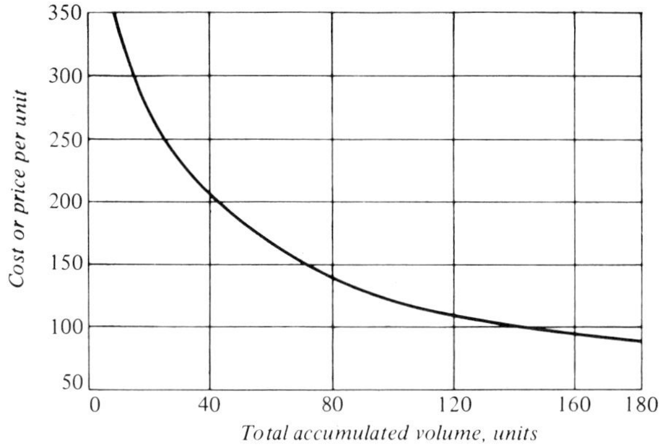

Exhibit 1 Representation of experience relationships graphically on a linear scale.

effect is not always considered by managers in assessing manufacturing performance. It is a vague or totally unfamiliar concept to a surprising number of senior managers who do not have a background in manufacturing or in the defense industry. Unfamiliarity takes on special significance, since the effect appears to depend somewhat on confidence that it exists![3]

In its most common form, the learning curve relates the direct-labor hours required to perform a task to the number of times the task has been performed. For a wide variety of activities, this relation has been found to be of the form shown in Exhibit 1, in which time to perform decreases by a constant percentage whenever the number of trials is doubled. Plotted on log-log scales, this relation becomes a straight line with a slope characteristic of the rate of "learning," such as that shown in Exhibit 2.

A 20 percent reduction in hours for each doubling of performance—or what is called an 80 percent curve—is typical of a very wide variety of tasks. The concept of continuing improvement "forever," which is apparent in Exhibit 2, is often disturbing. However, one must recall that the base of the curve is *not* time but trials and that the number of trials required to make a given percentage improvement grows enormously as learning occurs. Thus, for all practical purposes, learning in most instances eventually becomes so slow that it appears static. If the task lends itself to application of new technology or to partial mechanization, then the slope of the curve can become substantially steeper and 70 to 75 percent slopes are commonly observed.

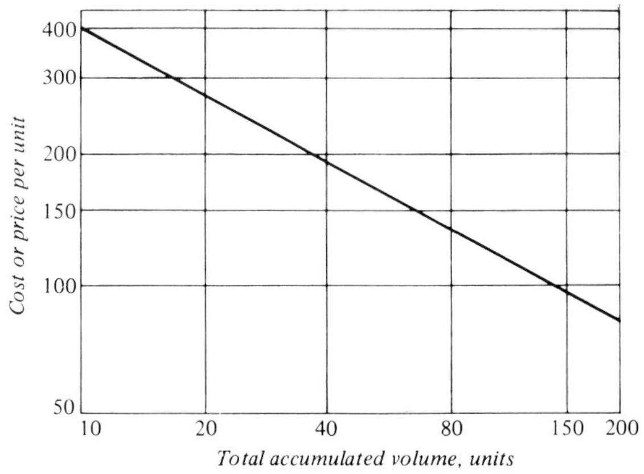

Exhibit 2 Representation of experience relationships graphically on a log-log scale.

The experience effect, quantitatively similar to the learning curve phenomenon, is not peculiar to manual direct-labor tasks but is quite general and seemingly applies to most of the activities undertaken within a corporation. In particular, it applies to the start-up of new plants and even to "automated" operations.

COST AS A FUNCTION OF LEARNING

Since experience increases the efficiency of an operation, it naturally reduces the cost of that operation. This fact has frequently been used for estimation and prediction.[5] In fact, observers have noted that costs go down *by a fixed percentage* each time the number of units produced doubles. Recent studies by The Boston Consulting Group serve to augment these observations. There is every reason to believe that each element of cost declines in such a way that total cost follows a composite "learning" curve.

In computing the precise relationship between costs and experience, one must be alert to certain factors that can distort the picture. If costs are measured in dollars, it is necessary to eliminate inflation when observations are made over a substantial period of time. Deflation of cost figures thus becomes more important when growth rates are slow, so the doubling of trials or units requires several years. One might also argue that material costs, when large and fixed, should be removed and the experience effect applied only to the value added. However, removing material costs turns out to be a relatively minor correction in most instances: in other instances, these costs are themselves subject to reduction through substitutions ("learning?").

The fact that the total cost of many products declines by a fixed percentage each time the cumulative number of units produced is doubled has been widely recognized and used for cost prediction and control.[3,6] However, cost data are usually proprietary and always mechanically difficult to obtain for individual products, so research on the subject requires a high degree of cooperation and assistance on the part of the manufacturer. A common problem encountered when one examines the historical cost of a particular product is a series of discontinuities in the data. The discontinuities are usually associated with changes in accounting methods and are expensive and tedious to rationalize. Also, since we are considering *total* costs, the method of allocating indirect costs becomes a factor in multiproduct companies, and traditional allocations may have to be adjusted to achieve the desired precision.

COSTS AND MARKET SHARE

In spite of long-standing awareness of the learning-curve phenomenon and its effect on costs, the broader experience effect and its obvious strategic implication seem until now to have been overlooked. If cost declines predictably with units produced, the competitor who has produced the most units will probably have the lowest cost. Since the products of all competitors have sensibly the same market price, the competitor with the most unit experience should enjoy the greatest profit. Furthermore, it should be clear that very substantial differences in cost and profit can exist between competitors having widely different unit experiences. Of course, this assumes that all competitors have equal access to resources and patents and that the competitors are all reasonably efficient.

Over a period of time when market positions are relatively stable, experience can be equated with market share. Thus market share and profitability are closely related, and competitive positions can become those shown in Exhibit 3. In the exhibit, competitor A is the marginal competitor, whereas competitor C dominates the market. Empirically (and perhaps theoretically), the market share of the dominant competitor in a stable, slowly growing market turns out to be about 50 percent. The next competitor typically has 25 percent; the third has 12 percent, and so on.[7] The 50-25

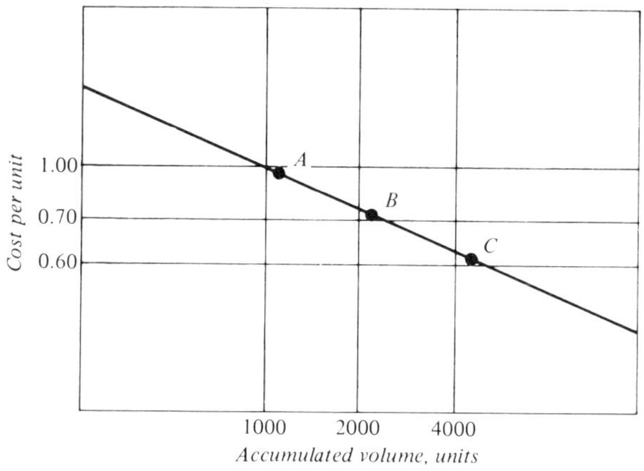

Exhibit 3 Market share and costs for three competitors

percent share distribution observed by Cohen may result more from a subconscious agreement among competitors than from the operation of random influences. In a mature market, stability is often in the best interest of all the competitors.

If the market is growing rapidly—say 15 percent or more annually in units—then market shares may be fairly fluid, and the dominant producer may have much more or even less than 50 percent of the market.

PRICE AND EXPERIENCE

Assuming that costs can be made to decline at a predictable rate such as that shown in Exhibit 2, we can examine the related price curves for possible correlation. In general, we find most price curves to have either the form shown in Exhibit 4 or that shown in Exhibit 5, with a strong predominance of the former type. In these idealized examples, as well as in the actual ones to be discussed later, we are plotting industry unit price (or weighted average unit price if several sizes or grades are involved) against total historical industry units on logarithmic scales. The costs shown are average industry costs, weighted by the unit production of each competitor. (If these prices are plotted with appropriate costs for the individual competitor's experience, the slope of the price line will *appear* to vary if the

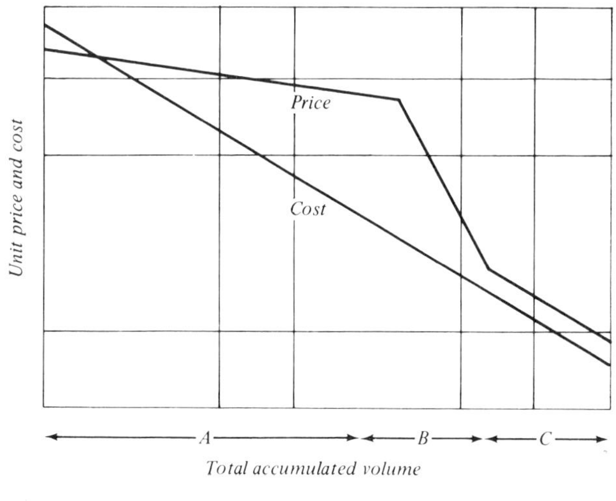

Exhibit 4 A characteristic pattern of costs and prices.

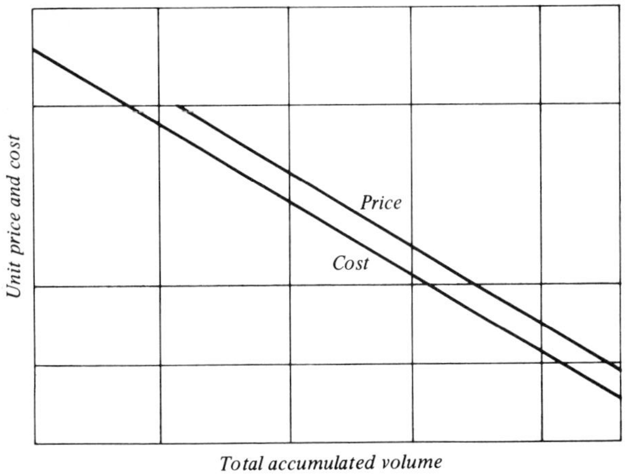

Exhibit 5 An alternative pattern of costs and prices.

competitor is gaining or losing market share substantially.)

In Exhibit 4, the constant-dollar price shows little or no decline during phase A, a steep slope of around 60 percent in phase B, and a moderate 70 to 80 percent slope in phase C. The relatively level price exhibited in phase A is associated with the introductory period in which price is set somewhat below initial cost and not changed as volume grows. If this price is held too long, competitors enter, and all add capacity until a "shakeout" price decline occurs in phase B. When prices reach a "reasonable" level above costs, they continue to decline with cost, as shown in phase C.

Characteristically, the dominant producer is losing his share of the market during phase A. During phase B, market shares may shift considerably as the more aggressive competitors struggle for dominance, using price as a major weapon. In phase C a stable competitive situation is again established with possibly a different dominant competitor than the one in Phase A.

In Exhibit 5, the price is brought down more nearly in parallel with cost—usually in an attempt to discourage the entry of competition. Although initial margins are less, final margins are usually greater.

There is nothing inherent in the price characteristics shown in Exhibits 4 and 5 that reveals one to be "better" than the other. One might expect a wide variety of patterns between the two types shown; however, such variation does not appear to occur in practical instances.

It must be remembered that these idealized curves are typical of those obtaining in uninhibited competition and are exclusive of the influence of inflation. One must also be certain to avoid thinking of them as plots against *time*. Although time increases with experience, the curves are plotted against *units produced* and may be quite irregular with respect to time.

OBSERVATIONS OF PRICE BEHAVIOR

Price data are relatively easy to acquire and, when adjusted by means of the GNP deflator,* they can be plotted as shown in Exhibits 6 through 10. These exhibits are typical of many, many similar ones for a very wide variety of products. Exhibits 6 and 7 show the two classical forms of price behavior in semiconductors. Exhibit 8 is considered typical of the chemical industry. Exhibit 9, for facial tissues, has an unusual break in the price pattern. This break shows what happened

*The GNP deflator is a factor used to correct prices for any given year to what they would have been in the base year by removing the average inflation in the gross national product.

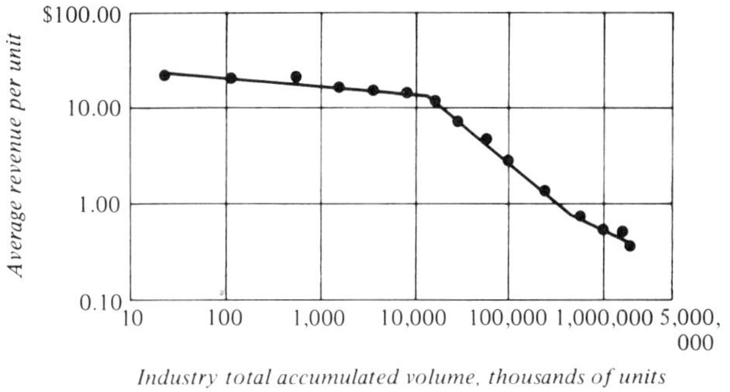

Exhibit 6 Revenue curve for silicon transistors during the period from 1954 to 1968.

when an element in the distribution chain was omitted and the factory picked up the eliminated unit's markup. Exhibit 10 shows the behavior of a very slowly growing product, free-standing gas ranges, over a very considerable period. In all of the cases, the data points in any one graph refer to equal intervals of *time*. Obviously, strong underlying laws are at work.

The 1965–1966 data for integrated circuits in Exhibit 7 are particularly remarkable, since each point represents an average *monthly*-price. The clustering of points, shown strongly in the progressive data at the high-volume end of Exhibit 9, is indicative of declining growth rate in the product. Such a decline (with its resulting cluster) is often the precursor of a price break when it occurs in the location of phase A of Exhibit 4.

From the data shown, as well as from the long-acknowledged behavior of costs, one can conclude that prices behave in a remarkably predictable and regular manner and that, in constant dollars, prices tend to decline. Break points are perhaps difficult to foresee, but they are associated with declining growth rates in the presence of a price "umbrella." Once again, the plots are in terms of total units produced and not in terms of time.

PRODUCT STRATEGY IMPLICATIONS

Since prices and costs tend to decline with units produced and since the producer with the largest stable market share eventually has the lowest costs and greatest profits, then it becomes vital to have a dominant market share in as many products as possible. How-

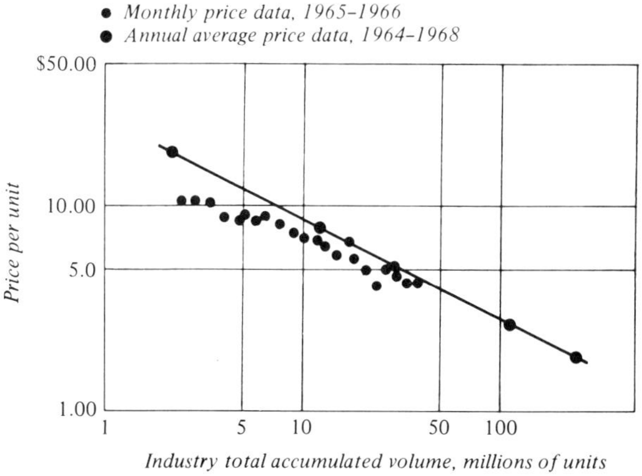

Exhibit 7 Price curve for integrated circuits.

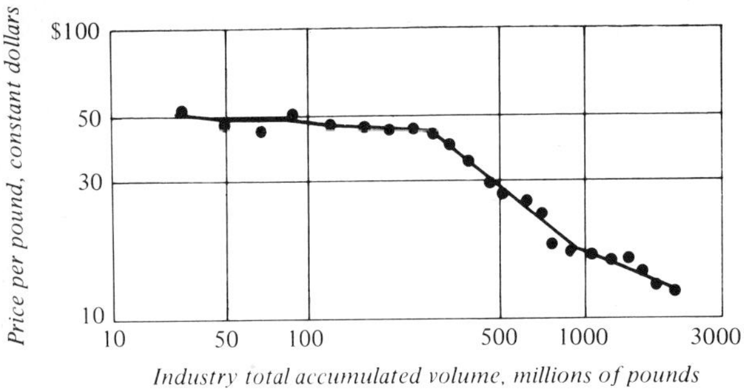

Exhibit 8 Polyvinyl chloride price curve (1946–1968).

ever, market share in slowly growing products can be gained only by reducing the share of competitors who are likely to fight back. It may not be worth the cost to wrest shares away from competent competitors in low-growth products. The value—in terms of improved cost and increased volume—of an increase in market share can be calculated with the aid of the experience curve. The investment required to increase one's share in the market can be compared with the calculated value, and, after suitable allowances for risk factors, the decision can be made. The company should remember, however, that most competitors will price at out-of-pocket cost rather than close a facility.

But all products at some time enjoy a period of rapid growth. During rapid growth, a company can gain share by securing most of the *growth*. Thus, while competitors grow, the company can grow even faster and emerge with a dominant share when growth eventually slows. The competitors, pleased with their own growth, may not stage much of a contest even when the company is compounding its market share at their eventual expense. At high growth rates—say 20 to 30 percent in units—it is possible to overtake a competitor in a remarkably few years.

The strategic implication is that a company should strive to dominate the market, either by introducing the product, by segmenting the market, or by discouraging competitors' growth in rapidly growing areas by preemptive pricing or value. Developing and introducing new products, though a good road to dominance, involve considerable cost and uncertainty. Similarly, it is difficult to identify a market segment that can be isolated from those segments in which competitors have more experience and lower costs. However, the history of business abounds with examples of successful segmentation. The key is to find a segment the company can protect over a long period of time. In contrast, the idea of preempting market by price or value concessions is intuitive in most business organizations. Although price competition is usually resisted, it is often cheaper than the more intangible weapon of added value.

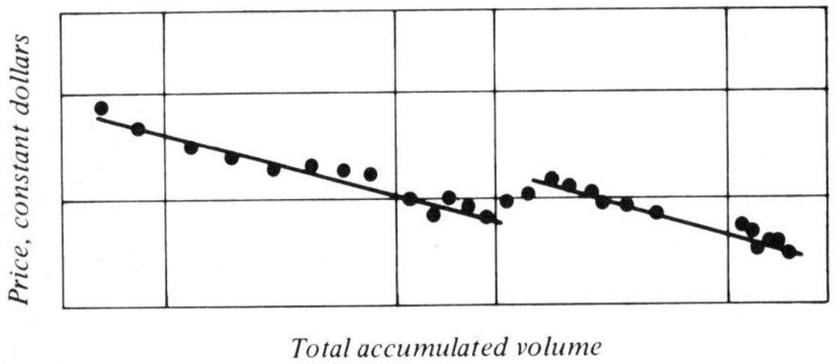

Exhibit 9 Price curve for facial tissues (for the years 1933–1955 and 1961–1966).

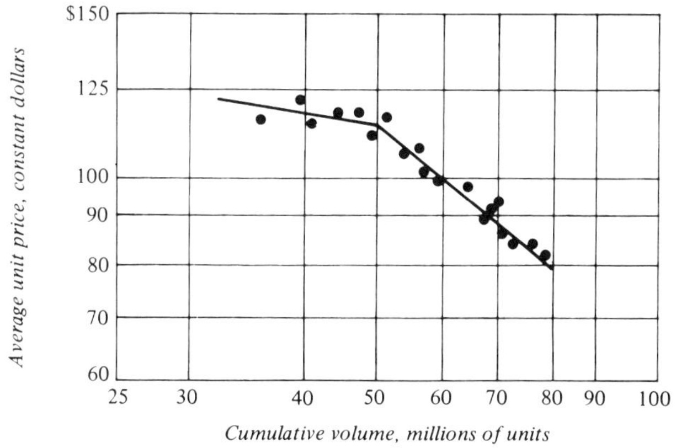

Exhibit 10 Price curve for free standing gas ranges.

THE PRODUCT PORTFOLIO

The products of a firm can be categorized into four groups in terms of market share and growth rate. Exhibit 11 depicts such a matrix.

Category 1: Products with a high market share but with low growth. Products in category 1—those whose growth is equivalent to the growth rate of the GNP—are *not* attractive areas for investment, but they are the main source of reported earnings and cash. They are usually products for which a dominant market share is held. Their good earnings are sometimes used inappropriately to justify continued investment in the hope that growth can be increased, whereas the proper objective is to maximize cash flow consistent with maintaining market share.

Category 2: Products with a high market share and rapid growth. Products in category 2 are those that, if dominant share can be maintained until growth slows, will become the high dollar earners of category 1. These products are heavy consumers of cash and earnings, and those for which leading market position must be maintained. To attempt to extract high earnings from these products during their growth phase will usually blight the growth and sacrifice the dominant position. If continued until growth slows, such "bleeding" will move the product into category 4 instead of into category 1.

Exhibit 11 Product Growth and Market Share

	High market share	Low market share
High growth rate	category 2	category 3
Low growth rate	category 1	category 4

Category 3: Products with a low market share but rapid growth. Category 3 includes products in which a dominant market share must be achieved before growth slows or a marginal position will be "frozen in." These products demand a heavy commitment of financial and management resources. Since such resources are limited, the number of such products in the portfolio must be limited. If resources are not available to move a product in this category into a dominant market position, then it is usually wise to withdraw from the market.

Category 4: Products with low market shares and slow growth. The final category comprises the "dogs"—products that consume far more than a just amount of management attention. They can never become satisfactorily profitable and should be liquidated in as clever and graceful a manner as possible. Outright sale to a buyer with different perceptions can sometimes be accomplished. Often pricing in a manner to upset competitors is a useful adjunct to liquidation. In any event, investment in such areas should be discontinued.

It is useful to examine a corporation's products and try to classify them into the foregoing categories. Lack of balance becomes rapidly evident and plans can be laid to add and drop products to achieve a more nearly satisfactory portfolio. It must be remembered that we are talking of products, not industries, although some industries are sufficiently simple in product diversity that they behave as single products.

An unbalanced product portfolio produces some typical cash-flow symptoms. If the company has too many dominant, slow-growth products, it will usually have a low growth rate coupled with excess cash and inadequate investment opportunity.

Having too many high-growth products will produce cash deficiencies as well as rapid growth. Too many low-share, low-growth products will result in inadequate cash *and* inadequate growth. With time, the balance of a product portfolio will automatically change if no deletions or additions are made.

CONTROL IMPLICATIONS

Market dominance by product is the key to profitability and it can be achieved by expenditures and investments during the rapid-growth phase for a given product. The source of the funds should be mature or slowly growing products in which dominance has already been achieved and in which expense and investment are no longer intense. It is important to avoid control procedures that stifle the rapid-growth phase; yet when growth slows, it is vital to secure maximum cash flow and avoid investment overshoot.

Budgeting and control systems should be quite different for the two categories, and different objectives should be set for the product managers. Clearly, the main objective in managing the rapidly growing product should be market penetration, whereas the goal for the dominant mature product should be to maximize cash flow. In both cases the total costs should be managed to follow the experience-curve slope appropriate to the industry. A control system that sets appropriately designed goals for market share, cash flow, and cost progress is more likely to produce continuing growth in reported earnings than a system that merely stresses product-line profitability.

To use the experience-curve effect in the control system and the management decision process, the company must have comprehensive data on costs and market share. If such data can be obtained, the company will have a powerful tool.

Needless to say, the successful implementation of a competitive strategy also depends upon the reaction of competitors. The route to a dominant share of a growing market lies in discouraging competitors from adding capacity or increasing their capability to produce the product. An estimate of the key competitors' decision processes is thus invaluable in planning competitive interaction.

FORECASTING

The use of the experience curve to forecast prices—both for products and for purchases—is obvious. Again, one must use care to deflate the raw data and reinflate the forecast. Use of the GNP deflator has been most satisfactory and, in particular, better than the sector deflator.* (If the sector defla-

*The sector deflator is a correction factor to be applied to prices in a particular sector of the economy—for example, chemicals—to adjust for the inflation that has occurred in that particular economic sector.

tor is used, one is likely to erase evidence of the effect sought.) Obviously, the resulting forecast carries a forecast of inflation rate that is included in the deflator projection.

The forecast of price-break points is much more difficult than projecting an existing trend—even in the presence of strong inflation, if capacity in the industry seems high and if prices appear soft, it may be wise to initiate the break, since the leader in a severe price decline usually is the gainer in market share.

CONCLUSIONS

The fact that manufacturing costs tend to follow an experience curve not only is useful for cost control and forecasting but also has a profound implication for prices and profits. In particular, it is strongly suggested that the producer of a particular product who has made the most units should have the lowest costs and highest profits. The potential profitability of a mature product should be closely related to the market share it enjoys in its particular segment.

The products of a company can be grouped by market share and growth rate in order to prescribe appropriate management of products in each group. Substantially different management objectives should be pursued in each of the four categories described. The important strategic issues of product selection, price policy, investment criterions, and divestment decisions can be more effectively addressed in the context of the experience curve than in other ways—*even if no actual data are ever collected or actual curves plotted.*

REFERENCES

1 Wright, T. P., "Factors affecting the cost of airplanes," *J. Aeron. Sci.*, vol. 3, pp. 122–128, Feb. 1936.

2 Billon, S. A., *Industrial Time Reduction Curves as Tools for Forecasting.* Ann Arbor, Mich.: University Microfilms, 1960.

3 Hirschmann, W. B., "Profit from the learning curve," *Harvard Business Rev.*, vol. 42, pp. 125–139, Jan.–Feb. 1964.

4 Perkins, J. H., and Enuendy, G., "Use of the learning curve to forecast trends of chemical prices," presented at the American Association of Cost Engineers 10th Annual Meeting, Philadelphia, Pa., June 20–22, 1966.

5 Cole, R. R., "Increasing utilization of the cost-quantity relationship in manufacturing," *J. Ind. Eng.*, pp. 173–177, May–June 1958.

6 Andress, F. J., "The learning curve as a production tool," *Harvard Business Rev.*, pp. 87–97, Jan.–Feb. 1954.

7 Cohen, J. E., *Model of Simple Competition.* Cambridge: Harvard University Press, 1966.

8 Council of Economic Advisers, "Economic report to the President," U.S. Government Printing Office, Washington, D.C., 1969.

Part Five

Putting the Marketing Plan into Action

The discussions in the previous section on marketing strategies naturally lead to discussions in this section of some of the most significant variables on putting the marketing plan into action: products and product lines; pricing; channels of distribution and physical logistics; personal selling and management of the sales force; and advertising.

All these variables are interdependent, and all can be implemented in countless ways. Each of these marketing areas is discussed in some detail.

The products and product line readings deal with the product life cycle, the "just noticeable difference," the shift from brand to product line marketing, the targeting of prospects for a new product, and a discussion of why new industrial products fail.

The pricing articles cover corporate pricing practices, techniques for pricing new products and services, and a decision-making structure for price decisions.

The materials on channels of distribution include discussions of functional spin-offs, a frame of reference for improving productivity in distribution, and the total-cost approach to distribution.

The readings on personal selling and management of the sales force deal with interactions and influence processes in personal selling; the computer, personal selling, and sales management; and reactions by the industrial salesman to role conflict.

Finally, the articles on advertising include a theoretical view of advertising communication, imagery and symbolism, an attitudinal framework for advertising strategy, and media approaches to segmentation.

A PRODUCTS AND PRODUCT LINES

20

Managing the Product Life Cycle

Donald K. Clifford, Jr.

The product life cycle concept has long permeated marketing decision making. It is—or can be—a valuable tool for effecting practical marketing plans; but the author indicates how this can be the case only if the concept is truly understood and correctly applied.

Not long ago, a leading marketer of consumer packaged goods was building a brand of toilet soap. Growth had been fair but not spectacular. Market tests suggested that an increase in advertising, backed by a change in copy, could enable the new brand to reach the "escape velocity" it needed to become a sales leader. But marketing management, feeling the funds would be better spent in launching a new detergent, vetoed the proposal. The detergent was a moderate success, but the promising soap brand went into a gradual sales decline from which it never recovered. Management had pulled out the props at a critical point in the product's growth period.

A supplier of light industrial equipment felt that his major product was not receiving the sales support it deserved. Unconvinced by the salesmen's claims that it was hard to sell, he developed new presentations and sales kits and persuaded sales management to run special campaigns. At year-end, volume had shown no improvement. In fact, the product had long since passed the zenith of its potential sales and profits, and no amount of additional sales support could have profitably extended its growth. Yet in order to give extra sales support to this problem case, management had cut into the marketing budgets of several highly promising products that were still in their "young" growth phase. In short, management had failed to consider each product's position in its life cycle.

As these two cases suggest, the concept of the product life cycle—familiar as it may be to most business executives—seems too frequently forgotten in marketing planning. Yet there appears to be conclusive evidence that companies can make far more effective marketing decisions if they take the time to: (1) find out where each of their products stands in its life cycle; (2) determine the overall mix or balance of life cycles in their product line; and (3) analyze the trends in their life-cycle mix and the long-term profit impact of these trends. Without this information, some products will receive neither their rightful *share* of marketing attention, nor the right *kind* of attention. With it, marketing management has a twofold opportunity:

- To reshape and control the life cycles of individual products.
- To raise long-term corporate profitability by improving the overall mix of life cycles in the company's product line.

The size and profitability of any business depend on the product life cycles that make it up. But while companies may continue to grow in sales and profits, no product escapes eventual maturity and decline. Allocating re-

Reprinted from Roland Mann (ed.) *The Arts of Top Management: A McKinsey Anthology*, pp. 216–226. At the time of writing the author was a director of McKinsey & Co., Inc.

sources so as to reconcile corporate aims and ambitions with the life cycles of the company's products is the objective of life-cycle management. My purpose here is to show how the classic life-cycle concept can be turned into an active profit-making tool, and to describe an approach to life-cycle analysis that has helped some companies make more profitable marketing decisions.

THE LIFE-CYCLE CONCEPT

The product life-cycle concept derives from the fact that a product's sales volume follows a typical pattern that can readily be charted as a four-phase cycle. Following its birth, the product passes through a low-volume introduction phase. During the subsequent growth period, volume and profit both rise. Volume stabilizes during maturity, though unit profits typically start to fall off. Eventually, in the stage of obsolescence, sales volume declines.

The length of the life cycle, the duration of each phase, and the shape of the curve vary widely for different products. But in every instance, obsolescence eventually occurs for one of three reasons.

First, the need may disappear. This is what happened to the orange juice squeezer when frozen juice caught on.

Second, a better, cheaper, or more convenient product may be developed to suit the same need. Oil-based paint lost its position in the home to water-based paint; plastics have replaced wood, metal, and paper in product categories ranging from dry-cleaning bags to aircraft parts.

Third, a competitive product may, through superior marketing strategy, suddenly gain a decisive advantage. This happened to competing products when Arthur Godfrey's personal charm got behind Lipton Tea, and again when Procter & Gamble secured the American Dental Association's endorsement of its decay-prevention claims for Crest toothpaste.

As the chart below shows, a product's profit cycle is shaped quite differently from its sales cycle. During introduction, a product may not earn any profit at all because of high initial advertising and promotion costs.

In the growth period, before competition catches up, unit profits typically attain their peak. Then they start declining, though total profits may continue to rise for a time on rising

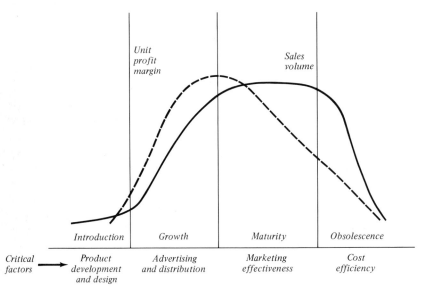

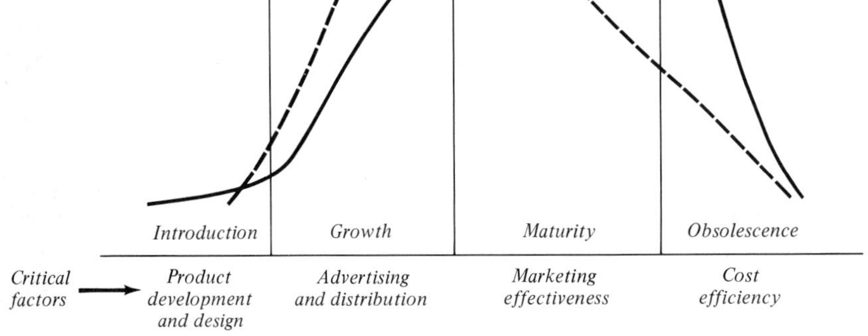

The product life cycle concept.

sales volume. In the chemical industry, for example, rapid volume increases often more than offset the effect of price reductions early in the growth phase.

During late growth and early maturity, increasing competition cuts deeply into profit margins and ultimately into total profits. For instance, as a result of drastic price cutting, general-purpose semiconductors, once highly profitable, now return so little unit profit that many companies have left the business.

Finally, in the period of obsolescence, declining volume eventually pushes costs up to a level that eliminates profits entirely.

In recent years, as most marketing men are aware, products have been maturing more rapidly and life cycles growing shorter. Indeed, this trend has been responsible for some of the major problems facing marketers today.

Razor blades are a classic example of accelerated maturity. For decades, with Blue Blades and thin blades, Gillette dominated the market and enjoyed steady growth. Ten years ago, Super Blue Blades arrived—a new product with greatly improved shaving qualities, which could normally have looked forward to a growth period of many years, if not decades. But in less than three years, the stainless steel blade was reintroduced into this country, and the Super Blue Blade started on its way to obsolescence, suddenly shifting from growth to maturity.

The trend to more rapid maturity can be observed in industrial products as well. In chemicals, the competitive advantage afforded by a new product such as nylon once ensured growing sales for a decade or more. But in recent years, the tempo of product innovation and substitution has quickened to the point where some companies, rather than risk heavy research investments on products that may mature within two or three years, now concentrate on exploiting present products and on rapidly copying the products introduced by market leaders.

Not only do products mature more rapidly, but product life cycles generally appear to be growing shorter. For more than 15 years—to cite one conspicuous example—the DC-3 held its place as the leading commercial airliner. But the DC-7, and later the turbo-prop Electra, were rendered obsolete in less than five years by the pure jet DC-8, the 707, and others like them.

The railroads of the United States stand out as a classic example of the first kind of failure, which I call the commodity illusion. For decades they viewed their service as a commodity, a changeless product that would forever meet a changeless transportation need. Only recently have the railroads begun to realize how much ground they have lost—and how much they are still losing—to air, water, and, particularly, over-the-road transportation.

A similar commodity illusion misled the many textile companies that failed to adapt their wool and cotton equipment and marketing capabilities to synthetic fibers in the decade following World War II. In product after product, market after market, companies that had regarded their traditional products as commodities went out of business or were absorbed by more wide-awake competitors.

The second cause of inadequate life-cycle management—neglecting to apply the life-cycle concept—may be illustrated by an electronics company whose products typically have life cycles of two years or less. Too much concerned with present problems, not enough with future opportunities and needs, this company had failed to assess the life-cycle mix of its product line.

As a result, it suddenly found itself with two products late in the growth phase, nine in the maturity or obsolescence phases—and none in introduction or early growth. New and improved products, the lifeblood of any organization in this industry, had simply been allowed to dry up. Had it failed to recognize its predicament in time, the company might well have been out of business in another two years. Fortunately, rapid development and acquisition programs were carried out in time to provide the new products it needed for survival.

FAILURE TO MANAGE THE LIFE CYCLE

Faced with the challenge of earlier maturity and shortening life cycles, few leading companies have seen the opportunity in life-cycle management, and fewer still have capitalized on it. Most have either (1) failed to recognize that their products have a life cycle, or (2) failed to apply the concept by analyzing the life cycles of their product lines in order to shape marketing strategy.

Such failures by management to fully understand or act on the changing requirements of the company's products and product mix are all too common. And as life cycles grow shorter and products mature more rapidly, the problem for many can only become more acute.

The classic life-cycle concept holds that marketing decisions should be largely determined by a product's position in its cycle, since—as the chart indicates—the critical factors affecting its profitability change with the four phases of its growth and decline.

In the introduction phase, product development and design are considered critical. For industrial goods, where customers have been slow to change from a proven product, technical superiority or demonstrable cost savings will often be needed to open the door. For consumer products, willingness to invest in future volume through heavy initial marketing expenditures may be critical.

During the growth period, consistent, reliable product performance must be regarded as essential to success for most industrial products—and for technically complex consumer products as well. A reputation for quality, backed by adequate production capability, can win a manufacturer the leading market position, as it did for Zenith in black-and-white TV. In contrast, for consumer packaged goods and other non-technical products, effective distribution and advertising have traditionally been the key factors.

The key requirements during maturity, though harder to define, usually come under the heading of "overall marketing effectiveness." Marketing skill may pay off in a variety of ways—for instance, generating incremental profits by reducing price so as to reach additional consumers; finding and promoting new uses for the product; or upgrading distribution channels to reach prime markets more efficiently.

During obsolescence, cost control becomes the key to generating profits. The product of the low-cost producer and distributor often enjoys a profitable "old age" long after its rivals have disappeared from the scene.

Though valid within their limits, the traditional generalizations about management decisions and the product life cycle do not really go far enough. They fail to take into account the all-important fact that *life cycles can be managed.*

THE DIMENSION OF CONTROL

Life-cycle management has two basic aspects:

- Controlling the mix of life cycles in the product line by: (1) planned new-product effort and product-line pruning, and (2) planned allocation of money and manpower among existing products and product groups according to the profit opportunity reflected by their respective life-cycle positions.
- Controlling individual product life cycles to generate added profits.

Experience indicates that there may be opportunities at any stage, except for the very end of the line, for marketing management to profitably alter the shape and duration of an individual product's life cycle. The introduction period, for example, can often be shortened by increasing marketing expenditures or securing national distribution more quickly. In the next phase, growth can be speeded and sales and profits ultimately pushed to higher levels by exploiting additional markets, by pricing the product to encourage wider usage, or by more vigorous advertising or sales efforts—in short, by more effectively planned and implemented marketing strategy.

The maturity stage usually offers marketing management the greatest opportunity to change the shape and duration of product life cycles. Has the product really approached obsolescence because of a superior substitute or a fundamental change in consumer needs? Or does obsolescence merely seem near because marketing management has failed to identify and reach the right consumer needs, or because a competitor has done a better marketing job? The question will be crucial, since often the supposed condition of "maturity" is misleading. The challenge may be rather to extend the product's youth by repackaging, physical modifications, repricing, appealing to new users, adding new distribution channels, or some combination of marketing strategy changes. Frequently, as subsequent examples will show, a successfully revitalized product offers a higher return on management time and funds invested than does a new product.

Of course, this will not always be possible. Maturity is forced upon some products by a basic change in consumer habits or the introduction of a greatly superior competitive item. In this event, determining when to cut back the investment of management time and money—and give higher priority to new or more active products—becomes the key marketing decision.

Finally, in obsolescence, marketing effectiveness becomes almost entirely a matter of knowing when to cut short the life of a product which has been demanding more than the small share of management attention that its profit contribution deserves.

CONTROLLING THE LIFE CYCLE

The tremendous impact of effective life-cycle management may be demonstrated by the success of several leading companies in directing the progress of both individual product cycles and the overall life-cycle mix. Consider these examples:

- Spurred by rapid technological change and by the trend toward packaging everything—a consequence of our self-service way of life—packaging has been a growth industry for well over a decade. One of the industry leaders has been E.I. du Pont de Nemours & Co. Du Pont has been strongest in cellophane, a product so well known it has become almost a synonym for transparent packaging.

With the end of World War II, flexible packaging, and cellophane in particular, entered a period of accelerated growth, but in the 1950s new products—notably polyethylene—began to meet certain packaging needs more effectively. Polyethylene film, for example, was less easily ruptured in cold weather—and in time, it also became lower in price. Consequently, cellophane began losing its share of the flexible packaging market. It became clear that sales volume would soon begin falling off unless strong corrective action was taken.

Faced with the immediate threat of obsolescence in a highly profitable product, Du Pont—followed by the two other cellophane manufacturers—introduced a series of modifications designed to maintain cellophane's growth and prolong its maturity. These included special coatings, new types, and lighter grades at prices more competitive with the newer packaging materials. In all, the customers' choice of cellophane types grew from a handful to well over 100.

The cumulative effect of these improvements had an impressive impact on cellophane sales. Contrary to widespread predictions of dramatic decline, cellophane maintained the bulk of its sales volume—of which the traditional grades now represent a relatively small fraction. With more than half of a $300 million market, Du Pont has been the primary beneficiary of this reversal of fortunes.

Further testimony to Du Pont's effectiveness in life-cycle management can be found in its control over the life-cycle *mix* of its flexible packaging products. Recognizing the maturity of cellophane, Du Pont developed a strong position in polyethylene and in other new packaging materials. While *maintaining* its leadership in flexible packaging by reshaping the life cycle of cellophane, the company also provided for *growth* by adding new products to strengthen its product mix.

• During the mid-1950s, Procter & Gamble's Gleem had attained a strong position in the toothpaste market. But the total market was growing at a slow rate, and P&G wanted to grow faster. Having introduced Crest as the first decay-preventive dentifrice, P&G found the way to explosive growth by obtaining endorsement of the new toothpaste by the American Dental Association—an achievement that had evaded other manufacturers for years. P&G thus reshaped the life cycle of the new dentifrice. Crest's share of the toothpaste market *quadrupled* between 1958 and 1963, while the sales curves of other brands of toothpaste showed strong signs of obsolescence, declining on the average more than 15 percent.

• Decades after the introduction of Jell-O, General Foods succeeded in converting it from a mature to a growth product by a revamping of marketing strategy. GF changed the Jell-O formula, repackaged the product and repriced it, found a host of new uses for Jell-O, and publicized them to the housewife through stepped-up advertising. Today, Jell-O remains one of GF's biggest selling and most profitable products.

• Aggressive life-cycle management was also demonstrated when International Business Machines introduced its "Series 360" computers early 1964. By the early 1960s, competition in this field had rapidly become severe. IBM controlled three-quarters of the computer business, but intensified competition was shortening the life cycles of its computer line. Management foresaw that the rapid growth it had enjoyed in the 1950s would soon slow down unless the company undertook a major shift in product and marketing strategy.

The solution adopted by IBM was to rapidly obsolete its own equipment—much of which had been on the market for less than four years. At the same time, the company moved to secure its entrenched position in computers by providing an expandable system that would make it uneconomic or inefficient for customers to switch to competing systems as their computer needs grew.

While there is no substitute for solid marketing judgment, these examples serve to suggest that the odds on making good decisions will be increased if management knows where its products stand—individually and collectively—in their respective life cycles.

LIFE-CYCLE ANALYSIS

One proven means of positioning a company's products in their life cycles—a way that has proven effective for some forward-looking companies—is life-cycle analysis. This may be described as a disciplined, periodic review resulting in (a) a formal audit that pinpoints each product's position in its life cycle, and (b) a profile of the life-cycle mix of the product line as a whole.

Although the steps followed by marketing management in carrying out the first part of a life-cycle analysis may vary among companies, the following are typical:

1 Develop historical trend information for a period of three to five years (longer for some products). Data included will be unit and dollar sales, profit margins, total profit contribution, return on invested capital, market share, and prices.

2 Check recent trends in the number and nature of competitors; number and market-share rankings of competing products, and their quality and performance advantages; shifts in distribution channels; and relative advantages enjoyed by competitive products in each channel.

3 Analyze developments in short-term competitive tactics, such as competitors' recent announcements of new products or plans for expanding production capacity.

4 Obtain (or update) historical information on the life cycles of similar or related products.

5 Project sales for the product over the next three to five years, based on all the information gathered, and estimate an incremental profit ratio for the product during each of these years (the ratio of total direct costs—manufacturing, advertising, product development, sales, distribution, etc.—to pretax profits). Expressed as a ratio—e.g., 4.8 to 1 or 6.3 to 1—this measures the number of dollars required to generate each additional dollar of profit. The ratio typically improves (becomes lower) as the product enters its growth period; begins to deteriorate (rise) as the product approaches maturity; and climbs more sharply as it reaches obsolescence.

6 Estimate the number of profitable years remaining in the product's life cycle, and—based on all the information at hand—fix the product's position on its life-cycle curve: (a) introduction, (b) early or late growth, (c) early or late maturity, or (d) early or late obsolescence.

DEVELOPING THE LIFE-CYCLE PROFILE

Once the life-cycle positions of all the company's major products have been determined, marketing management proceeds to develop a life-cycle profile of the company's entire line. Again, this involves a series of steps:

1 Determine what percentages of the company's sales and profits fall within each phase of the product life cycle. These percentage figures indicate the present life-cycle (sales) profile and the present profit profile of the company's current line.

2 Calculate changes in the life-cycle and profit profiles over the past five years, and project these profiles over the next five years.

3 Develop a target life-cycle profile for the company, and measure the company's present life-cycle profile against it. The target profile, established by marketing management, specifies the desirable share of company sales that should fall within each phase of the product life cycle. It can be determined by industry obsolescence trends, the pace of new product introduction in the field, the average length of product life cycles in the company's line, and top management's objectives for growth and profitability. As a rule, the target profile for growth-minded companies whose life cycles tend to be short will call for a high proportion of sales in the introductory and growth phases.

With these steps completed, management can assign priorities to such functions, as new-product development, acquisition, and product-line pruning, based on the discrepancies between the company's target profile and its present life-cycle profile. Once corporate effort has been broadly allocated in this way among products at various stages of their life cycles, marketing plans can be detailed for individual product lines.

21

The Marketing Importance of the "Just Noticeable Difference"

Steuart Henderson Britt
Victoria M. Nelson

Because substantial similarities prevail among many brands within the same product class, product differentiation is critical. But what constitutes a perceptual difference? The authors show that the use of a 100-year-old "law" can provide important insights into this problem.

In today's avalanche of closely competing products, a brand with a clearly perceptible difference stands a much better chance for success than another "me-too" product. And, after a time, even a very successful product needs the restaging boost of a perceptible improvement in the product itself, in its name, in its container, in its price, or in the methods of distribution, merchandising, sales or advertising. The key to product improvement is the word *perceptible.* This means perceptible to the consumer, who must perceive the improvement as truly better or different than before.

WEBER'S LAW

Most marketers do not know that two German physiologists of the nineteenth century discovered a guideline, called Weber's Law, that can be applied to product improvements in the last half of the twentieth century. It has already been demonstrated how this law can be applied to marketing.[1] Weber's Law states that the stronger the initial stimulus, the greater is the change in intensity required for the resulting stimulus to be perceived as different.

For example, anyone can perceive readily that a 10-inch line is longer than a 7-inch line, but the addition of 3 inches to a line measuring 25 feet may not be enough for the resulting 25 feet and 3 inches to be perceived as longer than the 25-foot line. As much as 2 feet in additional length might be required for the majority of people to perceive that the second line is longer than the first.

According to Weber's Law, an additional level of stimuli—known as the *just noticeable difference* or j.n.d.—is necessary for the majority of people to perceive that there is a difference between the resulting stimulus and the initial stimulus. This j.n.d. is not an absolute amount, but rather is relative to the intensity of the initial stimulus. Gustav Fechner, a colleague of Ernst Weber for whom the law is named, expressed this relationship in the mathematical ratio

$$\frac{\Delta I}{I} = k$$

where "k" is the constant ratio, "I" is the initial stimulus and "ΔI" is the j.n.d.

Happily, Weber's Law holds for all the

[1]Steuart Henderson Britt, "How Weber's Law Can Be Applied to Marketing," *Business Horizons* (February 1975), pp. 21–29.

Reprinted from *Business Horizons*, vol. 19, pp. 38–40, August 1976. Copyright 1976 by the Foundation for the School of Business at Indiana University. Reprinted by permission. At the time of writing, Steuart Henderson Britt was president of Britt and Frerichs Inc. Victoria M. Nelson was a recent graduate from the master's program in advertising, Medill School of Journalism, Northwestern University.

senses and for almost all intensities. Although it is not quite accurate or precise at extreme intensities, it does hold remarkably true in the middle range of intensities; and these are the ones to which consumers are most often exposed. The j.n.d. varies with the type of stimuli tested, but there is a j.n.d. for every type of stimulus that is sufficiently intense for the majority of individuals to perceive a noticeable difference.

THE CONSTANT STIMULI METHOD

Weber's principle can be applied to product improvement by using a research technique to find the correct j.n.d. This technique is the *constant stimuli method.* In this method, an individual is asked to compare increasingly intense stimuli with a standard set of stimuli until he reports that he perceives a difference between the current set of stimuli and the standard set of stimuli. The degree of difference between the standard stimuli and the final set of stimuli, then, is the just noticeable difference.

Applications to Product Improvement

How can this technique be applied to product improvement? Suppose that a luggage manufacturer wants to produce a suitcase that is perceived as lighter than his leading competitor's suitcase by the majority of women who travel.

The competitor's suitcase weighs 5 pounds. Women travelers individually and separately first pick up the 5-pound suitcase and then a case of identical appearance, but weighing 4 pounds 15 ounces, and each woman reports which is lighter.

Next, each woman picks up the 5-pound case, and then one weighing 4 pounds 14 ounces, and reports which is lighter, and so on. The order in which each woman lifts the cases is varied, of course, but the 5-pound case always represents the standard, that is, the constant stimuli.

This paired-comparison technique is continued until the majority of the women actually perceive the lighter case as being lighter. Let us suppose that at a weight of 4 pounds, over 50% of the women correctly identify it as the lighter case. Using Weber's Law we see that:

$$\frac{\Delta I}{I} = \frac{5 \text{ pounds} - 4 \text{ pounds}}{5 \text{ pounds}} = \frac{1}{5}$$

Thus, for this particular situation, the weight of the suitcase must be decreased by one-fifth of the original weight before the majority of women can perceive the change. If the suitcase manufacturer had decreased the weight by only one-half pound, his improvement would have gone undetected. If he had selected a 2-pound weight reduction, he probably would have sacrificed the durability and desirability of a heavier material.

Because Weber's Law holds true for most intensities, the manufacturer now knows what weight reduction will be required for his full line of luggage in order for the majority of women to perceive the lightness of his suitcases. For example, he must produce an 8-pound suitcase for the majority of women to perceive it as lighter than his competitor's 10-pound model.

$$\frac{\Delta I}{I} = \frac{10 \text{ pounds} - 8 \text{ pounds}}{10 \text{ pounds}} = \frac{2}{10} = \frac{1}{5}$$

As another example, a company has decided to manufacture a soap that is more economical than soaps of competitors, and will use the theme "lasts longer" to represent the product improvement. The marketing executive in charge of developing the new brand wants at least 50% of the consumers to perceive this new bar of soap as one that will last longer.

He finds that for an average family the company's present regular-sized bar lasts about 20 days. Using slightly harder mills, he has his company produce what are perceptibly the same kinds of bars, but ones that will last 21 days, 22 days, 23 days, 24 days and 25 days respectively.

In a series of experiments, he has individuals first use his regular-sized 20-day bar, then the 21-day bar, and report which lasts longer. Each person then compares the 20-day bar and the 22-day bar and reports which bar lasts longer. This process is continued until all the bars have been tested against the constant stimuli, that is, the 20-day bar of soap.

Suppose that only 25% of the individuals perceive the 23-day bar as lasting longer than the original bar, but that 53% of them perceive that the 25-day bar lasts longer.

$$\frac{\Delta I}{I} = \frac{25 \text{ days} - 20 \text{ days}}{20 \text{ days}} = \frac{5}{20} = \frac{1}{4}$$

The marketing executive now knows that the improved bar must last at least one-fourth of the time longer than the present bar for it to be perceived by the majority of users as improved. By finding this j.n.d. of 5 days, the soap company has isolated the minimum amount of time necessary to make its claim believable to the majority of consumers.

If the decision instead had been to make the bar last 30 days, a good deal of purchase frequency would have been sacrificed. Had the decision been that 3 extra days of product life would be sufficient, the improvement claim of "lasts longer" would not have been perceived as true by most consumers, thus possibly resulting in a loss of sales.

Similarly, the company now knows that the product life of its big 40-day bath-sized bar must be extended to 50 days in order for the improvement claim to be perceived by most consumers as true.

$$\frac{\Delta I}{I} = \frac{50 \text{ days} - 40 \text{ days}}{40 \text{ days}} = \frac{10}{40} = \frac{1}{4}$$

The ratios for Weber's Law vary, of course, among different individuals, in different stimuli ranges, and among different kinds of stimuli. But the fact remains that equal changes in stimuli intensity are not necessarily perceived as equal. By using the constant stimuli method, a marketer can ensure that his product improvement will be perceived as just noticeably different by the majority of his consumers or customers.

22

Shift from Brand to Product Line Marketing

Joseph A. Morein

How does a company react when, for example, its baby food sales begin to dwindle because of the country's much lower birth rate? Does it acquire a new but unrelated company? Does it sadly make plans to close its doors?

Neither of these options, according to the author, needs to be taken. Instead, he says, the trend seems to be away from brand marketing and toward product line

Reprinted from *Harvard Business Review*, vol. 53, pp. 56–64. At the time of writing, the author was Master Charge marketing manager at Citicorp.

marketing, a strategy that, to date, seems to come about more by accident than by planning. By developing a series of related products and marketing them under an established and respected name, a company can meet its investors' demands for growth.

The author reviews the differences between brand marketing and product line marketing and discusses some of the obstacles of the former. He then shows how product line marketing can successfully help to overcome these obstacles through a more efficient and coordinated marketing effort.

During the past 25 years, the development of sophisticated brand marketing has strongly influenced the consumer products field. Consumer packaged goods companies such as Procter & Gamble, Colgate, and General Foods have been regarded as the premier models of effective marketing. Their approach to brand marketing has been widely imitated, sometimes in categories far removed from consumer packaged goods.

However, recent trends indicate that the end of the era of brand marketing dominance may be in sight. In response to a complex and competitive business environment, a new method, product line marketing, is providing an alternative to the traditional brand approach. However, product line marketing is still in an early stage of development, and in most cases its implementation has been fortuitous, rather than a deliberate, planned strategy. The shift in strategy from brand to product line marketing has been achieved successfully, nevertheless, by some large companies.

Before discussing the benefits of a product line strategy, it would be helpful to summarize the characteristics of the brand marketing approach. Brand marketing is built around a simple concept. The "brand" is usually a single product, although it may have more than one model, size, or flavor. For the most part, it is marketed independently of other, even very similar, products in the parent company's line—even if some of the products compete with each other. Familiar examples of brands are Procter & Gamble's Tide and General Foods' Gainesburgers. Sharply focused advertising and promotion efforts support such brands, enabling them to maintain high levels of consumer awareness and acceptance despite significant internal and external competition.

The marketing effort for these products is managed by a brand group that is concerned almost exclusively with the sales and profit success of its brand. The brand group is generally led by a product manager, or in the case of a very large brand, a group product manager. Higher levels of management are responsible for the coordination needed to discourage any extremes of intracompany competition.

Brand marketing has been so successful for many companies in both maintaining and introducing products that it is rarely acknowledged that other approaches to packaged goods marketing exist. However, it is difficult to fit the following examples into the traditional view of brand marketing:

- Welch Foods (formerly the Welch Grape Juice Company) used to market primarily frozen and bottled grape juice. Recently the company has expanded its line to include powdered drinks, a chilled grape juice drink, grape soda, several cranberry products, and prune juice.
- Sara Lee, long a leader in frozen baked goods, has introduced a line of frozen meat entrées in a move to "dominate the frozen food cabinet in the prepared foods segment," according to a company spokesman. In the

same interview, he stated that "there is no way to go into new products without a strong traditional line."[1]

- Stouffer's Foods, similarly strong in frozen entrées, has introduced a line of frozen baked goods that are advertised as "a delicious alternative to Sara Lee."
- Castle & Cooke, now competing with Chiquita in the banana business, has been making its greatest progress since it put the Dole name on its product. Despite favorable market trends for its bananas under the brand name "Cabana," Castle & Cooke felt that "Dole was a stronger name to the consumer."[2]
- Merrill Lynch has long been the leading retail brokerage house, but recent advertising has stressed the wide variety of investment opportunities it offers. The company has shifted its emphasis from common stocks to the "29 ways" it can help the investor achieve financial security.

These illustrations suggest a marketing strategy that is more complex than brand marketing. They all involve the marketing of a series of related products under a common name and a coordinated marketing program. This new strategy is product line marketing.

Product line marketing differs from brand marketing in its approach to advertising, promotion, packaging, pricing, and marketing organization. It also has a significant effect on the interaction of the company with other organizations.

OBJECTIVES & OBSTACLES

Although brand marketing and product line marketing represent different strategies, they share the common objectives of growth and efficiency for new and established products. However, the new product ventures of Welch Foods, Sara Lee, and Stouffer's, the success of the Dole name, and the new opportunities offered by Merrill Lynch (relative to the bear market) are a reflection of changes in the marketing environment that make product line marketing an attractive option for consumer marketers.

Meeting the Demand for Growth

Consumer goods companies, like virtually all publicly held corporations in the United States, are under considerable pressure from their investors to show "performance," or growth in sales and profits. Unfortunately, many of the product categories that they compete in are simply not growth areas.

The demand for detergents does not grow at 10% a year, at least not any more; per capita consumption of coffee declines every year; price competition tends to lower profit margins for mature product categories. When conditions favorable to growth do not exist within a product category, a company is likely to look outside current product categories for growth opportunities.

In the past, growth by acquisition has been an important method of satisfying the performance objective. However, in recent years more aggressive government antitrust action, a depressed stock market, and the disappointing experiences of many companies that sought growth in areas beyond their expertise have cut off this avenue, particularly for large companies.

These political and economic conditions have left the growth-oriented company with a difficult task—to grow by exploiting new markets, primarily through internal resources. In addition to Welch, Sara Lee, and Stouffer's, another good example of a company that has shifted its marketing strategy is Gerber—a company that, until recently, proudly boasted that "babies are our business, our only busi-

[1]Valerie Adams, "Sara Lee broadens product lines in move to dominate freezer case," *Advertising Age*, January 1, 1973, p. 3.

[2]"Move Over Chiquita," interview with Bruce Paschal, vice president-marketing, Castle & Cooke Foods, *Media Decisions*, March 1974, p. 66.

Exhibit I Product Category Size Comparison for 1968 and 1972

	Number of advertised brands			Consumer expenditures (in millions of dollars)		
Product category	**1968**	**1972**	**% change**	**1968**	**1972**	**% change**
Deodorants, depilatories,	33	52	+ 58%	$ 285.4	$ 474.6	+66%
Shampoos	27	61	+126	266.6	441.6	+66
Toilet soap	25	28	+ 12	321.5	360.1	+20
Cigarettes	43	44	+ 2	7,125.2	8,737.2	+23
Soups	12	21	+ 75	617.7	689.7	+12
Cereals	79	91	+ 15	894.5	1,083.2	+21
Coffee, tea, cocoa	51	63	+ 24	2,709.1	3,420.5	+26
Heavy-duty detergents	32	45	+ 41	782.4	846.3	+ 8
Total	302	405	+ 34%	$13,002.4	$16.053.2	+23%

Sources: LNA Multi-Media Reports, Leading National Advertisers, New York, published for 1968 and 1972; Annual Survey of Consumer Expenditures, *Supermarketing*, September 1969, September 1973.

ness." A declining birth rate has forced Gerber to rethink its corporate strategy. This rethinking is evident in tests of peanut butter, ketchup, day care centers, insurance, and "singles" dinners under the Gerber name.[3]

Obstacles to Growth via Brand Marketing

Several factors are making effective brand marketing more difficult and the alternative of product line marketing more attractive. In particular, brand proliferation, the lessened impact of advertising, and the influence of consumerism have tended to decrease the effect of previously successful brand marketing techniques. Let us consider each of these obstacles in turn.

1 Brand Proliferation The proliferation of brands reflects the past success of brand marketing. But it has reached the point where fragmentation of many product categories is becoming counterproductive. One measure of brand proliferation is the increase in the number of advertised brands in a group of eight major drug and grocery categories (see *Exhibit I*). While sales in the listed product categories increased by an average of 23% over a period of four years, the number of separate brands that were being advertised increased by 34%.

To be certain that these figures did not simply reflect an increase in advertising activity for particular products, I compared them with the A.C. Nielsen Company's statistics on a similar group of product categories. Nielsen tracks all major brands, whether or not they are advertised. His figures show that the absolute number of brands in these categories increased from 394 to 453, a gain of 15% over four years.

Since an increase in brands in a category results in a smaller average brand market share, the expanding list of brand names spells trouble for companies' profits. The relationship between market share and profitability is explained in part by economies of scale, market power, and quality of management.[4] In the competitive world of consumer goods market-

[3]Valerie Adams, "Gerber woos adults with singles lines of heat-eat items," *Advertising Age*, April 1, 1974, p. 1; "The Lower Birth Rate Crimps the Baby-Food Market," *Business Week*, July 13, 1974, p. 44.

[4]See Robert D. Buzzell et al., "Market Share—A Key to Profitability," HBR, January-February 1975, p. 97, for a discussion of the relationship between market share and profitability.

ing, these factors are likely to be compounded by the difficulties of obtaining or maintaining distribution for low-volume brands and the ineffectiveness that usually results from low-level marketing budgets.

2 Lower Advertising Impact Advertising is often a critical factor in effective brand marketing. The ability to develop and maintain a positive image of a product in the mind of the consumer is often the difference between success and failure. Evidence is accumulating, however, that TV advertising, which is the major consumer marketing media vehicle, has become less powerful in recent years.

For one thing, consumers appear to be less influenced by television advertising. A study made by Daniel Starch and Staff indicates that recall of TV commercials declined significantly during the 1960s (see *Exhibit II*).[5] This decline may be due partly to the increase in the number of brands in product categories, which makes it more difficult for consumers to maintain a clear image of any given brand.

Another major factor hampering the effectiveness of TV advertising is commercial clutter. The Bureau of Advertising Research reports that during a representative three-week period in 1974, the total number of commercials increased by 61%, over an equivalent period in 1967.[6] This increase reflects a trend toward shorter, but more numerous, commercials. Another Starch study demonstrated the predictably lower recall scores for these shorter 10-, 20-, and 30-second message units. This lessened impact has reduced the ability of advertising to support existing products or successfully introduce new products.

Admittedly, Starch data for magazines suggest increased advertising recall during the same three-week period. However, television is clearly the dominant, growing medium. It accounted for three times as many ad dollars as did magazines in 1974. Similar ad effectiveness data are not available for radio, newspaper, or outdoor advertising.

Exhibit II Program Viewers Providing Correct Brand Associations in Selected Product Categories

Product category	1957/1960 % noted	1966/1968 % noted
Food	39%	17%
Soft drinks	32	18
Passenger cars	29	19
Cigarettes	27	16
Household supplies	26	19
Gas and oil	26	22

Note: Based on same evening telephone interviewing; customers given product category cue.

Source: Starch Custom TV Studies, Daniel Strach and Staff, Inc., Mamaroneck, N.Y., 1971.

3 Influence of Consumerism Consumerism has taken its toll on marketing in general and on advertising in particular. The impact has been twofold.

First, by raising questions about the quality and safety of well-known products, the consumerism movement has helped create a more skeptical consumer, one who is less likely to accept new products or believe advertising.[7]

Second, the movement has influenced both government and industry regulation of marketing practices, especially advertising. The tendency has been for consumerists to demand much more than they are likely to get. This technique often produces results, even when the government does not act directly. An example is the long-standing request to the FCC by Action for Children's Television

[5]*Some Observations and Thoughts Relating to Advertising Research*, Mamaroneck, New York, Daniel Starch and Staff, Inc., 1971, p. 12.

[6]Harry W. McMahan, "McMahan picks 100 best commercials of 1974," *Advertising Age*, January 27, 1975, p. 43.

[7]William P. Eckles, "Marketing Management Viewpoint," *Marketing News*, July 1, 1974, p. 3.

(ACT) for elimination of commercials on children's programs. While the request has not been granted, it has undoubtedly influenced industry to move on its own toward a more realistic presentation of products, reduced commercial time, and support of educational shows.

The government has also become more sensitive to consumer pressures. Much more attention has focused on the quality, quantity, and accuracy of information presented in consumer advertising, and regulations have reduced the latitude that marketers previously enjoyed.

Growing Efficiently

In entering new markets, a company obviously wants its product to become well known as efficiently—that is, as quickly and as cheaply—as possible. Consequently, the name of the new product is a significant concern. A company has the choice between launching a completely new brand name or using an established and respected one—Welch, Sara Lee, Stouffer's, and Gerber all chose the strategy of applying an existing name to a new product category.

This decision to use an existing, established name is one of the most important aspects of product line marketing. It reflects the goal of efficiency because, for one thing, it is so difficult to come up with a name for a new product that is not registered by someone else or that is not totally inappropriate. Anyone who has been involved in this type of effort can appreciate the problem it represents. It is very disappointing when, after brainstorming sessions with the advertising agency, employee contests, and computer runs of millions of possible combinations of vowels and consonants, a trademark search turns up information that an obscure company in eastern Montana has been selling pickles under the same name for 20 years!

In addition to the difficulty of coming up with an effective new product name, there is also the problem of successfully introducing a new brand—or even of supporting established ones. Companies that recognize the significance of the Starch scores, for example, will not be eager to add still another brand name to the list of those that customers cannot recall.

OVERCOMING THE OBSTACLES

To the company faced with the obstacles of traditional brand name marketing, the idea of product line marketing becomes highly attractive. It allows the marketer to concentrate an advertising and promotion budget that may currently be scattered among several products at levels too low to be meaningful; it permits entry into new categories with lower marketing expense; and it eliminates or reduces competition within the company (a common problem in multiple brand situations) by coordinating the total marketing program.

Although product line marketing can offer substantial opportunity, it also requires a number of changes from traditional techniques. Advertising strategy will probably be affected the most; the sales organization, which may already have been selling products as a line, may not need to be modified at all; package designs will have to be consistent with the image the company intends its products to project; and managers' responsibilities will have to be reorganized.

Advertising Modifications

Instead of a series of campaigns for individual brands, advertising to support entire lines must be developed. A variety of strategies are possible:

- *Multiple product.* Rising media costs encourage advertisers to mention a number of products in a single print ad or TV commercial. The limits on this technique are the consumer's ability to absorb the information and some media restrictions on combining unrelated products. Applications of multiple product advertising range from tag mentions of line extensions (Wonder English Muffins inserted at the end of a Wonder Bread commercial), through relatively straightforward multiple product sells (Gerber's combination baby food and baby care print ads), to the technique used by Del Monte of showing dozens of product packages in a series of quick cuts in TV commercials.

• *Corporate.* Advertising can focus on the glories of the parent company, giving a general assurance that all products sold under its name are high quality, economical, and so forth. This technique has not been used widely in packaged goods advertising. An example of a corporate approach to product line advertising in nonpackaged goods is a recent General Electric campaign. The advertising stressed the wide availability of GE service as a point to consider when buying a new appliance.

There are interesting possibilities for some of the large consumer goods companies that currently market a number of related products by using separate advertising campaigns. For example, General Foods sells at least seven pet food brands under the Gaines name, virtually all of which carry another brand name that is featured in advertising and packaging. GF spent $19.4 million in measured media supporting these products during 1974. This money (or even half this amount), concentrated in a corporate campaign, might be at least as effective as the present fragmented approach.

• *Line leader.* Advertising can concentrate on a particular product, relying on a "halo effect" to maintain awareness and interest in the rest of the line. The automobile industry has widely used line leader advertising; for example, a specially designed car (like Gremlins with denim upholstery or Golden VWs) is featured even though it may be available in limited quantities. This kind of advertising is less common in packaged goods advertising, although Gillette's advertising spending pattern in support of its razor and blade products seems to be a line leader approach. Between 1971 and 1974, spending in support of the Platinum Plus and Techmatic products went from over $6 million to less than $200,000 as the company concentrated funds behind the Trac II. It seems reasonable to expect the Trac II advertising to have a "halo effect" for the other Gillette razor products.

Any of these strategies, or some combination of them, may meet the needs of a product line marketer. However, measuring the effectiveness of product line advertising is likely to be more difficult than measuring that of brand advertising. Instead of simple awareness and attitude measurements of a single product, evaluation of product line advertising requires analysis of its impact on the previously established name as well as on the products being marketed under that name. In-market testing of product line advertising is likely to be similarly complicated.

In developing techniques for evaluating product line advertising, advertising researchers will have to study corporate and industrial advertising, areas where research and evaluation of impact have traditionally been the most tenuous. Advertising researchers will also have to develop new measuring techniques.

Packaging Alterations

The challenge in packaging is to give all products in the line a common look without causing them to lose their individual identities. Developing a new logo or increasing the prominence of an existing one can often provide unifying identification.

For greatest effectiveness, however, packaging must go beyond simple identification. Packaging should help create the product line image, reinforcing the basic message that the advertising communicates. Kraft has recently redesigned its traditional dinner line to match the best-selling macaroni and cheese package design. The new packaging also features a Kraft Dinner logo.

Product Line Consistency

The principle of internal consistency must apply to a product line. Since advertising and packaging are seeking to communicate certain things about an entire line, the products themselves must match this image. Whether the message is about economy, reliability, modernity, or high quality, any product that does not match the image can jeopardize the entire line.

This principle is of greatest importance when a company is developing new products or is entering new product categories. Consumer awareness of an established brand name can be of tremendous value in entering new categories, but only if the new product image is consistent with the established line.

This strategy of using an established brand name in new categories has been employed by Life Savers (gum), Gillette (shaving cream), and many others. Although in many cases the new entry has been treated as a separate brand, there is growing recognition of the need for a "fit" between the old and new products, since the parent brand may be weakened if there is no fit. William Mack Morris, executive vice president of Life Savers, Inc., directly addressed this issue in a *New York Times* article.[8] The company realized that the consumer would accept the concept of Life Savers Gum if the new gum delivered the same excellence in flavor, value, and quality as the parent brand.

Marketing Reorganization

Product line marketing places a different set of requirements on the marketing organization. The usual product manager areas of involvement—advertising, packaging, pricing, and promotion—require a far greater degree of coordination and integration in this kind of marketing than in the traditional brand management system. At least some of these functions, especially advertising, are likely to be taken completely away from the product manager, if in fact his position continues to exist. At the same time, there is no reason to believe that the actual amount of work involved in the marketing function will decrease. If anything, it may increase because of these two effects:

1 Activities associated with individual products diminish but continue to exist. Brand advertising and promotion disappear, but sales must still be tracked and decisions made on product quality, pricing, and cost reduction opportunities. These activities must be performed with a view to an overall product line strategy, one that has been developed above the product manager level.

2 Functional areas (advertising, promotion, pricing, packaging) become more important. The advertising budget is bigger, and evaluation and execution of creative ideas in the media become more complex.

Under the product line system the marketing manager or group product manager is likely to be the key individual. This person will be the one who develops strategies and coordinates functional areas. The former brand managers will have a combination of functional and product responsibilities.

This reduction in brand manager responsibility parallels an already-established trend in many companies that use a brand manager system. Brand managers frequently change from one brand to another, both within and between companies; so the system has been criticized for instilling a short-term outlook in brand managers, who know that they will not be assigned to a particular brand for very long. To counter this shortsightedness, many consumer goods companies have moved the decision making for advertising and other major areas farther up the organization chart.[9] This move suggests that even strongly brand-oriented organizations may be evolving toward a product line marketing approach.

SHIFTING RELATIONSHIPS

Product line marketing is also going to affect other organizations that are involved in con-

[8] William Mack Morris, "Advertising Point of View," *New York Times*, August 19, 1973, p. F13.

[9] "Marketing Observer," *Business Week*, February 10, 1973, p. 90.

sumer marketing, organizations such as advertising agencies and retailers.

The Advertising Agency

Product line advertising creates a number of challenges for the advertising agency. I have discussed the need to develop new strategic approaches and methods of measuring advertising effectiveness. If advertising agencies are going to maintain their traditional partnership position in consumer goods marketing, they are going to have to go well beyond simple measurements of advertising effectiveness. For one thing, the agency will need to advise clients on the limits and opportunities of product line marketing.

The shift to a product line approach means organizational changes on the agency as well as the client side. Just as responsibility is moved to a higher level in the company's marketing organization, the agency is likely to reorganize in a similar manner. The agency account executive, traditionally the individual with day-to-day responsibility for a brand account, will lose some of his freedom. The account supervisor and managers at higher levels in the agency will assume more direct control, while junior levels of agency management assume functional responsibilities similar to those in the client organization.

The Retailer

Although many large retailers have, in some sense, been using a product line approach for years, most do not appear to be conscious of what they are doing. However, a few are:

Sears, for example, has worked toward building its brand names as an umbrella under which a wide variety of products can be marketed. This umbrella permits the company to advertise and promote a relatively small percentage of products in the total line, knowing that a large number of other items will also benefit from this advertising.[10]

Supermarket chains have also used this approach in varying degrees. So far, however, most chains have tended to promote a number of unrelated, private-label names rather than trying to use their chain name as an umbrella. Private-label packaging and pricing have been similarly uncoordinated.

But there are signs that this uncoordinated system is beginning to change. The successful Pathmark chain is now using a uniform logo and packaging, and the brands are being supported by corporate-oriented advertising for the entire line.[11]

Conversely, A&P presents a prime example of a missed opportunity. A&P possesses manufacturing facilities and has had a long history of promoting its own brands. It has also had significant market share in many of the nations' major metropolitan areas. Despite these apparent strengths, the company has been in serious difficulty in recent years. Although the reasons for this go well beyond its deficiencies in marketing, a likely contributing factor is A&P's failure to market its private-label products effectively. Instead of using a single brand name, the company has almost as many brand names as products! Package design and product quality also appear to be inconsistent.

At a time when manufacturers' individual brand shares appear to be shrinking, many food retailers find themselves in a position where their share of local markets exceeds that of typical national brands. A retailer who makes effective use of product line marketing techniques may be able to create greater visibility for his brands than can a national manufacturer. Marketed more effectively, private-

[10] *Grey Matter*, 45, no. 6, New York, Grey Advertising, Inc., June 1974.

[11] Barbara Love, "More Image-Building, Ads Mark Revolution in Retailer advertising," *Supermarketing*, July 1973, p. 1.

label brands could be a more important factor in the future.

A CASE HISTORY

While many companies are utilizing at least parts of product line marketing, there is little indication that they are using it as a deliberate strategy. In most cases it appears to have evolved gradually, as individual responses to specific pressures on traditional brand marketing. The following case history shows this pattern.

Before: The company marketed a number of products within the packaged foods category. Each brand had a separate advertising campaign, so although the total budget was large, the dollars were spread out and the advertising impact was relatively low. Packaging for each brand had developed separately, partly because the brands had been introduced at different times. While all brands shared a common logo and the company name, neither was very prominent. Sales promotion activities were in the hands of sales-oriented product managers, who were relatively independent; the company provided little incentive to coordinate activities. Pricing decisions were also decentralized, and as a result pricing policies were often inconsistent from region to region.

After: Over a three-year period the company's marketing strategy and organization underwent substantial changes. Advertising was consolidated using a line approach that focused on the company name and featured multiple products in each commercial. Redesign of the packaging featured a more prominent logo to give the entire line a consistent look. Sales promotion activities were coordinated more closely, and pricing was gradually centralized, eliminating most of the inconsistencies. The company also considerably strengthened its marketing organization by developing a product group system whereby product managers were given brand, functional, and geographic responsibilities.

Evaluating the impact of these changes illustrates the difficulties of judging product line marketing in its present stage of development. Three circumstances characterize the evolution of the company's new marketing strategy:

1 The changes were implemented piecemeal and were not part of a deliberate strategy.

2 They occurred during a period that saw a price freeze, inflation, and major disruption of commodity markets.

3 Demographic trends resulted in a static market target.

While it is rarely easy to assess the impact of marketing programs on established products (even when single brands are involved), the company's results do suggest that product line marketing had a positive effect:

- Unit sales held up relatively well despite frequent price increases. The company was able to expand its geographic coverage while competitors retrenched.
- Commercial testing showed increases in consumer awareness and purchase interest after the line advertising campaign was substituted.
- Packaging tests, although inconclusive, were generally positive.
- Centralized pricing allowed the company to conduct pricing tests and to gain a better understanding of pricing relationships among the products.

BASIC QUESTIONS

This case history and the examples of Welch, Dole, Sara Lee, and others do indicate that a workable alternative to brand marketing does exist. However, for those who are ready to fire their advertising agency and turn their marketing organization upside down in pursuit of this latest cure for a group of sick products, here are some fundamental questions to consider:

- Is your product line really a line, or is it just a collection of different brands? Can you develop a common set of characteristics to create a line?
- Do you have or can you develop a brand name to support the entire line? Are you prepared to spend enough to register the brand image in the minds of consumers?
- Do you have or can you create an organization to implement this strategy? Will corporate management support the necessary changes?
- Are you prepared to implement these changes as a conscious, planned strategy?
- Most important, are you looking for long-term gains rather than short-term results?

If your answers to at least some of these questions are affirmative, then product line marketing is worth a try, at least for a few years. But in marketing, where change and innovation are the only constants, it is unlikely that product line marketing is the final answer.

23

Targeting Prospects for a New Product

Philip Kotler
Gerald Zaltman

Marketing managers are increasingly dissatisfied with launching a new product to the mass market or to heavy users only. Rather, they seek to identify those individuals or households with a high natural potential for purchasing the new product.

The authors try to provide insights into how a company can most effectively identify and reach the best potential early users of a product newly being introduced.

How can a company identify the best early-adopter prospects for a new product it is about to launch? Suppose its management has already:

1 found a product idea that appeared to be compatible with the company's objectives and resources;
2 developed alternative product concepts for the product idea, tested these concepts with a group of potential buyers, chose the best one, and was satisfied that this product concept had good sales and profit potential;
3 created a prototype that was faithful to the concept as well as packaging that reinforced the product concept;
4 given the prototype to a sample of potential consumers, who reported strong satisfaction but suggested further improvements;

Reprinted from *Journal of Advertising Research*, vol. 16, no. 1, pp. 7–18, February 1976. Copyright 1976 by the Advertising Research Foundation. At the time of writing, Philip Kotler was the Harold T. Martin Professor of Marketing, Graduate School of Management, Northwestern University. Gerald Zaltman was the Albert Wesley Frey Professor of Marketing, Graduate School of Business, University of Pittsburgh.

5 test marketed the product in a well-selected set of cities with strong results, giving the company the confidence to launch the product regionally;
6 selected a region with many ultimate customers and few competitors.

Having come this far, the company would like to launch the product so as to gain high early sales. The company attaches great importance to maximizing the speed of adoption of this new product because

1 some competitors might be shortly coming into the same market and the company would like to be deeply entrenched at the time of competitive entry;
2 the company would like to verify as soon as possible that market interest is truly strong for this product—it wants evidence of this before laying plans for expansion into the next set of regions;
3 the company's rate of return on its investment will be higher the faster its product penetrates the market for a given marketing budget.

The company would like to avoid certain techniques for stimulating rapid adoption and diffusion of a new product because they are costly and would not represent the marketing mix that it would normally use to enter each market—for example, (1) charging a lower than planned price to stimulate earlier trial and repurchase of the product; (2) distributing free samples of the product to acquaint the market as rapidly as possible with the product's existence and virtues; (3) offering price-off coupons or premiums to stimulate early trial; (4) using higher-than-planned levels of advertising expenditures to increase the rate at which consumers learn about the new product.

It is often the case that special incentives may simply precipitate early purchase among those who would ordinarily adopt the product anyway but at a later time. If the product is not a frequently purchased item, the company may gain little and, in fact, may lose money by offering special deals. However, there is a possibility, particularly where a product is radically different, that persons who have a propensity for early adoption in the product area or category may need an added incentive to activate it. Late adopters will be especially likely to adopt or reject the new product more on the basis of information obtained from early adopters than on the basis of special deals. Thus, the firm may wish to target incentives or deals in a special case only to early adopters. This increases the importance of studying early adopters from the special viewpoint to be advocated later. The issue here is whether early adopters (whose behavior is likely to be imitated by late adopters) need special stimulation or whether their natural propensity to adopt will be sufficiently active to make special deals, unusually high advertising, and so forth, unnecessary. At present, existing knowledge about this issue is insufficient to derive meaningful answers; the issue must be addressed on a case-by-case basis.

EARLY-ADOPTER THEORY

There is a body of theory known as early adopter theory that seems to provide the company with an answer to its problems. We shall state the antecedants of this theory, the theory as it stands today, and, finally, several of its weaknesses. Later, we shall prepare an alternative view of how to identify and reach the best potential early adopters for a specific new product.

Predecessors of Early-Adopter Theory

The mass-market approach, the earliest launching approach used by new-product marketers, consisted of distributing the product widely and informing everyone about it who might be a potential purchaser. For example, a manufacturer of a new cake mix might determine that women constitute the major market for cake mixes and would formulate a launching program to reach and inform as many women as possible. Most women, of course, would not buy the new cake mix; but, hopefully, enough women would buy it to return a satisfactory profit to the firm.

The mass-market approach, however, had at least two drawbacks: (1) it required a heavy marketing expenditure; and (2) it involved a substantial number of wasted exposures to nonpotential buyers. Its high cost led to a new stage of thinking about new-product introduction, that of heavy-user target marketing. Marketers became acutely aware that a small percentage of the users of a product typically accounted for a substantial share of all purchasing (Twedt, 1964). It followed that the marketer should attempt to identify the characteristics of the heavy users of the product class and then cast a narrow net designed to capture their specific interest in the new product. In the case of the new cake mix, the target would no longer be all women but rather women who were heavy users of cake mixes. An attempt would be made to identify their characteristics in terms of their distribution over social classes, family sizes, educational levels, media vehicles, and so on. Using volume segmentation, the marketer would rank different potential adopter classes. Thus it might be found that the heaviest users of cake mixes are housewives under 40 with families of three or more children and low income. It might be found that the next heaviest group of users are housewives under 40 with families of three or more children and medium income. The company would build its marketing plan to reach the first or first two target groups early and later plan to extend the message to the lighter-using groups.

Enter Early-Adopter Theory

But, it was noted, even within the group of heavy users of a product class, there would be a great difference in (1) how much interest individuals would show in new products and (2) the speed at which individuals would try them. For any new product, a handful of individuals (innovators) would be the first to notice and try the new product; they would be followed by a larger group (early adopters) who would try the product relatively early; others (early majority) would adopt the product after they had seen its growing use; still others (late majority) would come into the market relatively late; and, finally, a few remaining nontriers (laggards) would ultimately come into the market.

Observations in a wide range of contexts led to the hypothesis of a bell-shaped distribution of adoption times. It was further suggested that the first 2.5 percent of the adopters of a new product be called the innovators; the next 13.5 percent be called the early adopters; the next 34 percent be called the early majority; the next 34 percent be called the late majority; and the last 16 percent be called the laggards (Rogers and Shoemaker, 1971).

The import of this finding was that the new-product marketer ought to direct his communications not equally to everyone who might be an eventual adopter or a heavy user but rather to those persons who are most likely to adopt the product early. A theory, called the early-adopter theory, grew up around this view, whose premises might be stated as follows:

1 Persons within a well-defined target market will differ in the amount of time that passes between their exposure to a new product and their trial of the new product. Those who adopt the product early upon exposure may be called the early adopters.

2 Early adopters are likely to share some traits in common, which differentiate them from late adopters. That is, early adoption is not a fortuitous characteristic but rather associated with some common demographic, psychological, or situational factors. Early adopters are people who tend to be first in trying various new products in general or in particular product classes.

3 There exist efficient media for reaching early-adopter types.

4 Early-adopter types are likely to be high on opinion leadership and, therefore, helpful in "advertising" the new product to other potential buyers.

STATUS OF EARLY-ADOPTER THEORY

The premises of early-adopter theory have benefited from a considerable amount of research over the years. The two focal points of research have been premises 2 and 4. Accordingly, it will be useful here to review critically the literature related to these two premises.

There are several flaws with early-adopter research, two of which require special mention. One flaw arises from the way early adopters are most frequently identified. The method consists of introducing the new product in a test market or region and then obtaining the names of the first persons to buy the product. A sample of these people are interviewed and their common characteristics are noted. It might be found, for example, that they have a higher-than-average education. Then the marketing company assumes that early-adopter types have a higher-than-average education and undertakes to aim more of its communications at the higher-than-average educated group.

This information-collection design contains a major fallacy. It rates people on their time of adoption from the time of the product introduction, not their time of adoption from the time of their exposure. What the company really needs to identify are the group of people who responded early after exposure, not the group that responded in the early period. Virtually all research has been based on early adopters relative to the time the product or innovation is introduced rather than the time of first awareness. This distinction is of crucial importance in media planning. There should be more homogeneity between those who adopted early after exposure, and it is their common traits that should be identified. This means that greater attention must also be given to learning which media deliver messages more quickly to people. Media may differ in terms of whom they reach first. Also overlooked is why people rely on particular media and why this differs, if it does, between early and late adopters.

The second major problem concerns the magnitude and persistence of adoption. Almost totally absent in existing research is any consideration of the degree of commitment involved in adoption (as opposed to trial and evaluation) (Kiesler, 1971). Consumers, when trying to satisfy some need or desire, may vary from infrequently using a particular product brand, to using it often, to using it all the time. Media factors may be important here (Maloney and Schonfeld, 1973).

Other problems include:

1 a lack of attention given to interpersonal relations between early adopters and others (there is a need for more "relational analysis" where relationships, not individuals, are the unit of analysis) (Rogers, 1969 and 1973; Burnkrant and Cousineau, 1971);

2 an underemphasis on resistance or nonadoption and discontinuance relative to full adoption and the role of various channels of communication in creating resistance;

3 limited research on how the perception of different adopter categories differ (a) for perceived innovations versus noninnovations and (b) across different categories of innovations;

4 limited attention paid to the communications mix implications of feedback loops in adopter and resistor decision making;

5 limited research on whether particular media have differential effectiveness for innovations as compared to noninnovations and whether this varies by (a) stages of the adoption process, (b) adopter category, (c) product class, and (d) salient attributes of the product or service;

6 a lack of knowledge about the interaction effects between personal and mass-media channels of communication.

Research on the character and behavior of adopter categories has been extensive and is contradictory, probably due in part to the wrong use of exposure measures. Some of the contradictions will be pointed out here. Rogers and Shoemaker (1971), in their study of early adopters, observe that early adopters are no different in age than later adopters, although Arndt (1968) suggests that they may be younger and Bell (1964) suggests that they may be older. Early adopters have frequently been found to have more formal education than others, although there is evidence contradicting this too (Fliegel, 1965). Related to this is the finding that early adopters have higher social status (Zaltman, 1974). Cancian (1967), however, questions the validity of this finding. Many studies indicate that early adopters have larger businesses (Loomis, 1967) while other studies indicate that this is not necessarily true (Czepiel, 1972). Early adopters have been found to hold more positive attitudes toward the use of credit or other forms of borrowing (Dasgupta, 1966), but not in all circumstances (Havens, 1965).

Research is still scanty concerning the psychological states of early adopters, and the research reported is conflicting. Kivlin (1968), Zaltman (1971; and, with Pinson, 1974(a)), and others indicate that early adopters may possess greater empathetic ability, although this observation has not been confirmed in all studies (Rogers and de Ramos, 1965). There is considerable conflict among researchers as to whether early adopters are more (or less) dogmatic than late adopters. Jacoby (1971(a)) and Blake, Perloff, and Heslin (1970) suggest they are, while others (Robertson, 1967) argue the opposite position. The ability to think abstractly is believed to be associated with the early adoption of new products (Smith, 1968), and related to this is the observation in a few studies that early adopters may be more intelligent than late adopters. The propensity to take risk is generally believed to be a trait of early adopters (Boone, 1974; Robertson and Rossiter, 1968), although, again, not in all instances (Taylor, 1974) and not always in a positive way (Schiffman, 1972).

Many other traits have been studied in addition to those mentioned above, and in all cases there is debate as to what the set of conditions are that make a trait operative or inoperative as a causal factor in new-product adopters. Very briefly, these other traits are (1) attitudes toward science; (2) achievement motivation; (3) participation in social affairs; (4) orientations outside the immediate setting; (5) frequency of contact with salesmen; (6) mass-media exposure; (7) exposure to interpersonal communication; (8) information seeking; (9) knowledge of new products; and (10) the likelihood of early adopters being opinion leaders (Cohen and Golden, 1972; Robertson, 1971).

Much research needs to be done to clarify, explain, and, ultimately, help predict and control the functioning of the various social and psychological variables uniquely associated with early adopters. The following is a sample of research questions aimed at increasing our understanding of the role of early adopters in new-product marketing. After each question a reference is cited which either itself raises the research question or is its basis.

1 How do early adopters differ from late adopters in terms of the frequency of engaging in word-of-mouth behavior and in terms of the content of information exchanged (Belk and Rose, 1971; Uhl, Andrus, and Poulsen, 1970)?

2 To what extent are early adopters active-versus-passive opinion leaders in the communication process (Engel, Blackwell, and Kegerreis, 1969)?

3 How do early adopters use information

in formulating buying strategy and in deciding to seek or not seek additional information (Engel, Blackwell, and Kegerreis, 1969; Kohn and Jacoby, 1974)?

4 Is there a uniqueness motivation—i.e., a tendency to seek out the novel—that differentiates early adopters from late adopters in terms of their selection, processing, and retention of information (Fromkin, 1971, Lambert, 1972)?

5 How do personality variables for early adopters interact with attributes of new products, and how is this mediated by various communication channels (Goldberg, 1971; Zaltman and Pinson, 1974(b); Donnelly and Etzel, 1973)?

6 How valid are personality studies of early adopters (Myers and Robertson, 1974; Pizam, 1972; Reynolds and Darden, 1972)?

7 Do early adopters differ from late adopters in their perceptions of the new product because of greater experience with the new product (when other variables are held constant) (Zaltman and Pinson, 1974(b))?

8 When directing advertising to early adopters, should product attributes or should early-adopter ego and social factors be stressed (Jacoby, 1971(b))?

9 Can early adopters be "created" by altering communication strategies in the marketing plan (Mancuso, 1969)?

10 To what extent and by means of what variables can early buyers be identified (Darden and Reynolds, 1974; Ostlund, 1972)?

11 What are the sources of resistance among early rejectors (Zaltman and Dubois, 1971)? Do the same variables that cause rejection by some persons cause early adoption by others (Zaltman, Duncan, and Holbek, 1973)?

12 Are early adopters of optional new products (where not everyone in the home need use them) different from early adopters of mandatory new products (where everyone must use them) (Zaltman, Duncan, and Holbek, 1973; Rogers and Shoemaker, 1971)?

13 What are the differences between early adopters in consumer-goods settings and early adopters in industrial-goods settings (Schiffman and Gaccione, 1974)?

A careful analysis of the literature on early adopters, some of which has been mentioned above, and an examination of the assumptions and implications of the research questions cited leads to several important observations about the current state of early-adopter theory:

1 It is clear that early adopters, in some contexts at least, do differ from late adopters.

2 The underlying variables that account for a given difference between early and late adopters to display itself in one context and not in another still need to be identified.

3 The circumstances in which one particular early adopter trait rather than another becomes important still need to be identified.

4 Little explanation exists concerning the dynamic and causal impact that various sociological and psychological traits have on the "adopt now" or "adopt later" decision.

5 As a consequence of observations 1 to 4 above, the existing inventory of early-adopter knowledge and analytic techniques traditionally used for studying early adopters is inadequate for segmenting and predicting early adopters for given products or product categories.

6 However, a blending of the soundest early-adopter research findings with a bold new perspective and approach can overcome the inadequacies of the present way of segmenting and predicting the relevant early adopters.

7 The new approach we propose is highly promising in terms of aiding new-product management in developing strategies that will enhance its ability to shape or guide new-product adoption and diffusion.

THEORY OF THE BEST PROSPECT CHOICE

Early-adopter theory, particularly the perspective we feel necessary, holds that certain people characteristically are the first to adopt a new product upon exposure and that they should be identified and then exposed to the first communications about the product. But even allowing for the existence of early-adopter types, it would be wrong to equate this group with the best early prospects for a new product. Early-adopter types may not be the best prospects to target for a number of reasons. The trait of early-adoption propensity alone is neither necessary nor sufficient for warranting early targeting.

This can be shown through a simple theoretical model which combines all the criteria that relate to the value of a prospect. The model is offered as an aid to clear thinking about the variables that define the best target individuals for a new-product campaign. While it does not automatically translate into a practical model for media selection, for instance, it does clarify the considerations that should guide early-target selection.

The task is to define, at the time of launching, the value of different prospects for a new product. Let us assume that we could advertise a new product through a direct-mail campaign, that thousands of names of potential users of the product are available to us, but that we cannot advertise to all of them. The mailing-list supplier is able to answer up to four questions about the names on the mailing list. The four questions a marketer would want to ask should be:

1 What is the probability that the prospect would be an early purchaser of the product upon exposure? (Call this probability A = early-adoption propensity.)

2 How much is the prospect likely to buy per year if he tries the new product? (Call this amount Q = heavy-volume propensity.)

3 How much additional purchasing per year is this prospect likely to stimulate in others through interpersonal influence? (Call this amount I = influence propensity.)

4 What is the cost of an effective communication exposure to this person? (Call this cost C = cost of an effective communication exposure.)

We can combine the four factors into the following formula to find the value *(V)* of a prospect:

$$V = A(Q + I) - C$$

To illustrate this formula, let us assume that the first prospect on the list has a likelihood of only .05 of being an early buyer of this product upon exposure; if he buys, he will probably like it and buy \$5.00 worth a year; he is likely to stimulate another \$6.00 worth of purchases a year in others; and it will cost \$0.20 to communicate an effective message to him. According to the formula, this prospect would be worth:

$$V = .05\ (\$5.00 + \$6.00) - \$0.20$$
$$= \$0.35$$

Now consider a second prospect for whom the likelihood is .10 of being an early buyer of this product upon exposure; if he buys, he will probably like it and buy \$3.00 worth a year; he is likely to stimulate \$1.00 worth of purchases a year in others; and it will cost \$0.20 to communicate an effective message to him. According to the formula, this prospect would be worth:

$$V = .10\ (\$3.00 + \$1.00) - \$0.20$$
$$= \$0.20$$

Here we see that although the second prospect is twice as likely as the first to be an early adopter of the new product, he is a less valuable prospect because he will personally consume less and influence less than the first prospect. This is why we said earlier that being an early-adopter type is not automatically equivalent to being the best early prospect.

The reason that the two statuses have been confused is because it is commonly thought that early-adoption propensity *(A)* is positively correlated with heavy-volume propensity

(Q) and heavy-influence propensity *(I)*. To the extent that this is true in a particular product class, new-product marketers are correct in simply targeting their communications to early-adopter types. To the extent that the three variables A, Q, and I are uncorrelated or even negatively correlated, it does not make sense to look only at early-adoption propensity. Suppose it could be shown, for example, that early-adopter types buy less volume of a given new brand than late-adopter types because they are always trying out new brands and dropping the ones they just started using—that is, they are low loyals because of their need for variety. In this case, it can be questioned whether early-adopter types are the best target for new-product launchings.

Or suppose that the early adopters in a particular product class have average or weak social networks and another group of potential adopters, who would normally adopt later, have very strong social networks. Under these circumstances the marketer may prefer to first expose the new product to the slower adopter group along with incentives to encourage earlier-than-normal adopting behavior.

Or suppose the cost of reaching different prospects varies. Suppose it is costlier to communicate to early-adopter types—for example, they may be exposed to fewer or more expensive media. This would further vitiate the theory that early-adoption propensity is alone sufficient for determining whom to target for early communications.

Given that the value of a prospect is defined by the factors in formula (1), what subfactors underlie each of the major factors?

Early-Adoption Propensity

Early-adoption propensity is defined as the probability that a person would be an early purchaser of the product upon an effective communication exposure. Early-adoption propensity is a function of the following subfactors:

1 the extent to which the product has strong need-fulfillment potential for the person (call this F = need-fulfillment potential);
2 the extent to which the person has a new-product orientation (call this N = innovative disposition);
3 the extent to which the product is highly accessible to the individual (call this D = accessibility);
4 the extent to which the individual's income makes the price less important (call this Y = income sufficiency).

Each of these subfactors is important in assessing whether or not a person will have a high propensity toward adopting a particular new product. Let us assume that each factor can be scaled from zero to one. We would propose that these factors would combine in a multiplicative way to affect the early-adoption propensity:

$$A = F \times N \times D \times Y$$

For example, the highest early-adoption propensity would be found in a person who has a strong need for the new product, tends to search out new products, can easily acquire it without much effort, and can afford the price. The formula is multiplicative because if any factor is weak, the early adoption propensity drops considerably. It is not the case that the propensity would be high simply because two or three factors are very high.

Heavy-Volume Propensity

Heavy-volume propensity is the amount of the new product that the person is likely to buy per period if he tries it. This propensity depends on the following subfactors:

1 the probability that this type of person will be sufficiently satisfied with the new product upon trial to buy it again (call this T = trial-satisfaction probability);
2 the number of times per year that the

person makes a purchase in this product class (call this R = product-class re-purchase frequency);

3 the average amount purchased by this person per purchase occasion (call this K = average amount purchased per purchase occasion);

4 the likely share that the new product will enjoy of this person's purchases within the product class (call this S = new product's share of total purchases in the product class).

We would propose that these subfactors would combine in a multiplicative way to determine the person's heavy-volume propensity:

$$Q = T(R \times K \times S)$$

For example, suppose the person buys into this product class three times a year; he buys \$2.00 each time; and he buys the new brand half of the time. This would yield a new-product purchase volume per year of:

$$\begin{aligned} R \times K \times S &= 3 \times \$2.00 \times .50 \\ &= \$3.00 \end{aligned}$$

But will the individual be sufficiently satisfied as a result of trial to adopt the new product? Let us assume that this probability is .75. Then:

$$\begin{aligned} Q &= .75(\$3.00) \\ &= \$2.25 \end{aligned}$$

That is, the probability of sufficient trial satisfaction is used to scale down the value of his purchases if satisfied.

Influence Propensity

Influence Propensity is the amount of additional purchasing per year that the prospect is likely to stimulate in others through interpersonal influence. This propensity depends on the following factors:

1 the number of persons the individual interacts with on a conversational basis (call this M = the number of acquaintances);

2 the percentage of persons he influences during the year to try the product who would have not tried it otherwise (call this L = influence ratio);

3 the average volume an influenced person buys per year of the new brand (call this W = the influenced person's volume).

We would suggest that these subfactors also work in a multiplicative way:

$$I = M \times L \times W$$

The prospect's influence potential depends on the number of people he knows, the proportion of them he influences, and the average volume an influenced person buys. We will ignore the fact that the influenced person will, in turn, influence other persons to try the product during the year.

As a further refinement, the proportion of persons that the prospect influences *(L)* depends on three factors:

1 the person's new-product conversational propensity;

2 the percentage of his acquaintances who are potential purchasers of this product;

3 the degree to which other persons look upon this person as a new-product legitimator.

The prospect will show a higher influence propensity the more he tends to talk about new products he has tried, the more he talks to others who are interested in the product class, and the more he is seen as a legitimator of new-product ideas.

Prospect Communication Cost

Prospect communication cost is the cost of delivering an effective message with a given media vehicle to a given prospect. We can define this cost as some function of the following subfactors:

E_1 = the probability that the individual will be exposed to the message with the media;
E_1 = the probability that the individual will see the message;
E_4 = the probability that the individual will comprehend the message;
E_4 = the probability that the individual will be favorably impressed by the message;
0 = the actual cost of getting the given message exposed to the given individual with the given message.

The function will not be specified except to note that the real cost of communication (C) is higher than the actual cost (0) to the extent that the message-media combination is less than perfectly effective in exposing, informing, and motivating the prospect.

METHODOLOGICAL STEPS IN IDENTIFYING EARLY ADOPTERS

We now turn to the pragmatic problem facing a company that is readying the introduction of a new product and seeking to target its communications and distribution of the new product to the "best prospects." We will assume that the marketer has defined the characteristics of the ultimate target market and that his interest is to reach the best early prospects among them since he cannot make the product and communications instantly available to everyone in the ultimate market.

The perfect solution to this problem would exist if the marketer could turn to a comprehensive and unambiguous body of knowledge about the characteristics of early adopters, heavy adopters, and influential adopters without having to undertake additional research. This body of knowledge would define the demographics, sociographics, psychographics, and media habits of these groups and permit the determination of the best early prospects.

Of course, such a body of knowledge does not exist. As we saw earlier, there are too few solid findings available to the new-product marketer that reliably suggests the characteristics of early adopters, especially for a particular product class. Information on the characteristics of heavy adopters is usually better. Information on the characteristics of influential adopters is not very good. The new-product marketer has to rely mainly on a fresh investigation of the characteristics of these groups for each product class.

There are several stages in the product-development process where organized attention to the question of the characteristics of early adopters could yield useful information. We shall comment on two of these stages: the concept-testing stage and test-marketing stage.

Concept-testing Stage

The concept-testing stage is undertaken to test the appeal of a new product concept to a potential target user group. Various potential users are asked, among other things, to play back their understanding of the product concept, to express the degree of their interest in the concept, and to express the degree of their buying intent toward the product (Tauber, 1973). Usually missing are questions of the following nature:

1 If you intend to buy the product, how soon after its appearance are you likely to buy it?
  a ___ immediately
  b ___ within a week
  c ___ within a month
  d ___ within a year
2 How do you see yourself with regard to buying new products?
  a ___ as one of the first persons to buy new products
  b ___ as an early adopter of new products after a few others have tried them

c ____ as a late adopter of new products after a lot of people have bought them

3 If you liked the product, would you probably be:
a ____ a heavy buyer (more than ____ units per year)
b ____ a medium buyer (between ____ and ____ units per year)
c ____ a light buyer (less than ____ units per year)

4 If you liked the product, would you probably:
a ____ tell several other persons
b ____ tell a few other persons
c ____ not discuss

5 In what media or media vehicle do you think you would be likely to first learn about this product?
____

The first two questions would reveal those in the sample who are early-adopter types; the third question would reveal those who are heavy-buyer types; the fourth question would reveal those who are influential-adopter types; and the fifth question would reveal the media expectations of potential buyers. The questions will have to be refined through testing because they may either be insufficiently clear or be answered unreliably. Their basic intent is to reveal (1) the kinds of people making up each group and (2) the correlations that might exist among the various traits that are important in identifying the best prospects. This information would be verified as the product moves through subsequent stages of development. For example, the same or similar questions can be asked again of people who are exposed to the actual physical product in the product-testing stage.

Test-marketing Stage

If the company decides to place the new product in test markets before making the final launching decision, it can use the test-marketing stage to improve its knowledge of the characteristics of the best early prospects.

This is accomplished by having the marketer vary the channels of distribution, the media, and the messages to determine the level of sales associated with these variations. For example, he might advertise the new product to matched market areas using different media or he might use a succession of media vehicles in each of several weeks in the same market areas. He would then interview early buyers to learn how and when they were exposed to the new product, and would analyze those buyers who bought very soon after information exposure to see if some common characteristics could be identified. Such a set of common characteristics would provide the information he needs to direct his marketing efforts, including advertising copy design and media, to the best prospects for his product in the general population.

If the company skips the test-marketing stage and goes directly into a regional or national launch of the product, the same arguments apply as in the test-marketing stage—that is, as the product is launched in each new market, the marketer must attempt to observe those who buy the product first. He must also determine what factors under his control account for late exposure among other persons, particularly those who are good early-adopter candidates. By conducting marketing research into the characteristics of early adopters, he can keep current and improve the precision of his subsequent marketing efforts.

MEDIA IMPLICATIONS

A basic theme here is that many persons who have high early-adoption potential may be misclassified as late adopters or overlooked as potential early adopters because they adopt late relative to the time the new product was introduced. In fact, they may adopt quite soon after their initial exposure. That they do not become aware of the new product until well after it is introduced suggests that they may have communication patterns that differ from those of persons learning of a new product very soon upon its introduction. This has a very important implication in terms of media selection. Different media may have to be used to reach early those persons who are usually late knowers but otherwise early adopters. To the extent that different media may be necessary and that media and messages interact, it may also be necessary to use different message strategies. This is a second important implication. Unfortunately, information concerning both implications is scarce, and substantial research into this matter is necessary.

Another important media problem, one in which much more research is required, concerns the media behavior of early adopters beyond the considerations of identifying what their media exposure is. We need to study further the particular functions various media perform or services they provide for early adopters. Are some media perceived as "legitimators" of new products? Are some media perceived as "introducers"—that is, sources of initial but perhaps unreliable information?

Do some media affect volume of product usage more than other media? Are some media more effective in creating opinion leadership among early adopters? Many more such questions can be generated whose answers have important bearings on overall media strategy for introducing new products.

SUMMARY

We have concentrated on a key question that must be faced at the new-product launching stage but for which data must be collected in earlier stages: How can the company identify and effectively reach the best potential early adopters for a specific new product that is ready to be launched? Company marketers are no longer satisfied with launching a new product to the mass market or to the heavy users only. They want to identify the traits of those who would have a high natural propensity to adopt the new product early upon exposure.

We reviewed the literature on early adopters to discover that it has too few solid findings to guide the marketing planner. Contradictory findings exist about whether early adopters tend to be younger or older, more educated or less educated, of higher or lower social status, etc., than later adopters.

This literature will have to move into the next stage where the conditions under which various traits are associated with early adoption are thrown into better relief.

We also proposed that the most natural early adopters are not necessarily the best early prospects to target for a new product. The marketer, in choosing prospects early in the campaign, should consider four factors; (1) the prospect's early-adoption propensity; (2) the prospect's heavy-volume propensity; (3) the prospect's influence propensity; and (4) the cost of effectively reaching the particular prospect group. Early-adoption theory implicitly assumed that early adopters were also heavy users and high opinion leaders eithout confirming whether these relations were, in fact, true. A model of the subfactors underlying each of these major factors was developed.

Ultimately, the determination of the best prospects for a new product has to be researched as the product progresses through the various stages of new-product development. For example, questions asked during the concept-testing stage will indicate the types of people who think that they would buy the product early, buy in substantial volume, and influence others. An analysis of the first persons to buy the product upon exposure during its test marketing will reveal further information about the characteristics of best early prospects for the product. By organized probing during the preliminary stages of product development, the marketer should have a good idea of his best early prospects when he is ready to launch the product.

REFERENCES

Arndt, Johan. Profiling Consumer Innovators. In Johan Arndt (ed.). *Insights into Consumer Behavior*. Boston: Allyn & Bacon, 1968.

Belk, Russell, and Ivan Rose. An Investigation of the Nature of Word-of-Mouth Communication Across Adoption Categories for a Food Innovation. In David Gardner (ed.) *Proceedings of the Second Annual Conference, Association for Consumer Research*, 1971.

Bell, William E. Consumer Innovators: A Unique Market for Newness. In S. A. Greyser (ed.). *Toward Scientific Marketing: Proceedings of the 1963 Winter Conference of the American Marketing Association*. Chicago: American Marketing Association, 1964.

Blake, Brian, Robert Perloff, and Richard Heslin. Dogmatism and Acceptance of New Products. *Journal of Marketing Research*, Vol. 7, November 1970, pp. 483–86.

Boone, L. E. Personality and Innovative Buying Behavior. *Journal of Psychology*, Vol. 86, 1974, pp. 197–202.

Burnkrant, R. E., and A. Cousineau. Informational and Normative Social Influence in Buyer Behavior. Paper, School of Business Administration, University of California at Berkeley, 1974.

Cancian, Frank. Stratification and Risk-Taking: A Theory Tested on Agricultural Innovation. *American Sociological Review*, Vol. 32, 1967.

Cohen, J. B., and F. Golden, Informational Social Influence and Product Evaluation. *Journal of Applied Psychology*, Vol. 56, 1972, pp. 54–59.

Czepiel, John. The Diffusion of Major Technological Innovation in a Complex Industrial Community: An Analysis of the Social Processes in the American Steel Industry. Ph.D. Diss., Graduate School of Management, Northwestern University, June 1972.

Darden, William, and Fred Reynolds, Backward Profiling of Male Innovators. *Journal of Marketing Research*, Vol. 11, February 1974, pp. 79–85.

Dasgupta, Satadal. Village (or Community) Factors Related to the Level of Agricultural Practice. Paper presented at the Southern Sociological Society, New Orleans, 1966, p. 23.

Donnelly, James, and Michael Etzel. Degrees of Product Newness and Early Trial. *Journal of Marketing Research*, Vol. 5, August 1973, pp. 295–300.

Engel, James, Roger Blackwell, and Robert J. Kegerreis. How Information Is Used to Adopt an Innovation. *Journal of Advertising Research*, Vol. 9, No. 4, pp. 3–8.

Fliegel, Frederick C. Differences in Prestige Standards and Orientation to Change in a Traditional Agricultural Setting. *Rural Sociology*, Vol. 30, 1965, p. 288.

Fromkin, Howard. A Social Psychological Analysis of the Adoption and Diffusion of New Products and Practices from a Uniqueness Motivation Perspective. *Proceedings of the Second Annual Conference, Association for Consumer Research*, 1971.

Goldberg, Marvin. A Cognitive Model of Innovative Behavior: The Interaction of Product and Self-Attitudes. In David Gardner (ed.). *Proceedings of the Second Annual Conference, Association for Consumer Research*, 1971.

Havens, A. Eugene. Increasing the Effectiveness of Predicting Innovativeness. *Rural Sociology*, Vol. 30, 1965, p. 158.

Jacoby, Jacob. Multiple-Indicant Approach for Studying New Product Adopters. *Journal of Applied Psychology*, Vol. 55, No. 4, 1971(a), pp. 384–88.

Jacoby, Jacob. Personality and Innovation Proneness. *Journal of Marketing Research*, Vol. 8, May 1971(b), pp. 244–47.

Kiesler, Charles A. *The Psychology of Commitment*. New York: Academic Press, 1971.

Kivlin, Joseph E. *Correlates of Family Planning in Eight Indian Villages*. East Lansing: Michigan State University Diffusion of Innovations Research Dept., 1968, p. 38.

Kohn, Carol A., and Jacob Jacoby. Patterns of Information Acquisition in New Product Purchases. *Journal of Consumer Research*, Vol. 1, No. 2, 1974, pp. 18–22.

Lambert, Zarrel. Perceptual Patterns, Information Handling, and Innovativeness. *Journal of Mar-*

keting Research, Vol. 9, November 1972, pp. 427–431.

Loomis, Charles P. In Praise of Conflict and Its Resolution. *American Sociological Review*, Vol. 32, 1967, p. 25.

Maloney, John C., and Eugene P. Schonfeld. Social Change and Attitude Change. In G. Zaltman (ed.). *Processes and Phenomena of Social Change*. New York: Wiley-Interscience, 1973.

Mancuso, Joseph. Why Not Create Opinion Leaders for New Product Introductions? *Journal of Marketing*, Vol. 33, July 1969, pp. 20–25.

Myers, James, and Thomas S. Robertson. Stability of Self-Designated Opinion Leadership. In S. Ward and P. Wright (eds.). *Advances in Consumer Research*. Chicago: Association for Consumer Research, 1974.

Ostlund, Lyman. Identifying Early Buyers. *Journal of Advertising Research*, Vol. 12, No. 2, pp. 25–30.

Pizam, Abraham. Psychological Characteristics of Innovators. *European Journal of Marketing*, Vol. 6, No. 3, 1972, pp. 203–10.

Reynolds, Fred and William Darden. Predicting Opinion Leadership for Women's Clothing Fashions. *Combined Proceedings: Marketing Education and the Real World and Dynamic Marketing in a Changing World*. Chicago: American Marketing Association, 1972.

Robertson, Thomas S. Determinants of Innovative Behavior. Paper presented at the American Marketing Association, Washington, D.C., 1967.

Robertson, Thomas S. *Innovative Behavior and Communication*. New York: Holt, Rinehart & Winston, 1971, p. 100.

Robertson, Thomas S., and John R. Rossiter. Fashion Diffusion: The Interplay of Innovator and Opinion Leader Roles in College Social Systems. Unpublished paper, Graduate School of Business Administration, University of California, 1968.

Rogers, Everett M. *Family Planning Communication Strategies*. New York: Free Press, 1973.

Rogers, Everett M. *Modernization among Peasants*. New York: Holt, Rinehart & Winston, 1969.

Rogers, Everett M., and E. B. de Ramos. Prediction on the Adoption of Innovations: A Progress Report. Paper presented at the Rural Sociological Society, Chicago, 1965, p. 7.

Rogers, Everett M., and Floyd Shoemaker. *Communication of Innovations*. New York: Free Press, 1971.

Schiffman, Leon. Perceived Risk in New Product Trial by Elderly Consumers. *Journal of Marketing Research*, Vol. 9, February 1972, pp. 106–108.

Schiffman, Leon, and Vincent Gaccione. Opinion Leaders in Institutional Markets. *Journal of Marketing*, Vol. 38, No. 2, April 1974, pp. 43–53.

Smith, Donald R. A Theoretical and Empirical Analysis of the Adoption-Diffusion of Social Change. Ph.D. Diss., Baton Rouge, Louisiana State University, 1968.

Tauber, Edward M. Reduce New Product Failures: Measure Needs as Well as Purchase Interest. *Journal of Marketing*, July 1973, pp. 61–70.

Taylor, James. The Role of Risk in Consumer Behavior. *Journal of Marketing*, Vol. 38. No. 2, April 1974.

Twedt, Dik Warren. How Important to Marketing Strategy Is the "Heavy User"? *Journal of Marketing Research*, January 1964, pp. 71–72.

Uhl, Kenneth, Roman Andrus, and Lance Poulsen. How Are Laggards Different?: An Empirical Inquiry. *Journal of Marketing Research*, Vol. 7, February 1970.

Zaltman, Gerald. Introduction. In B. Sternthal and G. Zaltman (eds.). *Broadening the Concept of Consumer Behavior*. Chicago: Association for Consumer Research, 1976.

Zaltman, Gerald. New Perspectives on Diffusion Research. In David Gardner (ed.). *Proceedings of the Second Annual Conference, Association for Consumer Research*, 1971.

Zaltman, Gerald, and Bernard Dubois. New Conceptual Approaches in the Study of Innovation. In David Gardner (ed.). *Proceedings of the Second Annual Conference, Innovations and Organizations*. New York: Wiley-Interscience, 1973.

Zaltman, Gerald, and Bernard Dubois. New Conceptual Approaches in the Study of Innovation. In David Gardner (ed.). *Innovations and Organizations*. New York: Wiley-Interscience, 1973.

Zaltman, Gerald, and Christian Pinson. Empathetic Ability and Adoption Research. Paper, Northwestern University, 1974(a).

Zaltman, Gerald. Perception of New Product Attributes. Paper, Northwestern University, 1974(b).

24

Why New Industrial Products Fail

Robert G. Cooper

This article reports the results of an empirical investigation into why new industrial products fail. The results, based on a sample of 114 products, point to a very practical lesson for industrial firms.

INTRODUCTION

The high incidence of industrial new product failure plagues many corporations (Booz, Allen and Hamilton, 1965; O'Meara, 1961). Recent years have seen a proliferation of literature prescribing techniques aimed at remedying the problem. But the goal of reducing the risk of product and market development continues to be an elusive one for the majority of industrial firms.

Perhaps the best place to begin improving one's product development efforts is to study one's past failures. The research reported in this paper focusses on why new industrial products fail—the causes of failure and areas of weakness in the new product process. Previous research on this topic has suggested some general causes of product failure. An NICB study sought managers' opinions about the reasons for product failure in their own firms (National Industrial Conference Board, 1964). A variety of possible causes were identified, including inadequate market knowledge, technical defects in the product, bad timing, and poor marketing. However, these were general opinions, and were not based on a specific review of actual product failures. Konopa studied a sample of new products which had failed after passing the initial screen (Konopa, 1968). Here the sample size was quite limited, while the reasons cited tended to be fairly general ones. A recent study by Hlavacek (1974) investigated a sample of 21 ventures which had been terminated. Among the more frequent reasons cited for termination were: inadequate market size; distribution problems; internal conflicts, impatience and resistance; and bad marketing research [1].

To gain a more complete picture, an in-depth study of a large and representative sample of actual product failures which occurred after commercial introduction is needed. The present research aims at reporting on such a review. Its purpose is to identify the general and the specific causes of industrial new product failure and their relative importance. A second purpose is to reveal areas of deficiencies (latent causes) within firms which most frequently lead to these failures.

FRAMEWORK FOR THE STUDY

A conceptual scheme or preliminary structural model of new product failure was first developed. The purpose of the model was to suggest an exhaustive list of potential causes of failure in order to construct a detailed re-

Reprinted from *Industrial Marketing Management*, vol. 4, pp. 315–326, 1975, with permission of *Industrial Marketing Management*, copyright 1975. At the time of writing, Robert G. Cooper was assistant professor of marketing, Faculty of Management, McGill University.

search questionnaire. A second purpose was the development of categories of causes to permit their comparison and ranking. The model was based on information from previous research and from discussions with managers charged with new product development. As outlined in Fig. 1, the Causal Model of Product Failure has three main elements:

1 General Reasons for product failure.
2 Specific Causes of product failure.
3 Latent Causes of product failure.

The general reasons for failure are those which describe the outcomes of the product venture. In this research, a product failure is operationally defined as one which fell far short of profit expectations [2]. Various profitability measures suggest four outcomes which would result in financial failure:

1 Sales fell below expectations.
2 Percentage profit margins fell below expectations.
3 Development costs exceeded expectations.
4 Investment exceeded expectations.

These four outcomes constitute the general reasons for failure.

Corresponding to each of these general reasons are a number of fairly specific causes of product failure. In this research, specific causes of failure are defined as those which describe decisions and events which are immediately linked to the product venture's outcomes (Figure 1). A knowledge of these specific causes—for example, exactly what decision or event led to the outcome, low sales—provides a more complete picture of the failure, and is a vital concern of this research. For each outcome or general reason for failure, a listing of possible specific causes was developed as part of the model. These specific causes are listed in Tables II and V in abbreviated form.

Latent causes of product failure are those which are less visible and tend to underlie or precede the specific causes. That is, latent causes describe the elements of the product development process which result in the decisions and events considered to be the specific causes. Two types of latent causes of failure are included in the model:

1 Deficient Activities: activities commonly associated with the new product process (e.g. marketing research) were done poorly or mistakenly omitted.
2 Deficient Resources: resources which were vital to the product development (e.g. a strong and capable marketing research department) were missing or deficient in the firm.

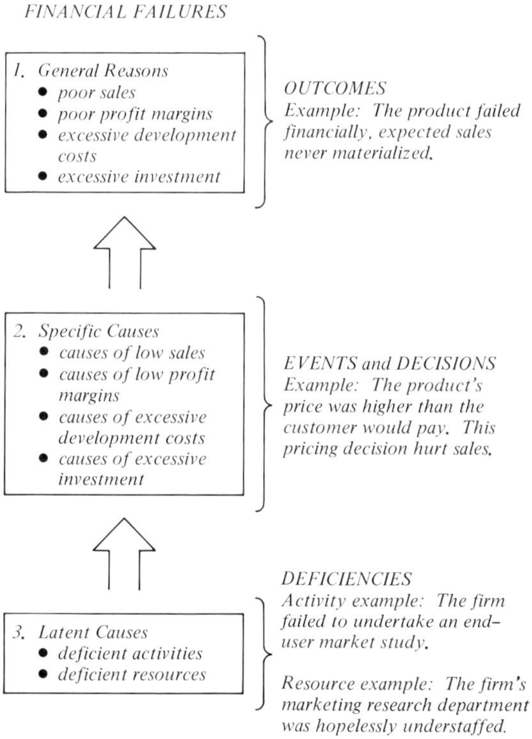

Figure 1 Causal model of product failure.

Figure 2 outlines the particular activities

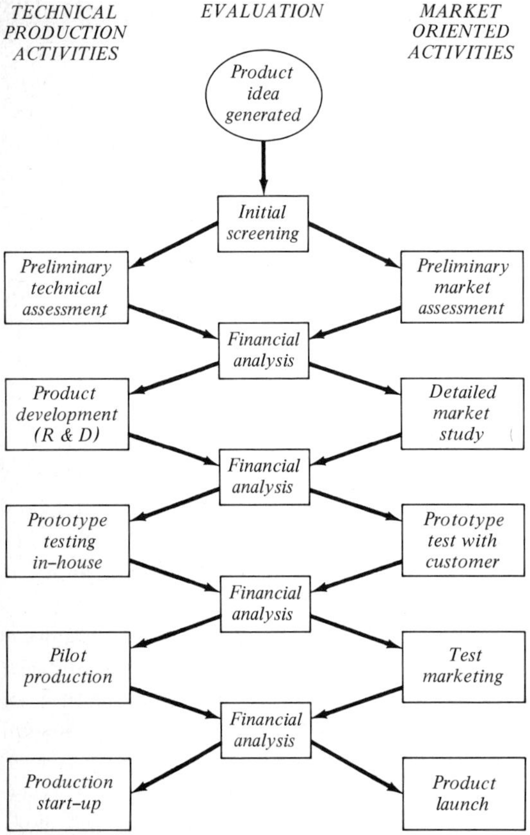

Figure 2 Sequential activities of the new product process.

considered which often are important to the successful development of a new product, while Table VI lists the various resource deficiencies which could prove detrimental to the new product process.

METHODOLOGY

A sample of 150 industrial product firms were contacted to provide the product failure information. These firms were located in Ontario and Quebec, Canada, and were known to be active in product development [3]. The sample included the larger and more obvious product developers as well as a random selection of smaller firms. This bias towards larger firms was deliberate in order to reflect their greater importance in a study of product development.

In each firm, the manager most likely to be familiar with his company's new product activities was contacted [4]. A questionnaire was mailed to each manager, who was asked to answer general questions about his firm and the nature of its business. Next he was requested to select two typical product failures—products which had been commercialized but had fallen far short of profitability expectations [5]. The criteria for selecting the two failures were:

- new products (new to the firm);
- recent failures (1965 or later);
- products developed by the firm in Canada;
- products typical to the firm.

For each product, the manager was asked to indicate why the failure occurred. This was accomplished first by presenting the list of general reasons for failure, and then requesting the respondent to indicate whether each was a main reason, a contributing reason, or not a reason for the product's failure. (An "other" category with space for comments was provided.) Depending upon how he answered this first question, the manager was then asked to review one or more of the lists of specific causes: causes of low sales; causes of low profit margins; causes of excessive investment; or causes of excessive development costs. The following response categories were used for each specific cause: a main cause, a contributing cause, or not a cause. Again, "other" categories and space for comments were provided.

In order to obtain an insight into the latent causes of failure, the manager was presented with a list of the new product development activities (outlined in Figure 2) and asked to rate how well each activity had been performed for each product failure. The response categories were:

- done more than adequately;
- done adequately;
- done inadequately;
- not done, but should have been;
- not applicable.

The manager was also shown a list of possible resource deficiencies, and asked to indicate how much each had contributed to the failure. The response categories were: very much, somewhat, or not at all.

The original sample of 150 firms was reduced to an effective sample of 101 [6]. A handful of firms were no longer in business. Another 46 firms actually had no recent product failures to discuss; in some cases, the firm was basically a one- or two-product firm, and simply did not undertake enough innovative product development to encounter failures; in other cases, the firm undertook product development on a contract basis (for example, aerospace), and once the contract was awarded, was assured of a profitable product development.

Of the sample of 101 firms which actually encountered product failures, 66 replied to the questionnaire for an effective response rate of 65%. Not all the firms were able to discuss two failures, and the eventual sample numbered 114 product failures. Thus, the sample of products is biased toward firms with more active product development programs. The sample of firms which responded represented a wide variety of industries, and ranged in size from very small companies to corporate giants [7].

RESULTS

General Reasons for Product Failure

The most important general reason for product failure was that anticipated sales never materialized. In 63.2% of the cases, the inability to achieve expected sales was cited as the main general reason for failure. In another 14.9% of the failures, poor sales was a contributing reason. In total, more than three-quarters of the product failures had poor sales as either a main or a contributing general reason for failure (Table I).

The other general reasons—low profit margins, excessive development costs and excessive investment—appeared to play a much

Table I General Reasons for Failure (N = 114)

General reasons	Percent of product failures: Main reason	Contributing reason	Main or contributing reason	Rating**
Sales fell below expectations	63.2 (1)*	14.9 (3)	78.1 (1)	70.7 (1)
Profit margins fell below expectations	21.1 (2)	23.7 (1)	44.7 (2)	33.0 (2)
Development costs exceeded expectations	19.3 (3)	21.1 (2)	40.4 (3)	29.9 (3)
Investment exceeded expectations	4.4	8.8	13.2	8.8
Other	4.4	0	4.4	4.4

*Numbers in parentheses indicate rank in each column.

**The rating score is weighted average of the frequencies (percents) of main and contributing reasons. Main reasons are scored 1.0 and contributing reasons scored 0.5 to yield a rating of 0–100%.

smaller role in product failure (Table I). For example, low profit margins, the next most frequently mentioned reason, was cited only one-third as often as poor sales as a main general reason for failure. However, low profit margins was clearly most important as a contributor to failure, being cited in almost one-quarter of the cases as a contributing reason. To compare the relative importance of these general reasons as both main and contributing influences, a weighted rating score (0—100%) was determined for each. This rating score was an arbitrary weighted average of the main and contributing frequencies cited, where a main reason was scored 1.0, and a contributing reason scored 0.5. Based upon these calculated ratings, the rank order and relative importance of the four general reasons for failure were:

General reason	Rating (in %)
Sales below expectations	70.7
Profit margins below expectations	33.0
Development costs excessive	29.9
Investment excessive	8.8

The fact that sales fell short of expectations in more than three-quarters of the failures strongly suggests that firms have the greatest difficulty with their external environment (the market place) rather than with internal environment. That internal reasons—development costs and investment—were so much less important that a poor sales performance also supports this view. Clearly industrial product firms must devote more effort towards reducing the uncertainties of the marketplace if they are to improve their new product performance record.

Specific Causes of Low Sales

That failure to achieve expected sales was cited most often as the general reason for product failure is not surprising. Of greater interest, however, are the specific causes of this poor sales performance. The most frequently mentioned specific cause of low sales was that "competitors were firmly entrenched in the market and it proved more difficult to break into the market than expected." This was the main cause for 36.4% of the low sales, and the contributing cause for another 13.6%. Table II shows the cited frequencies and ratings for each of the specific causes of low sales in order of decreasing importance. (Again, a main cause was scored 1.0 and a contributing cause scored 0.5 to yield a 0—100% rating.) "Potential users overestimated" and "technical deficiencies in product" were cited next as the main causes of low sales. These causes occurred with equal frequency as the main cause in 20.5% of the cases. The most frequently mentioned contributing cause was "price too high" (33.0%), followed by "inadequate marketing effort" (31.8%).

It is clear that most of the major causes of low sales were market ones and not technical inadequacies. When the frequencies of each cause are considered—both as a main and a contributing cause—the five most important causes of low sales based on their weighted rating scores were:

Specific causes	Rating (in %)
Competitors firmly entrenched in market	43.2
Overestimated number of potential users	35.9
Price too high	34.7
Technical difficulities with product	33.0
Misdirected marketing efforts	27.9

What is surprising in a review of the reported frequencies in Table II was to discover how unimportant certain causes of low sales appeared to be. The least important causes,

Table II Specific Causes of Poor Sales Performance (N = 88; 77.2% of Failures)

Specific cause	Percent of product failures: Main cause	Contributing cause	Main or contributing cause	Rating**
Competitors were more firmly entrenched in the market than expected	36.4 (1)*	13.6	50.0 (3)	43.2
The number of potential users was overestimated	20.5 (2)	30.7 (3)	51.1 (1)	35.9
The price was set higher than customers would pay	18.2 (4)	33.3 (1)	51.1 (1)	34.7
The product had design, technical or manufacturing deficiencies/difficulties	20.5 (2)	25.0 (5)	45.5 (4)	33.0
Selling, distribution or promotional efforts were misdirected	15.9 (5)	23.9	39.8 (6)	27.9
The product was the same as competing products . . . "a me too" product	14.8 (6)	25.0 (5)	39.8 (6)	27.3
Did not understand customer requirements; product did not meet his needs or specifications	13.6	26.1 (4)	39.8 (6)	26.7
Selling, distribution or promotional efforts were inadequate	9.1	31.8 (2)	40.9 (5)	25.0
A similar competitive product was introduced	10.2	22.7	33.0	21.6
Were unable to develop or produce product exactly as desired	11.4	19.3	30.7	21.1
Competitors lowered prices or took other defensive actions	12.5	13.6	26.1	19.3
Timing was too late	8.0	13.6	21.6	14.8
No market need existed for this type of product	5.7	18.2	23.9	14.8
Timing was premature	6.8	13.6	20.5	13.6
Government action/legislation hindered the sale of the product	2.3	3.4	5.7	44.0
Other	2.3	2.3	44.5	3.4

**Numbers in parentheses indicate rank in each column.
**See footnote to Table 1.

based on their rating scores were:

Government action/legislation (4.0)
Lack of market need (14.8)
Defensive actions by competitors (19.3)

The first two are frequently mentioned in marketing literature, yet did not play a key role in the sample of failures investigated. Premature timing and late timing were also seldomly cited on an individual basis (ratings of 13.6 and 14.8 respectively), but when considered together as "bad timing" became a fairly important category of failure causes.

A review of the specific causes of low sales and the response patterns of questionnaires suggested that many of these causes were closely related, and indeed might be explained by several underlying factors. Factor analysis was used to identify the underlying factors or dimensions of the causes of low sales (common factor analysis, varimax method, orthogonal rotation). Each of the variables included in this analysis—the causes of low sales in Table II—was treated as a continuous variable having values of 1.0 for "main cause," 0.5 for "contributing cause" and 0.0 for "not a cause" [8].

Six factors with eigenvalues greater than 1.0 were identified, and together explained 66.8% of the variance in the causes of low sales. Table III shows the important factor loadings—the loadings of specific causes on each factor—and provides an interpretation of each factor.

In order to assess the relative importance of each dimension or factor as a cause of low sales, the weightings of each product failure on each of the six dimensions were calculated. The proportions of failures most heavily weighted on each dimension were determined, and are shown in Table IV. These results suggest that all six dimensions of causes of low sales are approximately of equal importance, with the possible exception of Price Competition, which tended to be more a second than a first cause. Of greater interest is the fact that five of these six equally important dimensions describe a lack of understanding of the marketplace: customers, competition, and environment.

An attempt was also made to identify possible courses of corrective action. Asked what might have been done to avoid the low sales situation, 32.0% of the firms indicated "nothing at all"; another 32.0% suggested that better market information would have been the answer. A variety of other suggestions were made, but with much lower frequencies.

Other Specific Causes of Failure

Although low profit margins, excessive development costs and excessive investment were much less important as general reasons for

Table III Loadings of Specific Causes on Each Factor* (N = 88)**

Factor	Specific causes most heavily loaded on factor	Loading*	Interpretation
1	Technical difficulties with product	0.922	
	Could not produce product	0.616	Technical problems
	Inadequate selling effort (negative)	−0.292	
2	"Me too" product	0.728	
	Timing too late	0.703	Timing too late
	Competitors firmly entrenched	0.526	
	Timing premature (negative)	−0.289	
3	Lack of market need for product	0.678	
	Did not understand customer requirements	0.533	Lack of understanding of customers' needs
	Potential users overestimated	0.464	
4	Similar products were introduced	0.967	Defensive actions by competitors
	Competitive defensive actions	0.450	
5	Sales efforts misdirected	0.461	
	Government action/legislation	0.452	Lack of understanding of market environment
	Inadequate selling effort	0.276	
6	Competitive defensive actions	0.513	Price competition
	Price too high	0.446	

*Only the main loadings are shown.

**Only products where "low sales" was a general reason for failure are considered (N = 88).

Table IV Proportion of Failures Most Heavily Weighted on Each Factor (N = 88)

Dimension (Factor)	Percentage of failures when: Factor is first cause*	Factor is first or second cause*
Technical problems	21.2	18.2
Timing too late	17.7	13.9
Lack of understanding of customers' needs	20.0	18.8
Defensive actions by competitors	16.4	17.5
Lack of understanding of market environment	18.8	16.1
Price competition	5.9	15.5

*Based on the loadings of product failures on the six factors, i.e., the product locations on the six-dimentional map. First cause is the factor upon which the product is most heavily loaded; second cause is the factor upon which the product is next most heavily loaded.

failure, the specific causes leading to these types of failures were also investigated (Table V). In the case of products with low profit margins, clearly unexpectedly higher production costs were the main cause (49.4%), followed by low volume situations which resulted in higher per unit costs (25.0%). Where excessive development expenditures was the general reason for failure, the fact that firms underestimated the difficulty of development was the main cause (50.0%). The main cause of excessive investment was that firms simply erred in their estimates of the production facilities which would be required to manufacture the product (33.3%).

Latent Causes of Product Failure

A prime concern of the research was to identify some of the latent causes of product failure. Latent causes describe elements of the product development process which precede the specific causes of failure. Two types of latent causes were investigated: the lack of needed resources to undertake the venture; and inadequately undertaken activities during the development process.

Table VI summarizes the extent to which each resource deficiency contributed to the product failures. Again a weighted rating score was calculated to permit combining the "very much" and "somewhat" responses, where "very much" was scored 1.0, and "somewhat" scored 0.5. The single deficiency which contributed most often in a major way to product failure was a lack of marketing research skills or people, followed by a lack of selling resources or skills. Lack of general management skills along with lack of marketing research skills were cited most often as "somewhat" contributing to the failure. On the basis of the rating scores, the most important resource deficiencies which contributed to product failure were:

	Rating (in %)
Lack of:	
marketing research skills or people	43.2
general management skills	30.1
selling resources or skills	29.7

It is noteworthy that the lowest contributors to product failure were a lack of production resources and a lack of financial resources, with ratings of 12.2 and 14.2 respectively.

The second set of latent causes of failure included deficiencies in the activities undertaken during the development of the new product. Table VII summarizes the adequacies of the various activities undertaken in each product venture. The columns in the table indicate the percentage of cases where each activity was undertaken:

adequately (or better);
inadequately;
not done, but should have been;
not applicable.

Table V Other Specific Causes of Product Failure

Specific cause	Percent of product failures: Main cause	Contributing cause	Main or contributing cause	Rating*
Poor profit margins (N = 52)				
Production costs were greater than expected	40.4 (1)*	34.6 (1)	75.0 (1)	57.7
Volume was lower than expected, resulting in higher per unit costs	25.0 (2)	25.0 (2)	50.0 (2)	37.5
Price was overly optimistic; price was dropped	19.2 (3)	25.0 (2)	44.2	31.7
Competitive products was introduced; product's price was dropped	13.5	34.6 (1)	48.1 (3)	30.8
Selling, distribution or promotional costs were higher than expected	7.7	11.5	19.2	13.5
Other	0	0	0	0
Excessive development cost (N = 41)				
Underestimated development difficulties	50.0	36.9	86.9	68.5
Product concept was changed during development	36.9	36.9	73.8	55.4
Excessive investment (N = 12)				
Estimates for production facilities were too low	33.3	33.3	66.7	50.0
Expected manufacturing/production process was altered during development	16.7	41.7	58.4	37.6

*See Table I for footnotes.

Table VI Extent to Which Resource Deficiencies Contributed to Product Failure (N = 114)

Resource deficiency	Percent of product failures: Very much	Somewhat	Very much plus somewhat	Rating
Lack of financial resources	5.5	17.3	22.5	14.2
Lack of engineering skills or people	8.2	32.7 (3)	40.9	24.6
Lack of R & D skills or people	7.3	30.0	37.3	22.3
Lack of marketing research skills or people	21.6 (1)*	43.2 (1)	64.8 (1)	43.2 (1)
Lack of general management skills	9.0 (3)	42.1 (2)	51.1 (2)	30.1 (2)
Lack of production resources or skills	4.5	15.3	19.8	12.2
Lack of selling resources or skills	13.5 (2)	32.4	45.9 (3)	29.7 (3)

*Numbers in parenthesis indicate rank in each column.

The final column, "deficient," represents the percentage of ventures where the particular activity was undetaken "inadequately" or "not done but should have been," and is adjusted for the no response and not applicable responses.

There remains little question that the activities in which firms were most deficient are the market oriented ones. Those activities with the highest deficiency ratings were:

- detailed market study (74.0% deficient);
- test marketing (58.1% deficient);
- product launch (53.9% deficient).

These results can be compared to deficiencies in product development (R & D) and production start-up of 36.3% and 30.6% respectively. Deficiencies in financial analysis (51.5%) were also common.

Overall, every market oriented activity was reported to be much more deficient than its corresponding technical/production activity. A review of the deficiencies shows that each market activity was cited as deficient in 45% or more of the cases. On the other hand, not one of the technical/production activities was more than 40% deficient, and all but two were less than 35% deficient. The average for activities in each category reveals a similar picture: 56.5% deficient for market activities versus 33.8% deficient for technical/production efforts.

Table VII Activities during Product Development Process (N = 114)

	Percent of product failures				
Activity	Done adequately	Done inadequately	Not done	Not applicable	Deficient*
Market					
Preliminary assessment of market	50.0	36.6	8.9	4.5	47.7 (6)**
Detailed market study	24.1	46.4	22.3	7.1	74.0 (1)
Prototype testing with customer	42.9	29.5	11.6	14.3	48.9 (5)
Test marketing	27.7	25.0	13.4	28.6	58.1 (2)
Product launch	31.2	33.0	3.6	28.6	53.9 (3)
Average	35.2%	34.1%	11.9%	16.6%	56.5%
Technical/production					
Preliminary technical assessment	66.1	25.0	3.6	5.4	30.2
Product development (R & D)	58.0	29.5	3.6	88.9	36.3
Prototype testing—in house	51.8	25.9	6.3	15.2	38.3
Pilot production	50.9	12.5	13.4	18.8	33.7
Production start-up	38.4	11.6	5.4	40.2	30.6
Average	55.0%	20.9%	6.5%	17.7%	33.8%
Evaluative					
Initial screening	61.6	30.4	5.4	2.7	36.7
Detailed financial analysis	42.0	34.8	9.8	12.5	51.5 (4)
Average	51.8%	32.6%	7.6%	7.6%	44.1%

*Deficient includes "done inadequately" plus "not done but should have been", and is adjusted for no response and not applicable.

**Numbers in parenthesis indicate rank in the Deficient column.

SUMMARY AND CONCLUSIONS

The results of the research are consistent with previous investigations into new product failure. But the results go much further in identifying fairly specific causes of failure and problem areas within firms.

Clearly the main general reason for product failure was that sales failed to materialize. While this result is not surprising, it does imply that much more time, attention and money must be devoted to reducing market uncertainties. The main causes of low sales were chiefly market reasons and not technical ones. This result is quite provocative, particularly when one considers the relatively minor amounts spent on marketing research compared to the large sums spent on R & D. Underestimating competitive strength, overestimating the number of potential users, and overestimating the price customers would pay for the new product were the three major causes of low sales. The majority of the dimensions or factors which appeared to explain many of the causes of low sales were also market-related—a lack of understanding of the marketplace, the customer, and the competition.

Of great interest was the fact that in almost two-thirds of the product failures, a lack of marketing research skills or people was thought to have significantly contributed to the failure. Marketing launch resources and general management skills were also rated as weak. A review of activities which were poorly undertaken or mistakenly omitted altogether reveals a similar story. At every stage of the product development process, market oriented activities fared much worse than corresponding technical/production activities. By far the most deficient activity undertaken in these facilities was the detailed market study.

A closer look at the specific causes of low sales, the main reason for failure, reveals that industrial product firms in general suffer from an inward orientation. Many firms simply overlooked or dismissed the fact that competitors might have a stranglehold on the new product's market. It could be that undertaking a thorough analysis of competitive strengths and market positions is a very difficult task. But more likely, the new product firm sees its product as "so much better" that customers cannot help but "line up at their doors." The second main cause of low sales, overestimating the number of potential users, suggests a similar inward orientation. A relatively straightforward market study in many cases would have been sufficient to identify target markets and numbers of potential users. Overestimating the price customers would pay was another major cause of low sales. Once again, the firms' attention appears to be focused on the product and its attributes, rather than on customers' needs and their desire for a higher-priced, better product.

The message for industrial product firms is clear. A greater market orientation is required as part of the new product development effort. This means industrial goods firms must be prepared to balance their heavy R & D expenditures with research of another kind—marketing research.

ACKNOWLEDGEMENTS

This research was funded by the University Grants Program of the Canadian Department of Industrial, Trade and Commerce, Office of Science and Technology, Ottawa, Canada. The author thanks Dr. Stanley J. Shapiro, Dean, Faculty of Management, McGill University, and Professor Blan Little, School of Business Administration, University of Western Ontario, London, Ontario, for their assistance in this research.

NOTES

1 The Hlavacek study reviewed ventures which were organization "misfits" and not related to current operations. To the extent such cases were new business ventures, were undertaken in a venture management organizational system, and were terminated prior to commercialization, the reasons for failure can be expected to be different from the ones for the typical new product failure.

2 Thus a failure is defined from the point of view or perception of the firm involved, and in financial (rather than technological) terms. The fact that individual firms may differ in their financial/profitability criteria of success was not considered, each firm being free to judge financial success or failure as it saw fit.

3 Source: *Directory of Scientific Research and Development Establishments in Canada.*

4 All firms had been previously contacted in former research and hence a list of appropriate managers was available. In larger firms, the manager contacted was usually the corporate product development officer; in smaller firms, generally the president was the source of data.

5 An exact operational definition of a "product failure" was not possible in this research. However, to the extent the research focussed only on product failures (rather than matched pairs of successes and failures), an exact and dichotomous operational definition was not essential. Managers were merely instructed to pick ventures which were clear and obvious financial failures from their firms' point of view.

6 Based on information on returned questionnaires and discussions during telephone follow-up.

7 Industries included: electrical and electronic equipment (29%); light and heavy industrial equipment (11%); chemical (21%); automotive components, aircraft and agricultural equipment (21%); and miscellaneous (19%). Forty-one percent of the firms had annual sales of less than $10 million; 38% had sales between $10 million and $50 million; 21% had more than $50 million annual sales.

8 Although variables in reality were neither interval data nor normally distributed (and hence are not consistent with the assumptions of factor analysis) it should be noted that this statistical technique was not the primary method of analysis nor was it used for inferential purposes. Rather factor analysis was used here as an interpretational aid to supplement other methods.

REFERENCES

Booz, Allen and Hamilton (1965). *Management of New Products*, New York.

Directory of Scientific Research and Development Establishments in Canada (1969). Ottawa: Department of Industry, Trade, and Commerce.

Hlavacek, James D. (1974). "Toward More Successful Venture Management," *Journal of Marketing*, vol. 38, no. 4, pp. 56–60.

Konopa, L. J. (1968). *New Products: Assessing Commercial Potential, Management Bulletin #88*. New York: American Management Association.

National Industrial Conference Board (1964). "Why New Products Fail," *The Conference Board Record.*

O'Meara, J. T. Jr. (1961). "Selecting Profitable Products," *Harvard Business Review*, Jan.–Feb., p. 83.

B PRICING

25

The Myths and Realities of Corporate Pricing

Gilbert Burck

Business is sometimes accused of setting prices by using a simple formula: price equals costs plus overhead plus a predetermined profit. But it only *seems* to be doing so, says Prof. J. Fred Weston of UCLA, who spent a good part of two years discussing pricing with top executives. According to Professor Weston's research, large sophisticated companies necessarily decide on prices the way they do on investment, going through most if not all the same agonies.

Corporate profits may be recovering briskly this year, but resentment and suspicion of profits are rising briskly too. It is by now an article of faith in some sophisticated circles that the U.S. has become a corporate state, in which giant companies increasingly dominate markets and write their own price tickets regardless of demand by practicing "administered" and "target return" pricing. Ask ten campus economists whether prices will fall with demand in industries that are concentrated—that is, dominated by a few large firms—and nine of them will tell you that prices won't fall as much as they would if the industry were competitive. And almost everywhere the putative pricing power of big business is equated with the well-known monopoly power that organized labor exercises over wages.

So the pressure is mounting to police pricing practices and other "abuses" in concentrated industries. Senator George McGovern, for example, is denouncing oligopolies as responsible for most of the nation's inflation, and is sponsoring measures to break up big companies. Meanwhile, the notion that price controls should become a permanent American institution is certainly taken seriously by more and more people. The Price Commission itself, which has adopted the practice of regulating prices by relating them to profit margins of the past three years, seems to be leaning toward a theory of managed prices.

Yet all these passionately cherished attitudes and opinions are based at best on half truths and perhaps on no truth at all. The portentous fact is that the theory of administered prices is totally unproven and is growing less and less plausible as more evidence comes in. Always very controversial, it has lately been subjected to an extended counterattack of highly critical analysis.

Some of the best work on the subject is being done by the privately funded Research Program in Competition and Business Policy at the University of California (Los Angeles) Graduate School of Management, under Professor J. Fred Weston. For nearly two years now, Weston and his group have been taking a fresh, empirical approach to subjects like industrial concentration, profits, competition, and prices. Their techniques include asking businessmen themselves how they set prices and trying to find out why businessmen's formal statements about their price policies are usually so different from their actual practices.

The program, among other things, hopes to

Reprinted by special permission from *Fortune*, April 1972; At the time of writing, the author was a staff writer for *Fortune* magazine.

come up with a new theory of corporate profitability. "So far," Weston says, "we find that profit rates are not significantly higher in concentrated than in nonconcentrated industries. What we do find is that there is a relationship between efficiency and profits and nothing else." But a vast amount of work, Weston admits, needs to be done. As happens so often in the dismal science, the more economists find out about a subject, the more they realize (if they are honest) how much they still have to learn.

MR. MEANS SHOWS THE WAY

The argument about administered prices is now nearly forty years old; one philoprogenitive professor who took sides at the start is preparing to instruct his grandson on the subject. Few controversies in all economic history, indeed, have used up so many eminent brain hours or so much space in learned journals. Much if not most of the argument has been conducted on a macroeconomic level; that is, it has been concerned with analyzing over-all statistics on industrial concentration and comparing them with figures on prices. And that is exactly what was done by the man who started the argument by coining the phrase "administered price" in the first place. He is Gardiner Means, seventy-five, author (with the late Adolph Berle) of the celebrated book *The Modern Corporation and Private Property*, published in 1932.

Like a lot of economists in that day, Means was looking for reasons why the great depression occurred. He noticed that many prices remained stable or at least sticky, even when demand was falling. Thus demand was depressed still further and with it production and employment. Means's figures showed that wholesale prices fluctuated less in highly concentrated industries than in others; so to distinguish these prices from classic free-market prices, which are assumed to fluctuate with demand, he called them "administered" prices, or prices set by fiat and held constant "for a period of time and a series of transactions."

As an explanation for depression, Means's theory got some devastatingly critical attention over the next few years, but it did not fade away. In the middle 1950's it was revived as a major explanation for cost-push inflation, which Means calls administrative inflation; i.e., the supposed power of big business to raise prices arbitrarily. In 1957 the theory was taken up by Senator Estes Kefauver's antitrust and monopoly subcommittee, whose chief economist was John M. Blair, one of the nation's most energetic and passionate foes of industrial concentration. Ere long, dozens of the nation's eminent economists got into the argument, and many confected novel and often persuasive arguments in behalf of the theory of administered prices. Besides Blair, the advocates included the Johnson Administration's "new economists," such as James Duesenberry, Otto Eckstein, Gardner Ackley, and Charles Schultze, with "independent" savants like Adolph Berle and J. K. Galbraith helping out from time to time.

WHY DID THEY WAIT SO LONG?

The burden of proof, of course, is on the advocates of administered-price theory. They must do more than merely nourish a prejudice, particularly if their thesis is to provide a reliable guide for antitrust and other public policy (to say nothing of serving as a base for a new interpretation of the American economy, such as Galbraith vouchsafed to the world in his book, *The New Industrial State*). In other words, they must offer very convincing evidence they are right. That, it is fair to say, they have not done. In 1941 economists, Willard Thorp and Walter Crowder, in a study for the Temporary National Economic Committee, used a sophisticated analysis of price, volume, and concentration to conclude that there was no significant relationship between the level of seller concentration and price behavior and volume. Shortly afterward, Alfred Neal, now president of the Committee for Economic Development, argued that any measure of price inflexibility must consider cost changes, "a matter over which industries have little if any discretion." These and other attacks on Means's theory seemed to dispose of it as a proven cause of depression.

As a major explanation of cost-push inflation, the theory was also subjected to severe criticism. Murray N. Rothbard of the Polytechnic Institute of Brooklyn, for one, simply laughs at the theory of administered prices, and terms it a bogey. "If Big Business is causing inflation by suddenly and wickedly deciding to raise prices," he says, "one wonders why it hadn't done so many years before. Why the wait? If the answer is that now monetary and consumer demand have been increasing, then we find that we are back in a state of affairs determined by demand, and that the law of supply and demand hasn't been repealed after all."

Just two years ago the National Bureau of Economic Research printed a little book calculated to put an end to the argument. It was called *The Behavior of Industrial Prices*, and was written by George J. Stigler, a distinguished economist at the University of Chicago, and James K. Kindahl, of the University of Massachusetts. Stigler and Kindahl correctly observed that, owing to hidden discounts and concessions, a company's quoted prices are often very different from the prices it actually gets. So instead of using official figures compiled by the Bureau of Labor Statistics on sellers' quotations, as Means and others had done, Stigler and Kindahl used prices at which their surveys told them sales were made. These were then matched with figures on industry concentration. The Stigler-Kindahl findings for the period 1957-61 did not differ much from findings made with B.L.S. figures. But the findings for 1961-66 differed considerably, and Stigler and Kindahl at least showed that prices in concentrated industries were not as inflexible as some people thought. What is very important is that Stigler and Kindahl probably understated their case because their surveys did not manage to get at true selling prices. As most business journalists are well aware, companies neither record nor generally talk about all the "under the table" prices and other valuable concessions they make when the market is sluggish.

"NORMAL" PROFIT ISN'T SO NORMAL

While this macroeconomic analysis of price and concentration was going on, a few economists were beginning to take a microeconomic or close-up view of pricing. Why not ask businessmen themselves just how they really

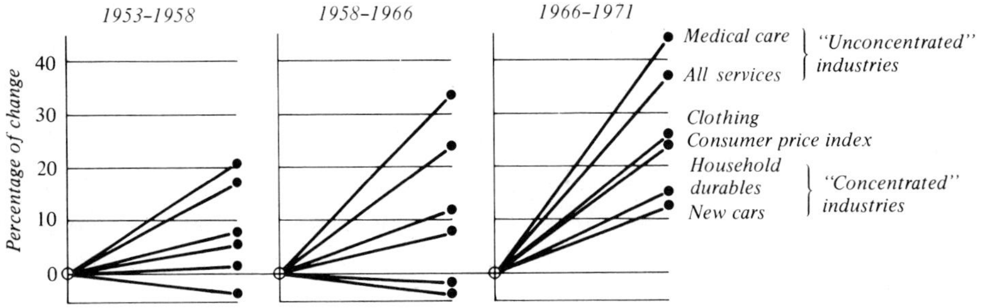

Adapted from *Fortune*.

price their products? This bright idea, however, proved not so easy to apply as to state. Classic economic theory says business should set prices to balance supply and demand—i.e., "to clear the market." But in 1939 two economists at Oxford University published a survey of thirty-eight British companies that found most of them tended to price their output pretty much on a stodgy cost-plus basis, almost as if they were accountants, or trying to behave like Gardiner Means's oligopolists.

It remained for Professor I. F. Pearce of the University of Nottingham to clear up the paradox. Pearce had been trained as a cost accountant, and understood why prices are not always what they seem. He pointed out that business almost universally bases prices on a cost figure, which in turn is based on both past cost data and future cost estimates; an economist would call this figure the long-term average cost. In most firms, moreover, a recognized profit margin remains stable over periods long enough to be significant, and is therefore considered normal. "What is less generally known, except to those who practice the art of price fixing," Pearce says, "is how often and for what a variety of reasons 'normal' profit is not in fact charged against any particular sale. . . . The informal adjustment of margins, since it is both informal and *ad hoc*, tends to be left out of any general discussion of price fixing routine, *and yet the issue really turns upon it*. Margins charged are highly sensitive to the market under normally competitive conditions, and the 'norm' is simply that figure around which they fluctuate."

To demonstrate what he meant, Pearce made an elaborate study of one medium-sized British manufacturing firm. He sent out questionnaires and conducted formal interviews, and made a record of quoted prices and actual selling prices. He found that a wide variation existed between the margins talked about in interviews and surveys and the margins actually achieved. "Normal" profit margins, in other words, were mere checkpoints in the company's planning process.

Of course, a significant minority of U.S. businesses actually do price on a cost-plus basis—the regulated monopolies like utilities, pipelines, and transportation companies, as well as a lot of military contractors. At first glance, many unregulated companies also seem to price on a cost-plus basis. This is only natural. Since they obviously cannot survive unless they take in more than they spend, the easiest way to think about a price is first to think like an accountant: price equals costs plus overhead plus a fair profit. Cost-plus, furthermore, is a useful ritual, with great public-relations advantages. A smart, prudent businessman would no more publicly brag about charging all the traffic will bear than he would publicly discourse on his wife's intimate charms. Recoiling from branding himself a "profiteer," he admits only to wanting a "fair" return. Ironically, this has made him a sitting duck for economists who accuse him of not striving to maximize his profits because he controls the market, and of changing his prices only when his planned return is threatened.

WHEN IT'S RIGHT TO CHARGE ALL YOU CAN GET

But no mechanical formula can guarantee a profit. Both cost and profit estimates depend on volume estimates; and volume, among many other things, depends on the right price, whether that price maximizes unit profit right away or not. A company with unused capacity and a growing market may well take the classical course of cutting prices and temporarily earning a smaller return on investment than it considers normal. But it may have equally cogent reasons for not cutting prices. The theorists of administered prices have pointed accusing fingers at business' behavior in the recession of 1957-58, when it raised prices somewhat in the face of falling demand.

What happened was that costs were increasing faster than demand was falling. According to the theory of pure competition, they should have raised prices. That they did, both small firms and large.

On the other hand, many companies, particularly those with new products, do charge all the traffic will bear, and so they should. It is not going too far to attribute the innovativeness and technical progress of the Western world to this kind of profit maximizing, and the innovative backwardness of the Soviet Union and East Europe to the absence of it. The hope of realizing extraordinary profits on their innovations, at least temporarily, is what drives capitalist corporations into risking money on research. DuPont's strategy for the best part of fifty years was to develop "proprietary" products and to charge all it could get for them as long as the getting was good. So with the giants in data processing, pharmaceuticals, machine tools, and other high technologies. But these proprietary profits inevitably fire up competition, which invades the market with innovations of its own. Thus the story of Western industrial progress is the story of the progressive liquidation of proprietary positions.

THE RAZOR BLADES WERE TOO CHEAP

This not to say that all or even most businesses are skillful practitioners of the art of pricing. Daniel Nimer, a vice president of a large Chicago company, has made an avocation of studying pricing and lectures and conducts surveys and seminars on the subject both here and abroad. Nimer believes that business in general is still far too inflexible in its pricing techniques and too prone to take a merely satisfactory return. The most frequent error, Nimer says, is to fail to charge what the traffic will bear, particularly when marketing a novel product. In 1961, Wilkinson Sword Ltd. brought out its new stainless-steel razor blades at 15.8 cents apiece. Overnight Wilkinson accumulated a staggering backlog of orders, the sort of thing that usually results in delivery delays and an expensive crash expansion program. Had Wilkinson started at 20 cents a blade, Nimer believes, it would have been much better able to fortify its position. Among Nimer's pearls of wisdom: (1) A big backlog is a nearly infallible indication of an underpriced product. (2) Always make decisions today that will help you tomorrow, and remember that it is easier to cut prices tomorrow than to raise them. (3) The key to pricing is to build value into the product and price it accordingly. (4) Above all, pricing is both analytical and intuitive, a scientific art.

SETTING A TARGET

The major if not the first case study of U.S. pricing was published in 1958 by the Brookings Institution in its book *Pricing in Big Business*. The authors were A.D.H. Kaplan (who was then a senior staff economist at Brookings and is now retired), Joel B. Dirlam of Rhode Island University, and Robert F. Lanzillotti of the University of Florida. Using questionnaires, interviews, and memos, the trio analyzed the pricing policies of twenty of the largest U.S. companies, including G.E., G.M., Alcoa, A&P, Sears, Roebuck, and U.S. Steel. Although the actual practices of the companies were predictably hard to describe and even harder to generalize about, the authors did manage to narrow the corporations' *goals* to five. The most typical pricing objectives, the authors decided, were to achieve (1) a target return on investment, (2) stable prices and markups over costs, (3) a specified market share, (4) a competitive position. Another objective, not so frequently cited, was to compete by taking advantage of product differences. The study's conclusion, written by Kaplan, was that many big, powerful companies seem not to be overwhelmingly controlled by the market, yet even they do not dominate the market. They do not have things their own way, with steady prices and rates of return, but are constantly forced to examine and change their policies.

Manifestly this study gives scant comfort to the administered-price theorists. Professor Lanzillotti apparently felt it was too easy on big business. Granted money to do further work on the data, he came up with a more critical interpretation of them in an article in the *American Economic Review* of December, 1958. Since Lanzillotti is now a member of the Price Commission and has been described as knowing "more about prices" than anyone else on that body, his thoughts are worth attending to. Lanzillotti devoted much of his thesis to the prevalence of so-called target-return pricing, which at that time was an almost esoteric concept.

When companies use target-return pricing, he explained, they do not try to maximize short-term profits. Instead they start with a rate of return they consider satisfactory, and then set a price that will allow them to earn that return when their plant utilization is at some "standard" rate—say 80 percent. In other words, they determine standard costs at standard volume and add the margin necessary to return the target rate of profit over the long run.

More and more companies, Lanzillotti argued, are adopting target-return pricing, either for specific products or across the board. He also concluded that the companies have the size to give them market power. Partly because of this power and partly because the companies are vulnerable to criticism and potential antitrust action, all tend to behave more and more like public utilities. Target-return pricing, with some exceptions in specific product lines, implies a policy of stable or rigid pricing.

Many of Lanzillotti's conclusions have already proved vulnerable to microeconomic analysis, most particularly at the hands of J. Fred Weston, who launched U.C.L.A.'s Research Program in Competition and Business Policy about two years ago. Prior to that, Weston studied finance and economics at the University of Chicago and wrote the three most popular (and profitable) textbooks on business finance. He got into pricing by a side door, having steeped himself in the literature on corporate resource allocation. He spent a considerable part of three years talking about that subject with executives—at first formally, then informally and postprandially. But he soon began to realize that he was also talking about the way prices were made. So he shifted his emphasis from financial to economic questions, and broadened considerably the scope of his work. Like others before him, he discovered that what businessmen formally say about their pricing and what they do about it are often very different. And their action is more consistent with classical theory than their talk.

In a major paper not yet published, Weston proceeds to apply his investigations to the three "popular" and related theories that were at the heart of the administered-price concept: (1) that large corporations generally try to realize a target markup or target return on investment; (2) that their prices tend to be inflexible, uncompetitive, and unresponsive to changes in demand; (3) that contrary to a fundamental postulate of classic economic theory, large, oligopolistic corporations do not maximize profits, but use their market power to achieve planned or target profit levels.

THE CONSTRAINTS OF THE MARKET

The concept of target pricing, Weston's research showed, was an arrant oversimplification of what actually happens in large companies. "The Brookings study," he explains, "focused on talking to top sales and marketing men, who take a target as given. If you talk to

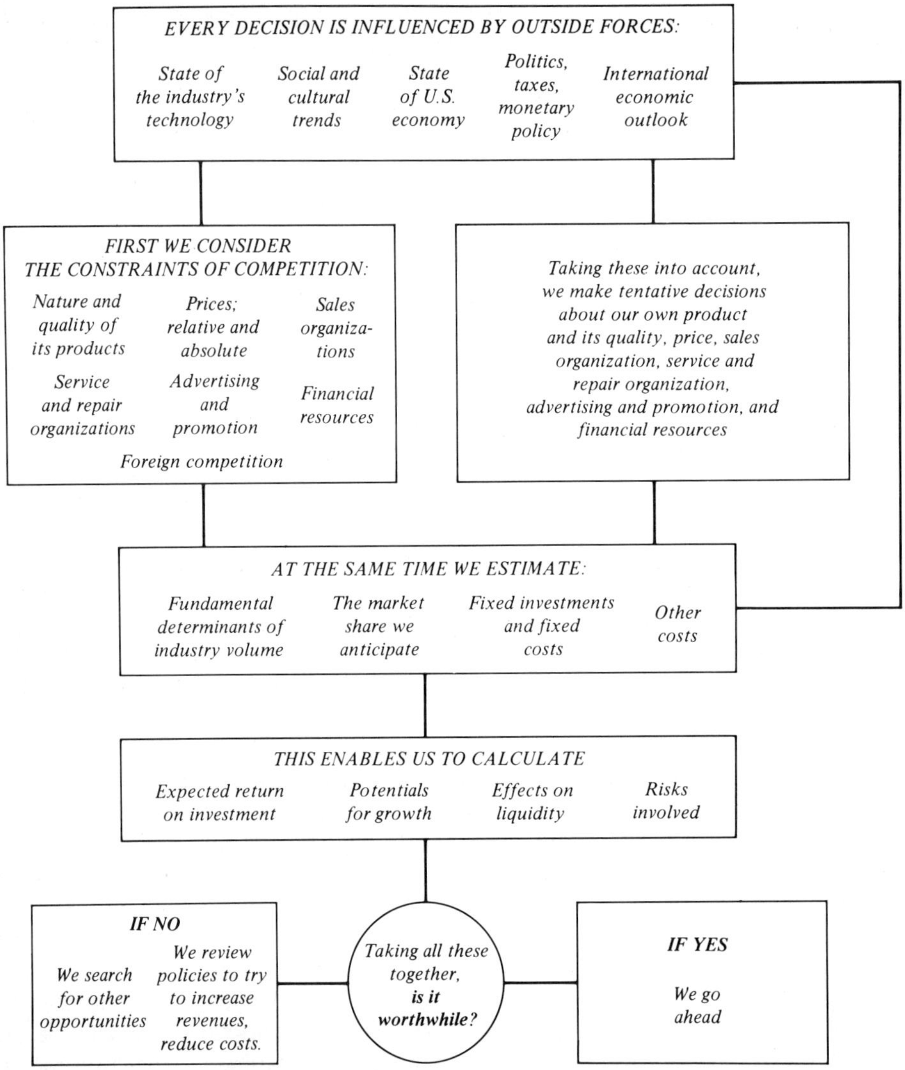

Pricing decisions cannot be separated from investment decisions.

top executives, you find they use the target as a screening device, a reference point." Pricing decisions, he found out, cannot be (and are not) made apart from other business decisions; price lists are based on long-run demand curves. In fact, as the drawing below suggests, all the considerations that go to make investment and other policies also go into pricing, either deliberately or intuitively.

Neither large nor small businesses have price "policies," Weston adds; pricing is too much interwoven with other factors to be formulated independently of them. And most of the people Weston talked to kept emphasizing the constraints of the market. In short, target-return pricing is not what the critics of business think it to be. If anything, it is an interim checkpoint set up by management to specify tentatively the company's potential.

Often, Weston argues, critics of corporate pricing condemn behavior as oligopolistic that does nothing more than follow modern accounting practices. Firms of all sizes use accounting budgets, plans, and controls to formulate performance objectives. Standard volume represents the firms' best judgment of the expected volume of operations, and standard cost is the unit cost at standard volume. And a technique called variance analysis compares management's actual performance with standard performance in order to evaluate and improve the former.

Economic textbooks, says Weston, have failed to keep up with such developments in the art of management, with the result that economists often fail to understand the nature and implications of business planning. In *The New Industrial State*, for example, Galbraith argues that planning by firms, aided by government, is eliminating the market mechanism. Nonsense, says Weston. Planning and control as management uses them do not eliminate the market or its uncertainties. Planning and control are what the market forces you to do. Since they provide a way of judging performance and spotting defects, a device to shorten the reaction time to uncertainty and change, they really increase the market's efficiency.

HOW DETROIT REACTS

The administered-price theorists have pointed to the auto industry as the archetype of a disciplined oligopoly whose prices are very rigid. This characterization is largely based on the industry's practice of setting dealers' recommended prices at the beginning of a model year. Actually, the auto companies change those prices, sometimes frequently and substantially, as the year rolls on and specific models demonstrate their popularity or lack of it. The price changes take a wide variety of forms: bonuses for sales exceeding quotas, bonuses for models not doing well, and so on. As Professor Yale Brozen of the University of Chicago analyzes the industry: "Competition in the auto market actually *makes* the retail price. If the retail price is low relative to wholesale prices, the dealers can't live, and the company must give them better margins; if the retail price is high, the dealers tend to get rich, and the company raises wholesale prices and steps up production."

Now that foreign competition has become so powerful, the auto companies find it harder than ever to price arbitrarily. "Take our Vega," a G.M. man says with some feeling. "If anything is the reverse of target-return pricing, that Vega is. We did not *make* its price. We had to *take* a price that was set by our competitors. Then the only way we could make a profit was to bring our costs down."

Summing up the alleged reluctance of large corporations to compete, Weston quotes Professor Martin Bailey of Brookings, who describes the idea as "a theory in search of a phenomenon."

The third allegation dealt with by Weston—i.e., that the large corporation, in formulating its price policies, does not seek to maximize profits—is a tough one to prove either way. "Management's approach to pricing is based upon planned profits," Lanzillotti has contended. "If we are to speak of 'administered' decisions in the large firm, it is perhaps more accurate to speak of administered *profits* rather than administered *prices*." To support his contention, Lanzillotti reexamined profit data on the twenty companies covered in the Brookings book. The data seemed to verify his belief that large firms are able to achieve their target returns on investment.

Weston noticed two major defects in the argument. One was that targets were specified for only seven of the twenty firms. The other was that Lanzillotti defined return on investment as the ratio of income before preferred-stock dividends to stockholders' net worth, including preferred stock, which makes the return look artificially large. But return on investment is normally and more realistically defined as the ratio of income (before interest payments) to total operating assets. On this basis, the figures show a big discrepancy between target and actual returns. And the Lanzillotti table included results for only the years 1947-55. When the figures were extended through 1967, there was an even larger discrepancy.

"WE JUST DON'T KNOW"

Moreover, the returns above target were consistent with a lot of contradictory theses—with target pricing, with random behavior, and with profit maximization; the returns below target were also consistent with a number of alternative theses. Weston's final conclusion: Studies by Lanzillotti and by others have established neither that large firms are able to "control" or plan profits, nor that they do not want to maximize or optimize profits. Case not proved: additional evidence and analysis needed.

"The third proposition probably cannot be answered anyway," Weston adds. "How do you know if firms are maximizing their profits? In an early draft I made the mistake of thinking that a company earning more than target was maximizing its profits. This isn't necessarily so. We just don't know. We are, however, finding out a lot of positive facts about other related things. It has always been assumed, for example, that there will be collusion in an industry with few firms. But the fact is that we are beginning to get solid evidence that competitive efficiency is an important characteristic of such industries." This finding, Weston points out, is consistent with the work of Professor Brozen, who has analyzed in detail the profitability of hundreds of companies. "Concentrated industries are concentrated because that, apparently, is the efficient way to organize those industries," says Brozen. "Unconcentrated industries are unconcentrated because that, apparently, is the efficient way to organize them."

THE BIG COMPANY AS COST LEADER

Standard textbook theory assumes that only "atomistic" industries—i.e., those with many companies and dominated by none—are perfectly competitive in price and highly responsive to changing tastes and technologies. But Weston contends that companies in concentrated industries can and do serve the consumer just as effectively. This view, incidentally, is persuasively set forth in a new book, *In Defense of Industrial Concentration*, by Professor John S. McGee, on leave from the University of Washington. The notion that concentration leads to the end of capitalism, McGee argues, springs from indefensibly narrow definitions of both competition and the aims of the economic system. Economic competition is best understood as an evolutionary process and not as a rigid structure or set of goals. But there is no necessary conflict between concentration and "competitiveness," even when the latter word is used in its narrow sense.

You can't explain the new competition with narrow textbook theory, Weston says. Big companies may be price leaders, but they are also cost leaders. Continually subjected to the efforts of rivals to steal business away, they deal with this uncertainty by reducing costs wherever they can. As Weston sees it, this kind of price leadership does not result in high prices and restricted output, as textbook theory says it should. What it does is to compel companies to try to strike a balance between growing as fast as possible and raising earnings per share as fast as possible.

ARE OLIGOPOLISTS MORE PROFITABLE?

Among the other provocative papers financed by the U.C.L.A. program is an unpublished dissertation on the relationship between industrial concentration and prices, by Steven H. Lustgarten, twenty-eight, who now teaches economics at the Baruch College of the City University of New York. His investigations show that during the period 1954-58, prices rose faster in concentrated industries. But the reason seems logical. Firms expanded plant and equipment at an abnormal rate. As production costs increased, prices did too. So Lustgarten could neither confirm nor reject the theory that 1954-58 was a period of profit-push inflation. For the years 1958-63, however, there was no relationship between concentration and price changes. The theory of administered prices, in other words, remained unproven.

A study of concentration and profits was done by Dr. Stanley Ornstein, thirty-three, a consultant to the program. He examined the traditional hypothesis that, as concentration increases, the likelihood of collusion or "weak competitive pressures" also increases and leads to higher profits in concentrated industries than in others. Not so, says Ornstein. Because stock-market prices represent the discounted value of expected future earnings, Ornstein used stock-market values to represent profitability over the long run. To eliminate false correlations, he also examined individual profit rates of the largest corporations in each industry, 131 companies in all, and subjected them to multiple regression analysis, a mathematical technique that is used to determine the relative influences of several variables.

"From 1947 through 1960," Ornstein observes, "the return on equity dropped from around 15 percent to 8 or 9 percent and in a continuous trend. Long-term fluctuations like this shouldn't occur if there is collusion or administered bias." Like Brozen, Ornstein finds no connection between high profits and concentration. On the contrary, he finds there is vigorous competition among so-called oligopolists. His conclusion, made after much analysis, was somewhat more cautious: "This study does not disprove the traditional hypothesis [that oligopoly is characterized by high profitability], any more than previous studies proved it. It does show, however, that prior conclusions have gone far beyond those warranted by economic theory."

REMEMBER THE NEW YORK YANKEES

One of the U.C.L.A. program's most distinguished participants is Professor Harold Demsetz, forty-one, on leave from the University of Chicago, where he taught for eight years. Demsetz' interests at present lie mainly in identifying the true sources of corporate efficiency. He maintains that when there is no real barrier to the entry of new competitors, concentration is not an index of monopoly power. Therefore, if a concentrated industry has a high rate of return, monopoly power is not the cause of it. Concentration results from the operation of normal market forces and from a company's ability to produce a better or cheaper product or both and to market it efficiently. Some companies are downright lucky, and some outperform others, while some are both lucky and superior performers.

Confirming Demsetz' belief, Professor Michael Granfield, twenty-eight, has tentatively concluded that differences in efficiency may account for most differences in profit levels and that high profits do not necessarily imply high prices but often quite the opposite—high volume and low prices. One way he accounts for efficiency is by what he calls Team Theory. "The old saw holds that the team outperforms its individual members; it may be right," says Granfield. "Although other companies are constantly hiring executives away from I.B.M., these companies never seem to do as well as I.B.M."

"Many managerial economies are not always evident," Ornstein adds. "The only way to get them is to get the whole team. The New York Yankees were a winning team for years; the technical skills responsible for their record accounted for only about 10 to 20 percent of the answer. What is really involved is managerial skills, and they can't be duplicated. To some extent a successful management is synergistic. By this I mean that there seem to be managerial economies of scale just as there are multi-plant economies of scale. If so, the argument that you can break up big business and not hurt the consumer is wrong."

It may not be long before the program staff develops a formal theory about what really makes enterprises excel and why the country is better off handling them with a certain amount of care instead of busting them up like freight trains in a classification yard, or subjecting them to permanent price controls.

STORED IN THE MINDS OF MILLIONS

The theory of administered prices, however, is not yet done for. Its new critics will doubtless find the going slow. Before their credo can hope to gain "popular" acceptance, it must first achieve standing in professional economic journals. And it has, for the moment, absolutely no political appeal. Thanks in large part to Ralph Nader, the big corporation is the whipping boy of the day. Indeed, George Stigler glumly predicts that the controversy will continue for another generation or more. "Administered-price theory," he says, "is like the Sacco-Vanzetti case. Whatever the jury's verdict, the defendants' innocence is stored in the minds of millions. So is the 'guilt' of administered prices and the businessmen who practice them."

The administered-price theorists are not resting on their oars, either. Gardiner Means, who started it all nearly forty years ago, now argues that the recent combination of inflation and recession can be explained *only* by his administered-price thesis. In the June, 1972, issue of the *American Economic Review*, he defines his theory and then tears into the Stigler-Kindahl book, which he says misrepresents his position.

What may be more important in its effect on public opinion, John Blair, he of the Kefauver committee, is publishing a monumental 832-page volume entitled *Economic Concentration—Structure, Behavior and Public Policy*. This opus contains something from almost everybody who has written about concentration and is complete with dozens of charts, as well as an introduction by Means. The fruit of more than thirty years of fighting big business, the work is larded with quotations and chuck-full of footnotes. Blair's mind is made up, and his book is passionately partisan; but that will probably not prevent it from being given glowing reviews in the popular press.

For all this, there seems no doubt that the case against the theory of administered prices will grow stronger. Groups like Weston's are being organized elsewhere. The University of Rochester, for example, has set up the Center for Research in Government Policy and Business in its Graduate School of Management and is looking around for private donations.

No matter what such groups find, it will be salutary. For the controversy about administered prices proves, among other things, how little Americans know about the inner workings of the big corporation, the country's most characteristic institution. And if present trends in research are any indication, the more that can be learned, the stronger will be the case for revising wrong notions about corporate behavior.

26

Techniques for Pricing New Products and Services

Joel Dean

Determining the price level of a new product or service is one of the most important and most difficult marketing problems faced by a manager. Although such pricing decisions are more of an art than a science and require experienced judgment, making them can be facilitated by the concepts and procedures suggested in this article.

Pricing a new product or service is one of the most important and puzzling of marketing problems. The high proportion of new products which fail in the marketplace is partly due to the difficulty of pricing them correctly.

A *new* product (or service)[1] is here defined as one which incorporates a major innovation. It is new to the world, not just new to the company. This means that its market is, at the outset, ill defined. Potential applications cannot be foreseen with precision. Pricing decisions usually have to be made with little knowledge and with wide margins of error in the forecasts of demand, cost, and competitors' capabilities.

This section deals with the price level, not the price structure; e.g., the average price per ton-mile of air freight, not the structure of price differentials by size of shipment, density, distance, etc.

The difficulty of pricing new products is enhanced by the dynamic deterioration of the competitive status of most new products, which is speeded by today's high rate of innovation. This makes the evolution of a new product's economic status a strategic consideration in practical pricing.

[1]Hereafter, the term "new product" will encompass new services as well.

DYNAMIC COMPETITIVE SETTING

A product which is new to the world, as opposed to being merely new to the company, passes through distinctive competitive stages in its life cycle. The appropriate pricing policy is likely to be different for each stage.

New products have a protected distinctiveness which is doomed to progressive degeneration from competitive inroads. As new competitors enter the field and innovations narrow the gap of distinctiveness between the product and its substitutes, the seller's zone of pricing discretion narrows. His distinctive "specialty" fades into a pedestrian "commodity" which is so little differentiated from other products that the seller has limited independence in pricing, even if rivals are few.

Throughout the cycle, continual changes occur in promotional and price elasticity and in costs of production and distribution. These changes call for adjustments in price policy.

Appropriate pricing over the cycle depends on the development of three different aspects of maturity which usually move in approximately parallel time paths: (1) *technical maturity,* indicated by declining rate of product development, increasing uniformity of competing brands, and increasing stability of manufacturing processes and knowledge about

Reprinted from *Handbook of Modern Marketing* by Victor P. Buell and Carl Heyel (eds.), pp. 5-51–5-61. At the time of writing, Joel Dean was president, Joel Dean Associates, Inc.

them; (2) *market maturity,* indicated by consumer acceptance of the basic service idea, by widespread belief that the products of most manufacturers will perform satisfactorily, and brands competently; and (3) *competitive maturity,* indicated by increasing stability of market shares and price structures.

The rate at which the cycle of degeneration progresses varies widely among products. What are the factors that set its pace? An overriding determinant is technical—the extent to which the economic environment must be reorganized to use the innovation effectively. The scale of plant investment and technical reaction called forth by the telephone, electric power, the automobile, or the jet airplane makes for a long gestation period as compared with even such major innovations as cellophane or frozen foods. Development comes fastest when the new gadget fills a new vacuum.

Monopoly Pricing

New product pricing, if the product is truly novel, is in essence monopoly pricing. Stark monopoly pricing, which is the core of new product pricing, considers only what the traffic will bear—the price which will maximize profits, taking into account the price sensitivity of demand and the incremental promotional and production cost of the seller. What the product is worth to the buyer, not what it costs the seller, is the controlling consideration.

The competitive setting of the new product has, however, peculiar features that modify monopoly pricing. The monopoly power of the new product is (1) restricted (i.e., buyers have alternatives in the form of products that compete indirectly), (2) ephemeral (i.e., subject to inevitable erosion by imitation and obsolescence), and (3) controllable (i.e., capable of some degree of expansion and prolongation by actions of the seller).

For example, Quanta Welding's new diffusion bonding system, based on a millisecond-shaped power pulse, is a patented monopoly. But its pricing power is restricted by alternatives. For supersonic aircraft, these are resistance-welding or riveting, which are candidate pricing benchmarks. The market power of Quanta's superior metals-joining process will be eventually eroded. Solid-state devices may make obsolete the mercury vapor tube that supplies the controllable massive pulses of electrical energy on which the process depends. Penetration pricing might discourage this competitive entry.

These peculiarities of the new-product monopoly introduce dynamism and uncertainty which call for dynamic modifications of monopoly pricing. Examples include:

1 Substitute ways to get the service. These set limits on the market power of a new product and hence serve as benchmarks for pricing it.

2 The perishability of the new product's wanted distinctiveness. This makes the timing of price, promotion, and capacity competition crucial (e.g., choice between skimming and penetration pricing).

3 The ability of influence the amount and the durability of the new products market power in some degree by specially planned pricing and promotion actions. This gives added weight to the effect of today's pricing upon tomorrows demand.

DEMAND SENSITIVITY OF VOLUME TO PRICE

Profitable monopoly pricing of a new product, even with these dynamic competitive modifications, requires an estimate of how price will affect sales. This relationship can be explored in two steps, by (1) finding what range of price will make the product economically attractive to buyers, and (2) estimating what sales volumes can be expected at various points in this price range.

Price Range

The price range is determined by the indirect competition of substitutes which set limits to the monopoly power of the new product. In this sense, no product is really new; the most novel product merely plugs an abnormally large gap in the chain of substitutes. This gap makes out the potential range of its price.

For industrial products, a relatively quick and cheap way to find this range is to "pick the brains" of professionals experienced in looking at comparative product performance in terms of buyers' costs and requirements—for example, distributors, prime contractors, and consulting engineers, as well as purchasing analysts and engineers of prospect companies.

For consumers' goods, different methods are needed. In guessing the price range of a radically novel product of small unit value, the concept of barter equivalent can be useful. For example, a manufacturer of paper specialites tested a dramatic new product this way: A wide variety of consumer products totally unlike the new product were purchased and spread out on a big table. Consumers selected the products they would swap for the new product.

Price-Volume Relationship

The effect of the price of the new product upon its volume of sales is the most important and most difficult estimate in pricing. We know in general that the lower the price, the greater the volume of sales and the faster its rate of growth. The air-freight growth rate is about 18 per cent; priced higher, it will grow more slowly. But to know the precise position and shape of the price-quantity demand schedule or how much faster sales will grow if the price is 20 per cent lower is not possible. But we must estimate.

The best way to predict the effect of price on sales volume for a new product is by controlled experiments: offering it at several different prices in comparable test markets under realistic sales conditions. For example, frozen orange juice was thus tested at three prices. When test marketing is not feasible, another method is to broaden the study of the cost of buyers' alternatives and include forecasts of the sales volume of substitutes (and other indications of the volume to customers of different categories). This approach is most promising for industrial customers, because performance comparisons are more explicit and measurable and economics more completely controls purchases. When buyers' alternatives differ widely in service value, the difficulty of translating this disparity into superiority premiums adds to the imprecision of this method of estimating price-volume relationships.

PRICING BENCHMARKS

The buyers' viewpoint should be controlling in pricing. For every new product there are alternatives. Buyers' best alternatives are usually products already tested in the marketplace. The new product will, presumably, supply a superior solution to the problem of some categories of buyers. The superiority differential over existing products differ widely among new products. The degree of superiority of any one new product over its substitutes usually also differs widely as viewed by different buyers.

Buyers' Alternatives

The prospective buyer of any new product does have alternatives. These indirectly competitive products are the benchmark for his appraisal of the price-performance package of a new product. This comparison with existing products determines its relative attractiveness to potential buyers. Such an analysis of demand can be made in the following steps:

1 Determine the major uses for the new

product. For each application, determine the product's performance characteristics.

2 For each important usage area, specify the products that are the buyer's best alternative to the new product. Determine the performance characteristics and requirements which buyers view as crucial in determining their product selection.

3 For each major use, determine how well the product's performance characteristics meet the requirements of customers compared with the performance of these buyers' alternative products.

4 Forecast the prices of alternative products in terms of transaction prices adjusted for the impact of the new product and translated into units of use. Estimate from the prices of these benchmark substitutes the alternative costs to the buyer per unit of the new product. Real transactions prices (after all discounts), rather than list prices, should be the benchmark in order to reflect marketplace realities. Prices should be predicted, after the introduction of the new product, so as to reflect probable competitive adaptation to the new product. Where eventual displacement of existing substitutes appears likely, short-run incremental cost supplies a Jeremiah forecast of defender's pricing retaliation.

5 Estimate the superiority premium; i.e., price the performance differential in terms of what the superior solution supplied by the new product is worth to buyers of various categories.

6 Figure a "parity price" for the product relative to the buyer's best alternative product in each use, and do this for major categories of customers. Parity is a price which encompasses the premium a customer would be willing to pay for comparative superiority in performance characteristics.

Pricing the Superiority Differential

Determining this price premium over benchmark products which the new product's superiority will most profitably warrant is the most intricate and challenging problem of new-product pricing.

The value to the customer of the innovational superiority of the new product is surrounded by uncertainties: whether the product will work, whether it will attain its designed superiorities, what its reliability and durability performance will be, and how soon it in turn will become obsolete. These uncertainties influence the price a customer would pay and the promotional outlay that would be required to persuade him to buy. Thus, customers' uncertainties will cost the seller something, either in price or promotion.

In essence, the superiority premium requires translation of differential performance characteristics into dollars, based on value analysis from the buyer's viewpoint. The premium will differ among uses, among alternative products, and among categories of customers. For some, it will be negative. Unless it proves practical to segment the market by application and to have widely discriminatory prices, the new product is likely to be priced out of some markets.

A simplistic, single-point premium reflecting "what the product can command in the marketplace" will not do. The customer-response pattern that is needed is the relationship between (1) a series of prospective superiority premiums and (2) the corresponding potential volumes.

What matters is superiority as *buyers* value it, not superiority as calibrated by technicians' measurements or the sellers' costs. This means that more and better promotion can raise the premium-volume schedule and make a higher superiority premium achieve the same sales volume or rate of sales growth as would a lower premium without the promotion. This premium-volume schedule will be kicked about by retaliatory pricing of displaceable substitutes as well as by the imitative and innovative new-product competition of rivals.

The optimizing premium—i.e., the price that would maximize profits in any specified time period—will depend upon future costs as well as upon the hazy and dynamic demand schedule. It will be hard to find. Uncertainty about the future thus makes the appropriate pricing strategy for the long run a matter of sophisticated judgment.

RATE-OF-RETURN PRICING

Application of the principles of economic pricing is illustrated by rate-of-return pricing of new capital equipment. Industrial goods are sold to businessmen in their capacity as profit-makers. The technique is different for a producer's good (e.g., a truck) than for a consumer's good (e.g., a sports car).

The difference is caused by the fact that the essential service purchased if a product is a producer's good is added profits. A product represents an investment by the customer. The test of whether or not this investment is a desirable one should be its profitability to the customer. The pricing guide that this suggests is rate of return on the capital a customer ties up by his investment in a product.

Rate of Return on Customer's Investment

Rate-of-return pricing looks at a price through the investment eyes of the customer. It recognizes that the upper limit is the price which will produce the minimum acceptable rate of return on the customer's investment. The added profits obtainable from the use of equipment differ among customers and among applications for the same customer.

Cutoff criteria of required return also differ, so prospective customers differ in the rate of return which will induce them to invest in a given product. Thus, the rate-of-return approach opens up a new kind of demand analysis for industrial goods. This analysis consists of inquiry into (a) the costs to buyers from displaceable alternative ways to do the job; (b) the cost-saving and profit-producing capability of equipment in different applications and for different prospects; and (c) the capital budgeting policies of customers, with particular emphasis on their cost-of-capital and their minimum rate-of-return requirements.

The rate-of-return-analysis just outlined is particularly useful in the pioneering stages of new products when the competition consists of only obsolescent ways of doing the job. At more mature stages in the life cycle of a new product, competitive imitation improves prospective customers' alternatives. These rival investment alternatives must then be taken explicitly into the analysis.

One way is to use a competitor's product as the benchmark in measuring the rate of return which a given product will produce for specified categories of prospects. The profitability from the product is measured in terms of its superiority over the best alternative new equipment offered by rivals rather than by its superiority over the customer's old equipment. Rate-of-return pricing translates this competitive superiority into dollars of added profit for the customer and relates this added profit to the added investment. In effect, one would say: "To be sure, buying my competitor's product will give you a 25 per cent rate of return, and that is better than keeping your old equipment but buying *my* product will give you a 30 per cent rate of return." For each customer category, rate-of-return analysis reveals a price for a given product that makes it an irresistibly good investment to the customer in view of his alternatives and at the same time extracts from the customer all that can safely be demanded.

Investigation of (1) the productivity of the buyers' capital invested in your new product and (2) the required rate of return of prospective customers has proven a practical way to predict the demand for industrial goods. It must be coupled with forecasts of costs to find the immediately most profitable price, and with considerations of competitive strategy for the longer run.

THE ROLE OF COST

To get maximum practical use from costs in new product pricing, three questions of theory must be answered: (1) Whose cost? (2) Which cost? and (3) What role? As to whose cost, three classes of costs are important: (1) those of prospective buyers, (2) those of existent and potential competitors, and (3) those of the producer of the new product. Cost should play a different role for each of the three, and the pertinent concept of cost will differ accordingly.

Buyers' Cost

How should costs of prospective customers be used in setting the price of a new product? By applying value analysis to prices and performance of alternative products to find the superiority premium that will make the new product attractive from an economic standpoint to buyers of specified categories. Rate-of-return pricing of capital goods illustrates this buyer's cost-approach, which is applicable in principle to all new products.

Competitors' Costs

Competitors' costs are usually the crucial estimate in appraisal of competitors' capabilities.

Costs of two kinds of competitive products can be helpful. The first kind are products already in the marketplace. The objectives are to estimate (1) their staying power and (2) the floor of retaliation pricing. For the first objective, the pertinent cost concept is the competitor's long-run incremental cost. For the second, his short-run incremental cost.

The second kind is the unborn competing product that could blight a new product's future or eventually displace it. Forecasts of competitors' costs for such products can help assess their crucial dimension of capability of prospective competitors and estimate the effectiveness of a strategy of pricing the new product so as to discourage entry. For this purpose, the cost behavior to forecast is the relationship between unit production cost and plant size as the new producer and his rivals move from pilot plant to small-scale test production plant to large-scale mass production. The cost forecasts should take into account technological progress and should be spotted on a time scale that reflects the potential head-start cost advantages that could be attained under a policy of penetration pricing and under skimming pricing.

Estimates of cost of unborn competitive products are necessarily rough, but evaluation of major differences between competitors' costs and the new producer's costs can nevertheless be useful. Thus cost estimates can help forecast a defending product's retaliation pricing and an invading product's conquest pricing.

Producer's Costs

The cost of the producer plays several roles in pricing a new product. The first is birth control. A new product must be prepriced provisionally early in the R&D stage and then again periodically as it progresses toward market. Forecasts of production and promotional costs at matching stages should play the role of forecasting its economic feasibility in determining whether to continue product development and ultimately to commercialize. The concept of cost relevant for this birth-control role is a prediction of full cost at a series of prospective volumes and corresponding technologies, and encompassing imputed cost of capital on intangible as well as tangible investment.

A second role is to establish a price floor which is also the threshold for selecting from candidate prices that which will maximize return on a new product investment over the long run.

For both jobs, the relevant concept is future

costs, forecast over a range of volume, production technologies, and promotional outlays in the marketing plan.

Two categories of cost require separate forecasts and have quite different impacts on new-product pricing: (1) Production costs (including physical distribution), and (2) Persuasion costs, which are discretionary and rivalrous with price.

The production costs that matter are the future costs over the long-run that will be added by making this product on the predicted scale (or scales) versus not making it. The added investment necessary to manufacture and distribute the new product should be estimated. Investment should include intangibles such as R&D, promotion, and launching outlays as well as increased working capital. Then the added costs of manufacturing and selling the product at various possible sales volumes should be estimated. It is important to calculate total costs (rather than unit costs) with and without the new product. The difference can then be assigned to the new product. Present overhead that will be the same whether or not the addition to the product line is adopted should be ignored. Future additions to overhead caused by the new product are alone relevant in pricing it. Two sets of cost and investment figures must be built up—one showing the situation *without* the new product and the other showing the situation *with* the new product added to the line, and at several possible volumes. High costs of pilot-plant production and of early small-scale production plants should be viewed as intangible capital investment rather than as the current operating costs. The losses of a break-in period are part of the investment on which a satisfactory return should be made.

Long-run future incremental costs, including costs of equity capital (i.e., satisfactory return on the added investment), supply the base line above which contribution profits of a new product should be maximized—not an impenetrable floor, but a calculation benchmark for optimization.

STRATEGY CHOICES

A major strategy decision in pricing a new product is the choice between (1) skimming pricing and (2) penetration pricing. There are intermediate positions, but the issues are made clearer by comparing the two extremes.

Skimming Pricing

Some products represent drastic improvements upon accepted ways of performing a service or filling a demand. For these products a strategy of high prices with large promotional expenditure in the early stages of market development (and lower prices at later stages) has frequently proved successful. This can be termed a "skimming-price" policy. There are four main reasons for its success:

1 Sales of the product are likely to be less sensitive to price in the early stages than when the product is "full-grown" and competitive imitations have appeared. In the early stages, the product usually has so few close rivals that cross elasticity of demand is low. Promotional sensitivity is, on the other hand, quite high, particularly for products with high unit prices, since it is difficult for the customer to value the service of the product.

2 Launching a new product with a high price is an efficient device for breaking the market up into segments that differ in price elasticity of demand. The initial high price serves to skim the cream of the market that is relatively insensitive to price. Subsequent price reductions tap successively more elastic sectors of the market. This pricing strategy is exemplified by the systematic succession of editions of a book, sometimes starting with a $50 limited personal edition and ending up with a 75-cent paperback book.

3 A skimming policy is safer, or at least it

appears so. Facing an unknown elasticity of demand, a high initial price serves as a "refusal" price during the stage of exploration. How much costs can be reduced as the market expands and as the design of the product is improved by increasing production efficiency with new techniques is difficult to predict.

4 High prices frequently produce a greater dollar volume of sales in the early stages of market development than are produced by low initial prices. When this is the case, skimming pricing will provide funds to finance expansion into the larger volume sectors of a given market.

Penetration Pricing

Despite its many advantages, a skimming-price policy is not appropriate for all new product problems. Although high initial prices may maximize profits during the early stages of product introduction, they may also prevent sales to many of the buyers upon whom you must rely for a mass market. The alternative is to use low prices as an entering wedge to get into mass markets early. This may be termed penetration pricing. Such an approach is likely to be desirable under any of these conditions:

First, when sales volume of the product is very sensitive to price, even in the early stages of introduction.

Second, when it is possible to achieve substantial economies in unit cost of manufacturing and distributing the product by operating at large volume.

Third, when a product faces threats of strong potential competition very soon after introduction.

Fourth, when there is no "elite" market—that is, no class of buyers willing to pay a higher price to obtain the newest and the best.

While a penetration pricing policy can be adopted at any stage in the product's life cycle, this pricing strategy should always be examined before a new product is marketed at all. Its possibility should be explored again as soon as the product has established an elite market. Sometimes a product can be rescued from premature death by adoption of a penetration price after the cream of the market has been skimmed.

One important consideration in the choice between skimming and penetration pricing at the time a new product is introduced is the ease and speed with which competitors can bring out substitute products. If you decide to set your initial price low enough, your large competitor may not feel it worthwhile to make a big investment for slim profit margins. The speed with which your product loses its uniqueness and sinks from its sheltered status to the level of just another competitive product depends on several factors:

1 Its total sales potential. A big potential market entices competitive imitation.

2 The investment required for rivals to manufacture and distribute the product. A big investment barrier deters invasion.

3 The strength of patent and know-how protection.

4 The alertness and power of competitors.

Although competitive imitation is almost inevitable, the company that introduces a new product can use price to discourage or delay the introduction of competitive products. Keep-out prices can be achieved quickly by penetration pricing.

Pricing in Maturity

To price appropriately for later stages in the cycle of competitive maturity, it is important to be able to tell when a product is approaching maturity. When the new product is about to slip into the commodity category, it is sometimes desirable to reduce real prices promptly as soon as symptoms of deterioration appear. Some of the symptoms of degeneration of competitive status toward the commodity level are:

1 Weakening in brand preference. This may be evidenced by a higher cross elasticity of demand among leading products, the leading brand not being able to continue demanding as much price premium as initially without losing position.

2 Narrowing physical variation among products as the best designs are developed and standardized. This has been dramatically demonstrated in automobiles and is still in process in television receivers.

3 The entry in force of private-label competitors. This is exemplified by the mail-order houses' sale of own-label refrigerators and paint sprayers.

4 Market saturation. The ratio of replacement sales to new-equipment sales serves as an indicator of the competitive degeneration of durable goods, but in general it must be kept in mind that both market size and degree of saturation are hard to define (e.g., saturation of the radio market, which was initially thought to be one radio per home and later had to be expanded to one radio per room).

5 The stabilization of production methods, indicated by slow rate of technological advance, high average age of equipment, and great uniformity among competitors' introduction technology.

PROMOTION AND DISTRIBUTION

Promotion

Closely related to pricing is promotional strategy. An innovator must not only sell his product, but frequently he must also make people recognize their need for a new *kind* of product. The problem is one of "creating a market."

Initial promotion outlays are an investment in the product that cannot be recovered until some kind of market has been established. The innovator shoulders the burden of educating consumers to the existence and uses of the product. Later imitators will never have to do this job; so if the innovator does not want to be simply a benefactor to his future competitors, he must make pricing plans to earn a return on all his initial outlays before his pricing discretion evaporates.

The basic strategic problem is to find the right mixture of price and promotion to maximize long run profits. A relatively high price may be chosen in pioneering stages, together with large advertising and dealer discounts, and the plan may be to get the promotion investment back early; or low prices and lean margins may be used from the very outset in order to discourage potential competition when the barriers of patents and investment in production capacity distribution channels, or production techniques become inadequate.

Channels of Distribution

Choice of channels of distribution should be consistent with strategy for initial pricing and for promotional outlays. Penetration pricing and explosive promotion call for distribution channels that promptly make the product broadly available. Otherwise advertising is wasted or mass-market pricing stymied. Distribution policy also concerns the role of the dealer is to play in pushing a given product, the margins he must be paid to induce this action, and the amount of protection of territory and of inventory required to do so.

Estimation of the costs of moving the new product through the channels of distribution to the final consumer must enter into the pricing procedure, since these costs govern the factory price that will result in a specified final price. Distributive margins are partly pure promotional costs and partly physical distribution costs. Margins must at least cover the distributors' costs of warehousing, handling, and order taking. These costs are similar to factory production costs in being related to physical capacity and its utilization; i.e., fluctuations in production or sales volume. Hence these set a floor to trade-channel discounts. But distributors usually also contribute promotional effort—in point-of-sale pushing, local advertising, and display—when it is made worth their while. These pure promotional costs are more optional.

Distributors' margins are best determined by study of distributors' alternatives. This does not mean that the distributor gross margin on a given product must be the same as that of rival products. It should instead produce a competitive rate of return on the distributors' investment (in inventory, shelf space and sales capacity).

SUMMARY

Pricing new products is an art. The important determinants in economic pricing of pioneering innovations are complex, interrelated, and hard to forecast. Experienced judgment is required in pricing and repricing the product to fit its changing competitive environment. This judgment may possible be improved by some pricing precepts suggested by the preceding analysis:

1 Corporate goals must be clearly defined. Pricing a new product is an occasion for rethinking them. This chapter has assumed that the overriding corporate goal is long-run profit maximization: e.g., making the stock worth the most by maximizing the present worth, at the corporation's cost of capital, of its per share earnings.

2 Pricing a new product should begin long before its birth. Prospective prices, coupled with forecast costs, should play the decisive role in product birth control.

3 Pricing a new product should be a continuing process of bracketing the truth by successive approximations. Rough estimates of the relevant concepts are preferable to precise knowledge of historical irrelevancies.

4 Costs can supply useful guidance in new-product pricing, but not by the conventional wisdom; i.e., cost-plus pricing. Three categories of costs are pertinent: those of the buyer, those of the seller, and those of the seller's rivals. The role of cost differs among the three, as does the concept of cost that is pertinent to that role: different costs for different purposes.

5 The role of cost is to set a reference base for picking the most profitable price. For this job the only costs that are pertinent to pricing a new product on the verge of commercialization (i.e., already developed and tested) are incremental costs; the added costs of going ahead at different plant scales. Costs of R&D and of market testing are now sunk and hence irrelevant.

6 The pricing implications of the changing economic status and competitive environment of a product must be recognized as it passes through its life cycle from birth to obsolescence. This cycle, and the plans that are made to influence it, are of paramount importance for pricing policy.

7 The product should be seen through the eyes of the customer and priced just low enough to make it an irrestible investment in view of his alternatives as he sees them. To estimate successfully how much a given product is worth to the prospect is never easy, but it is usually rewarding.

8 Customers' rate of return should be the main consideration in pricing novel capital goods. Buyers' cost savings (and other earnings) expressed as a return on his investment in the new product are the key to predicting the price sensitivity of demand and to pricing profitably.

9 The strategic choice between skimming and penetration pricing should be based on economics. The skimming policy—i.e., relatively high prices in the pioneering stage, cascading downward thereafter—is particularly appropriate for products whose sales initially are comparatively unresponsive to price but quite responsive to education. A policy of penetration pricing—i.e., relatively low prices in the pioneering stage in anticipation of the cost savings resulting from an expanding market—is best when scale economies are big, demand is price sensitive, and invasion is threatened. Low starting prices sacrifice short-run profits for long-run profits and discourage potential competitors.

SELECTED BIBLIOGRAPHY

Dean, Joel, *Managerial Economics,* Prentice-Hall, Englewood Cliffs, N.J., 1951 (especially pp. 419–424).

Harper, Donald, *Price Policy and Procedure,* Harcourt, Brace & World, New York, 1966.

Mulvihill, D. F., and S. Paranka, *Price Policies and Practices: A Source Book in Readings,* Wiley, New York, 1967.

Thompson, G. Clark, and M. M. MacDonald, "Pricing New Products," *Conference Board Record,* National Industrial Converence Board, New York, 1964.

27

A Decision-making Structure for Price Decisions

Alfred R. Oxenfeldt

Pricing practice remains largely intuitive and routine. To see why, the author examines critically some of the trends and gaps in the pricing literature and in pricing practice. A comprehensive and systematic guide to successful price setting is offered.

Until recently, almost all pricing decisions have either been highly intuitive, as in the case of new product introductions, or based on routine procedures, as in cost-plus or imitative pricing. The proportion of price decisions representing these extreme approaches seems to have declined substantially; yet, many business executives have not altered their pricing methods substantially.[1]

Research continues on how businesses should set prices. Most of these studies attempt to uncover the best methods rather than those in current practice. No researcher has completely overcome the enormous difficulties of learning the basis on which group decisions are made and the "sensitive" reasons underlying many price decisions.[2] This article examines some trends in pricing and the apparent gulf between pricing theory and practice. A pricing framework is presented to aid practitioners to structure their important pricing decisions.

[1]Professor F. E. Gillis writes in 1969, "Joel Dean opines that cost-plus pricing is the most common technique in the United States. The statement is too weak; it is almost universal." See his *Managerial Economics* (Reading, Mass.: Addison-Wesley, 1969), p. 254.

[2]A. A. Fitzpatrick, *Pricing Methods of Industry* (Boulder, Colo: Pruett Press, Inc., 1964); *Decision Making in Marketing—A Description of Decision Making Processes and Its Application to Pricing,* 1971, Report No. 525, National Industrial Conference Board; Kaplan, Dirlam and Lanzilotti, *Pricing in Big Business* (Washington, D.C.: The Brookings Institution, 1958); B. Fog, *Industrial Pricing Policies* (Amsterdam, Holland: North Holland Publishing Co., 1960); W. W. Haynes, *Pricing Decisions in Small Business* (Lexington, Ky.: University of Kentucky Press, 1962); and J. Fred Weston has been reported as directing a major study of this subject. See "The Myths and Realities of Corporate Pricing," *Fortune,* Vol. LXXXV (April, 1972), p. 85.

Reprinted from *Journal of Marketing,* vol. 37, pp. 48–53, American Marketing Association, January 1973. At the time of writing, the author was professor of business, Graduate School of Business, Columbia University.

THE GAP BETWEEN PRICING THEORY AND APPLICATION

The current pricing literature has produced few new insights or exciting new approaches that would interest most businessmen enough to change their present methods. Those executives who follow the business literature have no doubt broadened their viewpoint and become more explicit and systematic about their pricing decisions; however, few, if any, actually employ new and different goals, concepts, or techniques.

The gap between pricing literature and practice may exist because the authors lack extensive personal experience with the practical problems facing executives in a highly competitive and complex business environment. Other explanatory factors include: the number of products for which executives are responsible, the lack of reliable information on product demand, the dynamic nature of technology, and the unpredictable responses from competitors. Because of the large number of highly uncertain and variable factors, executives responsible for pricing closely adhere to methods that they have found to be effective in the past. Economists and practitioners have long recognized that price is a dangerously explosive and complex marketing variable.

This discussion does not suggest that those responsible for pricing should always adhere to traditional methods of setting price, or that those writing about pricing have contributed little of value. The point is that a significant gap exists between the two areas and that this gap must be closed if pricing is to continue to develop as a crucially important area of marketing theory and practice. Pricing specialists have suggested many helpful methods that have not been implemented in practice even after they have been demonstrated to be valid.

LITERATURE TRENDS: A CRITIQUE

The field of pricing remains largely the domain of economic theorists who discuss price primarily in relation to the analyses of specific market structures.

Much of the pricing literature deals with tactics and strategems for particular kinds of firms—wholesalers, manufacturers, franchisees, or joblot shops. Special corporate situations such as new product introductions, inflation, declining products, product-line pricing, price-structure problems, and price-cutting are also popular topics in the pricing literature.[3] The current literature on pricing, like that in most other areas of marketing, draws heavily on the behavioral sciences, quantitative tools, and detailed empirical research. Present-day writers employ simulation techniques and other computer applications much more than in the past, and are often concerned with cost computation and demand estimation. Pricing receives far more attention from marketing specialists today than it did when managerial economists such as Joel Dean, Jules Bachman, Arthur R. Burns, Donald Wallace, Edward Mason, Edwin Nourse, Walton Hamilton, Walter Adams, and Morris A. Adelman were the chief contributors to the field.

Recently, pricing specialists have channeled

[3]The best of these writings are to be found in several collections of articles and talks about pricing. These are: Elizabeth Marting, ed., *Creative Pricing* (New York: American Marketing Association, 1968); Almarin Phillips and O. E. Williamson, eds., *Prices: Issues in Theory, Practice and Public Policy* (Philadelphia: University of Pennsylvania Press, 1967); D. F. Mulvihill and S. Paranka, eds., *Price Policies and Practices: A Source Book of Readings* (New York: John Wiley, 1967); American Management Association, Management Report No. 17, *Competitive Pricing: Policies, Practices and Legal Considerations*, 1958; American Management Association, Management Report No. 66, *Pricing: The Critical Decision*, 1961; Donald Watson, ed., *Price Theory in Action: A Book of Readings* (Boston: Houghton Mifflin, 1965); and B. Taylor and G. Wills, eds., *Pricing Strategy* (London, 1969).

much of their research efforts into the development of approaches designed to aid the accuracy and efficiency of the decision maker. The most promising methods are: use of the computer;[4] simulation as a method for anticipating the effect of price changes on sales and for testing complex strategies;[5] research techniques for obtaining more reliable information about prospective customer responses to price change;[6] and the nature and determinants of price perception.[7]

Nevertheless, large gaps still remain in the pricing literature. Very little is said about reconciling the various price-optima; i.e., the prices that are best vis-à-vis costs, the ultimate customer, resellers, and rivals. Most authors deal with pricing problems unidimensionally, whereas businessmen must generally deal with price as one element in a multidimensional marketing program. Price is often dealt with as if it were completely separated from the other elements in the marketing mix. These authors tend to concentrate on the effect of price on immediate marketwide sales without adequately considering long-run or individual market effects. The writers dealing with pricing decisions typically identify variables that are sometimes not considered and suggest conceptual errors that are commonly made, but they typically treat only small, isolated parts of the problem faced by a business executive. Little has been written on innovative approaches to pricing—approaches designed to *increase* demand, rather than *adapt to existing* demand. This failing has been most common in writings that employ quantitative techniques. A price-setter must not merely view his responsibility as that of determining the various demand elasticities (price, promotion, assortment, quality, design, and place) and finding the price that best adapts to them. Attention must be given to measures that alter these elasticities in his firm's favor.

The setting of any price involves: (1) values that particular segments of customers place on a firm's offering; (2) consumer responses to price changes of the product; (3) competitive responses to any price changes; and (4) resellers' sensitivity to price changes. No one has yet developed a completely reliable method to measure the price elasticity of demand for a particular brand. Similarly, little is known about resellers' responses to margin changes or the sales support a brand will receive from distributors and retailers. The specific responses of competitors to both price and nonprice actions is still a matter of great uncertainty in almost all industries.

Pricing should be regarded as a field where the essential elements are quite clear and well known and where the concepts that need to be applied also are widely recognized and within reach of all executives. Practitioners face the problem of measuring a multitude of factors in many different specific situations; that is, they must attempt to quantify the response functions (elasticities) so they can be compared. One of the major problems in pricing is obtaining the data required to measure each of

[4]R. E. Good, "Using the Computer in Pricing," in *Creative Pricing*, Elizabeth Marting, ed. (New York: American Marketing Association, 1968), pp. 182–194.

[5]Arnold E. Amstutz, *Computer Simulation of Competitive Market Response* (Cambridge, Mass.: M.I.T. Press, 1967); and D. Kollat, R. Blackwell and J. Robeson, *Strategic Marketing* (New York: Holt, Rinehart and Winston, 1972), Chapter 19.

[6]A. Gabor and C. W. J. Granger, "On the Price Consciousness of Consumers," *Applied Statistics*, Vol. 10 (1961), pp. 170–188; idem, "Price as an Indicator of Quality: Report on an Enquiry," *Economica*, Vol. 33 (1966), pp. 43–70; and idem, "The Pricing of New Products," *Scientific Business*, Vol. 3 (1965), pp. 141–150.

[7]Nystrom, *Retail Pricing: An Integrated Economic and Psychological Approach* (Stockholm: Economic Research Institute of Stockholm School of Economics, 1970), especially Chapters 7 and 8; Brown and Oxenfeldt, *Misperceptions of Economic Phenomena* (New York: Sperr and Douth, 1972).

these response functions in different market contexts. Pricing specialists have made very few contributions to the solution of this problem.

CONSTRAINTS ON PRICING DECISIONS

Many vital price-related decisions made by top management deal with the following issues: Are we willing to drive competitors from business if we can? Should we inflict serious injury upon them when they have been struck by misfortune? Are we willing to violate the spirit or letter of the law to increase sales? At a different level of concern, pricing decisions are related to price strategy and general competitive policy by questions such as: "Should we seek price leadership for ourselves or foster a pattern of price leadership with some other firm as leader? Should we try to shake out the weak firms in the industry to achieve price stability and higher profitability? Should we foster a spirit of cooperativeness among rivals by an avoidance of price competition?"

These decisions are properly made by top executives and do not require a frequent revision. When they are not made explicitly, the executive responsible for pricing decision implicitly makes many of these decisions by default. A complete discussion of these constraints goes beyond the scope of this article.

To manage the complex nature of price-setting, practitioners need an effective, multidimensional model to guide their analysis. Such a pricing model would not only explicitly encourage systemized thinking, but also underscore the differential advantage available to the firm which strategically sets the prices of all of its products.

A FRAMEWORK FOR PRICING DECISIONS

The following discussion of price decisions employs a decision-making framework which identifies the following stages:

1 Recognize the need for a pricing decision.
2 Price determination.
3 Develop a model.
4 Identify and anticipate pricing problems.
5 Develop feasible courses of action.
6 Forecast the outcomes of each alternative.
7 Monitor and review the outcome of each action.

These seven stages overlap somewhat and are not strictly sequential.

Recognize the Need for a Pricing Decision

A firm's pricing difficulties and opportunities are related to its overall objectives. Only when a firm is explicit in defining its corporate objectives can the executive specifically evaluate the obstacles and opportunities confronting him. Table 1 provides a partial list of

Table 1 Potential Pricing Objectives

1. Maximum long-run profits
2. Maximum short-run profits
3. Growth
4. Stabilize market
5. Desensitize customers to price
6. Maintain price-leadership arrangement
7. Discourage entrants
8. Speed exit of marginal firms
9. Avoid government investigation and control
10. Maintain loyalty of middlemen and get their sales support
11. Avoid demands for "more" from suppliers—labor in particular
12. Enhance image of firm and its offerings
13. Be regarded as "fair" by customers (ultimate)
14. Create interest and excitement about the item
15. Be considered trustworthy and reliable by rivals
16. Help in the sale of weak items in the line
17. Discourage others from cutting prices
18. Make a product "visible"
19. "Spoil market" to obtain high price for sale of business
20. Build traffic

feasible pricing objectives. It is important to note that the objectives of profitability and growth constitute only a small part of this list. The pricing objectives of many different firms are listed below; however, *each firm* must evaluate and determine the priority of these objectives as they relate to the individual firm.

From this list of objectives, some of the pricing problems that firms face can readily be inferred. Among the more important are:

1 A decline in sales.

2 Prices are too high—relative to those charged by rivals, relative to the benefits of the product. (Prices might be too high in a few regional markets and very appropriate elsewhere.)

3 Price is too low, again in certain markets and not in others.

4 The company is regarded as exploitative of customers and not to be trusted.

5 The firm places excessive financial burdens on its resellers.

6 The price deferentials among items in the line are objectionable or unintelligible.

7 Its price changes are too frequent—or do not take account of major changes in market circumstances.

8 The firm's price reflects negatively on itself and on its products.

9 The price is unstabilizing the market which had finally become stabilized after great difficulty.

10 The firm is offering its customers too many price choices and confusing its customers and resellers.

11 The firm's prices seem higher to customers than they really are.

12 The firm's price policy attracts undesirable kinds of customers which have no loyalty to any seller.

13 The firm's pricing behavior makes customers unduly price sensitive and unappreciative of quality differences.

14 The company has fostered a decline in market discipline among sellers in the industry.

The list of pricing objectives in Table 1 and the illustrative list of pricing difficulties above suggest that prices and price changes do not simply affect current sales, but have more far-reaching effects.

To identify the problems listed, a firm requires a monitoring system or a means of empirically determining the existence of potential problems and opportunities. Table 2 presents indicators a firm might use to suggest the existence of pricing problems. It is evident that some of these indicators are very difficult to measure with accuracy.

Price Determination

A warning system will detect pricing problems and allow the manager to decide how much attention to give to each potential price problem and to whom to assign it. In assigning a problem for study, a decision-maker must determine whether to use his own staff or call upon outside resources. Some price problems

Table 2 Data That Might Be Used to Design a Price Monitoring System

1. Sales—in units and in dollars
   a. Previous year comparisons
   b. Different markets/channels comparisons
2. Rivals' prices
3. Inquiries from potential customers about the line
4. Company's sales at "off list" price
   a. Measured as a % of total sales
   b. Revenue as % of sales at full price
5. Types of customers getting the most and largest price reductions
6. Market shares—in individual markets
7. Marketing costs; production cost; production costs at nearly output
8. Price complaints
   a. From customers
   b. From salesmen
9. Inventories of finished goods at different levels
10. Customers' attitudes toward firm, prices, etc.
11. Number of lost customers (brand-switching)
12. Inquiries—and subsequent purchases
13. Marketing costs

are self-correcting, in which case the price setter should ignore the warning.

Develop a Model

The primary question that must be addressed here is: What models would help businessmen to best cope with pricing responsibilities? Models developed by economic theorists rarely direct a pricing executive's attention to the key variables. Behavioral science offers far more insight into the factors that determine how price changes will be perceived and reacted to by consumers. The influence of price extends far beyond current sales figures, and behavioral science helps us more fully understand the extensive effect of price decisions.

Some mathematical models deserve a brief mention, even though they are not widely used in practice. The multiple regression model is familiar to most economists and marketing specialists. Based on historical data, this technique determines a linear functional relationship between sales and factors such as price, advertising, personal selling, relative product quality, product design, distribution arrangements, and customer services.

Another technique is the experimental approach to pricing strategy. One type of experimental approach, which may be based on regression analysis, is simulation. Such models allow the pricing specialist to combine wide varieties of inputs (including price) to achieve desired results such as short- and long-run sales together with the costs incurred. The relative merits of different factor combinations can be tested and compared.

A third type of mathematical model emphasizes the situation-specific parameters of a strategy. This approach is referred to as adaptive modeling and combines historical analysis with different environmental situations. A given input mix may have widely divergent results for each situation. This type of approach is particularly helpful in assessing the merits of market expansion, segmentation analysis, and other decisions where contextual analysis is important.

These last two models deal with some fundamental characteristics of price. First, the interdependence and synergy of related model components become key issues in their effective use. Second, the proper mix of variables will differ from occasion to occasion, even for the same product or brand. Third, the outcome of any combination of marketing actions may be perceived differently by different consumers.

To completely understand how and when price works, an executive must understand how potential customers perceive, interpret, and evaluate price changes in making their purchase decisions. These decisions vary with the individual; therefore, an executive must also consider different market segments.

Identify and Anticipate Pricing Problems

When a firm encounters a pricing problem, its manifestations are generally not subtle and obscure; however, executives still have difficulty obtaining information that identifies the source of the problem. Information about customer reactions to a product are extremely difficult to interpret because the responses must be related to their particular market segments. A seller primarily seeks the opinions of those customer segments he wishes to serve, rather than of all perspective customers. Most research data, however, do not match customer responses with the corresponding market segment to which they belong.

Price-setters require an information system to monitor the effects of their pricing arrangements and thus to help make prompt and specific adaptive action in a fast changing market environment. Salesmen's reports, current sales experience, and individual favorite customers are the primary sources of information available to most firms.

Develop Feasible Courses of Action

Traditionally, price setters have considered only a very limited number of alternatives when faced with pricing difficulties. If their price seemed high, they would lower it, and if it was too low, they would simply raise it. Much more complex behaviors are available to most pricers which provide opportunities for novel approaches. In addition to varying the price level, the executive responsible for pricing may also change the following factors: (1) The timing of the price change; (2) the number of price changes (he is not limited to a single change); (3) the time interval to which the price change applies; and (4) the number of items whose price he changes (he could raise some prices while lowering others). In addition, the executive can combine a price change with other marketing actions. For example, he might change the product's package, advertising, quality, appearance, or the after-sale customer service. Even more important, he can change price in some markets and not in others, or change them in different ways. The price-setter may even modify his discount arrangement in such a way as to increase the effectiveness of the price change.

A price-setter must not regard his actions as simply shifting prices on individual product offerings. He must recognize that his firm sells a line of products in a wide variety of geographic markets, and that its offerings embrace many benefits of varying importance to customers. Price is only one of those consumer benefits. A firm rarely makes its very best reaction to a pricing problem or opportunity by simply altering price.

Forecast the Outcome of Each Alternative Action

Once a price-setter has selected the most feasible actions available, he must forecast their consequences to determine which will best achieve his goals. At this stage, the price-setter must be as specific as possible about the expected short- and long-term consequences of his decision.

Successful management of pricing information requires an understanding of the possible consequences of price changes. The more important of these include the effect of price changes on: the customer's ability to buy; the brand image and customers' evaluations of a product's quality; the value of inventories held by resellers; the willingness of resellers to hold inventory; the attitude of ultimate customers and resellers who recently purchased the product at a different price; the company's cash flow; and the need to borrow capital. Price changes can also disrupt or improve market discipline; foster or retard the growth and power of a trade association; instill the trust or suspicion of competitors in the integrity of one's business practices; or increase or reduce the probability of government investigation and criminal prosecution.

The effects of most business actions are extremely difficult to forecast, but an executive must attempt to forecast them. Before selecting an alternative, the executive should consciously consider all possible effects.

If the concept of price elasticity of demand has any value to price-setters, it is in forecasting the effect of price changes. Therefore, the following questions should be asked: Can price elasticity of demand be measured accurately? How much do such measurements cost? How long are such measurements valid? Does price elasticity apply to all geographic markets or only represent an average of all regions? Do elasticity measurements apply equally to all items in a firm's line of products? Is the elasticity of demand the same for all brands of the same product? The emphatic answer is that it is impossible to measure accurately the price elasticity of demand for any brand or product. However, executives responsible for pricing must continue to improve their understanding of the effects of price changes on sales.

Can a measure of demand be developed that is a better indicator than the price elasticity of demand? As implied above, past experience is an unreliable guide to present relationships. Rather than seek a quantitative measure of price elasticity, perhaps a different concept is needed. Businessmen will rarely change price alone, but ordinarily adopt a marketing program coordinated around the proposed price change. A marketing executive wishes to forecast the effects of the total marketing program, rather than the effect of price change alone.

Since most markets are highly dynamic and extremely complex, one cannot expect to develop reliable quantitative measures of the effects of different marketing programs on unit sales. How can a marketing executive forecast the results of alternative price strategies and marketing programs? He must intuitively estimate the effects of the program; however, he will rarely find precisely comparable circumstances in either his own firm's experience or in that of other firms. Specifically, the executive should consider the extent to which his price change will be perceived; the possible interpretations that customers and resellers can attribute to his price change; and the effects of customers' reactions to the price changes.

Select among Alternative Outcomes

When a price-setter forecasts the outcomes of alternative actions, he selects that alternative which best achieves his objectives. As indicated earlier, an executive actually pursues many objectives; therefore, the selection among alternatives is quite difficult in practice, although it is simple in principle. An index should be developed to indicate the extent to which any set of outcomes achieves the executive's multiple goals—weighing each one according to its importance. Various outcomes of each feasible course of action can then be forecast by assigning probabilities to each one. The action selected should represent the alternative that best realizes product, department, and corporate goals, while reflecting an acceptable amount of risk.

SUMMARY

Pricing involves far more than arriving at a dollar and cents figure for a single product. A price-setter is responsible for managing a complex function, even though pricing involves relatively little effort for the implementation of decisions. To manage the pricing function, a firm must develop a detailed hierarchy of objectives; a monitor system; explicit mathematical models; and, most importantly, new approaches to pricing management.

The corporate pricing function within a decision-making structure is a very complex process. Many components must be integrated and managed as a unit if the firm is quickly to capitalize on its pricing opportunities.

28

Functional Spin-off: A Key to Anticipating Change in Distribution Structure

Bruce Mallen

Building on the concepts of marketing functions and divisions of labor, this author develops an approach to help channel designers anticipate changes in distribution structure *before* such changes become obvious trends. He demonstrates that an understanding of how and why producers spin off marketing functions will, in turn, lead to an understanding of change in all dimensions of channel structure.

The purpose of this article is to suggest to anyone interested in understanding distribution channel change an approach whereby the channel designer may anticipate distribution change in his industry, *before* such change has developed into an obvious trend. The channel designer would then be in a position to incorporate this information in planning his distribution strategy and in adapting to his distribution environment.

To successfully complete his task, the channel designer must closely analyze five factors:[1]

1 The selected target markets
2 The rest of his marketing mix: price, product, promotion, physical distribution, etc.
3 His company's resources
4 Competition and other external forces
5 Current and anticipated distribution structures in his industry

Perhaps the most difficult of these factors to analyze is the future changes in distribution structure—those that have not yet developed into obvious trends. Typically, the channel designer must limit himself to reading futuristic type articles on distribution trends[2] and/or to surveying a cross-section of opinions in his industry. The problem with the first information source is that such articles are usually too general to be of direct benefit to the reader and are extrapolations of current obvious trends rather than anticipations of changes which have not yet developed into trends. The problem with an opinion study is that the consensus may be completely wrong—nothing more than the reflection of a common pool of ignorance.

This article does not attempt to provide a comprehensive explanation of distribution structure based on empirical research. Rather

[1]For a detailed description of the selection process, see Bruce Mallen, "Selecting Channels of Distribution for Consumer Products," in *Handbook of Modern Marketing*, Victor P. Buell, ed. (New York: McGraw-Hill, 1970), pp. 4–15 to 4–30.

[2]See, for example, William R. Davidson, "Changes in Distribution Institutions," *Journal of Marketing*, Vol. 34 (January 1970), pp. 7-10; and Philip B. Schary, "Changing Aspects of Channel Structure in America," *British Journal of Marketing*, Vol. 4 (Autumn 1970), pp. 133–147.

Reprinted from *Journal of Marketing*, vol. 37, pp. 18–25, American Marketing Association, July 1973. At the time of writing, the author was chairman of graduate studies, Faculty of Commerce and Administration, Sir George Williams University, Montreal, Canada.

it presents a sequence of relationships which can be used to aid in anticipating change.

THE CONCEPTUAL APPROACH

For approximately 60 years, economic and marketing scholars have recognized the concept of marketing functions and have related them in a more and more exact fashion to the determination of channel structure. Early contributions were made by Butler, Shaw, Weld, Cherington, Clark, Breyer, and Converse. More recently Stigler, Vaile, Grether, Cox, Alderson, and Bucklin have been major contributors to functionalism as it relates to channel structure.[3]

The basic message of all channel functionalists is as follows:

1 Marketing functions are the various types of job tasks which channel members undertake.

2 These functions can be allocated in different mixes to different channel members.

3 The functional mixes will be patterned in a way which provides the greatest profit either to the consumer (in the form of lower prices and/or more convenience) or the channel members with the most power (which depends on market structure).

4 Should one or more channel members (or potential members) see an opportunity to change the functional mix of the channel in order to increase his profits, he will attempt to do so.

5 Should the attempt be successful, and if the functional mix change is big enough, it will (by definition) change the institutional arrangement in the channel, i.e., the channel structure.

Thus, the channel functionalist attempts to answer two basic questions: What is the most efficient functional mix in a given situation, and how will this functional mix affect the channel structure?

There are four dimensions of distribution structure in which change can be anticipated:

1 The number of channel levels

2 The number of channels or whether one, two (dual), or more (multi) channel types will be used

3 The types of middlemen that will evolve

4 The number of middlemen that will develop at each level

Although the goal to attain market power and to manipulate demand is an important consideration in understanding structural change, the drive for efficiency is also of primary importance. The fundamental premise of this paper is that given a specific level of demand, firms will try to maximize profits by designing or selecting a channel which will generate the lowest total average costs for their organizations.

This drive for efficiency and its anticipated effects on the four dimensions of channel structure can be evaluated through the concept of "functional spin-off."

[3]Ralph S. Butler, *Selling and Buying,* Part II, *Advertising, Selling and Credits of Modern Business,* Vol. IX (New York: Alexander Hamilton Institute, 1911), pp. 276–277; Ralph S. Butler, H. F. Debower, and J. G. Jones, *Modern Business,* Vol. III, *Marketing Methods and Salesmanship* (New York: Alexander Hamilton Institute, 1914), pp. 8–9; Arch W. Shaw, *Some Problems In Market Distribution* (Cambridge, Mass.: Harvard University Press, 1915), pp. 4–28; L. D. Weld, "Marketing Functions and Mercantile Organization," *American Economic Review,* Vol. 7 (June 1917), pp. 306–318; Paul T. Cherington, *Elements of Marketing* (New York: MacMillan, 1920), pp. 44, 56–59; Fred E. Clark, *Principles of Marketing* (New York: Macmillan, 1922); Ralph F. Breyer, *The Marketing Institution* (New York: McGraw-Hill, 1934); P. D. Converse, *Essentials of Distribution* (New York: Prentice-Hall, 1936); George J. Stigler, "The Division of Labor is Limited by the Extent of the Market," *Journal of Political Economy,* Vol. 54 (June 1951), pp. 185–193; R. S. Vaile, E. T. Grether, and R. Cox, *Marketing in the American Economy* (New York: Ronald Press, 1952), pp. 121–133; Wroe Alderson, *Marketing Behavior and Executive Action* (Homewood, Ill.: Richard D. Irwin, 1957); Louis P. Bucklin, *A Theory of Distribution Channel Structure* (Berkeley, Calif.: Institute of Business and Economic Research, University of California, 1966).

The Basic Concept of Functional Spin-off

The basis for the functional spin-off concept is a 1951 article by Stigler.[4] In this article, Stigler provides a most important conceptual framework for measuring and anticipating channel structural arrangements. His approach to isolating the reasons why firms will "subcontract" some functions is to analyze or break down the average total cost curve of the firm by function rather than by the normal category of expense calculations such as salaries and interest. Included would be costs associated with functions such as ownership, promotion, information gathering, risk taking, negotiation, and so on. Each function will then have its own cost curve, and the sum of the cost curves for each function will be the total average cost curve of the firm.

These functional cost curves will have various shapes, and each may differ from the other to some degree. Average cost curves for some functions will increase with increasing volume whereas others will decrease with increasing volume. The average cost curves for some functions will assume a U-shaped design: they decrease with increasing volume and at some point start to increase with increasing volume. (Stigler assumes a U-shaped design for the total average cost curve.)

Functional Spin-off and the Number of Channel Levels It is economically beneficial to spin off to marketing specialists those distributive functions which have a decreasing curve as volume increases when the firm has a relatively small volume. When a firm enters or creates a new market, it typically produces a small volume in that market. Assuming the middleman specialist faces the same cost curve as the producer, the individual producer at this low volume will have a higher average cost for performing a function with a decreasing cost curve than the specialist who can combine the volumes of a number of producers and thus benefit from the economies that the performance of this particular function generates at higher volumes. If the middleman specialist passes on all or some of the lower costs, the producer's total average cost will decline as a result of this spin-off of the distributive function. In effect, the middleman has generated the basic *raison d'être* for his own existence by providing external economies to producer firms.

Although the falling functional cost curve is of most interest because it is probably the most common situation, the reverse curve also has implications for channel structure. With a rising functional cost curve, it would make sense economically to spin off certain functions to small specialists when the firm has achieved a high volume. These small specialists can perform the rising cost function at lower costs if they stay small and do not combine the volumes of too many producers. If they are competitive (a more likely event than in the falling cost functional curve situation) such savings will be passed on to the producer.

Some Qualifications At the beginning of the development of a new market, there may not be enough volume for a middleman to enter the market since there may not be enough producers from which the middleman can draw supplies to create the large volume required for a profitable operation. In this case, the producer will not have any middleman to whom he may spin off a high cost function. The situation may also occur during the declining stage of the product life cycle when industry volume has decreased to a point where insufficient total sales exist to justify a functional specialist. In the second case, vertical reintegration becomes necessary as middlemen leave the market.

As the market develops, more producers enter, industry volume increases, and it be-

[4] Stigler, same reference as footnote 3.

comes viable for middlemen to operate. It is possible that with even greater volume, a given spin-off function will in turn be broken down into several subfunctions, some of which may be spun off by existing middlemen to even narrower specialists; for example, import distributors might spin off certain types of selling to domestic wholesalers. Thus several levels and other types of middlemen may be added to the structural arrangement.

It should be noted that even if the middleman is a monopolist, he cannot exploit his situation completely. A producer will distribute directly if a middleman attempts to charge more for his services than the producer would have to pay with direct distribution. In other words, the middleman faces an elastic demand curve for his services. At most, he can take all of the efficiencies that he provides in the form of his own profits, but no more. The middleman monopolist is more likely to be present at the beginning of a new market situation, where volume does not warrant the entry of competitive middlemen. Eventually, however, with increasing volume and no artificial barriers to entry, competitive middlemen will enter the market.

It should also be noted that functions are not independent but are interrelated. Therefore, the spin-off of one function could have repercussions, up or down, for the cost of one or more other functions. For example, coordination costs may fall with the spin-off of a function. That is, if a given function is not being performed in a company, there is no longer the need for internal company communication between the people that would have been performing the function and the rest of the company.

Extensions of the Functional Spin-off Concept as Related to Channel Levels

U- or L-shaped Average Cost Function There are a number of important implications for industrial structure and, more specifically, channel structure on which Stigler did not elaborate. Perhaps the most important are the implications arising from a functional average cost curve which initially declines and then at some point starts to increase (really a U-shaped curve) or even flattens out.

If the cost curve does not continue to fall, at a high level of volume a point will be reached at which that producer can retake the function without losing economies. For example, in Figure 1 at volumes up to Q1 it will pay the producer to spin off to middlemen the function shown by the cost curve. Between Q1 and Q2, performance by the producer or spinning it off will provide the same economies. After volume Q2, however, it would be beneficial for the producer to resume performance of the function (unless middlemen split themselves up and form smaller firms or smaller middle-

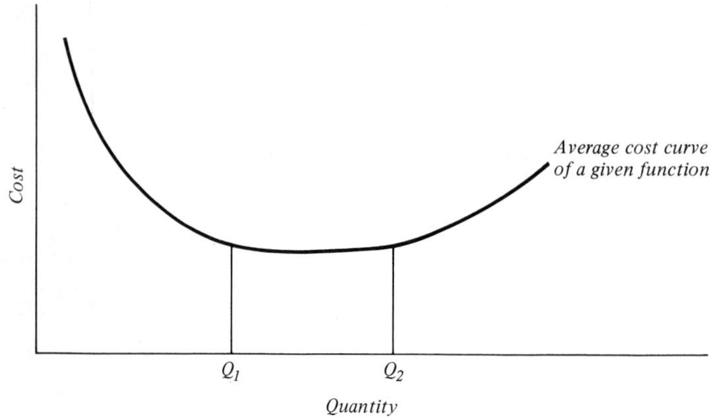

Figure 1 A U-shaped average cost curve for a given function faced by an individual producer or marketing middleman.

men are available in the market, so that a very large volume can be distributed among them). The resumption process can apply to any function. For example, the resumption of the ownership function removes the task from a merchant middleman and results in the producer selling direct to the market; self-performance of the advertising function means a producer will not use an advertising agency but relies completely on his own personnel, and so on.

Functions with Continually Decreasing Average Cost Curves Another extension of the Stigler model is that if the functional cost curve continually falls, the middleman industry, and perhaps individual middleman firms which result from this situation, will become bigger and bigger.

Stigler's model can also be reconstructed into a dynamic rather than a static one. If the channel's costs fall, prices fall; so that given an elastic demand curve, volume will increase. In other words, the market situation propels itself further along the various functional cost curves, with the implications depending on the shapes of these curves. For falling functional cost curves, another round of functional spin-offs, falling costs and prices, and increasing volume will take place. An implication of this last situation is that the middleman industry would become very large, perhaps creating extremely large firms. This process may have facilitated the rise of the mass merchandiser.

Extensions of the Functional Spin-off Concept as Related to Other Structure Dimensions

Multi-channel Structures The concepts employed here can also be useful in explaining the rationale behind dual-channel or multi-channel distribution systems. If the functional cost curves are analyzed by large retailer versus small retailer markets, it is possible for the same function to have different shapes in each market. For example, for the small retailer market the producer's functional cost curve at a given quantity may fall with increasing volume; whereas for the large retailer market the cost curve for that same function at the same given quantity may be flat or even increase with volume. This would occur if there were few economies associated with increasing volume in marketing to big retailers once any reasonable amount was sold to them; e.g., the selling effort and cost per unit which is required to sell X units to big retailers is the same as to sell 2X units.

If the above situation held true in a given case, it would be economically beneficial for the producer to spin off to a middleman the particular function involved in selling to the small retailer market and to sell directly to the large retailer market. Even if the shapes of the cost curves in each market were identical, say declining and then leveling off, the spin-off in the small retailer market would be beneficial if the quantity being sold was still small enough to be on the declining portion of the curve. Of course, if the situation was reversed, i.e., selling the small quantity to the large retailer market and large (flat portion of curve) quantity to the small retailer market, the spin-off would take place in the large retailer market. This would lead to indirect distribution to large retailers and direct distribution to small retailers.

Figure 2 portrays the possible situations. Qs (1 or 2) is assumed to be the quantity sold to the small retailer market and Qb (1 or 2) is the quantity assumed to be sold to the large retailer market by a given producer. In the cost curves shown in this figure, the reason for selling directly to retailers (large or small) at high volumes is shown, i.e., leveling cost curves at Qs2 or Qb2; as well as the reason for selling indirectly, i.e., falling cost curves at Qs1 or Qb1.

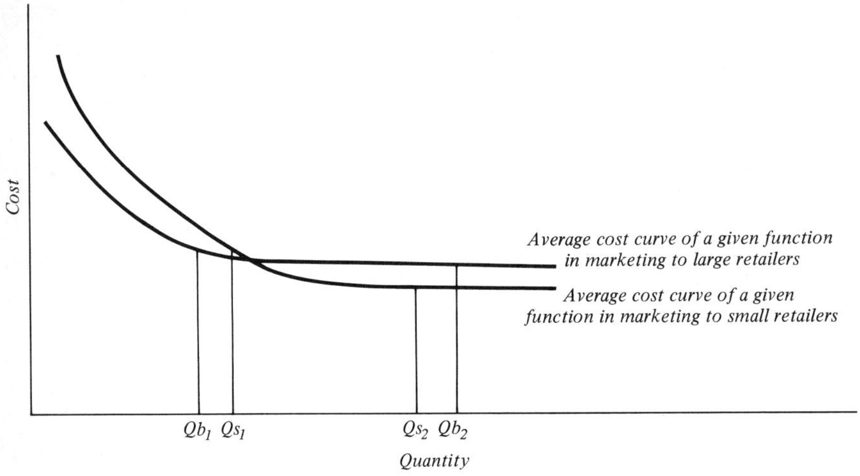

Figure 2 L-shaped average cost curves faced by individual producers or marketing middlemen in selling to a large retailer market and a small retailer market for the same given marketing function.

Assume four possible volume situations:

a Qs1 and Qb2
b Qs2 and Qb1
c Qs2 and Qb2
d Qs1 and Qb1

In the first situation, if the producer is selling Qs1 and Qb2 it can be seen that lower average costs for a given marketing function to small retailers can be obtained at higher volumes (e.g., Qs2). Hence, it makes economic sense for the producer to spin off the function of selling to small retailers to middlemen who, by combining the volume of two or more producers, can achieve these economies and, if competitive, pass them on to the producer. At Qb2 it is obvious that no further economies (or diseconomies) are available at this and higher volumes to the firm. Therefore, it would not be reasonable to spin off the function to middlemen in marketing to large retailers at that point.

In another situation, if a producer is selling Qb1 and Qs2 the reverse channel structure would result. The function would be spun off to middlemen in selling to large retailers and would be retained on a direct basis for small retailers.

Should the relevant volumes be Qb2 and Qs2, there would not be any multi-channels, i.e., there would be only direct distribution. Should the relevant quantities be Qb1 and Qs1, there would be spin-offs in both cases; and should the middlemen be the same firms in both cases, there would not be any multichannel distribution, but simply indirect single-channel distribution. If, on the other hand, distribution to the large retailer market and the small retailer market required different types of middlemen, there would still be multi-channel distribution although of a different nature.

Middlemen Types The types of marketing intermediaries that are created will be directly determined by the mix of functions spun off to them, inasmuch as part of the definition of a middleman depends on the functions he performs. For example, if part of the ownership function is spun off, then merchants are created; if a negotiation function is spun off, then agents are created; if advertising only, then advertising agencies; if marketing research only, then marketing research agencies; and so on.

Horizontal Channel Structure Up to this point the discussion has dealt with only three of the four dimensions of structure listed earlier: the number of levels, the determination of the number of patterns of distribution—single-, dual-, or multi-channels; and their type (as defined by functions performed). Insight into the determination of one other channel dimension—horizontal structure, or the number of middlemen at each channel level—may also be provided by the functional spin-off concept. However, integration of certain concepts from the field of industrial organization with the spin-off concept is necessary.

The basic force which will determine the number of channel members at a given level appears to be the size of the market in relation to the optimum scale of the firm.[5] The greater the market size is in relation to the optimum scale size, the greater the number of channel members that will evolve, and vice versa. The optimum scale size will itself change from industry to industry and over time as technology changes.

In addition to this fundamental determining relationship, there are a number of other factors. Most of these factors are closely associated with scale and market size, which also help to determine how many members will exist at a channel level. The forces which tend to create more firms at a given channel level include: diseconomies of medium or large scale plants and firms, only small inefficiencies at smaller than optimum scale of operation, growth of market size, high profit potentials, inability to agree on merger terms, legal barriers on merger or monopolization, and buyers wishing the convenience of many outlets.

The forces which tend to create fewer firms at a given channel level include: no diseconomies of large scale operations or diseconomies commencing at only extremely high output of plants and firms; only small inefficiencies at a larger than optimum scale of operations; decline in market size; low profit potential; monopolization practices brought about through collusion, predatory behavior, or barriers to entry; and "outside" financial considerations in effecting mergers.

Although most theoretical discussions normally view diseconomies as starting almost immediately after the optimum scale is reached, in practice there appears to be a rather broad range of possible scales—from a minimum optimum scale to some maximum (which in some cases could accommodate a monopoly)—which could provide the same optimum efficiencies.

> We will seldom if ever find firms with a single unique optimal scale. Diseconomies of very large scale are typically encountered, if at all, only at scales substantially greater than the minimum optimal scale of a firm. This is in spite of the fact that a priori theories of pricing and market structure have usually represented the scale curves of firms as having a U shape. . . .[6]
>
> . . . the bulk of evidence is consistent with the hypothesis that the gigantic firms are in general neither more nor less efficient than firms which are simply large.[7]

Hence, since diseconomies come slowly, if at all, a basic underlying trend could be toward fewer firms and, at the extreme, one (monopoly) channel member at a given level of a channel. In other words, it is conceivable that a channel level not only can be an oligopoly, duopoly, or even a monopoly and still operate, but *must* have that market structure in order to operate at an optimum scale.

This concept of a wide range of optimum scales when combined with the concept of functional spin-off has important implications for channel structure. It suggests the possibili-

[5]For an excellent detailed discussion of this concept (though not interpreted in a channel context) see Joe S. Bain, *Industrial Organization* (New York: John Wiley and Sons, Inc., 1968), Chapter 6.

[6]Same reference as footnote 5, p. 175.

[7]Same reference as footnote 5, p. 173.

ty of a structure which consists of all producers using direct channels, all using indirect channels, or some using direct and some using indirect. The first case is probable when all producers reach the minimum optimum point; the second is probable when none reach the minimum optimum point. The last case (of mixed structures) is most probable when some do and some do not reach this point; it is also optimally compatible when all reach the minimum optimum point, as in the first case.

Consider a hypothetical example of a market having a total volume of $10 million and a minimum optimum scale for distribution functions (whether undertaken by the producer or a middleman) of $1 million, with no diseconomies up to the total market. If no producer reaches this minimum, then it is probable that all will distribute indirectly with a total of one to ten middlemen in the market. If one producer reaches 100% of the market, he can distribute directly with no middlemen in the market, he can distribute completely through one to ten middlemen, or he can distribute directly in part and indirectly in part through one to nine middlemen (nine, if he lets $9 million go indirectly). If only one producer reaches $1 million in output, he may distribute directly or indirectly. If he distributes indirectly, then the other producers, who will probably distribute indirectly in any case, will do so through one to nine middlemen. If there are ten producers, and eight producers each reach at least $1 million in sales for a total of $9 million, some of the eight may distribute directly and others indirectly, or all may distribute one way or the other. If all decide to distribute directly, then the remaining two producers will probably distribute indirectly through one middleman.

Thus the minimum optimum scale point only indicates the maximum number of channel members that are compatible with maximum efficiency, and so leaves room for a number of other forces (not discussed here) which will determine the actual point in the optimum range that will be utilized by the firms in the industry, i.e., the actual outcome in terms of number of channel members at different levels. Further, firms may not even choose to (or cannot) operate within the optimum range because of some of the factors listed earlier. These factors include: only small inefficiencies at nonoptimum scales, a decline in market size, a high profit potential even without optimum operation, monopolization practices, inability to merge, and a desire for outlet convenience. In spite of these possibilities, one cannot ignore what is a very key determinant of the number of channel members that will exist at each level—market size in relation to the optimum scale of firm and the spin-off ability.

HYPOTHESES

The key hypotheses generated by the functional spin-off and industrial organization concepts for distribution structure are as follows:

As Related to "Number of Levels" Dimension

1 A producer will spin off a marketing function to a marketing intermediary(s) if the latter can perform the function more efficiently than the former. This will logically be the case when economies can be effected for that function by a change in volume from that of the producer. The greater the economies, the greater will be the incentive to spin off. If the majority of producers in a given industry are in or will be in a similar position, then the use of marketing intermediaries will characterize, or come to characterize, that industry.

2 If there are continual economies to be obtained within a wide range of volume changes, the middleman portion of the industry (and perhaps individual middlemen) will become bigger and bigger.

3 A producer will keep or resume a marketing function from a marketing intermediary(s) if the former can perform the function at least as efficiently as the latter. This will logically be the case when no economies can be effected for that function by a change in volume from that of the producer. If the majority of producers in a given industry are in, or will be in, a similar position, then the nonuse of marketing intermediaries (direct distribution) will characterize, or come to characterize, that industry.

4 If in performing a marketing function a marketing intermediary finds that for a part of that function (i.e., a subfunction) another perhaps more specialized marketing intermediary can perform it more efficiently, then he will spin off that subfunction to the latter. This will occur for the same reasoning presented in hypothesis 1 above. Similarly, the first marketing intermediary will keep or resume a subfunction if there are no economies to be effected by a spin-off.

As Related to "Number of Channels" Dimension

5 If a producer finds that in marketing to one (or more) of his markets a middleman can perform a given marketing function more efficiently for the reasons noted in hypothesis 1 above and for another (or others) of his markets he can perform the same function at least as efficiently for the reasons noted in hypothesis 3 above, he will spin off that function in marketing to the first market(s) and keep or resume the function in marketing to the second. If the majority of producers in a given industry are in, or will be in, a similar position; then the use of dual- or multiple-channels will characterize, or come to characterize, that industry.

As Related to "Middlemen Types" Dimension

6 If marketing intermediaries characterize an industry, their nature will be determined by the mix of functions and subfunctions spun off. For example, if the ownership function is a prevalent spin-off function, then the merchant will be a prevalent type of marketing intermediary in the industry.

As Related to "Number of Middlemen" Dimension

7 The greater the market size is in relation to optimum scale size (at each channel level), the greater the number of channel members that will come into being. With the growth of market size, and especially if there exist diseconomies or only very small economies of larger scale, more firms may be expected to enter the channel. With a decline in market size, and especially if there exist economies of larger scale, firms may be expected to leave the channel.

8 With a change in technology and the growth of optimum scale size, firms may be expected to leave the channel if there is no corresponding change in market size and vice versa.

IMPLICATIONS

Using the eight relationships hypothesized above, the channel planner is in a better position to anticipate trends in his industry by estimating relevant cost and market data. (It is beyond the scope of this article to describe a program of data collection or to suggest how to overcome the admittedly difficult, but not impossible, task of collecting competitive cost information.)

The channel planner must estimate the present and future total market volume, new technological changes which affect the optimum firm scale, and the volume and shape of the average cost curve for the key marketing functions of a representative sample of firms (producers and marketing intermediaries) in his industry. Fortunately, because his purpose is to gauge broad underlying trends, the data can be fairly rough without losing its usefulness. Trade associations often collect competitive cost data for use by their members. However, further estimates of different types of marketing costs by market being served would probably have to be made from such sources. He then can apply to his findings the structural results predicted by the eight hypotheses listed above.

For example, if he finds that producing firms in his industry in general have faced a declining average cost curve for the ownership function in the past but are now approaching a flat portion of the curve where no economies of scale are forthcoming, and further he predicts an increase in total market volume, he will anticipate in his channel strategy a general move by his industry to more direct ownership channels (see hypothesis 3 above). He will also anticipate more firms entering the market at the producer level (see hypothesis 7 above: note in this case that the market size may actually decline at the merchant middleman level because of the first conclusion). The exact change in number of channel members will depend on factors discussed earlier under the subtitle "horizontal channel structure." If, in the same example, the channel planner also finds that with the same volume increase the negotiation function cost curve declines sharply, he will also anticipate an increase in the number of agent middlemen.

The possible combinations of cost and market size changes are numerous. The channel planner by collecting the data and applying the concepts discussed here should be able to anticipate distribution structure changes before they become obvious trends.

The functional spin-off concept is a powerful conceptual tool for the marketer in understanding many of the aspects of channel structure (which itself is one of the most and perhaps *the* most fundamental contribution of marketing as a discipline)[8] and in predicting structural outcomes in specific industries. It is also useful, in a micro or managerial sense, to the channel selector or designer who is seeking to conceptually organize and understand the framework of underlying economic forces within which he must operate and make his decisions and to which he must adapt.

[8]R. Ferber, D. Blankertz, and S. Hollander, *Marketing Research* (New York: Ronald Press Company, 1964), p. 471. See also, Michael Halbert, *The Meaning and Sources of Marketing Theory* (New York: McGraw-Hill, 1965), p. 10.

29

A Frame of Reference for Improving Productivity in Distribution

Bert C. McCammon, Jr.
William L. Hammer

Because of the increasing importance of labor-intensive service industries, plus their effect on inflation, ways must be found to make them more productive. These authors analyze and evaluate recent productivity developments in both the retail and wholesale trades. Much of what is discussed can be applied to other service industries.

Reprinted from Ronald C. Curhan (ed.), *1974 Combined Proceedings* (Chicago: American Marketing Association, 1974), pp. 455–460. At the time of writing, Bert C. McCammon, Jr., was professor of business administration, University of Oklahoma; William L. Hammer was vice president and associate research director of Management Horizons, Inc.

INTRODUCTION

The service sector of the American economy is undergoing rapid expansion. Over the decade ahead, service industries will provide 86 percent of all new jobs created. Furthermore, by 1985, service workers will outnumber manufacturing employees by more than three to one.[1]

Unfortunately, many service industries, including retailing and wholesaling, tend to be labor-intensive. These industries have traditionally experienced severe productivity problems and have therefore been a major source of inflation. Between 1958 and 1972, for example, labor-intensity service industries accounted for 71 percent of total U.S. inflation while producing only 50 percent of the nation's output [1]. Clearly, this historical pattern must be reversed if inflationary pressures are to be contained during the decade ahead.

Improving productivity is much more than an inflation-fighting exercise, however. As Robert C. Scrivener points out, higher rates of productivity are required both to improve the quality of life and to compete more effectively in world markets [6]. In short, productivity is the cornerstone of continued economic and social development.

The balance of this report examines productivity developments in retail and wholesale trade. Many of the approaches and concepts discussed, however, can be applied in other service industries; thus, the analysis that follows should be of use to nondistribution executives.

THE PRODUCTIVITY CHALLENGE IN DISTRIBUTION

Labor Productivity Trends

In recent years, output per manhour in distribution has risen much less rapidly than in other sectors of the economy. Retailers, for example, increased their output per manhour at a rate of only .8 percent per year between 1968 and 1972, and wholesalers did only slightly better.

Table 1

Economic sector	Average annual increase in real output per manhour (1968-1972)
Agriculture	4.5%
Mining	3.9
Manufacturing	2.3
Wholesaling	1.7
Retailing	.8
Total economy	1.9%

Source: U.S. Department of Labor, U.S. Department of Commerce, and authors' calculations.

As a result of lagging productivity (and rising wages), retailing and wholesaling companies experienced sharp increases in their unit labor costs between 1968 and 1972. Consider the following labor cost comparisons between retailing, wholesaling, and manufacturing enterprises.

Table 2

Economic sector	Average annual increase in unit labor costs (1968-1972)
Manufacturing	3.0%
Wholesaling	5.1
Retailing	6.2

Source: U.S. Department of Labor, U.S. Department of Commerce, and authors' calculations.

This pattern of rising unit labor costs had significant impact on profit margins. IRS data indicate that retail profit margins declined from 1.4 percent of sales in 1968 to 1.0 percent of sales in 1972. Wholesale profit margins fell from 1.2 to 1.0 percent of sales during the same periods [3]. In summary, low rates of productivity, accompanied by upward wage

[1]For a careful analysis of these trends, see [2].

Table 3

Economic sector	Average hourly wage rate for operating employees 1968	1972	Average annual increase
Manufacturing	$3.01	$3.81	6.1%
Retailing	2.16	2.70	5.7
Wage Gap	$ .85	$1.11	6.9%

Source: U.S. Department of Labor.

Table 4

Economic sector	Net sales to total assets (times) 1968	1972
Wholesaling	2.9	2.8
Retailing	2.6	2.6

Source: Internal Revenue Service and authors' calculations.

pressures, exerted a major influence on retail and wholesale profits over the past five years.

The Wage Gap Cycle

Lagging productivity can result in a vicious, regenerative cycle. Lagging productivity, at some point in time, inevitably results in lagging wages. Lagging wages, in turn, eventually result in the recruitment of marginal personnel, which further depresses productivity. The ultimate consequence of this iterative process is a stagnant and depressed industry.

Recent trends suggest that retailers are already confronted by a wage gap problem. Consider the following comparison between manufacturing and retailing wage rates.

If the gap between manufacturing and retailing wages continues to widen, retailers will find it increasingly difficult to attract and retain productive personnel.

Capital Productivity Trends

Retailers and wholesalers have also experienced difficulty in improving their capital productivity ratios over the past five years. This trend is documented in Table 4.

The stagnant rates of asset turnover that prevail in the field of distribution acquire additional significance when viewed in the context of the strategic profit model. Such a model involves multiplying a company's profit margin by its rate of asset turnover and its leverage ratio to obtain its rate of return on net worth. Thus, the model combines the principal elements of a company's operating statement and balance sheet into a single profit planning equation.

As indicated, retailers and wholesalers achieved inadequate rates of return on net worth between 1968 and 1972. Since both types of organizations are already highly leveraged, improved results are most likely to be achieved by companies that simultaneously increase both their profit margins *and* their rates of asset turnover.

Figure 1

		$\left(\frac{\text{Net profits}}{\text{Net sales}}\right)$	×	$\left(\frac{\text{Net sales}}{\text{Total assets}}\right)$	×	$\left(\frac{\text{Total assets}}{\text{Net worth}}\right)$	=	$\left(\frac{\text{Net profits}}{\text{Net worth}}\right)$
Wholesaling	1968	1.2%	×	2.9X	×	2.4X	=	8.6%
Corporations	1972	1.0%	×	2.8X	×	2.6X	=	7.3%
Retailing	1968	1.4%	×	2.6X	×	2.3X	=	8.8%
Corporations	1972	1.0%	×	2.6X	×	2.5X	=	6.5%

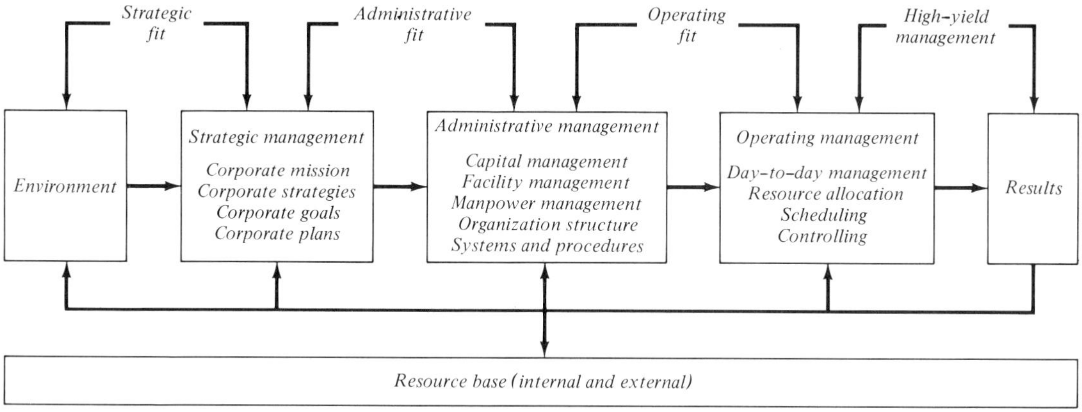

Figure 2 The total performance model.

Managerial Implications The performance mandate is clear. Retailers and wholesalers must significantly improve their labor and capital productivity ratios in the 1970's. In many cases, labor productivity increases of 6 to 8 percent a year will be required to offset rising wages and to improve profit margins.

Capital productivity ratios must be increased at a comparable rate, primarily through better management of inventories and through more intensive use of both equipment and physical facilities. In short, there must be a concerted attack on the productivity problem in distribution.

A FRAME OF REFERENCE FOR IMPROVING PRODUCTIVITY IN DISTRIBUTION

The total performance model is a new frame of reference for improving productivity in distribution. As specified in the model, management is the process by which strategic, administrative, and operating decisions are coordinated to achieve target results on a programmed and predictable basis.

Executives and management scientists have traditionally focused on improving administrative and operating efficiency with significant results. Consider, for example, the following vignettes in the field of distribution.

- John Wanamaker, a leading department store in Philadelphia, used short interval scheduling techniques to increase the productivity of sales personnel by 19.8 percent over a two-year period [4].
- A. T. Kearney developed a truck scheduling model that produced delivery savings of 32 percent in the linen supply field [7].
- Early adopters of COSMOS report that their direct product profits increased by 15 percent after this sophisticated inventory management and space allocation system was installed. They also reduced their out-of-stock ratios by 25 percent during the same period [5].
- A computer simulation model in the department store field increased a staple department's gross margin return on inventory investment (GMROI) by 11.8 percent [8].

Clearly, continued emphasis should be placed on management science programs in the field of distribution. In a growing number of cases, however, *strategic* breakthroughs will be required to achieve adequate results.

MAINSTREAM STRATEGIES FOR IMPROVING PRODUCTIVITY IN DISTRIBUTION

Retailers and wholesalers are currently employing *five* major strategies to improve productivity and profitability in distribution. The results achieved by U.S., Canadian, and European companies employing these strategies are shown in the Appendix. The strategies themselves may be described as follows.

Warehouse Retailing

Warehouse retailers have combined the economics of wholesaling and retailing to create a new low-cost form of distribution. Specifically, warehouse retailers achieve operating economies by occupying low-cost facilities, by utilizing vertical space intensively, and by employing modern materials handling and data processing techniques. In addition, they "escape" certain costs by shifting selected functions backward to suppliers or forward to consumers. As a result, warehouse retailers are able to underprice conventional merchants by 10 to 30 percent, which enables them to achieve unusually high sales per employee and per square foot of selling area.

The principal types of warehouse outlets currently in operation are furniture warehouse showrooms (Levitz, Leon's, Pascal, and Wickes); appliance and TV warehouse showrooms (Kennedy and Cohen, Luskin's, and Silo); catalog showrooms (Best Products, Consumers Distributing, and Service Merchandise); and hypermarches (Carrefour, Oshawa, and Wertkauf). Apparel, food and sporting goods warehouse have also begun to appear in numerous metropolitan markets.

As indicated in the Appendix, warehouse retailers expanded rapidly between 1969 and 1973. They also achieved unusually high rates of return on investment. As a result, many analysts contend that warehouse retailing will be to the 1970's what discount department stores were to the 1960's.

Supermarket Retailing

The supermarket concept is being used extensively to improve productivity in distribution. Toys R' Us and Oshman's currently operate toy supermarkets; Beaver Lumber, Builder's Emporium, and Handy Dan are vigorous proponents of the self-service, home improvement center concept; and both Long's and Skagg's operate massive super drug stores. Like their warehouse retailing counterparts, these merchants have achieved significant productivity breakthroughs.

Direct Marketing

Analysts agree that direct marketing could be the next revolution in retailing. Certainly, there are a sufficient number of prototypes to suggest that this could be the wave of the future. Beeline and Tupperware have been conspicuously successful in the party plan field; Avon and Shaklee are formidable direct selling organizations, and Fingerhut and New Process have achieved rapid rates of growth through catalog selling. Among the new arrivals on the direct marketing scene are Call-a-Mart, K-Tel, and Unity Buying Service.

Though the data are fragmentary, it is apparent that many forms of direct marketing are expanding two or three times more rapidly than total retail sales. This trend will undoubtedly accelerate in the 1980's when CATV retailing becomes a competitive reality.

Vertical Marketing Systems

Retailers affiliated with cooperative groups, voluntary groups, and franchise networks currently account for over 40 percent of total retail sales. Corporate chains represent another 32 percent of total retail sales. Corporate chains represent another 32 percent of the

Appendix Mainstream Strategies for Improving Productivity in Distribution

Strategic thrust	Company	Corporate profile	Strategic profit model ratios (1973)				Compound annual growth rates (1969–1973)		
			Net profits to net sales	Net sales to total assets	Total assets to net worth	Net profits to net worth	Net sales	Net profits	Earnings per share
Warehouse retailing	Carrefour	Carrefour is the leading hypermarche chain in Western Europe. In fiscal 1973, the company operated on a gross margin of 16.4 percent, which enabled it to underprice conventional retailers by at least 10.0 percent. As a result of its underpricing strategy, Carrefour generates unusually high sales per employee and per square foot of selling area. In 1973, Carrefour announced that it plans to enter the North American market on a joint venture basis.	3.0	5.0	2.0	30.0	53.6	54.2	52.6
	Levitz	Levitz pioneered the furniture warehouse showroom concept in North America. Available data suggest that the company underprices conventional furniture stores by 13.3 percent. In 1974, Levitz added carpets, consumer electronics, and major appliances to its merchandise mix by signing leased department agreements with Allen Carpet and Kennedy and Cohen respectively.	3.7	2.5	1.9	17.8	69.6	64.4	53.4

Appendix Mainstream Strategies for Improving Productivity in Distribution (*Continued*)

			Strategic profit model ratios (1973)				Compound annual growth rates (1969–1973)		
Strategic thrust	**Company**	**Corporate profile**	**Net profits to net sales**	**Net sales to total assets**	**Total assets to net worth**	**Net profits to net worth**	**Net sales**	**Net profits**	**Earnings per share**
	Consumers Distributing	Consumers Distributing is the major catalog showroom chain in Canada. In 1973, the company signed a joint venture agreement with May Department Stores to enter the U.S. market.	5.7	2.0	2.2	25.9	42.4	42.1	38.9
Supermarket retailing	Handy Dan	Handy Dan operates 52 home improvement centers in six states. A typical center generates $1.8 million in annual sales, contains over 40,000 square feet of space, and carries an inventory of 30,000 items.	2.9	2.8	2.3	18.4	35.9	40.7	23.6
	Standard Brands Paint	Standard Brands operates paint and decoration supermarkets in California and other Western states. At the present time, the company obtains 41 percent of its merchandise requirements from captive manufacturing facilities.	7.6	1.8	1.3	17.2	19.5	20.9	19.7
	Child World	Child World is a leading operator of toy supermarkets. A typical Child World unit contains 25,000 square feet of space and carries over 20,000 items in inventory.	3.4	2.9	1.5	14.8	35.4	37.6	15.7

Direct Marketing	Unity Buying Service	Unity Buying Service operates a unique direct mail program. Through the company's Factory Buying Club, consumers purchase merchandise from a 10,000 item catalog. The consumer's purchase price is factory cost plus a 6 percent service fee, taxes where applicable, and shipping costs. As of September 1973, the Club's active membership consisted of 781,000 consumers.	4.5	3.1	2.0	27.5	26.1	42.3	40.9
	K-Tel	K-Tel is one of the leading direct response marketing organizations in North America. The company markets records and other specialty products through saturation TV campaigns. The products are distributed through 20,000 retail outlets on a consignment basis.	7.6	2.1	2.1	33.5	66.8	47.6	48.2
Vertical marketing systems	Koffler Stores	Koffler is the largest franchiser of drug stores in North America. In 1972, the company signed a joint venture agreement with Steinberg's to open franchise stores in Quebec.	2.1	3.2	2.2	14.3	41.0	32.2	20.3

Appendix Mainstream Strategies for Improving Productivity in Distribution (*Continued*)

Strategic thrust	Company	Corporate profile	Strategic profit model ratios (1973)				Compound annual growth rates (1969–1973)		
			Net profits to net sales	Net sales to total assets	Total assets to net worth	Net profits to net worth	Net sales	Net profits	Earnings per share
	Canadian Tire	Canadian Tire is a large voluntary group wholesaler that supplies affiliated stores with a variety of lines, including automotive parts and accessories, hardware, housewares, small appliances, and sporting goods. A typical Canadian Tire outlet contains approximately 25,000 square feet of space and carries over 20,000 items in inventory.	5.2	1.9	1.6	16.2	19.5	27.4	25.1
Corporate diversification	Malone & Hyde	Malone & Hyde is a large voluntary group wholesaler in the food field. The company has pursued a vigorous diversification policy in recent years and currently obtains 34 percent of its earnings from company-owned stores and related ventures.	1.3	6.5	1.9	16.3	13.1	13.9	13.0
	Lucky Stores	Lucky Stores is the 8th largest food chain in the United States. The company also operates 115 discount department stores, 39 membership department stores, 39 home and auto stores, 29 drug stores, and 4 sporting goods stores.	1.5	4.2	3.0	19.7	17.9	20.6	14.8

market. If present trends continue, contractual groups and corporate chains could account for 85 percent of total retail sales by 1980.

More important, these vertical networks are becoming increasingly rationalized as productivity and profitability pressures intensify. Thus, they are still a viable strategy for improving results in the field of distribution.

Corporate Diversification

Finally, a growing number of companies have diversified in recent years to improve their overall results. A recent analysis of Value Line data indicates that diversified retailers performed much better than their conventional counterparts between 1968 and 1973. Jewell, Lucky, Malone & Hyde, Melville, and Zale are among the leading proponents of diversified distribution. All have achieved superior performance in the marketplace.

CONCLUSIONS

Retailers and wholesalers are currently confronted by *major* productivity and profitability problems. Over the decade ahead, they must improve their performance in both of these areas to fully satisfy stockholder expectations.

In addition, distribution organizations will be increasingly confronted by rising social pressures. Consumerism will become a more important force; product and environmental safety codes will proliferate; and zoning ordinances will become more restrictive. In this complex milieu, corporate acceptance of the new technology of management will become a prerequisite to survival. But, more important, new *strategies* must be devised to simultaneously respond to new social demands while maintaining an adequate rate of return on shareholders' equity.

REFERENCES

1 "Expanding Service Economy," *Quarterly Review of Economic Prospects,* 72–4 Part 2 (February, 1973), 12–3. (no author)

2 Fuchs, Victor R. *The Service Economy.* New York: National Bureau of Economic Research, Inc., 1968.

3 Internal Revenue Service, *Corporation Income Tax Returns,* 1968 and 1969 editions, and authors' calculations.

4 Lubinski, Stephen R. "A Program for Improving Productivity," *Retail Control,* 42 (September, 1973), 10–21.

5 "Manufacturers Ponder COSMOS Data," *Grocery Manufacturer* (September 1971), 1–4. (no author)

6 Scrivener, Robert C. "Productivity in a Modern Economy," *The Canadian Business Review* (Winter 1974), 18–20.

7 "Successful Savings with CARD," *Linen Supply News* (September 1973, 60–70. (no author)

8 Sweeney, Daniel J. "Improving the Profitability of Retail Merchandising Decisions," *Journal of Marketing,* 37 (January 1973), 60–8.

30

The Total Cost Approach to Distribution

Raymond LeKashman
John F. Stolle

Everyone agrees on the need for reducing distribution costs, yet this unanimity does not exist with respect to defining real cost of distribution. The authors spell out real cost and discuss the concept of the total cost approach: when to use it, how to use it, and its meaning to management.

The more management focuses the company's efforts on cutting distribution costs, the less successful it is likely to be in reducing the real costs of distribution. This apparent paradox is no abstract or armchair play on phrases. It explains why so many companies have diligently pruned distribution costs—in the warehouse and in inventory, in order processing and in transportation—only to find that these hard-earned savings are somehow not translated into improved profit margins. They have been watered down or actually washed out by increases in other costs scattered throughout the company.

It is these "other costs," motley and miscellaneous as they first seem, that turn out on closer analysis to be the *real* cost of distribution. (See Figure 1.) They never appear as distribution costs on any financial or operating report, but show up unidentified and unexplained at different times and in assorted places—in purchasing, in production, in paper-work processing—anywhere and everywhere in the business. When the gremlin-like costs are traced to their roots, however, one finds that they are, in fact, all intimately interrelated, linked together by one common bond. They all result from the way the company distributes its products.

It is this aggregation of distribution-related costs—rather than what managements usually mean when they complain about the cost of distribution—that represents the important and increasing drain of distribution on earnings. These are the costs—rather than those usually defined and dealt with as distribution costs—that have eluded even the most earnest cost-cutting drives. Because of its size and its elusiveness, this cost complex remains for many companies a promising profit-improvement potential.

THE TOTAL COST APPROACH

When to Use It

For earnings-minded managements, the dimensions of this profit potential, and a practical technique for tapping it, have now been tested and proved. A handful of companies have faced up to the across-the-board impact of distribution on costs and profits. They have accomplished this by applying an approach—we call it the "total cost approach"—that is designed to convert these intangible and intricate cost interrelationships into tangible dollar-and-cents improvements in profit margins.

Authors' Note: Harold Wolff of Booz, Allen and Hamilton, Inc., helped develop this article and prepared the material for publication.

Reprinted from *Business Horizons,* vol. 6, pp. 33–46, Winter 1965. Copyright 1965 by the Foundation for the School of Business at Indiana University. Reprinted by permission. At the time of writing, both authors were vice-presidents of Booz, Allen and Hamilton, Inc., management consulting firm.

A major food manufacturer, after applying effectively an assortment of rigid cost-cutting techniques, has found that this new approach is enabling the company to add 1.7 per cent to its margin on sales.

A major merchandiser, already enjoying the benefits of advanced distribution techniques, found that this same new approach could cut from its corporate costs an addition $7.5 million—3 per cent of the sales value of its products—while at the same time significantly improving service to customers.

At Du Pont, a company well known for its general management excellence, this same new approach underlies the announcement that programs recently instituted are expected to cut $30 million from its total cost, a 10 per cent reduction of the costs attributed to distribution.

These success stories shed some light on how distribution drains profits—and on what can be done about it:

The real impact of distribution on profits is much greater than most managements think. In companies in which distribution-connected costs have been studied, they turned out to be significantly greater than management estimated—as much as from a third to a half of the selling price of the product.

This untapped profit-improvement potential exists because these costs lie in a managerial no-man's land, where they can increase because they are outside the scope of responsibility or control of any operating executive. These distribution-related costs are not strictly the responsibility of the man in charge of distribution, because they are costs of purchasing, manufacturing, or some other function of the business. But they cannot be dealt with effectively by the executive in charge of these other functions because they are actually caused by distribution decisions, for which only the man in charge of distribution has any responsibility. They are the result of complex interrelationships involving all of the functions of the business. Distribution lies at the crossroad of these complex interactions, and that is what is so different about distribution. In no other function of the business can decisions made at the operating level look so right and be so wrong.

These costs will not respond to the usual cost-cutting approaches. Management has achieved near miracles in cutting costs in one function of the business after another, including costs within the distribution function, notably in warehousing, transportation, and order-filling. But conventional cost-cutting approaches are limited to costs that fall within any one operation of the business; for cutting these costs, management can hold some executive responsible. Distribution-related costs are organizational orphans, beyond the reach of even the most diligent, skillful cost-minded executives.

These costs will respond only to a high level across-the-board re-examination of how distribution affects the total costs and total profits of the business, and of what management action is necessary to tap this profit opportunity.

Thus the problem and the opportunity are deposited squarely on the desk of the chief executive. The pursuit of these added profits has to get its start, its support, and its sanctions at the top management level. With this high-level effort, even companies that have tightened and tidied their distribution operations can greatly increase earnings by a frontal attack on the basic framework of their distribution decisions and practices.

This broad, basic approach has a continuing payoff, for once the most profitable pattern of distribution has been defined for the present operations of the business, management has in its hands a yardstick for measuring the impact on total profits of any proposed management move. This makes it possible to define the impact on total profits of a new plant or a new product, or a cluster of new customers, and so makes it possible to determine what changes in distribution—if any—will ensure peak profits from these new ventures.

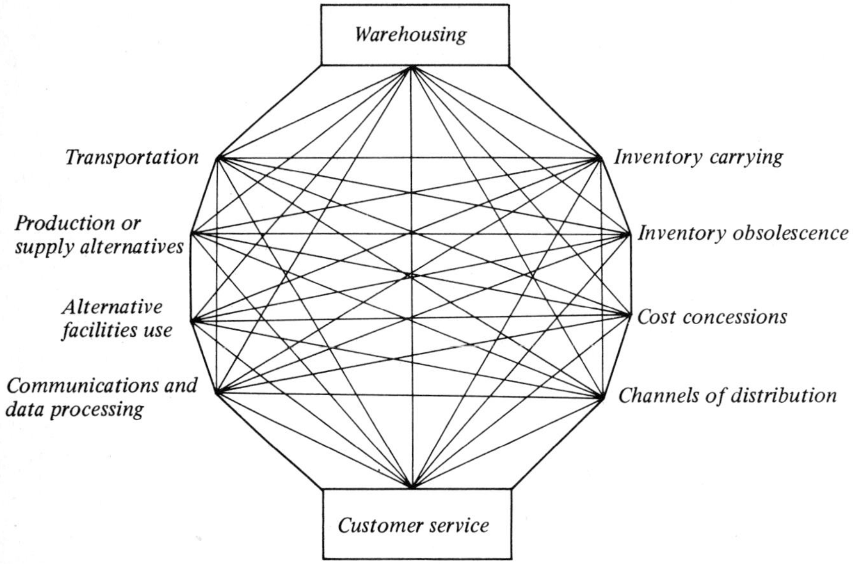

Figure 1 The real cost of distribution.

The real cost of distribution includes much more than what most companies consider when they attempt to deal with distribution costs. In a sense, any major distribution decision can affect every cost in the business and each cost is related to all the others. Our experience indicates that the following ten cost elements and interrelationships are the ones that are most likely to prove critical in evaluating the impact of alternative distribution approaches on total costs and total profits.

Warehousing. To provide service through the company's chosen channels of distribution, some warehousing is required, involving from one in-plant warehouse to a multiple-unit network dispersed across the country. Service usually becomes better as the number of warehouses is increased, at least up to a point. However, as the number of warehouses increases, their average size decreases; this will begin to reduce the efficiency of service to customers. Also, costs increase. Thus, any change in the three variables—number, type, or location or warehouses—will affect both service and costs.

Inventory carrying. The ownership of inventory gives rise to costs for money, insurance, occupancy, pilferage losses and custodial services, and sometimes inventory taxes. Depending on the business involved, this group of costs may range from 10 per cent to 30 per cent of average annual inventory value. Customer service will be improved by keeping inventory at many storage points in the field near to customers, but this will increase total inventory and the cost of carrying that inventory. Thus, inventory carrying cost is closely linked to warehousing cost and customer service.

Inventory obsolescence. If (at a given level of sales) total inventory is increased to provide better customer service, then inventory turnover is decreased. Also, the greater the "pipeline fill" in the distribution system, the slower the inventory turnover. This automatically exposes the owner to greater risks of obsolescence and inventory write-down. This is a particularly important cost for companies having frequent model changeovers, style changes or product perishability.

Production or supply alternatives. Production costs vary among plants and vary with the volume produced at each individual plant. Plants have different fixed costs and different unit variable costs as volume is increased. The decision of which plant should serve which customers must give weight not only to transportation and warehousing costs, but also to production and supply costs; these will vary significantly with the volume allocated to each plant.

Cost concessions. A special aspect of production or supply alternatives arises from the fact that distribution decisions can affect costs otherwise incurred by suppliers or customers. For example, when a retailer creates his own warehouses, this may free suppliers from packing and shipping small quantities or from maintaining small local warehouses in the field. A retailer who establishes

What is this total cost approach? What is new about it? Why have we not heard more about it?

The Approach Simply Stated

This approach sounds simple. First, analyze the distribution impact on each cost of the business, and select for more detailed study those activities the cost of which is significantly affected by distribution policies and practices. *Second,* develop the data necessary to measure the profit impact that alternative distribution decisions would have on each of these activities. *Finally,* determine which distribution decision will maximize profits.

Obviously, if it were as simple as it sounds, more companies would long ago have beaten a path to this better mousetrap. Three sets of facts explain why this has not been so:

1 The impact of distribution on costs is more difficult to unravel than is the effect of other business decisions. All functions of a business are somewhat interrelated, but distribution is more complexly intertwined with each. And it is these interrelationships—rather than the costs of the distribution functions *per se*—that are the cause of high distribution costs and the key to understanding and reducing these costs.

2 Because corporate accounting has historically been oriented to finance and production, rather than to marketing or distribution, the operating reports that guide managerial action do not tot up in any place the full impact of distribution on costs. The real cost of distribution never stares management in the face.

3 Even where managements have become aware of these costs and their impacts on profits, there was until recently very little that anyone could do about the pervasive effects of distribution. Even a relatively simple problem in distribution system design can involve hundreds of bits of information that interact in thousands of ways. So there was no way of dealing with the distribution cost complex until techniques were developed to manipulate this mass of material as a single integrated entity.

---

his own warehouse network may be able to recoup some of these costs by negotiation with the supplier.

Channels of distribution. The choice of distribution channels profoundly affects the nature and costs of a company's sales organization, its selling price and gross margin structure, its commitment to physical distribution facilities. These in turn will affect production and supply costs.

Transportation. Changing the number or location of warehouses changes transportation costs, sometimes in unanticipated and complex ways. For example, an increase in the number of warehouses may initially reduce total transportation costs; but past some determinable point, the cost trend may reverse because of the decreasing ratio of carload to less-than-carload tonnage.

Communications and data processing. These costs vary with the complexity of the distribution system and with the level of service provided, including costs for order processing, inventory control, payables, receivables and shipping documents. These costs rise as more distribution points are added to the system. Additionally, as the cycle time or response time of the communications and data processing system is shortened, costs of this service are increased.

Alternative facilities use. Changes in inventory requirements or in other aspects of the distribution operation will change space requirements and utilization in a plant-warehouse facility or a retail store. Space used for distribution may be convertible to selling space which yields incremental sales and profits. In the case of retail business, this is actually a variation of the customer service factor since it increases the availability of goods with which to fill customer requirements.

Customer service. Stock-outs, excess delivery time, or excess variability of delivery time all result in lost sales. Any change in the distribution system will influence these elements of customer service and therefore must either gain or lose sales for the company. These effects, while difficult to measure, must be considered part of the real cost of distribution.

This last is, in fact, the major reason why these distribution-related costs have continued to rise and to depress profit margins throughout our economy. And for that same reason the total cost concept remained until recently a topic for textbook discussion, theoretically provocative but of little practical use. But techniques have been developed to deal with information in these quantities and with interrelationships of such complexity. They have converted this sound but previously unworkable concept into a practical management approach.

The examples that follow are composites of a number of companies. The relevant facts and figures have thus been disguised without in any way changing the practical significance of the results. The first example traces the step-by-step process involved in the analysis of the factors that enter into the application of the total cost approach in a business engaged primarily in the retail distribution of a wide range of consumer products; the second shows how this complex array of information is analyzed and manipulated to provide management with profitable answers to some familiar distribution problems.

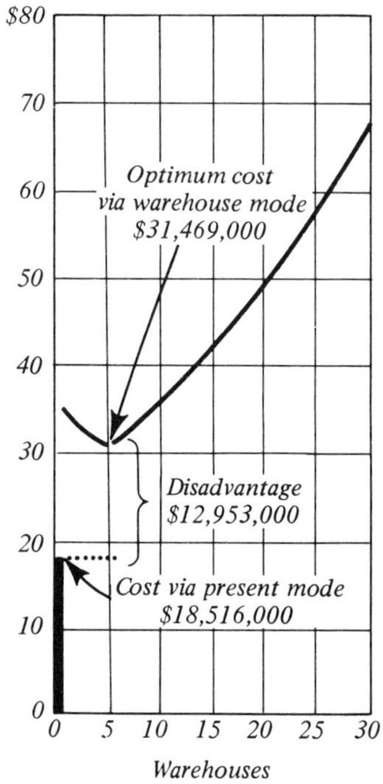

Figure 2 Distribution cost solution.

WHAT MAKES DISTRIBUTION DIFFERENT

Consider the problem facing the management of a large company whose business consists of a widely dispersed chain of retail stores and a few factories that produce some of the merchandise sold in these stores. This company has shipped directly from its suppliers and its factories to its stores, but wants to determine whether there would be any profit advantage in shifting to a national system of field warehouses.

When this company looked at the combined cost of warehousing and of transportation that would result from introducing various combinations of field warehouses, it appeared, as shown in Figure 2, that the lowest cost system was one with six warehouses. But this would *increase* its distribution costs by $12.9 million. Thus, on the basis of apparent distribution costs alone, there was no profit advantage in any field warehouse system.

However, when this study investigated how alternative distribution networks would affect other costs in the company, the answer was quite different. As shown in Figure 3, the most efficient warehouse system turned out to be one with five, rather than six, field warehouses. And this five-warehouse system would cut the total costs of the company by $7.7 million; an increase of 1.4 per cent on sales.

Looking at distribution from a standpoint of total costs, this company discovered an opportunity to increase its profits that it could not have identified or taken advantage of in any other way. What explains the difference? What legerdemain turned up this handsome profit potential that represented a 22.4 per cent

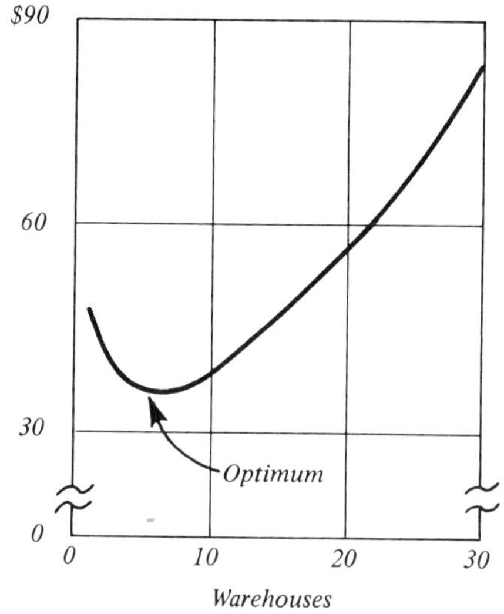

Figure 3 Total cost solution.

return on the investment required to design and install this field warehouse system? The answer, in this case as in other similar corporate experiences, involves following through the various steps of the total cost approach—that is, to determine the total cost of the present operation and then compare it with the total costs that would follow from alternative distribution systems.

At its very inception, the total cost approach is different in a number of ways from the traditional functional approach to distribution management. In the first place, it deals with the impact of distribution decisions on business costs wherever these costs appear. Secondly, many important cost factors and many critical relationships between distribution and other parts of the business are not usually translatable to quantitive terms. Customer service is a classic example.

The first step was to determine what distribution-related factors contribute significantly to total costs, trace the interrelationships of these factors, and then quantify both the factors and the interrelationships. This process has to be repeated anew for each company because of the important differences from industry to industry and even from one company to another in the same industry.

Then each of these have to be translated into a common denominator, so they can be measured and compared. If impact is measured in dollars, a unit that meets these requirements, it is possible to reduce all of the cost and profit considerations and all of these intricate interrelationships to one final total dollar cost for each alternative course of action.

The significance of this for management is seen in Figure 4; graphs show, for each major activity affected, the impact of different field warehouse systems (indicated by the numbers along the base of each graph) on the total cost of this operation. These graphs clearly show that for each factor of costs, a certain number of warehouses would yield the lowest costs and the maximum profit. Because each of these factors has its own built-in logic, each curve takes on its own configuration. The sum of all of these curves—each with its own optimum—is one final curve that defines the total cost. That in turn defines the optimum number of warehouses for this operation, when all considerations are taken into account. Except by chance coincidence, this point will differ from the optimum of each of the component curves. Obviously, a piecemeal approach to cost reduction will not yield the maximum profit impact achieved by this total cost approach.

These graphs show that even though one or several elements of distribution cost are cut to their lowest practical level, total costs may actually increase, and dealing with these costs one at a time will not produce the best result. They show the pitfalls of considering these various factors as single and static, instead of as interrelated and dynamic. The first and second graphs in the series make apparent the process whereby the consideration of distribution costs alone—the cost of warehouse

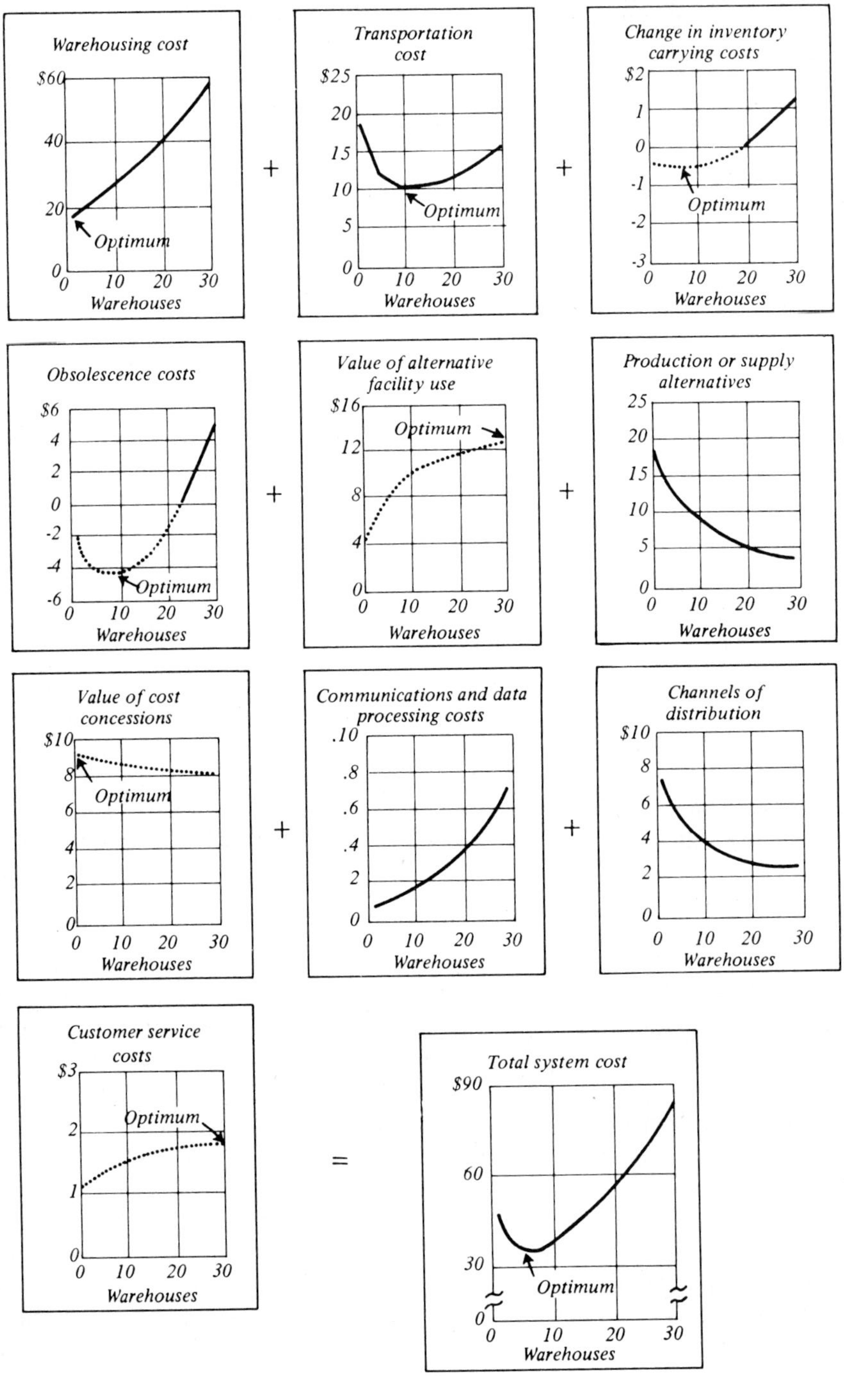

Figure 4 Total cost approach.

plus the cost of transportation—led to the conclusion that no change in distribution could add to the profitability of the business. Only the final graph, summing up all of the interacting factors involved, demonstrates unmistakably that a shift to the five-warehouse system would be a very profitable move for this management.

Actually, in this case as in so many others, a reduction in warehouse and transportation could in fact lead to increases in other distribution-related costs, with the result that total costs would be increased and this significant profit opportunity missed. Only by increasing these distribution costs could total expenses be cut and total earnings increased in this company. By this kind of trade-off the total cost approach brings a company closer to achieving its maximum potential profit. The actual figures from this company's calculations for the five-warehouse system are shown in Table I.

Table I Profit Impact of Distribution—Gains (Losses) (*in Millions of Dollars*)

Warehousing	(14.4)
Transportation	0.5
Total distribution costs	(13.9)
Inventory	
Carrying costs	1.4
Obsolescence costs	4.3
Value of alternative use of facilities	7.8
	13.5
Production and purchasing	
Production and raw materials costs	0.2
Reduced cost of purchased finished goods	6.7
	6.9
Data processing	(.02)
Marketing	
Channels of distribution	0.2
Customer service	1.4
	1.6
Total profit impact of distribution-related items	21.8
Pretax profit increase	7.9

It is difficult to conceive of a distribution problem in a company of any substantial size that could not show near-term benefits from this kind of analytical approach; the approach does much more than offer a one-time solution to what is actually a perennial problem. Because this company distributes mostly through its own retail outlets, the channels of distribution are not currently an important variable. They involve only the small amount of its product that it makes in its own factories but sells to other customers. The availability of field warehouses, however, would make it possible to sell and ship more of the output of these plants direct to customers rather than through local jobbers. As it turned out, the $200,000 it added to profitability was just about what it cost to design and engineer this whole new distribution system.

In this case, the company had good reason for considering the significance of distribution channels. Looking ahead, it could see the possibility of integrating backwards, then becoming more heavily involved in manufacturing. In that case, alternative channels of distribution might become more important. The point is that in this kind of analytical exercise it is essential to consider all possible directions for company growth. Otherwise, a new distribution system, however profitable it may be under present conditions, might freeze the company into a set of cost factors that would preclude an otherwise profitable growth opportunity. The total cost approach offers management this built-in flexibility in assessing alternatives.

Every time management makes a decision of any magnitude, it ought to be in a position to get an answer to the question, "How will it affect distribution costs throughout the company?" The total cost approach puts the company in a position to make continuing gains by applying a rigid yardstick to any proposed corporate venture. Whenever manufacturing management designs a new plant, develops a new production process, or turns to a new source of raw materials, the pattern of distribution-related costs will be changed throughout the business. Similar far-flung changes will take place whenever marketing management adds a new product or a promising new group of customers. The total cost approach enables management to define how these changes will interact with distribution to affect the company's total cost and its total profits. It tells management what distribution decisions need to be made to avoid the loss of potential profits, or to add to them. So both short-term and long-term benefits result from management's recognition of these complex cost and profit relationships.

FROM DATA TO DECISION

How these complex interrelationships and the mass of related data enable management to put a dollar value on alternative courses of action can be seen quite readily in the following case. The total cost approach was used by a division of a large manufacturing company. This division does an annual business of about $45 million, with over 3,000 customers located in every state. It has manufacturers and warehouses at five points across the country, shipping to customers via both rail and truck.

The profit problems this management posed have a familiar ring: some are long-range problems.

> Without any major investment, can we increase our profits by changing our distribution system?
>
> Can total costs be reduced by shifting some of our available equipment from one factory to another?
>
> Can we further reduce costs and increase profits by changing our marketing approach?
>
> Is there any profit advantage in changing the capacity of one or more of our present plants, or perhaps building a new facility at another location?
>
> Could we further improve profitability by changing our warehouse capacities or locations?

An analysis of this company's business showed quite readily what factors and what interactions determined the total profit of the product delivered to the customer.

Finding Relevant Facts

Every distribution study has to start with a definition of where the customers are located and what requirements they impose on their suppliers. In this case, some customers requested that products be shipped to them by rail, and others stipulated that they be served by truck. Some buy f.o.b., others at a delivered price. Options, consolidation requirements, or other ingredients of the customer service package are often relevant.

Different companies will have differing requirements for details. In this case, it was important that the data be broken down by sales districts. Therefore, it was determined for 160 sales districts what percentages of sales came into each district by rail and by truck, and percentages were found in each sales district for f.o.b. and delivered prices.

The company then knew where the products were going and how they were going to get there. Next, information was needed that would help determine from which of the five plants and warehouses each sales district should be supplied. This involved an indepth analysis of the cost of production and warehousing per unit in each of the plants and warehouses for various volume levels.

Figure 5 shows the total plant and warehouse cost of the Indiana installation of this division, for the amounts from 0 to 2,100,000 hundredweight. The total plant cost is built up by analyzing the cost for varying production volume of materials, inbound freight, direct labor, and plant overhead. Each of these cost elements will, of course, differ at each plant, even within the same company. Total ware-

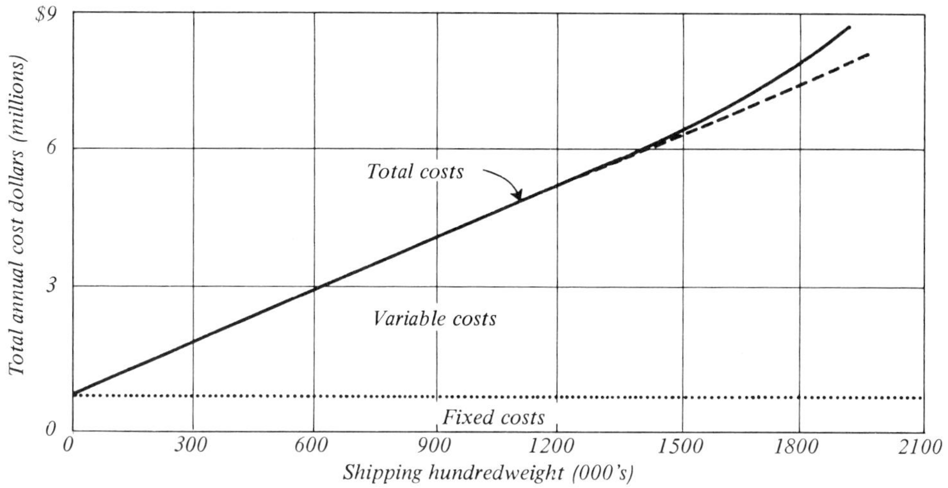

Figure 5 Total plant and warehousing cost, Indiana plant.

house costs over this same volume range were similarly analyzed. The same calculations were made for each of the company's five facilities.

Figure 6 shows these total cost curves for all of the plants and warehouses. These costs are, of course, different for each facility at each point on the curve. Not only does each curve start at a different point, reflecting different overhead costs, but the rate of increase is also different, reflecting different variable cost factors at increasing volumes of each installation. These cost differences play an important role in the calculations. It then became necessary to know the cost of shipping from each warehouse to each sales district, by train and by truck. This information is readily available, though gathering it often a time-consuming chore. Any other factors influencing profitability have to be studied similarly, in relation to each of the other cost factors. In this case, management, as a matter of policy, eliminated from consideration any changes in data processing, customer service, and channels of distribution, so these were held as constants. Under other circumstances these factors might have been evaluated as significant variables. Similarly, in other company situations, other cost factors might have required analysis so that their impact could be introduced into the final decision.

Manipulating the Data

At this point, available information showed for each unit of product and for each customer the profit contribution under all possible combinations of production and distribution. The problem that remained was to put all these possibilities together into a single solution that would maximize the company's total earnings.

While this could be done by a series of pencil and paper calculations in which each combination of factors could be worked out and the profitability of each pattern determined, it would represent an enormous and costly chore. That, of course, is the reason why the total cost concept has not found its way into management thinking until recently. To make the process practical requires a computer to process the data. And to introduce this data into the computer calls for a range of mathematical techniques known as nonlinear programming and simulation modeling. The technical aspects of these techniques are not

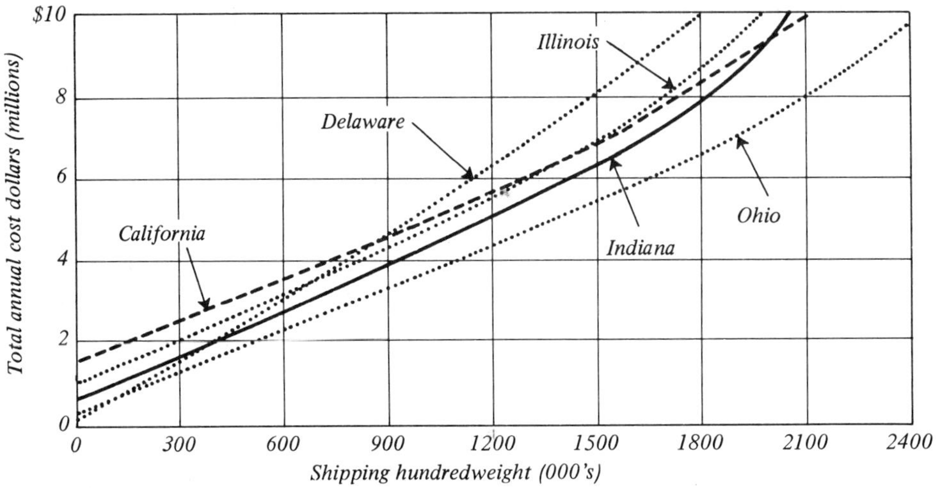

Figure 6 Total plant and warehousing cost, five plants.

important for their managerial implications. What is significant is that they do exist, that they do work, and that once the computer program has been written, this kind of distribution problem can be solved in a matter of minutes.

Concerning the questions confronting the management of this company, the total cost approach was able to provide a very precise answer to each of them.

1 *By rearranging the company's distribution pattern and making appropriate shifts in production and warehousing loads, it was possible without any change in facilities to increase this company's profits by $492,000 a year.* The largest ingredient in this change would come from reduced materials cost at $126,000, with warehouse savings contributing $138,000, direct labor saving in the plants adding $57,000, and plant overhead $27,000. Transportation, so often overstressed in distribution decisions, contributed only $54,000 to this total profit improvement package.

2 *Additional savings of $180,000 could be effected by shifting equipment from one plant to another at minor cost.* To determine this, it was necessary to develop new production cost curves for alternative arrangements of equipment and run these through the computer, comparing them with the most profitable way of using the equipment as presently located.

3 *Further savings of $447,000 a year would result if about half of the customers could be persuaded to shift from truck to rail delivery.* These reduced costs could be added to earnings or passed on to the customer, thus giving the company a competitively significant price advantage.

4 *It was determined that there was no plant addition that would provide an acceptable return on investment.* Although building a new plant in Michigan would result in lower production and warehousing costs amounting to $225,000, the return on the investments would be only 2 percent, and the "other costs" discussed above more than offset any possible gains, so that this investment would not be a wise one.

5 *On the other hand, an addition to the capacity of the warehouse at the Delaware plant would add $75,000 a year to profits and represent a sound investment.* This was determined by setting up new warehousing cost schedules and running them through the computer alongside the costs under existing conditions. The comparison showed that the investment in the added Delaware warehouse capacity would return almost 25 per cent a year.

The total addition to profits adds up to almost $750,000 a year, from changes in distribution and facilities, that were well within the company's capabilities. These would add 1.7 percent to this company's margin on sales. The important point is this: these profits could not have been generated by decisions based on the insight or the experience of the most competent line executive. Only the total cost approach could have established, for example, that the earnings of this business could be increased by supplying its customers in the Dakotas from a plant in Ohio rather than from a much nearer facility in Illinois. Yet when total profits were calculated, this turned out to be an element in the most profitable use of the existing facilities of this company.

Similarly, only a total cost calculation could provide the background for estimating the return on investment that could be expected from building a new facility in Michigan. Actually, that new plant would have reduced production and warehousing costs by an appreciable figure. However, other costs would be incurred in serving customers from this facility rather than from the present plant in Illinois; these other costs substantially reduced the potential savings and made the investment an unsound one. This ability to put precise price and profit tags on each pattern of alternatives makes the total cost approach a particularly effective management tool.

MAKING THE TOTAL COST APPROACH WORK

The successful applications of the total cost approach illustrated by these examples leave no doubt that this approach can, for many companies, uncover profit opportunities previously obscured by established ways of looking at distribution costs and by existing methods of managing distribution functions. But the experience of the successful companies also serves as a warning to those who are tempted to use the term "total cost" lightly. Understanding of many factors is required in order to undertake the kind of analysis required to define what all these costs are and what they really amount to, to develop a way to recover the profits they represent, and then to translate that solution into actual practice.

Though experience shows that the approach works out differently in every practical application, the sequence of steps that management has to take is always the same and it always involves the same inexorable logic:

To succeed, the total cost approach must have the active endorsement of top management. The total cost concept can be initiated at any place in the company, but unless it receives strong support from the top, it will not progress successfully, for the simple reason that only top management can insist that the real cost and profit impact of distribution be defined and measured, and at regular intervals. Only top management can see to it that there is a senior executive actively concerned with doing something about this impact of distribution on costs and on profitability. And only top management can assign to this executive the authority necessary to tackle this problem across organization lines, in order to identify and take advantage of this profit opportunity.

Only a carefully conceived feasibility study can determine whether or not a restructuring of the distribution system is likely to be profitable. This thorough kind of study requires a wide range of technical and managerial skills. The team that can do such a study has to include transportation, production, and materials handling specialists, warehousing and logistics experts, as well as analysts with backgrounds in economics, mathematical decision making and operations research.

Some companies have found it appropriate to assemble these skills within the company, while others have preferred to bring the necessary talent in from outside; this is a decision that management must make. But one fact cannot be avoided: this kind of study involves a much wider range of talents than is usually brought to bear on distribution problems as well as a broad experience in the application of these capabilities to these total cost problems.

A more substantial and more time-consuming study is then required to determine in detail what changes are indicated, what profits can validly be expected from alternative ways of effecting these changes, and what improvement in profits can be anticipated from the most practical solution.

To succeed in this effort the firm must develop quantitative information on the variables that affect each cost factor and the interrelationships among the various factors. Much of this information may be available in company records, and some of what is not available can usually be derived from existing reports. In most cases, it will be necessary to generate additional data.

Then, all of the significant interrelationships must be traced through the operation, the significant correlations defined and quantified, and all of this data subjected to mathematical analysis.

Next, the appropriate mathematical models must be constructed and then tested against past experience to validate their effectiveness. Then, alternative solutions to present and foreseeable problems have to be developed, and these studied by putting them through the model. This puts dollar values against each alternative and defines the optimum solution—the one that is most practical and most profitable.

Finally, the business implications of this solution need to be checked against organizational requirements, implications for competitive strategy, and ultimately for practicality in terms of timing and return on investment.

The final stage in the application of the total cost approach is the actual implementation of the solution. Initially, this involves putting into place the distribution system that matches the company's existing needs and its requirements for the short-term future. Since the business itself and its external environment are both changing inevitably with the passage of time, with changes in product and in marketing policies and practices, as well as in response to changes in competitive forces and strategies, it is likely to prove profitable to rerun the problem at regular intervals. This process will redefine optimum distribution decisions and adjust plant loads and shipping schedules.

The companies that have been successful in using this approach have found that along with this restructuring of their distribution system, certain additional steps are likely to be critical. The assignment of responsibility for distribution has to be clarified. An information system has to be developed that will provide data on distribution costs and performance to whomever is responsible for controlling these activities. The company's data-gathering and data-processing system must be adapted so that it will pick up routinely the necessary informational input. Procedures must also be established to feed into the information system intelligence concerning conditions in the marketplace, and notably a continuing reassessment of prevailing customer service levels.

Thus the accumulated experience not only confirms the practicality and profitability of the total cost approach, but it also defines some clear-cut guidelines for managements who propose to put this approach to work. Experience in applying this approach suggests, too, that a number of additional considerations need to be clarified.

The fact that this substantial profit opportunity exists in a company is no implicit criticism of its operating management. No traffic manager or transportation specialist can be expected to deal with a problem the roots of which extend far beyond his sphere into manufacturing and marketing. Nor can the best warehouse manager be expected to come up with solutions to problems the causes and conditions of which extend from purchasing and supplier relationships at one extreme, to customer service considerations at the other. Even those companies that have centralized distribution responsibility in the hands of a single high-level executive rarely can provide this executive with the wide range of supporting capabilities and in-depth experience necessary to deal with this profit potential.

Nor does the fact that the necessary action requires top management support mean that the chief executive has to become an expert in the complexities of the mathematical tools involved, any more than he has to become knowledgeable in computer technology or the relative merits of the hardware and software. No one intends to suggest that management has to do or know anything specific or technical about distribution. What is required is management's insistence that something be done, by someone with the appropriate capabilities and experience.

In this sense, the challenge of the total cost approach has another interesting management meaning. The relentless and increasing impact of distribution on profits is one of a growing category of management problems that are not going to be solved satisfactorily within the framework of traditional organizational and decision-making approaches. The most effective solution to any company's distribution problem requires looking at the company as a whole and dealing with the profitability of the entity. More and more, management is being faced with problems requiring the kind of the across-the-board attention.

At the same time new concepts, new techniques, and new technology are becoming available that are peculiarly able to cope with this very kind of problem. The more we learn about the computer and about such techniques as simulation, the more apparent it is that they are used to fullest advantage when they are used to deal with problems like these for which no other problem-solving technique is truly appropriate.

There is every reason to believe that with the increasing complexity of modern businesses and the mounting competitive pressures in their environment, the ability of companies to forge ahead and to grow profitably may have a direct relationship to the ability of management to put these new tools and their vast new capabilities to work. In the days ahead, competition between companies may in large measure reflect the skill with which competing managements take advantage of these new management tools.

D PERSONAL SELLING AND MANAGEMENT OF THE SALES FORCE

31

Interaction and Influence Processes in Personal Selling

Harry L. Davis
Alvin J. Silk

Behavioral research offers marketers a great deal of potentially useful material. The authors provide an extensive review of studies of interaction and influence processes in sales situations. Several important insights and implications for sales management are revealed.

Reprinted from *Sloan Management Review*, vol. 12, pp. 59–76. Winter 1972. At the time of writing, Mr. Davis was assistant professor of marketing in the Graduate School of Business at the University of Chicago, and Mr. Silk was associate professor in the Sloan School of Management at the Massachusetts Institute of Technology.

INTRODUCTION

When stock is being taken of the current state of marketing knowledge, one frequently hears it said that personal selling is a neglected area of study. The point is usually made that despite its generally greater significance as a marketing expense than media advertising, personal selling has been the object of much less model-building and empirical study. There are, however, indications that the situation is changing. The amount of attention being paid to sales force management problems in the management science/operations research literature appears to be increasing.[1] Sales operations are also the focal point of much of the work going on in the area of marketing information systems.[2]

This paper reviews some relevant developments of yet another sort—behavioral research on personal selling. A great deal of research on the behavior of salesmen has been conducted in the past, but most of it has dealt with psychological testing and the prediction of salesmen's performance. A quite different point of view is reflected in the material examined here. Our interest centers on efforts to apply social psychological knowledge about interaction and influence processes to selling problems.

The paper is organized as follows: We first consider investigations of customer-salesman interaction. We then consider their implications for sales force management. Work that treats selling as interpersonal influence is then discussed. Finally, findings are summarized and further applications of behavioral research are suggested.

SELLING AS INTERPERSONAL INTERACTION

A criticism sometimes made of behavioral science research is that after cutting through the specialized lingo and complex methodology, one finds in barely recognizable form, little more than an affirmation of what was already "obvious" to everyone—mere "truisms, platitudes, and tautologies."[3] Thus, the observation that the most fundamental aspect of personal selling is the "interaction" that goes on between a prospect and a salesman may well appear as yet another example of befuddling the commonplace with fancy verbiage. While it may seem self-evident that selling involves interaction, such a description implies a somewhat different view of the selling process than that which is generally stressed in the vast literature of this field. More important, some empirical studies of personal selling as interaction have begun to appear which offer fresh insights of practical significance into a number of thorny issues of long standing.

The Customer-Salesman Dyad

The person primarily responsible for stimulating the current interest in salesman-prospect interaction is Franklin B. Evans. Examining a sample of the abundant and diverse writings of practitioners on the subject of selling, Evans points out that "invariably these deal with only the salesman's point of view."[4] The customer is certainly not ignored in these conventional writings but the emphasis is, understandably, on how to sell. The typical discussion places the customer, at least implicitly, in a somewhat passive role. In prescribing such things as the personal characteristics required of the "successful" salesman, means of diagnosing and adapting to customer's needs, persuasive techniques, etc., salesmanship authorities naturally focus on how the salesman's behavior affects the outcome of a sales contact. As a consequence, analysis of the influence of the prospect on the process tends to be neglected.

[1]The December 1971 issue of *Management Science*, which is devoted entirely to marketing models, contains four papers dealing with sales force problems.

[2]See Smith *et al.* [35].

[3]See, for example, Henry [22]. For an opposing view on this issue see Lazarsfeld [25].

[4]See Evans [12], p. 76.

A similar imbalance characterizes most past empirical research on personal selling which is also voluminous—as Miner has observed, "there is little question but that the salesman is one of the most extensively studied men in the business world."[5] The focus of attention in most empirical research has been on the prediction of some measure of salesman performance from information about the salesman's background characteristics and a variety of personality, interest, and ability factors measured by psychological testing instruments.[6] The results of these attempts to discover criteria useful for recruiting and selecting salesmen have been quite mixed—sizeable correlations have been reported for certain sales occupations while in numerous other studies, few of which are ever published, no meaningful relationships have been found.[7] Even for its limited intended purpose (*i.e.,* to aid in making personnel decisions), the value of this work remains highly controversial and, as has been noted by others, it has contributed very little to our understanding of why or how a salesman becomes effective.[8] In attempting to predict sales performance, this research has concentrated almost entirely on the characteristics of salesmen and has failed to take explicit account of who the salesman interacts with in attempting to make a sale.[9] The assumption tacitly made is that differences among salesmen with respect to the types of prospects they contact are minimal, and hence variations in performance must be due to differences among the salesmen themselves. As we shall discuss below, such an assumption seems tenuous for many if not most types of selling. In contrast, Evans argues that the unit of analyses in personal selling research should not be the salesman alone but rather the *interaction dyad*—the salesman-prospect pair involved in a sales encounter.

Evans summarizes his position as follows:

> . . . the sale (or no sale) is the result of the particular interaction situation, the face-to-face contact of the given salesman and his prospect. The result of the contact depends not on the characteristics of either party alone but how the two parties view and react to each other.[10]

Interpersonal Attraction

Given such an orientation, what can behavioral science suggest about the nature of a prospect-salesman interaction and the chance of a sale being made? One source of relevant ideas is research on "interpersonal attraction."[11] The general question motivating work by social psychologists and sociologists in this area is: why is a person attracted to certain individuals and repelled by others? There is a considerable body of evidence to suggest that the answer lies in how similar the two individuals are. It has been repeatedly demonstrated in a long list of both experimental and correlational studies of such phenomena as friendship formation, mate selection, and survey interviewing that a strong positive relationship exists between interpersonal similarity and liking.[12] Various dimensions of similarity have been investigated including background characteristics (e.g., race, age, status, ethnicity, etc.), attitudes, interests, values, and personality. The proposition that similarity leads to liking can be derived from several theoretical positions such as those involving models of cognitive consistency[13] and social exchange[14]

[5]See Miner [31], p. 6.

[6]For a recent review of some of this work see Cotham [11].

[7]See, for example, Stevens [36].

[8]See Willett and Pennington [41].

[9]One of the methods for evaluating salesmen, reported by Chapple [10] some years ago, was a mechanical device which recorded the time pattern of responses of a subject as he interacted with an observer in a standardized interview.

[10]See Evans [13], p. 25.

[11]See Berscheid and Walster [6].

[12]Extensive reviews of various aspects of this literature are available. See Bramel [7], Byrne [9], Lindzey and Byrne [27], esp. pp. 496–509; Lott and Lott [28], and Marlow and Gergen [29], esp. pp. 621–637.

[13]See Heider [21] and Newcomb [32].

[14]See Homans [23] and Thibaut and Kelley [38].

but most emphasize the notion that interacting with others who are similar to, or agree with oneself provides rewards or need satisfaction.

Salesman-Customer Similarity

Drawing on these ideas, Evans hypothesized that "the more similar the parties in the dyad are, the more likely a favorable outcome, a sale."[15] Evans tested this hypothesis in a field study of life insurance selling.[16] The latter was chosen because it represented an area where the salesman (rather than the product offering and/or other promotion) appeared to be the critical factor determining whether or not a sale was made. A group of 86 experienced male agents were selected from three insurance firms. From records of all the face-to-face contacts they made during a four-week period, a random sample of 168 sold and 183 unsold prospects was chosen. On the average, personal interviews were conducted with the sample eleven weeks after the date of the salesman's visit. Care was taken to minimize the chance of respondents' making a connection between the sales call and the interview. Sold and unsold prospects responded to a questionnaire covering the following classes of variables: attitudes and knowledge of life insurance and life insurance salesmen in general; attitudes and perceptions of the "last" insurance agent who had called on them; management of personal finances; demographics, background, and physical characteristics; and personality needs. Essentially the same instruments were administered to the salesmen; however, they rated themselves on scales similar to those the prospects had used to describe the salesmen who had contacted them.

In general, the results supported the similarity hypothesis; the insurance agents were found to be more like the sold than the unsold prospects. Evans demonstrated that whether or not a prospect would buy insurance from a particular agent could *not* be predicted in any straightforward manner solely on the basis of knowledge of the prospect's attitudinal, personality, and demographic characteristics. As groups, the sold and unsold prospects were essentially similar in all the above respects.

However, when the three groups were compared to one another, the salesmen appeared to be more like the sold prospects than the unsolds. To illustrate, the difference in mean ages between the salesmen and sold prospects was 1.2 years while that for the salesmen and unsold prospects was 2.5 years. The same pattern manifested itself when similar comparisons were made with respect to numerous variables ranging from background and physical characteristics through personality needs. Furthermore, not only did objective measures of the variables indicate that the salesmen were more similar to the sold than the unsold prospects, but the sold prospects tended to *perceive* the salesmen as more like themselves than the unsolds did.

The basic notion underlying Evans' work is that the more similar a salesman and prospect are, the greater will be their mutual attraction which, in turn, enhances the likelihood of a sale being made—i.e., the more a prospect likes a salesman, the greater the chance that the latter will be able to influence the former. The findings summarized above indicated that the probability of a sale occurring was related to salesman-prospect similarity.

In addition, Evans investigated the intervening variable, liking. As expected, sold prospects evaluated the salesman more favorably than did the unsolds. Evans describes the differences between the sold and unsold prospects' reactions to the salesmen as follows: The successful salesman is seen by sold prospects as (1) an expert in insurance, (2) similar

[15]See Evans [12], p. 78.

[16]Only a brief, preliminary account of this work, by Evans [12], has appeared in the literature. We have relied here on a more extensive, but unpublished, report by Evans [13].

to themselves in outlook and situation, (3) as a person they'd like to know better, and (4) interested in them personally, not just as a source of revenue.[17]

The sold and unsold prospects held a common and quite negative stereotype of the "typical" insurance salesman as an aggressive, fast-talking, untrustworthy type. However, the two groups did not share the same view of the particular agents who had contacted them. Compared to the unsolds, the ratings of the particular salesmen given by sold prospects were more positive and closer to the salesmen's own evaluations of themselves. This would suggest that salesman-prospect similarity facilitated the development of a friendly relaxed interaction. Since Evans' study was basically a correlational one utilizing data obtained *after* the salesman-prospect contact had taken place, whether the sold prospects' greater liking of the salesmen preceded or followed the sale cannot be determined. Clearly, the similarity-attraction hypothesis would suggest that liking was the antecedent condition and the occurrence of the sale, the consequence. On the other hand, for a variety of reasons one would expect prospects to evaluate a salesman from whom they had bought an insurance policy more positively than one from whom they had declined to buy. For example, there is evidence that individuals tend to like persons who have influenced them.[18]

A similar question about causal priorities might also be raised concerning the relationship Evans observed between perceived prospect-salesman similarity and the occurrence of a sale. Although it has been frequently demonstrated experimentally that similarity leads to interpersonal liking, there is also a large body of evidence which indicates that persons tend to perceive other whom they like as similar to themselves.[19] Thus, an association between perceived similarity and purchasing could reflect causation in either direction. However, Evans found that not only did the sold prospects *perceive* the salesmen to be more similar to themselves than the unsolds but in fact they actually were when compared in terms of objective measures, such as physical and personality characteristics, which would remain unchanged before and after the sales transaction.

If one accepts the basic notion that salesman-prospect similarity affects the likelihood of a sale being made, then the practical question that naturally comes to mind is: with respect to what attributes is similarity critical? Two additional studies have been reported which provide some further support for Evans' views and are relevant to this question. Another study of life insurance selling carried out by Gadel[20] suggests that age may be a key factor. An analysis of some 22,000 policies revealed that agents' sales tended to be concentrated among persons who were in the same age group as themselves. This concentration was greatest for young agents and tended to decrease with years of experience. If salesman-prospect similarity affects sales success, salesmen are likely to develop an awareness of this condition. To the extent that insurance agents have some latitude in choosing prospects, one would expect them to seek out prospects similar to themselves. Clearly, their ability to do so is limited by what they can ascertain about a prospect before making a sales contact. Given the ways agents learn about prospects initially, it is probably easier to obtain a rough indication of the prospect's age and to use that as a screening criterion; rather than attempt to assess other personal characteristics. Of course, agents may well use more than one criterion.

[17]See Evans [13], p. xii.
[18]See Lott and Lott [28], p. 276.
[19]See Lott and Lott [28], p. 290.
[20]See Gadel [17].

A quite different aspect of customer-salesman similarity was investigated by Tosi in a study of middleman selling.[21] Here attention was focused on the extent to which customer and salesman share the same conception of the salesman's role. A group of 40 wholesale drug salesmen and 103 retail pharmacists whom the former contacted regularly were asked to indicate their perceptions of the "ideal" and "actual" behavior of salesmen on a set of predetermined scales. Differences between the salesman's and customer's responses on the "ideal" scales were taken as a measure of *role consensus*—the extent to which the salesman and customer agreed as to what the salesman's behavior should be. Discrepancies between the ideal and actual ratings given by either the salesman or the customer were used as indicators of *expectation level*—the degree to which the salesman's actual behavior was perceived to differ from that which was considered desirable.

Tosi hypothesized that both role consensus and expectation level would be related to sales performance. Two indices of the latter variable were employed: the share of a given customer's business placed with the salesman's firm, and the number of *other* suppliers also serving the customer. Contrary to the first hypothesis, no statistically significant relationship was found between role consensus and either measure of sales success. However, the buyers' expectation levels were shown to be related to the number of suppliers they purchased from but not to the share of business the salesmen obtained.[22]

That is, the less the discrepancy between buyer's conception of the "ideal" behavior of a salesman and his perception of how the particular salesman actually conducted himself, the fewer other suppliers the customer tended to deal with. Thus it appeared that agreement between the customer and salesman as to how the salesman *ought* to behave did not have any bearing on the latter's effectiveness; but the closer the salesman came to meeting the customer's expectations regarding how he should function, the smaller the number of competitors he would have to contend with.

[21]See Tosi [39].

[22]The salesmen's expectation level was also significantly related to the number of suppliers but in a nonlinear manner.

Selling Strategies

The studies of Evans, Gadel, and Tosi described above dealt primarily with the relationship between salesman-prospect similarity and sales performance. All three were correlational investigations based on data obtained after the sales contacts had been made. As such, they were not well suited to uncovering exactly what transpires between the salesman and prospect in the course of their encounters. The interpersonal attraction theory referred to above would suggest that salesman-prospect similarity is conducive to the occurrence of an amicable exchange between the two parties, thereby making it more likely that the salesman will be able to influence the prospect to buy.

Willett and Pennington made a detailed study of the content of customer-salesman interactions occurring in retail stores in connection with the purchase of certain appliances.[23] The interactions were tape-recorded in a seemingly unobtrusive way and content-analyzed using the scheme developed by Bales which distinguishes between task or instrumental behavior on the one hand, and socioemotional or affective behavior on the other.[24] Comparisons were drawn between "successful" and "unsuccessful" transactions involving 132 customers and 14 salesmen. The interactions that resulted in immediate purchases appeared to be characterized by more suggestion-seeking and giving and fewer displays of negative feelings than those interac-

[23]See Willett and Pennington [41].

[24]See Bales [4].

tions that were not culminated by a purchase. Although salesman-customer similarity was not examined, these data constitute evidence that interactions preceding a sale tend to be friendlier, more free-flowing exchanges than those which do not produce a purchase.

From a managerial standpoint, the important question about sales interactions is, of course, how the salesman's behavior affects the outcome. What can the salesman do to shape the course along which an interaction proceeds? Are certain selling strategies and techniques more effective than others in this regard? Consider the following problem. In selling paint to consumers, who will be more successful: the salesman who appears to customers to be more knowledgeable about using paint than they are, or one whom customers perceive as having about the same amount of experience (or lack thereof) as themselves? At first glance, most would probably opt for the prediction favoring the salesman who appeared more knowledgeable than his customers—i.e., the more experienced a salesman is perceived as being with respect to his product, the more likely it is that he can influence a customer to buy. Besides its common sense appeal, this proposition finds support in numerous experimental studies of communications source credibility which have been demonstrated that the effectiveness of a given message in changing attitudes varies according to the amount of expertise attributed to the source of the message.[25] However, application of the salesman-customer similarity hypothesis to this situation leads to just the opposite prediction. The amount of experience a salesman claims to have had with the product could affect the customer's perception of their similarity. For the typical consumer who is only an occasional painter, the more painting the salesman indicates he personally has done, the less similar he will appear to the novice buyer and hence, the less influence the salesman will have with the buyer.

The efficacy of these two competing factors, salesman expertise and customer-salesman similarity, was investigated in a field experiment conducted by Brock.[26] Over a five-month period, two part-time salesmen in the paint department of a retail store attempted to influence customers to purchase paint at a different price level from that which they initially selected. After a consumer indicated that he wished to buy a given amount of some variety of paint at a particular price, the salesman tried to alter his choice by delivering one of two predetermined appeals. Half the time the salesman represented himself as being similar to customers by emphasizing that the magnitude of his own recent paint consumption was the same as the amount being purchased by the customer. For the other half of the cases, the dissimilar or "expert" condition was applied by having the salesman portray himself as having just used twenty times the quantity of paint the consumer planned to buy. Attempts were made to influence some customers to buy at higher prices and others at lower prices than they originally intended. The results indicated that similarity was more important than expertise. While the dissimilar salesman was presumably perceived as more knowledgeable about paint, he was less effective than the salesman who identified his own paint consumption as similar to that of his customers. The differential effectiveness of the two approaches held up over attempts to persuade consumers to buy higher as well as lower priced paints.

Central to the view of selling as interpersonal interaction is the proposition that the more a prospect likes a salesman, the greater the influence the salesman will have on the prospect. This would imply that ingratiating consumers should be an effective selling tactic. Farley and Swinth performed an experiment

[25]See McGuire [30], pp. 182–187.

[26]See Brock [8].

bearing on this matter.[27] The main purpose of the study was to compare the impact of two different sales messages for a roll-up yardstick. One message, dubbed the "product pitch," emphasized a description and demonstration of the product's features. The other, a "personal pitch," featured a favorable personal discussion of the customer's role and stressed how the product was compatible with it. A group of 87 females served as subjects—about a third were undergraduates and the remainder were housewives. After hearing one of the presentations, subjects chose between the product and an equivalent sum of money ($0.75) and then rated the product and the salesman on a number of scales. The percentage choosing the yardstick over the money was slightly greater for the group hearing the personal rather than the product pitch. However, the difference was not statistically significant.

Paradoxically, subjects exposed to the product pitch evaluated both the product and the salesman more positively than those receiving the personal pitch. Regardless of which sales presentation they heard, those selecting the product had more favorable attitudes toward the product and the salesman than those who chose to take the money. Here again, the design of the study did not permit the direction of causal relations between attitudes and choice to be untangled. As Farley and Swinth note, the results suggest that an effective sales appeal alters the buyer's perception of the attractiveness of the product and the salesman and hence, *both* considerations require attention in designing sales messages.

IMPLICATIONS FOR SALES FORCE MANAGEMENT

We began the last section by suggesting that personal selling might be fruitfully viewed as salesman-prospect interaction. One stream of research from the small groups field was identified as being especially relevant to the problem of understanding the determinants of effective salesman performance—that dealing with the subject of interpersonal attraction. Applying the core idea of this work to personal selling suggests that the greater the similarity between a salesman and a prospect, the more the prospect will like the salesman and, therefore, the greater the salesman's influence. We then reviewed a handful of empirical studies that embrace the interactionist view of selling within the framework of this proposition. While the number of investigations available is limited and various kinds of methodological questions can be raised about them, significant relationships between several aspects of customer-salesman similarity and buying have been reported with considerable, but by no means total, regularity. Much remains to be learned about why and under what conditions this relationship occurs. For example, it would be useful to consider how not only similarity but also complementarity between salesmen and customers is related to sales success. While the old adage that "birds of a feather flock together" seems plausible enough, is there not also something in that other oft-repeated maxim about "opposites attracting?" In pursuing such questions the available behavioral literature should prove useful as a source of ideas for conditional propositions which can be tested so as to refine our knowledge about where a certain relationship does or does not hold. A theory of interpersonal *congruency* has been proposed which suggests that under certain circumstances attraction will be facilitated by dissimilarities as well as similarities.[28]

Research has scarcely begun on the question of how and to what extent the salesman can influence and/or control the direction a sales interaction takes by modifying his own

[27]See Farley and Swinth [14].

[28]See Marlow and Gergen [29], pp. 629–631.

behavior in appropriate ways. Nonetheless, Brock's provocative experiment dealing with customer-salesman similarity with respect to product experience is indicative of how a non-obvious relationship involving an important control variable suggested by the similarity-attraction hypothesis can be studied in a natural sales setting. An intriguing question raised by Brock's study is: in what types of selling situations will it be more effective to stress salesman-customer differences rather than similarities with respect to product expertise? Here again, the behavioral literature can offer some relevant insights. Recently a review has appeared which attempts to integrate research on interpersonal similarity and attraction with that bearing on source credibility and attitude change.[29]

Having discussed research on sales interactions at some length, we may now consider what practical implications it may have. This work is relevant to several aspects of sales force management.

Recruitment, Selection, and Manpower Planning

The notion that the outcome of a sales contact depends on customer-prospect similarity casts doubt on the usefulness of much research and practice in the area of salesman recruitment and selection, which is aimed at identifying a successful "sales type."[30] If a firm's potential customers are appreciably more heterogeneous than its sales force, it may be effectively excluding itself from penetrating certain market segments. Simple models of the size and composition of a sales force can be structured for manpower planning purposes to assure that sales forces will be matched to the markets they serve with respect to key characteristics.[31]

Sales Training Training for salesmen should focus on helping them develop the special skills they require to be effective in interacting with prospects.[32] For example, a familiarity with existing knowledge about how perceptions of others are developed might enable salesmen to discriminate better among prospects.[33] There is much room for improvement in this area. One study showed that salesman *failed* to perceive as ready to buy 69 percent of appliance shoppers who had previously indicated that they had definite purchasing plans.[34] Salesmen might be taught more reliable procedures for identifying the prospect status of shoppers.

Allocating Salesmen to Customers

A number of suggestions as to how a closer match between the characteristics of salesmen and prospects might be effected in the life insurance field have been made.[35] For example, a salesman who uncovers a prospect quite unlike himself could turn over the lead to another salesman who is more similar to the prospect and who, therefore, would have a better chance of making the sale. The notion that salesmen should be "compatible" with the customers they serve is certainly not new, but knowledge of what dimensions of similarity and differences are critical in a particular type of selling might lead to improved matchings.[36]

SELLING AS INTERPERSONAL INFLUENCE

In this section we shall consider some work in which selling is viewed as a *process* of influence and an attempt is made to apply behavioral knowledge about this phenomenon to problems of personal selling.

[29] See Simons *et al.* [34].
[30] See Evans [13].
[31] See Gadel [17].
[32] See Webster [40].
[33] See Taguiri [37].
[34] See Granbois and Willett [19].
[35] See Evans [13].
[36] See Stevens [36].

Influencing others via verbal communications is the salesman's basic stock and trade. At the same time, the study of communication and persuasion has long represented one of the major areas of interest to social psychologists.[37] In light of this, one might expect to find that the large body of behavioral science theory and research findings on this subject would have considerable use in dealing with problems of personal selling. While general discussions of "selling as communication" are readily available[38] and so-called "principles of persuasion" are sometimes presented in sales training programs,[39] the diligent reader of the marketing literature would be hard pressed to come up with a very extensive list of systematic applications of behavioral science knowledge about influence to issues of real concern to practitioners in the field of personal selling. Fortunately, examples of the productive utilization of behavioral science research on influence processes are available, and an examination of some of this work will serve to illustrate what behavioral scientists have to say about persuasion and how these ideas might be brought to bear on selling problems.

Using Group Pressure to Overcome Buyer Resistance

The most sophisticated and creative application of behavioral research on influence processes to personal selling that has come to our attention is a program developed by Jacoba Varela, a consultant in Uruguay.[40] The selling problem tackled was that faced by an upholstery firm in marketing fabrics to retailers. The firm's sales objectives conflicted with the established buying habits of both consumers and retailers. The product being promoted was ready-made curtains. Traditionally, however, Uruguayan housewives had their curtains custom-made. The firm's effort to sell retailers in the fall also ran contrary to the latter's customary practice of selecting new fabrics only in the spring. Furthermore, economic conditions were extremely adverse. Severe inflation had led to stringent government policies to curb consumer spending. To deal with this difficult set of circumstances, Varela designed a most elaborate and extensive selling program based on a number of concepts and propositions borrowed from social psychological research on influence. A few aspects of this work can be described here.

One phase of Varela's program made use of the results of Asch's classic experiments on group pressure and conformity.[41] Briefly, the typical Asch experiment is run as follows.

An unsuspecting person enters a laboratory with seven other persons who are confederates of the experimenter. The experimental task requires that each subject match a standard line with one of three other lines of varying lengths. All subjects report their judgements orally and in a particular order so that six of the seven confederates give their answers before the naive subject does. The correct answer is easily determined since the sizes of the lines are clearly presented. However, by pre-arrangement, the experimenter's confederates unanimously begin to give incorrect answers. Suddenly the subject finds that the judgements of all those around him completely contradict what he perceives to be the obviously correct answer. In this way, group pressure is exerted on the subject to modify his judgement in the direction of the majority. The experiment consists of several trials and

[37]A number of short, highly readable accounts of this research are available. See Karlins and Abelson [24] and Zimbardo and Ebbesen [42]. Undoutedly, the best and most complete review of the field is McGuire[30].

[38]See, for example, Webster [40].

[39]See, for example, Andelson [1].

[40]This discussion is based on descriptions of Varela's work given in Festinger [15] and Zimbardo and Ebbesen [42], pp. 114–122.

[41]See Asch [3].

on each the subject may either respond correctly or agree with the group of confederates and give the incorrect answer. Replications of this experiment, varying such things as the stimulus conditions and the size of the majority, have been made many times. The results show that about one third of the naive subjects yield to group pressure and alter their answers to be in accord with the majority.

Such an experimental finding would surely seem to be a prime candidate for the "interesting but irrelevant" category as far as suggesting anything applicable to personal selling. The subjects (college undergraduates), setting (artificial and highly controlled), and task (judging line length) bear little resemblance to selling curtains to retailers in South America. The dissimilarity between the real and laboratory worlds has led some to question the generalizability and hence the usefulness of marketing of this type of research.[42]

Varela largely circumvented this issue by skillfully manipulating the sales situation so that it essentially became a simulation of Asch's laboratory setting. Rather than have the company's salesmen sell the retailers in the stores, prospective buyers were invited to the company's offices. Buyers came in small groups. In the firm's own showroom, various facilities could be used which enabled the product line to be presented far more effectively than would have been possible in the retailers' stores. As an item was being presented, the salesmen made an assessment of how favorably impressed each of the prospective buyers was with the product. The salesmen had been trained to scan buyers' facial expressions and look for other cues that might reflect evaluations of the product. The buyer appearing most favorable was then asked for his opinion of the product and encouraged to explain why his reaction was positive. By this process the buyer was led to commit himself gradually and finally asked to place an order. In the meantime, the salesmen had been on the alert for indications of how the other buyers were reacting. The buyer identified as being next most positive was asked to express his views and the whole process was repeated. Thus the salesmen proceeded from the most to the least positive buyer and thereby took advantage of the opportunity of bringing to bear on those initially unfavorable the pressure of their peers who held more positive attitudes. In line with Asch's experimental results, a large percentage of resistant buyers are reported to have been successfully converted by this approach.

What has been described above represents only one phase of a much larger program developed by Varela which involved the ingenious use of numerous facets of social psychological knowledge about influence. For example, attention was given to the difficult persuasive task of convincing the retailer to come to the firm's showroom in the first place. To reduce their opposition, an approach referred to as the "foot in the door technique" was used. It has been demonstrated that once a person has carried out a small request, he is more likely to comply with a larger one.[43] Hence, before inviting the retailers to the showroom, Varela had the salesmen ask the retailers to display a small sign in their stores. If they agreed to this small favor, when the salesman returned a week later he asked them to come to the showroom. Having once made a small commitment to the salesman, the retailer was more likely to take the next, larger step on the path leading to a sale that had been carefully laid by Varela. The last phase of the selling strategy was aimed at developing their long-run loyalty. Techniques suggested by research on "immunizing" persons against counterpersuasion were employed in an effort to reduce the retailers' susceptibility to the

[42]See, for example, Greenberg [18].

[43]See Freedman and Fraser [16].

promotion of competitors.[44] From all indications, the total campaign developed by Varela was highly successful. Large sales increases were realized despite unfavorable economic conditions.

The Influence of Company Reputation on Salesman Effectiveness

An example of a somewhat different use of research on communication and influence processes may be found in Levitt's experimental study of the role of company reputation in industrial selling.[45] The basic issue studied by Levitt was whether the evaluations of a new product made by those involved in the purchase decision process of industrial organizations are influenced by the general attitudes they hold toward the producing firm. Industrial marketers have long debated the value of expenditures on such activities as media campaigns undertaken for purposes of building a favorable corporate image. One rationale sometimes put forth in support of such programs is that they make buyers more receptive to the firm's salesmen. Implementing the elaborate kind of experimental design needed to measure such an effect would be extremely difficult in an industrial market—especially in the absence of a model of the process to help guide the research in deciding what effects to look for. Levitt developed a framework for analyzing this problem using concepts suggested by communications research on the influence of source credibility on communications effectiveness.[46] He then carried out a laboratory experiment which enabled him to achieve the degree of control required to study the problem.

As we noted in the earlier discussion of salesman-customer similarity, it has been shown in a number of experiments that the same message will produce attitude change when it is ascribed to a source of high rather than low credibility. Competence and trustworthiness are the components of credibility that have been manipulated in these studies.[47] Levitt suggests that the effectiveness of an industrial salesman will be influenced by the general reputation, among buyers, of the firm he represents much in the same way that source credibility affects the impact of an impersonal communication. In the parlance of communications research, the salesman is the communicator, the material he presents constitutes the message, and the firm for which he sells is the source.

A second factor considered by Levitt was the quality of the salesman's presentation. He was interested, for example, in the question of whether a high quality sales presentation made by a salesman from a lesser known firm could be as effective as a lesser quality sales presentation made by a salesman from a better known firm. The final factor examined was the recipient of the sales effort. Levitt reasoned that persons in various management roles who became involved in the purchase decision process (purchasing agents and technical personnel) would evaluate a new product from different frames of reference and hence might be differentially affected by a given message from a given source. Thus, the overall impact of the salesman was hypothesized to be dependent upon the source he represents (company reputation), the quality of his sales presentation, and the type of audience he is dealing with (technical vs. purchasing personnel).

The experimental test of these ideas involved exposing subjects to one of four versions of a ten minute filmed sales presentation for a fictitious but plausible new product (a paint ingredient). In one version the salesman gave a careful, professional ("good") presentation while in the other the same salesman

[44]See McGuire [30], pp. 258–265.
[45]See Levitt [26].
[46]See Bauer [5].
[47]See McGuire [30], pp. 182–187.

delivered a less polished ("poor") presentation. Company reputation was manipulated by varying the name of the firm which the salesman was identified as representing. A significant feature of the study was that experienced business personnel were used as subjects. A group of 113 practicing purchasing agents and 130 engineers and scientists participated in the experiment. Immediately after viewing the film and again five weeks later, subjects filled out a questionnaire which asked, among other things, (1) whether they would recommend that the product be given further consideration by others in their organization, and (2) would they favor adoption of the product if such a decision were theirs to make. Levitt suggests that the decision implied in the second question involves more risk than that connected with the first. The expected effects of company reputation and quality of the sales presentation were observed with regard to the willingness of both the purchasing agents and the technical personnel to recommend the product to others. However, for the riskier choice of whether or not to adopt the product, the pattern of results was more complex. The intriguing finding that emerged was that company reputation influenced the propensity of technical personnel to adopt the product, but *not* that of the purchasing agents. Levitt offers two explanations for this unexpected result. It is possible that as a result of being frequently exposed to salesmen, purchasing agents become sophisticated in judging products from sales presentations and learn to discount the effect of company reputation. Alternatively, it may simply be that the purchasing agent wishes to encourage competition among his suppliers and, in so doing, may tend to favor less well-known companies. The principal implication would seem to be that a seller's reputation makes a difference to a salesman in getting a favorable first hearing for a new product with both purchasing and technical personnel but when it comes to making an actual purchase decision, the advantage of a good reputation only obtains with technical personnel.

Discussion

The above examples serve to illustrate two of the ways in which behavioral research on influence processes can be useful in dealing with selling problems. Levitt's study represents the kind of application which results in a better understanding of a previously ill-structured problem. The findings bearing on the differential responsiveness of the purchasing and technical personnel are examples of the kind of suggestive new insights which such efforts may produce. Follow-up research is needed to test and refine these ideas further.

In Varela's work, we saw an application of a different order. There, behavioral concepts were used to develop specific, operational selling procedures that apparently worked. This type of immediate and direct application rarely occurs. In assessing the applicability of behavioral science research findings to practical problems, a question frequently asked is whether the results produced in the comfort and control of a psychological laboratory can be extrapolated to the complexity of the real world. Perhaps the lesson worth remembering from Varela's work is that we should also consider what opportunities there may be to arrange our real world problem situation so that it begins to resemble the laboratory setting where our knowledge is more certain.

SUMMARY AND CONCLUSIONS

The studies reviewed above serve to illustrate the possibility of bringing knowledge about interaction and influence processes to bear on specific operating problems associated with personal selling. Research on interpersonal similarity and attraction suggests a set of variables and relationships that not only appear relevant to understanding variability in salesmen's performance but also have some immediate implications for policy issues surrounding the selection, training, and allocation of salesmen. Examples were also given where concepts borrowed from psychological research on influence processes had been used both to analyze problems pertaining to selling strategies and techniques, and to develop operational methods for solving them.

While behavioral research offers marketers a great deal of material that is potentially useful to them, the utilization of such knowledge in dealing with practical marketing problems is not a simple task. Successful applications would appear to require two critical ingredients. The first is the skills and knowledge of what Guetzkow refers to as a "social engineer or middleman"—"someone who knows how to transform basic knowledge into useable forms."[48] An unusual combination of talents is needed to perform this role effectively. On the one hand, such a person must have the training and background that gives him a firm grasp of a broad range of behavioral science subject matter. On the other hand, he must also be of both a creative and practical bent if he is to be able to interact with management personnel and identify their problems.

The other element needed is the kind of problem-oriented, programmatic approach to applying behavioral science notions to real world problems which Ray has proposed with reference to advertising.[49] To assure relevance, the starting point is a careful definition of the practitioner's problem. The next step is a search for applicable behavioral science knowledge. The key variables of the problem must be identified in theoretical terms and a model selected which interrelates them. Ideally, the latter should take the form of conditional propositions (or "micro-theoretical notions" to use Ray's terminology)—statements which not only describe relationships between variables but also specify qualifying or limiting conditions. Following that comes empirical testing and estimation and this involves a gradual movement from highly controlled (e. g., laboratory) to more natural (i.e., field) research settings. The final stops are production, implementation, and monitoring of results. Difficulties encountered at any stage require a re-cycling of activities. By such a systematic approach one hopes to avoid the failures and disappointments which plague efforts to transfer knowledge from the realm of behavioral science to the real world.

Most of the applications described in this paper essentially represent work at the beginning or middle stages of Ray's scheme. The task ahead is to carry forward through the subsequent stages those promising ideas that appear to have some practical payoff.

[48]See Guetzkow [20], p. 77.
[49]See Ray [33].

REFERENCES

1 Andelson, R. P. "Harnessing Engineers and Scientists to the Sales Effort." In J. S. Wright and J. L. Goldstucker (eds.), *New Ideas for Successful Marketing,* pp. 204–215, Proceedings of the June 1966 Conference of the American Marketing Association, Chicago.

2 Aronson, Elliot, and Lindzey, Gardner (eds.), *Handbook of Social Psychology,* 2nd ed. Reading, Mass., Addison-Wesley, 1968–69.

3 Asch, S. E., "Effects of Group Pressure Upon the Modification and Distortion of Judgements," In E. E. Maccoby, T. M. Newcomb, and E. Hartley (eds.), *Readings in Social Psychology,* 3rd ed. Holt, Rinehart, and Winston, 1958, pp. 174–183.

4 Bales, R. F. "A Set of Categories for the Analysis of Small Group Interactions," *American Sociological Review,* Vol. 15 (April 1950), pp. 257–263.

5 Bauer, R. A. "Source Effect and Persuasibility: A New Look." In D. F. Cox (ed.), *Risk Taking and Information Handling in Consumer Behavior,* pp. 559–578. Boston, Mass., Division of

Research, Graduate School of Business Administration, Harvard University, 1967.

6 Berscheid, E., and Walster, E. H. *Interpersonal Attraction.* Reading, Mass., Addison-Wesley, 1969.

7 Bramel, D. "Interpersonal Attraction, Hostility, and Perception," In Judson Mills (ed.), *Experimental Social Psychology,* pp. 1–120. New York, MacMillan, 1969.

8 Brock, T. C. "Communicator-Recipient Similarity and Decision Change," *Journal of Personality and Social Psychology,* Vol. I, no. 6 (June 1965), pp. 650–654.

9 Byrne, D. "Attitudes and Attraction." In Leonard Berkowitz (ed.), *Advances in Experimental Social Psychology,* Vol. 4, pp. 35–89. New York, Academic Press, 1969.

10 Chapple, E. D. "The Interaction Chronograph: Its Evolution and Present Applications," *Personnel,* Vol. 25 (January 1949), pp. 295–307.

11 Cotham, J. C. III. "Selecting Salesmen: Approaches and Problems," *MSU Business Topics,* Vol. 18, no. 1 (Winter 1970), pp. 64–72.

12 Evans, F. B. "Selling as a Dyadic Relationship," *American Behavioral Scientist,* Vol. 6, no. 9 (May 1963), pp. 76–79.

13 Evans, F. B. "Dyadic Interaction in Selling: A New Approach." Unpublished monograph, Graduate School of Business, University of Chicago, 1964.

14 Farley, J. U., and Swinth, R. L. "Effects of Choice and Sales Message on Customer-Salesman Interaction," *Journal of Applied Psychology,* Vol. 51, no. 2 (April 1967), pp. 107–110.

15 Festinger, L. "The Application of Behavioral Science Knowledge." Paper presented at the Sloan School of Management, Massachusetts Institute of Technology, Cambridge, Mass., Fall 1968.

16 Freedman, J. L., and Fraser, S. C. "Compliance Without Pressure: The Foot-in-the-Door Technique," *Journal of Personality and Social Psychology,* Vol. 4, no. 2 (August 1966), pp. 195–202.

17 Gadel, M. S. "Concentration by Salesmen on Congenial Prospects." *Journal of Marketing,* Vol. 28, no. 2 (April 1964), pp. 64–66.

18 Greenberg, A. "Is Communications Research Worthwhile?" *Journal of Marketing,* Vol. 31, no. 1 (January 1967), pp. 48–50.

19 Granbois, D. H., and Willett, R. P. "Patterns of Conflicting Perceptions Among Channel Members." In L. G. Smith (ed.), *Reflections on Progress in Marketing,* pp. 86–100. Proceedings of the Winter 1964 Conference of the American Marketing Association, Chicago, 1965.

20 Guetzkow, H. "Conversion Barriers in Using the Social Sciences," *Administrative Science Quarterly,* Vol. 4, no. 1 (June 1959), pp. 68–81.

21 Heider, F. *The Psychology of Interpersonal Relations,* New York, Wiley, 1958.

22 Henry, J. Review of "Human Behavior: An Inventory of Scientific Findings," by B. Berelson and G. A. Steiner, *Scientific American,* Vol. 211, no. 1 (July 1964), pp. 129ff.

23 Homans, G. C. *Social Behavior: Its Elementary Forms.* New York, Harcourt, Brace & World, 1961.

24 Karlins, M., and Abelson, H. I. *Persuasion,* 2nd ed. New York, Springer, 1970.

25 Lazarsfeld, P. F. "The American Soldier—An Expository Review," *Public Opinion Quarterly,* Vol. 13, no. 3 (Fall 1949), pp. 377–404.

26 Levitt, T. *Industrial Purchasing Behavior.* Boston, Mass., Division of Research, Graduate School of Business Administration, Harvard University, 1965.

27 Lindzey, Gardner, and Byrne, D. "Measurement of Social Choice and Interpersonal Attractiveness." In [2], Vol. 2, pp. 452–525.

28 Lott, A. J., and Lott, B. E. "Group Cohesiveness as Interpersonal Attractiveness: A Review of Relationships with Antecedent and Consequent Variables." *Psychological Bulletin,* Vol. 64, no. 4 (October 1965), pp. 259–309.

29 Marlow, D., and Gergen, K. J. "Personality and Social Interaction." In [2], Vol. 3, pp. 590–665.

30 McGuire, W. J. "The Nature of Attitudes and Attitude Change," In [2], Vol. 3, Chapter 21, pp. 136–314.

31 Miner, J. B. "Personality and Ability Factors in Sales Performance," *Journal of Applied Psychology,* Vol. 46, no. 1 (February 1962), pp. 6–13.

32 Newcomb, T. M. "An Approach to the Study of Communicative Acts," *Psychological Review,* Vol. 60, no. 6 (November 1953), pp. 393–404.

33 Ray, M. L. "The Present and Potential Linkages Between the Microtheoretical Notions of Behavioral Science and the Problems of Advertising: A Proposal for a Research System." In H. L. Davis and A. J. Silk (eds.), *Behavioral and Management Science in Marketing,* New York, Ronald (forthcoming).

34 Simons, H. W., Berkowitz, N. N., and Moyer, R. J. "Similarity, Credibility, and Attitude Change: A Review and A Theory," *Psychological Bulletin,* Vol. 73, no. 1 (January 1970), pp. 1–16.

35 Smith, S. V., Brien, R. H., and Stafford, J. E. (eds.), *Readings in Marketing Information Systems.* Boston, Houghton Mifflin, 1968.

36 Stevens, S. N. "The Application of Social Science Findings to Selling and the Salesman." In *Aspects of Modern Management,* Management Report No. 15, pp. 85–94. New York, American Management Association, 1958.

37 Taguiri, R. "Person Perception." In [2], Vol. 3, pp. 395–449.

38 Thibaut, J. W., and Kelley, H. H. *The Social Psychology of Groups,* New York, Wiley, 1959.

39 Tosi, H. L. "The Effects of Expectation Levels and Role Consensus on the Buyer-Seller Dyad," *Journal of Business,* Vol. 39, no. 4 (October 1966), pp. 516–529.

40 Webster, F. E., Jr. "Interpersonal Communication and Salesman Effectiveness," *Journal of Marketing,* Vol. 32, no. 3 (July 1968), pp. 7–13.

41 Willett, R. P., and Pennington, A. L. "Customer and Salesman: The Anatomy of Choice and Influence in a Retail Setting." In R. M. Haas (ed.), *Science, Technology, and Marketing,* pp. 598–616. Proceedings of the Fall 1966 Conference of the American Marketing Association, Chicago.

42 Zimbardo, P., and Ebbesen, E. B. *Influencing Attitudes and Changing Behavior.* Reading, Mass., Addison-Wesley, 1969.

32

The Computer, Personal Selling, and Sales Management

James M. Comer

This article is a brief review of the literature dealing with the integration of the computer into sales management planning, organizing, and control activities. It demonstrates how computers are increasingly being used for model building, as well as how a particular computer-based information system can be useful to a sales manager.

Several years ago an article entitled "The Salesman Isn't Dead, He's Different" was published.[1] It is now the sales manager's turn—he is not expendable, but he must become more sophisticated. He must learn to participate not only in the development, but also in the application, of new technology. The aggressive, knowledgeable sales manager must prepare *now* for what he soon will be required to do. One important aspect of that preparation must be a thorough knowledge of,

[1]Carl Reiser, "The Salesman Isn't Dead, He's Different," *Fortune,* November 1962.

Reprinted from *Journal of Marketing,* vol. 39, pp. 27–33, American Marketing Association, July 1975. At the time of writing, the author was chairman of the department of marketing, College of Commerce, DePaul University, Chicago.

and familiarity with, computer technology and the integration of the computer into his regular activities.

The purpose of this article is to review published reports of the integration of the computer into sales management planning, organizing, and control activities. This is done: (1) to demonstrate the logical, but not necessarily inevitable, progression of a firm from simple computer-based data collection and manipulation into model building; and (2) to point out when and under what circumstances a particular system is useful to a sales manager. This latter objective is especially important since complex computer-based systems are frequently touted as the "answer" to the sales manager's problems. Often these computer-based systems are not necessary and a less complex system will suffice, or a simple system must be instituted and operated successfully *before* a more complex system can be installed.

To facilitate the review, a categorization method is suggested that divides the literature on computer applications in sales management into two general areas: (1) sales reporting and analysis systems, and (2) planning-oriented systems.

SALES REPORTING AND ANALYSIS SYSTEMS

Firms have had sales reporting and analysis systems for decades. Reporting has been as informal as casual verbal exchanges or as stringent as daily written reports. Sales managers, in most cases, conducted analysis by reading call reports and comparing them with actual sales. They were then expected to draw vital conclusions about such things as salesmen abilities and performance and customer response to programs. They were also required to make rational decisions about sales territory design, sales force size, and so on. Given these kinds of responsibilities and the expansion of sales forces over wider geographic areas, it is not surprising that published accounts in the 1960s about the innovative introduction of the computer into sales management were glowing.[2]

The enthusiasm of the 1960s waxed over the computer's ability to digest, consolidate, and reorganize data into meaningful reports. The first applications were on the analysis of sales by product, by account, and by salesman or territory.[3] They were designed to facilitate sales management *ex post facto* product, market, and territory analysis. With this capacity, the mechanical aspects of sales analysis were performed routinely for sales management.

However, routinized computer sales analysis proved inadequate in many cases. This led to the development of the next stage—a system that would produce data not only on account sales but also on salesmen call allocations. The immediate objective of such a system was to relieve sales managers of their data-matching responsibility and give them more time for certain planning activities. Such a system was SOAR (Store Objectives and Accomplishments Report).

SOAR was a computer-based salesman reporting and analysis system developed at Pillsbury Company. It covered over 500 salesmen selling some 100 types, sizes, and flavors of products in 25 regions and five zones to over 40,000 retail stores plus direct accounts.[4] The impetus for the development of SOAR arose out of such problems as salesman control and the determination of which retail stores should be called upon, and how frequently, by the sales force. In system operation, the computer prints from a master cus-

[2]William T. Cullen, "Sales Reporting Systems," and John Lincoln, "Using the Computer for More Effective Sales Force Management," in "Marketing Harnesses the Computer," *American Management Association Bulletin*, No. 92, 1966, pp. 14–18 and 19–25. See also, Phyllis Daignault, "Marketing Management and the Computer," *Sales Management*, August 20, 1965, pp. 49–60.

[3]Cullen, same reference as footnote 2, p. 17.

[4]Lloyd M. DeBoer and William H. Ward, "Integration of the Computer Into Salesman Reporting," *Journal of Marketing*, Vol. 35 (January 1971), pp. 41–47.

tomer list a SOAR form for each account. The form contains such information as region, store name and address, dollar volume, advertising group, and the like. Each salesman receives a batch of these preprinted forms which corresponds to the accounts in his territory, with one form printed for each call the salesman is to make during a given retail selling period. The salesman then sets both dollar and quantity sales objectives, preferably by store, for the subsequent two- or three-month selling period. When the salesman makes his store call, he reports day and time in hours and minutes, presentations scanned, and the results compared with the salesman's projections. The system periodically condenses these results and sends them out to the individual salesman and his immediate supervisor.

At Pillsbury, SOAR was replaced in late 1974 by REACH (Retail Achievement Report).[5] Among other things, REACH puts more emphasis on other salesman activities (such as setting up displays) and on quarterly, rather than monthly, volume goals. An interesting aspect of these modifications is that the sales department did the redesign work. Here is a case where the user, once a system had proved its worth, took over the system, adapted it, and made it his own.

SOAR, REACH, and similar systems are not the ultimate in system development. Weiss has described a direct salesman-computer communication link-up in which salesmen carry a small mobile device that instantaneously records and transmits information to a central electronic facility.[6] The picture that Weiss paints is yet to be completed, and there are many technological and human problems to be solved before it is. In the interim, sales management must clearly define its needs and role in the development of firm-wide information systems. Dodge has made a start in this direction with his enumeration of three general rules for sales management to observe in developing information systems:

1 The marketing information system should be fitted to the existing organizational structure of sales management. . . .
2 The marketing information system should reflect the operational philosophy established for field sales. Accountability at a given organization level specifies the data parameters of output.
3 The marketing information system should be thoroughly understood and accepted by all personnel in sales.[7]

Several additional lessons have been learned in this area. For example, whenever an information system of any kind is designed and installed it must be recognized that the salesman's primary responsibility is to sell, not to collect data. Furthermore, any sales system must be useful and relevant to the people most concerned, the salesman and sales manager. Without their support and participation, the system will be useless.

Management Use of Computerized Sales Reporting and Analysis Systems

It is likely that most firms have some type of computerized sales analysis system. The question of whether the more advanced, SOAR-type system, should be adopted depends on the firm's resources and the conditions it faces in its market. This step should be taken if: (1) the firm has the technical and monetary resources to do so, (2) the market is complex and geographically extensive, (3) major decisions on sales force allocation and size are made frequently, (4) the redistribution

[5]From a conversation with Mr. William H. Ward at Pillsbury Company, Minneapolis, January 1975.

[6]E. P. Weiss, "The Salesman Gets Hooked into Information Systems," *Advertising Age,* June 14, 1965, pp. 84–87.

[7]H. R. Dodge, *Field Sales Management* (Dallas: Business Publications, 1973), p. 28.

system is complex, (5) the sales force is large and organizationally "distant" from management, (6) the product line is broad, and (7) the probability is high that some of these conditions will exist in the next five years. Two characteristics of these conditions are important: (a) they are independent of the nature of a firm's business, and (b) it is not necessary that all conditions exist in order for a firm to install such a system.

A computer-based system, if correctly designed, serves several purposes. First, it relieves both sales managers and the sales force of many of the onerous, repetitive reporting and summarization responsibilities. Second, it permits a fuller application of management by exception, since highly specific limits on sales performance can be established and monitored. Last, the routinization of control functions permits sales management and salespeople to allocate more time to planning and sales effort.

PLANNING-ORIENTED SYSTEMS

Some of the first analytical attempts at solving such sales management problems as call allocation relied on operations research (OR) techniques.[8] These early attempts were static, limited in scope, and designed solely to solve the specific problem at hand.[9] It was soon apparent that, in the dynamic environment of sales management, OR solutions might be outmoded as soon as they were discovered. The development of flexible planning systems that had the capacity to incorporate market dynamism was a solution to the static limitations inherent in OR-type approaches. However, useful planning systems are not instantaneously developed and made operational. A variety of preceding systems, perhaps analogous to SOAR, make them feasible. For example, a fully developed salesman reporting management analysis system functions as: a data source for the construction and operation of diverse aspects of the planning system, a monitoring or control device to insure salesmen observation of planning dictums, and a measurement of the validity and reliability of the underlying planning models.

To organize discussion of the various computer applications in this area, a two-way categorization has been devised: data base systems and model base systems. These two systems represent a progression in sophistication rather than a distinction; thus, this categorization is more an organizational device than an attempt to identify unique entities.

Data Base Systems

These systems rely on an aggregated or disaggregated data base for making certain sales management decisions. Normally, these data bases are but an aspect of the firm's computerized marketing information system. Sales management usually must devise its own data extraction and manipulation routines to solve its peculiar problems.[10]

In constructing a data base, the firm will use many sources both inside and outside the firm. The internal sources normally provide microdata such as customer billing records, salesmen call activities, consumer attitudes, and the like, as well as information on potential

[8]Arthur A. Brown, Frank T. Hulswit, and John D. Kettelle, "A Study of Sales Operations," *Operations Research,* Vol. 4 (June 1956), pp. 296–308; and Clark Ward, Donald F. Clark, and Russell Ackoff, "Allocation of Sales Effort in the Lamp Division of the General Electric Company," *Operations Research,* Vol. 14 (December 1956), pp. 629–647.

[9]For a discussion of operations research and personal selling, see David Montgomery and Frederick E. Webster, Jr., "Applications of Operations Research to Personal Selling Strategy," *Journal of Marketing,* Vol. 32 (January 1968), pp. 50–57.

[10]Two examples of methodologies that rely heavily on large data bases are: Walter J. Semlow, "How Many Salesmen Do You Need," *Harvard Business Review,* Vol. 27 (May–June 1959), pp. 126–132; and Walter J. Talley, Jr., "How to Design Sales Territories," *Journal of Marketing,* Vol. 25 (January 1961), pp. 7–12.

customers and competitive activities. Outside sources, for the most part, provide macrodata on industry performance and broad-based changes in the economy, and disaggregated microdata. The composition and construction of these data are beyond the scope of this article. What is of concern is how sales management uses a data base system. Several examples demonstrate this use:

- Prospect Identification. One firm identifies prospects for its salesmen by collating facts about sales territories from existing data, SIC information, and various product characteristics. These various data sets are combined into a matrix so that top prospects in a territory can be identified.[11]
- Customer Profiles. A firm profiles each customer in its data bank. This profile includes customer features and reasons for using a competitive product. It is the feeling in this company that not only is the salesman better prepared for his calls with this kind of information, but sales forecasting and product design problems are also more easily solved when customer needs are more clearly defined.[12]
- An NICB report detailed a number of specific sales management applications of a computerized data base. Some examples are: J. T. Ryerson and Son, Inc., redesigned its sales territory structure based upon marginal profit figures; Girdwood Publishing Company reorganized its sales force in both the line and staff functions; and Diamond Crystal Salt Corporation has a wide spectrum of applications, ranging from developing salesmen call policy through analyzing individual account profitability.[13]

[11]For these examples and others, the reader is referred to Thayer C. Taylor, ed., "The Computer in Marketing—Part II: Sales Force Management," *Sales Management,* March 15, 1969, pp. 71–78.

[12]Same reference as footnote 11.

[13]National Industrial Conference Board, "Allocating Field Sales Resources," *Experience in Marketing Management,* Vol. 23, 1970, pp. 20–34.

The foregoing are some of the applications of computer technology. These applications do not relieve either sales management or field sales personnel of many decision-making responsibilities; rather, they organize data in such a way as to facilitate decision making. On the other hand, a model base system does, in a sense, substitute computerized "decisions" for personal ones.

Model Base Systems

These systems have at their heart a model or series of models for data manipulation and output generation. Often these models are designed to solve one specific class of problems or assist in making a particular type of recurring decision. Whatever the situation may be, it is the independent verified model, which manipulates data and prescribes courses of action, that distinguishes this type of system.

Work done in this area can be divided in three groups: (1) call allocation determination, (2) sales territory design, and (3) salesmen routing.

Call Allocation Lodish, in a pioneering study, developed CALLPLAN: "an interactive computer system designed to aid salesmen or sales management in allocating sales call time."[14] The salesman or sales manager provides information for a territory on: the number of clients, prospects, and geographical subdivisions in the territory; the call length in hours; the sales response period; the effort period in months; and, for each effort period, the total number of half hours available for selling plus travel time, and the maximum number of calls to make on any account. Additional data on historical call patterns per client are used, as well as estimates of client

[14]Leonard M. Lodish, "CALLPLAN: An Interactive Salesman's Call Planning System," *Management Science,* Vol. 18 (December 1971), p. 25.

sales response if alternative call allocations are made. Output from CALLPLAN is a series of optimal call allocations to clients and prospects by geographic area, and a comparison of estimated sales from the optimal policy with those of the present policy. Lodish reported fourteen preliminary applications of CALLPLAN. In 1974, Lodish cited additional applications of his model as part of a larger procedure for allocating sales force effort.[15]

Armstrong has also developed an interactive system (SCHEDULE) for determining optimal call policy. Like Lodish's CALLPLAN, it has the individual salesman or sales manager provide certain values. These values are transformed via a mathematical programming model into a suggested call allocation policy by account along with expected return for the call allocation. Armstrong cited one application of SCHEDULE with a small sales force. He did not present any statistical evidence that SCHEDULE had improved the sales force call policy, but he did interview the salesmen after they used SCHEDULE. They "agreed that SCHEDULE-prepared call allocation plans . . . were significantly better than the plans they were currently using."[16]

The present author has developed and tested a system entitled ALLOCATE, which assigns effort to subsets of customers and prospects based on their progress toward the saturation state of their response curve.[17] It is a batch-processed system designed to be used by upper-level sales management either as an input device for sales management decisions, such as sales-territory-size, or as a vehicle for determining the effect of alternative call allocation strategies on territorial revenue over multiple time periods. The author tested ALLOCATE on the sales territories of a consumer products firm that was selling through a combination of wholesalers and direct retail accounts. In the test, ALLOCATE not only successfully replicated salesman behavior in selected sales territories, but also demonstrated its capacity to generate the effect of alternative call allocation strategies on revenue over time in those territories.

Sales Territory Design Xerox Corporation developed a salesman allocation model employing a market grid approach.[18] A grid of intersecting horizontal and vertical lines is laid over a sales area, thus generating a set of cells which contain customers. Each cell must contain data on the expected number of customers, the expected revenue from each customer, and the expected number of calls per day per salesman. The model then allocates calls sequentially to the customer with the highest revenue per call value until all accounts in a cell are called on and all potential realized. Additional cells are combined until the salesman's maximum time limit is reached. This set of cells then constitutes the salesman's territory.

Hess and Samuels have developed a salesdistricting model, GEOLINE, which they derived from research and application of a successful computer technique for legislative districting.[19] The model assumes an established territorial set and constructs a predetermined number of compact sales territories using an

[15]Leonard M. Lodish, "A 'Vaguely Right' Approach to Sales Force Allocations," *Harvard Business Review*, Vol. 52 (January–February 1974), pp. 119–124.

[16]Gary M. Armstrong, "SCHEDULE: An Interactive Computer Program for Determination of the Optimal Allocation of Personal Selling Effort," (Working paper. University of Illinois at Chicago Circle, 1973).

[17]James M. Comer, "ALLOCATE: A Computer Model for Sales Territory Planning," *Decision Sciences*, Vol. 3 (July 1974), pp. 323–339.

[18]Peter J. Gray, "Computers and Models in the Marketing Decision Process," in *Computer Innovations in Marketing*, Evelyn Konrad, ed. (New York: American Management Assn., 1970), pp. 158–167.

[19]Sidney W. Hess and Stuart A. Samuels, "Experiences with a Sales Districting Model: Criteria and Implementation," *Management Science*, Vol. 18 (December 1971), pp. 41–54.

integer formulation of a linear transportation program. The solution is not optimal, because the objective of GEOLINE is to design sales territories such that the sales activity measure among the territories is approximately equal. The sales activity measure may be territory potential, salesman workload, or some other relevant criterion. However, GEOLINE output is a set of sales territories realigned quickly, efficiently, and more accurately than by noncomputer methods. Hess and Samuels cited successful field applications by CIBA Pharmaceutical Company and the IBM World Trade Corporation. Since 1970, the system has also been put into operation in a number of pharmaceutical and oil companies.

One output of Lodish's CALLPLAN program was an estimate of the marginal profit of an additional hour of allocated salesman effort in a territory. Lodish has used CALLPLAN and its output as a basis for the development of a sales districing model.[20] It is a mathematical programming model that is heuristically solved so that the marginal profit figures for each salesman are approximately equal. Output defines: (1) which salesmen are to be assigned to which area, (2) the number of trips to be made by the salesman to each area, and (3) the amount of time to be spent in each area. Lodish notes that five companies realigned territories using his procedure, and they felt the computer procedure made a positive contribution to the improved results.

Salesmen Routing Truck routing and salesman routing are part of the operations research touring problem. Several attempts have been made to develop computerized routing models for salesmen and sales management.

Lazer et al. developed a simple computerized model, using Bayesian decision methodology, in which a "routing ratio" is constructed for each account on the basis of the expected value of sales from the account divided by the total time (travel, waiting, and sales) required for that account.[21] The model selects the route that maximizes the total expected value of a "trip" covering all selected accounts, subject to a time constraint. They tested their model by routing the salesmen for a wholesale liquor distributor. In the example provided, a salesman's route was improved from his selected route of $1.98 expected value per minute of selling time to an "optimum" value of $2.03.

A more complete routing system, TOURPLAN, has been developed by Cloonan.[22] TOURPLAN is a heuristic programming approach to the salesman tour problem. The TOURPLAN model employs two heuristics to arrive at an initial solution for the accounts under consideration.[23] An optimal solution is then determined using a combinatorial search routine. The system was first tested in two environments: first, in artificial territories with known and unknown optimal routings; and second, in real territories where salesman solutions were known but optimums were not. In the artificial territories, the system achieved efficiencies (ratio to optimum) of 99% to 100%. In real territories, a 90%+ efficiency rate was obtained where the corresponding field salesmen were operating at about 85% efficiency.

Shanker et al. have developed a computer-based procedure to solve simultaneously the

[20]Leonard M. Lodish, "Sales Territory Alignment to Maximize Profit," *Journal of Marketing Research*, Vol. 12 (February 1975), pp. 30–36.

[21]William Lazer, Richard T. Hise, and Jay A. Smith, "Computer Routing: Putting Salesmen in Their Place," *Sales Management*, March 15, 1970, pp. 29–35. See also, James H. Donnelly and John M. Ivancevich, *Analysis for Marketing Decisions* (Homewood, Ill.: Richard D. Irwin, 1970), pp. 252–262.

[22]James B. Cloonan, "TOURPLAN: A Sales Call Routing and Scheduling Program" (Working Paper 9-73, DePaul University, Chicago, 1973).

[23]The first heuristic is developed in James B. Cloonan, "A Heuristic Approach to Some Sales Territory Problems," in *Proceedings of the Fourth International Conference on Operations Research*, D. B. Hertz and J. Malese, eds. (New York: John Wiley & Sons, 1966), pp. 284–292.

sales territory design problem and the salesman call frequency problem.[24] It combines and extends the Hess and Lodish methodologies in several aspects. Input consists primarily of management estimates of various problem dimensions combined with an integer-programming–set-partitioning algorithm. It is an optimizing program whose solution specifies which customers should be called on by which salesman and prescribes the call frequency. A hypothetical situation was used to illustrate the effectiveness of the procedure.

Two other computer-based systems have been developed that may be adaptable for use by sales management. DETAILER, developed by Montgomery et al., was designed to allocate salesman time to product promotions on a sales call.[25] However, Montgomery describes DETAILER as being used by a product manager and not sales management. Winer's system is presented as a procedure for developing otpimal compensation plans.[26] However, it was designed to determine the best salary career path for salesmen, not to optimize sales or profit generated for the firm.

Planning Systems and Sales Management

The traditions of the sales fraternity maintain that the personal selling function is strictly a person-to-person relationship and that rigorous analysis should be suspect as unrealistic and academic. Although this view is far from accurate, it is a barrier to those far-sighted corporate and sales managers who have, or intend to develop, a computer-based planning system for their firms. The fears and prejudices of more traditional sales managers and salesmen must be assuaged, because an intricate system forcibly superimposed on a complex sales force can lead to permanent damage. The problem for the manager is to get the support and cooperation of the sales force and sales managers for system development.

Several suggestions are made:

1 It is a tenet of human relations theory that involving people in the formulation/design of a project tends to invoke commitment. So, in the system design stage, solicit salesmen/sales manager participation wherever possible.

2 The development and installation of any new system, especially one such as this, is bound to cause anxiety about job loss or fears of inadequacy in dealing with the "monster." Although there is no perfect solution, familiarity can help reduce fears and anxieties. Therefore, introduce the system slowly and carefully, and hold frequent training sessions to educate your personnel in system use.

3 In tests, Lodish and Armstrong had salesmen use the systems on their own territories. Both reported salesmen conclusions that the program allocated calls better than they could. The implication is that the salesmen developed favorable attitudes toward the system because they could, on their own initiative, construct better call routines. The message to management is clear: to maintain salesman morale when you are instituting changes using a system, whenever possible have the salesman see for himself the beneficial effects for his territory.

Planning Systems and Control

Once a firm has computerized planning systems in operation, two questions arise: "How do we know that the planned change is operating effectively?" and "How do we know when to rerun the model(s)?" Both questions reflect

[24] Roy J. Shanker, Ronald E. Turner, and Andres A. Zoltners, "Sales Territory Design: An Integrated Approach," *Management Science*, forthcoming.

[25] David B. Montgomery, Alvin J. Silk and Carlos E. Zaragoza, "Multiple-Product Sales Force Allocation Model," *Management Science*, Vol. 21 (December 1974), pp. 3–24.

[26] Leon Winer and Leon Schiffman, "Developing Optimum Sales Compensation Plans with the Aid of a Simulation Model," in *1974 Combined Proceedings*, Ronald Curhan, ed. (Chicago: American Marketing Assn., 1975), pp. 509–514.

the necessary development of control routines to complement the planning models. The first question may be answered in two parts. First, hard criteria for performance evaluation should be established before the change is made. Examples of criteria are average sales or cost per call and aggregate territory sales or cost. Second, after the planned changes are implemented, these changes must be monitored to ensure performance. The second question may be answered either by establishing a policy of rerunning the models at regular intervals or, in the mode of management by exception, rerunning only when behavior or events exceed certain predetermined tolerances. If management finds it is faced with consistent violations of standards, model validity may be questionable or the sales force may be playing the model instead of doing its job.

IMPLEMENTING SYSTEMS

A large-scale operating system takes years to develop. Therefore, if management wishes to have a useful system available in the future, it must start *now* to develop one. Three stages in the process can be identified: appraisal, design, and implementation.

Appraisal

Most firms who use personal selling have some type of reporting and analysis system. As there is a great diversity among firms, so too is there a broad range of complexity in system design. Each firm must weigh the pros and cons and decide which course of action it should select. Some factors to consider are: (1) the present state of sophistication of the firm's planning system, (2) current and projected product and market complexity, (3) the firm's technical and monetary resources, and (4) current and predicted competitor activities. If the firm decides to extend its present system, a gradual, carefully prepared implementation program is strongly recommended.

Design

A useful first step in system design is to identify the existing needs of your sales personnel. This can be accomplished through consultation with knowledgeable sales managers and salesmen. Succeeding steps should include an in-depth examination of the models discussed in this article to see if one or more of them is relevant, and the development of estimates of the costs and benefits of designing an original program peculiarly suited to the present and future needs of the firm.

Before full-scale implementation can occur, designed systems must be field tested for validity and reliability. In fact, part of system design should include the establishment of routine control procedures for insuring the maintenance of validity.

Implementation

In implementing a new system, the firm should proceed carefully in step-wise fashion, adding capability only after such factors as data bases are established and users are trained. Gradual implementation may be technical in nature, progressing from the less complex to the more sophisticated; or it may progress on a geographic basis, from territory to district, region, and ultimately to the national level. Obviously, a schedule that combines geographic and technical implementation is also possible. System implementation should include procedures for involving sales managers and salesmen in the process. Formal feedback systems on problems with system operation perform two necessary functions. First, the firm can check users to be certain they are utilizing the system efficiently. Often opportunities for new applications are identified here. Second, users may not feel as threatened by the system and, in fact, may make valuable contributions if they have a question and suggestion pipeline to designers and corporate management.

CONCLUSION

This article reviewed published accounts of the integration of the computer into reporting, analysis, and decision making in personal selling and sales management. It was shown that, contrary to tradition, the computer has applications in this area of marketing, but so far only a few problems have been attacked beyond the routine computer-based sales reporting and analysis systems. For a firm to take that additional step requires patient development geared to the capabilities and requirements of the user. Only when the user, be it sales representative or sales manager, accepts the system as relevant to his needs and integrates it into his routine can it be truly labeled a success.

33

Reactions to Role Conflict: The Case of the Industrial Salesman

Orville C. Walker, Jr.
Gilbert A. Churchill, Jr.
Neil M. Ford

Because industrial sales representatives often find conflicting demands made on them by organization superiors and customers, their personal well-being and job performance are sometimes adversely affected. These authors explain the factors which influence the sales representatives' reactions to incompatible demands, as well as the variables which affect their choices between conflicting company rules and customer requests.

For centuries we have honored unity of command as one of the inviolable principles of good management. The industrial salesman, however, frequently receives conflicting demands from many masters. He is often caught in the middle between the policies and programs formulated by his organizational superiors on the one hand, and the special requirements and demands of his customers and potential customers on the other. These incompatible demands adversely affect the salesman's personal well-being and his job performance. He must somehow "divide his loyalty between employer and customer, choosing between demands on his behavior which originate in both these domains."[1]

This paper examines the characteristics of

[1]Gerhard W. Ditz, "The Internal-External Dichotomy in Business Organizations," *Industrial Management Review* (Fall, 1964), p. 55.

Reprinted from *The Journal of Business Administration*, vol. 3, no. 2, Spring 1973. At the time of writing, Orville C. Walker, Jr., was an assistant professor of marketing, Graduate School of Business Administration, University of Minnesota. Gilbert A. Churchill, Jr., and Neil M. Ford were associate professors of marketing, Graduate School of Business Administration, University of Wisconsin, Madison.

the industrial salesman's role and the reasons why he is susceptible to conflicting expectations and demands. Particular attention is given to factors which influence the salesman's reactions to incompatible demands; the variables that affect his choice between conflicting company rules and customer requests.

I. CONFLICT IN THE SALESMAN'S ROLE

The salesman occupies one of many positions in his organization. A set of activities or desired behaviors is associated with each organizational position. These activities constitute the role to be performed by the individual who occupies that position.

The content of the role attached to an organizational position is defined by the expectations held by the role occupant and the occupants of the other positions. In the case of a salesman, many people, within and outside of the salesman's organization, depend on his performance as a source of rewards or as a precondition for the performance of their own roles. These members of the salesman's role-set, therefore, develop beliefs and attitudes about how the salesman should and should not behave. The salesman's sales manager, other organizational personnel, his customers and his family all expect him to perform his job in certain ways. The members of the role-set communicate their expectations, attitudes and demands to the salesman through their words and actions. These communications are aimed at getting the salesman to perform his role according to the sender's desires. The expectations communicated to the salesman by his role-set constitute his *objective sent role.*

The salesman performs his role in accordance with his perceptions of the pressures being sent by his role partners. He suffers *perceived role conflict* when he believes that the expectations of one member of his role-set are incompatible with the demands of some other member. He is uncertain about how to perform his role.[2]

Antecedents of Conflict in the Salesman's Role

There are several characteristics of the salesman's role that make it particularly susceptible to role conflict: (1) it is at the boundary of the firm, (2) its performance affects the occupants of a large number of other positions, and (3) it is an innovative role.

The Effect of a Boundary Position The salesman is likely to experience more role conflict than most other organization members because he occupies a position at the firm's boundary. Some members of his role set—his customers—are located in organizations outside of his own. As a result, the salesman receives demands from different organizations with diverse goals, policies and problems.[3] Since each role partner wants the salesman's behavior to be consistent with the attainment of his own goals, the demands they communicate to the salesman are also diverse and often incompatible.[4] A customer, for example, might request that a product be modified in order to make it more suitable for his particular needs, but the salesman's company may be unwilling to modify their products because of the additional design and production costs involved.[5] The salesman is caught in the mid-

[2]This discussion of the theory of role dynamics and role conflict is drawn from Robert L. Kahn, *et. al., Organizational Stress: Studies in Role Conflict and Ambiguity* (New York: John Wiley and Sons, Inc., 1964), pp. 11–35.

[3]Henry O. Pruden, "Interorganizational Conflict, Linkage, and Exchange: A Study of Industrial Salesmen," *Academy of Management Journal*, Vol. 12 (September 1969), pp. 339–350.

[4]James A. Belasco, "The Salesman's Role Revisited," *Journal of Marketing*, Vol. 30 (April 1966), pp. 6–8.

[5]J. M. Dutton and R. E. Walton, "Interdepartmental Conflict and Cooperation: A Study of Two Contrasting Cases," *Human Organization*, Vol. 25 (Fall 1966), pp. 207–220.

dle. In order to satisfy the demands of one role partner he must ignore or attempt to change the demands of the other.

Another problem arising from the salesman's boundary position is that his role partners in one organization often have no knowledge of or appreciation for the expectations and demands made by role partners in another. A customer, for example, may not know the policies of the salesman's company or the other constraints under which the salesman must operate. The salesman's superiors, on the other hand, may formulate some company policies without an adequate understanding of the particular requirements of some customers. Even when one role partner is aware of another's demands upon the salesman, he may not understand the reasoning behind them and, as a result, consider them arbitrary or illegitimate.[6]

The Effect of a Large Role-Set The industrial salesman's role-set includes a large number of diverse individuals. Hundreds of different customers each expect him to satisfy their particular needs and requirements. In addition, people in numerous departments within his own firm rely on him for the execution of company policies in dealings with customers and for the ultimate success of the firm's revenue producing efforts. All of these people hold definite beliefs about how the salesman should perform his job and they all pressure him to conform to their expectations.[7] The large number of different people from diverse departments and organizations who depend upon the salesman increases the probability that at least some of the role demands he receives will be incompatible.[8]

The Effect of an Innovative Role The industrial salesman's role is frequently an innovative one. He is often required to produce new solutions to non-routine problems. Innovativeness is particularly important, for example, when a salesman helps design products to customer specifications, when he sells engineered systems, or when he is cultivating new accounts.

Occupants of innovative roles tend to experience more conflict than other organization members because they require the flexibility necessary to try new and unusual approaches to the problems they face.[9] This need for flexibility often brings the salesman into conflict with the standing rules and procedures of his firm and with the expectations of organization members who desire to maintain the status quo.

II. THE EFFECTS OF ROLE CONFLICT UPON THE SALESMAN AND HIS ORGANIZATION

Most people experience some amount of role conflict occasionally. In small doses, role conflict may be good for the individual and his organization since conflict is often associated with adaptation and change. There is a "level of hostility" below which the processes of conflict may be benign but above which they will be malign.[10]

The industrial salesman, however, faces frequent, perhaps excessive, role conflict because of the nature of his position within his

[6]For a more complete discussion of boundary positions and role conflict see Kahn, *op. cit.*, pp. 99–124.

[7]R. E. Walton, J. M. Dutton, and H. G. Fitch, "A Study of Conflict in the Process, Structure, and Attitudes of Lateral Relationships," in Albert H. Rubenstein and Chadwick J. Haberstroh (eds.), *Some Theories of Organization*, rev. ed. (Homewood, Ill.: Richard D. Irwin, Inc., 1966), pp. 444–465.

[8]Harry A. Landsberger, "The Horizontal Dimensions in Bureaucracy," *Administrative Science Quarterly*, Vol. 6 (June 1961), pp. 299–328.

[9]Kahn, *op. cit.*, pp. 125–136.

[10]Kenneth E. Boulding, "The Economics of Human Conflict," in Elton B. McNeil (ed.), *The Nature of Human Conflict* (Englewood Cliffs, N.J.: Prentice-Hall, Inc. 1965), pp. 174–175.

company. Excessive role conflict can have dysfunctional consequences for the individual and his organization. A salesman faced with conflicting demands performs uncertainly. He worries about his work and he experiences more job-related tension. He becomes less satisfied with his job and he loses confidence in his superiors and his organization.[11]

Levels of job tension, satisfaction, and confidence in the organization and in superiors are "important components of employee morale and have been shown under certain conditions to have significant effects on work performance, absenteeism, and staff turnover."[12] The effects of role conflict on the salesman, therefore, may ultimately have dysfunctional consequences for his organization as the salesman's morale and performance deteriorate.

Several existing articles discuss the conflicts that salesmen face and attempt to find ways to reduce the level of conflict and its dysfunctional consequences for the selling organization.[13] Since the nature of the salesman's role makes it unlikely that role conflict can ever be eliminated, however, both sales managers and industrial buyers should attempt to understand how salesmen react to conflictful situations.

III. THE SALESMAN'S REACTIONS TO ROLE CONFLICT

When a salesman experiences role conflict he can respond in one of several ways: (1) he may attempt to withdraw from the situation; (2) he may honor one partner's demands while ignoring those of the other; (3) he may attempt to bring the conflicting demands to his role partners' attention and let them work out their differences; or (4) he may try to find a compromise course of action that he believes both role partners will accept.[14]

Withdrawal from Conflict Situations A salesman may attempt to reduce his feelings of stress and uncertainty by withdrawing from conflictful situations. He may withdraw *socially* by avoiding role partners who make conflicting demands. Many salesmen, for example, spend a large proportion of their time calling on customers who seldom make extreme demands and with whom they are "comfortable," while they call less frequently on new or demanding accounts.

When he is faced with an extremely high level of conflict, the salesman may withdraw *physically* by being frequently absent from work, spending less time calling on accounts, or by quitting his job entirely.[15]

When the salesman cannot avoid contact with role partners who make incompatible demands, he may reduce his stress by *psychologically* withdrawing from those individuals. He can do this by belittling the importance of their demands or minimizing the amount of power he attributes to them. In this way, their conflicting demands are made to seem less threatening.

While it is an almost universal human desire to withdraw from stressful situations, most salesmen are constrained from doing so. A change of jobs usually entails social and economic costs as well as a substantial amount of risk. Salesmen, therefore, are not likely to view physical withdrawal as a viable response unless attractive new job opportunities are

[11]Grady D. Bruce, Charles M. Bonjean, and J. Allen Williams, Jr., "Job Satisfaction Among Independent Businessmen: A Correlative Study," *Sociology and Social Research*, Vol. 52 (April 1968), pp. 195–204.

[12]Kahn, *op. cit.*, pp. 66–67.

[13]See, for example, Richard T. Hise, "Conflict in the Salesman's Role," in J. Allison Barnhill (ed.) *Sales Management: Contemporary Perspectives* (Glenview, Ill.: Scott, Foresman and Company, 1970), pp. 48–62.

[14]For a different classification of possible reactions to conflict, see Paul R. Lawrence and Jay W. Lorsch, "Differentiation and Integration in Complex Organizations," *Administrative Science Quarterly*, Vol. 12 (June 1967), pp. 1–47.

[15]Kahn, *op. cit.*, pp. 28–29.

readily available or the stress of conflict becomes great enough to outweigh the disadvantages of changing jobs. The less extreme forms of social and psychological withdrawal are probably employed to some extent by all salesmen. Since the salesman must produce sales in order to keep his job, however, he cannot completely escape conflict by continually avoiding his role partners or belittling their demands. He must eventually choose a course of action from among the incompatible expectations he faces.

The Choice between Conflicting Demands

The salesman may react to role conflict by honoring one partner's demands while completely ignoring those of the other. If the salesman's firm enjoys monopoly power, for example, or if he is dealing with a marginal customer, he may present his company's offer on a "take it or leave it" basis. When competition is intense, on the other hand, he may ignore company policies in order to satisfy a customer in the hope that his superiors will agree to the concessions rather than lose the sale.

Since the salesman has no formal authority to alter company policies and his customers usually have alternative sources of supply, however, he can seldom ignore all the demands of either role partner. He must usually seek a compromise course of action that both partners will accept.

Informing Role Partners of Inconsistencies in Their Demands Salesmen sometimes turn to their role partners for help in resolving their conflicts. When the salesman's superiors and customers are unaware that their demands are incompatible, each will press his own case. When the salesman informs them that their demands conflict, however, they may take the initiative and attempt to resolve their differences. When the salesman's role partners are willing to seek a compromise, negotiations between the two organizations climb the chains of command. Executives with the authority to adjust company policies will begin to negotiate directly with executives at corresponding levels in the customer's organization.[16] The salesman "can virtually become a bystander whose function it is to highlight the conflicting demands being made by members of his role-set."[17]

The salesman, however, remains his company's primary source of information about their customers and market conditions and his customer's primary source of knowledge about his firm and its policies. His ability to withhold, edit and interpret this information enables him to lend support to either his customer's or his company's expectations[18] and thereby influence their willingness to negotiate and the nature of the compromise they reach.[19]

Informing role partners of the conflicts in their demands is a viable response for the salesman when at least one partner is willing to consider changing his demands to accommodate some of the expectations of the other members of the role-set. Some customer-oriented firms, for example, even take the initiative by encouraging salesmen to provide feedback concerning customer demands and by establishing formal mechanisms, such as trade relations departments, for negotiations with customers at higher management levels. When some or all of the company's and customer's demands are non-negotiable, howev-

[16]Henry O. Pruden, "The Outside Salesman: Interorganizational Link," *California Management Review*, Vol. XII (Winter 1969), p. 63.

[17]Robert K. Merton, "The Role-Set: Problems in Sociological Theory," *British Journal of Sociology*, Vol. 8 (1957), p. 117.

[18]Gerald L. Albaum, "Horizontal Information Flow: An Exploratory Study," *Academy of Management Journal*, Vol. 7 (March 1964), pp. 21–33.

[19]See the discussion of "uncertainty absorption" in James G. March and Herbert A. Simon, *Organizations* (New York: John Wiley and Sons, Inc., 1958), p. 165.

er, communicating those demands to the parties involved does nothing to resolve the conflict.

Imposing a Compromise When the salesman cannot ignore either role partner's demands and when they are unwilling to resolve their differences, the salesman may attempt to impose a compromise by responding with behaviors he hopes will satisfy both the customer and his superiors even though they are not entirely consistent with either partner's expectations. He might, for example, violate delivery policies he feels are of minor concern to his superiors in order to overcome a customer's resistance to more strictly enforced price policies.

An attempt at imposing a compromise is a risky response for the salesman, however, since he is never certain that his behavior will be acceptable to either role partner. In order to help assure his success, therefore, he may try to convince both partners that his actions are consistent with their demands by engaging in a common "man-in-the-middle" tactic: "double-talk"—one story for the customer and another for his own company.[20]

FACTORS WHICH INFLUENCE THE SALESMAN'S REACTIONS TO ROLE CONFLICT

Unless the salesman can effectively withdraw from role conflict situations, all of his potential responses to conflict require him to evaluate each partner's demands and decide which should be satisfied and which can be safely compromised or ignored. He may decide to completely ignore one customer's demands, violate company delivery policies in order to satisfy another, and forcefully support a third customer's demands to his superiors in hopes that they will initiate action to satisfy the customer.

[20]Pruden, *op. cit.*, p. 64.

The major factor determining which role partner's demands will be assigned the greatest importance by the salesman is the relative amount of power he attributes to each partner. A role partner's power over the salesman can be defined as the net increase in the probability that the salesman will behave in a way desired by the role partner as a result of the pressures for compliance brought to bear by that role partner.[21] It follows that if two role partners make incompatible demands of a salesman, he is most likely to conform to the expectations of the partner with the greatest power.

Determinants of Attributed Power Textbooks contend that the firm's personal selling activities are a "controllable" element of marketing strategy. They implicitly assume that the formal authority of company executives is sufficient to guarantee the salesman's adherence to the firm's policies and procedures. While the salesman's customers do not hold formal authority over him, however they frequently hold other types of power sufficient to influence his behavior. Both customers and organizational superiors may have (1) legitimate power, (2) reward power, (3) coercive power, (4) expert power, and (5) referent power over the salesman.[22] The relative amounts of each kind of power the salesman attributes to his various role partners depends on their characteristics, the situation, and the manner in which they communicate their demands.

Legitimate Power Classical organization theories hold that organizational authority

[21]Dorwin Cartwright, "Influence, Leadership and Social Control," in James C. March (ed.) *Handbook of Organizations* (Chicago: Rand McNally and Company 1965), p. 11.

[22]J. R. P. French and B. Raven, "The Bases of Social Power," in Dorwin Cartwright (ed.) *Studies in Social Power* (Ann Arbor, Mich.: University of Michigan Press, 1959), pp. 150–167.

stems from resource ownership and is delegated from owners to lower organizational levels. Given this view, all the demands of a salesman's superiors should be considered legitimate, whereas demands emanating from outside the organization have no legitimacy unless they are consistent with the best interests of the firm and its owners.

The more recent concept of authority, beginning with Chester Barnard,[23] holds that the amount of authority or legitimate power a person holds depends on the willingness of his subordinates to accept his orders and decisions. The salesman, therefore, will not view all of his superior's demands as legitimate. Instead, he will adhere to some orders and policies and reject others on the basis of a rational evaluation of their merits and implications. The salesman will also accept some of his customers' requests and demands as rational and legitimate while rejecting others as unreasonable or capricious.

This political view of legitimate power suggests that the salesman is most likely to abide by his superiors' demands when they are fully explained to him and are supported by sound logic and factual information. He is even more likely to feel his company's policies are legitimate when he is allowed to participate in their formulation.[24]

A customer also holds legitimate power when the salesman feels his demands are reasonable and that he has a "right" to expect such demands to be satisfied. Customers, therefore, should support their requests and demands with detailed facts and logic whenever possible.

Reward Power Reward power is based on the salesman's belief that a role partner has the ability to mediate rewards for him and that he will deliver the reward if the salesman cooperates. The strength of the reward power increases with the magnitude of the rewards which the salesman perceives the role partner possesses.

The salesman's superiors possess substantial reward power through their control of financial and occupational remunerations. They can affect his rate of pay, his sales territory, his promotions, and so on. They also have additional power through their control of social rewards. These can take the form of social acceptance, compliments and recognition when the salesman performs his role in accordance with their wishes.

Many of the rewards granted by a salesman's superiors are in recognition of satisfactory job performance. Since his performance is largely judged by his volume of sales, however, his customers directly influence his ability to attain occupational rewards. Their willingness to purchase from the salesman determines his performance and his subsequent rewards. In addition, customers also control social rewards such as friendship and esteem.

The relative amounts of reward power a salesman attributes to his organization and his customers are moderated by the method of compensation employed by his company. When the salesman is paid on a straight commission basis, his customers possess great financial reward power. The salesman must satisfy the customer and obtain an order before he receives his pay. When the compensation basis is straight salary, on the other hand, the salesman is likely to attribute a greater amount of reward power to his organizational superiors since his financial rewards depend entirely upon his ability to satisfy them.

Coercive Power Coercive power exists when the salesman believes he will be punished by a role partner if he fails to conform to that partner's demands. The strength of the coercive power increases with the sales-

[23]Chester I. Barnard, *The Functions of the Executive* (Cambridge, Mass.: Harvard University Press, 1938).

[24]L. Coch and J. R. P. French, "Overcoming Resistance to Change," *Human Relations*, Vol. I (1948), pp. 512–533.

man's perceptions of the severity of the punishment.

Coercive power can be based on two forms of punishment. (1) A role partner may withhold, or threaten to withhold, rewards aspired to by the salesman. This form of coercive power accompanies reward power. Since the salesman's customers and superiors both have the ability to reward him they both can refuse to confer those rewards. His superiors, for example, can fail to promote him, deny a pay raise, refuse to transfer him to more desirable territories, and so forth. His customers can simply withhold orders or threaten to buy from his competitors. (2) The second form of punishment involves the threat or performance of overt negative acts. The salesman's superiors can ostracize him, demote him, transfer him to undesirable territories, or fire him. Customers can also resort to ostracism, give preferential treatment to competing salesmen, and so forth.

While the threat of punishment may be effective in gaining the salesman's compliance, the continued use of coercive power may be self-defeating. Continued punishment or overt threats of punishment will tend to lower the salesman's attraction for his role partners and increase the likelihood that he will withdraw from the situation.

Expert Power Expert power exists when the salesman perceives that a role partner possesses a high level of knowledge or skill in a particular area and that his demands are made in good faith on the basis of sound judgment. While expert power is closely associated with the political concept of legitimacy, expert power stems from the salesman's evaluation of the role partner himself rather than the content of his demands. The salesman is most likely to defer to the expectations of the role partner he considers to have the most expertise and best judgment.

Perceptions of expert power are influenced by the salesman's past experience with and evaluations of his role partners. Past deceptions or errors in judgment can undermine a superior's or customer's ability to win the salesman's compliance with his demands. This also suggests that a role partner will be most successful in influencing a salesman's behavior when his demands are related to areas in which he has demonstrated his competence.

Referent Power A role partner holds referent power when the salesman has had a satisfying association with him in the past and when he desires to continue that relationship. Referent power typically occurs with other forms of power. When a customer has consistently rewarded a salesman over time, for example, the salesman will no longer evaluate each individual demand by that customer. He will simply try to conform to those demands in order to continue the satisfying relationship.

The Relative Importance of Different Types of Power A role partner's power to control a salesman's behavior in conflictful situations flows from a combination of the five bases of power discussed above. One study indicates, however, that salesmen perceive some types of power as being more important than others.[25] The salesmen in this study rated legitimate power as the most important reason for complying with a superior's demands. Referent and expert power were rated as intermediate in importance, while reward and coercive power were held to be the least important reasons for compliance. These ratings were based on the subjects' self-reported perceptions of their superiors' sources of power and, therefore, may not be descriptive of the actual reasons for their adherence to their superiors' demands. The findings do suggest, however,

[25]J. C. Bachman, C. G. Smith and J. A. Slesinger, "Control, Performance and Satisfaction: An Analysis of Structural and Individual Effects," *Journal of Personality and Social Psychology*, Vol. 4 (1966), pp. 127–136.

that the most effective means for a role partner to influence the salesman's behavior when he is torn between conflicting demands may be to substantiate the legitimacy of his own expectations.

The perceived importance of different forms of power, however, may vary between individual salesmen. Gross, Mason and McEachern, for example, have found that individuals characterized by a "moral orientation" attribute the greatest importance to the legitimacy of demands in resolving role conflict. Other individuals with an "expedient orientation" give primacy to the relative amounts of reward and coercive power held by their various role partners.[26] A salesman's behavior in role conflict situations, therefore, is not only determined by the relative amounts of power he attributes to each role partner, but also by the relative importance he attaches to each type of power.

The Existing Empirical Evidence Research on the role conflict resolution process in nonselling situations indicates that reasonably accurate predictions of which role demands an individual will conform to can be made on the basis of measurements of his perceptions of (1) the *legitimacy* of each role partner's demands and (2) the negative sanctions controlled by each partner.[27] Perceived legitimacy is defined in these studies as the individual's belief that a role partner has a "right" to expect him to conform to his expectations, and it is consistent with the concept of legitimate power discussed above. Perceived negative sanctions are similar to the concept of coercive power. They are defined as the punishments one individual believes a role partner can employ if he fails to satisfy his demands.

Further research is necessary, however, to determine whether these findings can be generalized to include the responses of salesmen in conflictful situations. Further studies should also determine whether knowledge of the salesman's perceptions of the reward, expert and referent power of each role partner, in addition to legitimacy and negative sanctions, enables a fuller explanation and a more accurate prediction of his responses to conflict.

V. CONCLUSIONS

Textbooks assume that the salesman will abide by company policies and procedures and loyally represent his firm and its products in dealings with customers. The nature of the salesman's position, however, frequently places him in the middle between his superiors' expectations and policies on one hand and the customers' objectives and demands on the other. When the salesman is faced with this kind of conflict, the formal authority of his organizational superiors may not be sufficient to guarantee his loyalty to company policies. While his superiors' authority may impose a major constraint on his freedom of action, the salesman's choice among conflicting demands is largely determined by his perceptions of the relative power held by superiors and customers.

Instead of a totally controllable tool of his company, the salesman is an "influenceable" intermediary between company and customer. An understanding of the different sources of power, therefore, is important to sales managers and customers alike as they attempt to influence the salesman's behavior in the field.

[26] Neal Gross, W. S. Mason, and A. W. McEachern, *Explorations in Role Analysis* (New York: John Wiley and Sons, Inc., 1958), p. 289.

[27] *Ibid*, pp. 281–318. Delbert C. Miller and Fremont A. Shull, Jr., "The Prediction of Administrative Role Conflict Resolutions," *Administrative Science Quarterly*, (September 1962), pp. 143–160. H. J. Ehrlich, J. W. Rinehart, and J. C. Howell, "The Study of Role Conflict: Explorations in Methodology," *Sociometry*, Vol. 25 (March 1962), pp. 85–97.

E ADVERTISING

34

A Theoretical View of Advertising Communication

Joseph T. Plummer

It is proposed that advertising research be based less on one-way transmission models of communication and more on multivariate studies, with emphasis on receivers' contributions to communication outcomes. A four-level model of the process is presented; and several dimensions within each level are identified, based on recent research on the effects of TV commercials.

The four levels described, along with research, are (1) the unconscious level, (2) the immediate perceptual level, (3) the retention or learning level, and (4) the behavior level.

Most concepts or formalized models of advertising communication have implicitly stated some expression of a unidimensional, one-way, stimulus-response theory. Probably the most current model of advertising communications states that an effective television commercial should:

a attract and hold the attention of the target audience,
b communicate a message, explicitly or implicitly, about the brand,
c favorably affect attitudes toward the brand.

There can be little argument about the logic or the usefulness of this model for decision-makers intent upon evaluating the job accomplished by the communication stimuli. At the same time, this model does little to shed insights into the role of the receiver, except that he perform specific tasks. It places emphasis on what the communication does to people and has placed little emphasis on what people do to the communication. The purpose of this paper is to challenge this conception and to present an alternate view using as support some recent research conducted by the author and some of his colleagues.

Before presenting an alternate view, a few observations should be made on the model stated earlier and on another even simpler concept that "advertising builds sales." The sales effect notion and the three-step model are goals of advertising. But the true effect of advertising on sales is not known. Advertising helps, but in what ways and to what degrees have not been demonstrated empirically, except that advertising can increase brand awareness through manipulation of spending levels and that there is some correlation between basic measures of advertising—such as recall or pre-post scores—and sales. There is no clear picture of how the three-step model relates to sales, nor do we have very clear notions of the interrelationships of the three steps among themselves.

Factor analytic studies of commercial testing data show that recall measures and attitude measures seldom vary together and that they seldom rank order commercials in the same way [5, 13]. Finally, these are the goals and the related measurements made on a single commercial, at a single point in time. Overlooked are the effects of repeated exposures over time interspersed with actual experience with the product by consumers.

Reprinted from *The Journal of Communication*, vol. 21, no. 4, pp. 315–325, December, 1971, with permission of *The Journal of Communication*, copyright 1971. At the time of writing, the author was manager of copy and creative research at the Leo Burnett Company, Inc., Chicago.

In order to understand how advertising works as communication between source and receiver, it is necessary to examine *the process* of advertising communication. It is the purpose of this paper to propose one way of thinking about advertising as a communication process between visual and aural stimuli and the people experiencing these stimuli.

It will help to first consider the place of advertising in the total communications spectrum. At one end of the spectrum there is person-to-person communication. Farther along the spectrum is person-to-group communication and at the opposite end is mass communications—a message delivered to an unseen audience. Without discussing all the differences and similarities between the various forms of communication, it is important to the understanding of mass communications to state that immediate, observable feedback or "feed forward" is difficult to obtain in most mass communications except through research of some kind. Unlike a participant in person-to-person communication (in which it is difficult enough), the creator or sender of the mass media message has little or no opportunity to observe or get a sense of what hearers and viewers are understanding, structuring, accepting, rejecting, enjoying, intending to do, etc., except through some form of audience research. This makes the task of communicating rather difficult because the sender does not have first hand knowledge of who he is reaching or how this unknown receiver is reacting. This lack of feedback has made the gaining of real insights into the process of advertising communication very difficult.

There are three unique aspects of advertising as a form of communication that need to be recognized in a model of advertising communication. The first aspect is the *repetitive nature of advertising over time*. It is this aspect, technically called "wearout," into which research has shed very little understanding up to now. There have been a few research studies on the repetition aspect from the perspective of learning [7]. Another special aspect of advertising is the highly competitive nature of the environment where advertising messages exist. This competitive environment has been called "clutter" as it relates to television. In just four years, the average number of different network commercials per month increased from 1,990 in 1964 to 3,022 in 1968 [6]. Whether it is "clutter" or not, advertisers have seen day-after recall scores slowly declining over the past five years. Television advertising is very short—many messages are less than 30 seconds—which has given rise to the clutter. In order to get through this clutter then, television advertising needs to be more than straight transmission of hard product information unless the sender is saying something like "the product now costs five cents."

The third unique aspect of advertising communication is the role it plays in our culture. Because advertising has become an accepted part of our popular culture, things can be shown or said that outside of advertising would be rejected as absurd. As a result of this cultural role and the "addictive" nature of television, people probably "see" most television advertising, but the degrees of their interest, involvement, comprehension, retention, and responses vary significantly.

Given the above perspective, it is proposed that advertising communication be viewed as *a process that incorporates both the messages and the receivers, with major emphasis on the viewers' perspectives*. One way to think about the advertising communication process is to theorize that there are several dimensions within each of four levels of viewer response. These four levels are (a) the unconscious level, (b) the immediate perceptual level, (c) the retention or learning level, and (d) the behavior level.

The first level, unconscious response, is the most difficult to conceptualize, measure, and illustrate; but there is evidence that it probably does exist. One indication that unconscious responses to advertising communication take place may be seen in the physiological responses, such as galvanic skin response and heart beat rate, that have been measured in the laboratory. The present knowledge in this area is that reliable differences between stimuli effects can be measured. However, what the various differences mean are still equivocal.

A second level of response is seen in the immediate cognitive responses that a viewer has while viewing the commercial. This level relates to the feelings, emotions, personal experiences and attitudes the commercial arouses in the viewer. It has to do with how people perceive and affectively interpreted what they see and hear. Laughter, stimulation, empathy, dislike, etc., are the kinds of responses that make up this level of the communication process.

The third level of response is the level of learning that takes place as a result of experiencing the commercial. It is best conceptualized as the "filing" of elements from the communication experience in one's "filing system." Recall of specific elements or product claims is part of the retention process, but so are the attitudes and images stored and retrieved at a later time. This level of retention has been indicated by years of delayed recall research in advertising at varying time-delays, the most common being twenty-four hours. It appears that the amount a person is able to recall or play back is a function of many variables such as the interviewing time, the number of cues provided to aid recall, the interest of the person in the product category, etc. But there can be little question that retention and recall do take place and constitute a major response mode to advertising communication.

The final level of response is the action or behavior that takes place as a result of the communication experience. In most cases of advertising communication, this level of response is less traceable to a particular commercial and is farthest removed in time. Immediate behavior can take place as when a person goes to his refrigerator and gets a beer after experiencing a beer commercial. The primary behavior advertisers are interested in is product purchase, but there are other types of behavior, such as information seeking, that may be linked to the advertising communication. Another link is through a "two-step flow" in which people who view a commercial influence others to buy the product. Clearly, much purchase behavior is not just the result of a single commercial experience, but of many factors in addition, such as previous experience with the product, other promotional activity, and availability.

Each level of response by the viewer has some relationship to the other levels and to the various dimensions of the message presented to them. The important thing to keep in mind is that understanding how a commercial is communicating requires consideration of all levels of response.

The present understanding of the level of unconscious response as measured by physiological dimensions centers on two concepts: arousal and potential wearout. Neither of these concepts has been definitely proven, but accumulating evidence does suggest some validity for these concepts [2, 4]. Significant pupil and skin responses occur when the commercials present stimulating action, or extreme changes in the mood, tempo or volume of the commercial, or when there is some sexy event in the commercial. Further research and experience with this level of response—often overlooked—is clearly needed in advertising communication research.

In the last two years a great deal of research effort at the Leo Burnett Company has gone into the investigation of the second level of response—the immediate cognitive response to the commercial. Adjectives and descriptive sentences have been used to allow viewers to rate commercials immediately after exposure. Rating data from over four thousand respondents and over a hundred different commercials have been factor analyzed a number of times using principal components analysis and an orthogonal rotation procedure. In general, the results are quite similar with a few factors unique to the adjective data and a few factors unique to the sentence data. In-depth discussions of both procedures and the research development of them can be found in recent reports [12]. The factor analysis results indicate that the immediate cognitive response level is multidimensional and not merely a general evaluation.

A brief description of the various dimensions that emerged from the research and the kinds of commercials that relate to the responses on each dimension may provide an understanding of this response level. Seven independent dimensions emerged, accounting for over seventy percent of the total variance.

The dimension that accounted for the most variance might be called *entertainment* or *stimulation*. This dimension appears to measure the extent to which viewers enjoy and are positively stimulated by a commercial. Humorous ads often score high on this dimension as do those that portray warm, charming people. Among the ads that score high are those which feature well-liked characters, such as the Pillsbury "Doughboy" and the Green Giant elves, or which star popular entertainers. Another type of commercial that is seen as entertaining and stimulating is the contemporary, "swinging" commercial. In short, this dimension differentiates those commercials which are pleasureable and stimulating to watch and listen to and those which are not. A second dimension that appears to be the opposite response from the first dimension, but which does not co-vary with it, may be called *irritation*. This suggests that viewers are making a judgment of annoyance independent of an ad's stimulation. This dimension appears to relate to viewers' perceptions of ads as far-fetched, untrue in their implications, or insulting in manner. The negative feelings people have toward the characters or situations, particularly anxiety-producing ones, also seem to be reflected in this dimension.

The third dimension, which may be called *familiarity*, appears to measure the viewers' perception of ads as being familiar to them or being very unique and novel in their presentations. Very few commercials are perceived by respondents to be truly unique or novel. This response seems to relate to the total execution of the commercial rather than some specific element.

The fourth dimension seems to indicate the degree to which viewers say, in effect, "I am like or wish I were like" the people portrayed in the ads. One might call this dimension *empathy* or *gratifying involvement* as the commercials that score high on this dimension show attractive characters, cute children, warm family situations, beautiful spots like Hawaii, or meaningful adult social interactions that viewers can identify with or get involved with in an idealized fashion.

The fifth dimension, extent of *confusion*, relates to the degree to which viewers feel confused by a commercial. Respondents perceive most commercials to be relatively clear, but this does not mean that they truly understand everything nor that they grasp the point that the copywriter is trying to make. There are a few commercials that viewers do perceive to be more confusing than most, however. Commercials that utilize disconnected quick-cuts, that lack audio-video congruence or those that include distracting or obscurely related elements are likely to be perceived as less comprehensible.

The sixth dimension might be called *informativeness* or *personal relevance*. This dimension does not measure the content of the information, but only the extent to which something in the commercial was of interest and importance to viewers. It also appears to be a measure of the viewers' impression that the commercial was informative in nature. Most ads for new products perform at the high end of this dimension, as one would expect. The judgment of "how important, how relevant to me and my interest in this product was the information in the commercial?" is one of the major responses viewers make to commercials.

The final dimension might be called *brand reinforcement.* It relates to the degree to which respondents' brand attitudes and images are reinforced by the ad. It is important to note that viewers do respond to commercials in terms of pre-determined brand attitudes and images, yet few researchers try to measure this elusive dimension. However it did emerge from the research reviewed here and can be useful in spotting commercials that present an image deviant from the one that viewers bring to the commercial. It appears that the more similar the commercial's execution is to previous commercials, the more likely that brand reinforcement will take place.

These seven factors of response comprise the immediate cognitive response level in the proposed model. These dimensions provide insight into advertising communication experiences, which have been overlooked in advertising research.

Historically, emphasis in research has been on the third level in the model, the retention level. Most television commercial testing services operate on the level of retention and are of two basic types of measurement systems—24-hour proved recall and pre-post attitude shifting measures. Several correlational studies of the two types of measurement systems and several factor analytic studies of systems that include both of these measures indicate that commercials vary on proved recall effects independently of pre-post brand attitude shift measures. These data suggest that a commercial or elements of a commercial can be recalled without an accompanying "effect" on attitudes or choices of the advertised brand and vice versa. Clearly, there is some minimal recall required for some brand response, but the two do not go hand in hand. Nor does either measure alone provide an understanding of this third level of response.

Factor analytic studies [13] suggest three or possibly four dimensions in this retention response level. These dimensions are (1) *proved awareness of the commercial* in general, (2) *specific awareness of the intended message*, (3) *attitude toward the advertised brand*, and (4) *attitude toward the commercial.* The first dimension is a measure of the proportion of viewers who remember seeing the commercial when it was shown in a normal environment 24 hours earlier. The second dimension indicates the proportion of viewers aware of the commercial who retained the important product messages. Often a highly memorable character or personality can create high awareness, yet lead few people to retain what it was the character or personality was trying to say about the brand. The third dimension indicates how many viewers retained over time a positive or negative attitude attributed to the commercial. This attitude retention could be in the form of a reminder of previous attitudes, or creation of new attitudes. The fourth dimension appears less stable than the other three, but general liking or disliking of a commercial does appear to account for some of the variance.

This third level of response appears to be related to the extent and kind of learning (or forgetting) that takes place as a result of the advertising communication. Work by Leavitt [9] suggests that the major underlying construct operating on this third level is meaningfulness based upon organizational structure. Although rats can learn to recognize nonsense stimuli via conditioning, Leavitt's notion was that organized, meaningful stimuli which are relevant to viewers of advertising communication are recognized most quickly. This underlying construct of structure as an indication of meaningfulness does appear to relate to the three major dimensions in the retention level of viewer response. Experience with structure has generated some useful concepts about the kinds of communication variables that enhance retention.

In many cases, the inherent structure of the commercial is very similar to the structure viewers impose upon it. There are times, however, when viewers have trouble structuring or organizing the commercial either because it has little inherent structure or because the structure is too complex and meaningless. It is in these instances that very little information is retained over time. Such principles as shape in a commercial or the building and reduction of tension, congruence of audio and video, integration of the product into the storyline as high points of interest rather than at random, and visual dramatization of the product claim rather than mere statement of it, appear to enhance learning significantly. Some recent research[1] has indicated that commercials which viewers can organize easily around the product are retained by more people and deliver more specific information than those commercials which viewers cannot organize in their minds.

Another important construct that relates to this retention level is "the needs of the viewer." A person who has no need for nor interest in the product is much less likely to be aware of or to retain something from the commercial. In order to enhance learning it would seem best to start with some need or knowledge already shared by the viewer and build upon that rather than an abstract approach remote from the world of the viewer.

The final level of response, action, is extremely difficult to attribute solely to the communication. Part of the difficulty arises from the fact that the communication is received in the home while purchasing action occurs outside the home at a later time. Purchasing action is the result of many interacting variables or influences which challenge conceptualization and research. Very little conclusive work has been done on the subject of immediate or delayed action as it relates to advertising communication. Yet, this level is the most central to the question of communication effectiveness. Perhaps as more large scale experiments are conducted and the relationships of the levels of the model presented here are further explored, advances will be made in understanding of all kinds of communication and their relationships to behavior.

These advances will depend upon the abilities of people from all communication-related disciplines to join in their thinking and research. Leo Bogart [3] articulated the challenge very well when he stated, "The twilight areas of advertising research are precisely those of social psychology in general: 1) the relation between emotional arousal or affect and the transmittal of information; 2) the relation between learning information on a subject and acquiring certain opinions about it; 3) the conditions under which favorable opinions are translated into overt behavior."

It seems clear that a narrow view of the communication process or the manipulation of a single message variable offers little promise of new information about advertising communication. Through application of a conceptual model of various multi-dimensional levels, such as the four-level model presented here, some new insights into key questions may emerge.

[1]Reported by Fred Schlinger in a presentation on Structural Analysis in 1968.

REFERENCES

1 Agres, Stuart. "The Use of Skin Conductance in Predicting Commercial Effectiveness." In

house report. Leo Burnett Company, Inc., January 1968.

2 Agres, Stuart. "The Effect of Repeated Stimulus Exposure on the Structure of Verbal Responses." Working paper. Leo Burnett Company, Inc., 1969.

3 Bogart, Leo. "Where Does Advertising Research Go From Here?" *Journal of Advertising Research*, 9:3–15, 1969.

4 Cloverdale, Herbert L., Jr. "Pupil Response, GSR and Novelty: A Pilot Study." Unpublished report. Illinois Institute of Technology, September, 1968.

5 Cage, C., and J. Plummer. "A Look at Leo Burnett Commercial Test." In house report. Leo Burnett Company, Inc., 1968.

6 Gould, Jack. "Why Viewers Tune Out, or Plugged to Death." *New York Times*, January 4, 1971, p. D17.

7 Grass, R. C. "The Use of Research to Forecast the Effectiveness of Television Advertising." Paper presented to the Winter Regional Conference of the Division of Consumer Psychology, American Psychological Association, at West Point, New York, March 12, 1970.

8 Hess, E. H. "Attitude and Pupil Size." *Scientific American*, 212:46–54, 1965.

9 Leavitt, C. "Response Structure: A Determinant of Recall." *Journal of Advertising Research*, 8:3–6, 1968.

10 Leavitt, C. "Notes on Communication #2." Working paper. Leo Burnett Company, Inc., 1970.

11 Leavitt, C. "A Multidimensional Set of Rating Scales for Television Commercials," *Journal of Applied Psychology*, 54:427–429, 1970.

12 Leavitt, C., M. McConville and W. D. Wells. "A Reaction Profile for TV Commercials." *Journal of Advertising Research* (in press).

13 Plummer, J. "A Systematic Approach to Commercial Testing Evaluation." Working paper. Leo Burnett Company, Inc., 1970.

14 Plummer, J. and M. J. Schlinger. "Viewer Response Profile." Working paper. Leo Burnett Company, Inc., 1970.

35

Imagery and Symbolism

Sidney J. Levy
Ira O. Glick

The concept of *imagery* is important in marketing. The term is widely used, both casually and technically, and often in misleading ways. The purpose of this selection is to explain what imagery is and how it is conveyed and received. After imagery has been defined, the discussion will examine the role of this concept in marketing planning and communications. How symbolism functions in relation to imagery will then be explored, followed by analysis of imagery and symbolism from the viewpoints of participants in the marketing system.

Reprinted from Steuart Henderson Britt (ed.), *Marketing Manager's Handbook*, pp. 857–867. © 1973, The Dartnell Corporation. Used by permission of The Dartnell Corporation. At the time of writing, Sidney Levy was professor of behavioral sciences in management, Graduate School of Management, Northwestern University. Ira O. Glick was president, Ira O. Glick & Associates, Inc.

THE MEANING OF IMAGERY

The concept of brand image was introduced in 1955,[1] and was widely seized upon[2] because it aptly summed up the idea that consumers buy brands not only for their physical attributes and functions, but also because of the *meanings* connected with the brands.

The notion of imagery reminds us that action in the marketplace is based on impressions and interpretations that people derive from their experience of a broader sort than that which narrowly relates to the objects they buy or sell. They cannot learn all the facts available, and they cannot keep in mind all those they do learn. In addition, there are various influences pressing them to have one opinion or another about the product, service, and company, at issue.

The Content of Images

The image is a result of all these facts and influences, reduced to manageable proportions. Drawn from many sources, the image includes such ideas as these.

1 *Knowledge about technical matters* helps people define a brand. For example, the image of Volkswagen might include the fact that it has 4 cylinders; or the image of Jell-O might say it is high in protein.

2 *Awareness of other characteristics* that are somewhat more subjective, that seem like facts, but may or may not be supported by experience, is part of imagery. Here might be included the idea that a certain fabric will launder well, or that a certain movie is very funny.

3 *Beliefs about the value of the object* come to be part of its image. For example, the conviction that a Rolls-Royce is worth the cost, that Budweiser is indeed a premium beer, that Pepsi-Cola has a lot to give—such ideas become bound up in the image of those brands.

4 *Judgments about the suitability of the brand* are influences added to the image. Brands come to acquire a greater sense of appropriateness for some kinds of people than for others. It is part of the image, then, that one brand is thought to be a cigarette mainly smoked by men, a beverage preferred by teen-agers, a food too spicy for American tastes.

As these points suggest, imagery is a mixture of notions and deductions, based on many things. It is fundamentally subjective, a fact that troubles those who believe marketing decisions should be made only on hard facts and in accordance with their ideas about what is rational or economically sound. The harder fact is, however, that people live by their images and these are governed by their individual experiences, their values, and how they interpret what comes across to them.

Illusions and Facts

At times, the imagery is indeed largely an illusion—e.g., the belief that some product is highly nutritious when it is not, that a carrot will contribute significantly to improved vision, that a particular automobile make is near-perfect in quality or that another offers the degree of "functional" transportation believed to be the case. Other images are debatable: will a sports car enhance one's sexuality and youthfulness? Will ownership of a particular airplane brand imply a higher status level or a more attractive life style? No, say some, a deodorant or toothpaste will not make one more alluring to the opposite sex; on the other hand, say others, bad breath and dingy teeth *are* offensive and of no help in social relations, as the advertisements claim.

[1]Burleigh B. Gardner and Sidney J. Levy, "The Product and the Brand," *Harvard Business Review*, Vol. 33 (March–April, 1955), pp. 33–39.

[2]David Ogilvy, "The Image and the Brand," *Advertising Age*, Vol. 26 (October 17, 1955), p. 1.

The idea of imagery is not restricted (as often used) to mean only those aspects of products or communications that are misleading or which try to make things seem more attractive or valuable than they really are. It also refers to any inferences drawn about qualities that seem well-grounded—e.g., the image of diamonds as hard and durable, of prices as rising, of refrigerators as noisy, of candy as sweet, of tires as safer than they used to be, of Mercedes-Benz cars as socially impressive.

Long-Range and Short-Range Imagery Goals

There is much discussion among marketers about setting objectives, and planning has first to consider where the enterprise wishes to go. Commonly, however, objectives are thought of in concrete terms relating to sales volume, profit level, or getting customers to be aware of some facts about the product. More recently, marketing managers have been giving attention to what kinds of imagery goals they should have and how to achieve them.

There are many problems involved. Often, managers do not realize how some given action will affect the imagery about their brand or their company, as when an emphasis on stylishness or an upgrading of quality unexpectedly modifies customers' views of a product's value or desirability, or their feelings about a company's suitability to their own habits, tastes, and identities. Managers may not know how to bring about the imagery they want to present—what precise ideas to present, the context in which these are appropriately dealt with, the channels of communication where this might be best accomplished. Their imagery goals may have elements that are in conflict. An example of how inadvertent imagery might come about is the frequent running of sales, only to discover that the product is coming to be regarded as inferior in quality. When a brand creates imagery that boasts of the popularity of the brand, there may be difficulty in trying also to suggest it is an intimate brand. Brands that seem large tend thereby to seem impersonal.

Thus it is that a marketing action (running a sale, designing a package, selecting an advertising theme) is both a short-run effort and an investment in the long-run reputation of the brand. If short-run decisions are made without reference to long-run implications, as is commonly the case under competitive pressures and the varied demands of dealers, advertising agencies, and package designers, the results may be haphazard and confused so that over time the brand image is not well oriented to its market segments, or it turns out to be an image that is different from what the seller would like.

Corporate Imagery

An important instance of imagery is that which affects the company as a whole. The corporate image refers to the kinds of ideas and impressions people have of the organization in general. Reputation of its specific products and brands will play a role, but other factors are also relevant. Such knowledge, awareness, beliefs, and judgments are the size of the company, its personnel, incidents in its history, its value as a stock, its contribution to the life of the community or the country, and are used in reacting to the company.

The corporate image may be of significance to consumers of the specific products by reassuring them of the responsibility and quality of the manufacture. It affects the buyers of company shares; it influences the government in its relations with the enterprise; and suppliers to the company will be guided by their image of it.

Appreciation of the power of corporate imagery has led many companies to give special thought to communicating with their various publics. Public relations, institutional advertising, community-oriented programs, training programs, corporate literature, the name of the company and its logogram, and marketing activity within the trade are increasingly evaluated for their effects on the corporate image as well as their immediate practical functions.

Imagery and Symbolic Communication

An image is an interpretation, a set of inferences and reactions. It is a symbol because it is not the object itself, but refers to it and stands for it. In addition to the physical realities of the product, brand, or corporation, the image includes their meanings—that is, the beliefs, attitudes, and feelings that have come to be attached to them.

These meanings are learned or stimulated by the component experiences people have with the product, and these components are particular symbols whose significance is grasped. For example, part of the "real" experience of riding in a convertible is the wind blowing one's hair. This experience becomes symbolic of the convertible, a component with such meanings as freedom, youthfulness, and irresponsibility. As a rider, one feels a release from conventional restraints, and watchers see the riders visibly showing (probably flaunting) their disorderly hair.

Similarly, all other component symbols communicate aspects of the image, acting as messages to the observer. A new package design might be made to serve as a more efficient container than the old one. Symbolically, the new package could also imply a more modern product inside, a company concern with beauty, or an enhanced femininity, depending on the shape, colors, graphics, and illustrations.

Symbols in Advertising and Promotion

The symbolic actions in marketing are pervasive and inescapable. They are most noticeable and are given most specific attention in advertising and promotion. The structure of a company's office lobby plays a symbolic marketing role, but architects are commonly either unaware of or indifferent to that fact. However, people in promotional work are apt to be sensitive to the more intangible aspects of their efforts, the possible effects on imagery.

Advertising as an activity is itself symbolic. To advertise is usually understood as a way of being proud and boastful, as something one may do hard or softly. Advertising contrasts with personal selling by usually being some kind of public announcement, a fact that suggests an openness, a prevalence, a quality of being larger than life. It seems democratic, potentially for everyone, and often enjoyable because it is bold, colorful, fantasy-arousing, and exaggerated.

On the same grounds, it is adversely criticized because it may symbolize deception and distraction from the true facts: it seems demanding and intrusive or insufficiently informative.

Whether appreciated or demeaned, advertising is powerful in presenting symbols that help to form people's images. It does this even when the symbolism is resisted. Commercials that show white doves and white tornadoes in the kitchen, giant's fists in washing machines, white knights transforming laundry, crowns for eating Imperial margarine, are frequently criticized as meaningless and insulting to intelligence. At the same time, the symbolic vigor of these messages is pronounced, absorbs attention, arouses astonishment and amusement as well as irritation, and creates imagery concerning brand effectiveness.

Symbolic Form and Movement

Such results come about because people are not merely literal-minded, nor do they respond only to the most obvious, explicit statements in advertising. This is evident if one examines the various kinds of advertising symbolism and how they gain their effects.

Viewers of television commercials may

come to learn the messages well because they usually have several opportunities. In doing so, they are often especially influenced by such elements of form as animation, music, special word choices, particular forms and shapes, the sequence of events, their pace, and so on. Some of this influence is difficult to describe and to specify, attesting to the subtle symbolic factors at work. Examples might be the absurd charm of the Alka-Seltzer girl who served her husband the monstrous dumpling and the repellent quality felt by many about the Man from Glad.

The less deliberate or self-conscious reactions to symbolism are also demonstrated by the effects of movement. The kinds of movement used in television commercials are themselves a vocabulary, contributing to imagery in an intricate fashion. Some examples are:

1 *Rotation*, a movement that suggests the confining three-dimensional form of the television tube, and a showing off of all sides.

2 *Approach and retreat*, a movement indicating arriving and departing, bringing something to the viewer, or the yearning feeling elicted by a fading away.

3 *Unifying movement*, which occurs when parts are shown that come together to form a whole. The movement is dynamic, leading the audience to want to see the resolution.

4 *Staccato movement*, such as achieved by stop-motion photography. The effect is one of stylization, a quirkiness, a watch-and-wait idea that is sometimes annoying because viewers vary in their rates of ability to integrate such visual material.

The Manager's Point of View

The position of the marketing manager trying to promote his brand is not an easy one because the creation of a desired brand image is a complex activity. It draws upon all the symbolic elements discussed briefly above, in a situation that is in constant flux. There is no simple recipe for the symbolic mix that will produce a specific brand image. The problems vary: perhaps the brand is on the rise and needs to be kept aloft, conveying a sense of confidence, of having a sturdy place in the contemporary market, and a suitability for everyday life styles. Perhaps the brand is declining. This is an agonizing situation for marketers, since what is wrong is often not apparent, leading to some flailing around and blaming in all directions.

Introducing a new brand is an exciting challenge and opportunity. Customarily, the focus on the product is so great that the manager may neglect the fact that he is engaged in creating a brand image almost from scratch (almost, because he may be constrained by existing imagery about the company and by other products in the line). If he forgets to realize that pricing policy, channels of distribution, media employed, timing, and all the myriad marketing decisions will each be saying something about the brand, defining it and symbolizing it, as well as offering it in practical ways, he may miss his target audience.

The Buyer's Point of View

The world of marketing symbolism and imagery is composed of individual events—products, prices, coupons, advertisements, salesmen, media, and each is handled in some particular way when encountered. Together, these individual events come to form a substantial part of the daily environment. As people move through the day, the multitude of objects and messages that remind them about consuming and buying is almost inescapable and relentless. The manager's problem is to make himself seen, heard, and noticed among all the communications; the people being marketed to have the problem of sorting out their experience, learning from it, and finding in it the things and the meanings that will satisfy them. They constantly process the symbols they are exposed to, deciding how much attention to give to them, making inferences about the product and the form in which it is presented, and about how well it fits into their goals.

An example of how this goes on in a particular area of marketing is found in consumer incentives. Managers may not realize the extent to which housewives reason and draw imagery from different promotional approaches. When such devices as coupons, contests, premiums, and miscellaneous deals are used, these can be interpreted positively or negatively, not only as means of gaining advantage but for suggesting something about the company or brand. On the positive side, incentives have such meanings as these:

- A large, well-established company.
- An aggressive marketer.
- A generous, friendly company.

On the other hand, negative inferences may be drawn.

- The company is in trouble.
- The product is poor or overstocked.
- It is normally overpriced.

Additionally, each type of incentive has its own symbolic character and appeal. Samples are almost always welcome, seeming truly free and fair. Sweepstakes are fun and get large numbers of entries, but they seem frothy and are usually forgotten quickly and do little for the company.

Symbolism in Industrial Advertising

Imagery is often thought to be less important in industrial marketing than in consumer marketing. This is a misunderstanding that comes about when the image is taken to refer only to the "nonrational" mood aspects of communications. This view overlooks the fact that industrial organizations and their brands also have images, even if the content of those images has to do with reliability, service, delivery dates, and competitive pricing. Imagery is not merely frivolity, as a company can have a stodgy image as well as a stylish or even phony one.

Part of the imagery of industrial communication is a sense of dull technical emphasis, of old-line companies relying on their salesmen, being heavy and serious to the point of depression. Where advertising is used, it tends to be traditional, conventional messages with relatively straightforward reassurances that the company and product can provide the performance the user needs. The product is illustrated, or one of its applications is shown, and a request for inquiries winds it up. The people shown, if any, are often earnest, stiff representatives of the seller or users, or both, in "show and tell" situations.

Changing Imagery

Some organizations are discontent with this, feeling the result is an imagery that is static, old-fashioned, and false to the animated character of the company. As newer symbols are used to modify the industrial and commercial scene, the advertising becomes more "emotional" and colorful, the imagery changes toward greater subtlety. Humor has come to the fore, taking many forms. Verbal and visual puns are common. A bank in New York says to its commercial customers, "The American Capitalist. When his needs are financial, his reactions are Chemical." An ad for Canteen Corporation showed a drinking straw, with the headline, "Are you keeping this management pipeline open?" The sense of good humor starting to pervade industrial advertising may show R&D workers exaggeratedly achieving their marvels. It finds expression in cartoons, whimsy, and many kinds of fantasy. The purpose is to show that the company is not conventional and routine. The use of humor symbolizes that the company has some modern self-awareness, that it is "with it," that it is not just plodding along doing the same dull, unamusing things. An engineer shows his appreciation of more vital industrial advertising:

> The photograph is modern, the catch phrase is up to date, suggests a modern, today, ad approach. This all comes over to the company. . . . I'd expect to see cylinders and fittings—I've seen one that showed all the fittings that were available. I appreciate this. This is an eye-catcher. I like the unusualness of the ad. It's far from the workaday world ads.

Implications

From the point of view developed in this chapter, the main overall task of the marketihg manager is to relate all the symbols he can control to the general thrust of the company or his product responsibility. He can do this by asking and exploring the following questions.

1. What does he have to sell? The manager should *understand* what he sells, in a fundamental way. That is, he should learn about the symbolic significance of what he is offering in the marketplace. The meaning of his offering is the central message he sends out.

2. What is the symbolic suitability to the audience? In studying his markets, the manager needs to understand more than the conventional descriptions of market segments. Part of modern study is to learn about the life style of the customers, as the imagery of the brand will be seen through the eyes of people living in diverse ways.

3. What can the manager say? All that the manager has to present to his current and potential customers constitutes a repertoire of symbols from which he can draw in order to put together the image he would like to have. He has to work complexly with what his ideal imagery goals might be; what would be believable given his product, his history, and what the contemporary period allows; and what he can control in the face of his competition.

4. How do subsymbols relate to the goal? If the image the company offers of itself and its brands is a large symbol, the specific actions taken in the marketplace are subsymbols that comprise the total. The accumulation of symbolic meanings produces more intense imagery. Each action should be analyzed not only for its immediate value (e.g., reducing inventory, making more people aware of the name), but for what it contributes to the accumulating imagery.

SUGGESTIONS FOR FURTHER READING

Kenneth Boulding, *The Image*. (Ann Arbor: University of Michigan Press, 1968).

I. J. Dolich, "Congruence Relationships Between Self Images and Product Brands," *Journal of Marketing Research*, Vol. 6 (February, 1969), pp. 80–85.

Henry Dreyfuss, *Symbol Sourcebook* (New York: McGraw-Hill Book Company, 1972).

Erving Goffman, *The Presentation of Self in Everyday Life*. (New York: Doubleday Anchor, 1959).

Sidney J. Levy, *Promotional Behavior* (Glenview, Ill.: Scott-Foresman, 1971).

36

An Attitudinal Framework for Advertising Strategy

Harper W. Boyd, Jr.
Michael L. Ray
Edward S. Strong

Is it realistic to consider advertising strategy in terms of more than just levels on a "hierarchy of effect?" The authors report that it is. They present a five-alternative framework for advertising strategy based on attitude research which relates product and brand perceptions to consumer preferences.

Advertising and marketing researchers have developed a variety of new techniques for defining and measuring attitude and attitudinal change. These techniques have added much to the understanding of the communications process, but seldom have they been used in a comprehensive form to structure advertising strategies and tactics.[1] This article focuses on the nature of advertising objectives from an attitudinal perspective.

The proposed framework facilitates the formulation of a strategy of consumer attitudinal change and suggests that basically five advertising strategy alternatives are available to the decision maker. The nature of each of these strategy alternatives is discussed, but the framework also holds promise for meeting other marketing problems such as market segmentation and the development of product features and new products.

ATTITUDES AS ADVERTISING OBJECTIVES

The specification of advertising objectives is of critical significance for the formulation of advertising strategy. Therefore, it is important to select objectives that can be affected by advertising and that allow for efficient and continuous testing and evaluation.

The issue of objectives had been somewhat neglected in the advertising field until 1961 when the Association of National Advertisers published Colley's *Defining Advertising Goals for Measured Advertising Results*.[2] This book, and a subsequent monograph, suggested that the goals of advertising are most often goals of communication rather than those pertaining to sales.[3] These and similar publications essen-

[1]Lee Adler and Irving Crespi, eds., *Attitude Research at Sea* (Chicago: American Marketing Association, 1966) and *Attitude Research on the Rocks* (1968); Allan Greenberg, "Is Communication Research Really Worthwhile?" *Journal of Marketing*, Vol. 31 (January, 1967), pp. 48–50; and Charles K. Ramond, "Must Advertising Communicate to Sell?" *Harvard Business Review*, Vol. 43 (September–October, 1965), pp. 148–161.

[2]Russell Colley, *Defining Advertising Goals for Measured Advertising Results* (New York: Association of National Advertisers, 1961).

[3]Harry Deane Wolfe, James K. Brown, and G. Clark Thompson, *Measuring Advertising Results* (New York: National Industrial Conference Board, 1962).

Reprinted from *Marketing Management and Administrative Action* by Steuart Henderson Britt and Harper W. Boyd, Jr. (eds.), Section 5 E, pp. 541–552. At the time of writing, Mr. Boyd was Sebastian S. Kresge Professor of Marketing and Director of Continuing Education in the Graduate School of Business at Stanford University, Mr. Ray was associate professor of marketing in the Graduate School of Business at Stanford University, and Mr. Strong was assistant professor of marketing at INSEAD in Fontainebleau, France.

tially conceptualized the advertising process as a "hierarchy of effect."[4] Their view was that advertising's purpose was to affect some level of the hierarchy—such as awareness, comprehension, or conviction—and that this effect, combined with the effects of other variables in the marketing mix, would lead to the ultimate goals of sales and profits.

This "hierarchy" view was criticized on two fronts. First, quantitatively oriented researchers and managers argued that inasmuch as sales are the ultimate outcome of advertising efforts, sales should be measured.[5] Second, certain behavioral scientists contended that little evidence supported the hierarchy of effects itself; that is, learning does not necessarily lead to attitudinal change, nor does attitudinal change necessarily lead to behavioral change.[6] Thus, advertising goals formed on the basis of changes in intermediate variables—such as recall or comprehension—may be of questionable value.

Fortunately, this controversy about objectives created some insight and raised a number of significant issues. For example, one of the recent key developments in marketing research has been that of techniques for measuring attitude as a predispositional response—one that is indicative of future behavior.[7] Richard Reiser, executive director of the market research department of Grey Advertising, has commented:

> Our reason for selecting attitudes as our basic way of looking at a market is based on more than the fact that one function of advertising is to affect attitudes. There is considerable evidence to show that the way a person thinks and feels about a brand—his attitudinal set—determines how he will behave. His reasons for wanting a product determine his selection: we have always found a close relationship between opinion towards a product and probability of purchase.[8]

Maloney also concluded that consumer attitudes do relate to sales. He offers considerable evidence that ". . . consumer attitude data can become a focal point for defining marketing problems and determining marketing goals."[9]

Defining advertising goals in relation to attitudes and attitudinal change has considerable appeal. Attitudes have the operationally desirable quality of being measurable, albeit with difficulty and some lack of precision. Attitudes also have long been the object of investigation by behavioral scientists, and a considerable body of knowledge has resulted from their studies and models. Today's psychologists believe that attitude includes both perceptual and preferential components, i.e., attitude is an inferred construct. When one refers to an

[4]See for example, Rosser Reeves, *Reality in Advertising* (New York: Alfred A. Knopf, 1961); Darrell Blaine Lucas and Steuart Henderson Britt, *Measuring Advertising Effectiveness* (New York: McGraw-Hill, 1963), and Robert I. Lavidge and Gary A. Steiner, "A Model for Predictive Measurements of Advertising Effectiveness," *Journal of Marketing*, Vol. 25 (October, 1961), pp. 59–62.

[5]Kristian S. Palda, "The Hypothesis of Hierarchy of Effects: A Partial Evaluation," *Journal of Marketing Research*, Vol. 3 (February, 1966), pp. 13–24; Ramond, same reference as footnote 1; and Ambar G. Rao, *Quantitative Theories in Advertising* (New York: John Wiley & Sons, 1970).

[6]Leon Festinger, "Behavioral Support for Opinion Change," *Public Opinion Quarterly*, Vol. 28 (Fall, 1964), pp. 404–417; Jack B. Haskins, "Factual Recall as a Measure of Advertising Effectiveness," *Journal of Advertising Research*, Vol. 4 (March, 1964), pp. 2–8; and Herbert E. Krugman, "The Impact of Television Advertising: Learning Without Involvement," *Public Opinion Quarterly*, Vol. 29 (Fall, 1965), pp. 349–356.

[7]Alvin A. Achenbaum, "An Answer to One of the Unanswered Questions About the Measurement of Advertising Effectiveness," in *Proceedings of the 12th Annual Meeting of the Advertising Research Foundation* (New York: Advertising Research Foundation, 1966), pp. 24–32; George S. Day, "Using Attitude Measures to Evaluate New Product Introductions," *Journal of Marketing Research*, Vol. 7 (November, 1970), pp. 474–482; and John C. Maloney, "Attitude Measurement and Formation," paper presented at the AMA Test Marketing Workshop (Chicago: American Marketing Association, 1966), mimeo.

[8]As quoted in *Advertising Age*, December 19, 1966, p. 1.

[9]Maloney, same reference as footnote 7.

attitude he means that a person's past experiences predispose him to respond in certain ways on the basis of certain perceptions. Attitude, therefore, may be viewed as a variable which links psychological and behavioral components.[10]

Since attitudes reflect perceptions, they inevitably indicate predispositions. Thus, they permit advertising strategists to design advertising inputs which will affect perceptions and thereby change predispositions to respond or behave. This process is the foundation of the strategy suggestions contained in the following sections.

AN EMERGING FRAMEWORK

The possibility of linking perceptions and preferences in formulating advertising strategy has only recently occurred, because strategists and researchers have emphasized either perceptions or preferences to the exclusion of the other. Some have emphasized brand image with only vague regard to response; others have emphasized brand loyalty with little regard to the perception that led to that loyalty.[11]

Now, however, marketing has witnessed an active integration of research on the perceptual and the preference aspects of attitude. The Colley-DAGMAR and NICB books hinted at this integration.[12] Maloney suggested using both perceptions and preferences with his CAPP (Continuous Advertising Planning Program) research.[13] Smith described General Motors' advertising evaluation program as including measurement of consumer perceptions of automobile characteristics and the relating of these characteristics to automobile preferences or likelihood of purchase.[14]

Even more recently, technical advances have been made in marketing that further allow managers to link perceptions and preferences in order to make advertising plans. These technical advances have come from two areas. One is the area of research for new product developments which is typified by the market structure studies pioneered by Stefflre and others.[15] The other area is that of consumer behavior models. These models typically examine the nature of the changes in the perceptions and preferences of consumers as they move toward a buying decision. Although a number of such models exist, they are typified by Amstutz's microsimulation model which posits that consumers move through four major stages in the purchase process: development of perceived need, decision to shop, purchase, and post-purchase. While moving through these stages, consumers can experience alterations in attitudinal structure.[16] His concept is the primary basis for the framework for advertising strategy suggested in this article.

[10]See Martin Fishbein, ed., *Readings in Attitude Theory and Measurement* (New York: John Wiley & Sons, 1967); Marie Jahoda and Neil Warren, eds., *Attitudes* (Baltimore: Penguin Books, 1966); and Gene F. Summers, ed., *Attitude Measurement* (Chicago: Rand-McNally, 1970).

[11]Summers, same reference as footnote 10, pp. 227–234 and pp. 149–158; and Jacob Jacoby, "A Model of Multi-Brand Loyalty," *Journal of Advertising Research*, Vol. 11 (June, 1971), pp. 25–31.

[12]Colley, same reference as footnote 2; and Wolfe et al., same reference as footnote 3.

[13]Maloney, same reference as footnote 7.

[14]Gail Smith, "How G.M. Measures Ad Effectiveness," *Printers' Ink* (May 1965), pp. 19–29.

[15]Volney Stefflre, "Market Structure Studies: New Products for Old Markets and New Markets (Foreign) for Old Products," in *Applications of the Sciences in Marketing Management* (New York: John Wiley and Sons, 1968), pp. 251–268; and Alvin J. Silk, "The Use of Preference and Perception Measures in New Product Development: An Exposition and Review," *Industrial Management Review*, Vol. 11 (Fall, 1969), pp. 21–37.

[16]Arnold E. Amstutz, *Computer Simulation of Competitive Market Response* (Cambridge, Massachusetts: M.I.T. Press, 1967). For other micro-type consumer behavior models see John A. Howard and Jagdish N. Sheth, *The Theory of Buyer Behavior* (New York: John Wiley & Sons, 1964); Francesco M. Nicosia, *Consumer Decision Processes* (Englewood Cliffs, N.J.: Prentice-Hall, 1966), pp. 155–191; and James F. Engel, David T. Kollat, and Roger D. Blackwell, *Consumer Behavior* (New York: Holt, Rinehart & Winston, 1968).

Amstutz assumes that the consumer's attitudinal structure for any product class consists of a set of salient product class characteristics (choice criteria) and a set of brand perceptions regarding each of the salient product characteristics. That is, for a particular product class an individual considers a number of product characteristics to be salient. He also has a perception about what the ideal brand of this product would be like with respect to each of these characteristics or dimensions.

The consumer's choice criteria reflects his needs, values, prior product experience, and so on. In the case of mature products, the choice criteria are reasonably well defined. Such is not the case with many new products; therefore, the seller has the opportunity to play an important role in the building of attitudes toward the product class.

More specifically, the consumer is asked to indicate the extent to which each product characteristic is salient using a scale, say, of 0-10. The result is an attitudinal set which forms the consumer's choice criteria against which the individual brands belonging to the product class are evaluated. The consumer is then asked to rate the same product characteristics for each relevant brand again on a scale of 0-10. Conceptually, the consumer chooses a particular brand by comparing his ratings toward each brand with his ratings of the ideal brand. The brand which compares most favorably with the "ideal" has the highest probability of being chosen. This is the link between perception and preference.

For example, a housewife who did not believe that nutrition was a highly salient product characteristic for a ready-to-eat cereal would, of course, be unlikely to buy such a cereal type. On the other hand, the following product characteristics might be salient to a housewife who *is* considering the purchase of such a cereal type: protein, minerals, vitamins, and the absence of sugar. Assume that a housewife is asked for her ideal saliency ratings on these four product characteristics using a scale of 0-10. Further assume that the same consumer is asked to rate brands A and B in the same fashion with the results shown in Table 1.

Table 1 Hypothetical Example of Amstutz-Type Attitude Structure for Nutritional Ready-to-Eat Cereals

	Ratings		
Salient product characteristics	Product category	Brand A	Brand B
Protein	8	9	5
Minerals	5	7	5
Vitamins	9	8	4
Absence of Sugar	4	3	6

Based on such an attitudinal set the consumer would probably buy brand A over brand B. It should be stated that predictions of behavior based on such ratings are essentially probabilistic.

The above described perceptual structure holds considerable promise as a framework for advertising strategy formulation. Rather than assume that advertising's function is to affect sales directly or to have an effect on a level of the hierarchy, it would seem more functional to assume that advertising can maintain or shift attitudes with respect to salient product characteristics and their ratings. If such can be accomplished, it will lead to preference which affects sales and profits.

If advertising's overriding goal is to influence attitudinal structures such as those suggested in Table 1, then a manager can choose from among five broad strategy alternatives. He can seek to:

1 Affect those forces which influence strongly the choice criteria used for evaluating brands belonging to the product class;

2 Add characteristic(s) to those considered salient for the product class;

3 Increase/decrease the rating for a salient product class characteristic;

4 Change perception of the company's brand with regard to some particular salient product characteristic; or

5 Change perception of competitive brands with regard to some particular salient product characteristic.

The remainder of this article discusses these strategies.

STRATEGY ONE: AFFECT PRODUCT CLASS LINKAGES TO GOALS AND EVENTS

This strategy relates to the formulation of advertising which attempts to stimulate primary demand. Such a strategy would seek to enhance the saliency rating given one product class versus others with respect to obtaining certain goals. The framework is similar to that presented earlier in that the consumer has choice criteria which he uses to rate alternative product classes with respect to obtaining his goals.

If the advertiser knows (1) the goals of a given market segment with respect to (2) the choice criteria (salient product characteristics) used to evaluate the alternative product classes considered as ways of achieving the goals, and (3) the perceptions regarding each product class, he can better decide what action to take to stimulate demand for his product class. Inevitably he must link his product class to the relevant goals. But he must also seek to change the consumer's rating of his product class versus others with respect to the choice criteria involved.

The advertiser could seek to change the saliency of the consumer's goals and thus increase the demand for his product class. However, most of the change associated with goals comes about through environmental factors operating over long periods of time, although advertising can, no doubt, accelerate the trends.

Thus far no distinction has been made between "goals" and "needs." In the final analysis, products are judged on the basis of their function or role in helping the individual to attain some goal or in meeting a need. In the case of nutritional ready-to-eat cereal, the goal of many consumers is to maintain or improve health while not gaining (or losing) weight. Still other consumers might wish to achieve the goal of caring for their loved ones by ensuring that they receive their daily quota of minerals and vitamins. Many other goals could be outlined, but their importance lies, first, in that the goal(s) will partly determine what product class characteristics are salient (as well as how salient), and second, that the goal(s) will ultimately be reflected in the individual's attitudes toward alternative brands of the product. Thus, if goals are known—however imprecisely—they help to explain attitudinal ratings, or if salient product characteristics and ratings are known, goals may be deduced.

After the advertiser has differentiated individuals on the basis of goals and translated this differentiation into preference for one product class over another via saliency ratings, he now could try to alter these saliency ratings or product class choice criteria in the hope of attracting more consumers to *his* product class and ultimately to his brand. In the nutritional cereal example, at least one advertiser attempted to do this by making the appeal: "What's a mother to do . . . about vitamins. . . . Serve . . . . the only leading cereal with a whole day's vitamin supply. . . . Feel vitamin-safe all day." Another advertiser perceived another goal as instrumental and advertised: "Charge Up, Sleek Down . . . Feel Like a Healthy Animal." The first advertiser tied goals to product class choice criteria, while the latter simply stressed the goal to be obtained.

Other examples of attempting to change, influence, or create additional goals as they relate to the use of product classes or brands are safety in automobiles, health protection by eliminating oral bacteria and germs through the frequent use of a mouth wash, easing problems of mild insomnia by taking aspirin, reducing the financial burden of decentralized inventories through the regularized use of air freight, and the reduction in air pollution through the use of low-lead gasoline.

Once goals are set, the consumer will proceed to select products which will help him obtain his objectives. But there is an intervening consideration since most products are consumed as part of an "event"—that is, it is part of a situation which occurs at certain places at certain times and often involves the presence of more than one individual. The situation may be socially or work-oriented and often involves more than one product. The event is, of course, tied to the goal and is prescribed and constrained accordingly.

The possibility presented for strategy formulation at this level is the use of advertising to change the individual's attitude toward the use of a product class *within* a particular event. In other words, the salient product characteristics of alternative product classes will be judged according to how well they "fit" with the event to be pursued. The event itself is perceived by the individual as being associated with certain salient product class characteristics, and the decision process is similar to the notion of perception and brand choice. The advertiser seeks to change or modify the attitudes toward salient product class characteristics that the individual associates with the event in order to increase the probability that the product class of interest will be chosen.

It is at the event level of demand that social or group influence on the individual's choice of brand becomes more apparent. This is only natural, because social encounter is viewed as an "event" by individuals, whether people gather for some jointly agreed purpose (specific goal-related activities) or merely meet "by chance." Frequently, a modification or influence of attitude sets at the event level entails changing attitudes of the group or at least changing the individual's perception of attitudes held by the group. A prominent example of such attempted influence involves the social acceptability of women smoking small cigars in public. Others include the serving of margarine to guests, the serving of wine at family meals to bring greater enjoyment to a commonplace affair, and the drinking of milk after strenuous exercise to reduce body temperature.

The first broad strategy alternative is a complex one, and this article can only hint at how the strategy can be implemented. Nevertheless, goals and events are important to consider since they affect the way each product class is perceived and thus help to explain consumer response to the product class. Further, they provide the most appropriate communication setting in which the appeals are embedded and thus enhance their acceptability.

THE TWO PRODUCT CLASS STRATEGIES

The strategist who observes that his brand does not "fit" the ideal product class characteristics is faced with the alternative of either changing consumer attitudes toward his brand or changing consumer attitudes concerning the "ideal." These two approaches are discussed below.

Adding a Salient Characteristic—Strategy Two

Through advertising, a firm can make consumers aware of an attribute of a product class which has previously not been considered salient or which may not even have existed. Examples of this strategy's application include the use of additives to gasoline, the adding of fluorides to toothpaste, the adding of minerals to cereals, and the incorporation of light meters into cameras.

This type of strategy is most often attempted when a product is at the mature stages in its life cycle since by this time consumer attitudes pertaining to choice criteria have been well established. The advertising change is frequently combined with a product modification, although this may not be necessary. Clearly, research must show that the new characteristic has the potential of becoming salient; further, the advertiser must believe that his brand can attain a high relative rating on the new characteristic. Ideally, he would like to appropriate it so that competitors who followed would reinforce the claims made for his brand while simultaneously building the saliency of the product characteristics.

Altering the Perception of Existing Product Characteristics—Strategy Three

Increasing Salience The advertiser who observes that his brand rates well on a product class characteristic which consumers do not consider too salient may wish to try to effect an increase in its salience. This strategy is an extension of the previous one and requires careful research to determine how the advertiser's brand and competitive brands are positioned by market segment. This kind of comparative examination is important since research has indicated that changing the importance of a product class characteristic will not affect preference for it unless one brand rates high and competitive brands are low with respect to that characteristic.[17] For example, an airline company which noted that "on schedule" was not given a high saliency rating might seek to increase the rating of this product class characteristic provided that it felt that its "on schedule" performance was better than that of its competitors.

Changing the Optimal Range Underlying much of the above is an assumption of how advertising relates to brand and product perceptions and the way these relate to brand preference. Specifically, the purchase probability of any particular brand is the sum of the salient characteristics ratings multiplied by the brand ratings across all characteristics considered by a segment. In other words, the assumption is that the higher the brand is rated across all ideal characteristics, the more likely it is to be preferred and purchased.

This assumption probably holds true in only a few markets because, in order for it to be correct, consumers would have to desire an unlimited amount of any characteristic. More realistically, however, there may be optimal ratings below or beyond which preferences fall off. For instance, in the nutritional cereal example shown earlier, it is likely that for the characteristics "protein," "minerals," and "vitamins," the more a brand is perceived as having the characteristic, the more a consumer is likely to buy the brand. But, for the characteristic "absence of sugar," a point probably exists beyond which the consumer is not willing to go; that is, a cereal could have too little sugar. Possibly the relationships are also somewhat different on either side of the optimal point. In the case of the cereal example in Table 1, any deviation above the "4" ideal point on the characteristic "absence of sugar" may be enough to reject the brand. On the other hand, deviations below "4," however, may still be within the acceptable range.

These relationships can vary across the ideal characteristics within any given market. For instance, when price is considered as a variable, the ideal product rating usually rep-

[17]For further discussion of this subject see Joel B. Cohen and Michael Houston, "The Structure of Consumer Attitudes: The Use of Attribute Possession and Importance Scores," Faculty Working Paper Number 2, University of Illinois at Urbana, 1971; Martin Fishbein, "A Behavior Theory Approach to the Relations between Beliefs about an Object and Attitude Toward That Object," and "Attitudes and the Prediction of Behavior," in *Readings in Attitude Theory and Measurement*, Martin Fishbein, ed. (New York: John Wiley & Sons, 1967), pp. 382–389 and pp. 477–491; Jagdish N. Sheth and Wayne W. Talarzyk, "Relative Contribution of Perceived Instrumentality and Value Importance Components in Determining Attitudes," paper presented at the Fall Meetings of the American Marketing Association, Boston, 1970.

resents a maximum level above which the consumer may not move and below which the consumer would happily go. For "quality," on the other hand, the ideal rating is usually a minimum level with higher rated brands acceptable and lower rated brands not acceptable. Moreover, interactions between characteristics often occur; e.g., consumers will accept infinite drops in price so long as no clearly perceptible quality decrease occurs. A price drop in some instances will affect the consumer's perception of the product's quality.[18]

Consequently, a manager must consider the optimal product rating not only with regard to its relation to brand perception and preference, but also with regard to (a) the distribution of that relationship around the ideal point, and (b) the relationships between distributions for all of the characteristics considered to be important by consumers. While this may appear to be extremely complex, the process is simplified by the fact that few product characteristics seem to be utilized in any single product purchase decision.[19] Also, the characteristics by which products are identified and conceptualized are fairly stable over time. Further, managers have demonstrated their ability to understand and predict very well with the use of a few simple variables.[20]

Once the meaning of the saliency of product class characteristics is established, it is possible to consider the process which entails an attempt to change the nature of the acceptable distribution around the ideal point for a characteristic. If an advertiser is selling a higher priced product than his competitors, for instance, he may not be able to change the ideal rating a segment would give for price. But he may be able to get consumers to consider a range of prices *above* the ideal rating by affecting the price-quality relationship which is perceived by many. He could point out the quality that is possible only with the higher-priced product.

Similar strategy examples could be cited for all the negative relationships discussed above. Thus, for example, one could attempt to deal with the potential negative relationship between the perception of sweetness and nutrition for cereals, initial cost and upkeep for machinery, horse power and safety for cars, taste and the effectiveness of mouthwashes, and so on. The goal of advertising is to change the nature of the range around the ideal point. Typically, this is done with advertising using two or more of the product characteristics.

A substantial amount of research has been conducted by psychologists on latitudes of acceptance and rejection in attitude.[21] This article does not discuss such research, but it will suffice to emphasize that the research indicates the significant value of considering strategies not only in terms of points but also in terms of the distribution around the points.

TWO BRAND-LEVEL STRATEGIES

Changing Perceptions of Advertiser's Brand—Strategy Four

Whereas strategies 2 and 3 were concerned with changing consumer perceptions of the

[18]See Alfred Oxenfeldt, David Miller, Abraham Shuchman, and Charles Winick, *Insights Into Pricing* (Belmont, California: Wadsworth Publishing Company, 1961), Chapter 4; and Joseph M. Kamen and Robert J. Toman, "Psychographics of Pricing," *Journal of Marketing Research*, Vol. 7 (February, 1970), pp. 27–35.

[19]Same reference as footnote 15. Also see David Klahr, "A Study of Consumers' Cognitive Structure for Cigarette Brands," paper presented at the meetings of the Institute of Management Sciences, May, 1968.

[20]David B. Montgomery, "Initial Distribution: A Gate Keeping Analysis of Supermarket Buyer Divisions," paper presented at the Institute of Management Sciences fall meetings, Detroit, 1971.

[21]Carolyn W. Sherif, Muzafer Sherif, and Richard Nebergall, *Attitude and Attitude Change* (Philadelphia: W. B. Saunders, 1965); and George S. Day, "Theories of Attitude Structure and Change," in *Consumer Behavior: A Theoretical Source Book*, Scott Ward and Thomas Robertson, eds. (Englewood Cliffs, New Jersey: Prentice-Hall, 1973).

ideal brand, the present strategy focuses on changing consumer perceptions of an advertiser's brand. In both cases, the strategy objective is to develop a better "fit" between the "ideal" brand and the advertiser's brand.

Little can be said about this strategy that has not been said already. Several significant suggestions, however, come from recent attitudinal research. An obvious one is that advertisers should not attempt to change perceptions for their brand when the brand itself does not possess an adequate quantity of the characteristic in question. The basic assumption of the Stefflre product development system, for instance, is that the purpose of advertising is to communicate the characteristics which the brand actually has.[22]

The framework suggested here provides a clear and measurable set of criteria for selecting the particular brand perceptions to be emphasized. Analysis of the optimal points and ranges for the salient product characteristics can indicate those characteristics that are most crucial in their effect on preference—and can do so by segments. Indeed such a process would appear to be at the very core of any segmentation scheme. Within this set of characteristics, the advertiser should seek to emphasize those for which he has the most relative advantage. Ideally, these would be characteristics for which both he and his competitors have low brand perceptions. These characteristics provide an opportunity for a profitable change in brand perception. This is especially true for those characteristics that the brand possesses and which will be difficult for competition to copy.

These conditions—high salience of a characteristic and exclusive possession of it by one brand—occur so seldom in marketing that their presence constitutes good reason to believe that there is a substantial opportunity for product development. Much of the criticism that is leveled against advertising has to do with the use of trivial claims; i.e., those which the consumer cannot link to any salient product class characteristics.

Changing Perceptions of Competing Brands—Strategy Five

Under some conditions, success may be achieved by altering perceptions for a brand with regard to salient characteristics that are perceived as being possessed to a greater extent by a competitive brand. There are techniques which boost the advertiser's brand while pointing out the fallibility of competitive claims. Specifically, two-sided and refutational messages provide a vehicle for fairly presenting both sides of an issue while at the same time improving the perceptions of the brand being advertised.[23]

Examples are Avis and Hertz advertising dealing with the advantages of first or second position in the rental car industry; Volkswagen's refutation of the small and ugly car counterclaims; Bayer Aspirin's counterattacks against other forms of headache remedy; and, in the political arena, Mayor John Lindsay's messages which refuted claims of his alleged mishandling of New York City's affairs. The strategy of dealing with competitive claims also occurs in industrial selling through the presentation of comparative cost data or competitive laboratory findings.

Once again, however, these techniques must be used carefully. Some evidence suggests that if they are not, the advertising can

[22]Stefflre, same reference as footnote 15, p. 262.

[23]Carl I. Hovland, Irving Janis, and Harold H. Kelley, *Communication and Persuasion* (New Haven, Connecticut: Yale University Press, 1953); William J. McGuire, "Inducing Resistance to Persuasion: Some Contemporary Approaches," *Advances in Experimental Social Psychology*, Vol. 1 (1964), pp. 192–231; Percy H. Tannenbaum, "The Congruity Principle Revisited: Studies in the Reduction, Induction, and Generalization of Persuasion," *Advances in Experimental Social Psychology*, Vol. 3 (1967), pp. 272–320; and Michael L. Ray, "Biases in Selection of Messages Designed to Induce Resistance to Persuasion," *Journal of Personality and Social Psychology*, Vol. 9 (August, 1968), pp. 335–339.

boomerang by giving support to competitive brands and claims.[24] Further evidence indicates that, unless the audience is relatively sophisticated and highly involved with the product, they are unlikely to comprehend two-sided messages fully. And if the audience is sophisticated and involved, their attitudes may be quite difficult to change with any kind of message.

CONCLUSION

For many years controversy has arisen concerning the determination of appropriateness of advertising effectiveness measures. No single measure suggested, however, has provided a basis for the formulation of advertising strategy, which has remained more art than science. Also, over the last several years, several theories of consumer behavior have made the marketing community sharply aware of the need to consider consumer behavior as a complete system. Few of these models specify the linkages between components of consumer behavior in sufficient detail to be managerially useful except for broad conceptual relationships. This article has taken a perspective of consumer brand choice from the model developed by Amstutz and extended it to various levels of demand. The resulting framework serves as a useful tool for advertising decision makers in developing comprehensive strategies of attitudinal change.

[24]Michael L. Ray, Alan G. Sawyer, and Edward C. Strong, "Frequency Effects Revisited," *Journal of Advertising Research*, Vol. 11 (February, 1971) pp. 14–20; and Michael L. Ray and Alan G. Sawyer, "Behavioral Measurement for Marketing Models: Empirical Estimates of Advertising Repetition for Media Planning," *Management Science: Applications*, Vol. 17 (December, 1971), Part II, pp. 73–89.

37

Media Approaches to Segmentation

Albert V. Bruno
Thomas P. Hustad
Edgar A. Pessemier

A segmentation plan is presented which should enable a firm to undertake better marketing and media planning. The proposed approach is for media planners to pay more attention to the qualities of each audience in order to reflect the audience's relative potential for being influenced by selected offensive or defensive market communications.

This paper examines an approach to marketing and media planning that classifies consumers into segments meaningful to the firm's overall communication strategy. Traditional descriptors of media audiences are normally confined to cost per exposure of consumers

Reprinted from *Journal of Advertising Research*, vol. 13, no. 2, pp. 35–42, April 1973. At the time of writing, Albert V. Bruno was an assistant professor of marketing, Graduate School of Business, University of Santa Clara; Thomas P. Hustad was an assistant professor of marketing, Faculty of Administrative Studies, York University in Toronto; Edgar A. Pessemier was professor of industrial administration, Krannert Graduate School, Purdue University.

expected to purchase or use the product at various rates per unit of time. This paper will investigate an array of additional consumer characteristics that affect the potential net value of the audience of the media vehicle in the specific context of the brand seller's current or prospective marketing plans. For a mature brand with a large market share, one of several defensive strategies may be suitable to protect its position. For a young brand or one that has acquired a new feature or valued property, an offensive strategy designed to capture buyers currently purchasing competing brands may be far more appropriate.

In light of the need to deal with strategic issues such as those mentioned above, the analyst must often know more than product class usage rates, exposure patterns, and advertising costs associated with various media. Other useful descriptors of media deal with the audience's preferences for various brands, their innovativeness and opinion leadership qualities and any additional specific factors that can influence consumer responses to a brand's communications. In particular, media analysts are interested in the qualities of each audience that reflect its relative potential for being influenced by selected offensive or defensive market communications—the extent to which certain messages will be accepted, transmitted, and acted upon. When a full set of relevant audience measurement data are available, the media planner can develop a totally integrated profile of the value of typical exposures to the media vehicle as an element in his media plan. When used in conjunction with ancillary data and a media selection model, a full schedule can be developed which accounts for the dependent mix of media in the context of specific communication objectives supporting the brand's marketing strategy (Little and Lodish, 1969).

In this paper, efforts to develop and test a richer set of measures relating to the complete, integrated profile of media vehicles are discussed. To be of interest in this setting, the differences in the characteristics of the audiences of media vehicles must be managerially significant. The differences in effectiveness for the brand advertiser's purposes must be large enough to warrant collecting and using the data to appraise the cost effectiveness of media vehicles. Although this question cannot be addressed in complete form without a specific set of advertising objectives, brand shares, vehicle costs and related data, the ultimate objective of the analysis must be kept clearly in mind: to efficiently estimate the worth of media vehicles in a specific marketing context.

Late in 1970, a large survey was completed at Purdue University by Pessemier, DeBruicker and Hustad in which extensive activity and attitude measures were obtained for 912 husband and wife pairs. The sample was a representative demographic cross section of an upscale midwest industrial community in a productive agricultural environment. A detailed discussion of the design and the instruments employed is available elsewhere (Pessemier, et. al., 1971).

The analysis reported here deals with generalized measures as well as others specific to the toothpaste product category. In particular, the focus is on a small subset of variables relevant to the media segmentation problem already outlined, profiling media audiences by: (1) levels of exposure or readership; (2) brand preference within a single product category; (3) product class usage rates; (4) generalized and product specific innovativeness; and (5) generalized and product specific opinion leadership. The coding of the independent variables in the study is discussed in Bruno, et al. (1970).

PRIOR RESEARCH

The literature reporting on research conducted on activity, attitude, life-style, psychographic, and related topics is limited and largely of recent origin. Despite this fact, this literature provides more than a glimpse at the potential value of these measures to media planners. Several of these articles are particularly germane.

Bass, et al. (1969) indicated that groups with various total media exposure profiles to print media differ about as much in terms of activity and attitude factors as they do along demographic lines. In another paper, Tigert (1969) successfully developed differential activity, interest, and opinion (AIO) profiles of the readers of several pairs of print media, including the difficult *Time/Newsweek* and *Look/Life* pairs. Other relevant work has been published by King and Summers (1971) and Wells and Tigert (1971). In a recent paper, Tigert and Arnold (1970) summarized findings about the innovator and opinion leader components of media audiences, but they cast some doubt on the capacity to reach these segments through selective use of mass print media.

RESULTS USING PSYCHOGRAPHICS

Research in the literature provides ample impetus and general guidance for the measurements used in this study. Unlike prior studies, however, a representative cross section of print and television vehicles are compared for generalized and product context specific data. The toothpaste category is used as the product throughout the analysis.

In the case of the innovativeness and opinion leadership scales used in this study, the spirit but not the letter of work by King and Summers has been followed. Composite scores have been developed from responses to a six-point differential scale (strongly agree to strongly disagree) for the generalized and product specific statements related to opinion leadership and innovativeness. [See Bruno, et al. (1972) for a list of these statements and Tigert and Arnold (1970) for the recording procedures of the scales.]

Table 1 shows the extent to which generalized and product specific innovativeness and opinion leadership are associated with exposure to print media and specific TV shows. The levels of significance are shown in Table 2.

The print media data support Tigert and Arnold's conclusion that generalized innovativeness and opinion leadership are weakly associated with exposure. This conclusion is strengthened by examining the product specific case. For TV, however, the general innovator and the product specific innovator and opinion leader appear to differ more strongly in the degree to which they are heavily exposed to specific media vehicles. These vehicles also differ to the extent in which the heavily exposed portions of their audiences consist of these selected "behavioral" classes.

For example, in the case of generalized attitudes, 51 per cent of all innovators in the sample were heavily exposed to Marcus Welby whereas for Gunsmoke the corresponding figure was only 11 per cent. However, the heavily exposed portion of the Marcus Welby audience had about the same proportion of innovators as one finds in the Gunsmoke audience. This conclusion is no longer appropriate when comparing the audiences of The Galloping Gourmet to Gunsmoke. In other words, when generalized innovativeness is considered among heavily exposed consumers, important differences in media are apparent. They appear even though no striking difference can be found when simple exposure is used as the base for computation.

The percentage of the audience classified as generalized innovators ranges from 19 to 26 among viewers and from 18 to 31 among heavy viewers. The same figures for generalized opinion leaders are 12 to 15 and 11 to 23. Noting similar findings on product specific innovativeness, the percentage ranges among viewers and heavy viewers of TV run from 21 to 27 and 22 to 29, respectively. For product specific opinion leadership, the percentage

Table 1 Relationship between Media Exposure and Selected Generalized and Product Specific, Attitudinal Constructs for Toothpaste

	Generalized innovativeness			Generalized opinion leadership			Product specific innovativeness			Product specific opinion leadership		
Media vehicle	Percent of innovators heavily exposed to this media	Percent of all exposed individuals who are innovators	Percent of heavily exposed individuals who are innovators	Percent of opinion leaders heavily exposed to this media	Percent of all exposed individuals who are opinion leaders	Percent of heavily exposed individuals who are opinion leaders	Percent of product specific innovators heavily exposed to this media	Percent of all exposed individuals who are product specific innovators	Percent of heavily exposed individuals who are product specific innovators	Percent of product specific opinion leaders heavily exposed to this media	Percent of all exposed individuals who are product specific opinion leaders	Percent of heavily exposed individuals who are product specific opinion leaders
Glenn Campbell*	18.5	19.5	18.3	18.3	13.0	13.0	22.1	22.5	26.0	20.6	23.4	23.7
Hawaii Five-O	24.4	18.8	19.3	25.8	13.3	14.6	27.1	24.6	25.5	25.3	22.3	23.1
Carol Burnett	25.6	20.2	20.9	21.7	11.5	12.6	27.1	23.6	26.2	25.3	21.9	23.8
Marcus Welby	50.6	18.8	20.7	47.5	13.6	13.9	54.3	24.8	26.3	50.0	23.4	23.6
Dating Game	6.0	19.5	25.0	7.5	14.0	22.5	4.5	24.4	22.5	6.7	30.5	32.5
60 Minutes	13.1	20.0	19.3	14.2	13.2	14.9	12.6	27.2	25.3	9.3	25.7	18.2
Galloping Gourmet	16.7	20.9	30.4	8.3	12.6	10.9	34.2	24.3	25.1	32.0	23.3	22.9
Love American Style	14.9	19.3	25.0	10.0	11.8	12.0	23.6	24.6	24.2	25.8	24.0	25.8
Eddie's Father	23.2	20.7	22.8	19.2	13.7	13.5	39.2	21.1	25.0	36.1	21.1	22.4
Johnny Carson	13.7	20.0	22.3	15.8	13.2	18.4	15.6	25.1	29.0	13.4	22.8	24.3
Gunsmoke	10.7	19.4	18.2	12.5	14.6	15.8	13.6	23.6	23.7	12.4	21.1	21.1
Bold Ones	32.1	20.3	19.9	41.7	13.6	18.5	11.1	24.1	23.9	11.3	23.7	23.9
Laugh-In	24.4	20.8	21.1	22.5	12.6	13.9	12.1	25.7	24.0	17.0	26.2	33.0
Flip Wilson	35.7	19.5	19.2	29.2	13.5	11.2	22.1	22.7	25.7	25.8	26.7	29.2
As the World Turns	19.6	26.3	30.8	13.3	15.2	15.0	14.1	25.6	27.2	12.4	24.0	23.3
Lawrence Welk	12.5	19.8	18.8	14.2	13.2	15.2	12.6	22.3	22.3	14.4	26.1	25.0
Life	21.4	20.2	19.0	25.8	14.3	16.4	21.1	24.1	22.2	21.1	25.0	21.7
Reader's Digest	39.3	18.5	16.9	35.0	12.4	10.7	41.2	21.7	21.0	41.8	22.5	20.7
Time	16.1	20.1	19.9	18.3	17.4	16.2	13.6	21.2	19.9	12.9	21.9	18.4
Good Housekeeping	38.1	21.2	23.8	25.0	12.1	11.2	32.2	23.8	23.8	29.9	22.1	21.6
Glamour	5.4	31.7	33.3	4.2	18.3	18.5	3.5	27.5	25.9	5.2	30.0	37.0
Cosmopolitan	4.2	22.4	24.1	5.8	16.0	24.1	3.5	28.8	24.1	4.6	24.0	31.0
Pageant	1.8	24.3	42.9	0.8	13.5	14.3	1.0	18.9	28.6	1.0	32.4	28.6
Atlantic Monthly	1.2	25.0	40.0	0.0	25.0	90.0	0.5	10.0	20.0	0.0	5.0	0.0
Indianapolis Star	30.4	23.3	24.3	25.0	15.5	14.3	24.6	25.0	23.3	24.2	24.3	22.4

*Read: Exposure to the Glenn Campbell Show is significantly related to generalized innovativeness. Only 18.5% of all people classified as generalized innovators are heavily exposed to this show. Of all exposed individuals, 19.5% are innovators; however, innovators constitute only 18.3% of all heavily exposed individuals. Similar interpretations follow for other columns.

Table 2 Significance of Correlation of Exposure

	General		Product specific	
Level of sig.	Innovativeness	Opinion leadership	Innovativeness	Opinion leadership
		TV shows		
.001	0 of 16*	0 of 16	2 of 16	3 of 16
.01	3 of 16	0 of 16	7 of 16	7 of 16
.05	8 of 16	0 of 16	11 of 16	9 of 16
		Print		
.001	2 of 9	0 of 9	0 of 9	0 of 9
.01	2 of 9	1 of 9	0 of 9	1 of 9
.05	4 of 9	3 of 9	1 of 9	2 of 9

*Read: For 0 of 16 TV shows, exposure was significantly related to the consumer's self-designated degree of generalized innovativeness at the .001 level.

ranges are 21 to 31 and 18 to 33. The reader can review the results for print media, noting a few striking differences such as those for the readers of *Good Housekeeping* and *Glamour* along generalized innovativeness and generalized and product specific opinion leadership.

RESULTS USING USAGE RATES

The preceding section provides information that establishes links between certain life-style variables and media exposure levels. Another traditional approach has been to examine relationships between media exposure and product class usage rate. In reality, these should not be considered mutually exclusive approaches but complementary ones. Garfinkle (1970) emphasized this point by remarking:

> We are trying to develop research information that enables us to identify the target market for the particular brand. We know that some people are more responsive to that brand than other people. Generally, the best kind of information that we can use to identify the target group is direct rather than indirect information. Both demographics and psychographics, from a research standpoint, represent indirect information. Specific information on the consumer's usage of the product or his responsiveness to the brand is, on the other hand, direct information. . . . As I see the Seventies emerging out of the revolution that occurred in the Sixties, we will be using direct marketing information to identify our target groups rather than indirect information either in the form of psychographics or demographics. The only exception in the area of media selection will be when a new product is being introduced. . . . We can't identify for a new brand users of the brand or people who have responded to the brand.

In reality, marketers following an offensive strategy may seek to appeal to new targets even after the introductory phases of their product life cycle. This necessitates continued use of indirect information to monitor these groups. Although direct or usage rate data may be more useful in a defensive sense, the analyst is always searching for potential targets, the reasons for their existence, and how to address them. It is unlikely that direct measures will ever fully satisfy these information needs.

Turning to usage rate variables for the toothpaste product category, Table 3 summarizes the association between usage rates and media exposure characteristics for the same 25 media shown in Table 1.

In the case of print media, the significance levels (shown at the bottom of Table 2) and the range of the differences in percentages of heavy usage consumers among each medium's readers and heavy readers are great enough to warrant careful attention. The ranges of the differences in the percentage of heavy users are also pronounced for television shows, but the significance levels are far less reassuring. From these usage rate data, however, it is clear that media should be examined for differences in the product class usage rates and the consequent potential economic value of achieving a given communication task for the members of the audience in question.

RESULTS USING BRAND PREFERENCES

Garfinkle's remarks concerning the usefulness of brand purchase histories incorporate an approximate measure of brand preference.

Table 3 Results of Examination of Relationships between Media Exposure and Toothpaste Usage Rates

Media vehicle	Heavy users heavily exposed to media %	Total audience who are heavy users %	Heavily exposed who are heavy users %
Glenn Campbell	16.4	59.7	53.8
Hawaii Five-O	21.9	49.8	37.1
Carol Burnett	22.1	62.6	59.7
Marcus Welby	46.2	61.5	62.5
Dating Game	4.1	42.1	27.1
60 Minutes	9.5	58.8	53.5
Galloping Gourmet	29.1	60.3	59.2
Love American Style	22.1	63.3	63.4
Eddie's Father	33.8	59.8	60.3
Johnny Carson	10.6	56.1	55.1
Gunsmoke	13.1	63.7	64.0
Bold Ones	8.1	60.5	48.9
Laugh-In	11.0	63.4	61.0
Flip Wilson	19.6	62.3	63.7
As the World Turns	10.4	64.8	56.3
Lawrence Welk	11.3	60.1	56.3
Life	22.8	64.8	67.2
Readers' Digest	43.9	60.0	62.4
Time	15.8	70.8	64.7
Good Housekeeping	30.6	65.5	63.2
Glamour	2.9	66.7	59.3
Cosmopolitan	4.0	72.0	75.9
Pageant	0.5	54.1	42.9
Atlantic Monthly	0.4	70.0	40.0
Indianapolis Star	25.7	69.3	68.1

Preference, however, should not be tied to usage. Certainly brands not currently purchased may vary greatly as potential entries into the active purchase/use sets of consumers. The literature has little to offer in this regard, particularly in linking more sophisticated brand preference data to media exposure.

Because of their obvious relevance to choosing media to fit the offensive versus defensive components of a marketing strategy, the association of brand preferences with media exposure characteristics has been examined. For the toothpaste category and the collection of mass media examined here, statistical significance was not high enough to permit the use of brand preference measures as criteria for evaluating the worth of an audience. These exploratory findings lead to the conclusion that, in the majority of cases, the association of these variables will be insignificant or too low to be managerially useful. On the basis of this same evidence, however, this variable should not be dismissed as a measure of the worth of media for a variety of important marketing situations, including for example the "selling" of political candidates. Unfortunately, for many low salience, mass-marketed items, it is hard to make an *a priori* case for market differences in levels of brand preferences across the audiences of important mass media.

A partial summary of the results presented in the foregoing discussion appears in Table 4. This table points up the fact that media audiences vary significantly across a larger set of managerially-useful characteristics than the limited product usage rate and allied demographic measures traditionally employed in media planning. The number and type of these characteristics depends to an important degree on the nature of the marketing problems at hand, measurement capabilities of the behavioral sciences, and the skills of the research technologists who collect data for the firm. Quite aside from these issues, it seems clear that some expansion and refinement of the measures on media are needed to efficiently develop media plans in support of well-defined marketing strategies. It is instructive to note that the innovativeness, opinion leadership, and usage rate measures each identify difference patterns of "desirable" media.

MEDIA VEHICLE MODELS

Implicit in the above discussion is a formal procedure whereby the total mix of relevant media measures can be used to evaluate the potential value of a unit of a media vehicle in the context of the firm's marketing strategy. Given the limited scope of this discussion, less than full justice will necessarily be done to the subject. The model has been described in detail elsewhere by Bruno (1972).

In this paper, the model illustrates results based on the very modest data set for the toothpaste product class. At best, this product class has moderate salience to the mass of consumers. This fact very likely introduces a downward bias in the discriminatory power of the variables and the economic value of the extended media analysis.

The model, as shown in Figure 1, is formulated to express the audience value of a single unit of a media vehicle, building it up from two separate sub-evaluations.

The first term examines the defensive potential of the audience, the demand which may be retained among recent buyers and triers of the brand by increasing the probability that they will rebuy. Naturally, this evaluation must be based on a variety of side conditions which include the brand's characteristics, the expected competitive environment and the like. Such an evaluation must also be based on the number of potentially loyal buyers in the audience and their purchase rates. Therefore, factors like each brand's market penetration

Table 4 Effectiveness of Selected Media in Reaching Managerially Useful Market Segments

Basis for Market segmentation[a] Innovativeness	Frequency in sample population	Media with highest proportion of desired segment heavily exposed in audience[b]	Media with lowest proportion of desired segment heavily exposed in audience[b]
Generalized Innovator	18.4%	Dating Game	Reader's Digest
Innovativeness			
Generalized Innovator	18.4%	Dating Game Galloping Gourmet As the World Turns Glamour Cosmopolitan	Reader's Digest
Product Specific			
Innovators	21.8%	Glenn Campbell Carol Burnett Marcus Welby Johnny Carson As the World Turns	Time
Opinion Leadership			
Generalized Opinion Leaders	13.2%	Dating Game Johnny Carson Bold Ones Glamour Cosmopolitan	Carol Burnett Galloping Gourmet Love American Style Flip Wilson Reader's Digest Good Housekeeping
Product Specific			
Opinion Leaders	21.3%	Dating Game Laugh-In Flip Wilson Glamour Cosmopolitan	60 Minutes Reader's Digest Time
Usage Rate			
Heavy Users	61.1%	Gunsmoke Life Time Cosmopolitan Indianapolis Star	Glenn Campbell Hawaii Five-O Dating Game 60 Minutes Bold Ones

[a] The percentage of the heavy exposed segment of the show's audience that are in a basic segment; i.e., generalized innovators, can be found in Table 1.
[b] Only five highest ranking shows are included in this table.

of the various usage-rate segments must be considered. Finally, all the factors bearing on the potential effect of the communication on the audience are accounted for to obtain a single numerical evaluation.

A defensive component must be supplemented by the addition of the elements evaluated in light of the offensive phases of the brand's advertising strategy. Here, the marketer's concern is largely centered on attract-

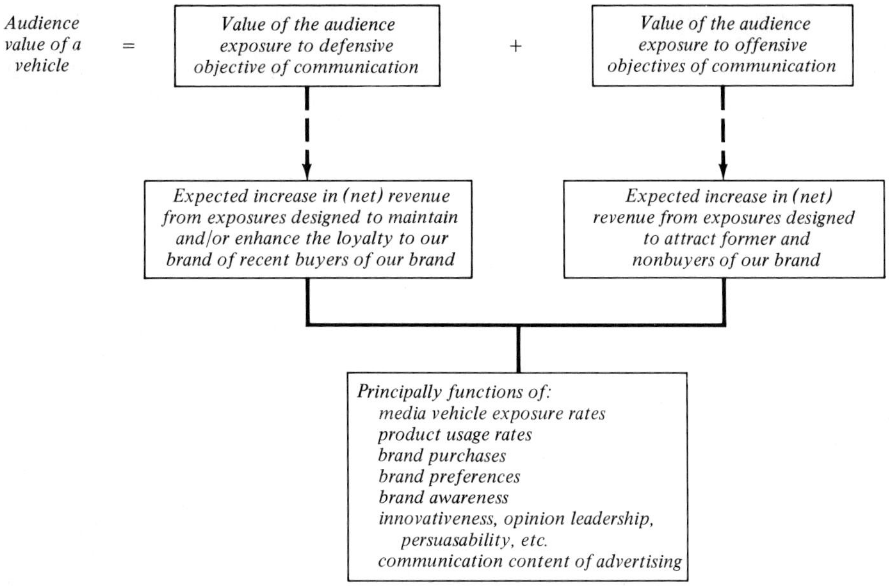

Figure 1 Model for assessing strategic values of media vehicles.

ing nonbuyers or buyers who are currently loyal to other brands in the product class. A brand's market position, maturity, and competitive qualities will all affect the evaluation of the audience as a target for offensively oriented elements in the marketing plan. Naturally, many situations will arise where a strategy is balanced with substantial emphasis placed on both the offensive and defensive components.

The overall value of the audience of a media vehicle is the sum of the values derived from the two objectives of attracting and keeping profitable customers for a particular brand. The offensive segment consists of former buyers and nonbuyers while the defensive one consists of loyal buyers and triers. The value of each is estimated as a function of differential preference, usage rates, and exposure specific to unique brand/media pairs. Needless to say, media costs enter the picture when the audience value is expressed in terms of its cost effectiveness. An indication of the model's structure and the brand specific efficiency of the very limited media vehicle measures which have been accumulated can be obtained from Bruno (1972). Because completely defined brand strategies or clear cut new product situations were not available for analysis, it was impossible to properly incorporate the innovator and opinion leadership elements in the above evaluations.

The intent of this analysis was to examine the degree to which the model components differed significantly across media employed. Both offensive and defensive elements of a strategy were considered for each of the brands studied in the toothpaste category. As noted earlier, the brand preference variables for toothpaste produced disappointing results due to their failure to discriminate among media vehicles; however, differences were significant for an offensive strategy for Close-Up and defensive strategies for Gleem II and Ultrabrite. Product class usage variables represented significant offensive elements in the model but had little value in the defensive component. As one would expect *a priori*, for all brands, the value of a media vehicle as an offensive or defensive element could be readily differentiated on the basis of usage times exposure levels. In summary, the media values for this analysis degenerate to functions of usage rates and exposure.

CONCLUSIONS

A media evaluation model with managerially meaningful components was briefly described in purely verbal terms. It was subjected to a very limited test using variables which were gathered in the context of a very general study. In practice, the model components will become more explicit and focused when a particular brand's marketing strategy is defined. Given the modest salience of the illustrative product category, the absence of fully defined competitive marketing and communication strategies, and the modest range of applicable attitudinal and behavioral measures, the results are inconclusive.

However, apparently useful attitudinal and activity variables describing media audiences were found to discriminate among the heavily exposed portions of audiences. As experience accumulates and measures become less primitive, predictive power should increase. The payoff from small marginal improvements in media selection may comfortably cover the added cost of collecting and analyzing the additional data needed to improve the capacity to judge the worth of individual media vehicles.

REFERENCES

Bass, Frank M., Edgar A. Pessemier, and Douglas J. Tigert. A Taxonomy of Magazine Readership Applied to Problems in Marketing Strategy and Media Selection. *Journal of Business*, July 1969, pp. 337–363.

Bruno, Albert V. The Media Audience Evaluation Model: An Empirical Test. *Santa Clara Business Review*, Vol. 3, No. 1, pp. 21–33.

Bruno, Albert V. An Explicit Model for Evaluating Television Audiences. Unpublished doctoral thesis, Purdue University, August 1971.

Bruno, Albert V., Thomas P. Hustad, and Edgar A. Pessemier. An Integrated Examination of Media Approaches to Market Segmentation. Unpublished working paper, Krannert Graduate School of Industrial Administration, Purdue University, January 1972.

Garfinkle, Norton. Facts or Fiction About Media in the Seventies, 61st Annual Meeting of the Association of National Advertisers, New York, October 1970.

King, Charles W. and John O. Summers. Attitudes and Media Exposure. *Journal of Advertising Research*, Vol. 11, No. 1, pp. 26–33.

Little, John D. C. and Leonard M. Lodish. A Media Planning Calculus. *Journal of Operations Research*, January-February 1969, pp. 1–35.

Pessemier, Edgar A., F. Stewart DeBruicker, and Thomas P. Hustad. *The 1970 Purdue Consumer Behavior Research Project*. Krannert Graduate School of Industrial Administration, Purdue University, June 1971.

Tigert, Douglas J. A Psychographic Profile of Magazine Audiences: An Investigation of Media Climate. Paper presented at the American Marketing Association Consumer Workshop, Columbus, Ohio.

Wells, William D. and Douglas J. Tigert. Activities, Interests and Opinions. *Journal of Advertising Research*, Vol. 11, No. 4, pp. 27–35.

Part Six

Marketing Information Systems

Closely related to the various aspects of putting the marketing plan into action—presented in the previous section with respect to products, pricing, distribution channels, selling, and advertising—is the relatively new and intriguing area of marketing information systems.

Development in the years ahead of ever-better marketing information systems is a surety. In the meantime, some important aspects of such systems are worthy of consideration here.

Accordingly, the first selection in the present section is an analysis of marketing information systems; followed by a presentation on modeling marketing phenomena; leading into a discussion of the use of environmental information systems for strategic marketing planning; and concluding with a brief selection on contingency planning.

38

Marketing Information Systems

Kenneth P. Uhl

This selection is concerned with evaluating marketing information systems and their relationships to marketing research. The author shows that information systems need to adapt to the user's dynamic environment, and he indicates how this can best be accomplished.

The focus of this chapter is on marketing information systems. The primary questions to be considered are:

1 What is a marketing information systems, and what are its objectives?
2 Are marketing information systems a replacement for marketing research?
3 What are the major parts and crucial dimensions of marketing information systems?
4 How should marketing information systems be organized and where should they fit in a company?

WHAT IS A MARKETING INFORMATION SYSTEM?

A definition that describes the concept of a marketing information system is:

> A structured, interacting complex of persons, machines, and procedures designed to generate an orderly flow of pertinent information, collected from both intra- and extra-firm sources, for use as the basis for decision-making in specified responsibility areas of marketing management [21].

This definition suggests the interdependence of the activities associated with the assembly, processing, and communication of marketing information. Just as the myriad activities can be viewed as subsystems within a marketing information system, in a larger context a marketing information system can be one of the several subsystems in a firm's total information system [26].

Figure 1 symbolizes a marketing information system, the major activities within it, and its relationships to the firm and the environment. The illustrated information system, as shown in the concentric circles, is composed of three subsystems: current awareness, in-depth crisis, and unanticipated information (which are defined and discussed in more detail later in this chapter).

The marketing information system is composed of and is dependent on the activities shown in the three outlying concentric rings. For example, models and model building, including simulation models, are used to formulate problems, to provide analysis, and to seek answers through all three subsystems. The next outlying concentric ring suggests that the model-building activities require data—data inputs which must be stored, retrieved, transmitted, and discarded. Finally, the outside ring shows many of the information assembly activities, the major ones being searching, scanning, filtering, evaluating, and abstracting.

Reprinted from *Handbook of Marketing Research* by Robert Ferber (editor-in-chief), sec. 1, chap. 3, pp. 1–31–1–43. At the time of writing, the author was professor of business administration, School of Commerce and Business Administration, University of Illinois at Urbana-Champaign, Illinois.

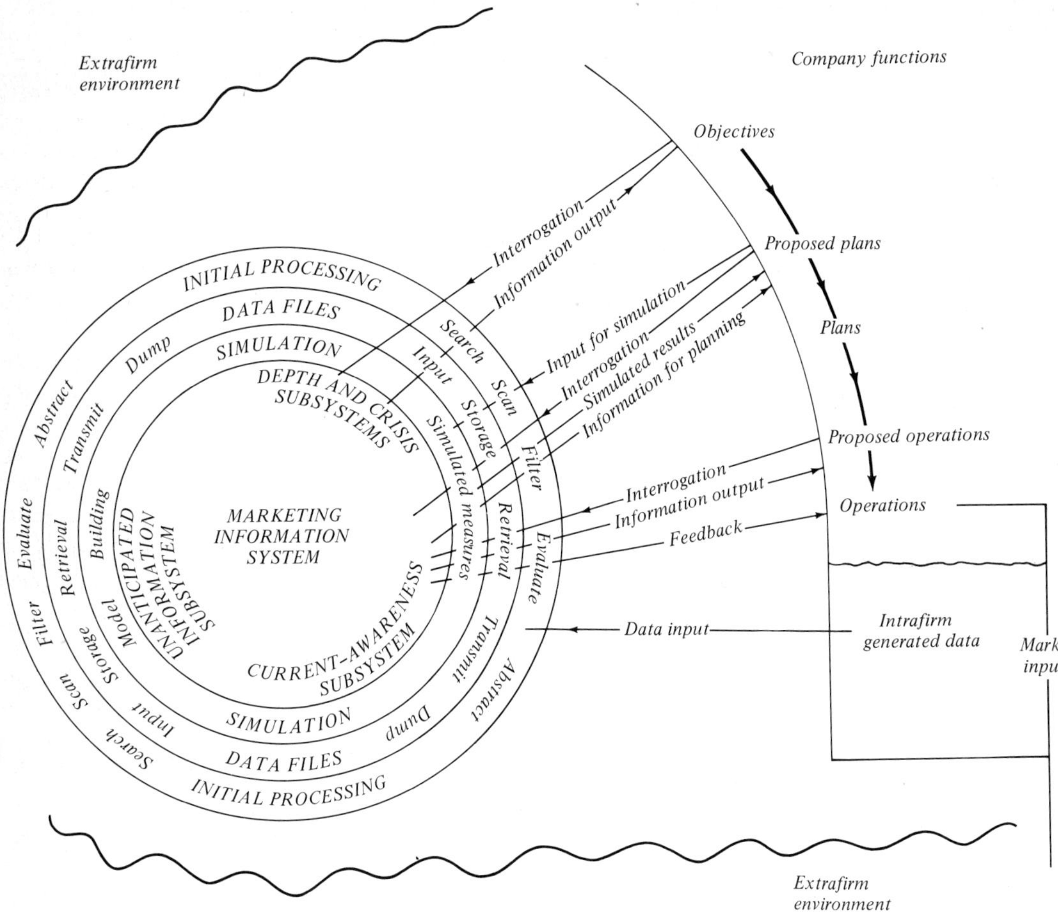

Figure 1 Marketing information system.

The marketing information system interfaces with the company's major functions: setting objectives, establishing plans, and operating the firm [27]. The straight lines between objectives and the information system indicate that management interrogates and gets information about proposed objectives from the system. At the next level, management gets information for planning and also uses the information system to simulate the outcomes of proposed plans. A similar arrangement is indicated for operations. In a continuing process, the system assembles and processes data on firm and market results and the environment and provides managers with information feedback.

Finally, the terms *marketing information system* and *computer system* are *not* synonymous. A marketing information system may make use of computer facilities, but a computer system is not an information system. A study of information systems is focused on how the organization communicates and processes information to maximize the effectiveness of management and to further the objectives of the organization [22].

OBJECTIVES OF MARKETING INFORMATION SYSTEMS

The fundamental objective of a marketing information system is to help managers make better decisions. To accomplish this, information systems must assemble, process, and communicate information that is used by managers to reduce uncertainty. The solution appears to lie with the creation of user-oriented systems which provide managers with information when they need it. These two notions, user orientation and information, provide key insights into the objectives of information systems.

User Orientation

A user-oriented system is not simply one that provides user-managers with all the information they may think they want. Examinations of operating systems [1] have suggested that:

1 Most systems suffer more from an overabundance of irrelevant information than from a lack of relevant information. This overabundance results in managers being burdened with information overload, both through the number of communications received and the redundancy within the communications. Such an overloaded system is not user-oriented. More consideration of data evaluation and aggregation is needed.

2 Most user-managers initially need help to know which information will help them to make better decisions. The system designer and information user, each left on his own, tend to oversupply and overask in order to be safe rather than sorry. To know which information helps reduce uncertainty, users *and* suppliers must be jointly aware of the decisions that *should* be made, and they must have models of them.

3 It is *not* enough to provide managers with information. User-managers, because of the complexity of decision processes, often need help in formulating decision rules or in performance feedback so they can gain experience and learn. User-oriented systems help provide this.

4 User-managers must understand their information system. It is a *mistake* to provide user-managers with only output information and assure them they need to know nothing about the system. Involvement helps users to understand their system and to make their views a part of the system. This, in turn, helps them to evaluate, control, and make the system more *adaptive* to their dynamic decision-making situations.[1]

Information

Relevance is a major criterion for including information in a system. Many information specialists, in fact, consider information as data which are relevant; that is, relevant information is a redundant term. To be relevant, data must:

1 Be different under available alternatives

2 Provide users with insight into their problems

3 Be reflected in some differences in the decisions made [12]

In other words, information is reduction of uncertainty. For example, data about last week's sales are relevant to a sales manager to the extent that they (1) reflect differences that could have influenced his decisions, (2) help him foresee the future (the past is beyond influence), and (3) bear on his future decisions.

Not all relevant data (information) should be part of a system. "Indeed, the fundamental question . . . may well be when to stop collecting data and developing the model and when to produce a recommendation for action" [18]. When the expected *cost* of information exceeds the expected *value* of that

[1]Readers wishing to explore adaptation and stability in systems should see [7].

information in terms of reduction of decision errors, the information should *not* be obtained. This also provides a rule for selecting among alternative items of information. The particular information set that is expected to yield the largest excess of value (largest reduction in decision errors) over the accompanying cost should be selected for inclusion in the system.

The costs of various information can be approximated. Values or benefits, in contrast, must ultimately be related to results arising from manager-users' decisions.[2] These benefits, while difficult to measure, are largely a function of:

1 The degree of uncertainty regarding the outcome of alternative courses of action
2 The economic consequences of *not* choosing the alternative which would lead to the "best" outcome
3 The amount by which the information, if obtained, is expected to reduce the initial uncertainty

ARE MARKETING INFORMATION SYSTEMS A REPLACEMENT FOR MARKETING RESEARCH?

The answer to this question is partly dependent on semantics. This statement, however, is not made merely to dismiss all substantive questions.

A frequently used definition of marketing research is "the systematic gathering, recording, and analyzing of data about problems relating to the marketing of goods and services" [5]. When marketing research means all this, as it does in this handbook, it can hardly be said that marketing information systems are a replacement for marketing research. A comparison of the two definitions also suggests that the objectives of both are essentially the same.

[2]For a good discussion of attaching values to information, see [19].

This being the situation, why should marketing information systems be developing? The general explanation seems to be that in practice, in many companies, the breadth of what has been called marketing research has fallen far short of the definition. In turn, management has been disappointed in marketing research.

The essence of the criticisms appears to be that marketing research has too frequently (1) produced data which were not relevant, (2) been concerned with research on nonrecurrent problems while it has virtually ignored current awareness information, and (3) failed to provide sufficient payoff-relevant marketing information.

These shortcomings arise largely because marketing research has been principally a series of independent, uncoordinated activities scattered throughout the complaining companies.

Marketing information systems are being viewed as the supplanters of unsatisfactory marketing research because they promise the very features that were not available through poor marketing research: *integrated, analytic, systematic approaches which will identify, assemble, process, and communicate payoff-relevant marketing information to decision makers.* The hope is that marketing information systems will serve to identify, establish, and integrate the various subfunctions so managers can work under the marketing concept.

THE MAJOR PARTS AND CRUCIAL DIMENSIONS OF MARKETING INFORMATION SYSTEMS

There is no one unique marketing information system that will serve all companies. Each management has unique information requirements because of its unique perspective on its environment and its company, along with a unique order of priorities and styles of management [13]. Furthermore, successful systems are a matter of evolution. Therefore in this handbook marketing information systems are discussed in terms of typical subsystems and their general dimensions.

The most obvious and also one of the fundamental aspects of existing marketing information systems is that they are composed of subsystems. Also, they typically have been built one subsystem at a time and have been managed in terms of subsystems. There are usually two or three major subsystems in mature systems and, despite wide variation in titles, the same two subsystems are commonly found in most marketing information systems.

One subsystem is usually designed to handle continuing current-awareness information. A second one usually handles in-depth information on special problems and areas of immediate, high-priority concern to users. Many companies have had the activities performed by this subsystem which has been available for years from their marketing research groups. When a third major subsystem is present, it tends to handle information and situations which do not fit into the other two subsystems but which seem to warrant attention [16]. Each of these three types of subsystems and their more crucial dimensions will be examined in some detail.

Current-Awareness Subsystems

Continuing flows of information for managers can be provided through a current-awareness information subsystem. A descriptive title frequently used for this kind of system is *selective dissemination subsystem.* Such subsystems can provide periodic (daily or otherwise) reports of company sales by products and by territories, total annual sales to date, comparative past sales data, and future forecasted values. They can also indicate changes in market share, competitive activities, and a host of other past and present information as well as estimates of future developments in internal matters, competition, and the environment.

This type of subsystem is usually computer-based and virtually requires that a firm have access to extensive and meaningful sources and supplies (banks) of data. Furthermore, a firm must be able to analyze, synthesize, match, and transfer information as managers need it. The more crucial dimensions of current-awareness subsystems are (1) information recency and aggregation levels, (2) computer systems' analytical sophistication and authority, and (3) transfer mechanisms.

Information Recency and Aggregation Current-awareness information can be no better than the data available in various sources or banks. Therefore, their constant feeding and care are of prime concern. Data sources are maintained by individual user companies and by commercial information companies. Generally, individual firms safeguard their own sales and costs and other internally generated data within their own data banks. Market data and other external and environmental data may be purchased from one or more outside sources or banks.

Aggregation refers to the detail in which data are available in a system. Data can vary from individual customer or product files, which record each transaction as it occurs, to massive aggregate files, which record measurements such as industry sales and market shares.

Data files are most useful when maintained in detailed time sequences, with new inputs maintained along with (not replaced or combined with) existing data. Such disaggregated files provide immediate advantages in that they allow data to be assembled, reshuffled, and, in general, to be more adaptive in many different ways than more aggregate files. Second, such disaggregated data files make information systems far more adaptive to future needs. If data files are initially aggregated to meet only first-stage system needs, later-stage system development, in response to managers' greater needs, may require complete file redevelopment. Such revisions are costly and, furthermore, aggregated data files may not be convertible [6].

Unfortunately, the more disaggregated the data files, the more costly they are to maintain as a data base. Therefore management must consider the cost of disaggregate data files against their present and probable future use.

Recency refers to the lapse of time between the occurrence of an event and the time at which it is reported in an information system. Data can be collected, analyzed, and transmitted periodically in batches of varying sizes (and aggregation levels) and time periods, or individual transactions can be noted and immediately transmitted and used without any batching. The latter, live-operation information is often called on-line, real-time (OLRT) information. *On-line* means compiling information instantaneously as events occur and maintaining instant access to the data in computer core. *Real-time* means managers use the information to control operations within the short or instantaneous period.

Many airlines use OLRT passenger reservation systems. With American Airlines' SABRE program, for example, each reservation request is transmitted directly to a computer and is either rejected or confirmed, with the "space available" figure in the memory unit adjusted accordingly. Another illustration is afforded by Bank of America, which keeps customers' balances OLRT. In both situations decisions are made in view of the knowledge of current conditions. The benefits from such systems are obvious. Other OLRT systems are used to control inventories, various facets of manufacturing operations, chemical process operations, and other reservation systems.

At present, the practicality of OLRT handling of masses of marketing information is questionable. There is the problem of the state of the art, both in terms of hardware and software. Costly computers with large storage capacities and random-access capabilities are required. Programming costs are also very high because systems must be sufficiently flexible to handle dynamic marketing situations.

To be practical, OLRT systems must provide sufficient benefits in the form of better decisions to justify the added costs as compared with batch-processing information systems. Three major factors currently limit the marketing benefits obtainable through the use of OLRT information. First, only incomplete parts of the total necessary decision information can be available in most open marketing system situations. Consequently, most of the real-time advantages are lost as decision makers wait for batched information. Second, most marketing *operations* are set up on a batch basis, so there is little advantage in reacting on an individual activity basis. The final customers, for example, may buy individual units, but channel orders, shipments, inventories, payments, and most other marketing operations are more economically handled on a batch basis.

Finally, there is little need to make decisions faster than a firm can respond [25]. For example, if shoes can be shipped to Dubuque only once a day, there is little point in making numerous decisions throughout the day. Instead, information should be batched until the one time at which the best decision can be made. In conclusion, the appropriate information recency in a situation depends on management's proposed use of the information along with consideration of the costs associated with various batch periods.

Computer Systems The typical current-awareness system has at its center a computer system. A computer is essential for rapid analysis, storage, and retrieval of information. The role of computers varies among current-awareness systems. Their relationships, however, can be described fairly well in terms of *analytical sophistication* and *computer authority*.

The degree of *analytical sophistication* of a computer system refers to the complexity of its models or structures. At the first level, a computer only identifies a specific file or record, retrieves it, and displays its information (this often presents horrendous problems). At the next level, a computer gathers data from one or more files and produces a subtotal or total. At the third level of sophistication, the computer is programmed to perform simple arithmetic operations such as computing differences and averages. The fourth level involves the computer in aggregating data by various classification schemes.

The fifth level introduces more complex analyses such as statistical best estimates, trend estimates, and analyses of variance. At the sixth level, the computer is programmed to "learn"; that is, to modify values of parameters and structures of models based on data inputs. At the most advanced level of analytical sophistication, simulation models are used in sufficient magnitude and detail to represent the real world. This permits management to test various combinations of variables in simulated environments [6].

The types of decisions a computer system is programmed to make without further man review or intervention determines its *authority* in a current-awareness system. At the elementary level, a computer is granted the authority only to store and retrieve certain information from designated locations. At the second level, the computer reviews (checks) the reasonableness of each file or record. The computer at the third level performs analyses on records and refers exceptions to managers for additional review.

At the fourth stage, the additional review noted at the third level is programmed for the computer and a *recommendation* for action is reported by the computer. At the fifth level, the computer is programmed to take *action* on all but the exceptional cases (as defined by managers) reported at the prior level. The final level of authority exists when the computer is programmed to predict. Involvement is greater here than at the prior levels in that predictions are used in future planning and commitments and not just in current activities [6].

Transfer Mechanisms In current-awareness information systems, a major matchmaking (adaptability) mechanism between data sources and manager-users is interest profiles of the managers. Individual managers (with the aid of information specialists) are responsible for describing the decisions they make and their optimal information sets. Furthermore, managers' interest profiles are changed over time in response to the actual information they use. These collective interest profiles are used to help determine what data will be collected and stored, how they will be analyzed, and which information will be disseminated to individual managers [10, 24]. These relationships are illustrated in Figure 2.

Data selection for inputs is of great concern since irrelevant or inaccurate data increase costs and overload users without providing payoffs. Payoffs can accrue only when decision makers receive and use information. Two of the complicating factors are (1) the continuing inflow of new data (some of which is from unstable processes) into data banks and (2) the changing needs of managers. The objective is to construct a sufficiently adaptable linkage through which relevant data can be selected and matched to decision makers.

The types of final communication linkage vary from those where managers directly in-

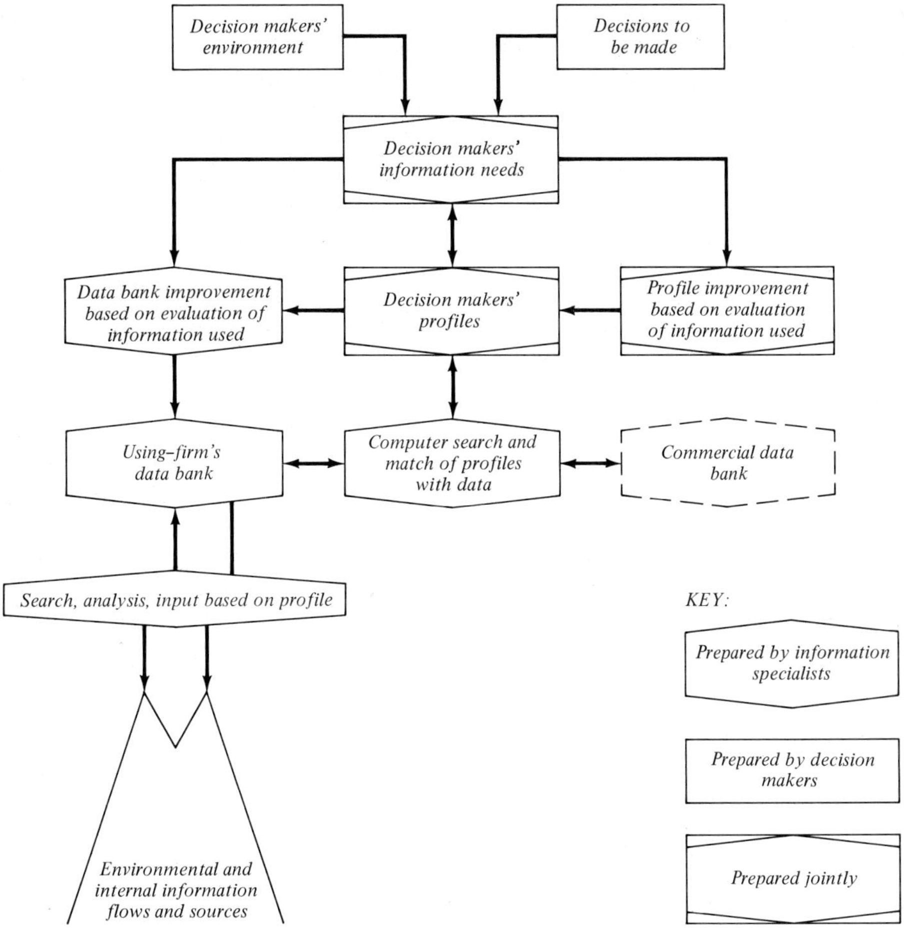

Figure 2 Selective dissemination subsystem.

terrogate the computer to those where the managers never interrogate it but instead look to information specialists who provide the linkage. With the first type of linkage, the managers must have very complete knowledge of the system, its contents, the forms in which the data outputs are available, and the language needed to communicate with the computer. In the second type of situation, managers need only a general understanding of the system and the available types and forms of information. Direct interrogation of data banks by managers will become increasingly common as more conventional communication languages and more advanced remote terminals become available [11].

In-Depth and Crisis Information Subsystems

In-depth and crisis information on special problems or on areas of immediate, high-priority interest to decision makers can be provided by a subsystem called a *retrospective search subsystem.* A company's current-awareness system, for example, may indicate deteriorating sales and profits for a major product line but may not provide insight into the causes and needed corrections. A retrospective search subsystem in such situations should be able to provide decision makers with detailed information and possible solutions to such special problems.

A situation faced by a brewery provides a case in point. The brewery bought a small but popular regional brewery. For about 14 months its current-awareness system indicated that market share and profit patterns were remaining constant. Suddenly, the current-awareness system reported declines in market shares followed by, at first, small declines in sales which were followed by larger losses in each of the following three months. Although management did get an early warning of trouble, it could not determine what caused the losses. The causes were finally ferreted out, but only after considerable in-depth research and information furnished through their retrospective search subsystem.

Structural Problem The successes of in-depth and crisis information subsystems are conditioned by the availability of flexible organizational structures capable of adapting to unique problems which present severe time constraints and often seem to occur at inappropriate times. Consequently, the highly structured, extensively staffed, routinized, and computer-centered organizations which serve well in current-awareness subsystems are particularly inappropriate for in-depth and crisis information subsystems.[3]

The concept of temporary organizations, originally advocated by Bennis, appears to be a promising structure to provide the needed flexibility. Instead of bureaucracy, temporary, specialized task forces are assembled to handle specific, unique problems as they are identified [8]. As new and unique problems are encountered, new groups, uniquely qualified for the task, are assembled, and upon solution the task forces are dissolved.

These problem-oriented task forces are composed of "relative strangers" with diverse skills appropriate to each situation. The task force used by the brewery, for example, was composed of a brewmaster, a market planning expert, a regional sales manager, and an advertising research specialist, and it was coordinated by a marketing research specialist. This diverse group was assembled because a preliminary investigation showed increased dissatisfaction with the taste of the beer among formerly loyal customers.

Under this concept, which still needs more testing, the administrators of the subsystem serve as "linking pins" among task forces, their special skills being (1) research—to help identify problems, (2) mediation—to get the best efforts from each task force, and (3) communication—both to help secure cooperation and ongoing adoption of task forces and their solutions.

In some respects, the temporary organization concept has received considerable testing and use. Over the years many companies have maintained only small in-house marketing research groups and have hired specific consulting groups, because of their expertise, to examine various problems. In these situations the consultants assembled the specialists, and a person within the hiring company served as the linking pin. The temporary organization made primary use of internal experts with supplementary help only when key insiders were not available.

Incidental Information Subsystems

Incidental and unsolicited information normally will not flow through either of the two subsystems discussed to this point. Those subsystems handle identified types and sources of information, or information for crisis or

[3]This does not suggest that data banks and computers are of no use. In fact, retrospective search subsystems are strengthened when data banks can be searched for information on similar problems and their solutions and when problems can be simulated on computers.

special problems. Some companies are developing *unsolicited information subsystems.*

These subsystems are unique both in terms of inputs and outputs. The *input* side is present to facilitate the collection, analysis, and synthesis of unsolicited, unanticipated, and incidental data which appear to warrant the attention of managers. In a sense, it is like a giant jigsaw puzzle assembly.

The *output* side concerns the communication to managers of what was unsolicited and incidental information. The output side also provides the information specialists a means of bringing managers together with unusual and unsolicited but relevant data which now can enter the system.

An illustration should help clarify and define the nature of unsolicited or incidental information. In this case a series of seemingly unrelated incidents provided the information. A draftsman for a writing instrument manufacturer received a complimentary sample of a Japanese-built sign pen. He used it, told a few close associates about it, and ordered a half-dozen of each of five colors. Later he reordered three dozen of each color. Almost simultaneously, two representatives of the same writing instrument company noted a Japanese-built sign pen in a few artist supply stores. One of them purchased a dozen for use around his home and office. About two months prior to these events a buyer in the purchasing department of the writing instrument company had heard about some new materials being used in the construction of writing instruments. He had no need for them and was not interested.

Less than one year after these seemingly unrelated events had occurred, the Japanese sign pen came to the unmistakable attention of the executives of the writing instrument company. Some of their pen lines were down in sales by as much as 12 percent due to broad market acceptance of the Japanese sign pen. The incidents experienced by a company draftsman, two salesmen, and a buyer provided a nucleus of incidental unsought information. Unfortunately, these particles of information were not treated as useful marketing information and their importance was not realized until it was too late.

Two major problems confront firms wishing to build and use this third type of marketing information subsystem. First, key personnel are often in contact with relevant data but neither recognize it as valuable nor collect and transmit it to appropriate places in their organizations. These failures are due largely to problems of selective exposure, perception, and retention.

The second problem is that key personnel do not know *where* and *how* to transmit the data; and prospective users do not know it is even available, let alone *where* it is to be found. These two problems are somewhat common to all information situations, but they are particularly oppressive to this subsystem because of the apparently incidental (that is, inconsequential) nature of the data.

Successful management of unsought and incidental information evolves around (1) the human element and (2) the organizational aspects [4].

The Human Element Identification and training of key information people are the first requirement. These should be people who have considerable contact with sources where needed data can be found. Salesmen, for example, are exposed to the general market, including both buyers and the salesmen who sell to competitors. These key people need to know how to search for and handle data. They must be *aware* of the need for broad exposure, critical perception, and data retention.

The second requirement is that key people be encouraged to seek and transmit data discoveries. When transmitters are subject to ridicule or find personal gains by holding back, few data flow [4].

Organizational Aspects A special framework is required. Basically, a structural framework should strive to (1) optimize securers' knowledge of what to do with secured data, (2) optimize the knowledge of decision makers as to the existence of information, (3) reduce the probability of information biases and distortions, (4) provide means whereby the data can be evaluated and related to company needs, and (5) reduce to the optimum the time required for relevant data to be initially secured, transmitted, analyzed, synthesized, and made available to decision makers [4].

A centralized control office appears to be virtually mandatory for accomplishing the preceding tasks. With one central office, securers know where to send data; at least they know there is only one receiver. Manager-users also know there is only *one* source, so they do not search among numerous units. Consequently, less time is wasted between securing and using the information. Direct handling also reduces distortions resulting from multiple transmitting, analysis, condensation, and so forth. Finally, the only way to fit jigsaw puzzle parts together and to know what parts are missing is to have a central staging and assembling location.

Subsystems do *not* exist and operate as separate information activities. They are managed as integrated analytic systems to discern, supply, and communicate needed marketing information to decision makers.

THE ORGANIZATION AND LOCATION OF MARKETING INFORMATION SYSTEMS WITHIN COMPANIES

It is not enough to say that marketing information systems are composed of and managed by subsystems. More specifically, the following question must be considered: Should there be one centralized marketing information system, or should there be a multiple number of independent divisional systems? Also, should marketing information systems be directed and controlled by marketing management or by nonmarketing management, perhaps as one subsystem with a companywide management information system?

In some companies, the overall organizational alignments are so distinctly and completely centralized or decentralized that marketing information system alignments obviously must fit the same patterns. In other companies, where some activities are centralized and others are not, the most advantageous alignment is often far from being clear. In this latter case, one centralized marketing information system is used mainly because (1) it minimizes duplication of personnel, space, and equipment; (2) it is more likely to permit full-time employment of a few extremely competent specialists; and (3) it facilitates companywide decision making. On the other hand, if information problems for regional, product, or customer divisions are radically different or if corporate staff is unacquainted with individual regions, product lines, or customers, divisional information systems may be advantageous.

The question of where marketing information systems should be located within companywide organizations has received very little attention. However, a basic question that should be considered is this: Should such systems (whether centralized or decentralized) be under the jurisdiction of marketing managers or under other personnel?

If marketing information systems follow the location patterns of marketing research offices, far more than half of them will report to marketing managers [23].

Prescriptive advice indicates that if information activities are limited to sales and marketing information, the information office should report to a marketing manager. The major explanation has been that such an information office works primarily with and for persons in the marketing division and, accordingly, it functions best in that division. When its activities are more inclusive and the office serves other parts of the company (finance, production, etc.), it should report to top-level *non*marketing management [17].

Several criteria which have been used to determine the placement of marketing research departments within companies also appear appropriate when marketing information systems are being considered. They should be located to provide (1) freedom from the influence of those whom their work affects, (2) maximum efficiency of operations, and (3) cooperation and support of managers to whom they report [17].

Organizational considerations will receive more attention in the following chapter. To date, the real-world experience with the organization of marketing information systems is scanty because, in general, attempts to integrate them are in their infancy.

SUMMARY

This chapter has dealt with marketing information systems and their relationship to marketing research. Marketing research, using the broadest definition, can perhaps be considered almost the equivalent of marketing information systems. However, marketing research as frequently practiced has not lived up to the popular definition. In turn, the systems' analytic approach is emerging as a reflection of the changing conceptual view of the payoffs available from marketing information.

Because of differences in managements, environments, and a host of other considerations, there does not appear to be any unique information system that will serve all companies. The most fundamental concept is that information systems need to be adaptive to users' dynamic environments. The most obvious dimensions are that information systems are composed of subsystems, usually two or three.

One subsystem is typically designed to provide current-awareness information and normally has at its center a computer system. A second subsystem provides in-depth and crisis information. This one typically evolves out of and is more akin to the marketing research function in the firm. A third subsystem, when present, typically handles information and situations which do not fit into the other two subsystems.[4]

REFERENCES

1 Ackoff, Russell L., " Management Misinformation Systems," *Management Science*, vol. 14, no. 4, pp. B-147–B-156, December 1967.

2 Albaum, Gerald, "Horizontal Information Flow: An Exploratory Study," *Journal of Academy of Management*, March 1964.

3 ———, "Information Flows and Decentralized Decision Making in Marketing," *California Management Review*, Summer 1967, pp. 59–70.

4 ———, "The Hidden Crisis in Information Transmission," *Pittsburgh Business Review*, vol. 33, no. 7, p. 2, July 1963.

5 Alexander, Ralph S., *Marketing Definitions*, Chicago: American Marketing Association, Committee on Definitions, 1963, pp. 16–17.

6 Amstutz, Arnold E., "The Marketing Executive and Management Information Systems," in R. Hass, ed., *Science, Technology and Marketing*, Chicago: American Marketing Association, 1966, pp. 69–86.

7 Ashby, Ross, *Design for a Brain*, New York: Wiley, 1960, pp. 44–70.

8 Bennis, W., "Changing Organizations," *The Journal of Applied Behavioral Science*, July–August–September 1966, pp. 247–262.

9 Cox, Donald, and Robert Good, "How to Build a Marketing Information System," *Harvard Business Review*, May–June 1967, pp. 145–154.

10 Craven, D. W., "Information Systems for Technology Transfer," in R. Hass, ed., *Science, Technology and Marketing*, American Marketing Association, 1966, pp. 47–60.

[4]For an illustration, see [2].

11 Diebold, John, "What's Ahead in Information Technology," *Harvard Business Review*, September–October 1965, pp. 76–82.
12 Feltham, Gerald A., "The Value of Information," *The Accounting Review*, October 1968, pp. 684–696.
13 Heany, Donald F., *Development of Information Systems; What Management Needs to Know*, New York: Ronald, 1968.
14 Hein, Leonard W., "The Management Account and the Integrated Information System," *Management Accounting*, June 1968, pp. 34–38.
15 Kostetsky, Oleh, "Decision Making, Information Systems, and the Role of the Systems Analyst," *Management Science*, October 1966, pp. C-17–C-20.
16 Liston, D., Jr., "Information Systems: What They Do, How They Work," *Machine Design*, July 21, 1966, pp. 190–197.
17 "Marketing Business and Commercial Research in Industry," *Studies in Business Policy 72*, New York: National Industrial Conference Board, 1955.
18 Morris, William T., *Management Science In Action*, Homewood, Ill.: Irwin, 1963, p. 113.
19 Rappaport, Alfred, "Sensitivity Analysis in Decision Making," *The Accounting Review*, July 1967, pp. 441–456.
20 Rhind, Ridley, "Management Information Systems," *Business Horizons*, June 1968, pp. 37–46.
21 Smith, S., R. Brien, and J. Stafford, ed., *Readings in Marketing Information Systems*, Boston: Houghton Mifflin, 1968, p. 7.
22 *The Use of Computers in Business Organizations*, Reading, Mass.: Addison-Wesley, 1966.
23 Twedt, D. W., ed., *A Survey of Marketing Research: Organization, Functions, Budgets, Compensation*, Chicago: American Marketing Association, 1963.
24 Uhl, Kenneth P., "Marketing Information Systems and Subsystems," in Robert L. King, ed., *Marketing and the New Science of Planning*, Chicago: American Marketing Association, 1968, pp. 163–168.
25 ———, and Bertram Schoner, *Marketing Research: Information Systems and Decision Making*, New York: Wiley, 1969.
26 Woods, Richard S., "Some Dimensions of Integrated Systems," *Accounting Review*, July 1964, pp. 598–614.
27 Zannetos, Zenon S., "Toward Intelligent Management Information Systems," *Industrial Management Review*, Spring 1968, pp. 21–38.

39

Modeling Marketing Phenomena: A Managerial Perspective

David B. Montgomery
Charles B. Weinberg

The authors discuss three major aspects of the use of marketing models. (1) Market models ought to be an aid to the decision-maker, not a replacement. (2) Such models now have evolved to a point where they should be classed as useful tools and not academic curiosities. (3) Marketing models can and ought to be useful to managers in many different ways.

Reprinted from *Journal of Contemporary Business*, Autumn 1973, pp. 17–22, with permission of the *Journal of Contemporary Business*, copyright 1973. At the time of writing, David B. Montgomery was professor of marketing and Charles B. Weinberg was assistant professor of marketing, Graduate School of Business, Stanford University.

In 1967, when one of the authors was asked by a Coca-Cola vice president at the beginning of a modeling project to "tell us about all the successful applications of marketing models," the answer did not take long. When the same question was asked by another executive last month, the answer ended only when the model builder was reminded that he had exceeded the time available.

The authors are currently revising *Management Science in Marketing* [20]. On a volume basis, the literature that has been published since 1967 easily doubles that which was available through 1967. On a content basis, the vast majority of the really managerially useful modeling work is post 1967.

A *Business Week* (24 May 1973) article summarized the marketing modeling work at Anheuser-Busch as follows:

> How often should a consumer-goods company advertise? In what media? With what kinds of ads to reach what types of customers? And what kind of response can the company expect? While nearly all consumer-goods companies puzzle over these questions, Anheuser-Busch is one of the few to come up with some answers, based on computer-modeling studies by Professor Russell Ackoff of the Wharton School's Management and Behavioral Science Institute. Every year Anheuser-Busch pays the university $200,000 to $300,000 for computer-modeling studies that explore everything from plant construction and utilization to what motivates the consumer. Under Ackoff's guidance, six to fifteen researchers work on anywhere from eight to twelve projects at a time—mostly in marketing and often in advertising. From studies on advertising level and frequency alone, Ackoff claims that Anheuser-Busch has cut its cost-per-unit-sold by 30 percent.

Marketing model systems which can be used by more than one company are available commercially for use by executives. MARKETPLAN [14] and BRANDAID [11] help a manager to prepare a marketing plan, CALLPLAN [13] and DETAILER [18] aid in allocating a salesforce to customers and products and MEDIAC [12] helps clients in preparing advertising media schedules. All these models, and others, have been purchased and used by companies other than the one in which or for which the model was developed, and most of them have been used in Europe as well as in the United States.

Marketing models are no longer an academic curiosity or an approach used by only one or two pioneering firms. Rather, although they still are in the early stages of their "product life cycle," they are well beyond the takeoff stage and into the growth stage. Consequently, marketing managers and their staffs would be well advised, at a minimum, to consider the use of such tools. Not to do so could deprive a company of a potential competitive edge.

The modeling of marketing phenomena may be viewed as having two main thrusts. The first is a scientific thrust and leads to greater understanding of marketing phenomena. Here the goal is to build either normative or descriptive models which advance knowledge. Aaker [1] recently has reviewed this approach. The second is a managerial thrust and is concerned with the capability of management science to aid marketing decision makers. The two thrusts are interrelated, and development in one area often spurs new effort in the other. In this article, we shall be concerned primarily with progress in modeling market phenomena as an aid to a corporate decision maker.

The remainder of this paper is divided into three major sections. The first is a general overview of the history of marketing decision models; the next section cites several case examples of the use of judgment-based models; and the final section examines the use of data-based models in the marketing of new, frequently purchased consumer products.

MARKETING DECISION MODELS

In order to provide perspective on current and potential developments in marketing decision models, it is useful to review briefly their history. Roughly, there have been three eras.[1]

Emulation of Classical Operations Research (1950-1964)

The earliest era of marketing models was characterized by techniques in search of problems. The emerging tools of operations research which were found to be very helpful in production and other operational problems were often applied blindly to marketing problems. The motto seems to have been "Have technique. Will travel."

A case in point was the rush to formulate the advertising media selection problem as a linear programming problem. The inherent difficulty was that by the time the media selection problem was mutilated in order to fit it into a linear programming format, most of the interesting and important marketing aspects were gone.

Although some excellent applications emerged during this era, for the most part, traditional tools of production-oriented operations research were of little use to the decision maker faced with the ill-structured, dynamic, nonlinear, uncertain, behavioral processes which constitute marketing.

Bigger and Better (1964-1970)

The reason for the lack of implementation success with most early marketing models appears to have been diagnosed as one of incomplete, overly simplified response functions in these models. Response functions are relationships which link controllable marketing activities, such as advertising expenditures or price, to some aspect(s) of market response, such as sales or market share.

The reaction to this diagnosis had its apex in the gigantic, theoretically elegant drug simulation developed by Claycamp and Amstutz [5]. This model was comprised of one thousand simulated doctors who engaged in simulated practice on simulated patients, whose symptoms and diseases were designed to match the actual incidence in the population. These simulated doctors not only practiced medicine, but also they read medical journals (ads), attended conventions, talked to one another about professional issues, received direct mail promotions and were called on by drug company salesmen (detailmen). They exhibited the behavioral phenomena of forgetting, selective perception and selective retention. In sum, the model was a very detailed, rich representation of the prescription pharmaceutical market.

The problem in the model was that it had far too much detail and was far too complex for continuing management use in market planning, the purpose for which the model was designed. The model was so complex that a manager would have to sacrifice much control over his or her own planning in order to use the model (to say nothing of the time investment required to provide inputs to the model and to then analyze its results).

Decision Calculus (1970-   )

Professor Little of MIT [10] has coined the term "decision calculus" to represent an approach to model building which leads to implementation and use of models to support management decisions. *A decision calculus is a model-based set of procedures for processing judgments and data to assist a manager in decision making.*

Experience has shown that such decision support models should satisfy a variety of criteria. First, they should be simple—not simple minded, but simple—and understandable. While all the important phenomena and variables should be included, users often generate considerable pressure on the model builder to increase complexity and detail. A model builder must resist this tendency until the user demonstrates that the increased level of detail can be handled. Parsimonious inclusion of variables and phenomena promotes ease of communication between the model

[1]This discussion parallels that in Montgomery [17].

builders and the users as well as ease of understanding on the part of the user.

Second, these models should be robust. The structure should constrain answers to a reasonable range of values and should be designed to make it difficult for implausible answers to result from inputs. Nothing will reduce a model's chances of successful implementation more than a stupid answer early in its stages of use.

Third, a decision calculus model should be easy to control. The user should be able to make the model respond in the way he or she wants it to; i.e., he or she should be able to set inputs in order to obtain nearly any outputs. What then is the model going to do for a manager? Doesn't this mean that the manager then simply will fudge inputs until the desired answer is obtained? In the general case, there are at least two countervailing factors. One is that experience suggests that most managers seem to honestly want help with their decision problems, and thus, they are unlikely to abuse this ability. Two, an important constraint on a manager's input assumptions is the fact that they are subject to review by others. When a model is used, the manager's assumptions are stated clearly so that everyone can examine them. While one would like to have objective inputs throughout the use of marketing models, this utopian state is realized frequently in practice. Marketing decision problems almost always involve major components of judgmental input. The next section discusses several examples of models whose inputs are entirely judgmental. The decision calculus notion, then, is that if management judgment is to be an important component, the manager should be left in control. The model structure and its parameterization should represent the world as the manager sees it. If he or she is not in some sense in control, a manager generally will be reluctant to use a model. The key is to provide the manager with a decision aid that actually will be used—not with a decision maker.

A fourth proposition is that a decision calculus model should be adaptive. It should be easy to change the parameters and the structure of the model as new insights and information become available. The notion is that of systems evolution.

Fifth, the model should be complete on important issues. In counterpoint to point one, that of simplicity, the model should be as complete as possible on important issues. The phenomena that the manager considers important must be capable of representation, either: (a) explicitly in the model structure or (b) as conditioning factors for specific parameter assumptions.

Finally, the model should be easy to communicate with—this usually implies the use of interactive computation.

The above desiderata for a decision calculus indicate that the focus is on providing the user with a decision-relevant tool. In contrast to earlier, more traditional approaches to models, the decision calculus focuses on *decision relevance* and *implementation* rather than on elegance. The authors do not want to imply that the decision calculus notion is the only way to develop relevant decision models which managers will use, but experience has shown that it seems to be a way that works very often, especially at this point in the development and use of marketing models.

Commercially available marketing modeling systems noted in the beginning of this article are examples of decision calculus models. Should a company want to "home grow" its own model, the following steps have been found useful in developing a decision calculus model.

- Determine the manager's "implicit model" of how the market works: This is to assure that the model will be relevant and understandable to the manager. This process will take advantage of the manager's knowledge and experience, will educate the model builder and will promote communication between the manager and the model builder. Another benefit is that this involves the manager in the model building process so that the resultant model will be his or her model rather than something presented by a staff group.

- Translate the manager's model into a formal structure: The model should represent in as simple a fashion as possible critical variables and processes which the manager has identified as important. At this stage, one should seek to identify inconsistencies in formulation and identify areas of incomplete and uncertain knowledge. This is likely to lead to iterative recycling with step one.
- Develop procedures for parameterizing the model: Naturally, whenever relevant objective data exist, they should be used. For those aspects of the model which require judgment, procedures must be developed which allow managers to quantify their judgments about market response. An important design issue at this stage is to phrase the questions relating to judgmental input in operational terms. For example, a manager may be able to make a reasonable judgment concerning the percent change in sales he or she would anticipate from a percent change in advertising, but there probably would be great difficulty in making a direct judgment of the advertising elasticity of sales.
- Develop an interactive program: Bring the model to the manager via an on-line, conversational computer program and a remote terminal.

Steps 1-3 above are likely to be performed iteratively as a project progresses: they also involve the most time in development. In a successful application to sales effort allocation across a multiproduct line, Montgomery, Silk, and Zaragoza [18] spent about 85 percent of their time on the first three steps and only about 15 percent on the computer programming.

JUDGMENT-BASED MODELS

"There's no point in attempting to model this problem, we simply don't have the proper data." While there are times when this is a well-reasoned evaluation, there is a tendency to overuse it as an excuse by management to avoid analytic reasoning which can provide a firm foundation for management decision. An examination of some case examples of judgment-based models will provide some evidence that such models, indeed, can be of significant assistance to marketing decision makers in many ways.

The first case example of a judgment-based model in action is the competitive bidding model developed at RCA [8]. It is a simple decision theoretic model which relies exclusively on management judgment and entails an underlying response relationship based on a limited number of inputs about competitive and customer behavior. The model thereby enables managers to evaluate large problems based on relatively few judgments.

The model is simple, but there is evidence that it can improve management decision making. The evidence is provided by a sequence of seven tests of the model solution versus the managers' unaided solution to the seven bidding problems (See Table 1.)

The test procedure was as follows:

- Managers used their traditional methods for arriving at a bid price in each bidding situation. They arrived at the bids with knowledge of results of previous bids. The managers' bid in each case is given in the second column of Table 1.
- In parallel with management determination of each bid, Edelman obtained management's judgmental inputs for the model analysis. It should be noted that the model relies exclusively on management judgment. The model-derived bid implied by management judgment is reported in the third column of Table 1.

The remainder of the table provides a comparison of the model solution versus the managers'. The fourth column reports the lowest competitive bid in each case. The seven test

Table 1 Seven Tests of the RCA Bidding Model

Test	Managers' bid	Model bid	Lowest competitive bid	Managers' bid: percent under (over) lowest competitive bid	Model bid: percent under lowest competitive bid
1	44.53	46.00	46.49	4.2	1.1
2	47.36	42.68	42.93	(10.3)	0.6
3	62.73	59.04	60.76	(3.2)	2.8
4	47.72	51.05	53.38	10.6	4.4
5	50.18	42.80	44.16	(13.7)	3.1
6	60.39	54.61	55.10	(9.6)	0.9
7	39.73	39.73	40.47	1.8	1.8

Source: Franz Edelman, "Art and Science of Competitive Bidding," *Harvard Business Review*, XXXIII (July–August 1965).

cases entailed bidding situations in which the lowest bid wins. Consequently, the managers' bids may be compared to the lowest competitive bid: this also is true for the model bid. The percent under (over) the lowest competitive bid is presented in columns five and six for managers and the model, respectively.

An examination of the table shows that the managers won only three of the seven bids, while the model-based analysis would have won them all. The reason that the managers won the last bid is that they used the model result. For the first six bids, managers averaged 7.4 percent under the lowest competitive bid in the two cases where they won, while the model-based analysis averaged 2.2 percent under in all the seven cases. Because the lowest bidder wins and the performance cost of the contract is not influenced by the price at which the contract is won, management obviously would prefer to be as little under the lowest competitive bid as possible. Hence, it appears that the model, which did not have any input other than from the manager—i.e., it is entirely judgmentally parameterized—has made better use of management judgment than the traditional bidding procedure.

A clue as to the mechanism whereby the model-based analysis enables managers to better utilize their judgment may be found in the fifth column. Notice that over time managers appear to be over-reacting to the result of the previous bid. In the first case, they undershot by 4.2 percent, so in the second case they overcorrected and were 10.3 percent over. This led to an adjustment in the third case which didn't quite make it—they were still 3.2 percent over. It appears that this led to a serious overcorrection in the fourth case, in which they are 10.6 percent under, which stimulated a bid 13.7 percent over on the fifth case. Hence, management appears to be over-responding to the most recent result. The simple model used to process judgments of the same managers appears to have provided a disciplined, stabilizing influence. An analogous set of results for production and manpower scheduling may be found in [3]. There, too, a simple, model-based reorganization of management judgment would have led to improved performance in three out of four cases.

In summary, it should be emphasized that the issue in this case is not men versus models. The model has no information which managers have not supplied. In fact, the success of the model in these seven cases is testimony to the managers' insight and understanding of the bidding situations. The model simply reorganized these judgments in a manner that made better use of their judgments. So, the issue is not men versus models, rather it is managers' unaided judgment versus managers plus an analytic tool designed to augment, but not replace, their judgment. The focus is on the process of combining and organizing the information that managers already have so as to enable them to take better advantage of this information.

While models often help managers make better use of their judgments, models also are harsh taskmasters because they require managers to articulate explicitly the bases for their decisions. The more disciplined analysis required by models places additional burdens on the manager. Consequently, an organization which is convinced that models can be of assistance must provide organizational incentives and support for their use.

An Additional Example

The need to provide organizational support if models are to be implemented and to continue in use is exemplified by the experience of an electronics firm with which the authors are familiar. This company developed a competitive bidding model, slightly more sophisticated than the RCA model discussed earlier, to help managers make a risk-return tradeoff in a bidding situation.[2] The model owed its existence and use to a particularly skilled operations research manager who assisted the managers in the process of providing judgments for the model. The company won twelve out of fourteen bids using the model. But, when the operations research manager became busy with other activities and the managers were left on their own to use the model, they reverted to the previous, less-disciplined bidding process. The company then lost three of the next four bids while not using the model. The apparent reason that managers stopped using this successful model was that the old fuzzy format was more comfortable and, after the OR manager went on to other things, they found it easier to go back to the old way. Further, top management did not insist on the use of the more thorough model-based analysis. In fact, largely because the OR manager left the firm and no one with comparable skill or stature sought to have the bidding model used, the model has not been used since then, despite its effectiveness. In contrast, strong top management support coupled with the requirement that output from a computer model accompany all marketing plans has led one consumer products company into the forefront of corporate marketing model users.[3] In summary, models require more from a manager and, consequently, steps must be taken to provide incentives and support for their use.

Models and Managers

Models can assist managers in their decision making by helping them find better solutions to their marketing problems. This can occur in three main ways. First, the availability of a computer model which provides a quick and convenient evaluation of an alternative allows managers to explore the anticipated consequences of a broad range of decision alternatives. The ease of evaluation of an alternative encourages a manager to consider more alternatives, and the time saved in computing the evaluation can be used to generate and compare alternatives. The Ayer model discussed in the next section is an example of this type of model which is designed to help the manager answer the question *"What* will be the outcome *if* this alternative is chosen?" A "what-if" model provides an evaluation of alternatives proposed directly by the manager. This ability to conveniently evaluate a broad range of decision alternatives should, in itself, enhance the likelihood of finding an improved solution.

Second, some models have a built-in ability

[2]The reader who wishes to examine this case in further detail should see the Nikoll Electronics Case in Day, et al. [7].

[3]For an example of one of the early planning models in this company, see Concorn Kitchens in Day, et al. [7].

to search for decision alternatives. In other words, these models not only evaluate alternatives, but also they search for better ones. An example of such a model is DETAILER, a judgment-based model designed to assist pharmaceutical companies in selecting the products in their product line that should receive salesforce (detailman) promotion [18].

DETAILER operates in two stages. The first stage is an interactive response model. Each product manager provides judgments on such variables as sales potential over the next few periods and the relative impact of alternative intensities of detailing for every product managed. From a few input judgments, the interactive model will enable a product manager to explore anticipated sales and profit implications of a wide range of potential detailing allocations to the product.

The second stage of DETAILER collects results from the first stage for all products and uses them in a search for an effective way to allocate limited manpower resources represented by the salesforce. The model generally begins with an initial management plan for detail allocation across products and time periods. The objective then is to see if the model can discover a potentially more profitable allocation.

The first application of DETAILER suggested a detailing plan expected to return $85,000 more in gross margin than management's initial detailing plan for that year. Because the estimated full commercial development cost of the model was about $25,000, the payback period on the model investment was less than 4 months. This first application was in a non-U.S. market; the second was in the domestic U.S. division of the same company. The results in this case were qualitatively similar to the first case, except that now the expected incremental gross margin was about one million dollars over a 2-year horizon due to greater total potential of the domestic U.S. market.

There are many other marketing models which search to discover very good, if not "optimum," decisions. For example, MEDIAC recommends how an advertising media budget should be allocated over media and time [12]. CALLPLAN utilizes a salesman's judgment as to how each customer and prospect will respond in terms of sales for different sales call intensities [13]. The CALLPLAN model seeks to discover a call strategy which will yield good results based on both the salesman's estimate of customer response and the travel time between customers. The model is appropriate to repetitive selling situations such as industrial chemicals, industrial plastics and selling bedding to retailers. It has been applied in more than ten situations. Two salesmen attributed actual sales increases of 15 percent and 39 percent due to their more efficient allocation of time using CALLPLAN. In most cases, expected sales increases run between 5 percent and 25 percent. It appears that the model is indeed effective in helping managers discover better marketing alternatives.

The third way in which models help managers find better solutions is to allow consideration of what might otherwise be politically unmentionable alternatives. As a case in point, consider the initial application of the DETAILER model. In aggregate, product managers usually want more detailing support than is available. This sets the stage for a bargaining session between the product managers, at which time available resources are allocated to each product. The process of compromise which usually occurs in such situations gives rise to a tendency to use extremes of the allocation spectrum rather sparingly, especially the heavy allocation end. For example, in this instance the company had settled on four potential levels of detailing support which a product could receive: nothing, one-quarter, one-half, or complete. The units of coverage were in terms of the percent of the doctors

Table 2 Managers' Policy Utilization versus DETAILER

	Policy			
	Complete	Half	Quarter	None
Managers'	0	13	14	9
DETAILER	4	4	16	12

called on who would hear a message for a given product. Table 2 compares the managers' and DETAILER's planned use of these policies for nine products over four quarters. The model utilized the more controversial complete and no coverage *more* and the intermediate or half-coverage alternative substantially *less* than management had. The reader should recall that the DETAILER plan had an anticipated extra profit of $85,000.

A further feature of DETAILER, which applies to many other models as well, is the fact that the model can be used to answer directly unanswerable questions such as "What's the value of a detailing (sales) force next year in terms of contribution margin?" Has the reader ever met a sales manager who could answer that question? Yet, using the product manager's judgmental parameterization of the response function for each product in the line, DETAILER may be used to obtain an answer to this question. The value of the sales force is ascertained by comparing sales and total gross margin contributions across the product line for the case of no sales effort for any product to the case of the best utilization of the salesforce across the product line which the model could discover. Hence, the model enables management to translate answers to answerable questions into an answer to a directly unanswerable question, thereby expanding management's capacity to analyze its decision situation. The authors would label this notion the concept of derived judgment.

DATA-BASED MODELS

Models can and have done more than work with managers' judgments. Models, when combined with the capacity of a computer, can take a large set of data and transform it into meaningful management information. The distinction between data and information is important. Many managers suffer more from too much irrelevant data and a lack of relevant information than from a lack of data per se [2]. One important use of models is to distill summary measures of market processes, dynamics and consequences of marketing actions from available data—i.e., to transform data into information. In brief, data only have value if the manager can use them. Models are a method to assign value to data.

Several data-based models dealing with the introduction of frequently purchased consumer products will be examined in this section. Although a number of data-based models are available in other marketing decision areas, a focus on a single important decision area, such as new products, can illustrate how data-based models can help provide relevant information for a manager.

New Products

An important problem in the introduction or test marketing of a new, frequently purchased consumer product is how to estimate the product's eventual market position based on relatively early market results. Products of this type generally experience over time sales curves of the form shown in Figure 1. Sales build up sharply at first, peak and then plateau at some level. In order to shorten the extent and to interpret early market returns from national introductions, managers would like to be able to project early market results in a way that will enable them to estimate whether the product will plateau at a high level (as in 1) or at a low level 2.

As the figure shows, simply extrapolating

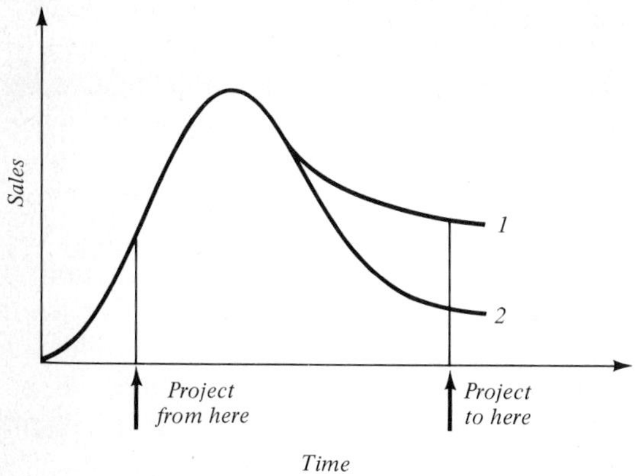

Figure 1 Typical sales curve for a new, frequently purchased consumer product.

early sales while they are still building would provide little relevant information for determining the ultimate plateau level. To help make this plateau projection, many companies utilize data from consumer diary panels in which participants record their brand purchases in the product class on a weekly basis. The early work of Fourt and Woodlock utilized panel data to develop estimates of the cumulative percent of the population which would try a new product [9]. They also developed estimates of repeat purchases which together with the cumulative trial estimates were then used to make forecasts of the product's future sales. Because ultimate sales levels are critically dependent on the product's ability to obtain both trial and repeat purchases, the Fourt and Woodlock model provided a mechanism whereby large blocks of panel data could be utilized by management. Several years later, Parfitt and Collins showed that forecasts could be improved if the model segmented the market according to when the trial purchase was made [21].

A More Sophisticated Model

Recently, Massy introduced a more sophisticated model of this type called STEAM (Stochastic Evolutionary Adoption Model) [15] which also makes use of consumer panel data but gleans greater information from it by further decomposing the structure into more basic components and by using more flexible statistical analysis. As in earlier models, STEAM uses estimates of the likelihood of a potential customer trying the new product and also accumulates information concerning the timing of conversion from a potential customer to a trier. Further, STEAM segments repeat buyers into depth of trial (DOT) classes. A DOT class consists of all panel members who have made a given number of purchases during the time period over which the panel is being analyzed. For example, DOT class two is made up of all panel members who have purchased the product at least twice. Statistics are accumulated on the likelihood that a panel member will convert from one DOT class to the next. In addition, the timing of these conversions is monitored. Specific functional forms are developed to utilize these elements, and statistical techniques are used to estimate parameters of these functions from the panel data.

After the parameters are estimated, STEAM forecasts the long-run position of the products by use of microanalytic simulation; i.e., each household's purchasing pattern over the forecast period is simulated by STEAM on a computer. The aggregate forecast is developed by summing the purchasing behavior of individual families.

An empirical application of STEAM will illustrate its potential use.[4] Panel data from the first 6 months of the product's introduction were used to forecast results over the next 2-1/2 years via the STEAM model (See Figure 2.) Although early sales results indicate a successful new product introduction, STEAM's analysis and projection of repeat

[4]The R^2 for each equation was over 0.7 and all factor weights were statistically significant except for Consumer Promotion Recall, Category Interest, Product Satisfaction and Category Usage.

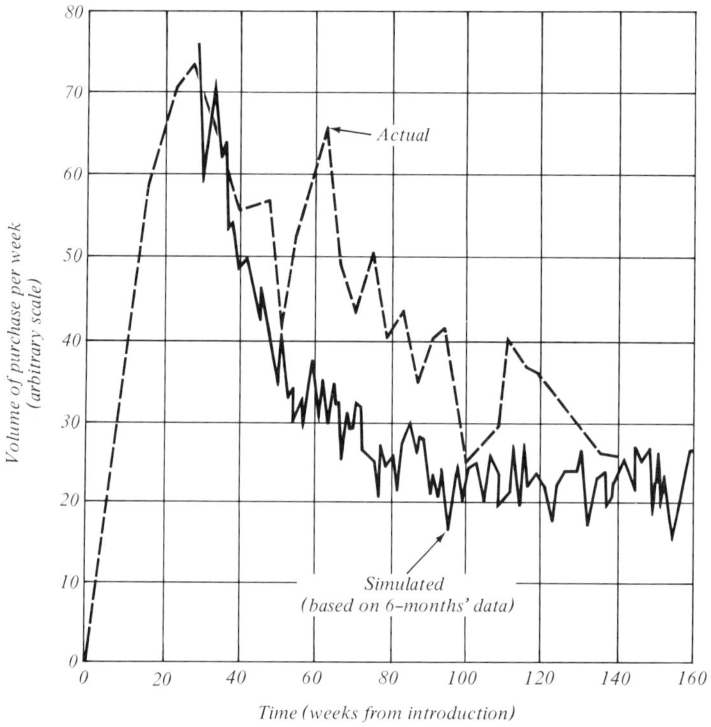

Figure 2 Actual vs. STEAM-projected sales.

rates and timing for different DOT classes suggest that sales will decline substantially and stabilize at less than half the peak value. When sales did drop considerably by week 50, an intensive promotional plan was introduced. Although this boosted sales temporarily, it did not change the underlying repeat purchase pattern, and by week 140, actual sales had fallen to the level projected by STEAM. Apparently, management's attempt to stem the tide of the sales decline with promotion only postponed the decline which STEAM had projected using just the first 6 months of consumer panel data.

Because the STEAM forecast did not take into account the intensive promotional program undertaken in week 50, the STEAM projection underestimates demand in weeks 50 to 100. This suggests another use for the STEAM projection. It can be viewed as a base line for sales, and the difference between actual sales and the STEAM projection in weeks 50 to 100 can be used as a measure of the effect of the promotional plan.

STEAM is a sophisticated model that utilizes much of the data reported in consumer diary panels and incorporates many factors that appear to be important in the new product situation. Although one cannot trace direct linkages with previous work, the development of STEAM draws on the efforts of many others (such as [9] and [21]) who have studied the same problem of making an early prediction of eventual sales level of frequently purchased supermarket products. Each of these models increased the amount of relevant information that could be gleaned from a set of data, and each also provided a stimulus for

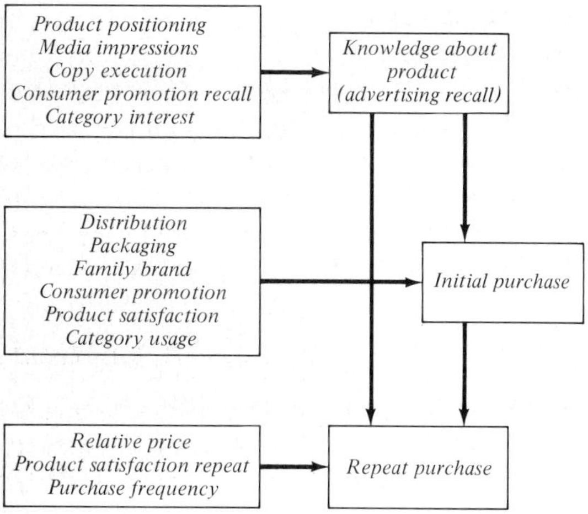

Figure 3 The Ayer new product model.

even more use of the data and a basis for deeper understanding of the new product introduction process.

The Influence of Marketing Efforts

Of course sales do not result independently of the marketing efforts of the firm. Sales depend, in particular, on the characteristics of the product and the method of marketing it. A manager introducing a new product might reasonably ask a model builder what he can learn from data about previously introduced new products. The model builder would then have at least three tasks: (1) to isolate the important explanatory variables, (2) to isolate the important dependent variables and (3) to develop and test relationships among these variables. If the efforts are successful, then the manager has an historic basis for a "conditional sales forecast"—i.e., a forecast of sales or another dependent variable conditional on the product and marketing mix.

The Ayer model, developed by Claycamp and Liddy, carries out the steps described above [6]. This model predicts two measures of the performance of a new brand after it has been on the market for 13 weeks. The measures are Advertising Recall (percentage of households in the potential market who can recall advertising claims) and Initial Purchase (percentage who buy at least once). As shown in Figure 3, the Ayer model consists of these two submodels which have been tested on data and a third untested one which predicts repeat purchase rate. The submodels are interrelated, and the Advertising Recall predicted by the first submodel is an input to the Initial Purchase submodel. The fourteen "critical factors" included were chosen after a review of the marketing literature and discussions with marketing executives.

An analysis of results for thirty-five low priced (less than $1.00), frequently purchased consumer items yielded the following relations:

(1) Advertising Recall

$$= -36 + 0.76\,(\text{Product Positioning}) + 2.12\,(\sqrt{\text{Media Impression} \times \text{Copy Execution}}) + 0.04\,(\text{Consumer Promotion Recall}) + 0.39\,(\text{Category Interest})$$

(2) Initial Purchase

$$= -16 + 0.37\,(\text{Predicted Advertising Recall}) + 0.19\,(\text{Distribution} \times \text{Packaging}) + 9.25\,(\text{Family Brand}) + 0.09\,(\text{Consumer Promotion}) + 0.02\,(\text{Product Satisfaction}) + 0.07\,(\text{Category Usage})$$

The specific numerical weights in (1) and (2) are the best summary weights for each critical factor for the thirty-five products which provided the basis for analysis.[4] The statistical analysis can also reveal the relative importance of the factors in explaining each of the measures of consumer response. (Although the weights in (1) and (2) are used to predict Advertising Recall and Initial Purchase, they do not reveal the relative importance. A related set of weights provides that information.[5]) Product Positioning and the interaction between Media Impressions and Copy Execution are, by far, the most important predictors of Advertising Recall, while Consumer Promotion, Family Brand and Predicted Advertising Recall are the three most important predictors of Initial Purchase, in that order. Hence, statistical analysis of the model using historical data can reveal the weights to use for each factor in predicting either Advertising Recall or Initial Purchase as well as their relative impact.

The next question is whether the best summary weights for each factor (e.g., a weight of 0.76 for the Product Positioning score) which were determined from the thirty-five new products also would be useful in predicting Advertising Recall and Initial Purchase for other new frequently purchased consumer products. The predictive ability of the model was tested on twenty-three additional products. The procedure used was: (1) to obtain values of each of the critical factors, such as Product Positioning, for a given new product (i.e., one of the twenty-three), (2) by using these values and the weights in equations (1) and (2) to predict Advertising Recall and Initial Purchase for the product, (3) to measure actual Advertising Recall and Initial Purchase for the product and compare them to the results obtained in step 2 and (4) repeat steps 1-3 for each of the twenty-three products. The results for Initial Purchase were that for thirteen of twenty-three products, the predicted value was within plus or minus five percentage points of the actual level; for Advertising Recall, the corresponding results were eight of the twenty-three. All other predictions were within ± 10 percentage points of the actual level. These are clearly good results, especially for the Initial Purchase variable.

The Ayer model seeks to relate inputs to outputs. Although it is a model which seeks to predict the value of two key variables based on a number of data points for selected independent variables, the role of executive judgment both in formulating and using the model should be noted. Variables to be included were based on judgment, and the values of the independent variables included are based on the interpretation of market research findings. A model, such as the Ayer one, which relates controllable variables to outcomes suggests that the model can be used to help a manager determine what the outcome would be if variables were set at certain levels. Such "conditional predictions" are important inputs to decision making.[6]

Diagnostics

Another usage of a data-based model of the type just described is as a diagnostic. A model developed at BBD&O called NEWS (New Product Early Warning System) emphasizes this capability [4]. (See Figure 4 for the structure of NEWS.) The NEWS system, when used as a diagnostic, takes data from very early in the test market and forecasts longer term (e.g., one-year) results. In addition, it shows in what areas a new product is below established norms for its category and how this shortfall will effect its long-term position. This is the diagnostic element—it suggests where management action should be taken.

A case example will illustrate how this diagnostic process is employed. A brand was introduced with a target share of 5 percent by one year after introduction. However, based on the early test market results and the planned advertising budget for the year, NEWS forecast a 2 percent market share.

[5]Technically, relative importance is determined by the standardized regression weights. Weights reported in (1) and (2) are the regression weights on the unstandardized variables.

[6]An example of the possible use of the Ayer model in a market planning system is provided in Day, et al. [7].

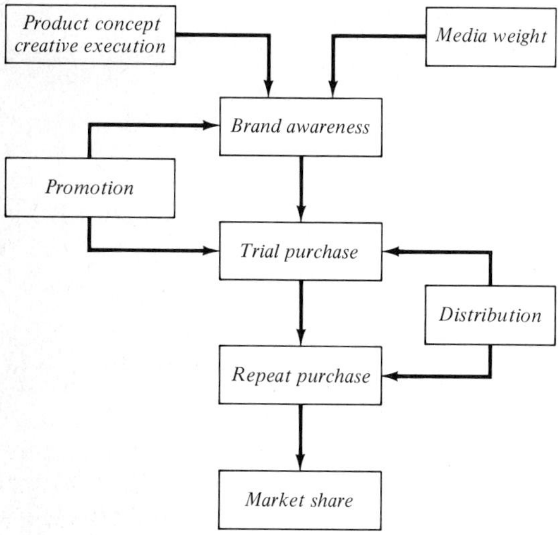

Figure 4 NEWS structure.

Further, the NEWS models indicated that while the trial-to-use and repeat measures were in an acceptable range, the attention-getting and awareness-to-trial measures were very much below the experience-based norms. After discussion, it was determined that these low measures were due to an inadequate advertising concept and that the concept would have to be strengthened if the brand were to succeed. Some revisions in promotion and distribution also were suggested and made. Thus, the use of the NEWS model helped to provide an evaluation of the marketing program, a diagnosis of problem spots and action recommendations.

The utility of the NEWS model as a predictive tool is illustrated by the results for seventeen cases. For these cases, covering test markets in which achieved actual share varied from 1 percent to 23 percent, the NEWS projection always was within ±1-1/2 percentage points of the actual results.

NEWS can also be used as a planning model before a test market by using anticipated values for variables in the model; i.e., instead of using observed test market data to make a projection, the model's projections may be based on anticipated values of the variables, such as percent distribution. When employed in this manner, the NEWS model serves a function similar to that of the Ayer model—both of these models seem to give accurate forecasts and both can be used for planning the marketing mix and as an aid to diagnosing test market results.

Implementation

The new product models just described are sophisticated and complex. As Urban and Karash [22] point out, the difficulties that occur in implementing these complex models "include (1) gaining management attention, understanding, and support (2) limited availability of data to support models (3) high risk because of large fund commitments, and (4) long model development periods which do not allow demonstration of short term benefits.

One way to overcome these difficulties is to adopt an evolutionary approach which starts from a simple model and becomes increasingly sophisticated as greater understanding of the problem and rapport with management is developed.

Urban's SPRINTER (Specification of Profits with Interdependencies) is a new product model which exists in three main evolutionary versions (Mod I, II and III). Mod I simply divides the population into four classes based on product usage experience. Sales predictions are based primarily on the number of persons in each class and the rate of movement from class to class. Mod II includes price and advertising as controllable variables, segments product experience classes by degree of awareness and increases the number of product experience classes. Although implementing Mod II (as compared to Mod I) requires considerably more data in order to represent the added descriptive and controllable variables, the model's ability to effectively use test market data is an important reason for its

Table 3 SPRINTER Cost Comparison of Evolutionary Stages

Item	Estimated costs		
	Mod I	Mod II	Mod III
Data collection cost; estimated thousands of dollars	0–10	25–50	50–75
Data analysis cost, thousands of dollars	0–5	10–15	15–25
Model acquisition cost, ratios	1	3	5

existence. Mod III continues this process of further disaggregating user classes and adding additional variables.

The costs of moving on to each subsequent stage are substantial. (See Table 3.) It costs about five times as much to build a Mod III model as a Mod I, and the data acquisition and analysis costs for Mod III can be as much as $100,000. However, the manager always has the option of not continuing if he or she does not believe that the benefits of having the model will be worth the cost of development. Further, the model interacts with the data collection process. The level of analysis to be carried out helps to determine both the data to be collected and the method of organizing it. Successful model implementation often turns out to be an evolutionary process, either through development of successively more complex[7] and data-demanding models, which also lead to greater understanding, or through the use of models to attack successively more difficult problems.

CONCLUSIONS AND SUMMARY

In summary, three aspects of the use of marketing models should be highlighted. First, marketing models are an *aid* to the decision maker, not a *replacement.* Marketing models often can help the manager make a better decision, but models do not make executive decisions by themselves. Second, marketing models have come to a point in their evolution where they should be viewed by managers as useful tools, not as academic curiosities. In particular, a model-building approach known as decision calculus seems well suited to operational needs of managers, especially those who have not yet used models. Third, model building in marketing covers a broad range of activities, and models can be useful to managers in many different ways. To review briefly, some of the ways in which the use of appropriate models can aid a marketing executive are the following:

- Helps to better utilize a manager's judgment.
- Limits a manager's tendency to overreact to pressures of the immediate and recent situation.
- Requires an explicit listing of input assumptions which leads to more informed discussion.
- Provides a method for quick and convenient evaluation of the consequences of alternative plans.
- Searches for improved plans or better solutions to problems.
- Allows the emergence of politically unmentionable solutions.

[7]Note that complexity alone does not guarantee greater understanding or control. One tries to understand a process with as parsimonious a model as possible.

- Expands the range of questions which can be answered by use of the notion of derived judgment.
- Distills from available data relevant information as in new product forecasting.
- Provides a basis for relating marketing inputs to market results and, hence, serves as basis for marketing planning.
- Diagnoses, based on early data, the adequacy of a market plan and locates areas needing improvement.

An impressive list of potential gains that can result from the use of models by managers has been delineated in this paper. However, this article must conclude with two cautionary points. First, successful models need to be custom fitted to organizations and management problems. Although a large collection of techniques and models are available to provide a basis for building a useful model, this collection should be used only as a foundation and must be coupled with considerable work to apply a model-building approach to a particular decision problem. The second cautionary point is a reminder that models are difficult to implement. One major reason for this difficulty is the often unsatisfactory nature of the manager-model builder interface. Often, neither party is willing to attempt to understand, learn and respect the other's problems and viewpoints. As a result, models that truly help managers do not get built as often as they might be. One objective of this paper is to help lower this communications barrier and thereby increase the probability of building managerially successful marketing models.

BIBLIOGRAPHY

1 Aaker, D. A., "Management Science in Marketing: The State of the Art," *Interfaces*, Vol. 3 (August 1973), pp. 17–31.

2 Ackoff, R. L., "Management Misinformation Systems," *Management Science* (December 1967), pp. 147–156.

3 Bowman, E. H., "Consistency and Optimality in Managerial Decision Making," *Management Science* (January 1963), pp. 310–321.

4 Brody, E., L. Pringle and R. Wachsler, "A Mathematical Model To Guide the Introduction of a New Brand (NEWS)" (New York: B.B.D. and O.), mimeographed paper.

5 Claycamp, H. J., and A. E. Amstutz, "Simulation Techniques in the Analysis of Marketing Strategy," in F. M. Bass, et al., eds., *Applications of the Sciences in Marketing Management* (New York: J. Wiley and Sons, 1968).

6 Claycamp, H. J., and L. E. Liddy, "Prediction of New Product Performance: An Analytical Approach," *Journal of Marketing Research*, Vol. 9 (November 1969), pp. 414–420.

7 Day, G. S., et al., *Cases in Computer and Model Assisted Marketing: Planning* (Cupertino, California: Hewlett-Packard, Inc., 1973).

8 Edelman, F., "Art and Science of Competitive Bidding," *Harvard Business Review* (July–August 1965), pp. 53–66.

9 Fourt, L. A., and J. W. Woodlock, "Early Prediction of Market Success for New Grocery Products," *Journal of Marketing* (October 1960), pp. 31–38.

10 Little, J. D. C., "Models and Managers: The Concept of a Decision Calculus," *Management Science: Applications* (April 1970), pp. 466–485.

11 Little, J. D. C., "BRANDAID: An On-Line Marketing-Mix Model," Working Paper 586–72 (Cambridge: M.I.T., Sloan School of Management, February 1972).

12 ———, and L. M. Lodish, "A Media Planning Calculus," *Operations Research* (January–February 1969), pp. 1–35.

13 Lodish, L. M., "CALLPLAN: An Interactive Salesman's Call Planning System," *Management Science*, Part II (December 1971), pp. 25–40.

14 Massy, W. F., "MARKETPLAN: A Marketing Mix Planning Model," mimeoed paper (MAC, Inc.).

15 ———, D. B. Montgomery and D. G. Morrison, *Stochastic Models of Buying Behavior* (Cambridge: MIT Press, 1970).

16 Montgomery, D. B., "The Outlook for MIS," *Journal of Advertising Research* (June 1973), pp. 5–11.

17 ———, "Marketing Information and Decision Systems: Coming of Age in the '70's," Research Paper No. 150 (Stanford University: Graduate School of Business, April 1973).

18 ———, A. J. Silk and C. C. Zaragoza, "A Multiproduct Sales Effort Allocation Model," *Management Science* (December 1971), pp. 3–24.

19 Montgomery, D. B., and A. B. Ryans, "Stochastic Models of Consumer Choice Behavior," in S. Ward, et al., *Consumer Behavior: Theoretical Sources* (Englewood Cliffs, New Jersey: Prentice-Hall, Inc., 1973).

20 Montgomery, D. B., and G. L. Urban, *Management Science in Marketing* (Englewood Cliffs, New Jersey: Prentice-Hall, Inc., 1969).

21 Parfitt, J. H., and B. J. K. Collins, "Use of Consumer Panels for Brand Share Prediction," *Journal of Marketing Research* (May 1968), pp. 131–145.

22 Urban, G. L., and R. I. Karash, "Evolutionary Model Building," *Journal of Marketing Research* (February 1971), pp. 62–66.

40

Environmental Information Systems for Strategic Marketing Planning

William R. King
David I. Cleland

This article describes an information system for providing externally generated data to support strategic marketing planning. Emphasis is placed on the strategy process through the gathering of data from generally defined sources.

A methodology consisting of the development of interrelated information subsystems is proposed.

Most complex organizations have developed sophisticated information systems to support their decision making and other managerial activities. Indeed, the term *management information systems* (MIS) has become so pervasive that it is now used to describe a wide variety of data processing systems, some of which are only indirectly related to the management process. Usually such systems—even the ones that support management decisions—are almost exclusively concerned with the *control function* as applied to the *operational activities* of the organization; few are directly focused on the *planning function* or the *strategic marketing decisions* that are so critical to the organization's future.

This emphasis on operations and control rather than planning and marketing has resulted in the creation of sophisticated systems for collecting, processing, and disseminating *internally generated information* such as costs, inventories, and personnel data; while relatively unsophisticated systems suffice for coping with critical *externally generated environmental information*. For instance, if one investigates the MIS development efforts of many

Reprinted from *Journal of Marketing*, Vol. 38, pp. 35–40, American Marketing Association, October 1974. At the time of writing, William R. King was professor of business administration, Graduate School of Business, University of Pittsburgh. David I. Cleland was professor of systems management engineering, School of Engineering, University of Pittsburgh.

firms, he finds that these efforts have begun by emphasizing cost and financial data systems and have evolved to incorporate other varieties of internal data. Usually only after these internal systems have been rather fully developed is attention given to the systematic collection and utilization of external information. Even then this function is usually performed in a narrow sales context that may not significantly encompass the wide variety of relevant environmental information that is potentially of critical value to the organization's strategic marketing planning.

Kelley, Kotler, and others have proposed designs and models for incorporating environmental information into marketing decision making.[1] However, these approaches have tended to concentrate on the information collection and processing aspects of the model rather than on the processes of utilizing environmental information in strategic marketing planning.

An organization's strategic planning effort is aimed at providing a sense of direction when approaching an uncertain future, the nature of which will only in part reflect the organization's own goals and choices. Forces in the environment—everything outside the organization itself—will also play an important role in determining the organization's future, so that effective strategic planning must operate to permit the organization to assess the environment, to forecast it, to develop strategies for taking advantage of it and, to the degree possible, to alter it.

Environmental information is, therefore, critical to effective strategic planning. However, most organizations base their strategic planning more on judgment, intuition, partial data, and ad hoc studies than on objective, systematic information that is routinely collected and analyzed for strategic purposes. This is the case, in part, because they have justified information systems largely on the basis of cost efficiencies rather than on increased organizational effectiveness and, in part, because of the conceptual and practical difficulties inherent in the definition of systems designed to support strategic decision making.

Indeed, it is possible to argue that truly strategic decisions are of such a unique and unstructured nature that it is not cost-effective to develop an information system to support them. While this may be true to some degree, the authors will attempt to demonstrate here that it is feasible, and even cost-effective, to develop information systems to support strategic planning *processes* (as opposed to individual strategic decisions).

The emphasis of this presentation is, therefore, on the informational support of a strategic marketing planning *process* through the gathering of information from generically defined *sources*. The methodology proposed is the development of interrelated information *subsystems*.

Table 1 depicts a strategic planning *process* in terms of a number of key phases, identifies a number of key *sources* of environmental information, and gives descriptive names to a number of environmental *information subsystems* that will be described in this article.

Several points must be made in explaining Table 1. First, there is no unique correspondence between the elements in each row; the various subsystems and information sources are interrelated, and each impinges on more than one phase of the planning process. However, there is a general primary relationship that is identified by the elements in each row.

Second, the various subsystems need not be developed as computerized information sys-

[1]William T. Kelley, "Marketing Intelligence for Top Management," *Journal of Marketing*, Vol. 29 (October 1965), pp. 19–24; Philip Kotler, "A Design for the Firm's Marketing Nerve Center," *Business Horizons*, Vol. 9 (Fall 1966), pp. 63–74; "Marketing Intelligence Systems: A DEW Line for Marketing Men," *Business Management* (January 1966), pp. 32, 34, and 68.

Table 1 Information Subsystems Relating Information Sources to the Planning Process

Strategic planning process	Environmental information subsystems	Strategic information sources
Situation assessment (What is our current situation?)	Image subsystem Customer subsystem	Customers
Goal development (What do we want our future situation to be?)	Potential customer subsystem	Potential customers
Constraint identification (What constraints might inhibit us?)	Competitive subsystem Regulatory subsystem	Competitors Government
Selection of strategies (What actions should we take to achieve our goals?)	Intelligence subsystem	

tems. The term *system* is used here to describe a systematic, continuous, and formal set of activities that provide decision-related information.

Also, no inference should be drawn that it is necessary, or even feasible, for a single firm to develop the total system described here. The framework of Table 1 will be explained in subsequent sections in terms of specific systems—all in industrial marketing contexts—in whose development the authors have participated. However, no single firm has, in fact, implemented all of these subsystems, and it may well not be cost-effective for any single firm to do so. The industrial marketing systems described here are illustrations of the kinds of environmental information systems that may prove to be useful and cost-effective to any given firm.

ENVIRONMENTAL INFORMATION SUBSYSTEMS

Image Information Subsystems

The most basic assessment made by the managers of an organization is summed up in the "Where are we now?" question. To function effectively, every organization must continually assess its status relative both to its history and its environment.

Such an assessment requires objective and subjective measurements. At the objective level, the necessary information is that which is readily obtainable from internal sources—data on profits, costs, the organization's financial status and, in general, historical performance data that are produced by the internal accounting and financial information systems.

These objective data can be readily complemented with subjective judgment data from internal sources. Whether this is done formally[2] or informally, internal judgments are often overly biased by the influence of the readily available objective data. More importantly, internally generated judgmental data do not provide critical information concerning the

[2]See William R. King, "Human Judgment and Management Decision Analysis," *Journal of Industrial Engineering*, Vol. 18 (December 1967), pp. 17–20, for an assessment of using formal assessments of human judgment in management; and William R. King, "Intelligent Management Information Systems," *Business Horizons*, Vol. 16 (October 1973), pp. 5–12, for a description of the incorporation of human judgmental data into information systems.

firm's external *image* as it is projected to and perceived by the customers and potential customers on whom the firm depends for its success.

The authors' experience with industrial marketers suggests that there are great discrepancies between a firm's image of itself and the image held by its customers. Often these discrepancies are less significant in their impact on the firm's current operations than in terms of their potential impact in the future. For instance, the firm that sees itself as technically superior in an era when cost is becoming more significant may find that its image of being high priced is more important to its future success.

A firm's image may be assessed in two general areas: product image (price, quality, reliability, etc.) and organizational image (quality of personnel, responsiveness, integrity, etc.). The basic techniques to use in the formal image survey are *structured and unstructured personal interviews* of key customer personnel. A questionnaire to serve as a guide for the conduct of these interviews can be developed and tested within the seller's organization. This in-house testing can be used as a basis to define and operationally describe the important dimensions of the product and organizational characteristics that are deemed to be important to the seller's image. For example, in one such survey conducted by the authors, the customer interviews centered around an evaluation of the following product and organization characteristics areas:

General characteristics
Personnel image
Ability to communicate with customers
Project management skills and capabilities
Ability to meet normal customer requirements
Responsiveness to customer's special requirements
Negotiating skills
Special capabilities
Product characteristics

The overall image that emerged in this case was surprising to the executives of the sponsoring organization. It depicted an honest and technically competent organization that lacked marketing aggressiveness. This lack of aggressiveness was reflected in the customers' perceptions of virtually all aspects of customer contact, from the bureaucratic lack of responsiveness to customer inquiries to the lack of contact of top management with customers. Such specifics as the failure to communicate to customers about key personnel changes in the organization and deficiencies in the technical proposals presented to customers were also pointed out. The seller's products were rated high in terms of operating characteristics—performance, reliability, and ease of maintenance—but customers raised serious questions about the seller's overall capability to manage a technical product development effort and still maintain cost and schedule credibility.

The image survey was also conducted internally by querying personnel within the sponsoring company. The contrast between customer perceptions and internal personnel perceptions led management to take a number of specific actions designed to have a short-run impact on the image as well as to formalize the incorporation of image considerations into the strategic planning activities of the firm. This led, for the first time, to specific concern with the image that the company wished to project and the actions that it could take to reach this image goal.

Such incorporations of image information as an integral and continuing part of the strategic planning process require that some type of formal information subsystem be established. In the case in point, the economic impracticality of continuing large-scale surveys led the firm to integrate the continuing image-monitoring activities into other information subsystems where image-related surrogate measures were monitored and assessed. In this firm, the overall image assessment is to be updated at two-year intervals.

Customer Information Subsystems

In most firms, the area of customer information is the best developed of all of the environmental information subsystems. However, much of the existing customer information is not systematically used for any decision purposes, much less for strategic planning.

Two types of customer information are most useful for strategic planning: aggregate information and trend information. Thus, while data on a specific customer may be useful in the short-term decisions of the sales manager, long-range decision making requires that sets of customers who form important market segments be identified and analyzed. Such segments are made up of customers who are homogeneous in some sense that is relevant to strategic planning—for example, a common industry, common behavior, common responses to changes in the business cycle, and the like.

Trend information, both in terms of individual customers and for market segments, is also important to strategic planning. For instance, is a given market segment likely to increase or decrease in importance in the future? Will a given segment be changing so that a different strategy will be required to retain them as customers? These are questions related to strategic planning that can only be answered through analyses of aggregates and trends.

Thus, the keys to creating customer information subsystems that are supportive of strategic planning are two-fold: first, new varieties of information in the form of aggregates and trends; and second, a built-in analytic capability that permits the objective analysis of the strategic customer information.[3] While many customer information systems are in existence, few have significant capabilities in these areas.

Potential Customer Information Subsystems

While most organizations have some form of organized information about current customers, few have similar information on potential customers. Yet, such information is of equal importance for the development of strategic goals, since potential customers represent the opportunities that will ultimately determine the organization's future. Information on potential customers permits the organization to make rational choices concerning its future products, services, and markets.

The development of a potential customer information subsystem is not a straightforward task for most organizations. The list of potential customers is infinite, so some rational culling of this list must be performed. This may be begun by using a criterion that reflects the potential of a particular segment of the overall market. For instance, one commercial bank determined that many small manufacturing firms in the local area could avail themselves of a variety of bank services. They began to construct a data base using commercially available services such as Dun & Bradstreet's State Sales Guides[4] and those provided by various manufacturers' associations. They then assessed the potential of various segments of the market through personal contacts made on a test basis.

Another firm, after having built the data

[3]The various levels of analysis that may form an intrinsic part of an information system are treated in William R. King and David I. Cleland, "Manager-Analyst Teamwork in MIS Design," *Business Horizons*, Vol. 14 (April 1971), pp. 59–68.

[4]Published for various states by Dun and Bradstreet, Inc., New York, New York 10008.

base and having identified high potential firms, developed a "clipping service" for collecting and assembling published references to these potential customers. In this way, a great deal of intelligence information concerning the performance, plans, new products, finances, and the like, of other organizations was obtained. Although this approach may seem naive to the uninitiated, it is the essence of any good intelligence function, and those firms that have tried it have often found it to be of surprising significance.

Competitive Information Subsystem

Few organizations have a great deal of nonhearsay information about competitors. Often the limited hearsay information that is available is misleading and, in any case, such unsystematic competitor information usually does not provide a sound basis for strategic planning.

One of the most useful tools in developing a competitive information system is a *profile* of each competitor. Such a profile should delineate the business "character" of the competitor. One company constructed profiles of all competitors to focus on such factors as:

a Background of key competitor personnel
b Characteristics of projects on which competitive proposals were made
c Characteristics of projects on which competitive proposals were not made
d Mix of competitor's in-house business
e Assessment of competitor's marketing strategy
f Assessment of relative value placed by competition on various performance measures—for example, product quality, service capability, and the like

From a compilation of basic public information and informed inferences about competitors emerged clear pictures that had not previously been perceived by the firm. For instance, one competitor clearly bid *only* on projects having a key common characteristic. Another was seen to be solidly in the control of managers with engineering backgrounds. The recent behavior of a third competitor was explained by the backgrounds of a number of nontechnical people who had recently moved into key executive positions. When these profiles were reported and discussed, some critical decisions were made concerning the company's future marketing strategy. The key to the strategy was the company's ability to identify a place for itself in the market—one that provided it with a comparative advantage over the competition.

The profile concept can be instituted as a regular part of the information system. It should be linked to a clipping service and updated on a continuing basis. In more advanced applications, it can be supplemented with competitive image assessments made parallel with the firm's own image assessment. Such information can form a data base when key questions or issues are being dealt with, as well as a source of valuable information that can be summarized for use in the ongoing strategic planning process.

Regulatory Information Subsystem

Every organization operates in an environment that imposes formal constraints on it and its activities. The most obvious such constraints are government regulations. Moreover, every organization has individuals who are knowledgeable about the existing regulatory environment. However, their knowledge is often used only in an informal way, and usually after commitments have already been made in ignorance of the constraints.

The basic nature of strategic planning—which involves *new* and unfamiliar areas for an organization—normally mitigates against such regulatory information being readily available to those who are doing the planning.

Managers may know the regulatory environment for the products and markets that they are used to dealing with, but they cannot be expected to be familiar with the regulations surrounding *new* areas. Thus, the strategic planning environment is fraught with the danger of expending planning and development resources in ignorance of crucial regulatory constraints. Such a situation cries out for a formalized data base with easy access by the many managers who participate in strategic planning.

The basic characteristic of a regulatory information subsystem is the same as that of any information retrieval system. The development of such a system requires that a taxonomy of the regulatory environment be developed. Then, key descriptors can be used by managers to access specific domains of the taxonomy. In this way, the regulations that are relevant to a particular product, industry, or political subdivision can be furnished to planners who have need for comprehensive regulatory information as it applies to a specific area for which planning is being accomplished.

While there are clearly no general truths concerning the desirability and feasibility of such a subsystem, it is the experience of the authors that it plays a less important role in the minds of planning executives than do the other subsystems discussed here. Perhaps this is because it deals with boundaries rather than opportunities, and thus constrains action rather than promoting it. Or perhaps the particular design requirements of such a system—roughly analogous to that of developing a useful library indexing system—present a major cost deterrent. In any event, the authors have found that such subsystems, while technically feasible, are generally considered only by those firms that already have been "burned" in the regulatory inferno. The current pervasiveness of such conflicts suggests that more attention may be paid to this area in the future.

Intelligence Information Subsystem

As used here, the term *intelligence* refers to specific facts or the answers to specific questions concerning happenings in the environment. For instance, the answer to a question concerning a competitor's intentions to bid or not bid on a project is an intelligence item, as is an assessment that a potential customer will soon be changing suppliers.

The usual definition of the term is broader than that used here. For instance, the competitor profiles and other aspects of the various information systems previously discussed also qualify under the more widely accepted military use of the term. Here, however, they are incorporated into other subsystems and specifically excluded from the intelligence subsystem.

The critical aspects of intelligence gathering are *organization* and *systemization.* It is not the purpose here to enumerate the myriad data sources and data collection requirements for a good business intelligence system,[5] but rather to establish the desirability of having a formalized intelligence system, and the authority and responsibility patterns that are appropriate for effective intelligence activities.

The critical point in the intelligence subsystem, as in the potential customer and competitive subsystems, is to gather intelligence systematically, to have it evaluated, aggregated, and analyzed by trained people, and *to ensure that it is distributed to those decision makers who can make use of it.* If this can be done in a parsimonious fashion to ensure that the great amount of redundant and irrelevant information already flowing around in the organization

[5]See, for example, David I. Cleland and William R. King, *Management: A Systems Approach* (New York, McGraw-Hill Book Co., 1972), Chapter 17.

is not merely made larger, the benefits can far outweigh the costs of such an operation.

In the development of a marketing intelligence system, the most important element is the people who will develop and implement it. Moreover, the most important factor in determining its effectiveness is the recognition that *everyone* in an organization is involved both in the marketing function and in the process of intelligence gathering. The engineer who discusses specifications with the customer is both a marketer and intelligence agent, as is the field marketing representative. Indeed, technical people can often have marketing impact of a far different and more significant variety than can the professional marketer or undercover agent. So, too, is top management involved both in marketing and in the collection of market intelligence. One of the most significant results of the image survey example described earlier was the recognition by the company that their top management, who had preached a customer-oriented marketing approach for years, were not themselves personally customer-oriented.

The ways in which nonprofessional marketers can be made aware of their marketing role and encouraged to perform as proficient marketers are diverse. Among those that the authors have successfully used are the conduct of joint technical-marketing seminars that begin with a discussion of image survey results and then go on to discuss each individual's role in remedying the problems that have been identified.

An effective approach to ensure that nonmarketers play their marketing intelligence roles is to specifically integrate them into the intelligence-gathering network. When engineers are to have customer contact, they must be made aware of the critical information that is needed and who in the customer's organization is likely to have it. Top management should be similarly briefed before their visits to customers and debriefed on return. In this way, a great deal of relevant information can be garnered and provided to those decision makers who are in need of it.

Of course, all of this presumes that an office in the organization has been set up for the collection and analysis of intelligence information. The analysis of intelligence involves a determination of the relevance, credibility, value, and appropriate dissemination of intelligence data. This central office can also perform the function of gathering together the key questions and identifying the voids in the knowledge necessary for effective strategic marketing planning. These questions can be asked in a routine fashion of field personnel and others who might be expected to have relevant information. Often, these people have the desired information in one form or another, but without a formalized intelligence system they have no way of getting it to the right people or of having it integrated with other information to form useful information aggregates.

This same intelligence organization—with its focus on analysis, eliminating redundancies, posing questions, and disseminating information to those who are in need of it—can also function as a part of the competitive and potential customer information subsystems. For example, data provided by clipping services require much the same analysis whether they relate to competitors or customers.

SUMMARY AND CONCLUSIONS

In describing the various information subsystems that can make up an overall environmental information system for the support of strategic marketing planning, the authors have related information sources to various phases of the strategic marketing planning process. However, these relationships are not unique; there are clearly many possible interrelationships among the supporting information subsystems.

The taxonomy chosen is one that the authors have found to be successful, whereas some other logical combinations have not worked well. For instance, the intelligence organization can play a role in the competitive and potential customer subsystems as well as in the intelligence subsystem. This suggests that the subsystems themselves might be combined. However, experience has shown that their differences in nature and function are more important than their commonalities. The competitive subsystem is designed to develop and maintain *overall profiles* of competitors. The intelligence subsystem is meant to develop *answers to specific questions* about competitors' activities and intentions. While the two are mutually supportive, they are quite different in their nature, objective, and in terms of the subsystem functions necessary to sustain them. Thus, it is concluded that the two are best designed to be separate, but overlapping, subsystems.

The important area of integration of the various subsystems is in terms of *output* rather than function. The output of the various subsystems must be compatible and available in the aggregate for use in decision problem analysis if new and more sophisticated varieties of information systems are to lead to more effective strategic decision making. The design of the overall system must ensure this after the firm has determined which of the various modules are to be developed and the sequence of development. Of course, many firms will not find it economic to develop the entire system, so that this design phase must necessarily be idiosyncratic.

By developing such an integrated environmental information system, a firm can begin to routinely provide objective information to support strategic marketing planning just as it provides objective data to support operational decision making. Since much of strategic planning is now based much more on judgment and intuition than on reliable information, the quality of the decisions that determine the company's future should be greatly enhanced.

41

Contingency Planning

Michael J. Clay

The author argues for the preparation of contingency plans to anticipate the occurrence of sudden situations which represent either a threat or an opportunity for a company. Such contingencies would include currency devaluation, a takeover bid, nationalization, shortage of raw materials, actions by a competitor (for example, a new product or a price war), and legislation.

A plan of action for generating a contingency plan is proposed, and also an appropriate organization possibility is suggested.

Reprinted from *Long Range Planning*, pp. 70–73, April 1971. Reprinted with permission from Michael J. Clay, title C, copyright April 1971, Pergamon Press Ltd. At the time of writing, Mr. Clay was manager of management services of a large British chemical company.

Many of the best features of industrial systems, plans and policies can be traced back to an origin in a closely related system, plan or policy of the armed services, of the United Kingdom before or after the industrial revolution and of other military bodies stretching back to classical times. This is only to be expected since when industry began to develop beyond the stage of cottage-based craft industries the armed services were the only model available. Furthermore the model had been tested over several thousand years and had to work effectively in far more demanding circumstances than industry had to face: such aspects as the sudden death of commanders, the annihilation of entire units and even the dramatic effect of new weapons were commonplace.

In view of this it is surprising that one of the best features of the military system, and one which is eminently suitable for use in industry and commerce has been almost completely ignored. This is the use of contingency planning which enables a war department to react defensively to sudden, undesirable situations created or threats, or offensively to suddenly desirable situations or *opportunities*. Industrial and commerical organisations do not usually do this. For many years those which did any planning produced a single budget of expected sales and costs. The best practice at the time was to compare draft budgets with desired levels and breakeven charts, and make alterations as necessary to achieve in the final budget as close a result as possible to the desired result. In the last few years an extension of this basic idea of budgeting has been developed. In the technique of profit planning companies consider alternative objectives, alternative strategies and alternative policies for several years ahead. After much *preplanning* the company settles for a single plan which is revised annually. From this point the procedure is almost identical to the older budgetary control.

In the budgetary control technique plans or budgets are prepared for all items of expense (materials, labour, direct expenses, cash, overheads, profit and loss, stocks, etc.) and are developed from a single sales budget.

In production planning, plans are prepared for production units and perhaps also for related stockholding, purchasing and distribution activities based on received or expected customer orders or the need to replenish stocks.

Three new terms are in use for new activities but the terms are often not used precisely and the activities covered apparently overlap. It is suggested that *corporate planning* is the preparation and execution of comprehensive plans related to total company activities (e.g., including management development, new product development, company growth and computer applications). *Long range planning* or long term planning relates to activities more than 5 years ahead (some authorities say 2 years ahead). A *strategy* is a plan covering the major features of the method to be used in the future to attain an objective and *strategic planning* is the process of creating sound strategies.

Corporate planning is thus a special type of strategic planning. But after some preliminary discussion of alternatives, both techniques become exclusively concerned with a single course of action . . . the *expected* course of action and the *expected* set of events. No prior attention is paid to unexpected events, whether favourable or unfavourable to the company's interests. Certainly attention may be paid to variances in a company's standard cost accounts, and the management by exception technique similarly highlights discrepancies from planned achievements, but both of these techniques are operating historically, on past events. It is the post mortem to establish the cause of death rather than the restorative to cure the ailment or the prophylactive to prevent its occurrence. If an unexpected situation occurs it is assumed that a 'professional' manager will instantly adapt himself to the changed position. It is a requirement of every manager that he should be flexible and capable of changing course from time to time. This argument contains truth but is not the whole truth.

In the first place we have to draw a distinction between two situations. Firstly there are unexpected events which it is reasonable to expect a capable manager to respond sufficiently quickly so as to maximise benefit to the company without killing himself and his staff in the process. Secondly there are situations in which the response required is so quick, the issues are so complex, or mistakes so likely that a manager who is unprepared cannot be expected to make the right response. In addition to all this we also must draw a distinction between threats and opportunities which may affect the company as a whole, as against those which are purely the internal affair of one or more departments. To make the whole thing more concrete, it is reasonable to expect the company to make an unprepared and instantaneous response to a flu epidemic which removes 20 percent of the staff; it may or may not be reasonable to expect an instantaneous and unprepared response to a currency devaluation; it is certainly unreasonable to expect a company to be able to mount an immediate and unprepared defence to a sudden take-over bid from a competitor.

The type of preliminary effort and organisation that is required to enable bodies to respond instantaneously, effectively and safely to suddenly presented opportunities and imposed threats is closely similar to the contingency planning carried out in the plans departments of the armed services and in some government departments.

The planning departments of the services exist in order to prevent their being caught napping either by an unexpected enemy move, or by an unexpected demand by the field commanders, war cabinet, chiefs of staff, etc. An extraordinary range of projects is tackled. In a situation in which *A, B, C* and *D* countries are at war with us, (*E*) the cabinet may wish to know the likely effect if a fifth country, *F*, declared war upon us. How would *F's* resources, physical location and other aspects affect the war? Would it make the outcome definite, or make little difference? This is a variation on the basic offensive and defensive strategic planning tasks undertaken. Again, a commander may conceive the idea of capturing a radar installation by a sudden raid and bringing selected components home. How many men, what ships, what timing and state of weather and tide would be needed? A plan may be called for on action in the event of an invasion. The planners would probably require more information before starting work, e.g., invasion by air or by sea, by how many troops, in what area and so on? No doubt many of the actions proposed by the planners would be set in train as a precautionary measure *before* an invasion materialised, e.g. bridge demolition contingency instructions to the territorial army or home guard. Another type of plan would be designed to answer a question on timing . . . How long could the nation hold out in the event of a complete stoppage of oil imports? The translation of the latter into industrial terms (how long can we carry on if the supply of major raw materials is interrupted?) is striking and immediate.

There is considerable experience in industry and other large organisations of a special case of contingency planning; this is the type of planning which is done as a threat gradually intensifies. Typical examples are the plans drawn up by industry in 1970 as the threat of a national dock strike emerged and intensified, and preparations made by motor manufacturers to counter probable strikes at component suppliers' factories.

Also oil companies built up strategic stocks of oil before the closure of Suez and this helped the British economy to continue functioning normally despite the immediate shortage of oil from the Middle East, which followed the Six Day War.

But in the more general form of the technique the preparatory work is done before an unplanned threat or opportunity emerges and here business organizations have apparently little or no experience.

But before we can recommend universal adoption of contingency planning by industry, we must be a little more certain about the nature of the costs and benefits of this type of planning, as applied to industry and of the problems entailed.

SUITABLE SUBJECTS FOR CONTINGENCY PLANNING

As a preliminary we can dismiss from the field an entire range of contingencies which is outside the scope of the present study.

The technique of *disaster control* has been devised to handle all those emergency conditions which can threaten the safety of human and other resources. In this technique contingency planning is applied to unlikely eventualities such as fire, flood, hurricane, subsidence, landslip, bursting of tanks, dropping of aerial objects, lunatic action, sabotage, riot and many other possible disturbances. The technique is applied by the safety officer.

The industrial analogue of military battles and campaigns is the performance battle (economics, productivity, profitability, etc.); our field of study, therefore, mainly relates to economic and commercial contingencies. However, it is not exclusively economic as in the case of anti-burglary action, before or after the event. Planning activities can be considered under two headings.

Defensive Contingency Planning

Several examples are given below of suitable subjects for contingency planning in many companies. Of course the list is not exhaustive. One may readily think of others, both threats which are standard throughout industry and those which are specific to one company.

a Possible litigation on public liability: patents, contracts, pollution, etc.

b Possible legislation on pollution: safety standards, conditions of employment, product specifications, terms of trade.

Some of the plans will require that specified actions are taken in the event of the materialisation of the threat. But there are many plans from which immediate actions flow, e.g., one has to establish a strategic stock for certain imported raw materials *before* the supply is interrupted. Similarly one takes out an insurance policy before trouble starts.

c A price war, started by a competitor.

d Sudden obsolescence of a principal product resulting from a new improved competitive product.

e A takeover bid or merger proposal.

f An accident which incapacitates all the Board at once.

g The need to withdraw suddenly a product that is being nationally marketed.

h The need to modify all models of product *X* currently on the market.

i The need to change an advertising campaign in the middle, owing to an unexpected unfavourable effect.

j Desire to prevent or minimise bad publicity for a sudden unfavourable event.

k An epidemic disease in the factory or offices.

l A strike of clerical and junior management grades.

m Destruction or loss of vital company records.

n Discovery of major fraud in progress, or corruption of senior management.

o A strike by engineers or operatives.

The second type of contingency plans can be called *offensive plans;* these are designed to improve the company's situation by taking advantage of opportunities, perhaps sudden short term, transitory or uncertain. Many of them have equivalents in the first category, for example:

a Litigation started by the company on others' liabilities: patents, contracts, pollution, e.g. of the company's fresh water intake from a river.

b A price war started by us.

c Sudden obsolescence of all products which compete with product *Y* resulting from own successful development work.

d A take-over bid or merger proposed.

e The need to mount an advertising or publicity campaign as an immediate reaction to some favourable news, e.g. if cigarette smoking is *proved* not to be harmful to health.

f The need to obtain £ *X* permanent short term capital for expansion, take over, etc., under favourable market conditions.

g The desire to send a team of experts overseas for 3–6 months to help an associate or customer in an emergency.

ORGANIZATION OF CONTINGENCY PLANNING

At this stage in the argument it does appear that there is extremely wide scope and many possible applications for a contingency planning function in a business. Given the need, the next question relates to the organization of the function. Who will run this function? Will it be part time or full time? To whom should the planner report? Who is empowered to demand that plans be prepared and who is allowed to study the highly confidential results?

Clearly, the staffing of this function, as of any other, depends on the workload imposed; a larger staff will be needed for a multidivisional international corporation than for a small jobbing joinery business. It is usually a safe policy to start a new function on a small scale, prove its value, then expand until the required standards of performance are achieved. In most firms contingency planning could be started as a part time job for a single middle manager. Ideally he would be a manager whose present job has a planning bias. The allied functions of profit planning, corporate planning and long term planning, all of which are recent innovations, are usually tied to an annual planning cycle and consequently are likely to have peak and trough workloads. A happy solution could be to enlarge the scope of the underloaded profit planners to include contingency planning responsibilities. An additional advantage of this arrangement is that the personnel are already concerned with planning on a companywide scale and are acquainted with most of the expected problems. The only essential difference between this activity and contingency planning is that the latter deals with activities and events which are less likely to materialise. Other planners such as production planners and project planners tend from the nature of their jobs to have a narrower outlook. To whom should the planner report? It is not necessary for the function to report to the Chief Executive although the latter will have a great influence on the type of work done. Contingency planning should report at a sufficiently high level so that all the confidential problems of the company can be freely discussed between the planner and his manager and so that the function remains a tool of the Board. All this suggests that the function should report to an official such as:

- The Company Secretary.
- The Administration Director.
- The Planning Director.
- The Head of Administrative Services.

There can be no single correct answer to the

question of who may call for a contingency plan to be prepared. Perhaps there should be no restriction on who could or should suggest the need for a plan (e.g. the insurance clerk in the Accounts Department may first realize the company's vulnerability in certain specialized areas such as public liability). Authorisation should, however, be restricted to the top manager to whom the contingency planning function reports. Once the plans are prepared the most severe restrictions must be placed on access to them. Each contingency plan must have a restricted circulation individually authorised to the top manager noted above. These will all include all Board members but beyond this the 'need to know' principle must be used, i.e., details are not disclosed to individuals unless they need to know. Such secrecy is essential since the plans concern the company's innermost thoughts, plans and policies on competition, and defending its position in the world.

FILING AND INDEXING

Safeguarding and referencing the planner's data efficiently is of the utmost importance owing to the importance and the secret nature of the information contained. It is suggested that each plan should be prominently numbered and only two copies made. One would be filed and locked away in the archives, a second filed and locked away in the manager's office. The top sheet of each plan should list the approved circulation and this should be signed by the manager. One suitable way of classifying plans is to place each in a folder, number both plan and folder serially and prepare a separate index, with cross references, of the material filed. Anyone on the approved circulation could borrow the file copy on signature; in the event of the contingency arising it may then be necessary to issue a photocopy of the relevant plan to each executive concerned. However, the *preparations* for any contingency could be carried out without each manager having a complete copy of the plan; a summary of the necessary actions would be enough.

All plans eventually become outdated. It will be necessary to include a system for keeping them permanently up to date. The front sheet of each plan should contain, in addition to the approved circulation, a control date at which time a revision would be necessary. Each plan would be reviewed annually. As a necessary compensation for the secrecy of the results it is advisable to be as open as possible about the need for and the existence of contingency plans. All managers should be encouraged to report on possible threats and opportunities which could perhaps be the subject of contingency plans.

It should be a part of the job responsibility of the contingency planner to talk to managers about possible but unexpected developments, as a means of increasing the chance that a plan will have been prepared when the event strikes. The planner must also exert a coordinating role over the actions which are thrown up by the plans. These are two types:

a actions needed immediately after the plan is ready, but before the contingency condition (let us call this the 'crisis').

b actions needed in the vent of the crisis.

The planner must ensure that everyone concerned knows that preliminary actions are needed (a) and that these are executed; he must also ensure that where secrecy does not render it inappropriate, everyone knows what actions he has to take if the crisis occurs. In these cases everyone concerned must read the contingency plan before it is filed away.

THE PLANNING PROCEDURE

Firstly a proposal is made to the top manager that a plan is advisable (e.g. if the only competitor on product *AB* 12 suffers a major fire or other catastrophe, creating the possibility of a sudden and largely temporary increase in sales). The top manager approves the proposal and asks the contingency planner to prepare a plan. The planner can work either alone, or through the efforts of a supporting section of department, or in a committee of experts which will differ for each plan. Whichever alternative is adopted a similar procedure is required.

The following notes highlight the most important aspects of this procedure:

a All assumptions made are carefully listed, and the source of all data is noted on working papers. The authority for any firm policy statement is also noted (e.g. Board Minute 35.12, or Sales Director verbal, or memo 11/6/70 from Works Manager). Where applicable the probable or possible error in information is also noted.

b A section of background comment containing the reasons for the selection of the particular course of action proposed and the rejection of alternatives is included, accompanied by any other explanatory remarks which are likely to be helpful.

c Preliminary action, i.e. action required prior to the crisis, is listed in step by step form with the name of the person responsible, a control date for completion and a statement of the action required. A contingency plan is, in this respect, no different from any other type of action plan as used in *management by objectives* or an implementation plan resulting from a profit improvement project.

d Contingency action, i.e. action required after the outbreak of the crisis is listed as far as possible in a similar way. The main difference here is that since the 'enemy's' or 'nature's' actions are uncertain one cannot always specify a single valid and binding course of action. Many of the actions must be conditional. For example, if the Sales Manager from ABC Ltd. (the firm whose factory has just burned down) requests us to supply our competitive product to his factory in completely plain containers we should stall for time, then refuse.

If the Sales Manager requests us to supply his customer, temporarily, with our own product direct, in our containers, we should agree.

The greater the number of successive steps that are planned the greater the number of conditional possibilities. A hint about the scale of this problem is shown in Figure 1, a decision tree.

This branching of conditional actions is what in the end limits the usefulness of contingency planning.

One way of restricting the number of alternatives is to phrase instructions in the form of attempting to reach specified objectives rather than stating exactly how to execute each minor task.

Whether the aim or whether the specific action to be taken is stated, the action statement should consist of four elements:

A code or item reference
An action statement, framed in the imperative mood
Time limits, e.g. start and complete dates
Personal responsibility, e.g. Chief Buyer

For example:

> 'Phase I Step 4, Invite union representative for preliminary discussion (Action, *BJK* before end of *C* day)'.

It would be a bold man who would assert that contingency planning has nothing to offer to his company. Such a statement is tantamount to saying that his company is not subject to contingencies. You have nothing to lose by trying it. Not the least of the technique's many virtues is the fact that it can be introduced without risk, without capital expense and at a sufficiently slow pace to match the available free time of one of the company's senior managers.

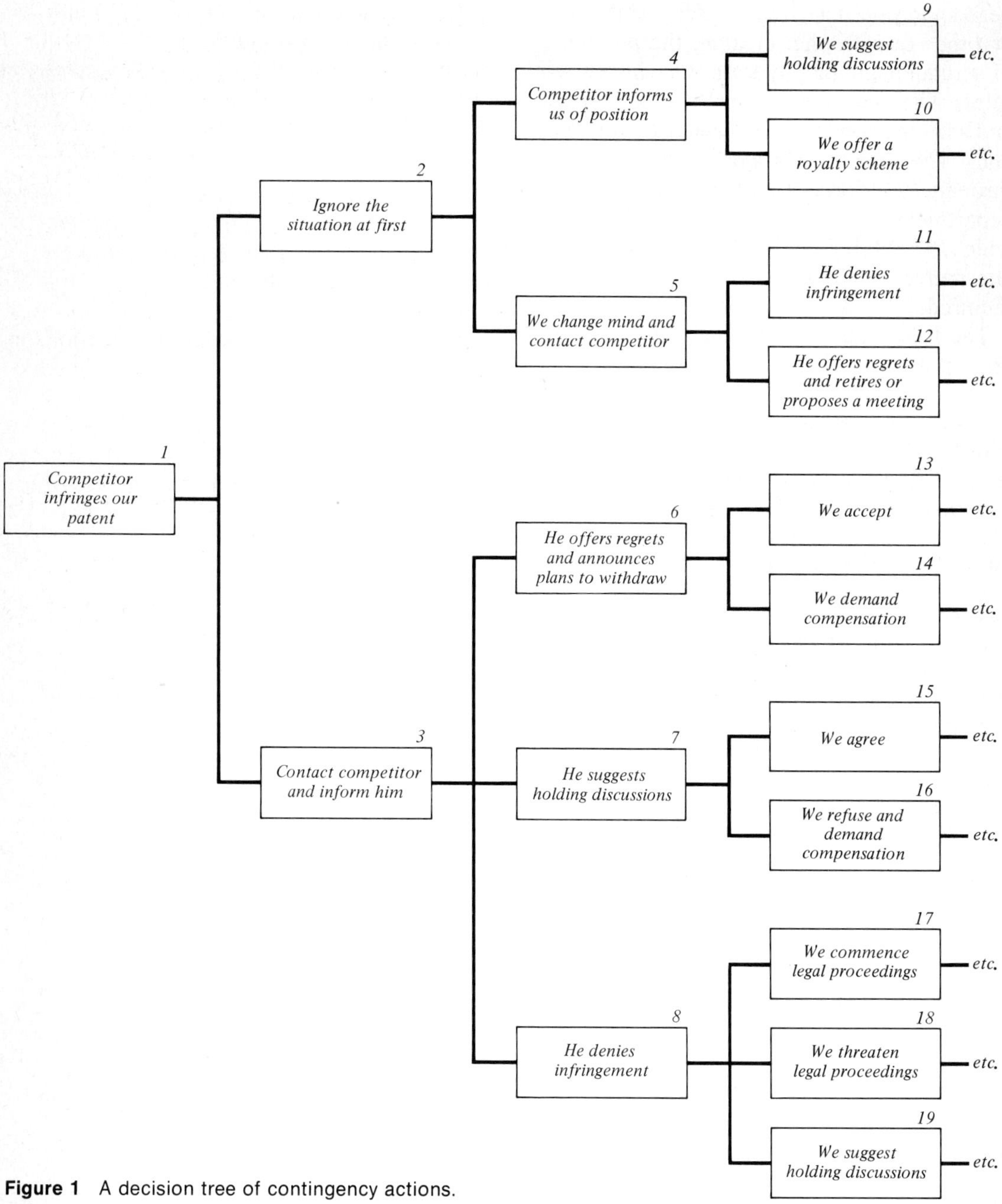

Figure 1 A decision tree of contingency actions.

REFERENCES

1. G. Donaldson, Strategies for emergencies. *Harvard Business Review,* Nov. 1969, pp. 67–79.
2. Robert J. Mockler, Theory and practice of planning (a review of milestones in planning literature). *Harvard Business Review,* Mar. 1970, pp. 148–150.
3. H. Igor Ansoff, *Corporate Strategy,* McGraw-Hill, New York (1965).
4. George A. Steiner, *Top Management Planning,* Macmillan, New York (1969).
5. James R. Collier, *Effective Long Range Business Planning,* Prentice-Hall, New York (1968).
6. Melville C. Branch, *Planning: Aspects and Applications,* John Wiley, New York (1966).
7. Bruce Payne, *Planning for Company Growth,* McGraw-Hill, New York (1963).
8. P. P. LeBreton and Dale A. Henning, *Planning Theory,* Prentice-Hall, New York (1961).

Name Index

A & P, 254, 286
Aaker, D. A., 424, 438*n.*
Abelson, H. I., 352*n.* 357*n.*
Abelson, Robert P., 140*n.*
Abernathy, William J., 210*n.*
Achenbaum, Alvin A., 390*n.*
Ackley, Gardner, 283
Ackoff, Russell L., 361*n.*, 422*n.*, 424, 438*n.*
ACT, (Action for Children's Television), 250, 251
Adams, Valerie, 248*n.*, 249*n.*
Adams, Walter, 304
Adelman, Morris A., 304
Adler, Lee, 389*n.*
Advertising Research Foundation, 106
Agne, Robert F., 9
Agres, Stuart, 381*n.*, 382*n.*
Albaum, Gerald, 371*n.*, 422*n.*
Alcibiades, 111
Alcoa, 286
Alderson, Wroe, 7, 9*n.*, 312
Alexander, Ivan, 180*n.*
Alexander, Ralph S., 136*n.*, 180*n.*, 422*n.*
Allen, Fred, 112
American Airlines, 416
American Dental Association, 238
American Marketing Association, 3
American Motors, 15
American Psychological Association, 104
Ames, Charles B., 180*n.*
Amstutz, Arnold E., 305*n.*, 391, 392, 422*n.*, 425, 438
Amtrak, 15
Andelson, H. P., 352*n.*, 356*n.*
Andress, F. J., 233*n.*
Andrus, Roman, 260, 269*n.*
Anheuser-Busch, 17, 424
Ansoff, H. Igor, 66, 70, 78*n.*, 209, 211*n.*, 455*n.*
Ansul Company, 36
Applewhite, P. B., 139*n.*
Aristotle, 4
Armstrong, Gary M., 363, 365
Arndt, Johan, 87, 260, 268*n.*
Aronson, Elliot, 356*n.*
Asch, S. E., 352, 356*n.*
Ashby, Ross, 422*n.*
Association of National Advertisers, 23–25, 27
Atkinson, J. W., 85
Auchincloss, Louis, 112
Avon, 324

Bachman, Jules, 304, 374*n.*
Bagozzi, Richard P., 7, 10*n.*
Bailey, Martin, 289
Bain, Joe S., 317*n.*
Bales, R. F., 348, 356*n.*
Bank of America, 416
Banks, Seymour, 158*n.*
Barnett, Norman L., 148*n.*, 150*n.*
Barnhill, J. Allison, 370*n.*
Bartels, Robert, 6, 10*n.*
Bass, Frank M., 145*n.*, 210*n.*, 400, 407*n.*
Bauer, Raymond A., 140*n.*, 152*n.*, 157*n.*, 354*n.*, 356*n.*
Baumwoll, Joel P., 154*n.*
BBD & O, 435
Beaver Lumber, 324
Becker, Boris W., 3, 8, 10*n.*
Beeline, 324
Belasco, James A., 368*n.*
Belk, Russell, 260, 268*n.*
Bell, William, 260, 268*n.*
Bennis, W., 419, 422*n.*
Berelson, B., 357*n.*
Berkowitz, Leonard, 357*n.*
Berkowitz, N. N., 358*n.*
Berle, Adolph, 283
Bernard, Chester I., 373*n.*
Bernhardt, Kenneth L., 3*n.*
Berscheid, E., 345*n.*, 357*n.*
Best Products, 324
Bieda, John C., 144
Billon, S. A., 233*n.*
Blackwell, Roger D., 84, 97, 187*n.*, 209*n.*, 211*n.*, 261, 268*n.*, 305*n.*, 391*n.*
Blair, John M., 283, 292
Blake, Brian, 260, 268*n.*
Blankertz, D., 320*n.*
Bogart, Leo, 381, 382*n.*
Bonjean, Charles M., 370*n.*
Boone, L. E., 260, 268*n.*
Booz, Allen, and Hamilton, 270, 281*n.*
Boston Consulting Group, 210*n.*, 212*n.*, 224*n.*
Boulding, Kenneth E., 369*n.*, 388*n.*
Bowman, E. H., 438*n.*
Boyd, Harper, Jr., 146, 148*n.*, 389
Bradley, M. F., 169*n.*
Bramel, D., 345*n.*, 357*n.*
Branch, Melville C., 455*n.*
Brandenburg, R. G., 78*n.*
Breyer, Ralph F., 312
Brien, R., 358*n.*, 423*n.*
British Airways, 123
Britt, Steuart Henderson, 244, 382, 389*n.*, 390*n.*
Brock, T. C., 349, 351, 357*n.*
Brody, E., 438*n.*
Brody, Robert P., 147, 148
Broun, Heywood, Jr., 112
Brown, Arthur A., 361*n.*
Brown, James K., 389*n.*
Brown, R. W., 85, 305*n.*
Brozen, Yale, 289–291
Bruce, Grady D., 370*n.*
Bruno, Albert V., 398–400, 404, 406, 407*n.*
Bucklin, Louis P., 312

Buckner, Hugh, 136*n.*
Budweiser, 166
Buell, Victor P., 23, 29, 293*n.*, 311*n.*
Builder's Emporium, 324
Bullock, Donald, 104
Burck, Gilbert, 282
Bureau of Advertising Research, 250
Burnett, Carol, 401, 403, 405
Burnett, Leo, Co., 378
Burnkrant, R. E., 259, 268*n.*
Burns, Arthur R., 304
Butler, Ralph S., 312
Buzzell, Robert D., 209*n.*, 210*n.*, 249*n.*
Byrne, D., 345*n.*, 357*n.*

Cadillac, 148
Cage, C., 382*n.*
Cagley, J. W., 136*n.*, 140*n.*
Call-a-Mart, 324
Callom, F. L., 136*n.*
Campbell, Glenn, 401, 403, 405
Canadian Tire, 328
Cancian, Frank, 260, 268*n.*
Cardozo, Richard N., 136*n.*, 170, 174, 180*n.*
Carman, James M., 146*n.*
Carmichael, Stokely, 167
Carmone, Frank J., 149, 150
Carroll, J. D., 169*n.*
Carson, Johnny, 401, 403, 405
Carter, E. Eugene, 209*n.*
Cartwright, Dorwin, 372*n.*
Castle & Cooke, 248
Catry, Bernard, 209*n.*
Central Data Corporation, 133, 134
Chambers, John C., 210*n.*
Chandler, A. D., Jr., 78*n.*
Chapple, E. D., 345*n.*, 357*n.*
Cherington, Paul T., 312
Chevalier, Michel, 209*n.*
Chevrolet, 106, 134, 145, 146
Child World, 326
Chomsky, Noam, 103
Churchill, Gilbert, 136*n.*
Churchill, Gilbert A., Jr., 367
CIBA Pharmaceutical Co., 364
Clark, Donald F., 361*n.*
Clark, Fred E., 312*n.*
Clark, Kenneth, 104
Clarkson, G. P. E., 78*n.*
Clay, Michael J., 447*n.*
Claycamp, Henry, 425, 434, 438*n.*
Cleland, David I., 439, 443*n.*, 445*n.*
Clewett, Richard M., 27, 31
Clifford, Donald K., Jr., 237
Cloonan, James B., 364*n.*
Cloverdale, Herbert L., 382*n.*
Coca-Cola, 36, 424
Coch, L., 373*n.*
Cochran, William G., 158*n.*
Cohen, Joel B., 260, 268*n.*, 395*n.*
Cohen, Joel E., 85, 92, 146, 233*n.*
Cohen, Kalman J., 209*n.*
Cole, R. R., 233*n.*
Coleman, Richard P., 114, 146*n.*
Colgate, 247
Colley, Russell, 389, 391
Collier, James R., 455*n.*
Collins, B. J. K., 432, 439*n.*
Comer, James M., 358, 363*n.*
Concorn Kitchens, 429*n.*
Conley, Patrick, 209*n.*, 224
Consumers Distributing, 324, 326
Continental Can's Metal Operations, 36
Converse, P. D., 312
Cooper, Robert G., 87, 88, 270
Copley, Thomas P., 136*n.*, 140*n.*
Cotham, J. C., III, 357*n.*
Cousineau, A., 259, 268*n.*
Cox, Donald, 114, 153*n.*, 157*n.*, 422*n.*
Cox, Gertrude M., 88, 158*n.*
Cox, R., 312*n.*
Cox, William E., Jr., 210*n.*
Craven, D. W., 422*n.*
Cravens, David W., 185
Crawford, C. Merle, 206, 211*n.*
Crespi, Irving, 389
Cross, J. S., 136*n.*, 180*n.*
Crowder, Walter, 283
Cullen, William T., 359*n.*
Cundiff, Edward W., 152*n.*
Cunningham, Ross M., 148
Cunningham, Scott M., 147, 153*n.*
Curhan, Ronald, 320*n.*, 365*n.*
Cyert, Richard M., 121, 122, 136*n.*
Czepiel, John, 260, 268*n.*

Daignault, Phyllis, 359*n.*
Darden, William, 261, 268*n.*, 269*n.*
Dasgupta, Satadal, 260, 268*n.*
Davidson, Thomas Lea, 8, 10*n.*
Davidson, William R., 311*n.*
Davis, Harry L., 113, 343, 358*n.*
Day, George S., 93, 96, 156*n.*, 193, 390*n.*, 396*n.*, 429*n.*, 435*n.*, 438*n.*
Dean, Joel, 293, 303*n.*, 304
DeBoer, Lloyd M., 359*n.*
Debower, H. F., 312*n.*
DeBruicker, Stewart, 399, 407*n.*
Demsetz, Harold, 291
Department of Defense, 72, 224
de Ramos, E. B., 260, 269*n.*
Dhalla, Nariman K., 151, 157*n.*
Diamond Crystal Salt Corporation, 362
Diebold, John, 423*n.*
Dietz, Stephen W., 23*n.*, 31, 211*n.*
Dirlam, Joel B., 286, 303*n.*
Ditz, Gerhard W., 367*n.*
Dodge, H. R., 360
Dodge, Robert H., 180*n.*
Dolich, I. J., 388*n.*
Donaldson, G., 455*n.*
Donnelly, James, 261, 268*n.*
Donnelly, James H., 364*n.*
Dreyfuss, Henry, 388
Dr. Strangelove, 103
Drucker, Peter F., 46, 54, 59, 209*n.*
Dubois, Bernard, 261, 269*n.*
Duesenberry, James, 283
Dun & Bradstreet, Inc., 443*n.*
DuPont, 71, 122, 241, 242, 286, 331
Dutton, J. M., 368*n.*, 369*n.*

Ebbeson, E. B., 352*n.*, 358*n.*
Eckles, William P., 250*n.*
Eckstein, Otto, 283
Edelman, Franz, 427, 428, 438*n.*
Ehrlich, H. J., 106, 375*n.*
Eisenhower, Dwight D., 167
Engel, James F., 8, 9, 84, 85, 88, 97, 268*n.*, 391*n.*
Enuendy, G., 233*n.*
Etzel, Michael, 261, 268*n.*
Etzioni, Amitai, 113
Evans, Franklin B., 111, 145*n.*, 146, 344–347, 351, 357*n.*

Family Brand, 435
Faris, Charles, 180*n.*
Farris, C. W., 136*n.*
Faust, 103
Fechner, Gustav, 244
Feltham, Gerald A., 423*n.*
Ferber, R., 320*n.*, 411*n.*
Festinger, Leon, 81, 92, 93, 106, 357*n.*, 390*n.*
Fine, I. V., 136*n.*, 138
Fire Safety Center, 35
Firestone, 123
Firth, Raymond, 10*n.*
Fishbein, Martin, 81, 86, 92–95, 97, 391*n.*, 395*n.*
Fitch, H. G., 369*n.*
Fitzpatrick, A. A., 303*n.*
Fliegel, Frederick, 260, 268*n.*
Fog, B., 303*n.*
Fogg, C. Davis, 211*n.*, 212
Ford, Henry, 102
Ford, Neil M., 367
Fourt, L. A., 432, 438*n.*
Fox, Karl A., 158*n.*
Fox, Leo B., 149, 150
Frank, Newton, 8
Frank, Ronald E., 145*n.*, 146–148, 152*n.*,–154*n.*, 158, 180*n.*
Frankenstein, 103
Fraser, S. C., 353*n.*, 357*n.*
Freedman, J. L., 107, 353*n.*, 357*n.*
French, J. R. P., 372*n.*, 373*n.*
Freud, Sigmund, 104
Fromkin, Howard, 261, 268*n.*
Frost, Robert, 104
Fruham, William E., 211*n.*
Fuchs, Victor R., 329*n.*

Gabor, A., 305*n.*
Gaccione, Vincent, 261, 269*n.*
Gadel, M. S., 347, 351, 357*n.*
Galbraith, J. K., 283, 289
Gale, Bradley T., 209*n.*, 210*n.*
Gallay, Ralph, 19*n.*
Gardner, Burleigh B., 383*n.*
Gardner, David, 269*n.*
Gemmill, Gary R., 31
General Electric, 35, 252, 286
General Foods, 34, 36, 38–41, 242, 247
General Motors, 45, 286, 289
Gergen, K. J., 345*n.*, 350*n.*, 357*n.*
Gerstner, Louis V., 209*n.*
Gillette, 239, 252
Gillis, F. E., 303*n.*
Gilmore, F. F., 78*n.*
Gimbel's, 148
Girdwood Publishing Company, 362
Gittler, Joseph B., 113
Glick, Ira O., 147, 382
Godfrey, Arthur, 238
Goffman, Erving, 388*n.*
Goldberg, Marvin, 261, 268*n.*
Golden, F., 260, 268*n.*
Goldstucker, J. L., 356*n.*
Golembiewski, Robert T., 139*n.*
Good, R. E., 305*n.*, 422*n.*
Goodyear, 123
Gould, Jack, 382*n.*
Grace, Peter, 71
Granbois, D. H., 351*n.*, 357*n.*
Granfield, Michael, 291, 292
Granger, C. W. J., 305*n.*
Grass, R. C., 382*n.*
Gray, Peter J., 363*n.*
Green, Paul E., 123, 124*n.*, 125*n.*, 132*n.*, 149, 150

Green Giant, 379
Greenberg, A., 353*n*., 357*n*., 389*n*.
Grether, E. T., 312
Gross, Neal, 114, 375*n*.
Gruen, W., 147
Guetzkow, H., 356, 357*n*.
Guttman, Louis, 169*n*.

Haas, G. H., 136*n*.
Haas, R. M., 358*n*., 422*n*.
Haberstroh, Chadwick J., 369*n*.
Halbert, Michael, 320*n*.
Haley, Russell I., 153*n*.
Hamilton, Walton, 304
Hamlet, 111
Hamm, B. Curtis, 152*n*.
Hammer, William L., 320
Hamm's, 166
Hanan, Mack, 34
Hancock, R. L., 140*n*.
Handel, Gerald, 146*n*.
Handy Dan, 324, 326
Harper, Donald, 303*n*.
Hart, B. H. Liddel, 211*n*.
Hartley, Eugene L., 12*n*., 356*n*.
Haskins, Jack B., 390*n*.
Havens, A. Eugene, 260, 268*n*.
Hawley, Cameron, 112
Haynes, W. W., 303*n*.
Hays, F. A., 136*n*.
Heany, Donald F., 209*n*., 423*n*.
Heider, F., 345*n*., 357*n*.
Hein, Leonard W., 423*n*.
Henderson, Bruce D., 210*n*., 211*n*.
Henning, Dale A., 455*n*.
Henry, Harry, 61
Henry, J., 344*n*., 357*n*.
Hertz, D. B., 364*n*.
Heslin, Richard, 260, 268*n*.
Hess, E. H., 382*n*.
Hess, Sidney W., 363, 365
Hewlett-Packard, 34
Heyel, Carl, 293*n*.
Hildegaard, Ingrid, 146*n*.
Hill, R. M., 136*n*., 180*n*.
Hirschmann, W. B., 233*n*.
Hise, Richard T., 364*n*., 370*n*.
Hlavacek, James D., 270, 281
Hollander, S., 320*n*.
Homans, G. C., 112, 345*n*., 357*n*.
Homans, Richard E., 8
Horney, Karen, 146
Householder, A. S., 169*n*.
Houston, Michael, 395*n*.
Hovland, Carl I., 114, 155*n*., 397*n*.
Howard, John A., 80, 81, 85, 86, 88, 92, 93, 95, 97, 136*n*., 137, 138*n*., 153*n*., 391*n*.
Howard, Ron, 119
Howell, J. C., 375*n*.
Hulswit, Frank T., 361*n*.
Humble, John W., 187*n*.
Humphrey, Hubert, 167
Hustad, Thomas P., 398, 399, 407*n*.

IBM, 133, 134, 292
IBM World Trade Corporation, 34, 38, 39, 242, 364
Imperial Oil, 102*n*.
IRS, 321
ITT, 42
Ivancevich, John M., 364*n*.

Jacoby, Jacob, 260, 261, 268*n*., 391*n*.
Jahoda, Marie, 391*n*.
Jain, Subhash C., 152*n*.
Janis, Irving, 397*n*.
John F. Kennedy Center of the Arts, 17
Johnson, Lyndon, 167
Johnson, Richard M., 130*n*., 161, 169*n*.
Johnson, Samuel C., 211*n*.
Johnson, Stephen C., 169*n*.
Jones, Conrad, 211*n*.
Jones, J. G., 312*n*.

Kahn, Robert L., 368*n*., 369*n*., 370*n*.
Kamen, Joseph, 147*n*., 396*n*.
Kaplan, A. D. H., 286, 303*n*.
Karash, R. I., 436, 439*n*.
Karlins, M., 352*n*., 357*n*.
Karmen, Joseph M., 147*n*.
Kassarjian, Harold H., 144, 147, 152*n*.
Katz, Elihu, 114, 115, 157*n*.
Kearney, A. T., 211*n*., 323
Kefauver, Estes, 283
Kegerreis, Robert J., 260, 261, 268*n*.
Kelley, H. H., 345*n*., 358*n*., 397*n*.
Kelley, William T., 440
Kennedy, John F., 167
Kennedy and Cohen, 324
Kettelle, John D., 361*n*.
Kiesler, Charles, 259, 268*n*.
Kindahl, James K., 284, 292
King, Charles W., 145*n*., 407*n*.
King, Martin Luther, 167
King, R. L., 136*n*., 423*n*.
King, William R., 439, 441*n*., 443*n*., 445*n*.
Kissinger, Henry, 102
Kivlin, Joseph E., 260, 268*n*.
Klahr, David, 396*n*.
Kline, C. H., 78*n*.
Kluckhohn, Clyde, 115
Knight, Frank, 120, 121
Kodak, 16
Koffler Stores, 327
Kohn, Carol A., 261, 268*n*.
Kollat, David T., 84, 97, 187*n*., 209*n*., 211*n*., 305, 391*n*.
Konopa, L. S., 270, 281*n*.
Koponen, Arthur, 146, 147
Kostetsky, Oleh, 423*n*.
Kotler, Phillip, 6, 7, 10, 17*n*., 145, 148, 256, 440
Krech, E. M., 136*n*.
Krueger, Lester, 146*n*.
Krugman, Herbert E., 390*n*.
Kruskal, Joseph B., 125*n*., 169*n*.
K-Tel, 324, 327

Lambert, Zarrel, 261, 268*n*.
Landsberger, Henry A., 141*n*., 142*n*., 369*n*.
Lanvin (Charles of the Ritz), 102*n*.
Lanzilotti, Robert F., 286, 287, 289, 303*n*.
Lavidge, Robert I., 390*n*.
Lawrence, Paul, 79, 370*n*.
Lazarsfeld, Paul F., 104, 113, 115, 157*n*., 344*n*., 357*n*.
Lazer, W., 136*n*.
Lazer, William, 364
Leavitt, C., 380, 382*n*.
LeBreton, P. P., 455*n*.
Leezenbaum, Ralph, 23*n*.
LeKashman, Raymond, 330
Lemay, Curtis, 167
Leonard, John, 103
Leon's, 324
Levitt, Theodore A., 59, 65, 71, 78*n*., 136*n*., 138*n*., 140*n*., 210*n*., 354, 355, 357*n*.
Levy, Sidney J., 3, 6, 7, 10*n*., 17*n*., 19*n*., 147, 156*n*., 382, 383*n*., 388*n*.
Lewin, Kurt, 12*n*.
Liddy, 434, 438*n*.
Life Savers, Inc., 253
Lincoln, John, 359*n*.
Lindsay, John, 167, 397
Lindzey, Gardner, 345*n*., 356*n*., 367*n*.
Linsky, Barry R., 209*n*.
Lipton Tea, 238
Liston, D., Jr., 423*n*.
Little, J. D. C., 399, 407, 425, 438*n*.
Lodish, Leonard M., 362*n*., 363*n*., 364, 365, 399, 407, 438*n*.
London, Perry, 12
Long's, 324
Loomis, Charles P., 260, 269*n*.
Lorsch, Jay W., 370*n*.
Lott, A. J., 345*n*., 347*n*., 357*n*.
Lott, B. E., 345*n*., 347*n*., 357*n*.
Love, Barbara, 254*n*.
Lubinski, Stephen R., 329*n*.
Lucas, Darrell B., 30, 390*n*.
Luce, R. Duncan, 169*n*.
Luck, David J., 6, 10*n*., 23*n*., 30
Lucky Stores, 328, 329
Lunn, J. A., 79, 81, 86, 89–92, 94, 96
Luskin's, 324
Lustgarten, Steven H., 291

McCammon, Bert C., 320
McCarthy, Eugene, 167
Maccoby, E. E., 356*n*.
MacDonald, M. M., 303*n*.
McEachern, A. W., 375*n*.
McGee, John S., 290
McGovern, George, 282
McGuire, W. J., 349*n*., 352*n*., 354*n*., 357*n*., 397*n*.
McKeon, James J., 169*n*.
McKinsey & Co., 27
McMahan, Harry W., 210*n*., 250*n*.
McMillan, James R., 136*n*., 138*n*., 140*n*.
McNeil, Elton, 369*n*.
Macy's, 148
Mahatoo, Winston H., 151
Malese, J., 364*n*.
Malinowski, Bronislaw, 115
Mallen, Bruce, 311
Maloney, John C., 259, 269*n*., 390, 391
Mancuso, Joseph, 261, 269*n*.
Mann, Roland, 237*n*.
Mann, Thomas, 112
March, B., 136*n*.
March, James C., 372*n*.
March, James G., 139*n*., 142*n*., 371*n*.
Market Facts, Inc., 130
Marketing Science Institute, 7
Marlow, D., 345*n*., 350*n*., 357*n*.
Marshall, Alfred, 120
Martineau, Pierre D., 147*n*.
Marting, Elizabeth, 304*n*., 305*n*.
Mason, Edward, 304
Mason, W. S., 375*n*.
Massy, W. F., 432, 438*n*.
Massy, William, 146, 148, 152*n*., 153*n*., 180*n*.
Mayer, Martin, 112
Means, Gardiner, 283–285, 292
Merrill Lynch, 248
Merton, Robert K., 371*n*.
Miller, David, 396*n*.
Miller, Delbert C., 375*n*.

Miller, Frank B., 113
Miller, G. A., 89
Miller, N. E., 85
Miller (brand name), 166
Miner, J. B., 345, 357*n.*
Misshauk, M. J., 139*n.*
MIT, 425
Mockler, Robert J., 455*n.*
Monsanto, 35
Montgomery, David B., 361*n.*, 365, 396*n.*, 423, 425*n.*, 427, 438*n.*, 439*n.*
Moore, C. G., Jr., 136*n.*, 138*n.*
Moran, Harry T., 210*n.*
Morein, Joseph A., 246
Morgenstern, O., 77, 78*n.*
Morin, B. A., 136*n.*, 144*n.*
Morris, William Mack, 253
Morris, William T., 423*n.*
Morrison, D. G., 438*n.*
Moyer, R. J., 358*n.*
Mullick, Satinder K., 210*n.*
Mulvihill, D. F., 303*n.*, 304*n.*
Myers, James, 94, 261, 269*n.*

Nader, Ralph, 292
National Bureau of Economic Research, 119, 284
National Cash Register, 36–39, 133, 134
Neal, Alfred, 284
Nebergall, Richard, 396*n.*
Nebergall, Roger E., 139, 154
Needham, Douglas, 210*n.*
Nelson, Victoria M., 244
Newcomb, Theodore M., 12*n.*, 345*n.*, 356*n.*, 358*n.*
New York Academy of Sciences, 103
Nicosia, Francesco M., 79, 82–84, 87, 88, 97, 111, 391*n.*
Nikoll Electronics Case, 429*n.*
Nimer, Daniel, 286
Nixon, Richard, 167
Nounse, Edwin, 304
Nowak, Theodore, 23*n.*

Ogilvy, David, 383*n.*
Oliver, Robert, 5, 10*n.*
O'Meara, J. T., Jr., 270, 281*n.*
Operations Research Society of America, 109
Ornstein, Stanley, 291, 292
Ostlund, Lyman, 261, 269*n.*
Oxenfeldt, Alfred R., 82, 303, 305*n.*, 396*n.*

Painter, John J., 111, 147*n.*
Palda, Kristine S., 390*n.*
Paranka, S., 303*n.*, 304*n.*
Parfitt, J. H., 432, 439
Parrish, Kirk, 102*n.*
Paschal, Bruce, 248*n.*
Pavlov, I. P., 104
Payne, Bruce, 455*n.*
Pearce, I. F., 285
Pearson, Andrall E., 27
Pennington, A. L., 345*n.*, 348, 358*n.*
PepsiCo, 27
Percy, Charles, 167
Perkins, J. H., 233*n.*
Perloff, Robert, 260, 268*n.*
Pernica, Joseph, 153*n.*
Pessemier, Edgar A., 145*n.*, 398, 399, 407*n.*
Phillips, Almarin, 304*n.*
Pillsbury Company, 359, 379
Pinson, Christian, 261, 269*n.*
Pizam, Abraham, 261, 269*n.*
Plummer, Joseph T., 376, 382*n.*
Pomeroy, James F., 23*n.*
Popper, Karl, 6, 10*n.*
Porter, Donald E., 139*n.*
Poulsen, Lance, 260, 269*n.*
PPG Industries, 35
Pringle, L., 438*n.*
Procter & Gamble, 34, 45, 238, 242, 247
Pruden, Henry O., 368*n.*, 371*n.*

Quanta Welding, 294

Rainwater, Lee, 145, 146*n.*
Ramond, Charles, 102, 105, 108, 109, 389*n.*
Rao, Ambar G., 390*n.*
Rao, Vithala R., 124*n.*
Rappaport, Alfred, 423*n.*
Raven, B., 372*n.*
Ray, Michael L., 356, 358*n.*, 389, 397*n.*, 398*n.*
Rayburn, Sam, 113
RCA, 49, 133, 427, 429
Reagan, Ronald, 167
Rector of Justin, The, 112
Reeves, Rosser, 390*n.*
Reiser, Carl, 358*n.*
Reiser, Richard, 390
Renard, G. A., 136*n.*
Revlon, 35
Reynolds, Fred, 261, 268*n.*, 269*n.*
Rhind, Ridley, 423*n.*
Rich, Stuart U., 152*n.*
Rinehart, J. W., 375*n.*
Robertson, Thomas S., 260, 261, 269*n.*, 396*n.*
Robeson, James F., 187*n.*, 209*n.*, 211*n.*, 305*n.*
Robinson, Joan, 158*n.*
Robinson, Patrick J., 136*n.*, 150, 180*n.*
Rockefeller, Nelson, 167
Rogers, Everett M., 258–261, 269*n.*
Rokeach, Milton P., 93, 95, 96, 107, 156*n.*
Rose, Ivan, 250*n.*, 260, 268*n.*
Rose, Sanford, 210*n.*
Rosenberg, 86, 94, 95
Rossiter, John, 260, 269*n.*
Rothbard, Murray N., 284
Rowe, David, 180*n.*
Royal Little, 71
Rubenstein, Albert H., 369*n.*
Ryans, A. B., 439*n.*
Ryerson, J. T., and Son, Inc., 362

Samuels, Stuart A., 363
Sara Lee, 247, 248, 251
Saunders, W. B., 396*n.*
Sawyer, Alan G., 398*n.*
Schary, Philip B., 311*n.*
Schiffman, Leon, 260, 261, 269*n.*, 365*n.*
Schlinger, Fred, 381*n.*
Schlinger, M. J., 382*n.*
Schlitz, 166
Schoeffler, Sidney, 209*n.*
Schoner, Bertram, 423*n.*
Schonfeld, Eugene P., 259, 269*n.*
Schultz, Randall, 8
Scrivener, Robert C., 321, 329*n.*
Sears, Roebuck, 123, 254, 286
Semlow, Walter J., 361*n.*
Service Merchandise, 324
Shable, J., 155*n.*
Shanker, Roy T., 364, 365*n.*
Shaw, Arch W., 312*n.*
Sherif, Carolyn W., 96, 154*n.*, 396*n.*
Sherif, Muzafer, 96, 154*n.*, 155*n.*, 396*n.*
Sheth, Jagdish N., 79–82, 85, 86, 88, 92, 93, 95–97, 135, 153*n.*, 391*n.*, 395*n.*
Shoaf, Robert F., 136*n.*, 138*n.*
Shoemaker, Floyd, 238, 260, 261, 269*n.*
Shuchman, Abraham, 396*n.*
Shull, Fremont A., Jr., 375*n.*
Silk, Alvin J., 343, 358*n.*, 365*n.*, 391*n.*, 427, 439
Simmonds, Kenneth, 211*n.*
Simon, Herbert A., 142*n.*, 371*n.*
Simons, H. W., 351, 358*n.*
Skinner, B. F., 103, 104, 107, 108, 110
Slesinger, J. A., 374*n.*
Sloan, Alfred, 34, 45
Smith, C. G., 374*n.*
Smith, Donald D., 210*n.*
Smith, Donald R. E., 269*n.*
Smith, Gail, 391*n.*
Smith, Jay A., 364*n.*
Smith, L. G., 357*n.*
Smith, S. V., 344, 358*n.*, 423*n.*
Smith, Wendell, 144, 158*n.*
Social Research Inc., 6
Sorrell, L. C., 74*n.*, 78*n.*
Springer, C. H., 209*n.*
Springer, Jack, 209*n.*
Stafford, J., 358*n.*, 423*n.*
Standard Brands Paint, 326
Starch, Daniel, 250
Stasch, Stanley F., 27, 31
Staudt, Thomas A., 136*n.*
Stefflre, Volney J., 150, 391, 397
Steiner, Gary A., 357*n.*, 390*n.*
Steiner, George A., 209*n.*, 455*n.*
Sternthal, B., 269*n.*
Stevens, S. N., 345*n.*, 351*n.*, 358*n.*
Stevens, S. S. 105
Steward, John, 211
Stigler, George J., 267, 275, 284, 292, 312, 313
Stobaugh, Robert B., 210*n.*
Stolle, John F., 330
Stouffer's, 248, 251
Strauss, George, 136*n.*, 138*n.*, 139*n.*, 141*n.*, 142*n.*
Strong, Edward, 389, 398*n.*
Sultan, Ralph G. M., 209*n.*, 210*n.*
Summers, Gene F., 391*n.*, 400
Summers, John O., 407*n.*
Sweeney, Daniel J., 329*n.*
Swinth, R. L., 349, 350, 357*n.*

Taguiri, R., 351*n.*, 358*n.*
Talarzyk, Wayne W., 395*n.*
Talese, Gay, 112
Talley, Walter J., Jr., 361*n.*
Tannenbaum, Percy E., 397*n.*
Tauber, Edward M., 269*n.*
Taylor, James, 260, 269*n.*
Taylor, Thayer C., 362*n.*
Terry, R. A., 169*n.*
Textron, 42, 71
Thackray, John, 210*n.*
Thibaut, J. W., 345, 358*n.*
Thompson, G. Clark, 303*n.*, 389
Thompson, J. Walter, 99, 104*n.*, 146–148
Thompson, Victor A., 141*n.*
Thorp, Willard, 283
Thucydides, 111

Tigert, Douglas J., 152*n.*, 400, 407*n.*
Tilles, S., 78*n.*, 211*n.*
Toman, Robert J., 396*n.*
Tosi, H. L., 348, 358*n.*
Townsend, Philip L., 210*n.*
Toys R' Us, 324
Tucker, Leydyard, 169*n.*
Tucker, William T., 5, 6, 10*n.*, 147*n.*
Tukey, John W., 124*n.*
Tupperware, 324
Turner, Ronald E., 365*n.*
TWA, 123
Twain, Mark, 111
Twedt, Dik Warren, 148, 258, 269*n.*, 423*n.*

Uhl, Kenneth, 260, 269*n.*, 411, 423*n.*
U. S. Steel, 286
Unity Buying Service, 324, 327
Univac, 133
Urban, G. L., 436, 439*n.*
Urban, Ozanne B., 136*n.*

Vaile, R. S., 312
Varela, Jacoba, 352–355
Vinson, Donald E., 136*n.*
Von Neumann, J., 77, 78*n.*

Wachsler, R., 438*n.*
Walker, Orville C., Jr., 367
Wallace, Donald, 304
Wallace, George, 167
Walster, E. H., 345*n.*, 357*n.*
Walters, S. G., 78*n.*
Walton, R. E., 368*n.*, 369*n.*
Wanamaker, John, 323
Ward, Clark, 361*n.*
Ward, Scott, 269*n.*, 396*n.*, 439*n.*
Ward, William H., 359*n.*, 360*n.*
Warren, Neil, 391*n.*
Watson, Donald, 304*n.*
Wayne, Kenneth, 210*n.*
Weber, Ernst, 105, 244–246
Webster, Frederick E., Jr., 136*n.*, 181*n.*, 351*n.*, 352*n.*, 358*n.*, 361*n.*
Weinberg, Charles B., 423
Weiss, E. B., 209
Weiss, E. P., 360*n.*
Weld, L. D., 312
Weldon, T. H., 120
Welk, Lawrence, 401, 403
Wells, William D., 110, 111, 152*n.*, 153*n.*, 400, 407
Westfall, Ralph, 111, 147
Westing, John, II, 136*n.*, 138*n.*
Weston, J. Fred, 282, 287–290, 292, 303*n.*
Wharton School's Management and Behavioral Science Institute, 424
Whyte, William Foote, 113
Wilding, John, 152*n.*
Wileman, David L., 31
Wilkie, William L., 154
Wilkinson Sword, Ltd., 286
Willett, R. P., 345*n.*, 348, 351*n.*, 357*n.*, 358*n.*
Williams, J. Allen, Jr., 370*n.*
Williamson, O. E., 304*n.*
Wills, G., 304*n.*
Wilson, Aubrey, 181*n.*, 210*n.*
Wilson, Flip, 401, 403, 405
Wilson, Thomas W., Jr., 27
Wind, Yoram, 123, 132*n.*, 136*n.*, 152*n.*, 170, 180*n.*
Winer, Leon, 365
Winick, Charles, 111, 396*n.*
Wolfe, Harry Deane, 389*n.*
Wolfe, Thomas, 112
Wolff, Harold, 330*n.*
Wood, James Playstead, 114
Woodlock, J. W., 432, 438*n.*
Woods, Richard S., 423*n.*
Woodside, Arch G., 152*n.*
Wright, J. S., 356*n.*
Wright, P., 269*n.*
Wright, Robert V. L., 46, 48*n.*
Wright, T. P., 233*n.*

Xerox Corporation, 34, 38, 133, 134, 363

Young, F. W., 169*n.*
Young, G., 169*n.*

Zacharias, Jerrold, 112
Zaltman, Gerald, 7, 10*n.*, 256, 260, 261, 269*n.*
Zannetos, Zenon S., 423*n.*
Zaragoza, C. C., 427, 439*n.*
Zaragoza, Carlos E., 365*n.*, 427, 439*n.*
Zenz, G. J., 136*n.*, 138*n.*
Zimbardo, P., 352*n.*, 358*n.*
Zoltners, Andres A., 365*n.*

Subject Index

Page numbers in *italic* indicate illustrations.

A priori approach to buyer behavior theory, 81–82
Absolute threshold, 122
Accessibility as market segmentation condition, 145, 148
Action of marketing plan, 235–407
Advertisement pretesting system, 91
Advertising:
  attitudes as objectives, 389–391
  communication, 376–382
  in communications behavior, 157
  competitive nature of, 377
  industrial, symbolism in, 387
  major and minor decisions in, *29*
  model of broadcast, 376
  role of, 28–30, 376–381
  specialist in, 30–31
  viewer response to, 377–383
Advertising recall, 434–435
Affect product class in advertising strategy, 393–394
Air carrier study, 128
Air travelers' utility functions, *129*
ALLOCATE, 363
Allocating salesmen to customers, 351
Allocation of resources, 32
Alternative facilities use, *333*
Analysis:
  cluster, 134–135
  computer, of utility data, *127*
  systems, 359–361
Anthropology, 115–116, 122
Anticipating change, 311–320
Approach(es):
  cost, to distribution, 330–343
  to market segmentation, *172*
  media, to segmentation, 398–407
Argonauts of the Western Pacific, 115
Argosy Magazine, 148
Attitude(s):
  as advertising objectives, 389–391
  behavior controversy, 92
  theory, 94
Attitudinal framework for advertising strategy, 389–407
Attributed power, 372
Attributes, importance of, 126
Autonomous versus joint decisions, 140
Axiom One, 117

Background of individuals as expectation factor, 139
Balance for multiindustry, 46
Bar soaps, designing of, 130
Bases of segmentation, *179*
Behavior:
  communications, 151
  industrial buyer, 135–144, *137*
  level response to advertising, 377–378
Behavioral sciences, 102–122
Beyond Freedom and Dignity, 103
Boundary position, 368
Brand level in advertising strategy, 396–398
Brand marketing, 246–256
Brand preferences in media approaches, 403–404
BRANDAID, 424, 438*n*.
Buddenbrooks, 112
Business manager:
  operation of, 42–45
  support available to, *43*
Business units, matrix for categorizing, *49*
Business Week, 424
Buyer(s):
  behavior, 135–144
  cost, 298
  as economic force, 117–120
  point of view of, 386–387
  resistance, 352
Buyer behavior theory:
  alternatives, 295
  approaches to, 81–82
  need for, and function of, 80–81
Buyer characteristics in market segmentation, 147
Buying style, 156

California Personality Inventory, 152
Call allocation, 362
CALL-PLAN, 362–364, 424, 430, 438
CARD, 329*n*.
Cars, buyers' judgments on, *134*
Cash flow share-gain plan, *222*
Categorizing business units, 49
Category Interest, 432*n*.
Category Usage, 432*n*.
Cattell's 16-Personality Factor Inventory, 152
Change:
  in distribution structure, 320–331
  when it's right, 285
Changing, imagery, 387–388
Channels:
  of distribution, 301, *333*
  horizontal structure, 316–318
Chicago beer market, *163*
Choices:
  consumer, 110
  managerial, 109–110